First Greek Course

First Greek Course

by Anne Mahoney

after W. H. D. Rouse

For PLK, who has maintained a lively interest in this project all along.

πείθεις δή μευ θυμόν, ἀπηνέα περ μάλ᾽ ἐόντα.

Odyssey 23.230

Contents

Preface to the Focus edition

This book is adapted from W. H. D. Rouse's *First Greek Course* (third edition, London, 1916). I have made the presentation of grammar more modern, removed the assumption that students know Latin before coming to Greek, fleshed out the conversation sections in the early chapters, added exercises, and added a great deal more reading. I have retained the sequence of grammatical concepts and the division into chapters, so that this new book still matches Rouse's classic reader *A Greek Boy at Home*, re-issued along with this textbook as *Rouse's Greek Boy*.

W. H. D. Rouse (1863-1950) was for many years headmaster of the Perse School in Cambridge (UK), where he introduced the Direct Method for teaching all foreign languages: French, Latin, and Greek. The Direct Method is nearly an immersion program, in which class is conducted as much as possible in the target language. Students at the Perse started Greek at age 14 or 15, after three years of Latin and five of French. They were thus already familiar with ideas like noun cases, verb moods, and agreement. Rouse exploited this background in his original textbook; for example, in chapter 8 we find "The Absolute Case in Greek is the genitive, as ἐμοῦ λέγοντος, 'as I was speaking.'" This is the *entire* discussion of the genitive absolute, and the Greek readings in the chapter contain no examples. For contemporary students, who may begin Greek before Latin, or relatively early in their study of Latin, this is inadequate, so I have replaced this one sentence with half a dozen paragraphs and two focused exercises.

The advantage of the Direct Method is that students use Greek actively: they don't just read, but also speak and write the language. On the other hand, it is difficult to provide intensive immersion in a college class meeting only three times a week. I have kept the conversation exercises, so that instructors may use as much oral work as they find appropriate and feasible. I have kept Rouse's composition exercises and added more; I have also included some simpler exercises in which students work with one sentence at a time, focusing on a single point of syntax or morphology. Thus an instructor who wants to encourage active use of Greek will find resources here, while classes working entirely on reading can, if they like, use the conversation scripts as additional texts or as written exercises.

Rouse was not particularly concerned about an organized presentation of vocabulary. Because he spoke and wrote classical Greek fluently, he could simply use the appropriate words for whatever he wanted to say, and trust to constant exposure to make the most common and useful words familiar to his students. The vocabulary lists in his textbook are a fairly arbitrary mix of necessary words and uncommon ones brought in for a particular reading, while some words introduced in the grammar sections don't appear in the vocabulary until several chapters later (for example, δίδωμι is taught and used in chapter 9, but appears in the vocabulary list for chapter 13). I have organized the vocabulary, so that words students should be held responsible for appear in the chapter lists, while words introduced only for a reading appear in notes to that reading. The chapter lists contain about 900 words, including the most common words in Xenophon's *Apology,* Plato's *Apology* and *Ion,* and Lysias speech 1: words in this book make up at least seventy percent of the running words in each of those texts.

The vocabulary also includes words related to farming, sailing, cooking, weather, and other basic concerns of the classical Greeks. All these words are used in classical literature, but their main value in the first-year course is that they allow conversation about concrete, real things, rather than an endless round of goddesses writing letters, poets educating men, and rulers sending shields to soldiers.

Readings include unadapted classical texts, slightly adapted texts, and newly written ones. Starting in chapter 7, the last reading of each chapter is about the Trojan War; this loosely connected series of readings covers the major incidents from the Judgement of Paris to the Nostoi, introducing stories that students will meet in epic and tragedy. *Rouse's Greek Boy*, the companion reader, is a single connected story of a year in the life of a fifteen-year-old Athenian boy, with chapters corresponding to the chapters of this textbook; this may be used as a narrative backbone for the year's work.

Rouse suggested that "it may be left as a pleasant exercise for those who use the book" to identify the readings taken from classical authors. Perhaps; but it seemed more useful to supply the references, so that students can see which readings are classical and which are new, and so that, if a text catches their fancy, they can find the rest of it. The readings range from Homer to Longus. As many teachers do, I ask beginners in Greek why they're taking the course and what authors they particularly want to read. I've used those lists as a guide to selecting readings to include; thus, Homer, Plato, Aristotle, Thucydides, Aristophanes, and the tragedians are all represented. I have also included one selection each from the Hippocratic corpus and Euclid. To Rouse's already generous selection from Middle and New Comedy, I have added a substantial passage from Menander's *Dyscolus,* a text which was not rediscovered until some years after Rouse's death. I have included two dialogues from Lucian, following Rouse's own edits (in his student commentary on Lucian) in the Ganymede dialogue.

Most of the shorter verse texts are accompanied by paraphrases in Attic prose, to help students understand and to demonstrate how the conventions of verse and prose differ. Once students start getting the idea, they may write their own paraphrases for verses that don't already have them.

The presentation of grammar is detailed, with a fair amount of linguistic background and terminology. While this is not directly relevant to acquisition of the language (in the strictest sense), it is often interesting to students, some of whom choose to study Greek because they are fascinated by language. Moreover, the textbook is the best place for this background material, so that students can read and absorb it at leisure, while class time can be spent on practice with the Greek language itself.

Appendices to the main text summarize morphology, both inflectional and derivational; syntax; rules for accentuation; and meter.

The ACL/APA *Standards for Classical Language Learning* articulate the goals of the language class as the "five Cs": communication, culture, connections, comparison, and communities. This textbook particularly supports goal 1, **communication,** with its oral and written exercises for active use of Greek. The materials in this book can bring students close to the intermediate level, as described in the *Standards*. Work on goal 2, **culture,** is supported by the readings and, even more, by *Rouse's Greek Boy*. The notes on cognates and derivatives in the vocabulary lists support work on goal 3, **connections,** as do the readings from scientific authors. Goal 4, **comparisons,** is supported by the explicit comparisons between Greek grammar and English, Latin, and Sanskrit throughout the book. Finally, work on goal 5, **communities,** is facilitated by the community of the classroom (as John Gruber-Miller argues in his introduction to *When Dead Tongues Speak*, APA Classical Resources no. 6, Oxford University Press, 2006, p. 16), and by some of the technological resources listed in the bibliography, Appendix 5.

I am delighted to acknowledge the contributions of the Tufts University students who spent a year working with this book in manuscript form: Karen Bustard, Colleen Chausse, Kwarteng Gyamfi, Jeffrey Luz-Alterman, Vanessa Miceli, Sara O'Donnell, and Erin Shanahan. Their comments have made this a better book.

I dedicate this book to my husband, Philip L. King, Jr., whose support and encouragement have been invaluable.

Boston, 29 March 2010

CHAPTER I

Introduction to Ancient Greek

I.1 The Alphabet

The Greek alphabet has 24 letters.

capital form	lower-case form	sound	Greek name	English name
A	α	ǎ (as in German *hat*), ā (as *father*)	ἄλφα	alpha
B	β	b	βῆτα	beta
Γ	γ	g (as in *good*, never as in *gel*)	γάμμα	gamma
Δ	δ	d	δέλτα	delta
E	ε	e (as in *wet*)	εῖ	epsilon, ei (pron. as in Greek, ěy)
Z	ζ	zd	ζῆτα	zeta
H	η	ē (like *a* in *say*, or better as in French *fée*, German *See*)	ἦτα	eta
Θ	θ	t (aspirated)	θῆτα	theta
I	ι	i (as in *machine*)	ἰῶτα	iota
K	κ	k	κάππα	kappa
Λ	λ	l	λάμβδα	lambda
M	μ	m	μῦ	mu
N	ν	n	νῦ	nu

capital form	lower-case form	sound	Greek name	English name
Ξ	ξ	x, ks	ξῖ	xi
Ο	ο	o (as in *pot*)	οὖ	ou, omicron
Π	π	p	πῖ	pi
Ρ	ρ	r	ῥῶ	rho
Σ	σ	s (as in *sing*, never as in *has*)	σῖγμα	sigma
	ς final		(σάν)	san or terminal sigma (used as final letter of a word)
Τ	τ	t	ταῦ	tau
Υ	υ	ü (as French *u* or German *ü*)	ῦ	upsilon, ü, hypsilon
Φ	φ	p (aspirated)	φῖ	phi
Χ	χ	k (aspirated)	χῖ	chi, khi
Ψ	ψ	ps	ψῖ	psi
Ω	ω	ō	ὦ	ō, omega

The names epsilon (ε), omicron (ο), hypsilon or upsilon (υ), and omega (ω) are late, and were not used by the Greeks of the classical age.

Observe the relation of the small letters to the line of writing:

αβγδεζηθικλμνξοπρστυφχψω.

Take α as a pattern: it sits directly on the line and has neither ascender nor descender, much like Roman *a*. These letters are like α in this regard: εικνοπστυω. These letters are taller, but do not go below the line: δθλ. These letters go below the line, but are not tall: γημρχψ. These letters are taller than α and also have tails below the line: βζξφ.

Pronunciation

It is difficult to learn pronunciation from a book. Follow your instructor's example; you will also find good examples on line at sites listed in the bibliography (Appendix 5).

Greek, like English, has **vowels** and **consonants**. The vowels are α, ε, η, ι, ο, υ, and ω. The names and sounds of the vowels are similar to those of most other European languages, for example *ah* for α, not the sound of English *a* in *cat*. English vowels used to have these sounds (and names) as well, but they changed as part of the transition from Middle English to Modern English, between about 1400 and 1600 (this is called the **Great Vowel Shift** in English). Thus ancient Greek vowel sounds are like those of Spanish, Italian, or Latin, different from English.

In particular, Greek vowel sounds are pure, single sounds. For example, ω is just "o," with no "w" (semi-vowel or glide) following after it. In English many vowels are pronounced as diphthongs, double sounds (see below): *go after* is pronounced like "go-w-after." In Greek this must be avoided.

One Greek vowel has a sound that does not occur in English: υ (= French *u*, or German *ü*). It should not be sounded *oo,* or it will be confused with ου. To make the Greek υ sound, say *ee,* then round your lips as for *oo.*

In addition to the pure single vowels, Greek does also have diphthongs. A **diphthong** is a double vowel sound, two vowels pronounced together as one sound in the same syllable. The second vowel will feel almost like a consonant, like English *y* or *w.* The Greek diphthongs are written with two vowel letters to show that they are double sounds:

> αι pronounced as in *aisle*
>
> ει pronounced as *ay* in *say*
>
> οι pronounced as in *foil*
>
> υι pronounced as *ouie* in *Louie,* or as French *oui*
>
> αυ pronounced as *ow* in *cow*
>
> ευ pronounced something like *pay you* but without the intervening *y* sound
>
> ηυ pronounced as ευ but longer
>
> ου pronounced as *oo* in *fool*

The so-called **improper diphthongs**, in which a long ᾱ η ω is followed by ι, were written αι ηι ωι, and pronounced as written. In modern books they are generally written ᾳ ῃ ῳ, with **iota subscript**. Remember that this iota is a real letter, even when it's written as a subscript! When an improper diphthong is the first sound in a capitalized word, the iota is always written **adscript**: a capital letter cannot have a subscript under it, so we write Αι, Ηι, Ωι. These diphthongs may also be pronounced α η ω simply, without the iota sound.

Quantity is important. Greek vowels may be **long** or **short**. A long vowel is held twice as long as a short vowel; you may think of the long vowels as quarter notes and the short ones as eighth notes. There is no other difference in sound between a long vowel and the corresponding short vowel: the *quality* is the same. (This is different from English, where we use the term "long vowel" to refer to a vowel that sounds different from its corresponding short, as in *cap, cape* or *not, note.*)

All diphthongs are long, and η and ω are always long. ε and ο are always short (when they are independent; if they are part of a diphthong, of course, that diphthong is long). The other three, α, ι, υ, are long in some words and short in others, and you need to learn this as part of the pronunciation of the word. In vocabulary listings, these vowels will be marked with a **macron** (ᾱ, ῑ, ῡ) when they are long; the macron is not part of the writing system but is included to help you pronounce the words correctly. We can also use a **breve** to specify that a vowel is short, as ᾰ, ῐ, ῠ.

Note that ω is long ο and η is long ε.

Breathings

When a word begins with a vowel sound, that sound may be aspirated or not. The vowel will be marked with the **rough breathing** if it is aspirated and the **smooth breathing** if it is not. The rough breathing sounds like English "h" and was originally represented by an H (which later came to be used as the vowel ἦτα). In rapid handwriting this came to be written like a sort of reversed comma on top of the vowel (as ἁ), and the smooth breathing was then written as an arc the other way (as ἀ). So: ἄλφα "alpha," smooth breathing, no aspiration; ὥρα "hōra" ("time, season"), rough breathing, aspirate sound. When a breathing is written over a diphthong, it is placed on the second letter: εἶ, οἰκία "house."

The rough breathing is always written over ρ when it is the first sound in a word, as ῥῶ "rho." This is why English words that come from Greek begin with "rh" rather than just "r."

The other letters denote consonant sounds. There are three kinds of consonant sounds in Greek: **stops**, **liquids**, and one **sibilant**. Stops have this name because the flow of air stops briefly when you say them; they are sometimes also called **mutes**. Liquids are sounds that "flow" in the sense that you can sustain them or sing through them. The sibilant sound is the hiss.

The stops are β, δ, γ, θ, κ, π, τ, φ, χ; more details on these are below.

The liquids are λ, ρ, μ, ν. Of these μ and ν are **nasal** sounds, because the sound comes through the nose. Greek has one more nasal sound, the sound of *ng* as in *sing*. This sound only occurs when the nasal sound ν would come before a guttural stop (see below). It is written with a γ before the other guttural, as γγ, γκ, γχ, γξ. For example, ἄγγελος "messenger" is pronounced *ang-ge-los*: the first γ is the nasal sound and the second has its own sound.

The sibilant is σ. This is always the unvoiced sound of English "s" in *sing*, never the voiced sound of English "z."

Learn the following organization of the stops or mutes:

Place of articulation	Manner of articulation		
	Unvoiced unaspirate	Unvoiced aspirate	Voiced
Labial (lips)	π	φ	β
Dental (teeth)	τ	θ	δ
Guttural or velar (throat or velum)	κ	χ	γ

The place of articulation is the point at which the sound is stopped. For labial consonants, the lips close (Latin *labia* means "lips"). For dental consonants, the tongue touches the front teeth (Latin *dentes* = "teeth"). For guttural or velar consonants, the stop comes at the back of your mouth, in your throat (Latin *guttur* = "throat") or at your soft palate or velum (also a Latin word).

As in English, Greek stops may be **voiced** or **unvoiced**. Voiced sounds are pronounced with vibration of the vocal cords, unvoiced sounds without this vibration. You can feel the vibration if you put your fingers on your throat at your larynx and say the sounds; try some examples in English, like *the big pig* or *we gab in the cab* or *you do, too*.

Greek also has a series of **aspirate** consonants, which are pronounced with a distinct puff of air. The difference between π and φ is this puff. Greek only has unvoiced aspirates, not voiced ones (voiced aspirate consonants do exist in other languages, such as Sanskrit, but not in Greek). In English, unvoiced consonants are aspirated when they are the first sound in a word or in a stressed syllable, but not when they are part of a cluster or at the start of an un-stressed syllable. Thus English speakers can make these sounds but do not normally recognize them. Consider the "p" sound in *pin, spin, princess, open*: most English speakers pronounce the first of these words with a φ sound and the other three with the sound of π. You can feel the aspiration if you hold the back of your hand in front of your mouth as you say the words.

Another way to think of aspirates is as if they combine the consonant sound with a rough breathing sound. Examples in English are *anthill, uphold*, and *lackhose*.

It is not difficult to learn to make the aspirate sounds. The hard part is making sure to make the *unaspirate* sounds, particularly in environments where English has automatic aspiration.

After the classical period, these sounds changed to **fricatives**, which is how they are still pronounced in Modern Greek. A fricative is a sound with friction, in which instead of cleanly stopping the flow of air, the articulating body parts buzz together. Some English speakers use the fricative sounds instead of aspirates in pronuncing classical Greek: φ like English "f," θ like "th" in "think," and χ like English "k" or like German or Scots "ch."

Double consonants must both be pronounced, as in English *tub-boat, black-cat, midday, full-liberty, home-made, ten-nights, stop-press, fur-rug, this-sort, that-time*. For example, ἄλλος "other" is pronounced "al-los" with two audible "l" sounds.

We have now accounted for 21 of the 24 Greek letters. The other three letters represent double consonant sounds: ξ = κσ, ψ = πσ, and ζ = σδ. These sounds are always written with these letters. That is, if a word whose stem ends in κ receives a suffix or ending beginning with σ, the resulting word will be spelled with ξ, never with κσ, and similarly for the other combinations. For example, many verbs take the suffix σ to form the aorist (the normal past tense), as λύω "release," root λυ-, aorist form ἐ + λυ + σα, ἔλυσα. The verb βλέπω "see" forms its aorist the same way, but we write ἐ + βλεπ + σα as ἔβλεψα, using ψ for the sound of π plus σ.

Accent

Every Greek word, except a few, has an **accent**, which originally marked the raising of the tone of voice, not stress as in English. It is possible, with careful practice from the first, to raise the pitch on these syllables (as little stress as possible being used) and to observe quantity at the same time.

There are three accent marks, the **acute** (ά), the **circumflex** (ᾶ), and the **grave** (ὰ). The acute simply sounds like a raised pitch: the syllable whose vowel has an acute accent is pronounced at a higher pitch than the rest of the word. The grave is used instead of the acute when the acute would be on the last syllable of a word and another (non-enclitic) word follows it, as καλή "beautiful" but καλὴ φωνή "beautiful voice" with grave accent.

The circumflex denotes a raising and lowering of pitch on one vowel, as in *no!* pronounced in a surprised tone of voice (*nô!*). This accent, therefore, can only stand on a long vowel or diphthong, because it involves two different pitches.

When a vowel has both an accent and a breathing, the breathing is written before the acute or grave accent and under the circumflex, as ὅ, ὃ "what" (relative pronoun), ὦ "oh" (used with the name of someone you are addressing by name). When a diphthong has an accent or breathing, it is written on the second vowel letter, as οὖ, οὔ, οὒ, οὐ.

Accents are a basic part of the sound system of ancient Greek and essential to the spelling, just as they are in French, Spanish, or Italian. As in those languages, there are sets of words in Greek that are the same except for their accent. For example, consider θέον, θεόν, θέων, and θεῶν. The first two of these have a short ŏ sound in the second syllable and the other two have a long ō. The first and third have an acute accent on the first syllable, while the other two are accented on the second syllable. They are all different: θέον "running," referring to a thing, like "running water"; θεόν "god," in the form used for the direct object; θέων "running," referring to a male person, like "running boy"; θεῶν "gods'," the plural possessive.

General rules for accents: The accent in a Greek word can only be on one of the last three syllables, never earlier. This rule is often called the **law of limitation**. The circumflex must be on one of the last two syllables; the acute may be on any of the last three. If the last syllable has a long vowel, the acute must be on one of the last two syllables; this is the **long vowel rule**. As noted above, if the last syllable has an acute accent, that accent will usually be written as grave.

You learn the accent of a word as part of the spelling and pronunciation of the word. Different forms of the same word may have different accents, to conform to the general rules. For example: ἄνθρωπος "person," in the nominative singular (form used for the subject), has an acute on its third-to-last syllable. The same word in the nominative dual is ἀνθρώπω. Because the last syllable of this form has a long vowel, the acute accent cannot remain on the third-to-last syllable, so moves to the second-to-last. Be careful to pronounce each form with its correct accent; this may be tricky because it's rare for English words to have different stress in different forms.

There are more specific rules, and patterns of accent, which you will learn as you go along; see chapter 4.

A few words are only used in combination with others which go before them. These have no accent, and are called **enclitics**. They generally throw an accent back upon the last syllable of the word before. For example, in παιδίον διδάσκαλός τε, "child and teacher," the word διδάσκαλος "teacher" gains a second accent from the following enclitic τε "and."

A few other words, standing first in a phrase, have no accent; these are called **proclitics** (as εἰ "if," εἰς "into," ἐν "in").

But a *normal* word, in *normal* circumstances, will have exactly one accent.

Punctuation. The punctuation marks in Classical Greek are (,) comma, (·) colon, (.) period or full stop, (;) question mark. They are used much as in English. Normally there is no capital letter at the start of a sentence. Quotation marks are usually not used, but are occasionally used in this book for clarity.

I.2 Exercises on the Alphabet

1. Learn the following poem, adapted from a fifth-century play called *The Alphabet Comedy*:

    ἔστ᾽ ἄλφα, βῆτα, γάμμα, δέλτα, καὶ τὸ εἶ,
    ζῆτ᾽ , ἦτα, θῆτ᾽ , ἰῶτα, κάππα, λάμβδα, μῦ,
    νῦ, ξῖ, τὸ οὖ, πῖ, ῥῶ, τὸ σῖγμα, ταῦ, τὸ ὖ,
    φῖ, χῖ τε καὶ ψῖ καὶ τὸ ὦ· τὰ γράμματα.

    > ἔστ᾽ short for ἔστι "there is"
    > καί "and"

τό "the," the definite article, neuter singular

τε "and," like Latin -*que*, often used in pairs or together with καί

τὰ γράμματα "the letters," plural of τὸ γράμμα

When a word ending with a short vowel, like ζῆτα in the second line, comes before a word beginning with a vowel, the first vowel is often omitted or **elided**, with an apostrophe to mark the **elision**.

2. Make up syllables combining a consonant and a vowel or diphthong, like this: βῆτα ἄλφα, βα. βῆτα εἶ, βε. βῆτα ἦτα, βη. βῆτα ἰῶτα, βι. βῆτα οὖ, βο. βῆτα ὔ, βυ. βῆτα ὦ, βω. βῆτα ἄλφα ἰῶτα, βαι. βῆτα εἶ ἰῶτα, βει. βῆτα οὖ ἰῶτα, βοι. and so on. Do the same thing with the other consonants. Practice writing and pronouncing these combinations. Practice them with accents as well: βά, βᾶ, and so on.

3. Alphabetical order. Each of the following groups of words has something in common. Put each group into alphabetical order, and see if you can determine what each group has to do with.

   Group 1: Ζεύς, Ἀθηνᾶ, Ἥρα, Δημήτηρ, Ἑρμῆς, Διόνυσος, Ἀφροδίτη, Ἀπόλλων, Ἄρτεμις, Ἥφαιστος, Ἄρης, Ποσειδῶν

   Group 2: λέων, μῦς, κύων, αἴλουρος, ἐλέφας, πάνθηρ, γαλῆ, ἵππος, πάρδαλις, ἄρκτος, βοῦς, αἴξ, ψιττακός

   Group 3: Σοφοκλῆς, Βακχυλίδης, Ὅμηρος, Ἀριστοφάνης, Μένανδρος, Θουκυδίδης, Εὐριπίδης, Αἰσχύλος, Πίνδαρος, Πλάτων

   Group 4: Μήδεια, Οἰδίπους, Προμηθεύς, Ἱππόλυτος, Ἀνδρομάχη, Ἠλέκτρα, Ἰφιγένεια, Ἀντιγόνη, Φιλοκτήτης, Αἴας

   Group 5: Ἀχαρνῆς, Ἱππῆς, Νεφέλαι, Σφῆκες, Εἰρήνη, Ὄρνιθες, Λυσιστράτη, Θεσμοφοριάζουσαι, Βάτραχοι, Ἐκκλησιάζουσαι, Πλοῦτος

I.3 Overview of the grammatical system

Greek is an **inflected language**. That means that words take on different forms when they have different grammatical functions. Modern English has a rudimentary inflectional system; Old English, before the Norman Conquest of 1066, had a much more elaborate system, similar to Greek. In Modern English, a noun may have four different forms: *child* (singular, the basic form), *children* (the plural), *child's* (singular possessive), *children's* (plural possessive). Pronouns also have varying forms, for example: *we* (used as the subject of a sentence), *us* (not the subject), *our* (possessive). A Greek noun may in principle have as many as fifteen different forms, for subject, possession, indirect object, direct object, and direct address (calling to someone), in singular, dual, and plural.

Similarly, Greek verbs take on more forms than English. An English verb may have as many as five forms: *sing* (the basic form, for the present tense and other uses), *sings* (used as present tense when the subject is singular), *sang* (the past tense form), *singing* (the present participle), *sung* (the past participle). A Greek verb has different forms for each of three persons (I or we; you; he, she, it, they), in each of three numbers (singular, dual, plural), six tenses (present, imperfect, future, aorist, perfect, pluperfect), three voices (active, middle, passive), and six moods (indicative, imperative, subjunctive, optative, infinitive, participle). Most English tenses are formed with auxiliary verbs: "she will sing" for the future, or "she had sung" for the pluperfect. Similarly, the English passive uses auxiliary verbs: "the song is being sung" (present), "the song was sung" (past). Greek (almost) never uses auxiliary verbs, instead using different forms of the main verb for different times and types of action.

Every word in Greek consists of a **stem** and an **ending**. Verbs have six different stems for the different tenses; nouns always have the same stem. The ending added to the stem tells you the particular function this word could have: third-person singular active voice (compare "sings"), direct object (compare "him"), or whatever it may be.

Thus, to determine what a Greek word is doing in a sentence, you need to look at its ending — βλέπε εἰς τὴν οὐράν, look at the tail!

The stem is formed from the **root**, which is the most basic form of the word. Sometimes different related words will be formed from the same root. To make a stem from a root, Greek may add a **prefix**, a **suffix**, or an **infix**, sometimes more than one. A prefix is something added at the beginning, a suffix at the end, and an infix is added inside the root. For example, the root λαβ means "take." The present tense of the verb "take," third person singular ("he takes"), is λαμβάνει, which is λαβ with infix μ, suffix αν, and ending ει. The past tense (the **aorist**, for which see chapter 5) in the same person and number ("he took") is ἔλαβε, which is the same root with prefix ἔ and ending ε. The noun meaning "handle" (what you use to take something with) is λαβή, again from the same root with the ending η (there's also a suffix, but it's invisible because it has been contracted with the ending vowel). The noun meaning "acceptance, receipt, act of taking" is λῆψις, with a stronger form of the root and the suffix σις to make an abstract noun.

I.4 Sketch of the history of the Greek language

The first written records of the Greek language come from the middle of the second millenium BC. These are clay tablets from archives in Mycenae, Pylos, and other cities. They are written not in the familiar alphabet but in a **syllabary** called **Linear B**; a syllabary is a writing system with one symbol for each syllable, not for each individual sound. The language is recognizably Greek, though not exactly the same as the classical Attic of about a thousand years later, nor the same as Modern Greek.

Greek belongs to the **Indo-European** language family, along with English, Latin, Sanskrit, Russian, Irish, and many other languages. These languages are called a family because they all descend from a common ancestor, called **Proto-Indo-European**, spoken in Eastern Europe, north of the Caspian Sea, roughly 6,000 years ago. There are other language families, such as Sino-Tibetan, including Chinese; Semitic, including Hebrew and Arabic; Bantu, including Swahili; Algonquian, including Mohegan and Cree; and many more. Linguists recognize a family because of a systematic pattern of correspondances among languages, one that cannot be accounted for by borrowing or language contact. Words that are descended independently from a common ancestor are called **cognate**. Examples of cognates in Indo-European are:

- Greek κύων, Latin *canis*, Sanskrit *śvan*, English *hound*
- Greek μῦς, Latin *mus*, Sanskrit *mūṣ*, English *mouse*
- Greek βοῦς, Latin *bos*, Sanskrit *go*, English *cow*

Although these words may not *look* similar at first glance, it turns out that there is a systematic set of **sound shifts** relating them. A sound shift is a change in pronunciation that affects a particular sound everywhere it occurs in a particular way (for example, whenever it is between vowels, or whenever it is the first sound in a word). Sound shifts are the main way languages change. The Great Vowel Shift in English, mentioned above, is one example.

Another important sound shift between Proto-Indo-European (normally abbreviated **PIE**) and English is **Grimm's Law**, a shift affecting consonants. This sound shift is the main reason English words look and sound different from their cognates in Greek. Grimm's Law says (roughly):

- Voiced aspirate consonants lose their aspiration: *bh, dh, gh* in PIE become *b, d, g* in English
- Voiced un-aspirate consonants lose their voicing: *b, d, g* in PIE become *p, t, k* in English
- Unvoiced unaspirate consonants become fricatives: *p, t, k* in PIE become *f, th, h* in English

Thus in PIE *kwon*, "dog," the initial sound becomes an "h" sound in English, while it does not change in Greek or Latin, and becomes a palatal sibilant in Sanskrit (a "sh" sound). The same shifts affect *every* word that has the inherited "k" sound.

Some English words are related to Greek because they have been "borrowed" from Greek, taken over unchanged or created within English from Greek elements. These are called **derivatives**. The word *cynic* is a derivative from Greek κύων: there were some philosophers who were called "dogs" (not by their friends!), and we have kept the name to refer to their attitude. More obviously, the word *canine* is a derivative from Latin *canis*. As a general rule, the Greek word will be more easily recognizable in its English derivatives than in its English cognates.

One pervasive feature of PIE which contributes to word formation in Greek is **ablaut**, a pattern of changes in vowels. In different forms of a word, or different words from the same root, the root vowel may appear in any of three different forms or "grades," called **e grade**, **o grade**, and **zero grade**. If the vowel is an *e*, we have e grade; if it's *o*, o grade; and if it's not there at all, we have zero grade. For example, the root *leip-* (originally *leikw-* but a sound shift in Greek changes the final consonant to *p*) means "leave, abandon." Greek has inherited a verb and an adjective from this root. The verb has e grade in the present tense, λείπει "he leaves." It has o grade in the perfect tense, λέλοιπε "he has left"; note the root syllable is the second syllable in this form, and between the λ and the ιπ we have o instead of ε. The verb has zero grade in the aorist (past) tense, ἔλιπε "he left": this time, there is nothing at all between the λ and the ιπ. The adjective λοιπός "left over, remaining" has o grade. This pattern is common: e grade in the present tense, zero grade in the past tense, o grade in the perfect tense and in nouns and adjectives. The same pattern is visible in Latin, for example *tegit* "he covers," a present-tense form with e grade, and *toga*, an o-grade noun meaning the clothing a Roman covers himself with. This pattern also stands behind English vowel alternations in forms like *sing, sang, sung* and the related noun *song*, though the details have been obscured by other changes in the history of English.

Greek itself has changed in the course of nearly 4,000 years of history. In this book we focus on classical Attic, the language of the Athenian city-state in the 5th and 4th centuries BC. The earliest attested Greek, as noted above, is from Mycenae and other cities, so it is often called **Mycenaean Greek**. The basic grammatical system is close to classical Attic, but several sound shifts are still in the future. The Mycenaean period of the Greek language lasts until about 1200 BC.

Archaic Greek includes the language of the great epics, the *Iliad* and the *Odyssey*, often called **epic Greek** or **Homeric Greek**. Other archaic poetry is composed in **Aeolic** and **Doric**. The Aeolic dialect comes from the northeastern islands, in particular Lesbos. Major poets in this dialect are Sappho and Alcaeus. The Doric dialect is associated with Sparta and the Peloponnese. Major archaic poets in Doric Greek include Tyrtaeus and Stesichorus.

At first, poets used their own local dialects, but by the 5th century BC, it was customary to use particular dialects for particular kinds of verse, imitating the canonical writers of the archaic period. Thus the spoken dialogue of drama is written in Attic, because drama is an Athenian invention. (Attica is the name of the territory whose principal city is Athens, so "Attic" roughly means "Athenian.") The songs in drama, however, are in Doric, because the greatest poets of choral song used Doric. And lyric for a single singer, including love poetry, party songs, and praise songs, is usually in Aeolic.

Later, as Greek civilization spread through the Mediterranean, a "common" or "shared" form of the language developed, normally called **Koine** from Greek κοινὴ γλῶττα "common language." This is the dialect used by the writers of the Christian *New Testament*. It is quite close to classical Attic. There are a couple of sound shifts that Attic has that Koine, like most other dialects, does not. For example the word γλῶττα "tongue, language" is an Attic form, corresponding to γλῶσσα in other dialects. There are also some small grammatical differences, for example the "OOO rule" no longer applies in Koine (see chapter 8). But once you can read Attic, you may not even notice the differences as you read Koine.

After the fall of the Roman empire, the Greek civilization that continued in the Eastern Mediterranean is called Byzantine, from its capital at Byzantium, and its variety of Greek is **Medieval Greek**. The Byzantine empire had a strong scholarly community who wrote in classicizing style, imitating classical Attic as closely as possible; their writing is also called **Byzantine Greek**. Compare the situation in Western Europe at roughly the same time, with classical Latin in use by scholars and the medieval Romance vernaculars developing in daily use. Scholarly Byzantine Greek, like Renaissance Latin, is essentially the same as the classical form of the language, while the language people spoke in ordinary life is different.

From AD 1453 the language is referred to as **Modern Greek**. The main outlines of the grammatical system are still recognizable, but there have been some changes, especially to the verb system. There have also been significant sound shifts, with the result that Modern Greek and Ancient Greek do not sound alike. The writing system has also changed just a little: Modern Greek no longer uses the three accent marks or the two breathing marks that are standard for classical Greek. But despite the changes, there is a clear family resemblance and a definite line of development directly from the Mycenaean Linear B tablets down to the present day.

I.5 Useful phrases

Here are some words and phrases you will use in the classroom. In later chapters you will learn how the phrases work and why they mean what they do; for now, simply learn them.

χαῖρε, ὦ διδάσκαλε	Hello, teacher/professor (when the teacher is male)
χαῖρε, ὦ διδασκάλη	Hello, teacher/professor (when the teacher is female)
χαίρετε, ὦ μαθηταί	Hello, students
χαῖρε καὶ σύ	Hello to you, too
ἀρχώμεθα	Let's begin
ναί	yes
οὔ *or* οὐχί	no
ἑλληνιστί	in Greek
ἀγγλιστί	in English
δῆλόν ἐστι	it is clear
ἆρα δῆλόν ἐστι;	is it clear? (do you understand?)
τί σημαίνει τὸ "…";	what does "…" mean?
τίς ὁ νοῦς;	what is the sense (of a passage)? what is the main idea?
τὸ ποιητέον ἔργον	homework
τὸ ἐπιτήδευμα *or* ἡ ἄσκησις	exercise, practice
ἀναγίγνωσκε *or* ἀνάγνωθι	read (instruction to one person)
ἀναγιγνώσκετε	read (to several people)
πόρρω	further, go on, keep going
γράψαι ἐν τῷ πίνακι	write on the board (instruction to one person)
γράψατε ἐν τῷ πίνακι	(to several people)
γράφω	I am writing
ἡ γύψος	chalk
αἶρε τὴν χεῖρα	raise your hand (to one person)
αἴρετε τὰς χεῖρας	raise your hands (to several people)
εὖ ἐποίησας	well done (to one person)
εὖ ἐποιήσατε	(to several people)
καὶ τὰ λοιπά	and so on, *et cetera*

CHAPTER II

Beautiful Helen

II.1 Questions and answers

As you saw in chapter 1, "yes" is ναί and "no" in answer to a question is οὔ or οὐχί. To negate a word within a sentence, use οὐ "not" (before unaspirated vowels οὐκ, before aspirated vowels οὐχ), the negative of plain denial (categorical negative); or μή "not," used in prohibitions, conditions, and abstract ideas. Thus, used alone, οὔ would mean "no," and μή "don't."

Most kinds of clauses and phrases are negated with οὐ, but some require μή; you will learn this as you learn each new kind of construction.

The difference among the three forms οὐ, οὐκ, and οὐχ is called **sandhi** (a Sanskrit word, pronounced "SUN-dee"). Sandhi refers to the way sounds change when they are put together. **External sandhi** is a change to a word depending on the form of a nearby word; **internal sandhi** is a change inside a word, for example to a root when it is combined with a suffix. Sandhi occurs in English as well: consider the difference between *a cat* and *an elephant*. The words "a" and "an" mean the same thing; they are in fact sandhi forms of the same word, one used before consonants and the other before vowels.

In this table are basic question words for reference; you will learn them in depth in chapter 4.

	Direct Question	Indirect Question	Relative	Indefinite
who	τίς	ὅστις	ὅς	τις, some one
where	ποῦ	ὅπου	οὗ	που, some where
whence, from where	ποθέν	ὁπόθεν	ὅθεν	πόθεν, some-whence
whither, to where	ποῖ	ὅποι	οἷ	ποι, some-whither
when	πότε	ὁπότε	ὅτε	ποτέ, some time
how	πῶς	ὅπως	ὡς	πως, somehow

	Direct Question	Indirect Question	Relative	Indefinite
how great	πόσος	ὁπόσος	ὅσος	ποσός, some size
what kind	ποῖος	ὁποῖος	οἷος	ποιός, some kind

Of these words, the first set, meaning "who," and the last two, meaning "how great, how big, how much" and "what kind," are pronouns or adjectives, so they have different forms in the different cases and numbers. The others are indeclinable adverbs.

ἆρα marks a sentence as a question; it goes first in its clause. Compare Latin *-ne*.

ἆρ᾽ οὐ marks a question whose answer should be "yes." Compare Latin *nonne*. In English we would use a **tag question** like "isn't it? don't you?" but in Greek we do not. So "You understand, don't you?" would be ἆρ᾽ οὐ μανθάνεις; in Greek.

Interrogative words always have the accent. The indefinite words are enclitic, so they usually have no accent; this is how you can tell them apart.

Here are some words useful in answering questions.

ἐνθάδε	here	νῦν	now
ἐνθένδε	hence	τότε	then
δεῦρο	hither	καί	and
εὖ	well	ἀλλά	but
κακῶς	badly	ὦ	O
ἐκεῖ	there	εἰ	if
ἐκεῖθεν	thence	ἐπεί, ἐπειδή	since, when, because
ἐκεῖσε	thither		

II.2 Nouns: first and second declension

There are three classes of Greek nouns, called **declensions**. The first declension comprises nouns whose stem ends in α or η; they are sometimes called **a-stem nouns** as a result. Most of them are feminine, with a few that are masculine and none that are neuter.

Nouns of the second declension have stems ending in ο, which may change to ε in some forms. These are thus the **o-stem nouns**. Most of them are masculine or neuter, but there are also a few that are feminine.

Finally, the third declension is the **consonant-stem nouns**, including also the nouns with stems in ι and υ. These can have any of the three genders, masculine, feminine, or neuter. You will learn the third declension in chapter 8.

There are three numbers: **singular, dual,** and **plural.** The singular is used for one thing. The plural is used for more than one, but when we speak of a pair of things, or of two things or people that are closely connected, we may use the dual. Thus "the child" is singular, τὸ παιδίον. "The children" is plural, τὰ παιδία. "The two children" may be dual, τὼ παιδίω, particularly if they are siblings or best friends.

There are three **genders**, masculine, feminine, and neuter. Usually words for people or animals have the appropriate gender, so for example θεός "god" is masculine and θεά "goddess" is feminine. But there are some exceptions, as παιδίον "child" is neuter. Words for things may be any gender. The gender of a noun determines the form of adjectives that modify it, as you will see in the next section. It is necessary to learn the gender of a noun as part of learning the word.

Nouns have five cases, **nominative, genitive, dative, accusative,** and **vocative,** each corresponding to a different group of grammatical functions. Learn the cases in this order. The following are the most basic functions of each case, though not an exhaustive list.

The nominative is used for the subject of a sentence. In a sentence like "The woman loves the child," "woman" would be nominative in Greek. The nominative is also used for the predicate nominative in copular sentences: in "The woman is a teacher," "teacher" would be nominative.

The genitive is used for possession, for separation, and for value. For example, "I see the woman's child." Here "woman" would be genitive in Greek. "I am coming out of the house" shows separation; "house" would be genitive. "I will buy the book for three obols" shows value; "obols" would also be genitive.

The dative is used for the indirect object, for place, and for an instrument. For example, in "I give the child a book," "child" is the indirect object and would be dative in Greek. "I am in the house" shows place and would use the dative form of "house." "I write with a pen" shows instrument; "pen" would be dative in Greek.

The accusative is used for the direct object and for motion toward something. Thus in "I give the child a book," "book" would be accusative in Greek because it is the direct object. "I am going into the house" shows motion toward; "house" would be accusative.

Although Greek has plenty of prepositions analogous to "of, out of, to, with, in" in English, many constructions that require prepositions in English are expressed with the case alone in Greek. English needs prepositions to clarify the relationship between two nouns, since English nouns have so few forms. Greek does not.

These are the forms of a first-declension noun: τύχη, "fortune, luck." This noun is feminine. Its stem is τύχη-.

Case	Form	Ending
singular		
nominative	τύχη	-η
genitive	τύχης	-ης
dative	τύχῃ	-ῃ
accusative	τύχην	-ην
vocative	τύχη	-η
dual		
nom., acc., voc.	τύχᾱ	-ᾱ
gen., dat.	τύχαιν	-αιν

Case	Form	Ending
plural		
nom., voc.	τύχαι	-αι
gen.	τυχῶν	-ῶν
dat.	τύχαις	-αις
acc.	τύχᾱς	-ᾱς

In the first declension, the vocative is always the same as the nominative.

These are the forms of a second-declension noun: ἄνθρωπος, "person, human being, man, woman." This noun is usually masculine, but can be feminine if it refers to a woman. Its stem is ἄνθρωπο-.

Case	Form	Ending
singular		
nominative	ἄνθρωπος	-ος
genitive	ἀνθρώπου	-ου
dative	ἀνθρώπῳ	-ῳ
accusative	ἄνθρωπον	-ον
vocative	ἄνθρωπε	-ε (the stem with e instead of o)
dual		
nom., acc., voc.	ἀνθρώπω	-ω
gen., dat.	ἀνθρώποιν	-οιν
plural		
nom., voc.	ἄνθρωποι	-οι
gen.	ἀνθρώπων	-ων
dat.	ἀνθρώποις	-οις
acc.	ἀνθρώπους	-ους

In the second declension, the vocative is almost always the same as the nominative. The exception is the masculine singular, when the vocative is the bare stem with **e grade** of the stem vowel (see chapter 1 section 4).

These are the forms of a second-declension neuter noun: παιδίον, "child."

Case	Form	Ending
singular		
nominative	παιδίον	-ον
genitive	παιδίου	-ου
dative	παιδίῳ	-ῳ
accusative	παιδίον	-ον
vocative	παιδίον	-ον
dual		
nom., acc., voc.	παιδίω	-ω
gen., dat.	παιδίοιν	-οιν
plural		
nom., voc.	παιδία	-α
gen.	παιδίων	-ων
dat.	παιδίοις	-οις
acc.	παιδία	-α

For all neuter nouns, of any declension, the nominative and accusative are the same. The ending for the neuter plural nominative and accusative is always -α. (This is true in Latin as well: compare Latin *bellum* "war," plural *bella*.)

In the vocabulary or in a dictionary, the entry for a noun will give its **principal parts**: the nominative singular, genitive singular, and definite article to show gender. (See below for the forms of the article.) To find out the stem of the noun, look at the genitive singular and remove the ending. To find out what declension the noun belongs to, look at what ending the genitive has: -ης for first declension, -ου for second, -ος for third (as you will see in chapter 8). **Principal parts** are a standard set of forms for an inflected word from which you can determine all of the word's stems. In Greek, nouns, adjectives, and verbs have principal parts.

Exercises

1. Write out the complete declension of ἀκοή, -ῆς, ἡ "hearing"; of θεός, -οῦ, ὁ "god"; and of βιβλίον, -ου, τό "book."

2. If you know Latin or Sanskrit, or can find the forms in a reference grammar, compare the endings for the first declension (Latin a-stems, like *femina* "woman"; Sanskrit ā-stems, like *senā* "army") with the Greek first declension endings. Do the same for the second declension (Latin o-stems, like *lupus* "wolf"; Sanskrit ă-stems, like *nara* "man"). Can you see a family resemblance?

II.3 Adjectives

Adjectives modify or qualify nouns. In English they are words like "good, strong, beautiful." In Greek, an adjective agrees with the noun it modifies, in number, gender, and case. Thus if you see a feminine genitive singular adjective, it must be modifying a feminine genitive singular noun. Normally, in prose, adjectives will be close to the nouns they modify.

Greek adjectives belong to the same declensions as nouns. Some adjectives are first-and-second declension, with first declension forms in the feminine and second declension forms in the masculine and neuter. Some are first-and-third declension, with first declension forms in the feminine and third declension for the other two genders. Some are purely third declension, and a few are purely second declension. In this chapter we will learn first-and-second declension adjectives.

The forms of adjectives are just like those of nouns of the same declension, so this chart, with the forms of καλός, "beautiful," also shows the forms of first and second declension nouns. The principal parts of an adjective are the three nominative singular forms.

Case	Masculine	Feminine	Neuter
singular			
nominative	καλός	καλή	καλόν
genitive	καλοῦ	καλῆς	καλοῦ
dative	καλῷ	καλῇ	καλῷ
accusative	καλόν	καλήν	καλόν
vocative	καλέ	καλή	καλόν
dual			
nom., acc., voc.	καλώ	καλά	καλώ
gen., dat.	καλοῖν	καλαῖν	καλοῖν
plural			
nom., voc.	καλοί	καλαί	καλά
gen.	καλῶν	καλῶν	καλῶν
dat.	καλοῖς	καλαῖς	καλοῖς
acc.	καλούς	καλάς	καλά

If you can, compare the Latin adjective *bonus, bona, bonum,* "good," or the Sanskrit *priya, priyā,* "dear."

One useful adjective is slightly irregular: πολύς "much." It is like καλός except in the nominative and accusative singular masculine and neuter:

Case	Masculine	Feminine	Neuter
nominative	πολύς	πολλή	πολύ
genitive	πολλοῦ	πολλῆς	πολλοῦ
dative	πολλῷ	πολλῇ	πολλῷ
accusative	πολύν	πολλήν	πολύ

The plural and dual are regular, with stem πολλ-.

The adjective agrees with its noun in number, gender, and case. This does *not* mean the noun and the adjective have to have the same ending! For example, καλὸς ἄνθρωπος "beautiful person, handsome man," but καλὴ ἄνθρωπος "beautiful woman" (remember that ἄνθρωπος can be either masculine or feminine).

II.4 The definite article and the relative pronoun

Case	Article ὁ, ἡ, τό			Relative pronoun ὅς, ἥ, ὅ		
	Masc.	Fem.	Neu.	Masc.	Fem.	Neu.
singular						
nominative	ὁ	ἡ	τό	ὅς	ἥ	ὅ
genitive	τοῦ	τῆς	τοῦ	οὗ	ἧς	οὗ
dative	τῷ	τῇ	τῷ	ᾧ	ᾗ	ᾧ
accusative	τόν	τήν	τό	ὅν	ἥν	ὅ
dual						
nom., acc.	τώ (all genders)			ᾧ (all genders)		
gen., dat.	τοῖν (all genders)			οἷν (all genders)		
plural						
nom.	οἱ	αἱ	τά	οἵ	αἵ	ἅ
gen.	τῶν	τῶν	τῶν	ὧν	ὧν	ὧν
dat.	τοῖς	ταῖς	τοῖς	οἷς	αἷς	οἷς
acc.	τούς	τάς	τά	οὕς	ἅς	ἅ

The **definite article** corresponds to English *the*. Nouns will have the article when they are definite, just like in English. They will also have them when they are general, as in French: οἱ ἄνθρωποι can mean "the people" (that we are talking about) or "people in general," much like *les hommes* in French. Proper names also have the article, particularly when the person being named is famous, or when he or she has been established as a character in the story: ὁ Ὅμηρος, Homer. But when a noun is indefinite, it stands alone: ἄνθρωπος "a person." There is no indefinite article in Greek.

A noun with its article (if it has one, as it usually does) make up a **noun phrase**. Adjectives, nouns in the genitive for possession, and other modifiers may be inside the noun phrase or outside it. When they are inside they are said to be in **attribute position** and when they are outside they are in **predicate position**. For example: ὁ καλὸς ἄνθρωπος has an adjective in attribute position, and ὁ ἄνθρωπος καλός has one in predicate position.

Modifiers in attribute position simply qualify the noun. They are part of the noun phrase, which is a complete sense unit.

Modifiers in predicate position add a new sense unit. In fact, a noun phrase plus a modifier in predicate position, or another noun phrase, make a complete sentence — there's no need for a linking verb like "is" or "was" to join them together. So: ὁ ἄνθρωπος καλός is a complete sentence telling you something about the man, and ἄνθρωπος ὁ Ὅμηρος tells you a fact about Homer. These are called **nominal sentences** because they're all noun, no verb. The subject is the noun phrase with the article (denoting "given" information, already known to the listener or reader) and the other modifier or noun phrase is the predicate. If both noun phrases have articles, the first one is the subject and the second is the predicate, for example ὁ ἄνθρωπος ὁ διδάσκαλος, "the (this) man is the teacher."

The possessive genitive also works as a modifier: τὸ τῆς ἀνθρώπου παιδίον is "the woman's child." Genitives, like adjectives, can be attributes or predicates: τὸ παιδίον τῆς ἀνθρώπου says "the child is the woman's," a nominal sentence whose predicate is a noun phrase in the genitive.

The definite article before a modifier alone makes that modifier into a noun phrase, with the noun omitted: ὁ καλός is "the beautiful (man, or other noun that is masculine in Greek)." In English we normally use a placeholder in constructions like this, "the beautiful one," but we can also use modifiers by themselves: "I'm going to Pat's" ("house" understood), "she's the best" (teacher, student, goalie, or whatever it is we're talking about), "the rich" ("people" understood). This construction is so common in Greek that it is sometimes hard to tell whether a word is a pure noun or an adjective with a noun understood. For example δοῦλος can be an adjective meaning "enslaved, serving" but it is so often used without ἄνθρωπος or another noun that it really acts like a noun itself, meaning "slave."

In fact, almost anything in Greek can become a noun phrase if it has the article in front of it, for example οἱ τότε, "the (ones living) then," ἡ ἐν τῷ κήπῳ, "the (woman) in the garden," τὸ ἐν τῷ βιβλίῳ, "the (thing/idea) in the book," and so on. The article was originally a demonstrative meaning "this," and in some of these phrases it still acts like a demonstrative. Note in particular ὁ μέν "this one" and ὁ δέ "that one, the other one," which can be used to introduce contrasting ideas: ὁ μὲν λέγει, ὁ δὲ ἀκούει: "this one (this man, person) speaks, that one (the other one) listens." Any form of the article can be used in this idiom, depending on what function the noun phrase has in the clause, for example: τὸ μὲν βιβλίον ὁρῶ, τὸν δὲ κάλαμον οὐχ ὁρῶ, "I see the book but not the pen." Or: τὸ μὲν ὁρῶ, τὸ δὲ οὔ, "I see this (thing) but not that (one)."

The **relative pronoun** joins together two sentences that refer to the same noun. One of the sentences becomes a subordinate clause, called a **relative clause**, with the relative pronoun in the place of the noun. For example: τὸ βιβλίον ὁρῶ. τὸ βιβλίον ἔχεις, "I see the book. You have the book." We may combine these into a single sentence: τὸ βιβλίον ὁρῶ, ὃ ἔχεις, "I see the book that you have." The relative pronoun replaces the noun in the subordinate clause. It is neuter singular, because βιβλίον is neuter singular. It is accusative, because it is the direct object of ἔχεις.

Further examples:

καλὸς ὁ ἄνθρωπος ὃν ὁρῶ.	The man that I see is handsome.
τὸν ἄνθρωπος ὁρῶ ὃς καλός ἐστι.	I see the man who is handsome.
ὁρῶ τὸν κάλαμον ᾧ γράφεις.	I see the pen with which you are writing, or I see the pen that you are writing with.
τῷ καλάμῳ γράφεις ὃν ὁρῶ.	You are writing with the pen that I see.

The noun that the pronoun replaces is called its **antecedent**. Every pronoun has an antecedent, which will always be the same gender and number, but may or may not be the same case. The antecedent of a relative pronoun is often a noun in the clause that the relative clause depends on, but for most other kinds of pronouns the antecedent generally is not even in the same sentence. For example: τίς γράφει; with the interrogative pronoun τίς, masculine or feminine nominative singular. Here the antecedent is the answer to the question: the speaker does not know who is writing. Or: ὁρῶ αὐτόν, "I see him" (see chapter 4 for the pronoun); here the antecedent is whatever man we have been talking about.

In English we often omit the relative pronoun: "The man I see is handsome" or "I see the man you gave the book to." In Greek the relative pronoun is never omitted.

The forms of the relative pronoun look very much like those of the definite article, except that the relative pronoun has a rough breathing where the article has τ, and the relative pronoun always has an accent.

Exercise

Write out all the forms of the noun phrases ὁ θεός "the god," ἡ διδασκάλη "the teacher," τὸ βιβλίον "the book," in all numbers and cases. Add a suitable adjective in attribute position.

II.5 The verb: present indicative active

These are the forms of the present indicative active: present tense, indicative mood, active voice. These forms are for action going on right now.

		(a) I loose	(b) I do	(c) I see	(d) I make clear
singular	1.	λύ-ω	ποι-ῶ	ὁρ-ῶ	δηλ-ῶ
	2.	λύ-εις	ποι-εῖς	ὁρ-ᾷς	δηλ-οῖς
	3.	λύ-ει	ποι-εῖ	ὁρ-ᾷ	δηλ-οῖ
dual	2.	λύ-ετον	ποι-εῖτον	ὁρ-ᾶτον	δηλ-οῦτον
	3.	λύ-ετον	ποι-εῖτον	ὁρ-ᾶτον	δηλ-οῦτον
plural	1.	λύ-ομεν	ποι-οῦμεν	ὁρ-ῶμεν	δηλ-οῦμεν
	2.	λύ-ετε	ποι-εῖτε	ὁρ-ᾶτε	δηλ-οῦτε
	3.	λύ-ουσι(ν)	ποι-οῦσι(ν)	ὁρ-ῶσι(ν)	δηλ-οῦσι(ν)

The **person** of a verb form indicates whether the subject is the speaker ("I, we" — **first person**), the hearer ("you" — **second person**), or someone else ("she, he, it, they" — **third person**). The subject answers the question "who?"; for a verb in the active voice, the subject is the one doing whatever the action is. The verb and its subject will always agree in person and number: if the subject is a single person, the verb is singular; if two, dual; if more, plural. The verb therefore indicates who the subject is, so λύω means "I loose" with no need to include a word for "I." Similarly, ποιεῖ means "he does" or "she does" or "it does," depending on the context, while ποιοῦσι is "they do." The subject, if included, will be in the nominative case.

The 3rd plur. -ν is used before vowels; this is another sandhi form.

There is no first person dual.

Notice how all the endings begin with -ε- or -ο-, either short or long. This is called the **theme vowel**, and the *e/o* alternation is **ablaut** (see chapter 1 section 4): some endings take **e grade** of the theme vowel and some take **o grade**. You will meet verbs without a theme vowel in chapter 9.

The first (λύω) is the ordinary type of verb; the other three are **contracted**. The endings are the same in all. In (*b*) the stem ends in -ε, which contracts with the endings: ποιέ-ω, ποιῶ, ποιέετον, ποιεῖτον. In (*c*) the stem ends in -α, which overpowers all endings except -ο. Thus α- and ω are the only vowels found in the contractions. In (*d*) the stem ends in -ο: δηλόομεν, δηλοῦμεν, etc. The complete table of vowel contractions is in Appendix 1, section 1. Observe the accent: when the first of the two vowels being contracted together has an acute accent (rising pitch, falling back down on the next syllable), the contraction has a circumflex (pitch rising and then falling on the same vowel).

In the vocabulary or in a lexicon, contracted verbs are written *without* contraction, so you can tell what the stem vowel is. You will see un-contracted forms in other dialects, but in Attic Greek these verbs are always pronounced and written with contraction.

Principal parts

Recall that the principal parts of an inflected word are a standard set of forms from which you can determine all the word's stems. A Greek verb has six principal parts, giving the stems for all the possible tenses and voices. Most of the time, the parts are predictable, but as there are several different patterns, you should learn all six principal parts whenever you learn a new verb.

Similarly in English: an English verb has only three principal parts, and they are *usually* formed in the standard way, but not invariably. The principal parts of an English verb are the present (the all-purpose form, used for first and second person singular and all plural forms of the present tense, and to form the infinitive), the preterite (the past tense form), and the past participle, as *love, loved, loved*. Usually the preterite and past participle are formed with *-ed*, but not always: consider *blink, blinked, blinked*, which is regular, but *think, thought, thought* and *drink, drank, drunk*. Although all three of these verbs have similar present forms, their other forms are different.

Just so, in Greek, *most* verbs have predictable principal parts, but not all, so you must learn the principal parts as part of learning the verb. The irregular or unpredictable verbs are some of the most common words in the language, so you will get plenty of practice with them.

The Standard Six Principal Parts of a Greek verb are all first-person singular indicative forms. They are:

- Present active
- Future active
- Aorist active (the aorist is a past tense; see chapter 5)
- Perfect active (the perfect is another tense; see chapter 14)
- Perfect middle/passive
- Aorist passive

Every form of the present tense, in all six moods and all three voices, is made from the stem of the first principal part. Forms of the future tense are made from the second principal part, and so on. Each principal part, and the forms built from its stem, can be called a **tense system**, so we have the **present system**, made up of forms made from the first principal part, the **future (active and middle) system** from the second, and so on.

The principal parts of λύω are: λύω, λύσω, ἔλυσα, λέλυκα, λέλυμαι, ἐλύθην. The corresponding stems are: λῡ-, λῡσ-, λῡσ-, λελυκ-, λελυ-, λυθη-.

Exercises

1. Write out the conjugation of γράφω, ἀκούω, and λέγω in the present indicative active.

2. Read the procedure for a **synopsis** of a verb in Appendix 1, section 5, and write a synopsis of βλέπω in 3rd singular.

II.6 Agreement

The form of a Greek word depends on its function and may also depend on other words that belong with it. A word **agrees** with another word if it must match that other word in one or more of the grammatical variables: case and number for nouns; gender, case, and number for adjectives and pronouns; person and number for verbs.

The Three Concords

- A verb and its subject agree in person and number.
- An adjective agrees with the noun it modifies in gender, case, and number.
- A pronoun agrees with its antecedent in gender and number.

These are the fundamental rules of agreement for Greek.

There is one exception to the first of the Three Concords. A *neuter plural* subject takes a *singular* verb. For example, we say τὰ παιδία γράφει, not τὰ παιδία γράφουσι.

II.7 Word order and syntax

In English, **word order** carries grammatical information. The difference between "the woman sees the teacher" and "the teacher sees the woman" is entirely in the word order: who sees whom depends on which noun phrase comes before the verb and which one comes after.

In Greek, this information comes from the endings of the nouns. The three phrases "the woman," "the teacher," and "sees" can be arranged in six different ways:

ἡ ἄνθρωπος τὸν διδάσκαλον βλέπει.

ἡ ἄνθρωπος βλέπει τὸν διδάσκαλον.

τὸν διδάσκαλον ἡ ἄνθρωπος βλέπει.

τὸν διδάσκαλον βλέπει ἡ ἄνθρωπος.

βλέπει ἡ ἄνθρωπος τὸν διδάσκαλον.

βλέπει τὸν διδάσκαλον ἡ ἄνθρωπος.

All six of them basically mean "the woman sees the teacher," because in all six of them "the woman" is in the nominative case, making it the subject, and "the teacher" is in the accusative case, making it the direct object. The case forms, not the word order, determine which noun is subject and which one is direct object.

Because word order does not carry *grammatical* information, it is free to do something else. In Greek, word order may have a **pragmatic** function, relating to how the sentence fits into the larger context. In general, what comes first is what the sentence is about, the **Topic** (the capital letter indicates that the word has its linguistic sense). Next is the essential new information the sentence is trying to convey, the **Focus**. And if we have not seen it yet, the verb comes next. Thus we can think of the basic word order as Topic, Focus, verb.

When there is an expressed subject, this is often the Topic. If the subject is the same from one sentence to the next, it is usually not repeated, so a new subject is usually new information. In a sentence like the third one above, the direct object comes first, so we assume this is the Topic, given information, and the subject is Focus, new information. This sentence might answer a question like "who sees the teacher?" — it's the woman who sees him, rather than the man. In the fourth sentence, the direct object is first again, but the verb is second, so we assume this is the essential new information, the Focus. This sentence might answer a question like "what is the woman doing with the teacher?"

In all six of these sentences, however, the woman is the subject and the teacher is the direct object: the basic meaning (who sees whom) is the same even though the order of the phrases is different.

Typically, the subject is not expressed unless it is new information, or unless there are several characters that need to be kept straight. When the same person is the subject of several successive main verbs, the subject will normally not be expressed, so for example if we have ἡ ἄνθρωπος τὸν διδάσκαλον βλέπει. βιβλίον οὐκ ἔχει, we assume it is the woman who doesn't have a book, because she's the current subject and nothing has told us otherwise.

In a more complicated sentence, there will be subordinate clauses or subordinate verb phrases. A **clause** is a finite verb with its subject (if explicitly expressed), object or other complement, and modifiers. A **verb phrase** is any verb along with its objects, complements, and modifiers, not including its subject. Every complete sentence has a **main clause**, in Greek just as in English.

Phrases and subordinate clauses stay together. That is, a noun phrase like ὁ ἀγαθὸς διδάσκαλος ("the good teacher") will not be interrupted by words belonging to other phrases of the sentence. If an adjective and a noun are separated, then they are not part of the same noun phrase but two different ones. For example: ὁ ἀγαθός ἐστι διδάσκαλος, "the good man is a teacher." Here ὁ ἀγαθός is one phrase, the subject, and διδάσκαλος is another, the predicate noun. Similarly, in the nominal sentence διδάσκαλος ὁ ἀγαθός, there are two noun phrases, once again subject and predicate noun.

One noun phrase may be part of another noun phrase, if it modifies or otherwise depends on the main noun. For example: τὸ τοῦ ἀνθρώπου παιδίον, "the man's child." Here the phrase τοῦ ἀνθρώπου, in the genitive case, modifies παιδίον: it is possessive. The phrase in the genitive is part of the larger phrase.

Similarly, subordinate clauses may be contained inside other clauses, including the main clause. For example: τὸ βιβλίον, ὃν γράφεις, ὁρῶ. The main clause is τὸ βιβλίον ὁρῶ, "I see the book." The subordinate clause is ὃν γράφεις, "that you are writing." This clause is contained inside the main clause because it modifies the noun βιβλίον, direct object of the main clause. (It answers the question "which book?" — the one you're writing.)

But clauses and phrases will not be interwoven: once a phrase or a subordinate clause starts, any other phrases or clauses that start within it must belong to it, must modify or depend on words in the higher-level phrase. Two clauses or phrases that do not have this kind of relationship will be separate.

For example, consider a sentence like this: ὁ διδάσκαλος ὃς βιβλία γράφει τὸν ἄνθρωπον βλέπει ὃς κάλαμον ἔχει. The sentence has one main clause and two subordinate clauses, one modifying each of the nouns in the main clause. The subordinate clause ὃς βιβλία γράφει ("who writes books") cannot be interrupted; once we see the relative pronoun ὃς we know that everything from here on must belong to the relative clause, until that clause is complete. Then we return to the still-incomplete main clause. When we see the next relative pronoun ὃς, we begin another, separate relative clause. Nothing inside the second relative clause can modify or depend on anything in the first relative clause, nor does anything in the first clause modify anything in this new one.

To **parse** a word in a Greek sentence means to explain its syntax: what function it has in the sentence. For a noun, this means why it is in a given case. For a verb, this means why it is in a given tense and mood. First identify what the form actually is, then say what it is doing.

To parse a noun, then, you first give its gender, case, and number, then its construction. For a pronoun, give gender, case, and number as for a noun, give the construction as for a noun, and indicate what noun is its antecedent. For an adjective, give gender, case, and number as for a noun, then say what noun it modifies and whether it is an attribute or a predicate. For example: ἡ κακὴ ἄνθρωπος τὸ βιβλίον τῷ ἄλλῳ ἀνθρώπῳ δηλοῖ. Parse the nouns as follows:

- ἄνθρωπος, feminine nominative singular, subject of δηλοῖ
- βιβλίον, neuter accusative singular, direct object of δηλοῖ
- ἀνθρώπῳ, masculine dative singular, indirect object of δηλοῖ.

Note how the articles and adjectives tell you what gender the forms of ἄνθρωπος are. To parse the adjectives in this sentence, say

- κακή, feminine nominative singular, modifies ἄνθρωπος in attribute position
- ἄλλῳ, masculine dative singular, modifies ἀνθρώπῳ in attribute position.

To parse a verb, give its person, number, tense, mood, and voice, then what kind of clause or phrase it belongs to. For example, οἱ διδάσκαλοι οἳ βιβλία γράφουσι τὼ ἀνθρώπω βλέπουσι ὣ κάλαμον ἔχετον. Parse these verbs as follows:

- γράφουσι, third person plural, present indicative active, verb of relative clause;
- βλέπουσι, third person plural, present indicative active, main verb of main clause;
- ἔχετον, third person dual, present indicative active, main verb of relative clause

And parse the pronouns in this sentence as follows:

- οἵ, masculine nominative plural, subject of γράφουσι, antecedent is διδάσκαλοι
- ὥ, masculine nominative dual, subject of ἔχετον, antecedent is ἀνθρώπω

Parsing is a way to demonstrate that you understand the grammar of a sentence. It is not as important as being able to read and understand the meaning of a paragraph.

II.8 Vocabulary

VERBS

ἀκούω, ἀκούσομαι, ἤκουσα, ἀκήκοα, – , ἠκούσθην, hear (cp. *acoustics*)

ἀπο-θνῄσκω, ἀποθανοῦμαι, ἀπέθανον, τέθνηκα, – , – , die

βλέπω, βλέψω, ἔβλεψα, βέβλεφα, βέβλεμμαι, ἐβλέφθην, see

γράφω, γράψω, ἔγραψα, γέγραφα, γέγραμμαι, ἐγράφην, write (cp. *graphic, telegraph*)

δηλόω, δηλώσω, ἐδήλωσα, δεδήλωκα, δεδήλωμαι, ἐδηλώθην, declare, make plain, show (cp. *psychedelic*)

ἔχω, ἕξω, ἔσχον, ἔσχηκα, ἔσχημαι, ἐσχέθην, have; with adverbs, used of a state, as εὖ ἔχω, I am well

λέγω, λέξω, ἔλεξα, – , λέλεγμαι, ἐλέχθην, speak, say

λύω, λύσω, ἔλῡσα, λέλυκα, λέλυμαι, ἐλύθην, loose, undo, annul

μανθάνω, μαθήσομαι, ἔμαθον, μεμάθηκα, – , – , learn (cp. *mathematics*)

ὁράω, ὄψομαι, εἶδον, ἑόρακα, ἑόραμαι, ὤφθην, see (cp. *optic*)

ποιέω, ποιήσω, ἐποίησα, πεποίηκα, πεποίημαι, ἐποιήθην, do, make (cp. *poet*)

φιλέω, φιλήσω, ἐφίλησα, πεφίληκα, πεφίλημαι, ἐφιλήθην, love (cp. *philanthropy*)

φωνέω, φωνήσω, ἐφώνησα, πεφώνηκα, πεφώνημαι, ἐφωνήθην, speak (cp. *telephone, phonetic*)

ἐστι, ἐστιν, is (cp. *is*, Latin *est*)

NOUNS

ἀκοή, ἀκοῆς, ἡ, hearing

ἄνθρωπος, ἀνθρώπου, ὁ, ἡ, human being (cp. *anthropology*)

βιβλίον, βιβλίου, τό, book (cp. *Bible*)

διδάσκαλος, διδασκάλου, ὁ, teacher; a female teacher is ἡ διδάσκαλος or ἡ διδασκάλη

θεός, θεοῦ, ὁ, ἡ, god (cp. *theology*)

κάλαμος, καλάμου, ὁ, pen

μεταβολή, μεταβολῆς, ἡ, change

ὀφθαλμός, ὀφθαλμοῦ, ὁ, eye (cp. *opthamology*)

παιδίον, παιδίου, τό, child (cp. *pedagogy*)

τύχη, τύχης, ἡ, fortune

φωνή, φωνῆς, ἡ, voice

ADJECTIVES

ἀγαθός, -ή, -ό, good

ἄλλος, ἄλλη, ἄλλο, other

δύστηνος, -ο, miserable

κακός, -ή, -ό, bad

καλός, -ή, -ό, fine, beautiful, noble (cp. *calligraphy*)

νέος, νέᾱ, νέον, young (cp. *new*)

ὅς, ἥ ὅ, who, which (relative pronoun; cp. *who*, L. *quis*)

ποῖος, ποίᾱ, ποῖον, of what kind?

πολύς, πολλή, πολυ, much

πόσος, -η, -ο, how large? (plural, how many?)

τι,(neuter of τίς), what?

τυφλός, -ῆ, -ό, blind

ADVERBS, CONJUNCTIONS, AND PARTICLES

εἰ, if

εὖ, well

καί, and, also, both

κακῶς, badly

πῶς, how?

τε, both, and (enclitic)

τοι, indeed, I tell you (enclitic)

Notes on the vocabulary

cp. means "compare." English and Latin words offered for comparison in the chapter vocabulary lists may be either **cognates** or **derivatives** of the Greek word; be sure to figure out which.

All six principal parts are given for verbs. For contracted verbs the first principal part is given in the *uncontracted* form so you can tell what the stem vowel is.

The verb ἀκούω takes a direct object when that object denotes a sound, as τὴν φωνὴν ἀκούει, but takes a genitive to indicate the source of the sound, or the person, animal, or object that is making the sound, as τοῦ διδασκάλου ἀκούει. Parse this as **genitive of source**.

In Attic Greek, original inherited long ā usually became η. This is why we call the first declension "a-stems" even though there does not appear to be an "a": it's still there in other dialects, but has changed in Attic. But after ε, ι, or ρ, the change did not happen. Thus the feminine forms of νέος have ā where those of καλός have η. You will meet some nouns that keep the ā in chapter 3.

Note the neuter nominative and accusative singular ἄλλο, ending in -o like the article τό rather than in -ον like most adjectives.

The difference between the two words for "and," καί and τε, is that καί comes between the two things it connects, like English *and,* but τε comes after. It is enclitic, just like Latin *que* and Sanskrit *ca* (which are cognates). So: κάλαμος καὶ βιβλίον, but κάλαμος βιβλίον τε. If the second item is a phrase, τε may go after the first word of the phrase, as ὁ κάλαμος τό τε βιβλίον. If two conjunctions are used together the effect is like English "both…and." In this case you might have καί both first and also in between the terms, or τε after each term, or τε after the first one and καί in between. For example, καὶ ὁ κάλαμος καὶ τὸ βιβλίον, κάλαμος τε βιβλίον τε, ὁ τε κάλαμος τό τε βιβλίον, ὁ τε κάλαμος καὶ τὸ βιβλίον, κάλαμος τε καὶ βιβλίον — these are five different ways to say the same thing.

II.9 Reading

The first three sentences are in verse, quoted from plays by Menander.

1. τυφλόν τε καὶ δύστηνόν ἐστιν ἡ τύχη.

2. τὸ τῆς τύχης τοι μεταβολὰς πολλὰς ἔχει.

>   Note the noun phrase τὸ τῆς τύχης, with no main noun: "fortune's thing," in the sense "what belongs to fortune."

3. ὃν οἱ θεοὶ φιλοῦσιν ἀποθνῄσκει νέος.

4. ἄνθρωπος ἔχει ἀκοὴν καὶ ἀκούει.

5. ἄνθρωπος ἔχει ὀφθαλμοὺς καὶ βλέπει.

6. ἄνθρωπος ἔχει ὀφθαλμοῖν καὶ βλέπει.

7. ἄνθρωπος ἔχει φωνὴν καὶ λέγει.

8. ἄνθρωπος ἔχει φωνὴν καὶ φωνεῖ.

9. ἔχομεν βιβλίον καὶ μανθάνομεν.

10. ἔχομεν κάλαμον καὶ γράφομεν.

11. τὰ παιδία καλάμους ἔχει καὶ γράφει.

　　　Remember that a neuter plural subject has a singular verb.

12. τοῖς ἀγαθοῖς βιβλίοις μανθάνομεν. εἰ ἄνθρωπος βιβλία μὴ ἔχει, παιδίον ἐστί. ἄνθρωπος ὃς βιβλία οὐκ ἔχει παιδίον ἐστί.

13. ὁ διδάσκαλος λέγει καὶ οἱ ἄνθρωποι ἀκούουσι.

14. τὸ παιδίον νέον, ὁ διδάσκαλος οὔ.

15. παιδίον ἐστὶ νέος ἄνθρωπος.

16. ὁ Οἰδίπους ἐστὶ παιδίον τῆς τύχης.

17. Ἑλένη ἐστι καλὴ ἄνθρωπος. καλὴ ἡ Ἑλένη. ὁ Ἀλέξανδρος τὴν Ἑλένην ὁρᾷ. φιλεῖ ὁ Ἀλέξανδρος τὴν καλὴν Ἑλένην. ἆρα ἡ Ἑλένη τὸν Ἀλέξανδρον φιλεῖ; τί ποιεῖ ἡ Ἑλένη; τί ποιεῖτον ἡ Ἑλένη καὶ ὁ Ἀλέξανδρος; ὁ Ὅμηρος λέγει.

18. τὸ βιβλίον τῷ παιδίῳ δηλῶ. τὸ παιδίον τὸ βιβλίον βλέπει. τὸ παιδίον τὸ βιβλίον ὁρᾷ. τὸ παιδίον τὸ βιβλίον βλέπει ὃ δηλῶ.

19. Μυρρίνη καὶ Νικόμαχος λέγετον.

　　Μυρρίνη· τί ποιεῖς, ὦ Νικόμαχε;

　　Νικόμαχος· βιβλίον γράφω, ὦ Μυρρίνη. εἰ εὖ γράφω, οἱ ἄλλοι ἄνθρωποι τῷ βιβλίῳ μανθάνουσι. τῷ βιβλίῳ τὴν τύχην δηλῶ. τὸ βιβλίον ἀγαθὸς διδάσκαλός ἐστι.

　　Μυρρίνη· καλῶς ποιεῖς, ὦ παιδίον. καλὸν βιβλίον γράφεις. τοῖς ἄλλοις τὴν τύχην δηλοῖς.

　　Νικόμαχος· τὰ ἀγαθὰ βιβλία οὐκ ἀποθνήσκει.

20. εἰ ὁ διδάσκαλος καλῶς λέγει, οἱ ἄνθρωποι μανθάνουσι. ἀλλὰ εἰ ὁ διδάσκαλος κακῶς λέγει, οὐκ ἀκούουσι. διδάσκαλος ὃς κακῶς λέγει κακὸς διδάσκαλός ἐστι. οὐ φιλοῦμεν διδάσκαλον ὃς κακῶς λέγει. οἱ ἄνθρωποι διδάσκαλον φιλοῦσι εἰ καλῶς λέγει, καὶ ἀκούουσι, καὶ πολλὰ μανθάνουσι.

21. ἄνθρωπος καλάμῳ γράφει. ἀνθρώπω καλάμοιν γράφετον. πολλοὶ ἄνθρωποι πολλοῖς καλάμοις γράφουσιν. τί γράφουσιν; βιβλία γράφουσιν.

22. ὁ δύστηνος ἄνθρωπος κακὴν τύχην ἔχει.

23. οἱ ἄνθρωποι ἀποθνήσκουσι. οἱ θεοὶ οὐκ ἀποθνήσκουσι. καλοὶ καὶ ἀγαθοὶ οἱ θεοί. οἱ θεοὶ ἀγαθοὺς ἀνθρώπους φιλοῦσι. κακοὺς ἀνθρώπους οὐ φιλοῦσι. εἰ ἀκούομεν τὴν τοῦ θεοῦ φωνήν, εὖ ἔχομεν.

24. ὁ Φίλιππος ἀγαθός ἐστι. κακοὶ ἄνθρωποι τὸν Φίλιππον ἔχουσι. ὦ Φίλιππε, δύστηνε, κακὴν τύχην ἔχεις! ὁρῶμεν τοὺς κακοὺς καὶ τὸν ἀγαθόν. βλέπομεν τὸν Φίλιππον καὶ τοὺς κακοὺς, οἳ Φίλιππον ἔχουσι. ἀκούομεν τὴν φωνήν. ἀκούομεν τὴν τοῦ Φιλίππου φωνήν. ὁ Φίλιππος λέγει, "κακῶς ἔχω!" τί ποιοῦσιν οἱ κακοί; οἱ κακοὶ τὸν ἀγαθὸν ἔχουσιν. λύομεν τὸν Φίλιππον. λέγομεν, "κακὸν ποιεῖτε, ὦ κακοί. ἀγαθὸς ὁ Φίλιππος." οἱ κακοὶ τὴν φωνὴν ἀκούουσι καὶ τὸν Φίλιππον λύουσι.

II.10 Conversation

The goals of the conversation exercise are to verify that students have understood the reading and to provide extra practice on the new vocabulary and forms. In the first few chapters sample exercises are written out in detail, but teachers should improvise and elaborate as necessary. Practice first with the vocabulary list and the readings, then close the book and review.

1. (compare readings 1, 2) ποῖόν ἐστιν ἡ τύχη; τυφλόν τε καὶ δύστηνόν ἐστιν ἡ τύχη. τί ἐστι δύστηνον; ἡ τύχη δύστηνόν ἐστιν. τί ἔχει ἡ τύχη; μεταβολὰς πολλὰς ἔχει ἡ τύχη. τί ἔχει μεταβολάς; ἡ τύχη ἔχει μεταβολάς. πόσας μεταβολάς; πολλάς.

2. (reading 12) τίσι μανθάνομεν; τοῖς ἀγαθοῖς βιβλίοις μανθάνομεν. ἆρα μανθάνομεν κακοῖς βιβλίοις; οὐχί, κακοῖς βιβλίοις οὐ μανθάνομεν. ποίοις βιβλίοις μανθάνομεν; ἀγαθοῖς. τίς ἐστι παιδίον; ἄνθρωπος ὃς βιβλία οὐκ ἔχει ἐστὶ παιδίον. εἰ ἄνθρωπος βιβλία μὴ ἔχει, τί ἐστι; ἔστι παιδίον. τί ἐστι ἄνθρωπος ὃς βιβλία οὐκ ἔχει; ἔστι παιδίον. τίς βιβλία οὐκ ἔχει; παιδίον βιβλία οὐκ ἔχει.

3. (reading 17) τίς ἐστι ἡ Ἑλένη; ποία ἐστὶ ἡ Ἑλένη; ἆρα καλή ἐστι; ἆρα κακή ἐστι; ἆρα θεός ἐστι;

   τίς ἐστι ἡ Ἑλένη; καλὴ ἄνθρωπος ἡ Ἑλένη. ποία ἐστὶ ἡ Ἑλένη; καλή ἐστι. ἆρα καλή ἐστι; ναί, καλή ἐστι ἡ Ἑλένη. ἆρα κακή ἐστι; οὐχί, οὐ κακή ἐστι, ἀλλὰ καλή. ἆρα θεός ἐστι; οὐκ ἔστι θεός, ἀλλὰ ἄνθρωπος.

4. (vocabulary) τί ἔχεις, ὦ παιδίον; ἀκοὴν ἔχω, ὦ διδάσκαλε. καὶ τί ποιεῖς ἀκοῇ; ἀκούω. πῶς ἀκούεις, ὦ παιδίον; εὖ ἀκούω, κακῶς ἀκούω. εἰ εὖ ἀκούεις, ποίαν ἀκοὴν ἔχεις; εἰ εὖ ἀκούω, καλὴν ἔχω ἀκοήν. εἰ κακῶς ἀκούεις, etc.

5. τί ἔχετον, ὦ Φίλιππε καὶ Μαρία; φωνὰ ἔχομεν, ὦ διδάσκαλε. λέγωμεν τοῖν φωναῖν. εἰ ὁ Φίλιππος λέγει, ἡ Μαρία ἀκούει. εἰ εὖ λέγετον, ποίαν φωνὰ ἔχετον; καλὰ φωνὰ ἔχομεν. καὶ ὁ Φίλιππος καὶ ἡ Μαρία καλὰς φωνὰς ἔχουσι.

   So with φωνή, ὀφθαλμός, βιβλίον, κάλαμος: e.g. τί ἄλλο ἔχεις; φωνὴν ἔχω, etc.

6. Chain Story Exercise. The first student makes a simple statement, such as ὁ διδάσκαλος βιβλίον ἔχει. The next student turns the previous main clause into a relative clause and adds a new main clause to advance the story, for example τὸ βιβλίον ὃ ὁ διδάσκαλος ἔχει κακόν ἐστι. The next student does it again, for example ὁ Σοφόκλης τὸ βιβλίον γράφει ὃ κακόν ἐστι. The connection between the previous student's statement (the new relative clause) and the new main clause can be as straightforward or silly as you like. To make a game of it, each student must repeat *all* the previous clauses, as in the nursery rhyme "The House that Jack Built." In this example we would have ὁ Σοφόκλης τὸ βιβλίον γράφει ὃ κακόν ἐστι ὃ ὁ διδάσκαλος ἔχει. A player who can't repeat the whole thing is out; last player left in wins.

II.11 Writing

1. Fill in the following to make complete sentences. You can choose any word that makes sense — serious or silly. You can use more than one word if you like.

   a. ὁ ἄνθρωπος τὴν φωνὴν _____.

   b. ἡ ἄνθρωπος τὸ παιδίον _____.

   c. ὁ διδάσκαλος τὸ βιβλίον _____.

   d. ἡ διδασκάλη τῷ παιδίῳ τὸ βιβλίον _____.

   e. τὸ παιδίον τὸν ἄνθρωπον _____.

   f. ὁ _____ τὴν φωνὴν ἀκούει.

   g. ὁ διδάσκαλος τὸ βιβλίον τῷ _____ δηλοῖ.

   h. ὁ διδάσκαλος τὸ _____ βιβλίον ἔχει.

   i. οἱ ἄνθρωποι τὴν φωνὴν _____.

   j. τὼ _____ τὴν _____ ἔχετον.

2. (The **change-number exercise**): In each of the following sentences, change the *main* verb to each of the other two numbers (where possible), and make the *minimum* number of other changes necessary for sense and grammar. For example, given ὁ ἄνθρωπος τὴν φωνὴν ἀκούει, whose main verb is singular, you would write one version in dual — τὼ ἀνθρώπω τὴν φωνὴν ἀκούετον — and one in plural — οἱ ἄνθρωποι τὴν φωνὴν ἀκούουσι. Since these make sense with τὴν φωνήν in singular, and there is no grammatical reason to change this noun phrase, this phrase stays the same in the revised sentences. Remember there are no first-person dual verb forms.

   a. ὁ ἄνθρωπος ἀποθνῄσκει.

   b. τὸ παιδίον βλέπεις.

   c. οἱ θεοὶ γράφουσι.

   d. τῷ καλάμῳ γράφω.

   e. τὸ παιδίον τὸν διδάσκαλον βλέπει.

   f. βιβλίον τῷ διδασκάλῳ δηλῶ.

   g. τὼ παιδίω πολλὰ βιβλία ἔχετον.

   h. ὁ ἀγαθὸς εὖ μανθάνει.

   i. τῇ φωνῇ λέγεις.

   j. κακὴ τύχη τοὺς ἀνθρώπους λύει.

   k. ἄνθρωπος τοῖν ὀφθαλμοῖν ὁρᾷ.

   l. ὁ κακὸς τοὺς θεοὺς οὐ φιλεῖ.

   m. ὁ ἄνθρωπος ὃν ὁρῶμεν εὖ μανθάνει.

   n. ὁ ἄνθρωπος ᾧ ὁ διδάσκαλος τὸ βιβλίον δηλοῖ εὖ μανθάνει.

   o. ὁ ἄνθρωπος ὃς βιβλία ἔχει εὖ μανθάνει.

3. Here are pairs of sentences containing the same noun. Turn them into complex sentences, making one the main clause and the other a relative clause. Make each of the two possible versions. For example, given ὁ ἄνθρωπος τὴν φωνὴν ἀκούει and τὸ βιβλίον τῷ ἀνθρώπῳ δηλοῦμεν, first make the first sentence the main clause: ὁ ἄνθρωπος, ᾧ τὸ βιβλίον δηλοῦμεν, τὴν φωνὴν ἀκούει. Then combine them the other way: τὸ βιβλίον τῷ ἀνθρώπῳ, ὃς τὴν φωνὴν ἀκούει, δηλοῦμεν.

    a. τῷ ἀνθρώπῳ φωνῶ. ὁ ἄνθρωπος εὖ ποιεῖ.

    b. τῷ ἀνθρώπῳ φωνῶ. τὸ παιδίον τοῦ ἀνθρώπου ὁρῶ.

    c. τῷ ἀνθρώπῳ φωνῶ. τὸ παιδίον τὸν ἄνθρωπον φιλεῖ.

    d. τῷ ἀνθρώπῳ φωνῶ. τῷ ἀνθρώπῳ τὸ βιβλίον δηλῶ.

    e. ὁ ἄνθρωπος τὸ παιδίον φιλεῖ. ὁ ἄνθρωπος κάλαμον ἔχει.

    f. ὁ ἄνθρωπος τὸ παιδίον φιλεῖ. ὁ διδάσκαλος τῷ ἀνθρώπῳ τὸ βιβλίον δηλοῖ.

    g. ὁ ἄνθρωπος τὸ παιδίον φιλεῖ. ὁ θεὸς τὸν ἄνθρωπον φιλεῖ.

    h. ὁ ἄνθρωπος τὸ παιδίον φιλεῖ. τὴν φωνὴν τοῦ ἀνθρώπου ἀκούομεν.

    i. ἡ Ἑλένη τοῖς ἀνθρώποις φωνεῖ. οἱ ἄνθρωποι καλάμῳ γράφουσι.

    j. οἱ ἀγαθοὶ ἄνθρωποι τὸ παιδίον φιλοῦσι. ὁ θεὸς τοὺς ἀγαθοὺς ἀνθρώπους φιλεῖ.

    k. τὼ ἀνθρώπω καλαμοῖς γράφετον. ὁ διδάσκαλος τὼ ἀνθρώπω βλέπει.

    l. οὐ φιλοῦμεν τὰς μεταβολάς. ταῖς μεταβολαῖς μανθάνομεν.

    m. οἱ θεοὶ τὸν ἄνθρωπον φιλοῦσιν. ὁ ἄνθρωπος ἀποθνήσκει νέος.

    n. οἱ θεοὶ ἄνθρωπον φιλοῦσιν. ὁ ἄνθρωπος τοὺς θεοὺς φιλεῖ.

    o. ἡ διδασκάλη τὸ βιβλίον γράφει. τὸ βιβλίον ἔχεις.

4. Write a paragraph in Greek on each of the following themes:

    a. A person's senses and what he or she does with them.

    b. A child's book and pen, and what he or she does with them.

Chapter III

Alexander, Son of Priam

III.1 Demonstrative pronouns

Two useful pronouns are οὗτος and ὅδε, which both mean "this." They can be used as pronouns by themselves, or as adjectives modifying a definite noun phrase. For example: τοῦτον ὁρῶ, "I see this (man, or other masculine idea)"; here τοῦτον is masculine accusative singular, direct object of ὁρῶ, and its antecedent is whatever masculine thing we have been talking about. Or: τοῦτον τὸν ἄνθρωπον ὁρῶ, "I see this man"; here τοῦτον is an adjective modifying the noun phrase τὸν ἄνθρωπον.

The forms of οὗτος:

Case	Masculine	Feminine	Neuter
singular			
nominative	οὗτος	αὕτη	τοῦτο
genitive	τούτου	ταύτης	τούτου
dative	τούτῳ	ταύτῃ	τούτῳ
accusative	τοῦτον	ταύτην	τοῦτο
dual			
nom., acc.	τούτω (all genders)		
gen., dat.	τούτοιν (all genders)		
plural			
nom.	οὗτοι	αὗται	ταῦτα
gen.	τούτων	τούτων	τούτων
dat.	τούτοις	ταύταις	τούτοις
acc.	τούτους	ταύτᾱς	ταῦτα

The forms are much like those of καλός, except that the nominative singular and plural have been influenced by the forms of the article.

Another word for "this" is ὅδε, ἥδε, τόδε, declined like the article with -δε affixed.

When they are adjectives, demonstratives need the article to be used with their noun: in Greek prose, they don't modify the naked noun, but the definite noun phrase. So οὗτος ὁ ἄνθρωπος or ὁ ἄνθρωπος οὗτος, "this man," but not οὗτος ἄνθρωπος without the article. The demonstrative is always outside the noun phrase, never in attribute position, so οὗτος ὁ ἄνθρωπος but not ὁ οὗτος ἄνθρωπος. This is true for both οὗτος and ὅδε, in all their forms.

Exercises

1. In each of the following sentences, replace one of the nouns or noun phrases by a demonstrative. For example, change τὴν φωνὴν ἀκούω to ταύτην ἀκούω.

   Sentences: ὁ ἄνθρωπος εὖ ποιεῖ. τὸ παιδίον μανθάνει. βιβλία καλάμῳ γράφομεν. ἡ τοῦ διδασκάλου τύχη ἐστὶ ἀγαθή. καλὼ τὼ τοῦ παιδίου ὀφθαλμώ. οἱ θεοὶ καλαῖς φωναῖς φωνοῦσιν. τὸ παιδίον τοῖς ἀνθρώποις βιβλία δηλοῖ.

2. Add demonstratives wherever possible in the following sentences. For example, change τὴν φωνὴν ἀκούω to τήνδε τὴν φωνὴν ἀκούω.

   Sentences: ὁ ἄνθρωπος ἀποθνήσκει. τὴν μεταβολὴν τῷ διδασκάλῳ δηλοῦμεν. ἡ τύχη πολλὰ κακὰ τοῖς ἀνθρώποις ποιεῖ. τὸ μὲν βιβλίον ἔχω, τὸν δὲ κάλαμον οὐχ ὁρῶ. οἱ θεοὶ τοὺς ἀγαθοὺς ἀνθρώπους φιλοῦσιν.

III.2 Nouns in ᾱ

In Attic Greek, -ᾱ- is used instead of -η after ε, ι, or ρ. (That is, the Attic sound shift from ᾱ to η did not happen after ε, ι, ρ, so the original ᾱ is retained unchanged.) For example:

ἡ θύρᾱ, door	τῆς θύρᾱς	τῇ θύρᾳ	τὴν θύρᾱν
ἡ οἰκίᾱ, house	τῆς οἰκίᾱς	τῇ οἰκίᾳ	τὴν οἰκίᾱν

and similarly in dual and plural.

Exercise

Write out the complete declension of ἡ ἀγαθὴ θύρᾱ and of ἡ καλὴ οἰκίᾱ in all cases and numbers, noting carefully how the endings of the nouns in -ᾱ differ from those of the adjectives in -η.

III.3 Present infinitive active

The present infinitive active is formed from the present stem by adding -ειν. With contracted stems this becomes -εῖν, -ᾶν, -οῦν, contracted from -έεεν, -άεεν, -όεεν respectively. Note that the usual ending -ειν is already a contraction, from original -εεν. This is why there is no iota in the infinitive of the α- and o-contract verbs.

λύ-ειν   ποι-εῖν   ὁρ-ᾶν   δη-λοῦν

The **infinitive** is a verbal noun: it is both a verb form and a noun. As a verb, it can have its own subject (which will be in the accusative case), object, or other complements, and it can be modified by an adverb. So: ἔχω εὖ ποιεῖν, "I can do well," with εὖ modifying the infinitive; φιλῶ βιβλία γράφειν, "I like to write books," with βιβλία as direct object of the infinitive.

As a noun, it is always neuter singular. It can be the subject of a sentence, object of a preposition, or anything else a noun can be. So: γράφειν ἐστὶ ἀγαθόν, "writing is good," with the infinitive as subject in the nominative case; μανθάνομεν τῷ γράφειν "we learn by writing," with the infinitive in the dative case as an instrument; τὸ ἀκούειν σοφώτερόν ἐστι τοῦ λέγειν "listening is wiser than speaking," with one infinitive in the nominative, subject of ἐστι, and the second in the genitive with the comparative (see below).

The infinitive is *both* verb and noun *at the same time,* so can have both verb-like characteristics and noun-like ones in the same sentence: βιβλία γράφειν ἐστὶ ἀγαθόν, "writing books is good," infinitive as subject (a noun) with a direct object (because it's also a verb). Or: μανθάνομεν τῷ εὖ γράφειν, "we learn by writing well," infinitive as dative of means (a noun function) modified by an adverb (as any verb can be).

When the infinitive is particularly noun-like, it has the article (always neuter singular, of course); this is called the **articular infinitive**.

The infinitive with verbs like φιλῶ "like to" or ἔχω "can, able to" is called a **complementary infinitive** because it *completes* the meaning of the main verb. Note the idiomatic use of ἔχω: the sense of ὁ ἄνθρωπος ἔχει γράφειν is "the person has (the power to) write, has (the capability of) writing," or more simply "can write."

We have now learned two of the six **moods** of the Greek verb. The moods are:

finite				non-finite	
indicative	imperative	subjunctive	optative	infinitive	participle
independent		subordinate			

Every verb form has tense, mood, and voice. A form can only have *one* of each of these categories: if it is present tense, it is not any other tense; if it is indicative mood, it is not any other mood; and so on.

As you already know, forms of the **finite** moods also have person and number, so for example λύει is "third person singular present indicative active." The **non-finite** moods are not *confined* to a single person and number, so for example λύειν is "present infinitive active"; if it has a subject at all, the subject could be any person and number. The non-finite moods straddle the boundary between verbs and nouns: the infinitive, as you've seen, is a verbal noun, and the participle is a verbal adjective (see chapter 8).

The so-called independent moods are most at home in main clauses, though as you've already seen the indicative can also be the verb of a subordinate clause, for example a relative clause or an if-clause. The dependent or subordinate moods are most at home in subordinate clauses, though the subjunctive and optative may also be the verbs of main clauses.

The present infinitive active is not the only infinitive form; Greek verbs have infinitives for each tense system and each voice. You will meet the aorist infinitive active in the next chapter.

Exercise

Form the present infinitive active of each of the following verbs: λέγω, ἀκούω, μανθάνω, ἔχω, φωνέω, φέρω "carry," βάλλω "throw," ἐθέλω "want," λαμβάνω "take," νικάω "conquer," ἀξιόω "think worthy," ἀποθνήσκω.

When you write a synopsis of a verb (see Appendix 1 section 5), from now on, include the present infinitive active in its proper place.

III.4 The verb εἶναι, "to be"

The verb "be" in Greek is somewhat irregular. This is its present indicative active:

	Singular	Dual	Plural
1st	εἰμί		ἐσμέν
2nd	εἶ	ἐστόν	ἐστέ
3rd	ἐστί	ἐστόν	εἰσί

All these forms except for εἶ are **enclitic**. This means they have no accent of their own, and cannot be first in the sentence; as you will learn (see chapter 4 and appendix 3), an enclitic may affect the accent of the word before it. But when a form of εἰμι is emphatic, or when it introduces something new (like English "there is, there are"), it is not enclitic: it will then have accent on the first syllable (as ἔστι, εἶσι) and will normally come first. Thus ἔστι ἄνθρωπος ὅς ... might be the beginning of a story, introducing a person we do not yet know that the story will be about, but ὁ ἄνθρωπός ἐστι διδάσκαλος is the normal pattern, with enclitic ἐστι just connecting the two noun phrases. With an infinitive as subject ἔστι means the action of the verb is possible, so ἔστι τὸν ἄνθρωπον γράφειν, "that the man writes is possible, it is possible for the man to write."

The third person singular and plural forms have the sandhi variants ἐστιν, εἰσιν before vowels.

The present infinitive active is εἶναι; it is not enclitic.

As you will see in the vocabulary list, εἰμι has only two principal parts, the first (present system) and the second (future system). It does not have an aorist or a perfect.

III.5 Comparison of adjectives

The comparative degree of an adjective is the "more" form, as "smaller, more small." The superlative is the "most" form, as "smallest, most small."

To form the comparative and superlative, change -ος to -ότερος -ότατος when the syllable before -ος contains a long vowel or ends in two consonants, -ώτερος -ώτατος if it has a short vowel followed by at most one consonant: —

μῑκρός, small   μῑκρότερος, smaller   μῑκρότατος, smallest
  (long vowel)

πῐκρός, bitter (vowel   πῐκρότερος, bitterer   πῐκρότατος, bitterest
  with two consonants)

σοφός, clever (short σοφώτερος, cleverer σοφώτατος, cleverest
vowel, one consonant)

These are the masculine nominative singular forms. Most of the rest of the forms are like those of καλός. The exception is the feminine of the comparative, which is like θύρα, and for the same reason: the original -ᾱ is retained after the -ρ-. Thus the nominative singular forms of the comparative of μῑκρός are μικρότερος, μικροτέρᾱ, μικρότερον and those of the superlative are μικρότατος, μικροτάτη, μικρότατον.

Adverbs are formed from adjectives in -ος by changing the ending of the genitive singular masculine to -ως, as καλός, gen. καλοῦ, adv. καλῶς. Comparative adverbs use the neuter singular of the adjective, superlative adverbs the neuter plural: σοφῶς, σοφώτερον, σοφώτατα "cleverly, more cleverly, most cleverly."

The standard of comparison, or the thing being compared to, can be given in the genitive, as τὸ παιδίον ἐστὶ μικρότερον τοῦ ἀνθρώπου, "smaller than the (adult) person." Parse this use as "genitive of comparison." It is also possible — and arguably easier — to use ἤ, much like "than" in English, and in this construction the two nouns being compared will be in the same case: τὸ παιδίον ἐστὶ μικρότερον ἢ ὁ ἄνθρωπος, or τὸ βιβλίον δηλῶ τῷ παιδίῳ μικροτέρῳ ἢ τῷ ἀνθρώπῳ. Here ἀνθρώπῳ can be parsed as "comparison."

Exercise

Form the nominative singular forms of the positive, comparative, and superlative in each gender (9 forms total) of each of the following regular first-and-second declension adjectives: νέος, τῠφλός, στρογγύλος "round," χρήσῐμος "useful," δίκαιος "just, fair."

III.6 Particles

One of the most characteristic features of Greek is the **discourse particles**, words like δέ, μέν, or τοι. Their major function is to connect sentences together.

While an individual word does have meaning all by itself (indeed, even a *part* of a word may have meaning, as the ending -ει means "third singular, active, present or future tense," or the ending -ους means "masculine accusative plural"), it's hard to express very much with isolated words. Words make more sense in complete sentences.

But even sentences are more meaningful when they have a context. Sometimes this context is in the real, extra-linguistic world: if you say "don't do that!" to a cat or a child, the antecedent of "that" is whatever the cat is doing (jumping on the table, say, or nibbling at a plant) and may never be put explicitly into words. Just as often, the context of a sentence may be the sentences that came before and will come after. In Greek, the connections between successive sentences are often made explicit by particles.

Particles are small indeclinable words; they can be classed as adverbs or conjunctions, if you want to group words by parts of speech. Almost all of them are **post-positive**, which means they must be positioned after (Latin *post*) another word. Typically (though not invariably) particles that are connecting clauses or sentences come second in their own clause or sentence. Particles can also mark a contrast, mark an idea as new information, or mark something as emphatic. In short, Greek uses particles for many of the sorts of things that English does with tone of voice. Of course Greek speakers probably also used tone of voice to color the meaning of a sentence, but it's all but impossible for us to find out how. It's therefore convenient that the particles are right there in the written texts. There is almost always a particle to show how a sentence fits in to its context; if you see a sentence that does *not* have a connecting particle, the lack should attract your attention.

Although Greek-English dictionaries and vocabulary lists try to give English glosses for the particles, it doesn't always make sense to do this: the idea of the particle may be something that English speakers would do with tone of voice or with an unusual word order. In other words, we can explain particles but cannot always find succinct English equivalents. You will learn how the particles work by reading and hearing examples.

These are the particles we have seen so far. All of them are post-positive (they cannot come first in a clause or sentence), though of this group only τοι is an enclitic (with no accent of its own).

τοι calls for the listener's attention, often marking the word it comes after as particularly important.

δέ marks a **Topic**. Think of δέ as something like a different camera angle or shot within the same scene: although the over-all subject of discussion continues, we consider first one point then another. If several characters are involved, δέ may mark a change of grammatical subject: ὁ διδάσκαλος ποιεῖ .... ὁ δὲ ἰατρός ποιεῖ .... And once it's clear who the characters are, the nouns may even be left out.

μέν marks contrast. If two parallel ideas are contrasted, they will be marked with μέν and δέ. For example, ἡ μὲν τύχη ἐστὶ τυφλή, οἱ δὲ θεοὶ ὁρῶσι. Although the same idea could be expressed with ἀλλά (as: ἡ τύχη ἐστὶ τυφλή, ἀλλὰ οἱ θεοὶ ὁρῶσι), it's more usual and more idiomatic to use μέν and δέ. If there are more than two ideas, δέ will appear with each one after the first.

γάρ says that this clause or sentence gives a reason for what has come before. Again, there are other ways to express this, for example using a subordinate clause introduced by διότι ("because") or by ἐπεί ("since, when, because, in the following circumstances"), but the particle is succinct and typically Greek.

III.7 Vocabulary

VERBS

εἰμι, ἔσομαι, be (present and future systems only)

NOUNS

δάκτυλος, -ου, ὁ, finger

δένδρον, -ου, τό, tree (cp. *rhododendron*)

δίφρος, -ου, ὁ, stool, chair

δωμάτιον, -ου, τό, room

ἕδρᾱ, -ᾱς, ἡ, seat

θεά, -ᾶς, ἡ, goddess

θελκτήριον, -ου, τό, charm, spell

θύρᾱ, -ᾶς, ἡ, door

ἰᾱτρός, -οῦ, ὁ, doctor, physician (cp. *psychiatrist*)

κῆπος, -ου, ὁ, garden

κλίνη, -ης, ἡ, lounge, couch (cp. *recline*)

λάχανον, -ου, τό, herb, vegetable

λόγος, -ου, ὁ, word, speech (cp. *dialogue, prologue*)

λύπη, -ης, ἡ, grief

νοῦς, νοῦ, ὁ, mind

οἰκίᾱ, -ᾶς, ἡ, house (cp. *economic*)

πέτασος, -ου, ὁ, hat

φάρμακον, -ου, τό, drug, medicine, remedy (cp. *pharmacy*)

ψῡχή, -ῆς, ἡ, soul, life (cp. *psychology*)

ADJECTIVES AND NUMERALS

δύο, δυοῖν, two

δέκα, ten

πέντε, five

ἀστεῖος, -ᾱ, -ον, nice, urbane

ἕκαστος, -η, -ον, each, every

μακρός, -ά, -όν, long

μῑκρός, -ά, -όν, small

μόνος, -η, -ον, alone

πικρός, -ά, -όν, bitter

σοφός, -ή, -όν, wise, clever

στρογγύλος, -η, -ον, round

χρήσιμος, -η, -ον, useful

PARTICLES, CONJUNCTIONS, ADVERBS, PRONOUNS

ἆρα, interrogative particle

γάρ, because, for (never first word)

δέ, particle making connection and marking Topic or contrast (never first word)

ἤ, or; can be used in pairs like English *either ... or*; also marks standard of comparison

μέν, particle marking first of contrasted items

ἐκτός, outside

ἐντός, inside

ὅδε, ἥδε, τόδε, this

οὗτος, αὕτη, τοῦτο, this

πάλαι, of old, in the olden times, long ago (cp. *paleography, paleolithic*)

τι, something

Notes on the vocabulary

The forms of νοῦς are contracted, much like the forms of δηλόω. The stem is νο-.

For more on the forms and use of τι see chapter 4.

III.8 Reading

1. λύπης ἰατρός ἐστιν ἀνθρώποις λόγος·
   ψυχῆς γὰρ οὗτος μόνος ἔχει θελκτήρια·
   λέγουσι δ᾽ αὐτὸν οἱ πάλαι σοφώτατοι
   ἀστεῖον εἶναι φάρμακον καὶ χρήσιμον.

   > A fragment from a play by Menander.

2. ψυχῆς ἰατρὸς τὰ γράμματα.

3. τὸ παιδίον τοὺς τοῦ διδασκάλου λόγους ἀκούει. πολλὰ παιδία τοὺς τοῦ διδασκάλου λόγους ἀκούει.

4. ἥδε ἡ οἰκία μακρὰν θύραν ἔχει. ἐντὸς δὲ δύο δωμάτιά ἐστι. τὸ μὲν μακρότερον δωμάτιον δίφρους, τὸ δὲ μικρότερον κλίνην ἔχει.

5. οὗτος ὁ ἄνθρωπός ἐστι διδάσκαλος. εἰ ἀκούομεν τοὺς τούτου λόγους, πολλὰ μανθάνομεν. χρήσιμος γὰρ καὶ σοφός ἐστι.

6. οἰκίαν ἔχομεν καλήν, ἐντὸς δ᾽ εἰσὶ δίφροι τε καὶ κλῖναι καὶ ἕδραι ἄλλαι, καὶ δωμάτια δέκα, καὶ κῆπον ἔχομεν, ἐντὸς δ᾽ ἐστὶ δένδρα καὶ λάχανα.

   > Note elision: δ᾽ ἐστι rather than δέ ἐστι. (For the accent see Appendix 3 rule 9.)

7. ἕκαστον παιδίον βιβλίον ἔχει καὶ κάλαμον. ἆρα μακροὶ ἢ μικροὶ οἱ τῶν παιδίων κάλαμοι; μικροί εἰσι. ποῖοί εἰτὶ εἰσι οἱ κάλαμοι; στρογγύλοι εἰσὶ καὶ μικροί. ἕκαστος κάλαμός ἐστι μικρός.

8. οἱ ἄνθρωποι ἔχουσιν ἕκαστος δύο ὀφθαλμώ, καὶ δέκα δακτύλους, ἔχουσι δὲ φωνὴν καὶ ἀκοήν καὶ νοῦν.

9. εἰ λύπην ἔχεις, κακῶς ἔχεις. εἰ δὲ λύπην μὴ ἔχεις, καλῶς ἔχεις. ἢ κακῶς ἢ καλῶς ἕκαστος ἔχει.

10. τίς ἐστι οὗτος ὁ τυφλός; Οἰδίπους ἐστί. πέτασον στρογγύλον ἔχει. ἡ ἄλλη τοί ἐστι Ἀντιγόνη, ἢ παιδίον τούτου ἐστί. τυφλὴ δὲ οὔκ ἐστι ἀλλὰ εὖ ὁρᾷ. πολλὰ δὲ τῷ ἀνθρώπῳ δηλοῖ. ἡ Ἀντιγόνη τοῦτον φιλεῖ. "ποῦ ἐσμέν;" λέγει ὁ Οἰδίπους. "τάδε τὰ μακρὰ δένδρα εἰσὶ τῶν θεῶν," λέγει ἡ Ἀντιγόνη. "ἕδραν ἀστείαν ἔχεις. οὐ μονοί ἐσμεν· αἱ θεαὶ γὰρ ἐντός εἰσιν."

11. καλὸν καὶ ἀστεῖόν ἐστι τόδε τὸ δωμάτιον. δίφρον μακρὸν καὶ ἕδραν μικρὰν ἐντὸς ὁρῶμεν.

12. τὸ γράφειν ἐστὶ χρήσιμον. εἰ ἡ διδασκάλη γράφει, οἱ ἀλλοὶ τοὺς λόγους βλέπουσι καὶ τοῖς λόγοις μανθάνουσι. καλὸν τὸ εὖ γράφειν, κακὸν δὲ τὸ κακῶς γράφειν ἢ τὸ κακὰ γράφειν. εἰ κακὰ γράφεις, κακὴν τύχην ἔχεις. εἰ δὲ κακῶς γράφεις, οἱ ἀλλοὶ τοὺς λόγους οὐ φιλοῦσι.

13. σοφός ἐστι ἄνθρωπος ὃς ἀγαθὸν νοῦν ἔχει. οἱ δὲ ἰατροὶ καὶ οἱ διδάσκαλοι σοφοί εἰσί. οἱ τῶν σοφῶν λόγοι χρήσιμοί εἰσι. φιλοῦμεν ἀκούειν τοὺς τῶν σοφῶν λόγους· σοφοὶ γάρ εἰσι οἵδε οἱ λόγοι.

14. εἰ σοφοὺς λόγους ἀκούετον, ὦ παιδίω, μανθάνετον. τῷ ἀκούειν μανθάνετον. τῇ ἀκοῇ μανθάνετον. εἰ μανθάνετον, σοφώ ἐστόν.

15. ἆρα φιλεῖς γράφειν; οὐχί. οὐ φιλῶ γράφειν· οὐ γὰρ εὖ γράφω. ἀγαθοὺς λόγους οὐ ποιῶ.

16. μακρόν ἐστι τοῦτο τὸ δένδρον. μακρότερόν ἐστι τῆς οἰκίας. ἡ οἰκία ἐστὶ μικρὰ καὶ τὸ δένδρον ἐστὶ μακρὸν. τόδε τὸ ἄλλο δένδρον ἐστὶ τὸ μακρότατον. μακρότερόν ἐστι τόδε τὸ δένδρον τούτου, καὶ μακροτέρω ἐστὸν τὼ δύο δένδρω τῆς οἰκίας. τόδε τὸ δένδρον ἐστὶ τὸ μακρότερον.

17. ὁ ἰατρὸς λάχανα ἔχει, οἷς φάρμακα ποιεῖ. ὁ ἰατρὸς φάρμακα λαχάνοις ποιεῖ. εἰ λύπην ἔχετε, ὁ σοφὸς ἰατρὸς χρήσιμον φάρμακον ποιεῖ, καὶ τὴν λύπην λύει. πικρὸν μὲν τὸ φάρμακον, χρήσιμον δέ. ὁ ἰατρὸς λύπην λύει τοῖς πικροῖς φαρμάκοις.

18. ὁ Πρίαμος καλὴν οἰκίαν ἔχει. ὁ Ἀλέξανδρος παιδίον ἐστὶ τοῦ Πριάμου. δύστηνός ἐστι ὁ Πρίαμος· κακὴν τύχην ἔχει. ὁ γὰρ Ἀλέξανδρος τὴν καλὴν Ἑλένην φιλεῖ. μακρός ἐστι ὁ τοῦ Πριάμου λόγος, ὃν λέγει ὁ Ὅμηρος.

19. ἐντὸς ἐμῆς κραδίας τὴν εὔλαλον Ἡλιοδώραν
    ψυχὴν τῆς ψυχῆς ἔπλασεν αὐτὸς Ἔρως

> Greek Anthology 5.155, by Meleager. **ἐμός, -ή, -όν**, my; in Greek, possessives are used only for emphasis or for contrast, so here *my* as opposed to anyone else's (see chapter 20). **κραδία, -ας, ἡ**, heart. This is a poetic form; in Attic prose the form καρδία is more usual. **εὔλαλος, -ον**, speaking sweetly, with a sweet voice. **ἔπλασεν** is third person singular aorist indicative active of πλάττω, to shape, form, or make; the aorist is the past tense (see chapter 5). **αὐτὸς Ἔρως** "Eros himself," nominative singular; see chapter 4 for the pronoun. A paraphrase in prose: ὁ θεὸς Ἔρως αὐτὸς ποιεῖ τὴν Ἡλιοδώραν, ἣ εὖ φωνεῖ, ψυχὴν τῆς ἐμῆς ψυχῆς, ἐν τῇ καρδίᾳ.

III.9 Conversation

1. (reading 1) τί ἐστι λύπης ἰατρὸς ἀνθρώποις; λόγος ἐστὶν ἀνθρώποις λύπης ἰατρός. τίνος (gen. sg. of τίς) ἐστιν ἰατρὸς λόγος; λύπης ἰατρός ἐστι λόγος. τίσιν (dat. pl. of τίς) ἰατρός ἐστι λύπης λόγος; ἀνθρώποις λύπης ἐστὶ λόγος ἰατρός. τί ἔχει; ψυχῆς ἔχει θελκτήρια. τίνος θελκτήρια; ψυχῆς. οὗτος μόνος ἢ καὶ ἄλλος; μόνος οὗτος. τί λέγουσιν αὐτὸν εἶναι οἱ σοφώτατοι; ἀστεῖον εἶναι φάρμακον λέγουσιν. ποῖον φάρμακον; ἀστεῖον φάρμακον καὶ χρήσιμον.

2. (reading 10) τίς ἐστι ὁ τυφλὸς ἄνθρωπος; ἔστι Οἰδίπους. τί ἔχει ὁ Οἰδίπους; πέτασον ἔχει καὶ παιδίον. ἆρα εὖ ὁρᾷ; οὐχί, οὐχ ὁρᾷ· τυφλὸς γάρ ἐστι. ποῖός ἐστι ὁ πέτασος;

στρογγύλος ἐστὶ ὁ πέτασος. τίς ἐστι τὸ παιδίον; ἔστι Ἀντιγόνη. ἆρα αὕτη τυφλή ἐστι; οὐχί, οὐ τυφλή ἐστι, ἀλλὰ εὖ ὁρᾷ. τίνα τῷ ἀνθρώπῳ δηλοῖ; δηλοῖ πολλά. πολλὰ τούτῳ δηλοῖ.

3. (vocabulary) ὦ παιδίον, ἆρ' ἔχεις οἰκίαν; ἔχω οἰκίαν, ὦ διδάσκαλε. καὶ ποίαν ἔχεις οἰκίαν; καλὴν ἔχω οἰκίαν. τί δ' ἐντός ἐστιν; δίφροι τ' ἐντός εἰσι καὶ κλῖναι καὶ ἕδραι. ἔστι δ' ἄλλο τι; κῆπός ἐστι, καὶ ἔχει λάχανα καὶ δένδρα.

4. τί ἔχει ἄνθρωπος ᾧ λέγει; φωνὴν ἔχει. πόσους δακτύλους ἔχει, πόσους ὀφθαλμούς, etc. ποῖόν τί ἐστιν ὁ ὀφθαλμός; στρογγύλος ἐστιν. καὶ δάκτυλος; μακρός.

5. τί φιλεῖς ποιεῖν, ὦ παιδίον; φιλῶ γράφειν, φιλῶ μανθάνειν. ἆρα φιλεῖς εὖ γράφειν ἢ κακῶς γράφειν; φιλῶ εὖ γράφειν. τί ἐστι σοφώτερον· τὸ εὖ γράφειν ἢ τὸ κακῶς γράφειν; τὸ εὖ γράφειν σοφώτερόν ἐστι.

III.10 Writing

1. Complete the following in as many ways as you can:

    a. ἡ οἰκία ἐστὶ _____

    b. τὼ ὀφθαλμώ ἐστον _____

    c. τὰ δένδρα ἐστί _____

    d. ἡ θύρα ἐστί _____

    e. οἱ δάκτυλοί εἰσι _____

    f. ἡ φωνή ἐστι _____

    g. μακρός ἐστιν _____

    h. χρησίμη ἐστὶν _____

    i. καλόν ἐστι _____

    j. μακροί εἰσιν _____

    k. τὸ παιδίον ἔχει _____

    l. τὸ παιδίον φιλεῖ _____

    m. τῷ καλάμῳ ἔχω _____

    n. τῇ φωνῇ ἔχω _____

    o. τῷ δακτύλῳ ἔχω _____

    p. ὁ μὲν θεὸς _____, ἡ δὲ θεὰ _____

    q. τὸ μὲν παιδίον _____, ἡ δὲ διδασκάλη _____

    r. ἐντὸς μέν ἐστι _____, ἐκτὸς δὲ _____

    s. τῇ μὲν φωνῇ _____, τῇ δὲ ἀκοῇ _____

    t. γράφει μὲν _____, λέγει δὲ _____

2. Each of the following sentences includes a comparison. Change the construction: if it uses ἤ rewrite with the genitive, or if it uses the genitive, rewrite with ἤ. For example, change τὸ παιδίον μικρότερόν ἐστι ἤ ὁ ἄνθρωπος to τὸ παιδίον μικρότερόν ἐστι τοῦ ἀνθρώπου, or the other way around.

   a. τὸ φάρμακον πικρότερόν ἐστι ἤ τὰ λάχανα.

   b. τὰ δωμάτιά εἰσι μικρότερα τῶν οἰκίων.

   c. λόγον ἀκούω δικαιότερον ἤ τόνδε.

   d. ὁ διδάσκαλος νεώτερός ἐστι τοῦ ἰατροῦ.

   e. τὸ ἀκούειν σοφώτερόν ἐστι τοῦ λέγειν.

3. Do the change-number exercise (chapter 2, ex. 2) with the following sentences:

   a. τῷ δακτύλῳ τὸ δένδρον δηλοῦσιν.

   b. τοῦτο τὸ δωμάτιόν ἐστι μικρόν.

   c. πολλοὺς δίφρους ἔχετε.

   d. ἡ διδασκάλη ἐστὶ σοφή.

   e. ὅδε ὁ ἄνθρωπος σοφώτερός ἐστι ἤ οὗτος.

   f. ὁ ἄνθρωπος ἔχει ἀκούειν.

   g. ὁ ἄνθρωπος ὀφθαλμὼ ἔχει οἶν ὁρᾷ.

   h. ὁ ἄνθρωπος ὀφθαλμὼ ἔχει καὶ ὁρᾶν ἔχει.

   i. τὸ πικρὸν φάρμακον οὐ φιλοῦμεν.

   j. οἱ θεοὶ τὰς μεταβολὰς ποιοῦσι.

   k. τὴν τοῦ θεοῦ φωνὴν ἀκούει.

   l. τὴν οἰκίαν ὁ διδάσκαλος ὁρᾷ.

   m. καλὸς καὶ ἀγαθὸς εἶ, ὦ ἄνθρωπε.

   n. μικρὰν θύραν ἔχει ἥδε ἡ οἰκία.

   o. λόγον χρήσιμον λέγω.

4. Write a paragraph in Greek on each of the following themes:

   a. The Medicine for Grief

   b. My House and its Garden

CHAPTER IV

The City of Troy

IV.1 Personal pronouns

Although subject pronouns are never grammatically required in Greek, they can be used for emphasis ("*I* did that"), for contrast ("*You* didn't do it, *I* did"), or for clarity. Pronouns in the other cases are often useful. Here are the forms for the first and second person:

	First Person (I, we)	Second Person (you)
singular		
nominative	ἐγώ	σύ
genitive	ἐμοῦ, μου	σοῦ, σου
dative	ἐμοί, μοι	σοί, σοι
accusative	ἐμέ, με	σέ, σε
dual		
nom., acc.	νώ	σφώ
gen., dat.	νῷν	σφῷν
plural		
nom.	ἡμεῖς	ὑμεῖς
gen.	ἡμῶν	ὑμῶν
dat.	ἡμῖν	ὑμῖν
acc.	ἡμᾶς	ὑμᾶς

The forms ἐμέ, ἐμοῦ, ἐμοί, σέ, σοῦ, σοί are emphatic. The forms με, μου, μοι, σε, σου, σοι are enclitic: they have no accent and cannot come first in a sentence. These are the more common forms.

All the plural forms have rough breathing. To keep the plural forms straight, it may help to remember that the "we" forms have a long *e* (η) and the "you" forms have *u* (υ).

Because there are no first-person dual verb forms, νώ takes a plural verb, as νὼ γράφομεν.

Next comes αὐτός, "him, her, same," a third-person pronoun.

	Masculine	Feminine	Neuter
nominative	αὐτός	αὐτή	αὐτό
genitive	αὐτοῦ	αὐτῆς	αὐτοῦ, and so on

The forms of αὐτός are much like those of the article or of οὗτος, and except for having no ν in the neuter nominative and accusative singular, are like the forms of καλός.

The *oblique* cases (but not the nominative) of this word are the normal third person pronoun, as: λύω αὐτόν "I loose him." But in attribute position (that is, inside a noun phrase with the article), this word means "the same" — ὁ αὐτός, ἡ αὐτή, τὸ αὐτό, or αὐτός, αὐτή, ταὐτό(ν) with **crasis** (see notes on vocabulary, below). Don't confuse αὑτή (crasis for ἡ αὐτή) and αὕτη (from οὗτος).

This can also be an emphatic pronoun, αὐτός λέγει, "he himself speaks." Compare Spanish *mismo* and French *même*, which have the same property: *el mismo hombre* "the same man," but *el hombre mismo* "the man himself, the very man"; similarly *le même homme* "the same man" and *l'homme même* "the man himself, the very man." You'll recognize this use because the pronoun will agree with a noun, but won't be inside the noun phrase (after the article), or because the pronoun will be nominative agreeing with the subject of the verb (whether that subject is expressed in the sentence or not).

Exercises

1. In each of the following sentences, replace one of the noun phrases — *not* the subject — with the appropriate form of the pronoun αὐτός.

   Sentences: ἐν τῷ δωματίῳ ὁρῶ ἕδραν καὶ κλίνην. ὁ διδάσκαλος τὸ βιβλίον δακτύλῳ τοῖς παιδίοις δηλοῖ. ὁ ἰατρὸς φάρμακα χρήσιμα ἔχει. ὁ τοῦ παιδίου δάκτυλός ἐστι μικρότερος ἢ ὁ τοῦ ἀνθρώπου. τὰ δένδρα τοῖν ὀφθαλμοῖν βλέπομεν.

2. In each of the following sentences, replace forms of ἄνθρωπος by forms of ἐγώ. Then replace them by forms of σύ. For example, from ὁ ἄνθρωπος λέγει make ἐγὼ λέγω and σὺ λέγεις.

   Sentences: οἱ ἄνθρωποί εἰσι σοφοί. τὸ παιδίον τοὺς ἀνθρώπους φιλεῖ. τὸ δένδρον μακρότερόν ἐστι τοῦ ἀνθρώπου. τῷ ἀνθρώπῳ τὸ βιβλίον δηλοῖ. ἡ διδασκάλη τοῖς ἀνθρώποις λέγει. τὼ ἀνθρώπω ἐν τῷ κήπῳ ἐστόν. ἡ ἄνθρωπος τὸ βιβλίον γράφει. τὸν ἄνθρωπον βλέπει ὁ ἰατρός.

IV.2 Interrogative pronoun

τίς, "who? what?"

	Masc./Fem.	Neuter
singular		
nominative	τίς	τί
genitive	τίνος	
dative	τίνι	
accusative	τίνα	τί
dual		
nom., acc.	τίνε	
gen., dat.	τίνοιν	
plural		
nom.	τίνες	τίνα
gen.	τίνων	
dat.	τίσι, τίσιν	
acc.	τίνας	τίνα

The nominative singular forms τίς and τί are the only words in Greek whose accent never becomes grave. Thus: τίς λέγει; "who is speaking?" with acute accent on the pronoun. The dative plural has the sandhi variant τίσιν, used before vowels.

The indefinite pronoun "some, any, a certain" is just like τίς except that it is enclitic, so has no accent or, sometimes, an accent on the last syllable. For this word the neuter nominative/accusative plural is ἄττα or τινα. When it is used with a noun, the indefinite pronoun comes after the noun it qualifies: ἔστι ἄνθρωπός τις "there is a certain man" (introducing a new character into the story); ἀνθρώπῳ τινὶ τὸ βιβλίον δηλῶ "I show the book to some person" (perhaps the speaker prefers not to specify who it is). The indefinite pronoun can also be used alone without a noun, for example τὸ βιβλίον τινὶ δηλῶ. Note the word order: because this pronoun is enclitic, it can never come first in the sentence.

The indefinite τις is typically used when the speaker knows who or what is referred to, but the listener doesn't. Either it doesn't matter ("some person, anybody") or the speaker is about to explain. Although the English indefinite article *a* can also be used in these ways, Greek τις is not equivalent to English *a*; in most circumstances where English would use *a*, Greek simply uses the unqualified noun by itself. For example, βιβλίον ἔχω is "I have a book," but βιβλίον τινά ἔχω is "I have a certain book, whose significance I'm going to explain to you."

The indirect interrogative ὅστις is declined like *both* the relative pronoun and the direct interrogative; that is, *both* parts of the word decline. Thus we have ἐρωτῶ ὅστις λέγει, ἐρωτῶ ὅντινα ὁρᾷς, ἐρωτῶ οὕτινος ἀκούεις, and so on, "I ask who is speaking, whom you see, whom you're listening to." The neuter nominative and accusative singular should be ὅτι, but to avoid confusion with a common conjunction (which you will meet in chapter 7), it is written ὅ τι.

IV.3 Cardinal numbers

The cardinal numbers are the counting numbers. See Appendix 1 section 3 for the ordinal numbers ("first, second, third" and so on) and the number adverbs ("once, twice, thrice" and so on).

εἷς, *one*, singular only

	Masc.	Fem.	Neu.
nom.	εἷς	μία	ἕν
gen.	ἑνός	μιᾶς	ἑνός
dat.	ἑνί	μιᾷ	ἑνί
acc.	ἕνα	μίαν	ἕν

δύο, *two*, dual only, same in all three genders

	Masc.	Fem.	Neu.
nom., acc.	δύο		
gen., dat.	δυοῖν		

τρεῖς, *three*, plural only

	Masc.	Fem.	Neu.
nom., acc.	τρεῖς		τρία
gen.	τριῶν		
dat.	τρισί, τρισίν		

τέτταρες, *four*, plural only

	Masc.	Fem.	Neu.
nom.	τέτταρες		τέτταρα
gen.	τεττάρων		
dat.	τέτταρσι(ν)		
acc.	τέτταρας		τέτταρα

The other numbers up to a hundred are indeclinable, starting with πέντε 5, ἕξ 6, ἑπτά 7, ὀκτώ 8, ἐννέα 9, δέκα 10. The rest are listed in Appendix 1 section 3.

The numeral adverbs, except for ἅπαξ, δίς, τρίς "once, twice, three times," are formed with the suffix -κις, as τετράκις "four times." This list is also in Appendix 1 section 3. The same suffix forms πολλάκις, "many times, often."

Exercise

Add numbers modifying as many as possible of the nouns in each of the following sentences. For example, οἰκίαν ἔχω might become μίαν οἰκίαν ἔχω. Sentences: παιδίω βλέπομεν. ἡ οἰκία θύρας ἔχει. ἐν τοῖς κήποις εἰσὶ λάχανα. ἕδραι εἰσὶ ἐν δωματίοις. τοὺς τοῖν διδασκάλοιν λόγους ἀκούουσι.

IV.4 First declension nouns in short ă

Some feminines end in nom. -ă: they are declined with those in -η or -ā except in the nom. and acc. singular:

nom., voc.	γλῶττα, tongue
gen.	γλώττης
dat.	γλώττῃ
acc.	γλῶτταν

The dual and plural are just like καλή.

Exercise

Write out the complete declension of ἡ μακρὰ καὶ καλὴ χλαῖνα, in all cases and numbers. Note that this phrase includes all three types of first-declension feminine forms. Where do they differ?

IV.5 The reflexive pronoun

The **reflexive pronoun** refers back to the subject of the sentence, as ἑαυτὴν ὁρᾷ, "she sees *herself.*" The forms of the reflexive pronoun are made by adding αὐτόν, "self" to the personal pronoun, like this: —

	First Person		Second Person		Third Person		
	Masc.	Fem.	Masc.	Fem.	Masc.	Fem.	Neu.
singular							
gen.	ἐμαυτοῦ	ἐμαυτῆς	σεαυτοῦ, σαυτοῦ	σεαυτῆς, σαυτῆς	ἑαυτοῦ, αὐτοῦ	ἑαυτῆς, αὐτῆς	ἑαυτοῦ, αὐτοῦ
dat.	ἐμαυτῷ	ἐμαυτῇ	σεαυτῷ, σαυτῷ	σεαυτῇ, σαυτῇ	ἑαυτῷ, αὐτῷ	ἑαυτῇ, αὐτῇ	ἑαυτῷ, αὐτῷ
acc.	ἐμαυτόν	ἐμαυτήν	σεαυτόν, σαυτόν	σεαυτήν, σαυτήν	ἑαυτόν, αὐτόν	ἑαυτήν, αὐτήν	ἑαυτό, αὐτό
plural							
gen.	ἡμῶν αὐτῶν		ὑμῶν αὐτῶν		ἑαυτῶν, αὐτῶν		
dat.	ἡμῖν αὐτοῖς	ἡμῖν αὐταῖς	ὑμῖν αὐτοῖς	ὑμῖν αὐταῖς	ἑαυτοῖς, αὐτοῖς	ἑαυταῖς, αὐταῖς	ἑαυτοῖς, αὐτοῖς
acc.	ἡμᾶς αὐτούς	ἡμᾶς αὐτάς	ὑμᾶς αὐτούς	ὑμᾶς αὐτάς	ἑαυτούς, αὐτούς	ἑαυτάς, αὐτάς	ἑαυτούς, αὐτούς

Dual forms are regular (made just like the singular, except with the usual dual endings), but not common. Note that the plural forms in first and second person are two words. All of these forms are made from a personal pronoun plus a form of αὐτός. The third person forms are built from an old third-person pronoun ἑ, obsolete in classical Attic prose but used in poetry. Both the second person and the third person have contracted forms: in the second person the forms may begin σεαυ- or σαυ-, and in the third they may begin ἑαυ- or αὑ-. Be careful of the difference between the contracted forms of the reflexive, which all have rough breathing, and the feminine forms of αὐτός, which are αὐτῆς, αὐτῇ, αὐτήν with smooth breathing.

There is no nominative because the reflexive cannot be the subject of the sentence: its antecedent will be the subject, but the reflexive pronoun is used when the person or thing that is the subject also has a different grammatical function in the same sentence. For example, in "she sees herself," the woman is both subject and direct object, so ἑαυτὴν βλέπει.

The following plural pronoun is sometimes used as an ordinary third person pronoun in poetry. Its oblique cases can be used to make reflexive forms, just as ἡμεῖς and ὑμεῖς are used for the first and second person plural; sometimes this pronoun is used alone as reflexive, without a form of αὐτός following. All three genders are the same.

nom.	σφεῖς
gen.	σφῶν
dat.	σφισί(ν)
acc.	σφᾶς

IV.6 Accent: the rules

First, recall the **law of limitation**: the accent must be on one of the last three syllables. If it's acute, it can be on any of the last three; if it's circumflex, it can only be on the last or second-to-last.

The key principles for accent are these:

- **Verbs**: In finite verb forms the accent goes back as far as possible.
- **Nouns**: In nouns, adjectives, and pronouns, the accent remains on the same syllable as in the nominative, unless this conflicts with the law of limitation.
- **Long Vowel**: If the *last* syllable has a long vowel, then the accent cannot be on the third-to-last syllable; if it belongs there, it moves forward to the second-to-last. And if the accent would be on the second-to-last syllable, it will be an acute, not a circumflex.

For example, ἀκούετε is a finite verb form, so it has its accent as far back as possible, on the third-to-last syllable. In ἀκούει the Long Vowel Rule applies, so the second-to-last syllable is as far back as the accent can go. Putting the accent as far back as possible is called **recessive accent**.

In the nominative παιδίον the accent is on the -ι- sound, so in the genitive παιδίου it stays there. In nominative ἄνθρωπος the accent is on the ἀν-syllable; in the accusative ἄνθρωπον it stays there, but in the genitive ἀνθρώπου it is forced to move by the Long Vowel Rule. Keeping the accent on the same syllable is called **persistent accent**.

The following details supplement these principles. The genitive plural of α-stems always has circumflex on the last syllable, so τύχη, τυχῶν, θύρα, θυρῶν, γλῶττα, γλωττῶν. If a first-declension (α-stem) or second-declension (o-stem) noun or adjective has its accent on its last syllable, then in the genitive and dative cases, singular, dual, and plural, the accent becomes circumflex. For example, καλός has genitive singular καλοῦ (masc., neut.) and καλῆς (fem.). This is because all these forms are originally contracted.

Also, final -οι and -αι, although diphthongs, and therefore long, are treated as short for the purposes of accent. Thus ἄνθρωποι may have its accent on the third-to-last syllable, because the vowel in the last syllable counts as short, so the Long Vowel Rule does not apply. (Compare the nominative dual, ἀνθρώπω.) When they are not the very last sound in the word, these diphthongs are long, as for example in ἀνθρώποις. (And these diphthongs count as long at the end of a verb in the optative mood; see chapter 8.)

Finally, the accent of contracted verb forms is placed *before* the contraction happens. The result is forms that may look like they contradict the general rule — but they really do conform. For example, ποιῶ starts out as ποιέω. When the vowel sounds contract, the pitch goes up (for the original ε sound) and then back down (for the original ω sound), both in the same syllable: therefore, the result is a circumflex. Similarly, ποιοῦμεν comes from ποιέομεν, a form accented in the regular way.

Non-finite verb forms (infinitives and participles) are accented like nouns. For the infinitives you learn the accent as part of the form, and the form does not change. Participles (see chapter 8) are verbal adjectives, and follow the same accent principles as ordinary adjectives.

See Appendix 3 for additional details, including the rules relating to enclitic words.

Exercise

The following words are incomplete; write them out *with* the proper accent.

Verbs: ἀκουε, μανθανουσι, ποιει, μανθανειν, ἐχετε, λυε, λεγομεθα, μανθανομεθα.
Nouns: θελκτηριοις, φαρμακων, τυχαις, τυχων, ψυχαις, ιατρῳ, κηπον, κηπου.

IV.7 Vocabulary

VERBS

πράττω, πράξω, ἔπραξα, πέπρᾱχα, πέπρᾱγμαι, ἐπράχθην, do (cp. *praxis*)

τρέφω, θρέψω, ἔθρεψα, τέτροφα, τέθραμμαι, ἐτράφην, feed, rear, nourish

φέρω, οἴσω, ἤνεγκα, ἐνήνοχα, ἐνήνεγμαι, ἠνέχθην, carry, bring, wear (clothing) (cp. *bear, metaphor*, L. *fero*)

NOUNS

ἀπορίᾱ, -ᾱς, ἡ, difficulty

ἀρβύλη, -ης, ἡ, boot

γεωργός, -οῦ, ὁ, farmer (cp. *George*)

γλῶττα, -ας, ἡ, tongue (cp. *polyglot*)

εἰρήνη, -ης, ἡ, peace

ἔργον, -ου, τό, work (cp. *work, ergonomic*)

ἱμάτιον, -ου, τό, cloak

κεφαλή, -ῆς, ἡ, head

πεδίον, -ου, τό, plain

πέτρᾱ, -ᾱς, ἡ, rock (cp. *petrify*)

πόλεμος, -ου, ὁ, war (cp. *polemics*)

φυτόν, -οῦ, τό, plant (cp. *phytochemical*)

χλαῖνα, -ας, ἡ, cloak, over-all

ὦμος, -ου, ὁ, shoulder

ADJECTIVES

ἐλεύθερος, -ᾱ, -ον, free (cp. L. *līber*)

λευκός, -ή, -όν, white (cp. *leucocyte*)

χρηστός, -ή, -όν, good, honest

PRONOUNS

αὐτός, same, self; him, her in oblique cases

ἑαυτοῦ, himself, herself, itself

ἐγώ, I

ἐμαυτοῦ, myself

ὅστις, ἥτις, ὅ τι, whoever, who, what

σεαυτοῦ, yourself

σύ, you

τίς, who

τις, some one

PARTICLES, PREPOSITIONS, ADVERBS, CONJUNCTIONS

ἀεί, always (also spelled αἰεί)

ἄρα, then, so that's how it is; marks inference (post-positive)

οὖν, therefore, marks a conclusion drawn from what's gone before (post-postive)

γε, marks emphasis or limitation; enclitic, merges with some pronouns, as ἔγωγε

δή, connecting particle, stronger than δέ (post-positive)

ἐκ, ἐξ, (preposition with genitive), out, out from

ἐν, (preposition with dative), in; κἀν = καὶ ἐν

ἐπί, (preposition with genitive), upon

μάλιστα, especially, very much

μάλιστά γε, yes, certainly

ἐπεί, because, since, when

Also learn the number words.

Notes on the vocabulary

φέρω has highly irregular principal parts, made from different roots. This is called **suppletion**, and a word that exhibits suppletion is **suppletive**. An example of a suppletive verb in English is *be*, which has forms from 3 different roots (*be*, cognate with Greek φύω, Latin *fui*, Sanskrit *bhavati*; *is*, cognate with Greek ἐστι, Latin *est*, Sanskrit *asti*; *was*, cognate with Sanskrit *vartate*; all these forms are from verbs meaning "be"). Very few Greek verbs — and almost no nouns — are as suppletive as φέρω; normally, all the principal parts are formed fairly predictably from the same root.

When you learn a new first-declension noun ending in -α, pay attention to whether it is a long -ᾱ or a short -ᾰ. If the previous sound is *not* ε, ι, or ρ, then the alpha must be short. The accent may also help show you: nouns in -ᾰ will be accented on the third-to-last syllable if the word is three or more syllables long, while nouns in -ᾱ cannot be accented there by the Long Vowel Rule.

Don't confuse the question word ἆρα and the declarative particle ἄρα, which is related.

ἐκ has the sandhi variant ἐξ, used before vowels.

κἀν = καί + ἐν by **crasis**, which is a contraction between words, when the first word ends with a vowel and the second one begins with one. The two words are normally part of the same phrase and the first word is often less important: the article, the conjunction καί, sometimes a particle. The resulting contraction is a long vowel and always marked with a breathing even if it is *not* the first sound of the resulting contracted form, for example ταὐτό, τὸ αὐτό. Thus if you see a breathing *inside* a word, after an initial consonant, you know the "word" is really two words, merged by crasis.

The conjunction ἐπεί indicates that the subordinate clause is relevant to the main clause, but without specifying exactly whether there is a causal relation, a temporal relation, or some other relation between them.

Although εἷς, μία, ἕν looks suppletive, actually all the forms come from the same root, *sem-*. The neuter nominative singular shows this most clearly; the initial *s* became a rough breathing, a sound shift that happened quite early in Greek, and the final *m* became ν, another regular Greek sound shift. The masculine has a third-declension nominative ending (see chapter 8), and the feminine has zero grade of the root and a feminine suffix -ια, much like οἰκία.

IV.8 Reading

1. κἀν ταῖς ἀπορίαις ἔσθ' ὁ χρηστὸς χρήσιμος.

2. τὰ χρηστὰ πράττειν ἔργον ἔστ' ἐλευθέρου.

3. ὁ νοῦς γὰρ ἡμῶν ἐστιν ἐν ἑκάστῳ θεός.

4. ἀεὶ μὲν εἰρήνη γεωργὸν κἀν πέτραις
τρέφει καλῶς, πόλεμος δὲ κἀν πεδίῳ κακῶς.

Passages 1-4 are in verse; they are lines from lost plays by Menander.

5. ἡ μὴν εἰρήνη ἐστὶ καλή, ὁ δὲ πόλεμος κακός.

6. δένδρα καὶ λάχανά ἐστι φυτά, ἀλλὰ πέτραι οὔκ εἰσι.

7. ὁ ἄνθρωπος πέτασον μὲν ἐπὶ τῆς κεφαλῆς ἔχει, ἱμάτιον δὲ ἐπὶ τῶν ὤμων.

8. εἰ τὰ ἔργα εὖ πράττεις, χρήσιμος ἄνθρωπος εἶ. εἰ δὲ μή, κακὸς εἶ. ὁ μὲν χρήσιμος ἄνθρωπος εὖ πράττει, ὁ δὲ κακὸς κακῶς.

9. ὁ γεωργὸς τὰ παιδία λαχάνοις τρέφει.

10. πολλαὶ πέτραι εἰσὶ ἐπὶ τοῦ πεδίου.

11. εἰ κάλαμον μὴ ἔχεις, ἀπορίαν τοῦ γράφειν ἔχεις. οὐκ ἔχεις γράφειν. κάλαμος γὰρ χρήσιμός ἐστι τῷ γράφειν· γράφομεν τοῖς καλάμοις.

12. οἱ γεωργοὶ ἀρβύλας ἔχουσιν. ἆρα ἐπὶ τῆς κεφαλῆς τὰς ἀρβύλας φέρουσιν; οὐχί· οἱ πέτασοί εἰσι ἐπὶ τῶν κεφαλῶν. ὁ μὲν πέτασος ἐπὶ τῆς κεφαλῆς ἐστι, αἱ δὲ ἀρβύλαι οὔ.

13. τὰ μὲν φυτὰ χρήσιμα, αἱ δὲ πέτραι οὔ. οὐκ ἄρα φιλοῦμεν πετρὰς ἐν τῷ κήπῳ ἔχειν. εἰ πετρὰς ἔχομεν ἐν τῷ κήπῳ, ἐκ τοῦ κήπου αὐτὰς φέρομεν.

14. τὸ μανθάνειν φαρμακόν ἐστι τῆς ἀπορίας.

15. φονῶμεν τῇ φωνῇ καὶ τῇ γλώττᾳ.

16. ἐν τῇ κεφαλῇ εἰσι τὼ ὀφθαλμὼ καὶ ἡ γλῶττα. δύο μὲν ὀφθαλμὼ ἔχω, μίαν δὲ γλῶτταν.

17. ἐγὼ μὲν ἱμάτιον φέρω. σὺ δὲ τὸ αὐτὸ ἱμάτιον φέρεις, ἐπεὶ αὐτὸ οὐ φέρω. εἰ ἐγὼ τὸ ἱμάτιον φέρω, σύ γε οὐκ ἔχεις αὐτὸν φέρειν. ἐπεὶ δὴ ἄλλο ἱμάτιον λαμβάνεις, καὶ ἐγὼ καὶ σὺ ἔχομεν ἱμάτια φέρειν. εἰ δύο ἱματίω ἐστόν, νὼ γέ τοι αὐτὼ φέρειν ἔχομεν.

18. πόσοι εἰσὶ οἱ θεοί; ἆρα εἷς θεός, ἢ πολλοί; εἴσι πολλοὶ θεοὶ Ἑλληνικοί· ὁ Ζεὺς ἡ Ἀθηνᾶ ἡ Ἥρα ὁ Ἀπόλλων καὶ πολλοὶ ἄλλοι. δώδεκα θεοὶ οἰκίας ἔχουσι ἐπὶ τῷ Ὀλύμπῳ.

19. ὁ Φίλιππός ἐστι γεωργός. ὁ δὲ Μάρκος ἐστι ἰατρός. ἀγαθὼ ἐστον τὼ ἀνθρώπω. ὁ μὲν τοὺς ἄλλους τρέφει, ὁ δὲ τὴν λύπην λύει. τὸ αὐτὸν ἔργον οὖν οὐ πράττετον. ὁ μὲν λάχανα τοῖς ἄλλοις φέρει, ὁ δὲ φάρμακα. εἰ ὁ Φίλιππος λύπην ἔχει, ὁ Μάρκος αὐτῷ εἰρήνην φέρει. ὁ δὲ Φίλιππος τῷ Μάρκῳ λάχανα φέρει καὶ αὐτὸν τρέφει.

20. ὁ Ἴλιος μακρὸς καὶ καλός ἐστι. ὁ μὲν Ἴλιός ἐστι πόλις (city). ἡ δὲ Ἰλιάς ἐστι βιβλίον. οἱ τοῦ Ἰλίου ἄνθρωποι ἐλεύθεροί εἰσι. εἰρήνην ἔχουσι. Πρίαμος Ἑκάβη τε τὸν Ἴλιον ἔχουσι καὶ τοὺς ἀνθρώπους φιλοῦσιν. ἀλλὰ οἱ Δαναοὶ πόλεμον πράττουσι τοῖς τοῦ Ἰλίου ἀνθρώποις. τίνες εἰσὶ οἱ Δαναοί; εἴσι οἱ Ἕλληνες.

“ὑμεῖς, ὦ Τρωικοί, τὴν Ἑλένην ἔχετε. κακόν ἐστί. κακῶς φέρομεν,” λέγουσιν οἱ Δαναοί.

“οὐ λύομεν τὴν Ἑλένην. ἡ Ἀφροδίτη αὐτὴν εἰς τὴν Τροίαν φέρει. ὁ δὲ Ἀλέξανδρος αὐτὴν φιλεῖ. ἡμεῖς γε ταύτην τὴν ἄνθρωπον οὐ λύομεν,” λέγουσιν οἱ τοῦ Ἰλίου ἄνθρωποι.

“πόλεμον οὖν πράττομεν. ὑμεῖς μὲν ἀποθνήσκετε, ἡ δὲ Ἑλένη ἐλεύθερά ἐστι,” λέγουσιν οἱ Δαναοί. μακρὸς οὖν ἐστι ὁ Τρωικὸς πόλεμος.

IV.9 Conversation

Carefully note the order of words in question and answer.

1. (readings 1, 2) πότε ἐστὶν ὁ χρηστὸς χρήσιμος; τί ἐστιν ἐν ἀπορίαις ὁ χρηστός; τίς ἐστι χρήσιμος ἐν ἀπορίαις; τί ἔργον ἐστὶν ἐλευθέρου; τίνος ἔργον ἐστὶ τὸ πράττειν τὰ χρηστά; τί πράττειν ἔργον ἐστὶν ἐλευθέρου; τίς ἐστι θεὸς ἐν ἡμῖν; τί καλῶς τρέφει τὸν γεωργόν; τίνα καλῶς τρέφει; τί κακῶς; ποῦ;

2. (reading 20) ποῖος ἐστι ὁ Ἴλιος; ποῦ εἰσι οἱ ἄνθρωποι ἐλεύθεροι; ἆρα οἱ τοῦ Ἰλίου ἄνθρωποι ἐλεύθεροι; ἆρα εἰρήνη ἐστὶ ἐν τῷ Ἰλίῳ; τίνες ἔχουσι τὸν Ἴλιον; τίς ἐστι ἡ Ἰλιάς; ἆρα ὁ Ἴλιος καὶ ἡ Ἰλιάς εἰσι οἱ αὐτοί; οὐχί· ὁ μὲν γάρ ἐστι πόλις, ἡ δὲ βιβλίον. τίνες πόλεμον πράττουσι;

3. (vocabulary) ποία ἐστὶν ἡ οἰκία σου; μικρά ἐστιν ἡ οἰκία μου. μικρὰν ἄρα ἔχεις οἰκίαν. μάλιστά γε, ὦ διδάσκαλε, μικράν.

   On the same model: ποίω τὼ ὀφθαλμώ ἔστον; ποῖοι δὲ οἱ δάκτυλοι; ποῖά ᾽στι τὰ δένδρα;

   Note the **prodelision** in ποῖά ᾽στι. You have already seen **elision** of a short vowel at the end of a word, like τοῦτ᾽ ἐστί. Sometimes instead it's the first vowel of the second word that is elided; because this is an elision from the front of a word it is called "pro-elision" (the "d" is for sandhi). Elision of whatever type usually only happens when the words belong together.

4. ἔστι μοι κλίνη καλή· ποία δὲ σοί; κακὴ ἔμοιγε. πέντε ἔχω ἐγώ· σὺ δὲ πόσας; δέκα ἔγωγε.

   Also ἔστον μοι κακὼ τὼ ὀφθαλμώ· ποίω δὲ σοί; ἐμοὶ μὲν μακροὶ οἱ δάκτυλοι· σοὶ δὲ ποῖοι;

5. τί φέρεις ἐπὶ τῶν ὤμων; χλαῖναν φέρω ἐπὶ τῶν ὤμων. ποία δέ σοι ἡ χλαῖνα; λευκὴ ἔμοιγε ἡ χλαῖνα.

   So also τί φέρεις ἐπὶ τῆς κεφαλῆς;

6. τί ἔστι σοι ἐν τῷ κήπῳ; δένδρα ἐστ᾽ ἐν τῷ κήπῳ. καὶ τί ἄλλο; φυτά ἐστι καὶ λάχανα. ποῖα δή; καὶ μικρὰ καὶ μακρά.

   So τί ἐστιν ἐν τῇ οἰκίᾳ, τῷ δωματίῳ;

IV.10 Writing

1. In each of the following sentences, replace one of the noun phrases by a suitable third-person pronoun. For example, τὸ βιβλίον ὁρῶ — αὐτὸ ὁρῶ.

   a. τῷ δακτύλῳ ἕδραν δηλοῖ.

   b. οἱ τῶν διδασκάλων λόγοι εἰσὶ χρήσιμοι.

   c. ὁ γεωργὸς πέτασον φέρει ἐπὶ τῆς κεφαλῆς.

   d. τὼ δένδρω ἐπὶ τοῦ κήπου βλέπομεν.

   e. ὁ ἰατρὸς πολλὰ φάρμακα ἔχει.

   f. τὰ δένδρα νοῦν οὐκ ἔχει.

g. ἡ τῆς μικρᾶς οἰκίας θύρα μακρά ἐστι.

h. τοῖς δέκα δακτύλοις ὁ ἄνθρωπος γράφει.

i. τὸν ἄνθρωπον βλέπομεν, ὃς τὰ λάχανα οὐ φιλεῖ.

j. εἰ λύπην ἐν τῇ ψυχῇ ἔχεις, κακῶς ἔχεις.

2. In the sentences of exercise 1, replace one of the noun phrases by an interrogative pronoun, making a question. You will have to adjust the word order. Then invent a suitable answer to the question, *different* from the original sentence. For example, τὸ τοῦ διδασκάλου βιβλίον ὁρῶ — τίνος βιβλίον ὁρῶ; τὸ τοῦ ἰατροῦ βιβλίον ὁρῶ. or τί τοῦ διδασκάλου ὁρῶ; τὸν τοῦ διδασκάλου πέτασον ὁρῶ.

3. Do the change-number exercise with the following sentences. When one of the affected nouns is modified by a numeral, you'll need to replace it with a different one. For example: εἷς ἄνθρωπος γράφει. In dual, δύο ἀνθρώπω γράφετον — the number clearly must be 2. In plural, choose anything: ἕκατον ἄνθρωποι γράφουσι.

   a. τὰ ἔργα ἀεὶ πράττομεν.

   b. ἡμεῖς μέν ἐσμεν καλοί, ὑμεῖς δὲ κακοί ἐστε.

   c. οἱ ἀγαθοὶ τὰ παιδία εὖ τρέφουσι.

   d. οὗτος ὁ ἄνθρωπος οὐκ ἔχει ἑαυτὸν τρέφειν.

   e. ἡμᾶς αὐτοὺς τρέφομεν.

   f. οἱ τέτταρες γεωργοὶ πόλεμον πράττουσιν.

   g. ὁ ἄνθρωπος ἱμάτιον φέρει καὶ αὐτὸ φιλεῖ.

   h. εἰ ὁ διδάσκαλος τὰ παιδία μὴ βλέπει, ταῦτα τὴν αὐτοῦ φωνὴν οὐκ ἀκούει.

   i. τὴν μὲν εἰρήνην φιλεῖ ὁ γεωργός, τὸν δὲ πόλεμον οὔ.

   j. πέντε πέτραι εἰσὶν ἐν τούτῳ τῷ πεδίῳ.

   k. ὁ ἀγαθὸς λευκὸν πέτασον ἐπὶ τῆς κεφαλῆς φέρει.

   l. εἰ ταῦτα τὰ φυτὰ εὖ τρέφετον, ὦ ἀνθρώπω, χρήστω ἔστον.

   m. εἰ τρεῖς χλαίνας ἔχετε, καὶ τέτταρας ἄλλας ποιεῖτε, ἑπτὰ οὖν ἔχετε.

   n. πόλεμον οὐ φιλῶ· εἰρήνην οὖν ἐμαυτῇ ποιῶ.

   o. οἱ ἓξ διδάσκαλοι ἐννέα βιβλία γράφουσιν.

   q. μία ἄνθρωπος δύο παιδίω τρέφει.

4. Write a paragraph about what a person has in the house, in the garden, or on his or her person. Write the same thing in all persons and numbers.

CHAPTER V

Socrates: Examining One's Life

V.1 Past tenses: overview

Greek has three different past tenses: the **imperfect**, the **aorist**, and the **pluperfect**. The aorist is the normal past tense.

The past tenses have different endings from the present. Each is formed from a different tense stem: the imperfect from the present stem, the aorist from the aorist stem (third principal part), and the pluperfect from the perfect stem (fourth principal part, coming in chapter 14). All past-tense indicative forms have the **past indicative augment** as a prefix, usually called just "the augment" for short. The augment is ἐ- added before the stem. When the stem begins with a consonant we just have ἐ-, called the **syllabic augment** because it adds a syllable to the verb. When the stem begins with a vowel, the augment contracts with it to form a long vowel, called the **temporal augment** because it is a temporally longer form. For example, from λύω we form imperfect ἔλυον, which is ἐ + λυ + ον. But from ἀκούω we form ἤκουον, ἐ + ἀκου + ον. The augmented form has the same breathing as the original vowel has.

These are the contractions of the augment with an initial vowel:

stem vowel	augmented
α, ε	η
ο	ω
ι	ῑ
υ	ῡ
αι	ῃ
οι	ῳ
ευ	ηυ

But a small number of common verbs beginning with ε- have ει- for the augment, notably ἔχω, imperfect εἶχον. Usually the aorist will be the same way, so you can recognize these verbs because their third principal part will begin with εἰ- instead of ἠ- — though in fact ἔχω is an exception to this tendency, as its aorist is ἔσχον.

When a verb has a prefix, like ἀπο-θνήσκω, the augment always goes directly on the verb stem, after the prefix. For example, the third person singular imperfect indicative active of this verb is ἀπέθνησκε, and the third singular aorist indicative active is ἀπέθανε.

The past indicative augment is only used for past tense forms in the indicative mood. It is never used in the present, future, or perfect tenses (unlike in Latin, the perfect is not really a past tense in Greek). It is never used in the other moods — imperative, subjunctive, optative, infinitive, participle. Although it's normally just called "the augment," remembering the full name will help you remember where it is and is not used.

Verbs can form their aorist in any of three different ways. The **first aorist** is also called the **weak aorist** or the **sigmatic aorist**; we will discuss this in the next chapter. The **second aorist** or **strong aorist** can easily be learned now because it uses the same endings as the imperfect. The third kind really should be called "third aorist," but in fact it is conventionally called **root aorist**; only a few verbs have this, and you will see them in chapter 13. You learn which kind of aorist a verb takes as you learn its principal parts. If the third principal part ends in -ον, like ἔμαθον from μανθάνω, then the verb has a second aorist. If the third principal part ends in -α, like ἔλυσα from λύω, then the verb has a first aorist; these are more common. There is no difference in meaning; the difference between first and second aorist is similar to the difference between strong and weak preterites in English, like *write, wrote* (strong) as opposed to *love, loved* (weak). Here **strong** means that the verb stem conveys the appropriate meaning all by itself, while a **weak** form is one that needs the help of a suffix (like the -σ- of a Greek weak aorist, or the -*ed* of an English weak preterite).

Thus when a verb has a strong aorist, the aorist stem is the plain root of the verb, and the present stem is usually somehow lengthened or otherwise changed. For example, μανθάνω "I learn," ἔμαθον "I learned." The root of this verb is μαθ-. The aorist stem is just the root, with augment in the indicative; the present stem is μανθαν-, with an extra -ν- inside the root and a suffix -αν- after it. Some verbs have the plain root in both the present and the aorist; in these verbs, the present will have e grade and the aorist will have zero grade. An example is λείπω, "leave, abandon." Its root is λειπ- and you can see the e grade in the present tense; its aorist is ἔλιπον, with zero grade of the root. The present stem and the aorist stem will always be different in some way.

The imperfect tense is used for continuing or habitual action in the past. In fact, all the forms from the present system denote continuing action. You might think of this as an action viewed as a process rather than an event.

The aorist tense is the ordinary past, viewing an action as a single event or point. All the forms from the aorist system have this single-point meaning.

The difference between the process/continual/durative view and the single-point view of an action is called **aspect**. We may say that forms from the present system have **durative aspect** or **imperfective aspect**, while forms from the aorist system have **punctual aspect** or **aoristic aspect**. *Imperfect* comes from a Latin word meaning "not completely finished," and imperfective aspect focuses on the action while it is continuing, before it's over. *Aorist* is ἀόριστος "unlimited, unqualified," from ὅρος "boundary, limit." The aorist tense is the simple past tense, without any qualifications, restrictions, or limitations about what *kind* of past action it is. It is the usual past tense for telling what happens in a story, while the imperfect can be used for setting up the background.

The present stem has two tenses in the indicative mood, the present and the imperfect. In all the other moods there is only one form from the present stem, traditionally called "present infinitive, present imperative," and so on. Arguably these non-indicative forms should really be called "*imperfect* infinitive" and so on, because they all have imperfective aspect, but (depending on the mood and the construction) may or may not refer to present time. As you will learn in chapter 14, the perfect system also has two tenses in the indicative, not the other moods. The aorist system and the future system (chapter 5) both have only one indicative tense: there is no "punctual-aspect present indicative" formed from the aorist stem, only a "punctual-aspect (or unspecified-aspect) past indicative." All these forms can also exist in the various voices, active, middle, and passive, as you will see in chapter 10.

If you're wondering about the *second* principal part, it forms the future active system, and we will work with it in the next chapter.

V.2 Forms of the imperfect indicative active

These are the forms of the imperfect indicative active, from the present stem (first principal part): note the augment and the endings.

	λύ-ω	ἀκού-ω	εἰμί
singular			
1st	ἔ-λῡ-ον	ἤκου-ον	ἦν or ἦ
2nd	ἔ-λῡ-ες	ἤκου-ες	ἦσθα
3rd	ἔ-λῡ-ε(ν)	ἤκου-ε(ν)	ἦν
dual			
2nd	ἐ-λύ-ετον	ἠκού-ετον	ἦτον
3rd	ἐ-λῡ-έτην	ἠκου-έτην	ἤτην
plural			
1st	ἐ-λύ-ομεν	ἠκού-ομεν	ἦμεν
2nd	ἐ-λύ-ετε	ἠκού-ετε	ἦτε
3rd	ἔ-λῡ-ον	ἤκου-ον	ἦσαν

The endings of the imperfect are called the **secondary endings**, while those of the present are the **primary endings**. The primary endings are used for **primary tenses** in the indicative (present, future) and for the subjunctive mood, while secondary endings similar to those of the imperfect are used for **secondary tenses** in the indicative (imperfect, aorist) and for the optative mood. As you will see in chapter 10, there are also primary and secondary endings for the middle and passive voices.

Note that the 1st singular and 3rd plural are identical (for regular verbs, though not for εἰμι). This seems confusing, but in practice context virtually always tells you which form you have. The 3rd plural originally had a final -τ, making for example ἔλυοντ, but this cluster was simplified at the end of the word. (This is the same third-person plural ending as Latin *amant.*) In fact, the present tense ending is similar: it was originally λύοντι, but the -ντ-cluster was simplified to -σ- and the previous vowel was lengthened to "make up" for the lost sound — thus λύουσι. This "making up" is called **compensatory lengthening**: making a vowel long as if to make up or compensate for a lost sound after it.

Not surprisingly, the forms of εἰμι are irregular. In the imperfect this verb is *not* enclitic: every form has a circumflex except the third-person dual, which has acute accent.

In contracted verbs, the imperfect personal endings contract with the stem: ἐποίει = ἐ + ποιε + ε, ἐδήλου = ἐ + δηλο + ε, ἐτίμᾱ = ἐ + τιμα + ε. The rules for contraction are the same as in the present tense; the complete vowel chart is in Appendix 1 section 1. Note that the accent is put into position before contraction, just as in the present, so ἐποιεῖτε in second person plural, contracted from ἐποιέετε. Contracted verbs never have a second aorist, and no verb has contracted forms in the aorist system.

Here are the forms of the imperfect indicative active of contracted verbs:

		τῑμάω, τῑμῶ	ποιέω, ποιῶ	δηλόω, δηλῶ
singular				
	1st	ἐ-τίμ-ων	ἐ-ποί-ουν	ἐ-δήλ-ουν
	2nd	ἐ-τίμ-ᾱς	ἐ-ποί-εις	ἐ-δήλ-ους
	3rd	ἐ-τίμ-ᾱ	ἐ-ποί-ει	ἐ-δήλ-ου
dual				
	2nd	ἐ-τῑμ-ᾶτον	ἐ-ποι-εῖτον	ἐ-δηλ-οῦτον
	3rd	ἐ-τῑμ-ά-την	ἐ-ποι-είτην	ἐ-δηλ-ούτην
plural				
	1st	ἐ-τῑμ-ῶμεν	ἐ-ποι-οῦμεν	ἐ-δηλ-οῦμεν
	2nd	ἐ-τῑμ-ᾶτε	ἐ-ποι-εῖτε	ἐ-δηλ-οῦτε
	3rd	ἐ-τίμ-ων	ἐ-ποί-ουν	ἐ-δήλ-ουν

Exercise

Form the imperfect indicative active of the following verbs:

λέγω, τρέφω, λύω, μανθάνω, θιγγάνω "touch," τυγχάνω "chance, happen to" κτείνω "kill," βάλλω "throw," βλέπω, ἐλπίζω "hope," ᾄδω "sing," αἰσχύνω "disgrace," θνήσκω "die."

And form the imperfect indicative active of the following verbs, which are contracted:

ὁρῶ, φιλῶ, φωνῶ, ἀξιῶ (ἀξιόω) "ask, consider worthy."

V.3 Forms of the second aorist

These are the forms of the aorist indicative active, for a verb with a second aorist. These forms come from the third principal part, take the past indicative augment, and have the same endings as the imperfect. Example: λαμβάνω "take," whose root (and also second aorist stem) is λαβ-.

	Singular	Dual	Plural
1st	ἔ-λαβ-ον		ἐ-λάβ-ομεν
2nd	ἔ-λαβ-ες	ἐ-λάβ-ετον	ἐ-λάβ-ετε
3rd	ἔ-λαβ-ε(ν)	ἐ-λαβ-έτην	ἔ-λαβ-ον

Note the sandhi form ἔλαβεν for third person singular, before vowels.

The verb εἰμι "be" has no aorist at all. In fact, it has only two principal parts, εἰμι, ἔσομαι, and has only a present system (only in the active voice) and a future system (only in the middle voice).

Exercise

The following verbs have strong aorists (second aorist); write out the aorist indicative active for each. See the previous section for glosses.

Strong aorist from τυγχάνω (stem τυχ-), βάλλω (stem βαλ-), θιγγάνω (stem θιγ-), κτείνω (stem κταν-), μανθάνω (stem μαθ-), θνῄσκω (stem θαν-).

V.4 Aorist infinitive active

To form the second (strong) aorist infinitive, use the aorist active stem *without* the past indicative augment; add ending -εῖν, always with a circumflex accent. For example, from ἔλαβον, the infinitive is λαβεῖν. Note the accent: the present infinitive active is accented before the -ειν, as γράφειν, but the second aorist infinitive active is accented on the -εῖν.

The difference between these two infinitives is their aspect. Both are verbal nouns, but the present (imperfective, durative) infinitive considers the action as on-going, as a process, or as taking place at the same time as the main verb of the sentence, while the aorist (punctual or unspecified) infinitive considers the action either as a single unit or as taking place prior to the main verb of the sentence. For example, in ὁ διδάσκαλος τοῖς παιδίοις κελεύει τὰ γράμματα μανθάνειν, the teacher is telling the children to form the habit of learning literature, but in ὁ διδάσκαλος τοῖς παιδίοις κελεύει τὰ γράμματα μαθεῖν he is telling them to learn the specific lesson on a specific occasion.

Exercise

1. Write out the present infinitive active and the aorist infinitive active for all the verbs in the exercise of the previous section.

2. Write some synopses (see Appendix 1 section 5) including the aorist active forms.

V.5 Vocabulary

VERBS

βάλλω, βαλῶ, ἔβαλον, βέβληκα, βέβλημαι, ἐβλήθην, throw (cp. *ballistic*)

ἐλπίζω, ἐλπιῶ, ἤλπισα, – , – , ἠλπίσθην, hope, expect

ἐξετάζω, ἐξετῶ, ἐξήτασα, ἐξήτακα, ἐξήτασμαι, ἐξητάσθην, examine, test

ἔφη, said he, said she (from φημι, chapter 9)

κελεύω, κελεύσω, ἐκέλευσα, κεκέλευκα, κεκέλευσμαι, ἐκελεύσθην, order, command

λαμβάνω, λήψομαι, ἔλαβον, εἴληφα, εἴλημμαι, ἐλήφθην, take, grasp

τιμάω, τιμήσω, ἐτίμησα, τετίμηκα, τετίμημαι, ἐτιμήθην, honor

NOUNS

ἀξίᾱ, -ᾱς, ἡ, worth, value

δοῦλος, -ου, ὁ, slave (cp. *hierodule*)

δραχμή, -ῆς, ἡ, drachma, a silver coin about the size of a US dime

ἡμιμναῖον, -ου, τό, half-mina

μνᾶ, μνᾶς, ἡ, mina, a weight, or a sum of money equal to 100 drachmae

ὀβολός, -οῦ, ὁ, obol, a small coin

τάλαντον, -ου, τό, talent, a large weight of silver, about 26 kilograms or 57 pounds

φίλος, -ου, ὁ, friend

ADJECTIVES

ἄξιος, -α, -ον, worth, worthy

ὁπόσος, -η, -ο, so great, so much, how much

ADVERBS, CONJUNCTIONS, PARTICLES

εἴγε, if (= εἰ + γε)

οὐδέ, not even; can be used in pairs like English "neither ... nor"

οὐκοῦν, then

που, somewhere, I suppose, doubtless; enclitic particle expressing scepticism or softening a statement

τήμερον, today

χθές, ἐχθές, yesterday (cognate with *yesterday* and with L. *heri*)

ὥσπερ, as, like

Notes on the vocabulary

One drachma was roughly a day's wages for a skilled laborer in classical Athens. There were six obols to the drachma, 100 drachmae to the mina, 60 minae to the talent. An obol was a small amount of money and a talent was a huge fortune.

V.6 Reading

1. ἤκουσα δέ ποτε καὶ ἄλλον αὐτοῦ λόγον, ᾧ ἐκέλευσεν ὁ Σωκράτης ἕκαστον ἐξετάζειν ἑαυτόν, ὁπόσου τοῖς φίλοις ἄξιός ἐστιν. ἆρ᾽, ἔφη, εἰσὶν ἄξιαι φίλων, ὥσπερ δούλων; τῶν γὰρ δούλων ὁ μέν που δυοῖν μναῖν ἄξιός ἐστιν, ὁ δὲ πέντε μνῶν, ὁ δὲ καὶ δέκα, ὁ δ᾽ οὐδ᾽ ἡμιμναίου. Ναί, ἔφη ὁ Ἀντισθένης. οὐκοῦν, ἔφη ὁ Σωκράτης, εἴ γε ταῦτ᾽ ἐστὶ τοιαῦτα, καλῶς ἔχει ἐξετάζειν ἑαυτὸν ἕκαστον ἄνθρωπον, πόσου ἄρα ἐστὶ τοῖς φίλοις ἄξιος.

   The passage comes from Xenophon's *Memorabilia*, 2.5.

   ἤκουσα is aorist of ἀκούω; see chapter 6. This form is first person singular aorist indicative active.

   Remember that an adverb with ἔχω expresses a state, so καλῶς ἔχει is "it is well, it's going well."

2. τὸ μὲν τάλαντον ἔχει ἑξήκοντα μνᾶς, ἡ δὲ μνᾶ δραχμὰς ἑκατόν, ἡ δὲ δραχμὴ ὀβολοὺς ἕξ.

3. τάδε τὰ βιβλία εἰσὶ ἄξια δραχμῆς ἕκαστα. εἰ δραχμὴν ἔχω, βιβλίον λαβεῖν ἔχω. δραχμὴν δὲ οὐκ ἔχω· βιβλίον οὖν οὐ λαμβάνω.

4. χθὲς δοῦλος ἦν, ἀλλὰ τήμερον ἐλεύθερός εἰμι. χθὲς μὲν ὅδε ὁ ἄνθρωπος ἐμοὶ ἐκέλευε, τήμερον δὲ οὔ. οἱ ἄνθρωποι ἐλευθεροῖς οὐ κελεύουσι.

5. ὁ διδάσκαλος ἡμᾶς κελεύει μανθάνειν. τήμερον ἡμᾶς ἐξετάζει. εἰ εὖ ἐμανθάνομεν, ἄξιοί ἐσμεν καὶ ὁ διδάσκαλος ἡμᾶς τιμᾷ. εἰ δὲ μή, ὁ διδάσκαλος ἡμᾶς οὐδὲ τιμᾷ οὐδὲ φιλεῖ.

6. ἐπεὶ οἱ ἀγαθοὶ τὴν τῆς διδασκάλης φωνὴν ἤκουον, κακός τις τὸ βιβλίον ἔλαβε καὶ εἶπε, "χθὲς μὲν εἰς τὸ βιβλίον ἔβλεπον, τήμερον δὲ εἰς τὸ βιβλίον βλέπω, ἀλλ᾽ οὐ μανθάνω. σοῦ ἀκούω, ὦ διδασκάλη, ἀλλ᾽ οὐ μανθάνω. ἆρα δοῦλος εἰμι;"

   "οὐχί," ἔφη ἡ διδασκάλη. "οὐδὲ δοῦλος εἶ οὐδὲ χρήσιμος ἄνθρωπος. νοῦν οὐκ ἔχεις. πέτρα γέ τοι ἡ κεφαλή."

   οἱ δὲ ἄλλοι εἶπον, "κακὸς μέν ἐστι, ἀλλ᾽ οὐ πέτρα. φίλος ἡμῶν ἐστί. ἐπεὶ ταῦτα λέγεις, ὦ διδασκάλη, κακὴ εἶ. οὐ τιμῶμεν τοὺς κακούς."

   ἡ δὲ διδασκάλη τοῖς παιδίοις ἐκέλευσε πολλὰ γράφειν. "οὐκ ἔγωγε κακή εἰμι," ἔφη, "ἀλλ᾽ ὑμεῖς." ἆρα ἀγαθὴ διδασκάλη ἦν;

   ἐκέλευσε is aorist of κελεύω.

7. γεωργός τις πολλὰ καὶ καλὰ φυτὰ ἔτρεφε. δύο παιδία εἶχε, τὸ μὲν χρηστόν, τὸ δὲ κακόν. τὸ μὲν χρηστὸν παιδίον ἐν τῷ κήπῳ πολλὰ ἔπραττε καὶ τὰ τοῦ γεωργοῦ φυτὰ εὖ ἐφίλει. τὸ δὲ ἄλλο τὰ φυτὰ οὐκ ἔτρεφε. "οὔκ εἰμι δοῦλος," ἀεὶ ἔλεγε. ὁ δὲ γεωργὸς ἔλεγε, "εἴ τοι τὸ τῶν φυτῶν ἔργον μὴ πράττεις, πέτραις οὖν σαυτὸν τρέφεις!"

8. ὁ μὲν Φίλιππος ἓξ ὀβολοὺς ἔχει, ὁ δὲ Ἀλέξανδρος ἑπτά, ὁ δὲ Μάρκος ὀκτώ. πόσους ὀβολοὺς ἔχουσι; εἴκοσι καὶ ἕνα ὀβολοὺς ἔχουσι, ἓξ γὰρ καὶ ἑπτὰ καὶ ὀκτώ εἰσι ἕν καὶ εἴκοσι. πόσας δραχμὰς ἔχουσι; ὁ μὲν Φίλιππος μίαν δραχμὰν ἔχει, ἓξ γὰρ ὀβολοὺς ἔχει, καὶ ἓξ ὀβολοί εἰσι δραχμή. ὁ δὲ Ἀλέξανδρος δραχμὰν καὶ ὀβολὸν ἔχει, ὁ δὲ Μάρκος δραχμὰν καὶ δύο ὀβολὼ ἔχει. οἱ ἄνθρωποι οὖν ἔχουσι τρεῖς δραχμὰς καὶ τρεῖς ὀβολούς.

9. ἄνθρωπός τις πέτραν ἔλαβε καὶ αὐτὴν ἔβαλε. ἤλπιζε τὴν πέτραν ἐκ τοῦ πεδίου βαλεῖν. αἱ γὰρ πέτραι οὐ χρήσιμαί εἰσι. ἀλλὰ τῇ πέτρᾳ ὁ ἄνθρωπος τὸν φίλον ἔκτανε. πολλὰς οὖν λύπας εἶχε· εἰ γὰρ ὁ φίλος ἀποθνήσκει, λύπην αἰεὶ ἔχομεν. "κακός εἰμι," ἔφη, "φίλον γὰρ πέτρᾳ ἔκτανον. κακῶς ἔχω. ὁ φίλος ἐμοὶ ἀξιώτερος ἦν ἢ ἔκατον τάλαντα."

10. τίς ἐστι ἡμιμναῖον; ἡμιμναῖόν ἐστι πεντήκοντα δραχμαί. ἔστι οὖν τριακόσιοι ὀβολοί. δύο ἡμιμναῖόν εἰσι μνᾶ. μνᾶ μακρότερά ἐστι ἡμιμναίου, ἀλλὰ τάλαντον μακρότερόν ἐστι μνᾶς.

11. ἓξ μνῶν ἓξ φιάλας Κροῖσος βασιλεὺς ἀνέθηκεν
    δραχμῇ τὴν ἑτέρην μείζονα τῆς ἑτέρης.

> Greek Anthology 14.12. **φιάλη, -ης, ἡ** bowl, drinking cup. **βασιλεύς** king, nom. sg.; see chapter 16 for forms of this noun. **ἀνέθηκεν**, 3rd sg aorist indicative active of ἀνα-τίθημι, here "dedicate." **ἕτερος**, other, usually when there are only two things in question; here we are comparing each one to the next in the set. **μείζονα**, bigger, irregular comparative form, here fem. acc. sg. Puzzle: how much is each φιάλη worth?

V.7 Conversation

1. (reading 1) τί ἤκουσε τὸν λόγον; ἐν τούτῳ τῷ λόγῳ τί ἐποίει ὁ Σωκράτης; τί ἐκέλευσεν ὁ Σωκράτης; τίσι ἐκέλευσεν ὁ Σωκράτης; τί ἐξετάζομεν; ἆρα ἀξίαι φίλων εἰσὶν ὥσπερ ἀξίαι δούλων; ἆρα οἱ φίλοι ἀξιοί εἰσι μιᾶς δραχμῆς ἢ δυοῖν; τί λέγει ὁ Ἀντισθένης; ἆρα σὺ ἄξιος πέντε μνῶν τοῖς φίλοις;

2. (reading 4) ἆρα ὁ ἄνθρωπος, ὃς λέγει, δοῦλός ἐστι; ἆρα δοῦλος ἦν; πότε ἦν δοῦλος; (see question words, chapter 1) ἆρα τοῖς ἐλευθέροις ἀνθρώποις κελεύομεν; τίσι κελεύομεν; τίς ἐκέλευε τῷ ἀνθρώπῳ;

3. (reading 11) τίς τὰς φιάλας ἀνέθηκεν; τὰς φιάλας ὁ Κροῖσος ἀνέθηκεν. τίς ἐστι ὁ Κροῖσος; βασιλεὺς ὁ Κροῖσος. τί ἀνέθηκεν ὁ Κροῖσος; ὁ Κροῖσος ἓξ φιάλας ἀνέθηκεν. πόσαι φιάλαι εἰσί; ἓξ φιάλαι εἰσί. ἆρα αἱ φιάλαι αἱ αὐταί; οὐχί· αὐτὴ μείζων ἐστί τῆσδε. ἆρα ἡ πρώτη φιάλη ἐστὶ ἀξία δυοῖν μνῶν; ποσῶν δραχμῶν ἀξία ἐστὶ ἡ φιάλη;

4. (vocabulary) ἆρα δοῦλος εἶ, ὦ φίλε; οὐχί, οὐκ ἔγωγε. ἐλεύθερός εἰμι. ἆρα οὗτός ἐστι δοῦλος; οὔκ ἐστι. ἆρα οὗτός ἐστι φίλος; ναί, ὁ Μάρκος ἐμοὶ φίλος ἐστί. ἆρα ὁ Μάρκος καὶ ἡ Μυρρίνη φίλω ἐστόν; ναί, φίλω ἐστόν. τίνες φίλοι εἰσί; τίνες ἄξιοί εἰσι;

τί ἐλπίζεις ποιεῖν τήμερον; ἆρα ἐλπίζεις βιβλίον γράφειν; ἆρα ἐλπίζεις δραχμὰς λαμβάνειν; ἆρα ἐλπίζεις μανθάνειν; ἆρα ἐλπίζεις πέτρας βάλλειν εἰς τὰ δένδρα; ὁ Φίλιππος ἐλπίζει τοὺς φίλους βλέπειν. τί ἐλπίζει πράττειν ὁ Φίλιππος; τίνας ἐλπίζει βλέπειν; ἡ Ἑλένη ἐλπίζει τοὺς φίλους βλέπειν, ὥσπερ ὁ Φίλιππος. τί ἐλπίζει ποιεῖν; ἆρα ὁ Φίλιππος καὶ ἡ Ἑλένη ταὐτὸν ἐλπίζετον πράττειν;

V.8 Writing

1. Rewrite the sentences of chapter 4, writing exercise 3, in the imperfect tense.

2   Rewrite the following in the aorist tense:
   a. τὰς πέτρας βάλλει.
   b. τὸ βιβλίον τοῖς δακτύλοις θιγγάνουσι.
   c. ὁ πόλεμος πολλοὺς κτείνει.
   d. τοῖς βιβλίοις πολλὰ μανθάνομεν.
   e. οὗτος ὁ ἄνθρωπος νέος ἀποθνήσκει.
   f. τὸ τοῦ διδασκάλου βιβλίον λαμβάνεις.
   g. τὼ παιδίω οὐ μανθάνετον.
   h. τοὺς πετάσους βάλλετε.
   i. τὸν φίλον οὐ κτείνω.
   j. αἱ ἄνθρωποι τὰ παιδία ἐκ τοῦ κήπου λαμβάνουσι.

3. Rewrite each of the following sentences in the imperfect *and then* do the change-number exercise with the resulting sentence. For example, from δοῦλον βλέπει you would make: δοῦλον ἔβλεπε, δοῦλον ἐβλέπετον, δοῦλον ἔβλεπον. When the verb has a second aorist, *also* write in the aorist, in all three numbers.
   a. φέρω τὸν πέτασον ἐπὶ τῆς κεφαλῆς.
   b. μανθάνεις τὰ χρηστὰ ἐν τῷ βιβλίῳ.
   c. λέγουσι τοῦτο εἶναι καλὸν λύπης φάρμακον.
   d. γράφομεν ἕκαστον ἐν τῷ βιβλίῳ.
   e. ἀκούετον χρηστὰ τῇ ἀκοῇ.
   f. ἐλπίζω χρήσιμον εἶναι τὸν χρηστόν.
   g. βλέπω τοῖς ὀφθαλμοῖς ἕκαστον.
   h. ὁ διδάσκαλος τοῖς παιδίοις κελεύει βιβλία λαβεῖν.
   i. φιλοῦμεν καλοὺς λόγους ἀκούειν.
   j. ὀβολὸν τῷ δούλῳ βάλλω.
   k. οὗτος ὁ δοῦλος ἐστὶ φίλος τοῦ παιδίου.
   l. ἀξιοὶ καὶ ἀγαθοί ἐσμεν.
   m. ὁ φιλόσοφος κελεύει τὸν ἄνθρωπον ἑαυτὸν ἐξετάζειν.
   n. ὁ δοῦλος ἐλπίζει ἐλεύθερος εἶναι.
   o. ὁ νέος τὴν πέτραν λαμβάνει καὶ βάλλει.

4. Rewrite reading 1 from Socrates's point of view, so that Socrates is telling the story.

5. Rewrite reading 1 so that Antisthenes is telling the story.

Chapter VI

Cleobis and Biton

VI.1 The future system

The future stem comes from the second principal part. It is normally formed from the present with the suffix -σ-, as λύω, λύ-σ-ω or βλέπω, βλέπ-σ-ω = βλέψω. The endings of the future are always just the same as for the present (in all moods).

singular

1st	λύ-σ-ω	βλέψ-ω
2nd	λύ-σ-εις	βλέψ-εις
3rd	λύ-σ-ει	βλέψ-ει,

dual

2nd	λύ-σ-ετον	βλέψ-ετον
3rd	λύ-σ-ετον	βλέψ-ετον

plural

1st	λύ-σ-ομεν	βλέψ-ομεν
2nd	λύ-σ-ετε	βλέψ-ετε
3rd	λύ-σ-ουσι(ν)	βλέψ-ουσι(ν)

The future infinitive active is also just like the present: λύσειν, βλέψειν.

Only the active and middle voices of the future come from the second principal part; as you will see in chapter 12, the future passive comes from the sixth principal part.

When a verb's second principal part ends in -ῶ with circumflex, as βαλῶ from βάλλω, the verb has a contracted future, and the forms are like the present of ποιέω. All contracted futures are ε-contracts. So the future indicative active of βάλλω is βαλῶ, βαλεῖς, βαλεῖ, and so on. See further chapter 18.

The future tense, in any mood, refers to something that has not yet happened. Forms from the future system do not have a particular aspect: there is no way in Greek, in general, to distinguish between viewing a future event as a single incident (punctual or aoristic aspect) and viewing it as a process (durative or imperfective aspect). All you can say is that it hasn't happened.

VI.2 The first aorist

As you know, the aorist is the ordinary past tense, and the aorist active is formed from the third principal part. You have already learned the second or strong aorist. The first or weak aorist (α-aorist) stem normally looks much like the future stem; its suffix is also -σ-. The first aorist indicative is formed from the aorist stem by prefixing the augment and adding the proper endings. The characteristic vowel of the endings is α, which is found in all except the 3rd singular. The first aorist, just like the second aorist, has the past indicative augment in the indicative, but not in any other mood. A verb has *either* a first aorist *or* a second aorist (with a couple of exceptions), not both, just as in English verbs form their preterite either with -*ed* or with a vowel change, not both. The third principal part is the first person singular aorist indicative active. If it looks like ἔμαθον the verb has a second aorist; if it looks like ἔλυσα the verb has a first aorist.

These are the forms of the first aorist indicative active.

singular

1st	ἔ-λῡ-σ-α	ἔ-βλεψ-α
2nd	ἔ-λῡ-σ-ας	ἔ-βλεψ-ας,
3rd	ἔ-λῡ-σ-ε(ν)	ἔ-βλεψ-ε(ν)

dual

2nd	ἐ-λῡ́-σ-ατον	ἐ-βλεψ-ατον
3rd	ἐ-λῡ-σ-άτην	ἐ-βλεψ-ατην

plural

1st	ἐ-λῡ́-σ-αμεν	ἐ-βλεψ-αμεν
2nd	ἐ-λῡ́-σ-ατε	ἐ-βλεψ-ατε
3rd	ἔ-λῡ-σ-αν	ἐ-βλεψ-αν

From contracted verbs the future stem and the first aorist stem are generally formed with a long stem vowel, then the -σ- suffix, like this:

- ε-verbs have -ησ-: ποιῶ, ποιήσω, ἐποίησα
- α-verbs also have -ησ-: τιμῶ, τιμήσω, ἐτίμησα
- ο-verbs have -ωσ-: δηλῶ, δηλώσω, ἐδήλωσα

But not every verb has predictable forms, so you need to learn the principal parts for new verbs.

The aorist infinitive active is: λῦσαι, βλέψαι. Its accent is always on the second-to-last syllable, as ἀκοῦσαι; because the final -αι counts as short for accentuation, the accent on the second-to-last syllable will be a circumflex if the vowel is long. Be careful: there are two other forms that are just like this except for their accent: ἄκουσαι is second singular aorist imperative middle (chapter 11) and ἀκούσαι is third singular aorist optative active (chapter 8).

The aorist active and middle come from the third principal part; the aorist passive, like the future passive, comes from the sixth, as you will see in chapter 13.

Exercises

1. The following verbs have regular future and first aorist forms. Form the third person singular, dual, and plural, future indicative active and aorist indicative active (six forms total), for each one: λέγω, γράφω, πιστεύω "believe," ἄρχω "begin," πέμπω, κλήω, παύω, τάττω (stem ταγ-), φιλέω, ἀριστάω "eat breakfast," ἀξιόω "think worthy," κελεύω "order, command."

2. Form the future infinitive active and the aorist infinitive active for these same 12 verbs.

VI.3 Syntax of motion

Generally speaking, motion towards is expressed by the accusative, motion from is expressed by the genitive, rest at is expressed by the dative, and prepositions with these meanings take these cases (though ἐπί with the genitive in the sense "on, resting on" is an exception). In prose the Greeks preferred to use prepositional phrases, rather than the case alone, for motion, but in verse you will often see the cases used by themselves.

VI.4 Vocabulary

VERBS

ἀριστάω, ἀριστήσω, ἠρίστησα, ἠρίστηκα, – , – , eat breakfast

εἶπον, said (second aorist to λέγω)

ἐλαύνω, ἐλῶ, ἤλασα, ἐλήλακα, ἐλήλαμαι, ἠλάθην, ride, drive

ἕλκω, ἕλξω, εἵλκυσα, εἵλκυκα, εἵλκυσμαι, εἱλκύσθην, draw, drag, pull, row (cp. L. *sulcus*)

θαυμάζω, θαυμάσω, ἐθαύμασα, τεθαύμακα, – ἐθαυμάσθη, wonder, be amazed (cp. *thaumaturgy*)

θεραπεύω, θεραπεύσω, ἐθεράπευσα, – , – , ἐθεραπεύθην, tend, care for (cp. *therapy*)

κλήω, κλήσω, ἔκλησα, κέκληκα, κέκλημαι, ἐκλείσθην, shut (cp. L. *claudere*)

παύω, παύσω, ἔπαυσα, πέπαυκα, πέπαυμαι, ἐπαύθην, stop (cp. L. *pausa*)

πέμπω, πέμψω, ἔπεμψα, πέπομφα, πέπεμμαι, ἐπέμφθην, send

τάττω, τάξω, ἔταξα, τέταχα, τέταγμαι, ἐτάχθην, fix, arrange (cp. *tactics, syntax*)

τίκτω, τέξω, ἔτεκον, τέτοκα, – , ἐτέχθην, produce, bring forth, give birth (cp. *thane*)

φεύγω, φεύξομαι, ἔφυγον, πέφευγα, πέφυγμαι, – , flee (cp. L. *fugo*)

PREPOSITIONS

ἀνά, up, along (+ acc.)

ἀπό, from (+ gen.)

διά, on account of (+ acc.); through (+ gen.)

εἰς, ἐς, into, to (+ acc.)

ἐπί, upon (+ gen. or dat.); to (+ gen.); against (+ acc.)

κατά, down to (+ acc.); down from (+ gen.)

μετά, after (+ acc.); with (+ gen.); among (+ dat.)

παρά, along, up to, within (+ acc.); from (+ gen.); beside (+ dat.)

περί, around, about (+ gen., dat., or acc.)

πρό, before, in front of (+ gen.)

πρός, towards, for (+ acc.); besides (+ dat.)

ὑπό, under, to under (+ acc.); under (+ dat.); from under, by the agency of (+ gen.)

NOUNS

ἄγγελος, -ου, ὁ, messenger (cp. *angel*)

ἀγορά, -ᾶς, ἡ, market-place (cp. *agoraphobia*)

ἀδελφός, -οῦ, ὁ, brother (cp. *Philadelphia*)

ἅμαξα, -ης, ἡ, cart, carriage

βίος, -ου, ὁ, life (cp. *biology*)

βλάβη, -ης, ἡ, harm

διαθήκη, -ης, ἡ, will, testament

δίκη, -ης, ἡ, lawsuit, justice (cp. *theodicy*)

ζυγόν, -οῦ, τό, yoke (cp. *yoke*, L. *iugum*)

ἡμέρα, -ας, ἡ, day (cp. *ephemeral*)

θάλαττα, -ης, ἡ, sea

ἵππος, -ου, ὁ, horse (cp. L. *equus*)

κληρονόμος, -ου, ὁ, heir

κώμη, -ης, ἡ, village

σχολαστικός, -οῦ, ὁ, a scholar, pedant, student

χρόνος, -ου, ὁ, time (cp. *chronic*)

ᾠόν, ᾠοῦ, τό, egg (cp. *oocyte*, L. *ovum*)

ADJECTIVES

ἐκεῖνος, ἐκείνη, ἐκεῖνο, that

κοινός, -ή, -όν, common to all, shared

ὅμοιος, -α, -ον, like, alike, similar (also ὁμοῖος)

φιλάργυρος, -ον, miserly

ADVERBS

αὔριον, tomorrow

εὐθύς, right away, immediately

ἡδέως, pleasantly

μάλα, very (much)

οἴκοι, at home

οἴκοθεν, from home

οἴκαδε, homewards

οὔτε, neither, and not

οὕτως, so

ὡς, as, how

Notes on the vocabulary

Although λέγω can use the regular first aorist ἔλεξα, the suppletive second aorist εἶπον is more common. You will also learn a suppletive future for this verb, ἐρῶ, in chapter 18.

παύω is a transitive verb, meaning to make something stop, or make someone stop what he or she is doing. It often takes a genitive complement rather than an accusative direct object. Thus we can say either πολέμου παύω or πόλεμον παύω, "I stop the war." In the intransitive sense, "I cease (doing something)," we must use the middle, with a supplementary participle; see chapter 15.

δίκη refers to justice in the abstract, but also to a trial or lawsuit. Idioms include δίκην φεύγειν, be a defendant in a trial; δίκην διδόναι, incur punishment, pay a penalty (see chapter 9 for this verb); δίκην λαμβάνειν, punish someone (in the genitive).

There is no difference in sense between εἰς, the usual Attic form, and ἐς; both remain in use because it's convenient for poets to have a choice between a long and a short vowel.

ἐκεῖνος is a demonstrative like οὗτος, so its neuter nominative and accusative singular ends in -ο rather than -ον, and it modifies a definite noun phrase rather than modifying a noun alone.

ἐκεῖνος is the third major demonstrative pronoun/adjective in Greek, alongside οὗτος and ὅδε. It is often contrasted with οὗτος, in that οὗτος points to something near the speaker, ἐκεῖνος to something farther away. Note the neuter nominative/accusative singular in -ο like a pronoun rather than -ον like an ordinary adjective.

φιλάργυρος has the same forms for masculine and feminine; this is normal for adjectives that are compound words.

οὔτε can be used in pairs, as οὔτε θεὸς οὔτε ἄνθρωπος, "neither a god nor a person."

VI.5 Reading

1. ὁ κοινὸς ἰατρός σε θεραπεύσει χρόνος.

2. ἐγὼ μὲν ἠρίστησα καὶ μάλ᾽ ἡδέως.

3. ἐγώ τε καὶ σὺ ταὐτὸν ἕλξομεν ζυγόν.

4. δίκη δίκην ἔτικτε καὶ βλάβη βλάβην.

   These first four are lines from lost comic plays, in verse.

5. σχολαστικὸς ἀδελφοὺς δύο ὁρᾷ· ἐθαύμαζεν δέ τις ὡς ὅμοιοί εἰσιν· ὁ δ᾽ ἔλεξεν, οὐχ οὕτως ὅμοιός ἐστιν οὗτος ἐκείνῳ, ὡς ἐκεῖνος τούτῳ.

6. φιλάργυρός τις διαθήκην ἔγραψε, καὶ ἑαυτὸν κληρονόμον ἔταξεν.

7. Ἐξηκίας ἔγραψε καὶ ἐποίησέ με. Τλῆσον ὁ Νεάρχου ἐποίησε.

   These are signatures from vases. Note the idiom for "the son of."

8. κοινὰ τὰ τῶν φιλῶν.

9. ἦλθον, εἶδον, ἐνίκησα.

   This sentence may be more familiar in the original Latin: *veni, vidi, vici.* Plutarch quotes it in his life of Caesar (section 50), saying that it sounds better in Latin than in Greek. ἦλθον from ἔρχομαι "come"; νικάω "conquer" has predictable principal parts.

9. ἐπεὶ ὁ ἵππος ἔφυγε, τί κλήεις τὴν θύραν;

10. εἰ τοῦ πολέμου παύομεν, τὴν εἰρήνην ἕξομεν. εἰ δὲ μή, οἱ ἄνθρωποι ἐκ τῆς κώμης φεύξουσι. πέμψομεν οὖν ἄγγελον πρὸς τὴν κώμην ὃς λέξει "τοῦ πολέμου παύσομεν."

11. ἦν ποτε ἄνθρωπος ὃς μάλιστα κακῶς εἶχε. οἱ ἀδελφοὶ γὰρ αὐτὸν οὐκ ἐφίλουν. τὰ τοῦ ἀνθρώπου ἀεὶ ἐλάμβανον. βλάβην τῷ ἀνθρώπῳ ἔπραττον.

    τήμερον ὁ ἄνθρωπος ἡδέως οἴκοι ᾠὰ ἠρίστησε καὶ εἰς τὴν ἀγορὰν ἐλαύνειν ἐθέλει. ἀλλὰ ποῦ ἐστι ὁ ἵππος; εἰ ἵππον μὴ ἔχει, οὐκ ἔχει εἰς τὴν ἀγορὰν ἐλαύνειν. εἰ ἐν τῇ ἀγορᾷ μή ἐστι, οὐκ ἔχει λάχανα λαμβάνειν. εἰ λάχανα μὴ ἔχει, οὐχ ἑαυτὸν τρέψει. ὦ δύστανε! θάλατταν κακῶν ἔχεις.

12. Κροῖσος ὁ βασιλεὺς τῷ Σόλωνι εἶπε· "φιλόσοφος εἶ, ὦ ξένε Ἀθηναῖε. ἆρά μοι λέγεις ὅστις ἐστὶ ὀλβιώτατος ἀνθρώπων;" ἤλπιζε δὲ εἶναι ὀλβιώτατος.

    ὁ δὲ Σόλων εἶπε, "Κλέοβίς τε καὶ Βίτων, ἀδελφοὶ Ἀργεῖοι, ὀλβιώτατοί εἰσι. τούτοις γὰρ ἦσαν βίος τε ἀγαθὸς καὶ ῥώμη μεγάλη. ἀθλοφόροις ὅμοιοι ἦσαν. ὅδε ἐστὶ ὁ λόγος·

    ἡμέρα τινὶ ἦν ἑορτὴ τῇ Ἥρῃ. ἡ τῶν ἀδελφῶν μήτηρ ἦν ἱέρεια τῆς θεᾶς καὶ πρὸς τὴν ἑορτὴν ἐν ἁμάξᾳ ἤλαυνε. ἀλλὰ ποῦ ἦσαν οἱ ἵπποι; οὐκ ἦσαν παρὰ τῇ ἁμάξᾳ. πῶς πέμψομεν τὴν ἱέρειαν πρὸς τὴν ἑορτήν;

    τὼ δὲ ἀδελφὼ αὐτὼ ὑποδύνετον ὑπὸ τὸ ζυγόν. οἱ ἄλλοι θαυμάζουσι. τί πράττετον; ὁ Κλέοβίς τε καὶ ὁ Βίτων τὴν ἄμαξαν πρὸς τὴν ἑορτὴν ἕλκετον. "ἀγαθοὺς ἀνθρώπους ἔτεκες," λέγουσι οἱ Ἀργεῖοι. ἡ μήτηρ χαίρει. "ναί, ἀγαθοί εἰσι," λέγει. "ἐλπίζω τὴν Ἥρην ἀγαθὴν τύχην αὐτοῖς πέμψειν."

    οἱ ἀδελφοὶ εὐθὺς ἀπέθανον.

Adapted from Herodotus 1.31. βασιλεύς, king, a third declension noun (see chapter 16). ὄλβιος, -α, -ον, blessed, fortunate. ξένος, -η, -ον, foreign, stranger, guest. ῥώμη, -ης, ἡ, strength. μέγας, μεγάλη, μέγα, large, great. ἀθλοφόρος, -ου, ὁ, prize-winning athlete. ἑορτή, -ῆς, ἡ, festival. μήτηρ, mother, a third declension noun (see chapter 15). ἱέρεια, -ας, ἡ, priestess. ὑποδύνω, slip under, slip into; also used for putting on clothing. χαίρω, rejoice.

13. θαυμάζειν μοι ἔπεισιν, ὅπως Βύτος ἐστὶ σοφιστὴς
    οὔτε λόγον κοινὸν οὔτε λογισμὸν ἔχων.

> Greek Anthology 11.435, by Lucian.

> ἔπεισιν from ἔπειμι, ἐπί + εἶμι, "approach, come to"; this is 3rd singular present indicative active. A σοφιστής is one in the business of being σοφός. λογισμός is computation, reasoning, or rational thought. ἔχων is the present participle active, masc. nom. sg., from ἔχω. Prose paraphrase: θαυμάζω ὅπως σοφιστής ἐστι ὁ Βύτος, ὃς οὔτε λόγον κοινὸν οὔτε νοῦν ἔχει. ὁ δὲ Βύτος ἐστὶ σοφιστὴς ἀλλ᾽ οὐ σοφός. We do not know who Βύτος is; the name seems to be made up.

VI.6 Conversation

Begin as usual with questions on the readings; here are examples.

1. (reading 1) τίς ἐστι ὁ κοινὸς ἰατρός; τίς σε θεραπεύσει; ἆρα ὁ χρόνος σε θεραπεύσει; ἆρα ὁ χρόνος ἰατρός ἐστι; τίνων ἐστὶ ὁ χρόνος ἰατρός; τί ποιήσει ὁ χρόνος; τίνα θεραπεύσει ὁ χρόνος; τίς ἐστι ὁ χρόνος;

2. (reading 10) πῶς τὴν εἰρήνην ἕξομεν; πότε τὴν εἰρήνην ἕξομεν; εἰ τοῦ πολέμου παύομεν, τί ἕξομεν; εἰ τοῦ πολέμου μὴ παύομεν, τί ποιήσουσιν οἱ ἄνθρωποι; εἰ τοῦ πολέμου μὴ παύομεν, ποῦ φεύξουσιν οἱ ἄνθρωποι; τίς ἄγγελον πέμψει; τί λέξει ὁ ἄγγελος ὃν πέμψομεν;

3. (vocabulary) Pay attention to the order of words and resulting connections between question and answer: πέμψω ἄγγελον. πόθεν; οἴκοθεν. ποῖ; ἐς τὴν κώμην. πότε; αὔριον. τί πράξεις ἄρα; πέμψω ἄγγελον αὔριον οἴκοθεν ἐς τὴν κώμην. πότε; αὔριον πέμψω ἄγγελον οἴκοθεν ἐς τὴν κώμην. ποῖ δή; ἐς τὴν κώμην αὔριον πέμψω ἄγγελον. πόθεν; οἴκοθεν ἐς τὴν κώμην ἄγγελον πέμψω αὔριον. τίνα πέμψεις; ἄγγελον ἐς τὴν κώμην οἴκοθεν αὔριον.

4. In the following, complete sentences should be required for answers, and may be used for the questions. In other words, flesh out the minimal answers given here.

> ἔπεμψα παιδίον. πόθεν; οἴκοθεν. ποῖ; ἐς τὴν ἀγοράν. πότε; ἐχθές. τί ἔπραξεν; ἔφερέ μοι ᾠά. πόσα; δέκα. τί ἐποίησας; ἠρίστησα.

The same with πέμψεις, ἔπεμψα, ἐπέμψαμεν, or other forms.

Similarly for the following sentences: break them down into pieces and turn each piece into a question and answer.

   a. ἐλαύνω ἵππον νῦν ἐκ τῆς κώμης πρὸς τὴν θάλατταν.

   b. ἔκλῃον τότε τὴν θύραν τὴν ἐν τῇ οἰκίᾳ.

   c. ἠλαύνομεν τοὺς ἵππους ἀπὸ τῆς ἀγορᾶς ἐχθές.

   d. ἔπεμψάς ποτ᾽ ἀγγέλους ἀπὸ τῆς θαλάττης οἴκαδε.

VI.7 **Writing**

1. Each of these sentences is in aorist, present, or future tense. Change the main verb to each of the other two tenses, making all other changes necessary for grammar or sense.

   a. ὁ διδάσκαλος βιβλία γράφει.

   b. οἱ ἀδελφοὶ κελεύουσι τὸν ἄνθρωπον ἀκούειν.

   c. πολλοὺς καὶ ἀξίους φίλους ἔχω.

   d. τῆς βλάβης ἐπαύσαμεν.

   e. ἀγαθὰ παιδία ἔτεκες.

   f. τὸν πόλεμον οὐ παύσομεν.

   g. οἱ ἵπποι ᾠὰ οὐ τίκτουσι.

   h. ὁ σχολαστικὸς ἐν τῇ ἀγορᾷ λέγει καὶ οἱ ἄλλοι θαυμάζουσι.

   i. τοὺς φίλους ἡδέως θεραπεύσεις.

   j. ἐκεῖνοι τοὺς φίλους ἐφίλησαν.

2. Do the change-number exercise with each of the following.

   a. μάλ᾽ ἡδέως ὁ διδάσκαλος ἠρίστησε.

   b. ὁ φίλος δίκην φεύγει.

   c. ἄγγελος εἰς τὴν ἀγορὰν ἵππῳ ἤλασε.

   d. τήμερον τὼ φίλω εἰς τὴν κώμην ἐλαύνετον.

   e. τὸν Φίλιππον ἄγγελον τάξεις καὶ πρὸς τοὺς φίλους πέμψεις.

   f. ἐκεῖνοι οἱ ἀγαθοὶ ἵπποι τὴν ἅμαξαν εἵλκυσαν.

   g. τὴν θύραν κλήσουσι.

   h. τὴν θύραν ἔκλησαν.

   i. εἰ ᾠὸν εὖ θρέψεις, πέτρας οὐ τέξει.

   j. ὁ ἀδελφὸς ὅμοιός ἐστι ἐμοί.

3. Complete each of the following sentences in any way you like.

   a. τήμερον μὲν ἡ ἄνθρωπος _____, αὔριον δέ _____.

   b. οἴκοι μὲν _____, ἐν δὲ τῇ ἀγορᾷ _____.

   c. _____ ἡμῖν βλάβην τάττει.

   d. _____ μὲν θεραπεύω, _____ δ᾽ οὔ.

   e. ὁ σχολαστικὸς ἐν τῇ ἀγορᾷ _____.

   f. αὕτη μὲν _____, ἐκείνη δέ _____.

4. Write a paragraph telling a story based on this situation: A cart pulled by two horses runs away into the sea. A messenger returns to the village, and tells all to the people in the market-place.

5. Write a paragraph telling what happens next to the man in reading 11.

CHAPTER VII

The Judgement of Paris

VII.1 Masculine α-stems

There are a few masculine nouns in the first declension (the α-stem nouns), mostly **agent nouns** (name of the person who does the action of a verb) and proper names. They have -ς in the nominative singular and have the genitive singular in -ου like the second declension, but otherwise are like the feminines. As always, the vowel is α when it follows ε, ι, or ρ (traditionally called **α pure**); otherwise η by the regular Attic sound shift. Note the vocative forms.

	νεᾱνίᾱς youth, young man	πολίτης citizen	Χαρμίδης (proper name)
stem	νεᾱνιᾱ-	πολῑτᾱ-	Χαρμιδᾱ-
singular			
nom.	νεᾱνίᾱς	πολίτης	Χαρμίδης
gen.	νεᾱνίου	πολίτου	Χαρμίδου
dat.	νεᾱνίᾳ	πολίτῃ	Χαρμίδῃ
acc.	νεᾱνίᾱν	πολίτην	Χαρμίδην
voc.	νεᾱνίᾱ	πολῖτα	Χαρμίδη
dual			
nom., acc., voc.	νεᾱνίᾱ	πολίτᾱ	
gen., dat.	νεᾱνίαιν	πολίταιν	
plural			
nom., voc.	νεᾱνίαι	πολῖται	
gen.	νεᾱνιῶν	πολῑτῶν	
dat.	νεᾱνίαις	πολίταις	
acc.	νεᾱνίᾱς	πολίτᾱς	

Proper names are typically only used in the singular, but if a dual or plural is ever needed it is formed just as for the other nouns. Proper adjectives, of course, can be any number, for example οἱ Πέρσαι, "Persians."

Exercise

Write out the full declension of: κριτής, ποιητής, Πέρσης, στρατιώτης, ταμίας, βορέας "north wind," Νῑκίας. See the vocabulary for glosses.

VII.2 Contracted nouns

A few contracted nouns are found in the first and second declensions. Their endings may be seen from the adjective given below. Notice the neuter nominative/accusative/vocative plural: it has the ordinary ᾰ ending, but this contracts with the stem vowel resulting in *long* -ᾱ.

Examples are:

- ἡ γῆ, earth
- ὁ πλοῦς, voyage
- ἡ Ἀθηνᾶ, Athena (contracted from α-α)
- ὁ Ἑρμῆς, Hermes
- ὁ νοῦς, mind
- τὸ ὀστοῦν, bone

χρῡσοῦς, "golden"

	Masc.	Fem.	Neu.
singular			
nom., voc.	χρῡσοῦς	χρῡσῆ	χρῡσοῦν
gen.	χρῡσοῦ	χρῡσῆς	χρῡσοῦ
dat.	χρῡσῷ	χρῡσῇ	χρῡσῷ
acc.	χρῡσοῦν	χρῡσῆν	χρῡσοῦν
dual			
nom., voc., acc.	χρῡσώ	χρῡσᾱ	χρῡσώ
gen., dat.	χρῡσοῖν	χρῡσαῖν	χρῡσοῖν
plural			
nom., voc.	χρῡσοῖ	χρῡσαῖ	χρῡσᾱ
gen.	χρῡσῶν	χρῡσῶν	χρῡσῶν
dat.	χρῡσοῖς	χρῡσαῖς	χρῡσοῖς
acc.	χρῡσοῦς	χρῡσᾱς	χρῡσᾱ

VII.3 Attic declension

There are also a few second-declension nouns and adjectives, some of them fairly common, with stems in -εω. They have the normal second-declension endings, though the vowels (and accents) don't look quite right for reasons explained below. These nouns look like the stem plus -ς, -ν, or -ι (which is always subscript) wherever a normal second-declension noun would end in those sounds, except for the neuter nominative/accusative plural which has the usual -α ending and *no* -ω-.

ἵλεως, "propitious"

	Masc./Fem.	Neu.
singular		
nom., voc.	ἵλεως	ἵλεων
gen.	ἵλεω	
dat.	ἵλεῳ	
acc.	ἵλεων	ἵλεων
dual		
nom., voc., acc.	ἵλεω	
gen., dat.	ἵλεῳν	
plural		
nom., voc.	ἵλεῳ	ἵλεα
gen.	ἵλεων	
dat.	ἵλεῳς	
acc.	ἵλεως	ἵλεα

So also νεώς "temple"; λεώς "people." In these the accent on the ultima is always acute, not circumflex.

The accent in these words appears irregular, because the last syllable has a long vowel but the accent is on the third-to-last syllable. This is because the forms were originally ἵληος and so on, with ordinary second declension endings. The vowel quantities have "changed places" — long-short to short-long — after the position of the accent was fixed. The change of places is called **quantitative metathesis**; you will learn another group of nouns with quantitative metathesis (and resulting irregular-looking accents) in chapter 12. These second-declension nouns with quantitative metathesis are sometimes called the **Attic declension**.

Exercise

Write out the declension of the following phrases (all cases and numbers): ὁ χρυσοῦς νεώς, ἡ ἵλεως Ἀθηνᾶ, ὁ δεινὸς ποιητής, τὸ λευκὸν ὀστοῦν.

VII.4 Reported speech

To say what someone said, a writer has two choices: quote directly, or quote indirectly. Direct quotation simply reports the speaker's exact words: *Socrates says, "The gods are good."* Indirect quotation does not: *Socrates says that the gods are good.*

In Greek, direct quotation works just as in English: ὁ Σωκράτης λέγει, "οἱ θεοί εἰσιν ἀγαθοί." There are two ways to express an indirect quotation, one much like English and the other much like Latin. The "English-ish" way uses ὅτι or ὡς to introduce the quotation. While "that" can be omitted in an English sentence ("Socrates says the gods are good"), the subordinating conjunctions are never omitted in Greek: either ὅτι or ὡς will always be there to tell you where the indirect quotation begins. First-person forms change just as in English: compare direct ὁ Σωκράτης λέγει, "βιβλία οὐ γράφω" with indirect ὁ Σωκράτης λέγει ὅτι βιβλία οὐ γράφει, using a third-person verb for the subject Socrates.

The original verb tense of the direct statement *stays the same* even if the verb of saying is past: ὁ Σωκράτης ἔλεγε ὅτι βιβλία οὐ γράφει. This is different from English, which **back-shifts** all verb forms to the past when they're subordinate to a past-tense main verb to produce **tense harmony**: we would have to say "Socrates said he was not writing," with a past tense in the quotation.

If Socrates actually says γράφω, an indirect quotation of this statement in Greek will always have a present tense verb: ὁ Σωκράτης λέγει ὅτι γράφει. ὁ Σωκράτης λέγει (αὐτὸν) γράφειν. (S. says he is writing); ὁ Σωκράτης εἶπε ὅτι γράφει. ὁ Σωκράτης εἶπε γράφειν. (S. said he *was* writing, with English tense harmony). If what he says is ἔγραψα, the Greek indirect quotation will have a past-tense verb: ὁ Σωκράτης λέγει ὅτι ἔγραψε. ὁ Σωκράτης λέγει γράψαι. (S. says he wrote); ὁ Σωκράτης εἶπε ὅτι ἔγραψε. ὁ Σωκράτης εἶπε γράψαι. (S. says he *had* written, had been writing, used to write, with "past-in-the-past" pluperfect tense in English for harmony). In other words, the tense inside an indirect statement in Greek is always the same as the tense of the direct statement, whereas in English, the tense of the indirect quotation changes if the main verb is past tense.

It is sometimes convenient to remind the reader or listener that a passage is quoted, however, so Greek allows a change of *mood*. When the main verb is in a past tense (also called a **secondary tense**), the verb of the quotation may be optative, keeping the same tense as in the direct speech. That is, the rule for indirect quotation with ὅτι or ὡς is "keep the same tense; keep the same mood, or optional optative in secondary sequence." This is the first of several constructions you will meet for which such a change of mood is possible; we call the choice of mood **sequence of moods** and the rule is the **Or Optional Optative** rule, or **OOO Rule** for short. You will meet the optative in chapter 8.

The "Latin-ish" form of indirect quotation uses an infinitive for the verb of the quotation. Just as in the other form of indirect quotation, the tense remains the same as in the direct quotation; only the mood changes, from indicative (or whatever) to infinitive. The subject of an infinitive is always in the accusative case. There is no subordinate conjunction, just the infinitive by itself. Thus ὁ Σωκράτης λέγει τοὺς θεοὺς εἶναι ἀγαθούς. (Parse this infinitive as "verb of indirect quotation introduced by λέγει.")

When the subject of the quoted sentence is the same as that of the main sentence, however, it stays in the nominative; you may, if you like, think of this subject as staying in the main clause, not being repeated in the quotation. Thus: ὁ Σωκράτης λέγει, "ἐλεύθερός εἰμι" could be expressed as ὁ Σωκράτης λέγει ὅτι ἐλεύθερός ἐστι in the first form, or ὁ Σωκράτης λέγει ἐλεύθερος εἶναι in the second. (Note that this is *different* from the rule in Latin, where the subject is accusative even if it's the same as the main subject: *Socrates dicit se liberum esse.*)

The general rule for indirect quotation in Greek, then, is that the *tense* that the speaker used is always retained, but the *mood* may change — to optative, if the OOO rule is applicable and the quoting writer chooses to exploit it; or to infinitive, if the quoting writer uses this method of quoting.

Indirect quotation may be called **indirect statement**, **indirect discourse**, or **oratio obliqua** (Latin for "indirect discourse"). There are also indirect questions, which work just the same way as indirect statements, though they are introduced by a special set of indirect question words which you first met in chapter 1, all beginning with ὁ-: for example, ὁ Σωκράτης ἐρωτᾷ ὁποῖοί εἰσι οἱ θεοί, "Socrates asks what the gods are like," or ὁ Σωκράτης ἐρωτᾷ ὅστις ἀγαθός ἐστι, "Socrates asks who is good." Because indirect questions need the question word, they can't use the infinitive construction; the OOO rule applies to them as well. When an indirect question does not have an interrogative pronoun or adverb (one of the ὁ-words), it may begin with ἆρα as a direct question may, or with εἰ exactly as we could use "if" in English: ὁ Σωκράτης ἐρωτᾷ εἰ πάντες οἱ ἄνθρωποί εἰσιν ἀγαθοί, "Socrates asks if/whether all men are good."

We have compared the two forms of indirect statement in Greek to the way such sentences are expressed in English and in Latin. The astute reader may well wonder why we have not also compared Sanskrit. In fact, Sanskrit almost never uses indirect quotation at all.

VII.5 Prepositions

You have met several prepositions so far. A preposition takes a noun (or, more usually in Greek, a noun phrase) as its object to make a **prepositional phrase** which may modify a noun (like an adjective) or a verb (like an adverb). Each preposition takes one or more cases, genitive, dative, or accusative, for its object; no preposition takes a nominative or vocative object. If a preposition can take more than one case, often there is an idea of separation or motion away associated with the genitive, of position or place with the dative, and of motion toward with the accusative.

This table summarizes the most important prepositions in Greek with their cases. A dash means the preposition cannot take that case. Glosses give the major senses, but you will learn the breadth of meaning or the idiomatic uses by experience.

Preposition	with Gen.	with Dat.	with Acc.
ἀμφί	about, concerning	around	around, to around
ἀνά	—	—	up, along
ἄνευ	without	—	—
ἀντί	instead of, in return for	—	—
ἀπό	from	—	—

Preposition	with Gen.	with Dat.	with Acc.
διά	through, out from	—	through, because of
εἰς	—	—	into
ἐκ, ἐξ	out of	—	—
ἐν	—	in	—
ἐπί	on, near, in the course of	on, against	towards, extending over
κατά	down from, opposed to	—	down to, among, according to
μετά	among, with	with (poetic)	coming among, after
παρά	from alongside	alongside, beside	to, beyond, beside, except
περί	about, having to do with	around	around, near
πλήν	except for	—	—
πρό	in front of, earlier	—	—
πρός	from, on the part of	near, next to	toward, to do with
σύν	—	with	—
ὑπέρ	over, above	—	over, beyond
ὑπό	from under; by the agency of	under	under, to under

VII.6 Vocabulary

VERBS

ἄγω, ἄξω, ἤγαγον, ἦχα, ἦγμαι, ἤχθην, lead (cp. *demagogue, act*, L. *agere*)

ἁμαρτάνω, ἁμαρτήσομαι, ἥμαρτον, ἡμάρτηκα, ἡμάρτημαι, ἡμαρτήθη,err, make a mistake

γελάω, γελάσομαι, ἐγέλασα, – , γεγέλασμαι, ἐγελάσθην, laugh, laugh at

δουλεύω, δουλεύσω, ἐδούλευσα, δεδούλευκα, δεδούλευμαι, – , serve, be a slave

ἐθέλω, ἐθελήσω, ἠθέλησα, ἠθέληκα, – , – , wish, want to (+ complementary infinitive)

ἐρωτάω, ἐρωτήσω, ἠρώτησα, – , – , – , ask (a question)

καλέω, καλῶ, ἐκάλεσα, κέκληκα, κέκλημαι, ἐκλήθην, call (cp. L. *clamare, clamor*)

κρίνω, κρινῶ, ἔκρῑνα, κέκρικα, κέκριμαι, ἐκρίθην, judge (cp. *critic, crisis*)

νικάω, νικήσω, ἐνίκησα, νενίκηκα, νενίκημαι, ἐνικήθην, conquer

νομίζω, νομιῶ, ἐνόμισα, νενόμικα, νενόμισμαι, ἐνομίσθην, believe, think

πιστεύω, πιστεύσω, ἐπίστευσα, πεπίστευκα, πεπίστευμαι, ἐπιστεύθην, believe

χωρέω, χωρήσομαι, ἐχώρησα, κεχώρηκα, κεχώρημαι, ἐχωρήθην, hold, contain

CONJUNCTIONS AND ADVERBS

διότι, because

ὅθεν, whence, from where

ὅτι, that (conjunction introducing indirect statement)

πάλιν, back again

ὡς, that (conjunction introducing indirect statement)

NOUNS

ἀδελφή, -ῆς, ἡ, sister (fem. of ἀδελφός)

ἀργίᾱ, -ας, ἡ, sloth, idleness

γῆ, γῆς, ἡ, earth, land (cp. *geography*)

γραμματικός, -οῦ, ὁ, pedant, student

δεσπότης, -ου, ὁ, master (cp. *despot*)

ἔλαιον, -ου, τό, oil

ἐλευθερίᾱ, -ᾱς, ἡ, freedom, generosity

Ἰνδός, -οῦ, ὁ, Indian (from Asia, not Native American)

κριτής, -οῦ, ὁ, judge (cp. *critic*)

λεώς, λεώ, ὁ, people, populace

λήκυθος, -ου, ἡ, a little flask

Λῡδός, -ου, ὁ, Lydian

μαθητής, -ου, ὁ, student

μαρτύριον, -ου, τό, evidence (cp. *martyr*)

νεανίας, -ου, ὁ, youth, young man

νεώς, νεώ, ὁ, temple

οἶνος, -ου, ὁ, wine (cp. L. *vinum*)

ὀστοῦν, -οῦ, τό, bone (cp. *osteoporosis*)

Πέρσης, -ου, ὁ, Persian

ποιητής, -οῦ, ὁ, poet

πλοῦς, -οῦ, ὁ, voyage

πολίτης, -ου, ὁ, citizen

στρατηγός, -ου, ὁ, general (cp. *strategy*)

στρατιᾱ́, -ᾶς, ἡ, army

στρατός, -οῦ, ὁ, army

στρατιώτης, -ου, ὁ, soldier

ταμίᾱς, -ου, ὁ, steward

τέκνον, -ου, τό, child

φιλοσοφίᾱ, -ᾱς, ἡ, philosophy

χρηματισμός, -οῦ, ὁ, money-making

ADJECTIVES

ἄδικος, -ον, unjust, wicked

ἀμφότερος, -α, -ον, both

ἀνδρεῖος, -α, -ον, brave

ἀργός, -όν, idle, useless (from ἀ + ἔργον)

δειλός, -ή, -όν, cowardly

δεινός, -ή, -όν, terrible, clever (cp. *dinosaur*)

δίκαιος, -α, -ον, just, upright

ἐργαστικός, -ή, -όν, energetic, hard-working

ἐσθλός, -ή, -όν, good, honest

ἵλεως, ἵλεων, propitious, favorable, well-disposed

ὁπότερος, -α, -ον, which of the two (relative adj/pron)

ὅσος, -η, -ον, (as much) as (relative adj/pron)

πεντακότυλος, -ο, holding 5 measures (about 2 1/2 pints)

πότερος, -α, -ον, which one? (of two alternatives)

τοσοῦτος, -η, -ο, so much, that much, so large

χρυσοῦς, -ῆ, -οῦ, golden

PREPOSITIONS

ἀμφί, around (+ gen., dat., acc.)

ἄνευ, without (+ gen.)

ἀντί, instead of, in return for (+ gen.)

πλήν, except for (+ gen.)

σύν, with (+ dat.)

ὑπέρ, over (+ gen., acc.)

NUMERALS

εἴκοσι, twenty (εἴκοσιν before vowels)

ἑκατόν, a hundred

χίλιοι, -αι, – , a thousand

μύριοι, -αι, – , ten thousand

Notes on the vocabulary

Compound adjectives have the same forms in the masculine and the feminine. Compounds include words like πεντακότυλος "five-measure-ish"; all adjectives that have the negative prefix ἀ- (cognate with Germanic *un-* and Latin *in-*); and all the adjectives compounded with εὐ- and δυσ-. Thus we may have ἡ ἄδικος τύχη. Adjectives that are the same in masculine and feminine are sometimes called "adjectives with two endings," because they only have two distinct nominative singular forms, in other words only two principal parts.

The word λήκυθος is one of the few feminine nouns of the second declension. Others include ὁδός, -οῦ, ἡ, "road"; νόσος, -ου, ἡ, "sickness"; νῆσος, -ου, ἡ "island"; and σορός, -οῦ, ἡ, "coffin, burial urn."

To keep the military words straight, note: ὁ στρατηγὸς τὴν στρατιὰν ἄγει (the -αγο- element in the noun is from same root as the verb), and στρατιά, like φιλοσοφία and many other nouns in -ια, names an abstraction.

Α κοτύλη is both a kind of cup and the amount of liquid it holds, very much like *cup* in English (and about that large).

The adjectives πότερος and ὁπότερος belong to the family of question words and subordinators, just like ποῦ and ὅπου, πότε and ὁπότε, and all the rest. The neuter accusative πότερον can be used by itself to introduce a "one-or-the-other" question: πότερον γράψαι ἐθέλεις ἢ εἰπεῖν;

VII.7 Reading

1. Σιδώνιος γραμματικὸς ἠρώτα τὸν διδάσκαλον· "ἡ πεντακότυλος λήκυθος πόσον χωρεῖ;" ὁ δὲ εἶπεν· "οἶνον λέγεις ἢ ἔλαιον;"

   Σιδώνιος, -ου, ὁ a Sidonian, man from Sidon in Phoenicia. The anecdote is told by Philogelos.

2. οἱ Ἀβδηρῖται ἐκάλουν τὸν Δημόκριτον Φιλοσοφίαν. ἐγέλα δὲ ἀεὶ ὁ Δημόκριτος, ὅθεν καὶ Γελασῖνον αὐτὸν ἐκάλουν οἱ πολῖται.

   Aelian 4.20. **Ἀβδηρίτης, -ου, ὁ** a man of Abdera, the city on the Thracian coast where Democritus was born. **ὁ Γελασῖνός** ἐστι ἄνθρωπος ὃς γελᾷ, ἢ γελαστής.

3. Σωκράτης ἔλεγεν ὅτι ἡ ἀργία ἀδελφή ἐστι τῆς ἐλευθερίας. καὶ μαρτύριον ἔλεγεν ἀνδρειοτάτους καὶ ἐλευθερωτάτους Ἰνδοὺς καὶ Πέρσας, ἀμφοτέρους δὲ πρὸς χρηματισμὸν ἀργοτάτους εἶναι· Λυδοὺς δὲ ἐργαστικωτάτους, δουλεύειν δέ.

4. ἡ γῆ ἐστι ἡ κοινὴ οἰκία. πάντες ταμίαι ἐσμὲν τῆς γῆς. ἡ φιλοσοφία ἡμῖν λέγει ὅτι τέκνα τῆς γῆς ἐσμεν. πολῖται μέν ἐσμεν τῆς πατρίδος, τέκνα δὲ τῆς γῆς.

   πατρίς, πατρίδος, ἡ, native land, fatherland

5. ὁ νεὼς οἰκία ἐστὶ τοῦ θεοῦ. οἱ Ἀθηναῖοι μέγαν νεὼν ἐποίησαν τῇ θεᾷ Ἀθηνᾷ. αὕτη γάρ ἐστι θεὰ τῶν Ἀθηναίων, οἳ αὐτὴν φιλοῦσιν. οὗτος ὁ νεὼς ἐστι ὁ Παρθενών. ὁ νεὼς ἐστι ὑπὲρ τὴν πόλιν ἐπὶ τῇ Ἀκροπόλει. ὅτε ὑπὸ τῷ νεῷ ἐσμεν, ἐν τῷ νεῷ ἔχομεν ὁρᾶν μέγαν χρυσοῦν ἄγαλμα τῆς θεᾶς. ἀμφὶ τῷ τῆς Ἀθηνᾶς ἀγάλματι ἀεί

εἰσι πολλοὶ Ἀθηναῖοι οἳ εἰς τὸ ἄγαλμα βλέπουσι. οἱ γὰρ Ἀθηναῖοι ἐλπίζουσι τὴν θεὰν αὐτοῖς ἵλεων εἶναι. εἰ ὁ λεὼς τοῖς θεοῖς εὖ πράττει, οἱ θεοὶ τῷ λεῷ εὖ πράξουσιν. ἀλλ᾽ ἄνευ τῶν θεῶν, οὐδὲν ἔχομεν πλὴν τοῦ κακοῦ.

> ἄγαλμα, ἀγάλματος, τό, statue, third declension. πόλις, πόλεως, ἡ, city, also third declension. οὐδείς, οὐδεμία, οὐδέν, nothing.

6. πολλὰ τὰ δεινά, ἀλλ᾽ οὐδὲν ἀνθρώπου δεινότερόν ἐστι.

> This line is adapted from Sophocles' *Antigone*; you can read the original version in chapter 20, reading 4.

7. ἡ φιλοτιμία ἐστὶ ἄδικος θεά.

8. ἀεί με ἐρωτᾷς ὁπότερος ἀδελφὸς σοφώτερός ἐστι. ὁ μὲν μαθητής ἐστι, ὁ δὲ στρατιώτης. λέγω τὸν νεώτερον σοφώτερον εἶναι. σὺν τοῖς ἀδελφοῖς περὶ πολλῶν λέγω καὶ ἀεὶ μανθάνω. ποτέρου δὲ ἀδελφοῦ ὁ νοῦς δεινός; ἀμφοτέρω μὲν περὶ τῆς φιλοσοφίας λέγουσι, ὁ δὲ στρατιώτης ἄδικος, ὁ δὲ μαθητὴς ἐσθλός ἐστι. ἀντὶ τοῦ πολέμου ὁ μαθητὴς φιλοσοφίαν ποιεῖ. οὗτος ὁ ἀδελφὸς οὖν σοφώτερός ἐστι τοῦ ἄλλου. οὐκ ἐθέλω πολλὰ λέγειν πλὴν τούτου· ὅτι ἔγωγε σοφώτατός εἰμι πάντων.

9. μνῆμα μὲν Ἑλλὰς ἅπασ᾽ Εὐριπίδου, ὀστέα δ᾽ ἴσχει
   γῆ Μακεδών, ᾗπερ δέξατο τέρμα βίου.
   πατρὶς δ᾽ Ἑλλάδος Ἑλλάς, Ἀθῆναι· πλεῖστα δὲ Μούσαις
   τέρψας ἐκ πολλῶν καὶ τὸν ἔπαινον ἔχει.

> Epitaph for Euripides, possibly written by Thucydides.

> μνῆμα, μνήματος, τό, memorial; for third-declension forms see chapter 8. Note uncontracted ὀστέα, neuter accusative plural. ἴσχω = ἔχω. ᾗπερ = ᾗ with emphatic enclitic -περ; here dative of place. δέχομαι, receive; δέξατο is 3rd sg aorist indicative middle, without its augment as sometimes happens in poetry. Subject is ὁ Εὐριπίδης. τέρμα, τέρματος, τό, end, boundary. πατρίς, πατρίδος, ἡ, native land, fatherland. πλεῖστα = μάλιστα. τέρψας, τέρψασα, τέρψαν, delighting, causing pleasure; actually aorist participle active from τέρπω. ἔπαινος, -ου, ὁ, approval, praise.

> Prose paraphrase: πᾶσα ἡ Ἑλλάς ἐστι τὸ τοῦ Εὐριπίδου μνῆμα, ἀλλὰ ἡ γῆ Μακεδὼν τὰ ὀστᾶ ἔχει, διότι ἐν ταύτῃ τῇ γῇ ὁ ποιητὴς ἀπέθανε. Ἀθηναῖος ἦν. αἱ Μοῦσαι αὐτὸν μάλιστα ἐφίλουν καὶ πολλοὶ αὐτὸν ἐτίμων.

10. ἐπεὶ ὁ Πλάτων νεανίας ἦν, ἤθελε ποιητὴς εἶναι. λόγους πολλοὺς καὶ ποιήματα πολλὰ ἔγραφε, ἀλλὰ οἱ Ἀθηναῖοι τὰς τοῦ Πλάτωνος τραγῳδίας κακὰς ἐνόμιζον. ἡμέρᾳ τινὶ ὁ Πλάτων τὸν Σωκράτην εἶδε. ὁ δὲ Σωκράτης περὶ τῆς φιλοσοφίας ἔλεγε. ὁ δὲ Πλάτων αὐτοῦ ἤκουσε. ὁ μὲν Σωκράτης τοῖς ἄλλοις πολλὰ ἠρώτησε. οἱ δὲ μαθηταὶ πάντα ἐξήτασαν ἃ ἐπίστευον καὶ ἐνόμιζον. ὁ δὲ Σωκράτης πάλιν ἠρώτα. ὁ δὲ Πλάτων ἐθαύμασε. ποιητὴς μὲν εἶναι οὐκ ἤθελε, ἀλλὰ φιλόσοφος. ἑαυτὸν οὖν μαθητὴν τοῦ φιλοσόφου ἐποίησε.

> Adapted from the life of Plato by Diogenes Laertius.

11. οἱ Λακεδαιμόνιοι ποτὲ πόλεμον ἐποίουν πρὸς τοὺς Τεγεήτας. οἱ μὲν Τεγεῆται ἐνίκησαν, οἱ δὲ Λακεδαιμόνιοι ἠθέλησαν πάλιν πόλεμον πρᾶξαι. ἀγγέλους οὖν ἔπεμψαν πρὸς τὴν τοῦ Ἀπόλλωνος οἰκίαν οἳ ἐρωτήσουσι ὅπως νικᾶν ἔχουσι. ὁ

δὲ θεὸς εἶπε, "εἰ τὰ ὀστᾶ τὰ τοῦ Ὀρέστου φέρετε εἰς τὴν Λακεδαίμονα, ἕξετε τοὺς Τεγεήτας νικᾶν." οἱ ἄγγελοι τοῖς ἄλλοις Λακεδαιμονίοις τοὺς τοῦ θεοῦ λόγους εἶπον. πάντες ἐνόμισαν, "πῶς ἔχομεν τὰ τοῦ Ὀρέστου ὀστᾶ λαβεῖν; ποῦ εἰσι; ὁ γὰρ Ὀρέστης τέκνον ἦν τοῦ Ἀγαμέμνονος. οὐκ ἦν Λακεδαιμόνιος. τὰ δὲ ὀστᾶ οὔκ ἐστι ἐν τῇ Λακεδαίμονι."

ἡμέρᾳ τινὶ Λίχης, Λακεδαιμόνιός τις, εἰς τὴν Τεγέην ἦλθε. ἐργαστικὸς Τεγεήτης αὐτῷ εἶπε, "χαῖρε, ὦ Λίχης. ἆρ᾽ ἐθέλεις δεινὸν ὁρᾶν; θαυμάσεις. τὰ ἔργα ἐποίουν χθὲς ἐν τῷ κήπῳ καὶ μεγάλην σορὸν ἔτυχον, ἐν ᾗ ἐστι μεγάλα ὀστᾶ." ὁ δὲ Λίχης ἐθαύμασε. "εἴ μοι δηλοῖς ταύτην τὴν σορόν, πολὺ χαιρήσω. ποῦ ἐστι;" ὁ δὲ ἐργαστικὸς τῷ Λίχῃ τὴν σορὸν καὶ τὰ ὀστᾶ ἐδήλωσε. ἐστι τὰ τοῦ Ὀρέστου ὀστᾶ. ὁ δὲ Λίχης αὐτὰ ἔλαβε καὶ πάλιν εἰς τῇ Λακεδαίμονι ἤνεγκε. οἱ Λακεδαιμόνιοι πόλεμον ἔπραξαν καὶ ἐνίκησαν.

Adapted from Herodotus 1.67-68. **σορός, -οῦ, ἡ,** coffin or burial vessel

12. *περὶ τοῦ Τρωικοῦ πολέμου, πρῶτον μέρος*

Θέτις ἦν καλὴ νύμφη. αἱ νύμφαι εἰσὶ θεαὶ τῆς θαλάττης. Πηλεὺς ταύτην τὴν νύμφην ἔγημε· ἄνθρωπος μὲν ἦν, ἀνδρεῖος δὲ καὶ ἀγαθὸς. ἄξιος οὖν ἦν τῆς Θέτιδος. πάντες οἱ θεοὶ καὶ πᾶσαι αἱ θεαὶ πρὸς τοὺς γάμους ἦλθον καὶ ἔχαιρον. ἐφίλησαν γὰρ τὴν Θέτιδα. μία δὴ θεὰ οὐκ ἔχαιρε, ἡ Ἔρις. ἐκείνη μῆλον βάλλει εἰς τὸ δωμάτιον ᾧ πάντες χαίρουσι. τὸ μὲν μῆλον λέγει "τῇ καλλίστῃ· αἱ δὲ θεαὶ λέγουσι "καλλίστη ἔγωγε." τίς ἐστι ἡ καλλίστη θεά; τίς ἔχει κριτὴς εἶναι;

ὁ δὲ Ζεὺς ἐκέλευσε τὸν Ἀλέξανδρον κρίνειν. ὁ δὲ Ἀλέξανδρος υἱός ἦν τοῦ Πριάμου, ὃς βασιλεὺς ἦν τοῦ Ἰλίου. αἱ οὖν θεαὶ πρὸς τὸν Ἀλέξανδρον ἦλθον.

"δίκαιος εἶ, ὦ Ἀλέξανδρε," ἔλεγε ἡ Ἥρα τῷ νεανίᾳ. "ἡμεῖς μὲν σοὶ πιστεύομεν· σὺ δὲ δικαίως κρίνεις ἥτις ἡμῶν καλλίστη ἐστί."

ὁ δὲ Ἀλέξανδρος ἐγέλασε. "ἐν ἀπορίᾳ εἰμί," εἶπε. "τί κρίνω μετὰ ταῖς θεαῖς; εἰ ἁμαρτάνω, ἀποθνήσκω. ἔγωγε νομίζω ὑμᾶς πάσας καλὰς. οὐκ ἐθέλω κριτὴς θεῶν εἶναι."

ἡ δὲ Ἥρα εἶπε, "εἰ κρίνεις ἐμὲ καλλίστην εἶναι, σὲ ποιήσω δεσπότην πάντων." ἡ δὲ Ἀθηνᾶ, "εἰ κρίνεις ἐμὲ καλλίστην εἶναι, στρατιὰν ἀγαθὴν ἕξεις καὶ ἀεὶ νικήσεις." ἡ δὲ Ἀφροδίτη, "εἰ κρίνεις ἐμὲ καλλίστην εἶναι, καλλίστην ἄνθρωπον ἕξεις, ἣ σὲ φιλήσει."

ὁ δὲ Ἀλέξανδρος ἑαυτῷ εἶπε, "δεινόν ἐστι. τί ποιήσω; ἡ μὲν Ἥρα με δεσπότην ποιήσει, ἡ δὲ Ἀθηνᾶ στρατηγός, ἡ δὲ Ἀφροδίτη ἐραστήν." τέλος δὲ ταῖς θεαῖς εἶπε "νῦν ἐκρίνησα. σύ, ὦ Ἀφροδίτη, καλλίστη εἶ." ἡ δὲ Ἀφροδίτη ἔχαιρε. "εὖ ἐποίησας, ὦ Ἀλέξανδρε. εὖ ἐκρίνησας. νῦν ἕξεις τὴν Ἑλένην."

ὁ δὲ νεανίας στρατὸν ἔταξαν καὶ πλοῦν πρὸς τὴν Σπάρτην ἐποίησε. ἡ γὰρ Ἑλένη Σπάρτῃ ἦν μετὰ τοῦ Μενελάου. ὁ δὲ Μενέλαος τὸν Ἀλέξανδρον εἰς τὴν οἰκίαν ἤγαγε καὶ εἶπε φίλον εἶναι. ἀλλ᾽ ἐπεὶ ὁ Μενέλαος εἰς Κρήτην πλοῦν ἐποίησε, ὁ Ἀλέξανδρος τὴν Ἑλένην ἔλαβε καὶ ἦλθον οἴκαδε πρὸς τὴν Τροίαν.

ὁ Μενέλαος οὐκ ἔχαιρε. μετὰ τοῦ ἀδελφοῦ Ἀγαμέμνονος στρατιὰν ἔταξε. ὁ δὲ Ἀγαμέμνων ἦν στρατηγὸς ὃς τὴν στρατιὰν ἤγαγε πρὸς τὴν Τροίαν.

μέρος, -ους, τό, part, **τέλος, -ους, τό,** end; these are third-declension s-stem nouns, for which see chapter 11. **πᾶς, πᾶσα, πᾶν,** all (chapter 8). **γάμος, -ου, ὁ,**

marriage, wedding. **γαμέω**, marry (with predictable principal parts). **χαίρω**, rejoice. **ἔρις, ἔριδος, ἡ**, strife, quarreling, here personified as a goddess. **μῆλον, -ου, τό**, apple. **υἱός, -οῦ, ὁ**, son. **βασιλεύς, -εώς, ὁ**, king, a third-declension u-stem noun (chapter 16). **ἐραστής, -οῦ, ὁ**, lover, from **ἐράω** (present system only), love.

VII.8 Conversation

1. Questions and answers about the readings. For example, τί ἠρώτα ὁ Σιδώνιος; πόσον χωρεῖ ὁ λήκυθος; ἆρα ὁ λήκυθος πλείονα οἴνου χωρεῖ ἢ ἐλαίου; Similarly for the other passages.

2. Dialogues based on the vocabulary: τίς εἶ σύ; στρατιώτης εἰμί. ποῖος δὲ στρατιώτης εἶ; ἀνδρεῖός εἰμι στρατιώτης. So with ταμίας, δοῦλος, and so on, each having a suitable adjective.

3. τίς ἐστιν οὗτος; οὗτος μὲν στρατιώτης, ἐγὼ δὲ στρατηγός. τί δέ σοι ποιεῖ ὁ στρατιώτης; ὅσα ἐγὼ κελεύω ποιεῖ ὁ στρατιώτης. τίς οὖν ἐστι στρατηγός; ὁ στρατηγός ἐστι πρῶτος τῶν στρατιωτῶν. πότερός ἐστι στρατηγός; οὗτος μέν ἐστι στρατηγός, ἐγὼ δὲ στρατιώτης. So with ταμίας, δοῦλος, and δουλεύω, ταμιεύω, etc.

4. τί ἐποίεις νῦν δή; ἐγέλων. διὰ τί ἐγέλας; ὅτι ἐκάλουν με Γελασῖνον. Vary persons and numbers.

5. ἆρα δουλεύεις; δουλεύω. τίνι δὴ δουλεύεις; τῷ δεσπότῃ δουλεύω. Similarly in imperfect, and different numbers and persons.

6. ἆρα στρατός ἐστιν οὗτος; ἔστιν. πόσων δὲ στρατιωτῶν; δέκα στρατιωτῶν. τί λέγεις, ἄρ᾽ οὐχ ἥμαρτες; ἥμαρτον δή· καὶ γάρ ἐστι χιλίων στρατιωτῶν ὁ στρατός. εὖ λέγεις νῦν· οὕτως καὶ ἐγὼ ἐνόμιζον.

   So with ἑκατόν, μύριοι, πέντε, εἴκοσιν.

7. ὁ ποιητὴς λέγει ὅτι δεινός ἐστιν. τίς λέγει τοῦτο; ὁ ποιητὴς λέγει τοῦτο. ἀλλὰ τί λέγει; ὅτι δεινός ἐστι λέγει. πότερον δεινός ἢ δειλός ἐστι; δεινός ἐστι, ὥσπερ λέγει.

   So: οἱ κριταὶ ὁρῶσιν ὅτι κακῶς κρίνεις σύ.

   οἱ πολῖται ἔλεγον ὅτι ἀγαθώ ἐστον τὼ ἀνθρώπω.

   ὁ στρατηγὸς ἔλεγεν ὅτι οὔκ ἐστιν ἀνδρεῖος ὁ δοῦλος.

   τὸ παιδίον ἔλεγεν ὅτι ἐγέλα.

8. οὗτοι οἱ νεανίαι δέκα μέν εἰσιν, εἰκόσι δ᾽ ἔχουσιν ὀφθαλμούς.

   So with οἰκίαι _____ θύρας, παιδία _____ δούλους, κόραι _____ κεφαλαί, πολῖται _____ ἄμαξαι, κῶμαι _____ ἀγοραί.

VII.9 Writing

1. Each of the following sentences is an indirect quotation; rewrite as direct. For example, ὁ διδάσκαλος λέγει ὅτι οἱ μαθηταί εἰσι ἀγαθοί. becomes ὁ διδάσκαλος λέγει, "οἱ μαθηταί εἰσι ἀγαθοί."

   a. ὁ ποιητὴς λέγει ὅτι οἱ στρατιῶται εἰσι ἀνδρεῖοι.

   b. λέγω ὡς ὁ ἀδελφὸς πολλοὺς φίλους ἔχει.

   c. ὁ μαθητὴς νομίζει ὅτι ὁ διδάσκαλος ἁμαρτάνει.

   d. λέγεις ὅτι τοὺς ἀδίκους οὐ φιλεῖς.

   e. ἐρωτῶμεν ὅστις τῷ κριτῇ δουλεύει.

   f. ὁ μαθητὴς εἶπε ὅτι ἡ λήκυθος ἔλαιον χωρεῖ.

   g. ὁ μαθητὴς λέξει ὅτι τὴν φιλοσοφίαν οὐ φιλεῖ.

   h. εἴπομεν ὡς τὴν ἅμαξαν εἰς τὴν ἀγορὰν ἕλκομεν.

   i. εἴπομεν ὡς τὴν ἅμαξαν εἰς τὴν ἀγορὰν ἕλξομεν.

   j. ὁ ποιητὴς λέγει τὸν πόλεμον κακὸν εἶναι.

   k. λέγω τὴν λήκυθον οἶνον χωρεῖν.

   l. ὁ διδάσκαλος ἐρωτᾷ ὅπου ἐστὶ ὁ μαθητής.

   m. ὁ δοῦλος νομίζει τοὺς ἀγαθοὺς τὴν ἐλευθερίαν ἔχειν.

   n. ἄνθρωπός τις λέγει τοὺς Πέρσας πόλεμον ποιεῖν.

   o. ὁ δοῦλος εἶπε τὸν δεσπότην ἁμαρτάνειν.

   p. ὁ δοῦλος εἶπε τὸν δεσπότην ἁμαρτεῖν.

   q. εἶπες ἡμᾶς ἄγγελον πέμπειν.

   r. εἶπες ἡμᾶς ἄγγελον πέμψειν.

   s. εἶπες ἡμᾶς ἄγγελον πέμψαι.

   t. ὁ νεανίας εἶπε τὸν νέων καλὸν εἶναι.

   u. ὁ διδάσκαλος ἐρωτᾷ ὁποτέρου μαθητοῦ ἐστι τὸ βιβλίον.

   v. οἱ ἄνθρωποι ἐρωτῶσι ὁπότερα στρατία νικήσει.

   w. ἐρωτῶμεν τοὺς δούλους ὁποτέρῳ δεσπότῃ δουλεύουσι.

2. Each of the following sentences is a direct quotation; rewrite as indirect using ὅτι or ὡς. For example, ὁ διδάσκαλος λέγει, "οἱ μαθηταί εἰσι ἀγαθοί." becomes ὁ διδάσκαλος λέγει ὅτι οἱ μαθηταί εἰσι ἀγαθοί.

   a. ἄνθρωπός τις λέγει, "οἱ κριταὶ εὖ κρίνουσι."

   b. ὁ δοῦλος λέγει, "τῷ δεσπότῃ δουλεύω."

   c. ὁ δεσπότης λέγει, "ὁ κριτὴς ἁμαρτάνει καὶ κακῶς κρίνει."

   d. ὁ νεανίας λέγει, "ἡ στρατία εἰρήνην ποιεῖ."

   e. ὁ στρατιώτης λέγει, "ὁ λεὼς ἐλευθερίαν ἔχει."

   f. ὁ νεανίας λέγει, "τὸν ἀδελφὸν φιλῶ."

   g. οἱ νεανίαι λέγουσιν, "εἰ οἱ ἀδελφοὶ δίκαιοί εἰσι, αὐτοὺς φιλοῦμεν."

   h. ἡ καλὴ λέγει, "ὁ ποιητὴς ἐμὲ τιμᾷ."

   i. ἡ διδασκάλη ἐρωτᾷ, "ἆρα οἱ μαθηταί εἰσι ἐργαστικοί;"

   j. ὁ ταμίας ἐρωτᾷ, "τίς τὴν λήκυθον ἔχει;"

   k. ὁ στρατηγὸς ἐρωτᾷ, "πότερος στρατιώτης πρὸς τὴν κώμην ἵππῳ ἐλαύνει;"

   l. αἱ ἀδελφαὶ ἐμὲ ἐρωτῶσι, "πότερον ἁμαρτάνεις ἢ νικᾷς;"

3. Turn each of the following sentences into an indirect quotation: add a form of λέγω with a suitable subject, in present tense, and use ὅτι or ὡς. Then rewrite the sentence with the main verb in the aorist tense (using the appropriate form of εἶπον), leaving the verb of the indirect quotation in the *same* tense as before.

   a. δοῦλός ἐστιν ἐργαστικός.

   b. δοῦλος ἦν ἐργαστικός.

   c. ὁ κριτής εὖ κρίνει.

   d. τὸ ἔλαιον ἦν καλόν.

   e. ὁ Ἰνδὸς πιστεύει τῷ Πέρσῃ.

   f. οἱ ἀνδρεῖοι πολῖται τὸν πόλεμον θαυμάζουσιν.

   g. τῷ δεινῷ οὐ πιστεύομεν.

   h. ἡ ἐλευθερία τοὺς ἀνθρώπους δικαίους ποιεῖ.

   i. ὁ τῶν Ἰνδῶν στρατὸς ἀνδρειότερός ἐστι τοῦ ἄλλου.

   j. αὗται μὲν αἱ λήκυθοι οἶνον χωροῦσι, ἐκεῖναι δὲ ἔλαιον.

4. Rewrite each of the indirect quotations you wrote in 2 and 3 above with the infinitive construction, if possible. Note which sentences *cannot* use it.

5. Write a paragraph on the theme of an army: its numbers, their servants and friends, their characters, what each does and where he lives.

Chapter VIII

The Mustering of the Heroes

VIII.1 Third declension: stems in -οντ

The third declension in Greek contains nouns whose stems end in a consonant, or in ι or υ. All third-declension nouns have the same endings, but internal sandhi may make those endings hard to recognize. The third declension includes nouns of all genders.

The first group of third-declension nouns we will look at are the stems ending in -οντ-. These include ordinary nouns like λέων, λέοντος "lion" and also a large group of **participles**, verbal adjectives. We begin with the present participle active of εἰμί, which is a third-declension -οντ-stem in masculine and neuter, and a first-declension short-a stem in feminine.

	Masc.	Fem.	Neu.
singular			
nom., voc.	ὤν, being	οὖσα	ὄν
gen.	ὄντος	οὔσης	ὄντος
dat.	ὄντι	οὔσῃ	ὄντι
acc.	ὄντα	οὖσαν	ὄν
dual			
nom., voc., acc.	ὄντε	οὔσᾱ	ὄντε
gen., dat.	ὄντοιν	οὔσαιν	ὄντοιν
plural			
nom., voc.	ὄντες	οὖσαι	ὄντα
gen.	ὄντων	οὐσῶν	ὄντων
dat.	οὖσι(ν)	οὔσαις	οὖσι(ν)
acc.	ὄντας	οὔσᾱς	ὄντα

Conveniently, the forms of ὤν are just the suffix and endings for all present and future active participles. That is, the present and future participles are formed from the tense stems with the addition of -οντ- to produce an adjective stem for the masculine and neuter, or -ουσ- to produce a stem for the feminine, then the regular third-declension endings. The result is much like adding the forms of ὤν to the present or future tense stem. See the chart in section 2 below.

Nouns of the -ντ- stem group have sometimes a special vocative form, but are otherwise like the participles, including the sandhi variant in the dative plural:

singular

nom.	λέων, lion	γίγᾱς, giant
gen.	λέοντ-ος	γίγαντ-ος
dat.	λέοντ-ι	γίγαντ-ι
acc.	λέοντ-α	γίγαντ-α
voc.	λέον	γίγαν

dual

nom., voc., acc.	λέοντ-ε	γίγαντ-ε
gen., dat.	λεόντ-οιν	γιγάντ-οιν

plural

nom., voc.	λέοντ-ες	γίγαντ-ες
gen.	λεόντ-ων	γιγάντ-ων
dat.	λέουσι(ν)	γίγᾱσι(ν)
acc.	λέοντ-ας	γίγαντ-ας

The stems of these nouns are λέοντ- and γίγαντ-; the endings, everything after the stem, can be applied to any third declension stem. As with all nouns, the stem is more easily visible in the genitive singular than in the nominative singular; simply remove the genitive ending -ος and what is left is the stem of the noun. You will meet more groups of third-declension nouns in chapters 11, 12, 14, 15, and 16.

Some adjectives have α in their endings, but are otherwise just like ὤν and λέων. These include πᾶς πᾶσα πᾶν "all" and the aorist active participle of verbs with a first aorist, such as λύσᾱς λύσᾱσα λῦσαν from λύω. The genitive singular forms are πάντος and λύσαντος (M. and N.) and πάσης, λῦσάσης (F.) respectively, and the rest follow the pattern.

The adjectives μέλᾱς "black" and τάλᾱς "wretched, miserable" are similar but without -τ- and with a different stem in the feminine, like this:

	Masc.	**Fem.**	**Neu.**
singular			
nom., voc.	τάλᾱς	τάλαινα	τάλαν
gen.	τάλανος	ταλαίνης	τάλανος
dat.	τάλανι	ταλαίνῃ	τάλανι
acc.	τάλαν	τάλαιναν	τάλαν
dual			
nom., voc., acc.	τάλανε	ταλαίνᾱ	τάλανε
gen., dat.	ταλάνοιν	ταλαίναιν	ταλάνοιν
plural			
nom., voc.	τάλανες	τάλαιναι	τάλανα
gen.	ταλάνων	ταλαινῶν	ταλάνων
dat.	τάλασι(ν)	ταλαίναις	τάλασι(ν)
acc.	τάλανας	ταλαίνα-ς	τάλανα

Comparison: τάλας, ταλάντερος, ταλάντατος

Although you might expect μέγας, "big, great," to have the same declension, it does not. It is suppletive, using the stem μεγα- in masculine and neuter nominative and accusative singular, and μεγαλο-, μεγαλη- everywhere else. The feminine is μεγάλη exactly like καλή; the masculine and neuter are like καλός except for nominative and accusative singular. Thus its principal parts are μέγας, μεγάλη, μέγα and its genitive singular forms are μεγάλου, μεγάλης, μεγάλου. The masculine accusative singular is μέγαν and the neuter accusative singular, as always, is the same as the neuter nominative singular. All the other forms are regular, like καλός, using the stems you see in the genitive singular. The comparative forms are also suppletive: μείζων "bigger," a third-declension form coming in chapter 14, and μέγιστος "biggest," declined like καλός.

Exercise

Form the three masculine accusative forms (singular, dual, and plural) for the nouns ἀνδριάς, -άντος, ὁ "statue," γέρων, -οντος "old man," δράκων, -οντος "dragon, serpent," ἐλέφας, -αντος "elephant."

VIII.2 Participles

A **participle** is a verbal adjective: it is both a verb and an adjective at the same time (just as an infinitive is a verbal noun). When a participle modifies a noun (or a pronoun, or an understood noun), it shows that the person or thing denoted by the noun is doing, or has done, or will do the action represented by the verb. So: βλέπομεν τὸν γράφοντα διδάσκαλον says that we see the teacher, and at the same time (present participle) he is writing. We might also have βλέπομεν τὸν γράψαντα διδάσκαλον, if he wrote something in the past. Or βλέπομεν τὸν γράψοντα διδάσκαλον, if he is going to write.

The tense of the participle normally indicates time relative to the time of the main verb. If we have ἐβλέπομεν τὸν γράφοντα διδάσκαλον, this doesn't mean that the teacher is writing now, but that he was writing at the time we saw him: the present participle indicates action going on at the same time as the main verb, so the seeing and the writing happen at the same time. Similarly, ἐβλέπομεν τὸν γράψοντα διδάσκαλον says that the writing comes after the seeing, but this sentence doesn't say anything about whether the writing has happened yet at the time of speaking. If we saw him two hours ago, and he wrote whatever it was one hour ago, the Greek sentence would be appropriate; if we saw him two hours ago and he is still intending to write but hasn't done it yet, the same Greek sentence would also be appropriate.

Just like infinitives, participles can take direct objects and other complements: we might have, for example, βλέπομεν τὸν βιβλία γράφοντα διδάσκαλον, where βιβλία is the direct object of the participle.

A participle has tense and voice just as an infinitive does. Because participles are a non-finite mood, they do not have person or (verbal) number; because they are adjectives, however, they have gender, case, and (nominal) number. The noun that a participle modifies is its **subject**. Just as for finite verbs, the subject of a participle may be implicit: γράφουσι, they (some people clear from context) write; οἱ γράφοντες ἀκούουσι, the people writing listen. There's no need to say οἱ γράφοντες ἄνθρωποι ἀκούουσι just as there's no need for an explicit noun or pronoun subject in the sentence γράφουσι. While the subject of a finite verb (if expressed) is in the nominative case, and the subject of an infinitive (if expressed) is in the accusative, the subject of a participle may be in any case, depending on its function in its own clause. Thus: τὰ τοῦ γράφοντος βιβλία ἔχω, μετὰ τοῖς γράφουσί εἰμι, τὸν γράφοντα ὁρῶ, and so on.

The following participles are -οντ- stems: the present participle active, the future participle active, and the second aorist participle active. The first aorist participle active is an -αντ- stem. The participles look like the appropriate tense stem plus the forms of ὤν, so for example the masculine accusative singular of the future participle active is λύσ-οντα, and the feminine nominative plural of the present participle active is λύσ-ουσαι. Strictly, to form the participles add -οντ- to the present, future, or second aorist tense stem to make the masculine and neuter participle stem, for example λυοντ-. Add -αντ- to the first aorist tense stem for verbs with a first aorist, for example λυσαντ-. Then add the regular third declension endings. The feminine forms of these participles are first-declension adjectives; add -ουσα- to the tense stem for present, future, or second aorist, and add -ασα- for first aorist. Then use the same endings as γλῶττα.

This table gives the nominative singular forms for the present, future, and aorist participles active.

present	λύ-ων	λύ-ουσα	λῦ-ον
future	λύσ-ων	λύσ-ουσα	λῦσ-ον
1st aorist	λύσ-ᾱς	λύσ-ᾱσα	λῦσ-αν
2nd aorist	λαβ-ών	λαβ-οῦσα	λαβ-όν (note the accent)

Note that the masculine and neuter dative plural of the present participle active is identical to the third person plural present indicative active: λύουσι. Similarly for the future. Context will tell you which mood the form is in any given sentence.

Remember that the past indicative augment is only used in the indicative mood, so aorist participles do *not* have the augment.

The active participles in Greek are formed in just the same way as the present participle active in Latin, such as *amans*, masc. acc. sg. *amantem*, from *amare* "love," and also in Sanskrit, such as *gacchan*, masc. acc. sg. *gacchantam*, from *gam* "go."

For contracted verbs, the present participle active is:

α	ε	ο
τιμῶν τιμῶσα τιμῶν	ποιῶν ποιοῦσα ποιοῦν	δηλῶν δηλοῦσα δηλοῦν
τιμῶντος, etc.	ποιοῦντος, etc.	δηλοῦντος, etc.

Of course the future and aorist participles of contract verbs are formed from their tense stems in the regular way, as ποιήσων, ποιήσας.

Exercise

Write the three nominative singular forms of the present, future, and aorist participles active of each of the following verbs: φιλῶ, γράφω, λέγω, ἔχω, πέμπω, ἄγω, ἐρωτῶ. Be careful about which kind of aorist they have.

VIII.3 Remaining finite moods

The remaining moods of the Greek verb are the imperative, the subjunctive, and the optative. The **imperative** is used for giving orders. It exists in the second and third persons only, not the first. It exists in the present and aorist tenses, not the future or the perfect. The **subjunctive** is used for certain subordinate clauses, often to generalize — whoever, whenever, and so on. It exists in the present and aorist, not the future; the perfect subjunctive does exist, but is rare. The **optative** is also used in certain subordinate clauses, often to mark subordination to a past-tense main verb. In addition to the present and aorist, the optative also exists in the future tense (and in the perfect, which is rare). Both the subjunctive and optative may also be used in main clauses, though this is less common than their various uses in subordinate clauses.

These are the forms of these moods in the present tense and active voice.

	Imperative	Subjunctive	Optative
singular			
1st	—	λύ-ω	λύ-οιμι
2nd	λῦ-ε	λύ-ῃς	λύ-οις
3rd	λῦ-έτω	λύ-ῃ	λύ-οι

	Imperative	Subjunctive	Optative
dual			
2nd	λύ-ετον	λύ-ητον	λύ-οιτον
3rd	λῡ-έτων	λύ-ητον	λῡ-οίτην
plural			
1st	—	λύ-ωμεν	λύ-οιμεν
2nd	λύ-ετε	λύ-ητε	λύ-οιτε
3rd	λῡ-όντων	λύ-ωσι(ν)	λύ-οιεν

The second person singular present imperative active is the bare stem, including the e grade of the theme vowel. The second person dual and plural present imperative active are identical to the corresponding indicative forms, so it's necessary to pay attention to context. This is only a problem in the present, because the aorist indicative and imperative are easy to tell apart by the augment.

The imperative forms are similar to those in Latin, for example *lege, legito*, second and third person singular, *legite, legunto*, second and third person plural, from *legere* "speak." The Sanskrit forms are also similar, for example singular *vada, vadatu*, dual *vadatam, vadatām*, and plural *vadata, vadantu* from *vad* "speak."

The subjunctive forms are like those of the indicative, except with a longer vowel: compare third singular λύῃ and λύει, or first plural λύωμεν and λύομεν.

All the optative forms have -ι- in their endings. Notice the accent of the third person singular optative: here, and nowhere else in Greek, the -οι at the end of the word is treated like the diphthong it is. If the verb had more than one syllable the accent would have to be on the second-to-last, as for example λαμβάνοι.

For contract verbs, these moods use the same endings, which contract with the stem vowel, just as the endings of the present and imperfect indicative do. The rules for contraction are the same as everywhere else in the verb system; see Appendix 1 section 1 for the chart. These are the forms of the singular, to give you the idea:

	Imperative	Subjunctive	Optative
α	τίμᾱ, τιμάτω	τιμῶ, τιμᾷς, τιμᾷ	τιμῴην, τιμῴης, τιμῷ
ε	ποίει, ποιείτω	ποιῶ, ποιῇς, ποιῇ	ποιοίην, ποιοίης, ποιοίη
ο	δήλου, δηλούτω	δηλῶ, δηλοῖς, δηλοῖ	δηλοίην, δηλοίης, δηλοίη

Note that the subjunctive of α-contracts is the same as the indicative. The optative forms in the singular are different from those of non-contract verbs (though the expected forms like ποιοῖμι sometimes occur), but the dual and plural use the regular endings (for example, third plural ποιοῖεν).

For verbs with a second aorist, the aorist imperative, subjunctive, and optative are formed from the aorist stem exactly as the present imperative, subjunctive, and optative are formed from the present stem, because second aorist forms always use the same endings as present forms. As always, these non-indicative moods do not have the past indicative augment. For example, the third-person singular forms from λαμβάνω are: aorist imperative active λαβέτω, aorist subjunctive active λάβῃ, and aorist optative active λάβοι.

Five verbs have accent on the ending in the second singular aorist imperative active: εἰπέ (from εἶπον, suppletive to λέγω), ἐλθέ (from ἦλθον "came"), εὑρέ (from εὑρίσκω "find"), ἰδέ (from εἶδον, suppletive to ὁράω), and λαβέ. All the rest of the second aorists have the normal accent for this form, like βάλε.

For verbs with a first aorist, the imperative and optative use the characteristic aorist vowel α, and the subjunctive uses exactly the same endings as the present subjunctive. Of course there is no augment here either. Note the unusual second person singular imperative, ending in -ον. If you are familiar with the traditional Latin liturgy of the Roman Catholic Mass, perhaps from its many musical settings, you can remember this form from the one Greek prayer in that ritual, κύριε, ἐλέησον (κύριος, -ου, ὁ, lord, master; ἐλεέω, be merciful, show mercy).

	Imperative	Subjunctive	Optative
singular			
1st	—	λύσ-ω	λύσ-αιμι
2nd	λῦσ-ον	λύσ-ῃς	λύσ-αις, λύσ-ειας
3rd	λῦσ-άτω	λύσ-ῃ	λύσ-αι, λύσ-ειε
dual			
2nd	λύσ-ατον	λύσ-ητον	λύσ-αιτον
3rd	λυσ-άτων	λύσ-ητον	λυσ-αίτην
plural			
1st	—	λύσ-ωμεν	λύσ-αιμεν
2nd	λύσ-ατε	λύσ-ητε	λύσ-αιτε
3rd	λυσ-άντων	λύσ-ωσι(ν)	λύσ-αιεν, λύσ-ειαν

Just as for the -οι of the present and second aorist optative, the -αι of the first aorist optative counts as a real diphthong for accenting. Thus λύσαι has an acute instead of a circumflex, and the accent cannot go back to the third-to-last syllable, so we have κελεῦσαι for example.

Watch out for accents: κελεῦσαι, κελεύσαι, and κέλευσαι are all different. The first of these is the aorist infinitive active, as you learned in chapter 6. The next is the 3rd singular aorist optative active. The third form is the 2nd singular aorist imperative middle, which you will meet in chapter 11.

The imperative, subjunctive, and optative of εἰμί "be" are a bit irregular; they are in chapter 13.

We have now seen all six of the moods in the present active, aorist active, and future active. As you remember, the moods are:

finite				non-finite	
indicative	imperative	subjunctive	optative	infinitive	participle
independent		subordinate			

The finite moods have person and number; the non-finite moods do not. The infinitive is a verbal noun, always neuter singular; the participle is a verbal adjective which may be any gender, case, and (nominal) number. The indicative and imperative are called independent moods because they are most at home in independent clauses (main clauses), though the indicative also occurs in many kinds of subordinate clauses. The subjunctive and optative are called subordinate moods because their most common uses are in subordinate clauses, though they may be used in main clauses as well.

Exercise

Write out the following verbs in the given tenses and moods: φέρω, present subjunctive active; ἀκούω, present optative active; ἔχω, present imperative active; μανθάνω, aorist subjunctive active; πέμπω, aorist subjunctive active; λαμβάνω, aorist optative active; πράττω, aorist optative active; γράφω, aorist imperative active; βάλλω, aorist imperative active.

From now on, when you write a synopsis of a verb (see Appendix 1 section 5), you will include all the moods in the present, future, and aorist active.

VIII.4 Uses of the imperative

The imperative gives an order: γράψον, "write!" The third-person imperative expresses an order to someone other than the person you are speaking to: τὸ παιδίον, ὦ ἄνθρωπε, γραψάτω "Sir, your child must write," or "I order your child to write," or even "he'd better write!"

Tense in the imperative mood is entirely for aspect, not for time. A command, after all, always denotes something that will be happening in the future (perhaps the *immediate* future): it's not possible to give commands about the past. So the present imperative orders habitual or continuing action, while the aorist imperative orders a single action, or an action considered as a single unit. Thus the aorist is the normal imperative, and the present is used when the durative aspect of the action is important.

That is, γράφε can imply something like "write, and don't stop until I tell you" or "get in the habit of writing" or "write, and it's going to be a long job of it." But γράψον is just "write that one thing" or "do this one bit of writing" or even simply "write" without specifying anything about aspect.

Because the tense of an imperative denotes aspect, this mood only exists in the present and aorist, the tense systems most strongly marked for aspect. There is no future imperative or perfect imperative.

The negative with a command is μή, so μὴ φύγε, "don't run away." This can sometimes help you distinguish the ambiguous forms: μὴ παύετον is imperative but οὐ παύετον is indicative; similarly with παύετε.

VIII.5 Uses of the subjunctive

Two major uses of the subjunctive are **purpose clauses** and **general clauses**.

A **purpose clause** answers the question "why? with what intention?" — "why is he doing that?", "why did you do that?", or the like. It is not the same as a **reason clause**, though this can also answer a why-question; as you already know, these are clauses introduced by διότι, ἐπειδή, or ἐπεί, with the verb in the indicative. In Greek a purpose clause is always a clause with a finite verb, introduced by one of the subordinating conjunctions ἵνα, ὡς, or ὅπως. The verb is normally in the subjunctive, but the **OOO rule** applies — that is, the verb may be optative if the main verb is in a secondary (past) tense. The tense of the purpose clause denotes aspect: present subjunctive for continuing action or process, aorist for an action considered as a single unit.

For example, τὸ βιβλίον λαμβάνει ἵνα μανθάνῃ, "he takes the book so that he can learn," or more simply "he takes the book to learn." Here the learning is considered an on-going process, so the purpose clause has present subjunctive. If this were a narrative about the past, we could have τὸ βιβλίον ἔλαβε ἵνα μανθάνῃ or, equally possibly, τὸ βιβλίον ἔλαβε ἵνα μανθάνοι. Writers may use the subjunctive to keep the "purpose" notion fresh in your mind, and to make the character's intention vivid to you, or they may use the optative to make sure you realize that the clause is subordinate; see below for more on this optional optative.

The negative for purpose clauses is μή.

Purpose and reason are distinct in Greek exactly as in English. Compare: ἡ διδασκάλη ἀγαθοὺς λόγους λέγει διότι σοφή ἐστι giving a reason; ἡ διδασκάλη ἀγαθοὺς λόγους λέγει ὅπως οἱ μαθηταὶ ἀκούσωσι giving a purpose. Sometimes both reason and purpose are stated, as ἡ διδασκάλη ἀγαθοὺς λόγους λέγει ὅπως οἱ μαθηταὶ ἀκούσωσι· σοφὴ γάρ ἐστι.

English typically uses the infinitive for purpose ("he takes the book *to learn*"). Latin, too, though it has a subordinate purpose construction like Greek (*librum capit ut discet*), can use its verbal nouns and adjectives for purpose (gerund, *librum capit ad discendum*; gerundive, *epistulam capit ad eam legendam*, "he takes the letter to read it"; supine, *in bibliotecam it libros captum*, "he goes into the library to take some books"). Greek *does not* use the infinitive (verbal noun) for purpose constructions (as a rule). This will not give you any trouble in reading, because purpose clauses are always clearly marked with one of the appropriate conjunctions, ἵνα, ὡς, ὅπως. In your own writing and speaking, however, be careful to express purpose as a Greek writer would, not as in English.

The other key subjunctive construction is the **general clause**. The particle ἄν marks any kind of subordinate clause as general, much like English "ever." This particle is post-positive: it must *not* be first in its clause, and normally comes either second or next to the verb.

For example, compare ὃς βιβλία λαμβάνει εὖ μανθάνει and ὃς ἄν βιβλία λαμβάνῃ εὖ μανθάνει. The first sentence is a plain statement of fact about a particular situation: someone is taking books and that person is becoming erudite. The second is a general truth: *whoever* picks up books learns well, not just in a particular case. Similarly, ὅτε τὸν ποιητὴν ἀκούομεν, θαυμάζομεν is a specific statement about a particular time when we're listening, but ὅταν τὸν ποιητὴν ἀκούωμεν, θαυμάζομεν is general: *whenever*, not just on some particular occasion.

The particle ἄν merges with εἰ, ἐπεί, ἐπειδή, and ὅτε, in a sort of crasis, giving ἐάν, ἐπήν, ἐπειδάν, ὅταν.

Generalizing relative clauses may use the ordinary relative pronoun, as ὃν ἄν ὁρῶ, αὐτῷ λέγω, but may also use ὅστις, the same pronoun that can introduce indirect "who?"-questions. Remember that *both* parts of this word decline, so ὅντινα ἄν ὁρῶ, αὐτῷ λέγω. There is no difference in meaning; both of these sentences mean roughly λέγω πᾶσι.

The **OOO rule** (below) applies here as well, *but* the particle disappears if the writer uses the optative. So: ὃς ἄν βιβλία λαμβάνῃ εὖ ἐμάνθανε with subjunctive, ὃς βιβλία λαμβάνοι εὖ ἐμάνθανε with optional optative.

VIII.6 Uses of the optative

Two main uses of the optative mood are **wishes** and **potential** or hypothetical statements; here the optative is the only choice. The third major use of the optative is as a substitute for an indicative or subjunctive, to mark subordinate clauses as secondary.

A wish can be expressed by the optative alone, as λέγοιμι "I wish I could speak." The particles εἴθε and εἰ γάρ may also be used: εἴθε λέγοιμι or εἰ γὰρ λέγοιμι. In this use, the optative is the main verb of the main clause.

The name of the optative mood comes from this construction: Latin *optare* is "to wish."

Be careful with εἰ γάρ, which can also mean what it looks like, a conditional (εἰ) being given as a reason for something else (γάρ); if so, then the εἰ clause will be subordinate to the conclusion of the conditional. Thus: κελεύεις με μὴ λέγειν. εἰ γὰρ λέγοιμι, σὺ ἂν ἀποθνῇσκοις — the speaker says the reason the other person orders him to keep silent is that his speech would be fatal to the one giving the order.

The second use is the **potential optative**, for hypothetical statements or conditions. In a statement (in a main clause) the force is that something could or might happen, so λέγοιμι ἄν "I could say, I would say, I might say" — always with the particle ἄν in the main clause. In a conditional, the optative proposes a hypothesis which could be true, but seems unlikely. The main clause will probably also be a potential optative clause. For example, εἰ ὁ διδάσκαλος τὸ βιβλίον ἐκ τοῦ δωματίου βάλοι, οἱ μαθηταὶ γελάσαιεν ἄν — although it is unlikely that the teacher would treat his book this way, this is how the students would react if he did. The potential particle appears only in the main clause, not the condition clause.

The potential optative can be used as a softer or more polite equivalent for an imperative, as for example γράψοις ἄν, "you could write." There is no word in Greek corresponding to English "please" with an imperative or request; to be polite or deferential, a classical Greek would use this optative construction.

The third use of the optative is optional: writers may choose to substitute an optative for another mood in certain kinds of subordinate clauses, when the main verb is in a past tense. The choice of mood depending on the tense of the main verb is called **sequence of moods**. If the main verb is present, future, or perfect tense, it is called a **primary tense** and the sentence is said to be in **primary sequence**. In this case the subordinate clause will use its normal mood. If the main verb is imperfect, aorist, or pluperfect (and sometimes also perfect), it is called a secondary tense and the sentence is in secondary sequence. Now the writer may replace the verb in the subordinate clause with an optative.

When the optative is used this way it can be called an **oblique optative**, and when the ordinary indicative or subjunctive is used, it is sometimes called **retained indicative** (or **retained subjunctive** as the case may be). The general principle is that a type of clause, for example an indirect statement with ὅτι or a purpose clause, takes a particular mood, or optional optative in secondary sequence — thus, we call this the **OOO rule**, for "Or Optional Optative."

Writers will use the optative if they want to emphasize that the clause is subordinate. This can be useful with indirect quotations, where it otherwise might not be clear which parts of the sentence are part of the quotation and which are part of the outer main clause. On the other hand, they may use the ordinary mood (whichever is appropriate for the kind of clause) to make the subordinate clause more vivid, perhaps indicating that this information is immediately relevant to the hearer or listener.

The OOO rule does not apply to all subordinate clauses; for example, it does not apply to ordinary relative clauses. As you learn each new construction you will learn whether the rule applies. Of the subordinate clause types you know so far, the rule applies to indirect statement with ὅτι or ὡς, indirect question, purpose, conditionals, and general subjunctive clauses (relative type and conditional type). It does not apply to ordinary relative clauses or to clauses introduced by ἐπεί or διότι. See Appendix 2 section 4 for the list of clauses to which the OOO rule applies.

Here are some examples.

> οἱ μαθηταὶ λέγουσι ὅτι ἡ διδασκάλη ἁμαρτάνει. Everything is in the present: right now, we hear ἁμαρτάνεις, ὦ διδασκάλη. Suppose it was yesterday: χθὲς οἱ μαθηταὶ εἶπον ὅτι ἡ διδασκάλη ἁμαρτάνει, or χθὲς οἱ μαθηταὶ εἶπον ὅτι ἡ διδασκάλη ἁμαρτάνοι. In the first version, perhaps the listener is particularly concerned with the teacher's ability. In the second version, perhaps the speaker wants to stress that it's the students, not the speaker himself, who accused the teacher of a mistake.

> ἄγγελον πέμπω ἵνα εἰρήνην ἔχωμεν. Here is a purpose clause in primary sequence: I'm sending the messenger now. Again, suppose this was yesterday: then either χθὲς ἄγγελον ἔπεμψα ἵνα εἰρήνην ἔχωμεν (subjunctive) or χθὲς ἄγγελον ἔπεμψα ἵνα εἰρήνην ἔχοιμεν (optative). As in the previous example, the first version is more vivid, perhaps emphasizing that the "we" includes the listener, while the second version might be more appropriate if the listener is a third party (for example, if I am telling the Corinthians that I, an Athenian, sent a messenger to conclude peace between Athens and Boeotia).

> ὁ διδάσκαλος, ἐὰν δραχμὴν ἔχῃ, βιβλία ἀγοράζει. This is a general conditional statement telling us how the teacher always spends his money. In a memoir or biography of a long-ago teacher, we might have ὁ διδάσκαλος, ἐὰν δραχμὴν ἔχῃ, βιβλία ἠγόραζε, or, applying the OOO rule, ὁ διδάσκαλος, εἰ δραχμὴν ἔχοι, βιβλία ἠγόραζε. Note that ἄν disappears when the subordinate verb becomes optative: it has to, because an optative with ἄν means a potential, something that *might* happen, but here we need a generalization, something that *always* happens.

Thus while the particular subordinating conjunction generally tells you what kind of clause you have — ἵνα for purpose, ὅτι for indirect statement, εἰ for a condition, and so on — the mood of the verb within the subordinate clause may add a nuance.

VIII.7 Genitive absolute

Greek has a construction called the **genitive absolute** in which a phrase in the genitive case, often a noun modified by a participle, is attached to a sentence. The noun generally does *not* appear elsewhere in the sentence — if it did, the participle could simply modify it there. The absolute phrase has a logical connection with the rest of the sentence, but not a grammatical connection: it is "absolved" of grammatical connection, thus called "absolute."

The genitive absolute seems odd to English speakers because English normally insists that the connection between a subordinate clause or phrase and the main clause be explicit. In the Greek genitive absolute, however, the logical connection is left to the reader's imagination. It may be obvious from context, it may not be important, or the writer simply may not want to specify it. After all, if the writer *wants* to make the logical connection clear, there are plenty of ways to do that, with explicit subordinating conjunctions (like ὅτε "when" or διότι "because") or other constructions (like a purpose clause). The genitive absolute allows a degree of vagueness, saying that the subordinate idea is somehow in the background of the main one, a circumstance relevant in some way, but leaving the relationship undefined. This is quite foreign to English: you may even feel that genitive absolute phrases are similar to dangling modifiers in English, as perhaps they are, but in Greek this construction is not only grammatically acceptable but common, used in any style, in both prose and verse, and in both formal and informal language.

Here are some examples. τοῦ διδασκάλου λέγοντος, οἱ μαθηταὶ ἔγραφον. This sentence tells us that there is a connection between the teacher's speech and the students' writing, but not what it is. Perhaps they are going on at the same time; perhaps the teacher is dictating; perhaps on the other hand the students are passing notes rather than listening! To be more explicit, we could have said ὅτε ὁ διδάσκαλος ἔλεγε, οἱ μαθηταὶ ἔγραφον, which says the connection is that one happens while the other is going on. Or ταῦτα ἃ ὁ διδάσκαλος ἔλεγε οἱ μαθηταὶ ἔγραφον, where we're told the speaking and the writing involve the same words. Or οὐκ ἀκούοντες ἃ ὁ διδάσκαλος ἔλεγε, οἱ μαθηταὶ ἔγραφον, which clarifies that the students are writing rather than listening. The original sentence with the genitive absolute could mean *any* of these, depending on the larger context.

Another example: τοῦ δεσπότου ἀποθανόντος, οἱ δοῦλοι ἐλευθερίαν ἔχουσιν. The connection between these two ideas is sufficiently obvious that it doesn't need to be made explicit; the idea is οἱ δοῦλοι ἐλευθερίαν ἔχουσιν, ὁ γὰρ δεσπότης ἀπέθανε. The participle is aorist to indicate that the action of the genitive absolute phrase takes place before that of the main clause.

In this sentence the participle is still aorist, because it's before the time of the main verb, even though it is objectively in the future: τοῦ δεσπότου ἀποθανόντος, οἱ δοῦλοι ἐλευθερίαν ἕξουσιν. This is the sort of sentence that Latin (or even English) might express with the future perfect tense, but in Greek the aorist participle can indicate something anterior to the main verb, whether the main verb itself is past, present, or future.

The negative of the genitive absolute is normally οὐ. When you read or hear μή with a genitive absolute phrase, the phrase is like a conditional, so τοῦ διδασκάλου μὴ λέγοντος, οἱ μαθηταὶ ἔγραφον is roughly equivalent to εἰ ὁ διδάσκαλος μὴ λέγει, οἱ μαθηταὶ ἔγραφον rather than to any of the other possibilities.

This is an ancient construction, for Latin and Sanskrit also have absolute constructions that work the same way, though not with the genitive: Latin uses the ablative case and Sanskrit the locative.

VIII.8 Compound verbs

Many prepositions and adverbs can be used as prefixes to verbs. For example, you have already seen ἀπο-θνήσκω, which is the simple verb θνήσκω ("die") with the prefix ἀπό; compare English "die off." Verbs with prefixes are called **compound verbs**. Usually the prefix adds something similar to its adverbial or prepositional meaning, as ἀποφέρω is "carry *away*," or περιφέρω is "carry *around*." Sometimes the prefix makes little difference, as in ἀποθνῄσκω or ἀποκτείνω, which both mean much the same with or without ἀπο-. Sometimes the meaning of the compound verb is only vaguely related to that of the simple verb, as γιγνώσκω "know" and ἀναγιγνώσκω "read."

Attic Greek prose generally prefers a compound verb to a simple verb if the meaning is roughly the same; in verse, however, the simple verb is usually used. Thus ἀποθνῄσκω is prosaic and θνῄσκω is more poetic. Sometimes the compound verb has taken over, pushing the simple verb almost entirely out of use. For example, καθεύδω "sleep" is rather more common than εὕδω.

The prefix and the verb form may undergo sandhi changes. If the prefix ends in a vowel, and the verb form begins with a vowel, the vowel at the end of the prefix is elided, *not* contracted. So from ἐπί + ἄγω we form ἐπάγω "lead to, lead on, apply." The prefix σύν, which ends in a consonant, is assimilated to a consonant at the start of the verb form, as σύν + λέγω, συλλέγω, σύν + χωρέω, συγχωρέω, σύν + πέμπω, συμπέμπω. The prefix ἐκ becomes ἐξ before a vowel, exactly as the preposition ἐκ does, so ἐξεῖπον.

Note, therefore, that a prefix may look and sound different in different forms of the same verb, since it may have one form before a vowel and another before a consonant. For example, the imperfect of συλλέγω is συνέλεγον, with unassimilated prefix.

In compound verbs, the past indicative augment goes on the simple verb, with the prefix at the very beginning of the word. As always, if the prefix ends in a vowel, that vowel is elided, *not* contracted. So ἀποθνῄσκω has imperfect ἀπ-έ-θνησκον and aorist ἀπ-έ-θανον. The accent in finite forms goes as far back as possible, as for any other verb, except that in past indicative forms the accent never goes back beyond the augment. Thus from ἀπο- + ἦλθον we have ἀπῆλθον, with the accent on the second-to-last syllable even though the final syllable has a short vowel: the third-to-last syllable is before the past indicative augment.

There are two exceptions to the elision rule for prefixes. The final ι of περι- is not elided, so περι-αιρῶ, περι-ῄρουν "take away." And the ο of προ- often contracts with the past indicative augment, as προύβαινε, 3rd sg. imperfect indicative active of προ-βαίνω.

When the verb begins with a rough breathing, that breathing is retained in augmented forms, as αἱρέω "take," imperfect ᾕρουν, or εὑρίσκω "find," imperfect ηὕρισκον. When there is a prefix, if the prefix has an unvoiced consonant, that consonant is aspirated by the rough breathing, so ἀπο + αἱρέω becomes ἀφαιρέω ("take away, carry off"): elide the final -ο of the prefix, then aspirate the consonant. This also happens in augmented tenses, as ἀφῄρουν.

In compound verbs, sometimes the augment is not obvious, because it's buried between the prefix and the stem. If you see or hear a verb form beginning with ἐπ-, this could be a past-tense form of a verb beginning with π- or it could come from a verb with the prefix ἐπι. If you see a form beginning with ἐφ-, similarly, it could be an augmented form of a verb starting with φ- or a verb with prefix ἐπι- where the plain verb starts with a rough breathing. Mentally run through these possibilities if you don't immediately recognize a verb form: it will usually turn out to be a familiar verb in disguise.

Because the principal parts of a compound verb are exactly the same as those of the base verb, except that the prefix is added at the beginning, dictionaries and vocabulary lists will not show them all. Given the first principal part, you can determine all the others.

Exercises

1. Identify the following verb forms and give the first principal part of the verb in question. For example, εἰσπέμπουσι is 3rd pl. pres. indic. act. of εἰσ-πέμπω. Forms: εἰσήγαγε, ἀπέκρινον, εἰσεβάλετε, ἐπεγέλασε, μετέβαλε, ἐξελαύνει, ἀπέπεμψα, ἐξέταξε, ἐφέλκει.

2. Give all the principal parts of the following compounds, noting how the prefix changes and where the past indicative augment comes. διαλέγω, ἐκλέγω, συλλέγω, ἐμποιέω, προσποιέω, περιποιέω, καταλαμβάνω, παραλαμβάνω, ἀναλαμβάνω, διαφέρω, συμφέρω, ἐπιφέρω.

VIII.9 Vocabulary

VERBS

ἀγοράζω, ἀγοράσω, ἠγόρασα, ἠγόρακα, ἠγόρασμαι, ἠγοράσθην, buy

ἀξιόω, ἀξιώσω, ἠξίωσα, ἠξίωκα, ἠξίωμαι, ἠξιώθην, ask, claim; think worthy

ἀμελέω, ἀμελήσω, ἠμέλησα, ἠμέληκα, – , – , neglect, disregard

ἀπ-αντάω, ἀπ-αντήσομαι, ἀπ-ήντησα, ἀπ-ήντηκα, – , – , meet, go to meet (+ dat.)

ἀπο-δημέω, be away from home (usually only present system)

ἀπο-κτείνω, ἀπο-κτενῶ, ἀπ-έκτεινα, ἀπ-έκτονα, – , – , kill

ἔρχομαι, εἶμι, ἦλθον, ἐλήλυθα, – , – , come, go

ἐπ-αν-έρχομαι, return (like ἔρχομαι)

πωλέω, πωλήσω, ἐπώλησα, – , – , ἐπωλήθην, sell, put up for sale (cp. *monopoly*)

παρα-λαμβάνω, receive, find

NOUNS

ἀλήθεια, -ας, ἡ, truth

γίγας, γίγαντος, ὁ, giant

δεῖγμα, δείγματος, τό, specimen, example (cp. *paradigm*)

δικαστής, -οῦ, ὁ, juror

δῶρον, -ου, τό, gift

ἐπιστολή, -ῆς, ἡ, letter (cp. *epistle*)

ἑταῖρος, -ου, ὁ, companion, comrade

ζῷον, -ου, τό, animal (cp. *zoology*)

λέων, λέοντος, ὁ, lion

πλοῦτος, -ου, ὁ, wealth (cp. *plutocrat*)

χάρις, χάριτος, ἡ, favor, thanks, grace (cp. *charisma, yearn*, L. *hortor*)

ADJECTIVES

ἑκάτερος, -α, -ο, each of two, either (Lat. *uterque*)

μέγας, μεγάλη, μέγα, big, great

μέλᾱς, μέλαινα, μέλαν, black (cp. *melancholy, melanoma*)

μῶρος, -α, -ον, foolish (cp. *sophomore*)

πᾶς, πᾶσα, πᾶν, all (cp. *pantheon*)

τάλᾱς, τάλαινα, τάλαν, wretched, miserable

τοιοῦτος, τοιαύτη, τοιοῦτο(ν), such

ADVERBS AND CONJUNCTIONS

ἄν, particle marks general or hypothetical clause

διότι, because (from διὰ + ὅ τι)

ἐάν, if (contraction of εἰ + ἄν, so takes subjunctive)

εἴθε, particle introducing a wish

ἵνα, so that, in order that

καθάπερ, just as, like as (= κατὰ + ἅ + περ)

μά, (swearing) by, with accusative

ὅτε, when (subordinating conjunction)

Notes on the vocabulary

ἀμελέω normally takes a genitive complement, so we have τοῦ ἔργου ἀμέλει for "he neglects his work." It may take an accusative object particularly in the sense "overlook, slight," so τὸν διδάσκαλον ἀμέλει is "he slights the teacher, disrespects him." When it has an accusative object and a participle agreeing with the object the sense is "overlook, permit," as τὸν μαθητὴν γελῶντα ἀμέλει "he overlooks the student's laughing, lets the student laugh, lets the student get away with laughing."

ἀπαντάω takes a dative complement rather than an accusative direct object: one says ἀπαντῶ αὐτῷ for "I meet him."

The future of ἔρχομαι is athematic, in other words it belongs to the other major group of Greek verbs. You will learn this verb in chapter 15. The present does not have active forms, only middle; you will learn middle forms in chapter 10. Thus for the moment you can use this verb only in the aorist. The second aorist and perfect are suppletive (that is, they use a different stem from the present), but aside from this they are regular.

The noun δεῖγμα has the same endings as any other third declension noun, with stem δειγματ-. Only the nominative and accusative singular are different: because it's a neuter noun, it has no ending in those cases, and the final -τ has dropped because Greek words do not end in this sound.

ζῷον ultimately comes from the same root as βίος.

VIII.10 Reading

1. Σχολαστικῷ ἑταῖρος ἀποδημῶν ἔγραψεν ἐπιστολήν, ἵνα αὐτῷ βιβλία ἀγοράσῃ. ὁ δὲ ἀμελήσας, καὶ ἐπανελθόντι αὐτῷ ἀπαντήσας, εἶπεν, "ἡ περὶ τῶν βιβλίων ἐπιστολή, ἣν ἔγραψας, οὐκ ἦλθεν." ἆρα σοφὸς ὁ σχολαστικός; οὔκ, ἀλλὰ μῶρος.

2. Σχολαστικῷ τις ἀπαντήσας εἶπεν· "ὃν ἐπώλησάς μοι δοῦλον, ἀπέθανεν." "μὰ τοὺς θεούς," ἔφη, "παρ' ἐμοὶ ὅτε ἦν, οὐδὲν τοιοῦτον ἐποίησεν."

3. Σχολαστικῷ ἀποδημοῦντι φίλος ἔλεγεν· "ἀξιῶ σε δύο δούλους ἀγοράσαι μοι, ἑκάτερον πεντεκαίδεκα ἐτῶν." ὁ δὲ εἶπεν· "ἐὰν τοιούτους μὴ λάβω, ἀγοράσω σοι ἕνα τριάκοντα ἐτῶν."

   > ἐτῶν is gen. pl. of the neuter noun ἔτος "year," an s-stem noun whose forms you will learn in chapter 11.

4. ὁ πλοῦτος ἡμᾶς, καθάπερ ἰατρὸς κακός,
   πάντας βλέποντας παραλαβὼν τυφλοὺς ποιεῖ.

   > A fragment from a play by Antiphanes.

5. Σχολαστικὸς οἰκίαν πωλῶν λίθον ἀπ' αὐτῆς ὡς δεῖγμα περιέφερεν.

   > λίθος, -ου, ὁ = πέτρα.

6. τοῦ ἀδελφοῦ γελῶντος, τὸ παιδίον ἦλθε πρὸς τὸν ἄνθρωπον. "τάλας εἰμί," ἔφη. "ὁ ἄδικος ἀδελφὸς γελᾷ καὶ λέγει ἐμὲ μῶρον εἶναι." τοῦ ἀνθρώπου οὐκ ἀκούοντος, τὸ παιδίον τὸν ἀδελφὸν πέτραις ἔβαλε. τοῦ ἀδελφοῦ φυγόντος, τὸ παιδίον εἰρήνην εἶχε.

7. Ἕκτωρ Αἴαντι ξίφος ὤπασεν, Ἕκτορι δ' Αἴας
   ζωστῆρ' · ἀμφοτέρων ἡ χάρις εἰς θάνατος

   > Greek Anthology 7.151.

   > For the story see *Iliad* 7.303-305 and chapter 15 below. ξίφος, -ους, τό, sword. ὀπάζω, cause to follow, give as a companion or follower. ζωστήρ, ζωστῆρος, ὁ, sword-belt. θάνατος, -ου, ὁ, death.

8. εἴμι δ' ἐγὼ θεράπων μὲν Ἐνυαλίοιο ἄνακτος
   καὶ Μουσῶν ἐρατὸν δῶρον ἐπιστάμενος

   > θεράπων, -οντος, ὁ, attendant, helper, servant. Ἐνυάλιος is an old name for a war god, and Ἐνυαλίοιο is an old form of the genitive singular. ἄναξ, ἄνακτος, ὁ, lord. ἐρατός, -ή, -όν, lovely, lovable. ἐπιστάμενος, -η, -ον, understanding, knowledgeable; this is a present participle middle. The couplet, by Archilochus, is probably a complete poem.

9. αἴλινον αἴλινον εἰπέ, τὸ δ' εὖ νικάτω.

   > This is a refrain in the opening choral song of Aeschylus' *Agamemnon*.

10. χάρις χάριν τίκτει.

11. πάντων χρημάτων μέτρον ἄνθρωπος, τῶν μὲν ὄντων ὡς ἔστιν, τῶν δὲ οὐκ ὄντων ὡς οὐκ ἔστιν.

This dictum is attributed to Protagoras. Note that the subject of ἔστιν each time it occurs is (understood) τὰ χρήματα, neuter plural with singular verb.
μέτρον, -ου, τό, measure, standard of measurement.

12. ἦν ποτε λέων ὃς ἀεὶ ἐδίωκε τὰ ἄλλα ζῷα. ἡμέρᾳ τινὶ σκόλοπα εἰς τὸν πόδα ἔλαβε. ὁ λέων οὖν λύπην εἶχε. "ὦ τάλας ἐγώ," ἐνόμισε. "ἐκεῖνος ὁ σκόλοψ με βλάπτει. διὰ τὴν λύπην οὐκ ἔστι με ἄλλα ζῷα διώκειν. τοῖς δὲ ἄλλοις ἐμαυτὸν τρέφω. εἰ μὲν τὰ ἄλλα ζῷα μὴ διώκω, οὐκ ἔξω ἐσθίειν. ἐὰν δὲ μὴ ἐσθίωμεν, ἀποθνήσκομεν. οὐκ ἐθέλω ἀποθανεῖν. ἀλλά, δακτύλους οὐκ ἔχων, πῶς τὸν σκόλοπα ἐκ τοῦ ποδὸς ἐξέλκω;"

ὁ δὲ λέων οὕτως λέγων ἄνθρωπόν τινα εἶδον, Ἀνδρόκλεα ὀνόματι. πρὸς αὐτὸν ἐλθὼν ἔσαινε καὶ εἶπε, "χαῖρε, ὦ ἄνθρωπε. ἔγωγε μὲν σε οὐ βλάψω, σὺ δὲ με ὠφελεῖν ἔχεις. σκόλοπα γὰρ ἔχω ἐν τῷ ποδί. ἆρα ἄν μοι αὐτὸν ἐξέλκοις;

"ναί," ἔφη ὁ Ἀνδρόκλης, "ὦ λέων, σὲ ὠφελήσω." λαβὼν οὖν τὸν τοῦ λέοντος πόδα τὸν σκόλοπα εἶδον. "μέγας μὲν οὗτος ὁ σκόλοψ, μεγάλη δέ σοι ἡ λύπη, ὦ τάλας λέον. ἰδού, τὸν σκόλοπα ἐξεῖλξα." ὁ δὲ λέων ἔχαιρε καὶ ἀπὸ τοῦ Ἀνδρόκλους ἀπῆλθε.

μετὰ δὲ τρία ἔτη, ὁ Ἀνδρόκλης δίκην ἔφυγε. ἄδικον οὐκ ἔπραξε, ἀλλὰ οἱ δικασταὶ τὸν λόγον πιστεύσαντες εἶπον, "ὁ Ἀνδρόκλης ἀποθνησκέτω. λαβὲ αὐτὸν πρὸς τὸν ἀγῶνα ἵνα οἱ λέοντες αὐτὸν ἀποκτείνωσι."

οἱ δὲ πολῖται τὸν Ἀνδρόκλης πρὸς τὸν ἀγῶνα οὖν ἔλαβον, ὅπου ὁ Ἀνδρόκλης μέγαν λέοντα εἶδε. "ὦ τάλας ἐγώ," ἐνόμισε. "ἐκεῖνος ἐστι γίγας, οὐ ζῷον. οὐκ ἔχω φυγεῖν. τί ποιήσω;"

ἀλλὰ ὁ λέων, πρὸς τὸν ἄνθρωπον ἐλθών, σαίνων, "ῤῤῤ" ἔλεγε, ὥσπερ μικρὸς αἴλουρος. οὐκ ἔβλαψε τὸν Ἀνδρόκλεα· ἦν γὰρ ὁ αὐτὸς λέων. ὁ μὲν Ἀνδρόκλης ἔχαιρε, ὁ δὲ δικασταὶ ἔχαιρον, ἐπεὶ οὐκ ἀληθείᾳ ἤθελον αὐτὸν ἀποθνήσκειν.

ὁ Ἀνδρόκλης ὅ τε λέων τὴν αὐτὴν οἰκίαν εἶχον πάντα τὸν βίον. ὁ μὲν Ἀνδρόκλης τὸν λέοντα, ὁ δὲ λέων τὸν ἄνθρωπον ἀεὶ ἐφιλεῖ.

The story is adapted from Aulus Gellius.

διώκω, chase. **σκόλοψ, σκόλοπος, ὁ**, thorn. **ὄνομα, ὀνόματα, τό**, name. **πούς, ποδός, ὁ**, foot. **βλάπτω**, hurt. **ἐσθίω**, eat. **σαίνω**, wag the tail, nuzzle as a dog does, fawn on. **ὠφελέω**, help, assist. **ἰδού**, here, look (interjection). **ἔτη** is accusative plural of ἔτος, year (chapter 11). **ἀγών, ἀγῶνος, ὁ**, contest, game. **αἴλουρος, -ου, ὁ**, cat.

13. ὁ Ποσειδῶν δύο τέκνω εἶχε, Ὦτον καὶ Ἐφιάλτην, γίγαντε ὄντε. τὼ παιδίω πόλεμον ἐπραξάτην πρὸς τοὺς θεούς. ὄρος δὲ Πήλιον ἐβαλέτην ἐπὶ τῷ ὄρει Ὄσσᾳ ἵνα ἔλθητον ὅπου εἰσὶν οἱ θεοί. ἡ δὲ Ἄρτεμις αὐτὼ ἀπέκτανε· ἀλλάξασα γὰρ ἑαυτὴν εἰς ἔλαφον μετὰ τοῖν γιγάντοιν ἦλθε. ἕκαστος γίγας, λίθῳ βάλλων τὸν ἔλαφον, τὸν ἀδελφὸν ἀπέκτανε.

ὄρος, ὄρους, τό, mountain, an s-stem noun (chapter 11). **ἔλαφος, -ου, ὁ, ἡ**, deer.

14. *περὶ τοῦ Τρωικοῦ πολέμου, δεύτερον μέρος*

τοῦ Ἀλεξάνδρου τὴν Ἑλένην κλέψαντος, ὁ Μενέλαος οἴκαδε ἦλθε. μεγάλην λύπην εἶχε· ἐφίλει γὰρ τὴν Ἑλένην. πάντες τοι οἱ Δαναοὶ τὴν Ἑλένην ἐφίλουν καί, ἐπεὶ νέα ἦν, ἤθελον αὐτὴν γαμῆσαι. ὅρκον ἐποίησαν ὅτι, εἰ ὁ Μενέλαος τὴν Ἑλένην γαμεῖ, οἱ ἄλλοι αὐτὸν βοηθήσουσι τὴν Ἑλένην φυλάττειν.

— τί ποιήσω; ὁ δὲ Ἀλέξανδρος τὴν Ἑλένην μου ἔκλεψε. τίς μοι βοηθήσει;

— μὴ κλαίῃς, ὁ Μενέλαε, εἶπε ὁ Ἀγαμέμνων.

οἶνόν τοι, Μενέλαε, θεοὶ ποίησαν ἄριστον
θνητοῖς ἀνθρώποισιν ἀποσκεδάσαι μελεδῶνας.

πῖνε οὖν καὶ εἰπέ μοι ὅτι ἐθέλεις ποιεῖν.

— τὴν Ἑλένην πάλιν λαβεῖν ἐθέλω. πόλεμον τοῖς Τρωικοῖς ποιήσω. διὰ τὸν ὅρκον, ἔχω τοὺς ἄλλους Ἕλληνας καλέσαι οἵ μοι βοηθήσουσι.

τὼ ἀδελφὼ οὖν τοὺς ἄλλους Δαναοὺς ἐκάλεσαν. ἦλθον Φιλοκτήτης, Πρωτεσίλαος, Αἴας, Τεῦκρος, Διομήδης, πολλοί τε ἄλλοι.

ὁ δὲ Ὀδυσσεὺς οὐκ ἦλθε. "οὐκ ἔστι ἐμοῦ ἡ Ἑλένη. διὰ τί οὖν ἐθελοίμην ἂν πόλεμον πράττειν περὶ τῆς τοῦ Μενελάου γυναικός;" ἐρωτήσας, οἴκοι ἔμεινε.

ὁ δὲ ἄλλοι πρὸς τὸν Ὀδυσσέα ἐλθόντες, "ἔλθε μεθ᾽ ἡμῶν, ὦ Ὀδυσσεῦ," εἶπον. ὁ δὲ οὐκ ἤκουσε. "ἆρα μανίαν ἔχεις; ἆρα οἱ θεοί σοι τὸν νοῦν ἐξέλαβον;" ἠρώτησαν. ὁ δὲ Ὀδυσσεὺς τὸν ἀγρὸν ἤρουν, οὐδὲν λέγων. ὁ μὲν Ἀγαμέμνων τὸ τοῦ Ὀδυσσέως παιδίον λαβὼν παρὰ τῷ ἀρότρῳ ἔβαλε. εὐθὺς ὁ Ὀδυσσεὺς τοῦ ἔργου ἔπαυσε· οὐκ ἠθέλησε τὸ παιδίον βλάψαι.

— οὐκ ἄρα μανίαν εἶχες! ἔλθε οὖν μεθ᾽ ἡμῶν ἵνα πόλεμον πράξωμεν.

ὁ δὲ Ὀδυσσεὺς ἦλθε μετὰ τῶν ἄλλων. πάντες οἱ Δαναοὶ πρὸς τὴν θάλατταν ἦλθε ἵνα πρὸς τὸν Ἴλιον ἔλθωσι.

> **κλέπτω, κλέψω, ἔκλεψα, κέκλοφα, κέκλεμμαι, ἐκλάπην**, steal. **ὅρκος, -ου, ὁ**, oath. **βοηθέω, βοηθήσω, ἐβοήθησα, βεβοήθηκα, βεβοήθημαι, –** , help. **φυλάττω, φυλάξω, ἐφύλαξα, πεφύλαχα, πεφύλαγμαι, ἐφυλάχθην**, guard. **κλαίω**, weep, cry. **θνητός, -ή, -όν**, mortal. **ἀποσκεδάσαι**, scatter, aorist infinitive active of an athematic verb. **μελεδώνη, -ης, ἡ**, care, sorrow. **πίνω, πίομαι, ἔπιον, πέπωκα, πέπομαι, ἐπόθην**, drink. **γυνή, γυναικός, ἡ**, woman, wife. **μανία, -ας, ἡ**, madness. **ἀρόω, ἀρόσω, ἤροσα, –, –, ἠρόθην**, (to) plow. **ἄροτρον, -ου, τό**, (the) plow.
>
> The verse comes from the *Cypria*, an epic poem surviving only in fragments. In it the form ἐποίησαν appears without its augment, as sometimes happens in epic Greek. A prose paraphrase: οἱ θεοὶ ἐποίησαν οἶνον τοῖς θνητοῖς ἀνθρώποις, ἄριστον τὰς λύπας λῦσαι. The infinitive limits the adjective, in the sense *best at scattering*.

VIII.11 Conversation

1. (reading 1) ποῖός τις ἦν ὁ Σχολαστικός; μῶρος ἦν. τίς ἔγραψεν πρὸς αὐτὸν ἐπιστολήν; ἑταῖρος. ἵνα τί ποιῇ; ἵνα ἀγοράσῃ βιβλία. ἆρ᾽ ἠγόρασε τὰ βιβλία; οὔκ, ἀλλ᾽ ἠμέλησεν. ἐπανελθόντος δὲ ἑταίρου τί εἶπεν; ὅτι οὐκ ἦλθεν ἡ ἐπιστολή.

2. (reading 2) τίς ἀπέθανεν; τί ἐποίησεν ὁ δοῦλος; τίνος δοῦλος; τί εἶπεν ὁ Σχολαστικός;

3. (reading 3) ἀποδημοῦντος αὐτοῦ τί ἠξίου ὁ φίλος; πόσους δούλους; πόσων ἐτῶν; τί εἶπεν ὁ Σχολαστικός; ἆρα τοῦτ᾽ ἠξίου; οὔκ, ἀλλ᾽ ἄλλο τι. ἆρ᾽ οὔκ ἐστι ταὐτόν; οὔκ ἐστι. ἄλλο μὲν γὰρ δοῦλος τριάκοντα ἐτῶν, ἄλλο δὲ δύο δοῦλοι ἑκάτερος πεντεκαίδεκα ἐτῶν.

4. (reading 4) ποῖός ἐστιν ὁ πλοῦτος; τί ποιεῖ; ποίους παραλαβών; τίνας;

5. (imperatives) λαβὲ τὸ βιβλίον. τί ἐκέλευσα; ἐκέλευσας ἐμοὶ τὸ βιβλίον λαβεῖν. κέλευε τῷ ἑταίρῳ τὸ αὐτό· ὦ ἑταῖρε, λαβὲ τὸ βιβλίον. κέλευε τοῖν ἄλλοιν τὸ αὐτό· ὦ ἑταίρω, λάβετον τὸ βιβλίον. Similarly for γράψον τὸ ὄνομα, δήλωσον τὴν θύραν, βάλε τὸν κάλαμον, and so on. Of course the various commands should be obeyed.

6. Chain Story Exercise. See chapter 2 section 10 exercise 6. The first student makes a simple statement, such as ὁ διδάσκαλος βιβλίον ἔλαβε. The next student turns the previous main clause into a genitive absolute and adds a new main clause to advance the story, for example τοῦ διδασκάλου τὸ βιβλίον λαβόντος, οἱ μαθηταὶ τοὺς καλάμους ἔλαβον. The next student does it again, for example τῶν μαθητῶν τοὺς καλάμους λαβόντων, ὁ διδάσκαλος λόγον ἐκ τοῦ βιβλίου εἶπε. The connection between the previous student's statement (the new genitive absolute) and the new main clause can be anything at all, straightforward or silly.

VIII.12 Writing

1. Do the change-number exercise with the following sentences.
   a. ὁ γίγας, πέτραν φέρων, ἦλθε πρὸς τὸν νέων.
   b. ὁ διδάσκαλος, τὴν ἀλήθειαν εἴπων, οὐχ ἁμαρτάνει.
   c. τὸν δοῦλον πωλοῦμεν, οὐκ ἄξιον ὄντα.
   d. τὸν δοῦλον ἐπωλήσαμεν, οὐκ ἄξιον ὄντα.
   e. τὸν δοῦλον πωλοῦμεν, αὐτὸν οὐκ ἀξιῶντες.
   f. τὸν δοῦλον ἐπωλήσαμεν, αὐτὸν οὐκ ἀξιῶντες.
   g. ὁ ἄνθρωπος νομίζει τὸν στρατὸν νικήσοντα.
   h. λαβὲ τὸ βιβλίον, ὦ παιδίον, καὶ ἐλθὲ εἰς τὸ δωμάτιον.
   i. οἱ μαθηταὶ μανθανόντων.
   j. τὸ βιβλίον ἐπωλήσαμεν ἵνα τρεῖς δραχμὰς ἔχωμεν.
   k. τὸ βιβλίον πωλήσομεν ἵνα τρεῖς δραχμὰς ἔχωμεν.
   l. εἴθε νοῦν ἀγαθὸν ἔχοις.
   m. ἐὰν ἡ διδασκάλη γράφῃ, οἱ σχολαστικοὶ τὴν ἀλήθειαν μανθάνουσιν.
   n. ἐὰν ἡ διδασκάλη γράφῃ, οἱ σχολαστικοὶ τὴν ἀλήθειαν ἐμάνθανον.
   o. ὁ μαθητὴς ἐθέλει βλάπτειν τοὺς ἑαυτὸν γελῶντας.
   p. δῶρα τῷ ἡμᾶς αὐτοὺς νικήσαντι πέμπομεν.
   q. τὸ τοῦ ἀμελοῦντος ἀνθρώπου παιδίον ἦν τάλαν.
   r. ἀεὶ τῷ δεσπότῃ εὖ δούλευε, ἵνα μὴ σέ πωλήσῃ.
   s. εἰ ὁ στρατὸς πόλεμον πράττοι καὶ νικήσειε, πάντες χαίροιμεν ἄν.
   t. ὅταν ὁ στρατὸς πόλεμον πράττῃ, πάντας νικᾷ.

   u. ὅταν ὁ στρατὸς πόλεμον πράττῃ, πάντας ἐνίκησε.

   v. ὅτε ὁ στρατὸς πόλεμον πράττοι, πάντας ἐνίκησε.

   w. τοῦ γίγαντος ἐλθόντος, τὼ ἀδελφὼ ἐφυγέτην.

2. Rewrite the following sentences, turning the participial phrases into subordinate clauses. You may need to determine what kind of clause is appropriate. For example, from ὁ μαθητής, σοφὸς ὤν, εὖ μανθάνει you might make ὁ μαθητὴς εὖ μανθάνει, ἐπεὶ σοφός ἐστι.

   a. τὴν ἀληθείαν ἀκούουσα μανθάνω.

   b. ἀξιῶμεν τὸν φιλόσοφον τὴν ἀληθείαν λέγοντα.

   c. ἠξιώσαμεν τὸν φιλόσοφον τὴν ἀληθείαν λέγοντα.

   d. τιμῶμεν τὸν φιλόσοφον τὴν ἀληθείαν λέγοντες.

   e. ὁ ἑταῖρος τὴν οἰκίαν πωλήσας ἄλλην ἀγοράσει.

   f. λέοντες, ζῷα ὄντες, οὐκ ἔχουσιν εἰπεῖν.

   g. πολλὰ δείγματα δηλώσας, ὁ διδάσκαλος τοὺς μαθητὰς ἐξήτασε.

   h. τὸν φίλον ἰδών, ὁ ἄνθρωπος αὐτῷ ἀπαντᾷ.

   i. τὸν ἄδικον ἰδών, ὁ ἄνθρωπος αὐτὸν φεύγει.

   j. τὸν ἄδικον ἰδών, ὁ ἄνθρωπος αὐτὸν ἔφυγε.

   k. δῶρα τῷ ὑμᾶς αὐτοὺς νικήσαντι ἐπέμψατε.

   l. τὸ τοῦ ἀμελοῦντος ἀνθρώπου παιδίον ἐστὶ τάλαν.

   m. τὸ τοῦ ἀμελοῦντος ἀνθρώπου παιδίον ἦν τάλαν.

3. Rewrite the following sentences, using participles instead of subordinate clauses. For example, from ὁ μαθητὴς εὖ μανθάνει, ἐπεὶ σοφός ἐστι make ὁ μαθητής, σοφὸς ὤν, εὖ μανθάνει.

   a. ἐπεὶ τὸ τέκνον ἔτεκε, ἡ ἄνθρωπος αὐτὸν ἔτρεφε.

   b. σοφὸς εἶ, ὦ ἑταῖρε, διότι πολλὰ βιβλία ἔχεις.

   c. ὁ γίγας, ὃς πέτραν φέρει, ἦλθον πρὸς τὸν νέων.

   d. διότι ὁ δοῦλος οὐκ ἄξιός ἐστι, ὁ δεσπότης αὐτὸν πωλήσει.

   e. διότι ὁ δοῦλος οὐκ ἄξιος ἦν, ὁ δεσπότης αὐτὸν ἐπώλησε.

   f. οἱ ἐν τῇ κώμῃ δῶρα τῷ στρατηγῷ πέμπουσι, ὃς αὐτοὺς ἐνίκησε.

   g. οἱ ἐν τῇ κώμῃ δῶρα τῷ στρατηγῷ ἔπεμψαν, ὃς αὐτοὺς ἐνίκησε.

   h. ὅτε ἐπιστολὴν ἔγραψας, πρὸς τὸν φίλον αὐτὴν πέμπεις.

   i. εἰ πλοῦτον παραλαβεῖν ἐλπίζει, ὁ ἰατρὸς τοὺς ἄλλους εὖ τρεφέτω.

   j. διότι λέων ζῷόν ἐστι, οὐκ ἀληθείᾳ λέγειν ἔχει.

4. Each of the following sentences contains a genitive absolute phrase; rewrite the sentence using a suitable clause with a finite verb. For example, from τοῦ στρατοῦ νικήσαντος, ὁ λεὼς χαίρει, you might make ἐπεὶ ὁ στρατὸς ἐνίκησε, ὁ λεὼς χαίρει.

   a. τοῦ διδασκάλου πολλὰ δείγματα δηλώσαντος, οἱ μαθηταὶ πάντα ἔμαθον.

   b. θεῶν τρεφόντων, εὖ ἔξομεν.

   c. τῶν ἵππων τὴν ἅμαξαν ἑλκόντων, εἰς τὴν κώμην ἦλθε ὁ πολίτης.

   d. τοῦ ἰατροῦ τὸ τέκνον θεραπεύσαντος, ὁ ἄνθρωπος θαυμάζει.

   e. τοῦ ἵππου φυγόντος, διὰ τί κλήεις τὴν θύραν;

   f. τοῦ Πλάτωνος γράψαντος, πολλὰ μανθάνομεν περὶ τοῦ Σωκράτους.

   g. τῆς Ἑλένης καλῆς οὔσης, οἱ Ἕλληνες καὶ οἱ Τρωικοὶ πόλεμον ἔπραξαν.

   h. τῶν μαθητῶν ἀκουόντων, ὁ διδάσκαλος πάντα ἐδήλωσε.

   i. τοῦ ἱματίου ἐπὶ τοῖν ὤμοιν ὄντος, ὁ γεωργὸς εἰς τὴν ἀγορὰν ἦλθε.

   j. ἐλευθέρου ὄντος, τὰ χρηστὰ πρᾶττε, ὦ τέκνον.

5. Combine each of the following pairs of sentences into a single sentence, making one of the original sentences into a genitive absolute phrase. For example, given ὁ διδάσκαλος λέγει. ὁ μαθητὴς οὐκ ἀκούει. you might write τοῦ διδασκάλου λέγοντος, ὁ μαθητὴς οὐκ ἀκούει.

   a. ὁ στρατηγὸς τὴν στρατιὰν πρὸς τὴν κώμην ἐλαύνει. οἱ ἄνθρωποι φεύγουσι.

   b. τὰ παιδία κακὰ πράττουσι. γελῶμεν.

   c. τὰ παιδία κακὰ ἔπραττον. ἐγελῶμεν.

   d. ἡ τύχη πολλὰς μεταβολὰς ἔχει. οὐκ ἀεὶ δυστήνως ἕξομεν.

   e. ἡ δίκη τυφλὴ ἐστι. οἱ πλοῦτον ἔχοντες ἑαυτοὺς ἐξεταζόντων.

   f. τὼ τέκνω ἀκούετον. μὴ τὰ ἄδικα λέγε.

6. Each of the following sentences shows what someone wants or intends to do. Rewrite each one with a purpose clause. For example, given τὸ βιβλίον λαμβάνει διότι ἐθέλει μανθάνειν, you might write τὸ βιβλίον λαμβάνει ἵνα μανθάνῃ.

   a. εἰς τὴν ἀγορὰν λήκυθον φέρει διότι ἐθέλει οἶνον ἀγοράσαι.

   b. εἰς τὴν ἀγορὰν λήκυθον φέρει οἶνον ἀγοράσων.

   c. εἰς τὴν ἀγορὰν λήκυθον ἤνεγκε οἶνον ἀγοράσων.

   d. ὁ νεανίας δῶρον τῇ καλῇ ἀνθρώπῳ πέμψει διότι ἐθέλει αὐτὴν ἑταίραν ἔχειν.

   e. ὁ νεανίας δῶρον τῇ καλῇ ἀνθρώπῳ ἔπεμπε διότι ἐθέλει αὐτὴν ἑταίραν ἔχειν.

   f. ὁ νεανίας δῶρον τῇ καλῇ ἀνθρώπῳ πέμψει διότι ἐθέλει αὐτὴν ἑαυτὸν φιλεῖν.

   g. τὴν ἀλήθειαν λέγομεν διότι ἐθέλομεν πάντας ἡμῖν πιστεύειν.

   h. οἱ ἄνθρωποι τοῖς θεοῖς δουλεύουσι διότι ἐθέλουσι τοὺς θεοὺς τοὺς ἀνθρώπους θρέψαι.

7. Write an answer to each of the following questions using a purpose clause (as opposed to a reason clause). For example, given διὰ τί ἦλθε ὁ ἄνθρωπος εἰς τὴν ἀγοράν; you might write ὁ ἄνθρωπος ἦλθε εἰς τὴν ἀγορὰν ὅπως ἱμάτιον ἀγοράζῃ.

   a. διὰ τί τοῦ διδασκάλου ἀκούεις;

   b. διὰ τί οὐκ ἀμελεῖ ὁ ἄνθρωπος τῶν παιδίων;

   c. διὰ τί ἀπαντῶμεν τοῖς φίλοις;

   d. διὰ τί ὁ φιλόσοφος τὴν ἀλήθειαν εἶπε;

   e. διὰ τί ὁ γίγας τὸν ἄνθρωπον βλάβη ἐποίησε;

8. In each of these sentences, the OOO rule has been applied. Rewrite with the "retained" mood. For example, from εἶπον ὅτι γράφοις make εἶπον ὅτι γράφεις.

a. ὁ σχολαστικὸς τὸ βιβλίον ἐπώλησε ἵνα πέντε ὀβολοὺς ἔχοι.

b. εἰ ὁ διδάσκαλος γράφοι, πάντες οἱ μαθηταὶ τὰ ἀγαθὰ ἐμάνθανον.

c. ὁ Σωκράτης ἠρώτησε ὅστις τὴν ἀλήθειαν λέγοι.

d. ὁ Σωκράτης ἠρώτησε οἵτινες τὴν ἀλήθειαν λέγοιεν.

e. ὁ Σωκράτης ἠρώτησε ὁπότερον τὴν ἀλήθειαν λέγοις.

f. ὁ Σωκράτης ἠρώτησε ὁπότερον τὴν ἀλήθειαν εἴποις.

g. ὁ σοφὸς εἶπε ὅτι ὁ Σωκράτης τὴν ἀλήθειαν ἀεὶ λέγοι.

h. διδάσκαλοι, ὅτε βιβλία γράψειεν, πρὸς τοὺς φίλους αὐτὰ ἔπεμπον.

i. ὁ Ξενοφῶν εἶπε ὡς λόγον ἀκοῦσαι περὶ τοῦ Σωκράτους.

j. ὁ διδάσκαλος ἠρώτησε ὁπότερον ἡ λήκυθος οἶνον ἢ ἔλαιον χωροίη.

9. Each of these sentences contains a clause to which the OOO rule may apply. Change the main verb of the sentence to an appropriate past tense, and apply the OOO rule to the subordinate clause. For example, from λέγω ὅτι γράφεις make εἶπον ὅτι γράφοις.

a. ὁ ἄνθρωπος λέγει ὅτι τὸ παιδίον τὸν λέοντα φεύγει.

b. οὗτος λέγει ὅτι ὁ μαθητὴς τὰ βιβλία εἶχε.

c. ἐὰν σαυτὸν εὖ τρέφῃς, μακρὸν βίον ἕξεις.

d. ὅταν οἱ διδάσκαλοι λέγωσι, οὗτος ὁ μαθητής, ἀγαθός ὤν, ἀκούει.

e. τὼ ἑταίρω τοῦ φιλοσόφου ἀκούετον ὅπως μάθητον.

f. ὁ ἄνθρωπος ἐρωτᾷ ὅπου τὸ τέκνον τὸ βιβλίον ἔχει.

g. ἄλλος ἄνθρωπος λέγει ὡς τὸ τέκνον τὸ βιβλίον ἐν τῷ δωματίῳ ἔχει.

h. ὅστις ἂν βιβλία γράφῃ θάλατταν κακῶν ἔχει.

i. τέκνα τίκτουσι οἱ ἄνθρωποι ἵνα αὐτοὺς φιλῶσι.

10. For the sentences you wrote in 2, 4, and 6 above, say whether the OOO rule applies, and explain; then, if it does apply, write the sentence with the "retained" indicative or subjunctive and also with the optional optative (one of these will be the version you've already written, of course). For example, given τὸ βιβλίον ἔλαβε διότι ἤθελε μανθάνειν, in exercise 6 you would have written τὸ βιβλίον ἔλαβε ἵνα μανθάνῃ. In the present exercise you will say that the OOO rule does apply, because the subordinate clause is a purpose clause and the main verb is a secondary tense, and you would then form τὸ βιβλίον ἔλαβε ἵνα μανθάνοι.

11. Isolated sentences are not as meaningful or interesting as sentences in context. Choose at least five of the sentences from the exercises in this section, and write a coherent story incorporating them.

CHAPTER IX

Aulis

IX.1 Verbs in -μι: present system

A few common verbs form their present system differently from the verbs we have already had. Their first principal part (first person singular, present indicative active) ends in -μι, so they are usually called the **μι-verbs**, and the others are ω-verbs.

The following chart gives the present indicative active of several common μι- verbs, followed by the present infinitive active and present participle active. For the imperfect indicative, the other moods of the present system, and the aorist active system, see chapter 16. For the aorist middle, see chapter 20.

	ἵστημι, root στα-, place, set up	τίθημι, root θε-, put	δίδωμι, root δο-, give	ἵημι, root ἑ-, send
singular				
1st	ἵστημι	τίθημι	δίδωμι	ἵημι
2nd	ἵστης	τίθης	δίδως	ἵης
3rd	ἵστησι(ν)	τίθησι(ν)	δίδωσι(ν)	ἵησι(ν)
dual				
2nd	ἵστατον	τίθετον	δίδοτον	ἵετον
3rd	ἵστατον	τίθετον	δίδοτον	ἵετον
plural				
1st	ἵσταμεν	τίθεμεν	δίδομεν	ἵεμεν
2nd	ἵστατε	τίθετε	δίδοτε	ἵετε
3rd	ἱστᾶσι(ν)	τιθέᾱσι(ν)	διδόᾱσι(ν)	ἱᾶσι(ν)

111

	ἵστημι, root στα-, place, set up	τίθημι, root θε-, put	δίδωμι, root δο-, give	ἵημι, root ἑ-, send
pres. inf. act.	ἱστάναι	τιθέναι	διδόναι	ἱέναι
pres. part. act. nom. sg.	ἱστάς, ἱστᾶσα, ἱστάν	τιθείς, τιθεῖσα, τιθέν	διδούς, διδοῦσα, διδόν	ἱείς, ἱεῖσα, ἱέν
gen. sg.	ἱστάντος, ἱστάσης, ἱστάντος	τιθέντος, τιθείσης, τιθέντος	διδόντος, διδούσης, διδόντος	ἱέντος, ἱείσης, ἱέντος
dat. pl.	ἱστᾶσι(ν), ἱστάσαις	τιθεῖσι(ν), τιθείσαις	διδοῦσι(ν), διδούσαις	ἱεῖσι(ν), ἱείσαις

The participles are declined as first-and-third declension adjectives, like λύσας.

Another important μι-verb is φημί "say." Like εἰμί, this verb is enclitic in the present indicative. Its root is φα-, which is φη- in the forms with long vowel by the familiar Attic sound shift. Thus in the present indicative active the forms are φημί, φής, φησί(ν), φατόν, φατόν, φαμέν, φατέ, φᾱσί(ν).

IX.2 Thematic and athematic verbs

There are two major differences between the μι-verbs and the ω-verbs. First, the former add their endings directly to the stem, while the latter have a vowel between the stem and the endings. That vowel is always o or ε; it is called the **theme vowel**. Compare ἵστα-μεν, without theme vowel, and λύ-ο-μεν, with o between the present stem λυ- and the ending -μεν. Similarly ἵστα-τε and λύ-ε-τε, with **e grade** of the theme vowel. Therefore the μι-verbs are also called **athematic verbs** and the ω-verbs are **thematic verbs**. Note that this applies only in the present system.

The second major difference is that in athematic verbs, the present stem varies: it has a long vowel in some forms, like τίθημι, and a short vowel in others, like τίθεμεν. The long vowel forms are the singular of the present and imperfect indicative active and the second person singular of the present imperative active. The rest have the short form of the stem vowel, though it may contract with the vowel of the ending to produce a long vowel in the actual inflected form. For example, the present infinitive active is τιθέναι with short vowel, but the masculine nominative singular of the present participle active is τιθείς contracted from τιθε-ες.

Aside from the present system, thematic and athematic verbs are alike. The future is always thematic, for example δώ-σ-ω from δίδωμι is exactly like λύ-σ-ω from λύω. Athematic verbs sometimes have a first aorist, sometimes a **root aorist**, but there are also a few thematic verbs that have root aorists like athematic verbs. Athematic verbs may form their perfect stem differently from thematic verbs, but given the stem they form the tenses and moods of the perfect system the same way (you will learn the perfect system in chapter 14).

Many athematic verbs form their present stem by **reduplication**. In reduplication, the first consonant is doubled, with a vowel in between to form a new syllable. For example, from the stem δο-, we make the reduplicated form δι-δο-. Here the δ sound is repeated, using ι in between. Reduplicated presents always use ι for the vowel; as you will see in chapter 14, reduplication also happens in the perfect system, and there the vowel of the new syllable is always ε.

If the stem begins with a single non-aspirate consonant, as δο- does, then the reduplication syllable is just that consonant plus ι, as δι-δο-. If the stem begins with an aspirate consonant, however, the reduplication syllable starts with the corresponding *un-aspirate* consonant. This is called **dissimilation of aspirates**: Greek prefers not to have aspirate sounds starting successive syllables. As a result, we do not have θί-θη-μι but rather τί-θη-μι.

If the stem begins with σ, the reduplication syllable uses rough breathing. This is a special case of a more general phenomenon. Early in the history of Greek, the *s* sound at the start of a word by itself (not in a cluster with another consonant) turned into an *h* sound. For example, ἕπτα originally began with *s*, just like its cognates *seven*, Latin *septem*, and Sanskrit *sapta*. In the case of verb roots like στα-, this change happened after the reduplicated present stem was created, so instead of σίστημι we have ἵστημι.

Not every athematic verb has a reduplicated present; you will meet a fair-sized group in chapter 16 that are not reduplicated, including for example δείκνυμι "point out." And not every reduplicated present is athematic: there are also thematic reduplicated present stems, like γιγνώσκω "know," μιμνήσκω "remind," or γίγνομαι "be, become."

IX.3 Compounds of μι-verbs

The following list gives some of the most common compounds of the athematic verbs. As with any other compounds, these have the same principal parts as the simple verbs, with the prefix added at the beginning, and the augment, when present, is always after the prefix, right next to the stem. Thus we have principal parts ἀνίστημι, ἀναστήσω, ἀνέστησα, ἀνέστηκα, ἀνέσταμαι, ἀνεστάθην for the first verb in the list, ἀνά + ἵστημι.

ἀν-ίστημι, raise up

ἀφ-ίστημι, put away, remove

δι-ίστημι, separate

ἐφ-ίστημι, set over

καθ-ίστημι, place, set up. ἐς φόβον κ., frighten, throw into fear (φόβος, -ου, ὁ)

μεθ-ίστημι, remove

παρ-ίστημι, set beside, compare

προ-ίστημι, set before

συν-ίστημι, set together, associate

ἀνα-τίθημι, set up, hang up (an offering at a god's temple)

δια-τίθημι, distribute, separate; manage, treat

ἐπι-τίθημι, place upon

κατα-τίθημι, put down

παρα-κατα-τίθημι, deposit (funds)

παρα-τίθημι, put beside

προσ-τίθημι, hand over, deliver

συν-τίθημι, put together

ὑπο-τίθημι, put under, put down as deposit

ἀπο-δίδωμι, give up, give away; in middle, sell

δια-δίδωμι, distribute

ἐν-δίδωμι, give in, lend

ἐπι-δίδωμι, contribute

μετα-δίδωμι, give a share (of something: use genitive)

παρα-δίδωμι, hand over

ἀφ-ίημι, send away

συν-ίημι, send together; understand

ἄπ-ειμι, be away

ἔπ-ειμι, be on, be additional

πάρ-ειμι, be near

πρό-ειμι, be in front of

πρόσ-ειμι, be added to

σύν-ειμι, be with

IX.4 Vocabulary

VERBS (see also the compounds of μι- verbs, above)

διαφέρω, differ, be superior

δίδωμι, δώσω, ἔδωκα, δέδωκα, δέδομαι, ἐδόθην, give (cp. L. *do*)

ἐκπεράω, ἐκπερήσω, ἐξεπέρησα, ἐκπεπέρακα, – , – , cross, go over

ἔοικε(ν), it seems (defective verb, normally only 3rd sg)

ἐσθίω, ἔδομαι, ἔφαγον, ἐδήδοκα, ἐδήδεσμαι, – , eat (cp. *eat, macrophage*, L. *ĕdo*)

εὑρίσκω, εὑρήσω, εὗρον, εὕρηκα, εὕρημαι, εὑρέθην, find (cp. *heuristic*)

θύω, θύσω, ἔθῡσα, τέθῡκα, τέθῡμαι, ἐτύθην, sacrifice

ἵημι, ἥσω, ἧκα, εἷκα, εἷμαι, εἵθην, send

ἵστημι, στήσω, ἔστησα, ἔστηκα, ἔσταμαι, ἐστάθην, place, set up; aorist ἔστησα is transitive, ἔστην is intransitive (cp. *stand*, L. *sto*)

οἰκέω, οἰκήσω, ᾤκησα, ᾤκηκα, ᾤκημαι, ᾠκήθην, dwell, inhabit

ὀνομάζω, ὀνομάσω, ὠνόμασα, ὠνόμακα, ὠνόμασμαι, ὠνομάσθην, name, call by name (cp. *onomastic*)

πεινάω, πεινήσω, ἐπείνησα, πεπείνηκα, – , – , hunger, starve (intransitive)

πλουτέω, πλουτήσω, ἐπλούτησα, πεπλούτηκα, πεπλούτημαι, ἐπλουτήθην, be rich

τίθημι, θήσω, ἔθηκα, τέθηκα, – , ἐτέθην, put, place (cp. *do*, L. *facio*)

ὑγιαίνω, ὑγιανῶ, ὑγίανα, – , – , – , be healthy

φημι, φήσω, ἔφησα, – , – , – , say (cp. L. *for*)

χρῄζω, lack, need; be poor (present system only)

NOUNS

Ἀθῆναι, -ῶν, αἱ, Athens

Ἀθήναζε, to Athens

Ἀθήνηθεν, from Athens

Ἀθήνησι(ν), at Athens

ἄρτος, -ου, ὁ, loaf (of bread)

αὖρα, -ας, ἡ, breeze (L. *aura* is a derivative)

ἐλπίς, ἐλπίδος, η, hope (cp. *will*, L. *voluptas*)

θηρίον, -ου, τό, beast, wild animal

κόρη, -ης, ἡ, girl

κόρος, -ου, ὁ, young man

ὀδούς, ὀδόντος, ὁ, tooth (cp. *orthodontia, tooth*, L. *dens*)

παῖς, παιδός, ὁ, ἡ, child

πατρίς, πατρίδος, ἡ, fatherland, native land, homeland

πέδον, -ου, τό, ground

πεῖνα, -ης, ἡ, hunger

σκόλιον, -ου, το, drinking-song

ὑγίεια, -ης, ἡ, health (cp. *hygiene*)

ADJECTIVES

ἁγνός, -ή, -όν, holy

αἰσχρός, -ά, -όν, ugly, shameful

ἄριστος, -η, -ον, best (irregular superlative of ἀγαθός)

ἑκών, ἑκοῦσα, ἑκόν, willing

κλεινός, -ή, -όν, famous

μουσικός, -ή, -όν, musical, artistic (cp. *music*)

ὀξύ-πεινος, -ον, quick to hunger

ὀρθός, -ή, -όν, straight, right (cp. *orthopedic, orthogonal*)

ῥᾴδιος, -α, -ον, easy; superlative ῥᾷστος, adverb ῥᾷστα

ADVERBS

αὖ, αὖθις, again, moreover

ἔπειτα, then, next after

εἴτε, or, either (often in pairs, often for disjunctive questions)

καίπερ, even though, although (always modifying a participle)

μᾶλλον, comparative of μάλα

μέντοι, particle marking emphasis or contrast

οὗ, where (subordinating conjunction)

πάνυ, entirely, totally

χαμαί, on the ground

Notes on the vocabulary

See also the list of compound verbs in section 3.

Augmented forms of εὑρίσκω may start with either εὑ- or ηὑ-.

Several forms of θύω show dissimilation of aspirates. This is expected in the perfect τέθυκα, but in the aorist passive (see chapter 13), the suffix keeps its aspirate and the beginning of the root is changed — ἐτύθην.

ἵστημι has two different aorists, a first aorist ἔστησα and a root aorist ἔστην. The first aorist, like the present active, is transitive, meaning to stand something up, set it up; the root aorist, like the present middle, is intransitive, meaning to be standing, be upright.

πεινάω has -η- instead of -α- in contracted forms; see further chapter 17.

The noun ἐλπίς has stem ἐλπιδ- and takes the regular third-declension endings. Similarly for παῖς, though its accent is on the ending in the genitive and dative (all three numbers): τῷ παιδί and so on.

κόρη looks like an exception to the rule that Attic Greek has -α after -ρ-. In fact, the word was originally κόρϝα, and the Attic sound shift from -ᾱ to -η took place before the -ϝ- sound was lost. (The letter ϝ is called **digamma** and it sounds like English *w*.)

A *skolion* is a drinking song. The name comes from the adjective σκολιός, "crooked," because as different guests at a dinner party took turns singing verses, the song would move back and forth around and across the room.

ἄριστος is not related to ἀριστάω "eat breakfast"; the adjective has a short α while the verb has a long one. The verb comes from an adverb ἦρι (or ἄρι in other dialects) meaning "early," while the adjective is ultimately from a root meaning "fit together."

The adverb μάλα "much" has the irregular superlative μάλιστα (which you met in chapter 4) and comparative μᾶλλον.

IX.5 Reading

1. ὁ τὸ σκόλιον εὑρὼν ἐκεῖνος, ὅστις ἦν,
τὸ μὲν ὑγιαίνειν πρῶτον ὡς ἄριστον ὂν
ὠνόμασεν ὀρθῶς, δεύτερον δ᾽ εἶναι καλόν,
τρίτον δὲ πλουτεῖν, τοῦθ᾽, ὁρᾷς, ἔχρῃζέ που·
μετὰ τὴν ὑγίειαν γὰρ τὸ πλουτεῖν διαφέρει·
καλὸς δὲ πεινῶν ἐστιν αἰσχρὸν θηρίον.

> The *skolion* referred to is in chapter 18. This passage comes from a play by Anaxandrides, quoted by Athenaeus (15.49).

2. Ζῆθον μὲν ἐλθόνθ᾽ ἁγνὸν ἐς Θήβης πέδον
οἰκεῖν κελεύει· καὶ γὰρ ἀξιωτέρους
πωλοῦσιν, ὡς ἔοικε, τοὺς ἄρτους ἐκεῖ·
ὁ δ᾽ ὀξύπεινος· τὸν δὲ μουσικώτατον
κλεινὰς Ἀθήνας ἐκπερᾶν Ἀμφίονα
οὗ ῥᾷστ᾽ ἀεὶ πεινῶσι Κεκροπιδῶν κόροι
κάπτοντες αὔρας, ἐσθίοντες ἐλπίδας.

> **κάπτοντες** from κάπτω, "bite"; **Κεκροπίδης** means "son of Cecrops," that is, Athenian; it is a first-declension masculine noun. The passage comes from a play by Eubulus called Ἀντιόπη.

3. ὅστις ἂν πείνην ἔχῃ ἐθέλει φαγεῖν. οὗτος δὲ οὐκ ἔχει οὐδὲ ἄρτον οὐδὲ λάχανα οὐδὲ οἶνον. πεινῶν οὖν καὶ χρῄζων οὐχ ὑγιαίνει. ἐλπίζει δὲ ἄρτον εὑρεῖν ἵνα φάγῃ καὶ ὑγιάνῃ. ὅντινα ἂν εὑρίσκῃ, τοῖς ὀδοῦσι λαβὼν ἑκὼν ἐσθίει.

4. τί ἐσθίεις μᾶλλον, ὦ παῖ· τὰ λάχανα ἢ τὰ ᾠα; ὁ παῖς λέγει, "καίπερ πεινῶν, οὐκ ἐθέλω τὰ λάχανα ἐσθίειν. ἐσθίω τὰς πέτρας μᾶλλον ἢ τὰ λάχανα." ὁ δὲ παῖς τῆς ὑγιείας ἀμελεῖ, ὡς ἔοικε. ἠρώτησα εἴτε τὰ λάχανα ἐσθίοι εἴτε τὰ ᾠα, καὶ εἶπε τὰς πέτρας ἐσθίειν.

5. Ἀθήνησι οἱ πολῖται μέγαν νεὼν τιθέασι τῇ Ἀθηνᾷ. τὸν δὲ νεὼν ὀνομάζουσι Παρθενὼν διότι ἡ Ἀθηνᾶ παρθένος ἐστι. παρθένος δέ ἐστι κόρη ἢ γάμους οὐκ ἔσχε. εἰ μὲν δῶρον τίθης ἐν τῷ νεῷ, ἡ θεά σοι ἀγαθὴν τύχην ἥσει. εἰ δὲ μή, κακὰ δώσει. ταῦτα γέ φησι οἱ Ἀθηναῖοι. πάντες οὖν Ἀθήναζε δῶρα φέρουσι, καὶ τῇ θεᾷ ζῷα θύουσιν παρὰ τῷ νεῷ. κλεινὸς μὲν ὁ νεώς, κλεινὴ δὲ ἡ θεὰ παρθένος, κλειναὶ δὲ αἱ Ἀθῆναι. πολλοὶ μὲν Ἀθήνηθεν τὴν θάλατταν ἐκπερῶσι ἵνα οἰκῶσι ἄλλας γᾶς, πολλοὶ δὲ τὰς Ἀθήνας οἰκοῦσι οὗ τὸν τῆς Ἀθηνᾶς νεὼν ἀεὶ ὁρῶσι.

6. **Πενθεύς·** πρῶτον μὲν οὖν μοι λέξον ὅστις εἶ γένος.
Διόνυσος· οὐ κόμπος οὐδείς· ῥάδιον δ᾽ εἰπεῖν τόδε.
τὸν ἀνθεμώδη Τμῶλον οἶσθά που κλύων.
Πενθεύς· οἶδ᾽, ὃς τὸ Σάρδεων ἄστυ περιβάλλει κύκλῳ.
Διόνυσος· ἐντεῦθέν εἰμι, Λυδία δέ μοι πατρίς.
Πενθεύς· πόθεν δὲ τελετὰς τάσδ᾽ ἄγεις ἐς Ἑλλάδα;
Διόνυσος· Διόνυσος ἡμᾶς εἰσέβησ᾽, ὁ τοῦ Διός.
Πενθεύς· Ζεὺς δ᾽ ἔστ᾽ ἐκεῖ τις, ὃς νέους τίκτει θεούς;
Διόνυσος· οὔκ, ἀλλ᾽ ὁ Σεμέλην ἐνθάδε ζεύξας γάμοις.

> Euripides, *Βάκχαι* 460-468. In this scene, Pentheus does not know that the person he is speaking to is Dionysus.
>
> **γένος, -ους, τό**, family, race; here accusative, where prose might also use dative. **κόμπος, -ου, ὁ**, boast, vaunt. **οὐδείς, οὐδεμία, οὐδέν**, nothing. **ἀνθεμώδης, -ες**, flowery. **οἶσθα** is 2nd sg and **οἶδα** 1st sg from οἶδα "know," a verb with only a perfect system; see chapter 17. **ἐντεῦθεν**, from there. **κλύω** = ἀκούω. **ἄστυ, ἄστεως, τό** = πόλις, μεγάλη κώμη. **τελετή, -ῆς, ἡ**, mystic rite, ritual, initiation. **εἰσέβησε** is 3rd sg aor indic act of εἰσ-βαίνω; the present and root aorist mean "go in" but the first aorist is causative, "send in, bring in." **ζεύξας** is aor ppl active, m nom sg, of ζεύγνυμι, yoke together, harness. **γάμος, -ου, ὁ**, marriage, wedding.

7. **Σωκράτης·** τί δὴ αὖ λέγεις τὸ ὅσιον εἶναι καὶ τὴν ὁσιότητα; οὐχὶ ἐπιστήμην τινὰ τοῦ θύειν τε καὶ εὔχεσθαι;

Εὐθύφρων· ἔγωγε.

Σωκράτης· οὐκοῦν τὸ θύειν δωρεῖσθαί ἐστι τοῖς θεοῖς, τὸ δ᾽ εὔχεσθαι αἰτεῖν τοὺς θεούς;

Εὐθύφρων· καὶ μάλα, ὦ Σώκρατες.

Σωκράτης· ἐπιστήμη ἄρα αἰτήσεως καὶ δόσεως θεοῖς ὁσιότης ἂν εἴη ἐκ τούτου τοῦ λόγου.

Εὐθύφρων· πάνυ καλῶς, ὦ Σώκρατες, συνῆκας ὃ εἶπον.

Σωκράτης· ἐπιθυμητὴς γάρ εἰμι, ὦ φίλε, τῆς σῆς σοφίας καὶ προσέχω τὸν νοῦν αὐτῇ, ὥστε οὐ χαμαὶ πεσεῖται ὅτι ἂν εἴπῃς. ἀλλά μοι λέξον τίς αὕτη ἡ ὑπηρεσία ἐστὶ τοῖς θεοῖς; αἰτεῖν τε φὴς αὐτοὺς καὶ διδόναι ἐκείνοις;

Εὐθύφρων· ἔγωγε.

Σωκράτης· ἆρ᾽ οὖν οὐ τό γε ὀρθῶς αἰτεῖν ἂν εἴη ὧν δεόμεθα παρ᾽ ἐκείνων, ταῦτα αὐτοὺς αἰτεῖν;

Εὐθύφρων· ἀλλὰ τί;

Σωκράτης· καὶ αὖ τὸ διδόναι ὀρθῶς, ὧν ἐκεῖνοι τυγχάνουσιν δεόμενοι παρ᾽ ἡμῶν, ταῦτα ἐκείνοις αὖ ἀντιδωρεῖσθαι; οὐ γάρ που τεχνικόν γ᾽ ἂν εἴη δωροφορεῖν διδόντα τῷ ταῦτα ὧν οὐδὲν δεῖται.

Εὐθύφρων· ἀληθῆ λέγεις, ὦ Σώκρατες.

> An excerpt from Plato's *Εὐθύφρων*, 14c-14e.
>
> **ὅσιος, -α, -ον** = ἁγνός. **ὁσιότης, ὁσιότητος, ἡ**, holiness, piousness. **ἐπιστήμη, -ης, ἡ**, knowledge, understanding. **εὔχεσθαι** is present infinitive middle of εὔχομαι, pray. Euthyphro's first response, ἔγωγε, is one possible way of agreeing or saying "yes" to a question. **δωρεῖσθαι** = δῶρα διδόναι. **αἰτέω**, ask, request. **αἴτησις, -εως, ἡ**, request. **δόσις, -εως, ἡ**, act of giving; both of these nouns are third-declension vowel stems, for which see chapter 12. **εἴη** is 3rd sg. present optative active of εἰμι (see chapter 13). **ἐπιθυμητής, -οῦ, ὁ**, eager person, one who desires. **σός, σή, σόν**, your (possessive adjective, chapter 20). **σοφία, -ας, ἡ**, wisdom, intelligence, skill. **προσέχω τὸν νοῦν**, pay attention. **πεσεῖται** is 3rd sg fut indic middle of πίπτω, fall; the verb only has middle forms in the future. **ὑπηρεσία, -ας, ἡ**, help, assistance. **δεόμεθα**, 1st sg pres indic middle of δέομαι, ask for; δεόμενοι is the present participle passive and δεῖται is 3rd sg pres indic middle. **τυγχάνω**, happen to be, with participle: ὧν ἐκεῖνοι τυγχάνουσιν δεόμενοι παρ᾽ ἡμῶν = ταῦτα ἃ οἱ θεοὶ ἀκούουσι ὅτι δεόμεθα παρ᾽ ἐκείνων, ταῦτα ἃ αἰτοῦμεν παρὰ τῶν θεῶν. **ἀντιδωρεῖσθαι** = πάλιν διδόναι. **τεχνικός, -ή, -όν·** ὅστις ἂν τέχνην ἔχῃ τεχνικός ἐστι. **δωροφορεῖν** = δῶρα φέρειν, δῶρα διδόναι.

8. *περὶ τοῦ Τρωικοῦ πολέμου, τρίτον μέρος*

τοῦ στρατοῦ ἐν Αὐλίδι ὄντος, ἔθυσαν οἱ Ἕλληνες τῷ Ἀπόλλωνι. ἔπειτα δράκων ἐκ τοῦ βωμοῦ ἐξῆλθε πρὸς δένδρον τινὰ ἐν ᾧ ἦν οἰκία ὀρνίθων. ὁ δὲ δράκων τὴν ὄρνιθα καὶ τοὺς ὀκτὼ παῖδας ἀποκτείνας ἔφαγε. ὁ δὲ Κάλχας, μάντις ὤν, εἶπε σημεῖον εἶναι τῆς τοῦ Διὸς βουλῆς. ἐννέα μὲν εἶναι τοὺς ὄρνιθες, ἐννέα δὲ ἔτη πόλεμον ἕξειν, ἀλλὰ ἐν τῷ δεκάτῳ ἔτει τὴν πόλιν νικήσειν.

ὁ δὲ Ἀγαμέμνων ἐπὶ θήρας ἔλαφον βαλὼν εἶπε ἑαυτὸν διαφέρειν καὶ τὴν Ἄρτεμιν. ἡ δὲ θεὰ ἐμήνιε τῷ Ἀγαμέμνονι. χειμῶνα οὖν ἔπεμψε ἵνα οἱ Ἕλληνες τὸν πλοῦν μὴ ποιεῖν ἔχωσι.

"τί ποιήσωμεν;" ἠρώτησε ὁ Ἀγαμέμνων τῷ Κάλχαντι. "θεός τις ἡμῖν χειμῶνα ἵησι, ὡς μηνίων. τοῦ χειμῶνος ὄντος, οὐκ ἐκπερήσομεν τὴν θάλατταν πρὸς τὸν Ἴλιον."

ὁ δὲ μάντις εἶπε, "ἡ Ἄρτεμις σοὶ μηνίει. ἵνα τὴν μῆνιν λύσῃς, θῦε τὴν παῖδα Ἰφιγένειαν. ἔπειτα οὖν ἡ θεὰ, ἵλεως οὖσα, ἡμῖν αὔρας ἀγαθὰς δώσει."

ὁ δὲ Ἀγαμέμνων ἐθαύμασε. "ἆρα τὸ τέκνον θύσω; ἄδικον μὲν τὸ τέκνον θῦσαι, ἄδικον δὲ τοὺς φίλους οἴκαδε πέμψαι ἄνευ τῆς Ἑλένης. τὴν δὲ Ἰφιγένειαν φιλῶ· οὐ τοῦτον ποιήσω."

ὁ δὲ Μενέλαος καὶ ὁ Ὀδυσσεὺς αὐτῷ εἴπετον, "εἰ τὴν Ἰφιγένειαν μὴ θύεις, οἱ στρατιῶται μέντοι καὶ αὐτὴν καὶ σὲ ἀποκτανόντες πρὸς τὸν Ἴλιον ἐκπερήσουσι. ἡ Ἰφιγένεια ἀποθνῄσκει ἢ σοῦ ἑκόντος ἢ μή."

ὁ δὲ Ἀγαμέμνων, αὐτοῖν πιστεύων, ἐπιστολὴν ἧκε πρὸς τὴν Κλυταιμήστραν ἵνα τὴν Ἰφιγένειαν λαβοῦσα τὴν Αὐλίδα χωρήσῃ. ἐπεὶ ὁ Ἀγαμέμνων αὐτὰ ἔβλεψε, εἶπε, "χαιρέτω. σφὼ μὲν φιλῶ, τὸν δὲ ἀδελφὸν τιμῶ. σέ, ὦ Ἰφιγένεια, τῇ Ἀρτέμιδι θύσω."

"μὴ τὴν παῖδα θῦσον," ἐκέλευσε ἡ Κλυταιμήστρα.

"μὴ ταῦτα λέγε," εἶπε ἡ Ἰφιγένεια. "ἀποθνῄσκω μὲν, σώσω δὲ τὴν Ἑλλάδα, πατρίδα οὖσαν κοινὴν ἡμῶν πάντων. ἑκοῦσα οὖν ἀποθνῄσκω."

ὁ δὲ Ἀγαμέμνων τὴν Ἰφιγένειαν παρὰ τῷ βωμῷ ἵστησι. "σοί, ὦ Ἄρτεμις, ταύτην τὴν κόρην δίδωμι. μὴ ἡμῖν μηνίοις ἄν," εἶπε καὶ τὴν κόρην ἔθυσε. ἡ δὲ στρατία πρὸς τὸν Ἴλιον τὸν πλοῦν ἔπραξε.

> **δράκων, -οντος, ὁ,** snake, serpent, dragon. **βωμός, -οῦ, ὁ,** altar. **ὄρνις, ὄρνῑθος, ὁ, ἡ,** bird. **σημεῖον, -ου, τό,** sign, indication. **μάντις, -εως, ὁ,** prophet, seer. **βουλή, -ῆς, ἡ,** will, plan. **ἔτος, -ους, τό,** year. **θηρά, -ᾶς, ἡ,** hunt. **ἔλαφος, -ου, ὁ, ἡ,** deer (not to be confused with ἐλέφας). **μηνίω,** become angry. **χειμών, -ῶνος, ὁ,** storm. **μῆνις, εως, ἡ,** anger, wrath. **σῴζω, σώσω, ἔσωσα, σέσωκα, σέσωμαι, ἐσώθην,** save.

IX.6 Conversation

1. (reading 1) τί εὗρεν ἐκεῖνος; τί ὀνομάζει πρῶτον ὡς ἄριστον ὄν; τί δὲ δεύτερον, τί τρίτον; ποῖόν τι ἐστι τὸ ὑγιαίνειν; ποῖον δὲ τὸ πλουτεῖν; ποῖός ἐστιν καλὸς πεινῶν; etc.

2. (reading 2) ποῖ ἐλθεῖν κελεύει τὸν Ζῆθον; ἵνα τί ποιῇ; διὰ τί; ποῦ εἰσιν οἱ ἄρτοι ἄξιοι; τί δ᾽ ἄξιον Ἀθήνησιν; ποῖ ἐλθεῖν κελεύει τὸν Ἀμφίονα; and so on.

3. (reading 6) τίνω λέγετον; τί πρῶτον ἐρωτᾷ ὁ Πενθεύς; τίς ἐστι ἡ τοῦ Διονύσου πατρίς; ποῖός ἐστι ὁ Τμῶλος; ποῦ ἐστι;, etc.

4. (vocabulary) ἆρ᾽ ἔχεις βιβλίον; ἔχω δή (showing it). τί ποιεῖς; δίδωμί σοι αὐτό. καὶ ἐγὼ λαμβάνω μέν, δίδωμι δέ σοι πάλιν. εὖ ποιεῖς, ὦ διδάσκαλε, καὶ λαμβάνω ἑκών. Similarly in dual or plural, or with other objects.

5. ἆρ᾽ ἔχεις πέτασον; ἔχω δή. τί δὲ ποιεῖς; τίθημι ἐπὶ τῆς κεφαλῆς. So with ἱμάτιον, δίφρος· ἵστημι χαμαί. One student may describe what another one is doing: τί ποιεῖ ὁ Φίλιππος; τὸ πέτασον ἐπὶ τῆς κεφαλῆς τίθησι, and so on.

IX.7 Writing

1. Do the change-number exercise with the following sentences.

    a. ὁ διδάσκαλος τῷ μαθητῇ βιβλίον δίδωσι.

    b. πέτραν ἵστης παρὰ τῇ θύρᾳ.

    c. τὸν κάλαμον λαβοῦσα χαμαὶ τίθημι.

    d. τὸν παῖδα ἵεμεν Ἀθήναζε ἵνα πολὺ μανθάνῃ.

    e. ὁ στρατηγὸς αὐτὸν τῷ νικήσαντι παραδίδωσι.

    f. οἱ κόροι τὸν λόγον συνίασι.

    g. τρεῖς ὀβολοὺς τῷ πεινῶντι δίδομεν.

    h. τὰ δῶρα εἰς τὴν ἅμαξαν τιθεῖσα δραχμὴν εὗρε.

    i. χάριτα δίδοτε τῷ ὑμῖν χάριτα διδόντι.

    j. τὴν οἰκίαν ἱστὰς ἐν ᾗ οἰκήσει, ὁ ἄνθρωπος θύρας καὶ δωμάτια ποιεῖ.

    k. ἱέντες αὔραν τοῖς τὴν θάλατταν ἐκπερῶσι, οἱ θεοὶ ἐλπίδα διδόασιν.

    l. τὼ ἰατρὼ τῇ κόρῃ φάρμακα δίδοτον ἵνα ὑγιαίνῃ.

    m. ὁ ἀγαθὸς πολίτης ἐθέλει τὰ χρήσιμα τῇ πατρίδι διδόναι.

    n. τοῦ διδασκάλου ἀπόντος, οἱ μαθηταὶ τὰ ἔργα οὐ πράττουσι.

    o. μεθίστασα τὸ ἱμάτιον τῶν ὤμων, ἡ ἄνθρωπος αὐτὴν τοῖς ἄλλοις δηλοῖ.

    p. ὁ πεινῶν παῖς ἐσθίει ἅττα δίδομεν.

    q. οὐκ ἔχομεν τὰς τέτταρας δραχμὰς τήμερον ὑποτιθέναι.

    r. οἱ στρατιῶται δῶρα ὡς τὸν στρατηγὸν ἰέναι ἐθέλουσι.

    s. τὰς κλίνας ἱστάναι ἐν τῷ κήπῳ σε κελεύει ὁ δεσπότης.

    t. τὸ σκόλιον ἀκούσαντες, οἶνον λαμβάνομεν.

2. Rewrite the following sentences, using a clause with a finite verb instead of the genitive absolute.

    a. τοῦ κόρου ὑγιαίνοντος, ὁ ἰατρὸς οἴκαδε ἦλθε.

    b. τῶν θηρίων ὀξυπείνων ὄντων, ᾠά τε καὶ λάχανα εἰς τὸν κῆπον τίθημι.

    c. τῆς κόρης δῶρα διδούσας, χαίρομεν.

    d. τῶν παιδίων τὰ τοῖς θεοῖς δῶρα εἰς τὸν νεὼν ἀνατιθέντων, ὁ διδάσκαλος ἐθαύμασε.

    e. τοῦ διδασκάλου ἄρτον εὑρόντος, τὰ παιδία οὐκ ἐπείνησε.

3. Fill in the following to make complete sentences.

    a. ὁ μὲν αἰσχρός _____, ὁ δὲ καλός _____.

    b. εἴ σοι βιβλίον δίδωμι, _____.

    c. ὁ δεσπότης τοῖς δούλοις κελεύει τιθέναι _____.

    d. οὗτος ὁ ἄνθρωπος, ὡς ἔοικε, _____.

    e. εἰ πλουτεῖς καὶ μὴ ὑγιαίνεις, _____.

    f. εἴτε τῷ θεῷ _____ δίδως, εἴτε _____ ἐν τῷ νέῳ τίθης.

4. Rewrite reading 6 as a prose narrative instead of a dramatic dialogue. Do not, however, simply put ὁ Πενθεὺς λέγει, ὁ δὲ Διόνυσος λέγει in front of the existing lines. Instead, use indirect statement, or different ways of expressing what they say, and add as much connecting narrative as you like.

5. Explain briefly (in Greek, of course) the definition of τὸ ὅσιον that Socrates and Euthyphro are formulating in reading 7.

6. Write a paragraph on the theme of the best things in the world.

CHAPTER X

Philoctetes

X.1 Voices of the verb

In Greek, a verb has tense, mood, and **voice**. Voice tells the relationship between the grammatical subject and the action. The three voices are **active**, **middle**, and **passive**. In the active voice, the subject does the action: ὁ ἄνθρωπος γράφει. In the passive voice, the subject receives, suffers, undergoes, or puts up with the action: τὸ βιβλίον γράφεται. We can say the same thing in two different ways, active or passive: ὁ ἄνθρωπος τὸ βιβλίον γράφει means pretty much the same as τὸ βιβλίον ὑπὸ τοῦ ἀνθρώπου γράφεται. The difference is in emphasis: the passive sentence makes the book more important, as if we are explaining the situation from its point of view. Active and passive in Greek are similar to active and passive in English (or Latin, or Sanskrit, or many other languages).

The middle voice, however, does not exist in English or Latin (though Sanskrit has it). It means that the subject is doing the action for himself or herself, or arranging the action for his or her own benefit. It is also sometimes used for action done *to* oneself, or reflexive action, like λούομαι "I wash myself," although it is also possible to express reflexive action with an ordinary active verb and a reflexive pronoun, just as in English, λούω ἐμαυτήν. More usually, the subject and object of a middle verb will be different. For example, consider the two sentences ὁ ἄνθρωπος τὸ βιβλίον γράφει (active) and ὁ ἄνθρωπος τὸ βιβλίον γράφεται (middle). In each case, the person is writing the book, but in the second sentence he is more closely connected with the action: perhaps it is his autobiography.

Every tense and mood can be formed in all three voices. In the present system and the perfect system, the middle and the passive are the same. In the aorist system and the future system they are different. The aorist passive and future passive are formed from the sixth principal part; you will meet them in chapters 12 and 13.

X.2 Forms of the middle and passive

The endings for the middle and passive are different from those of the active. Here are the present and imperfect middle and passive indicative for thematic verbs. As always, the imperfect has the past indicative augment.

	Present	**Imperfect**
singular		
1st	λύ-ο-μαι	ἐ-λῡ-ό-μην
2nd	λύ-ῃ, λύ-ει	ἐ-λύ-ου
3rd	λύ-ε-ται	ἐ-λύ-ε-το
dual		
2nd	λύ-ε-σθον	ἐ-λύ-ε-σθον
3rd	λύ-ε-σθον	ἐ-λῡ-έ-σθην
plural		
1st	λῡ-ό-μεθα	ἐ-λῡ-ό-μεθα
2nd	λύ-ε-σθε	ἐ-λύ-ε-σθε
3rd	λύ-ο-νται	ἐ-λύ-ο-ντο

Be particularly careful of the first person singular secondary ending: do not confuse ἐλυόμην, with long -η-, 1st sg imperfect indicative middle, and ἐλύομεν, with short -ε-, 1st pl imperfect indicative active.

For contract verbs the forms can be worked out in the regular way: the endings are as for ordinary verbs, and the vowels contract. Here are the forms:

α-stems		**ε-stems**		**o-stems**	
Present	**Imperfect**	**Present**	**Imperfect**	**Present**	**Imperfect**
τῑμῶμαι	ἐτῑμώμην	ποιοῦμαι	ἐποιούμην	δηλοῦμαι	ἐδηλούμην
τῑμᾷ	ἐτῑμῶ	ποιῇ, ποιεῖ	ἐποιοῦ	δηλοῖ	ἐδηλοῦ
τῑμᾶται	ἐτῑμᾶτο	ποιεῖται	ἐποιεῖτο	δηλοῦται	ἐδηλοῦτο
τῑμᾶσθον	ἐτῑμᾶσθον	ποιεῖσθον	ἐποιεῖσθον	δηλοῦσθον	ἐδηλοῦσθον
τῑμᾶσθον	ἐτῑμᾶσθην	ποιεῖσθον	ἐποιείσθην	δηλοῦσθον	ἐδηλούσθην
τῑμώμεθα	ἐτῑμώμεθα	ποιούμεθα	ἐποιούμεθα	δηλούμεθα	ἐδηλούμεθα
τῑμᾶσθε	ἐτῑμᾶσθε	ποιεῖσθε	ἐποιεῖσθε	δηλοῦσθε	ἐδηλοῦσθε
τῑμῶνται	ἐτῑμῶντο	ποιοῦνται	ἐποιοῦντο	δηλοῦνται	ἐδηλοῦντο

Finally, here are the present middle/passive infinitives and participles:

infinitive	participle
λύεσθαι	λῡόμενος
τιμᾶσθαι	τιμώμενος
ποιεῖσθαι	ποιούμενος
δηλοῦσθαι	δηλούμενος

The participles are first-and-second declension adjectives, declined like καλός.

The present subjunctive, optative, and imperative middle and passive are formed as you would expect; you will learn them in the next chapter.

The future indicative, infinitive, and participle middle are formed from the second principal part and use the same endings as the present, for example λύσομαι. A verb whose second principal part ends in -ομαι has a future middle instead of a future active, as ἀκούσομαι from ἀκούω.

Athematic verbs use the short-vowel form of the stem and the same endings as thematic verbs (without the theme vowel of course) to form their present middle/passive, so δίδομαι or τίθεμαι; you will meet these forms in chapter 20.

Exercise

Write out the present indicative middle/passive of κελεύω, βλέπω, φιλέω, ἀξιόω, and ὁράω, and the imperfect indicative middle/passive of ἀκούω and ἔχω. Write out the present infinitive middle/passive and the three nominative singular forms of the present participle middle/passive for the same seven verbs.

X.3 Aorist middle

The second aorist middle is formed just like the imperfect middle, from the aorist stem of course, so ἐλαβόμην, ἐλάβου, ἐλάβετο, and so on. The infinitive is accented on the ending, just like the second aorist infinitive active, rather than on the stem like the present infinitives, so λαβέσθαι (compare λαμβάνεσθαι). The participle is accented λαβόμενος just like the present middle participle.

The first aorist uses similar endings but with the characteristic α of the aorist rather than the theme vowel of the present system:

singular	
1st	ἐ-λῡσ-άμην
2nd	ἐ-λύσ-ω
3rd	ἐ-λύσ-ατο
dual	
2nd	ἐ-λύσ-ασθον
3rd	ἐ-λῡσ-άσθην
plural	
1st	ἐ-λῡσ-άμεθα
2nd	ἐ-λύσ-ασθε
3rd	ἐ-λύσ-αντο

Note the second person singular: the ending -ω looks like the ending of the first person singular of the present indicative active, but watch for the augment.

The infinitive is λύσασθαι and the participle is λυσάμενος.

The remaining moods of the aorist middle are also formed from this stem, and are in the next chapter. The aorist passive and future passive are formed from the sixth principal part; you will meet them in chapters 12 and 13.

When the third principal part ends in -άμην, as for example ἡγησάμην from ἡγέομαι, the verb has a first aorist, and has middle forms but not active in the aorist. When the third principal part ends in -όμην, as ἐγενόμην from γίγνομαι, then the verb has a second aorist, and no active aorist forms.

Exercises

1. Write out the aorist indicative middle of κελεύω, μανθάνω, γράφω, εὑρίσκω, and λαμβάνω. Write out the aorist infinitive middle and the nominatives singular of the aorist participle middle for the same verbs.

2. Look at the verbs in the chapter vocabularies and tell whether each one has active or only middle (or passive) forms in the present, in the future, and in the aorist, and whether it has a first aorist or a second aorist. For example, ἀκούω has a present active, a future middle, and a first aorist active.

X.4 Syntax of the middle and passive

Since the present middle and passive are identical, how does one tell the voices apart? In the middle, a verb takes its normal direct object or other complement, but a passive verb will not have an object. Thus ἡ ἀδελφὴ τὸν ἀδελφὸν βλέπεται must be middle.

When the verb is passive, the **agent** may be specified or omitted. One reason to use the passive, in Greek as in English, can be to omit the doer of the action: consider the difference between τὸν ἄγγελον πέμπει and ὁ ἄγγελος πέμπεται. In the first, the active verb must have a subject, which must be clear from context if it's not explicitly included in the clause. Thus this sentence doesn't only tell us about the dispatch of the messenger, but also tells us who is responsible for it. In the second sentence, however, the subject of the verb is the messenger, the recipient of the action. There's no grammatical need to include the agent or doer of the sending. If that information isn't important, or if the speaker wants to conceal it, the passive voice can be useful.

But if the speaker does want to include the agent with a passive verb, the construction is ὑπό with genitive. Thus the following pairs of sentences mean roughly the same thing: ὁ Φίλιππος τὸν ἄγγελον πέμπει. ὁ ἄγγελος ὑπὸ τοῦ Φιλίππου πέμπεται. ὁ ἄνθρωπος δοῦλον πωλεῖ. ὁ δοῦλος ὑπὸ τοῦ ἀνθρώπου πωλεῖται. τὸν λόγον ἀκούομεν. ὁ λόγος ὑφ' ἡμῶν ἀκούεται. ἡμᾶς βλέπετε. ὑφ' ὑμῶν βλεπόμεθα.

Thus if you see a form that could be either middle or passive, and there is an accusative object, the verb is middle; if there is a ὑπό agent phrase instead, the verb is passive.

A verb in the passive, like any other Greek verb, agrees with its subject, which in this instance is *not* its agent: οἱ ἄγγελοι ὑπὸ τοῦ Φιλίππου πέμπονται requires a plural verb, because the subject is ἄγγελοι, while the corresponding active sentence has a singular subject and thus a singular verb: ὁ Φίλιππος τοὺς ἀγγέλους πέμπει.

It's not possible to make a passive sentence whose subject is the original indirect object. Consider ὁ ἄνθρωπος δοῦλον τῷ φίλῳ ἀγοράζει. In English, we can make two different passive equivalents for this sentence: "a slave is sold to the friend by the man," and "the friend is sold a slave by the man." In Greek only the first is legitimate: δοῦλος τῷ φίλῳ ὑπὸ τοῦ ἀνθρώπου ἀγοράζεται. There is no way to make a passive equivalent of this sentence with ὁ φίλος as subject, because τῷ φίλῳ is not a patient, undergoer, or recipient of the action in the original sentence (not a direct object).

Finally, some verbs have idiomatic uses in the middle. For example, γράφεται means "indict, charge." Some verbs have only middle forms in certain tense systems, or only passive forms. Sometimes a verb will have no active forms at all, like γίγνομαι "become." Other verbs have all three voices in some tenses, but are lacking the active in others. For example, ἀκούω is normal in the present, aorist, and perfect, but has no future active: its second principal part is ἀκούσομαι. Occasionally a verb has no passive and a different verb is used instead: for example, instead of a passive formed from ἀποκτείνω "kill," Greek uses ἀποθνῄσκω.

The verb εἰμι has no middle or passive forms in the present, and has only middle forms in the future, from second principal part ἔσομαι.

Exercise

In each of the following sentences, identify whether the main verb is middle or passive, and explain. Is it always possible to tell without a fuller context? τὴν φωνὴν ἀκούεται. ἡ φωνὴ ἀκούεται. λέγεται ὑπὸ τοῦ διδασκάλου. λέγεται τῷ διδασκάλῳ ὁ λόγος. λέγεται ὁ διδάσκαλος τὸν λόγον. τὸ παιδίον φιλεῖται. τὸ παιδίον τοὺς ἵππους φιλεῖται. τὸ παιδίον ὑπὸ τοῦ φίλου φιλεῖται. ὁ ἄνθρωπος ἔρχεται. ἡ στρατιὰ νικᾶται. ἡ στρατιὰ ὑπὸ τῶν Περσῶν νικᾶται. ἡ στρατιὰ ὑμᾶς νικᾶται.

X.5 Syntax: "the same"

As you recall, the pronoun/adjective αὐτός has three different uses:

- as part of the compound reflexive pronouns, as ἡμᾶς αὐτοὺς φιλοῦμεν "we love ourselves" (two-word compound), or ἑαυτὴν φιλεῖ "she loves herself" (one-word compound with the obsolete pronoun stem).

- to mean "self" in the emphatic way, as αὐτὸς λέγω "I say it *myself*" or κτείνουσι τὸν ἄνθρωπον αὐτόν "they kill the man *himself*" (English might prefer "they kill that very man"). Here the pronoun modifies a noun, or the subject of the verb, in predicate position, without being inside its noun phrase.

- to mean "the same," as ὁ αὐτὸς ἄνθρωπος, "the same man." Here the adjective is inside a noun phrase, in attribute position.

To say "the same *as*," Greek uses the dative, for example οὗτος ἐστὶν ὁ αὐτὸς ἐκείνῳ, "this man is the same as that one." Any word meaning "like" or "same" will use the dative in this way.

X.6 Vocabulary

VERBS

αἴρω, ἀρῶ, ἦρα, ἦρκα, ἦρμαι, ἤρθην, raise, lift (cp. *artery*)

ἀνα-σπάω, ἀνα-σπάσω, ἀνέσπασα, ἀνέσπακα, ἀνέσπασμαι, ἀνεσπάσθην, pull up

ἀνα-χωρέω, go away, go back, withdraw, retire

ἀπο-κρίνομαι, answer, reply

γίγνομαι, γενήσομαι, ἐγενόμην, γέγονα, γεγένημαι, – , become, be (cp. *kin*, *generate*, L. *genus*)

δια-θέω, run about (other tenses normally not used)

δοκέω, δόξω, ἔδοξα, – , δέδογμαι, ἐδόχθην, seem, think

εὐφημέω, εὐφημήσω, ηὐφήμησα, – , – , – , utter words of good omen, pray fairly; also, be silent (not say anything ill-omened) (cp. *euphemism*)

ἡγέομαι, ἡγήσομαι, ἡγησάμην, – , ἥγημαι, – , think, suppose; lead, be in charge (cp. *hegemony*)

καθ-ίημι, let down

κατα-λείπω, leave behind

λείπω, λείψω, ἔλιπον, λέλοιπα, λέλειμμαι, ἐλείφθην, leave (cp. *twelve*, L. *linquo*)

μάχομαι, μαχοῦμαι, ἐμαχεσάμην, – , μεμάχημαι, – , – , fight, contend

περι-άγω, pull round

πλέω, πλεύσομαι, ἔπλευσα, πέπλευκα, πέπλευσμαι, – , sail (cp. *float*)

τρέχω, δραμοῦμαι, ἔδραμον, δεδράμηκα, δεδράμημαι, – , run (cp. *tramp*, *hippodrome*, *velodrome*)

χαίρω, χαιρήσω, ἐχαίρησα, κεχάρηκα, κεχάρημαι, ἐχάρην, rejoice

NOUNS

ἄγκῡρα, -ας, ἡ, anchor

ἀναγωγή, -ῆς, ἡ, launching

ἄνεμος, -ου, ὁ, wind (cp. *anemometer*, Lat. *animus*)

εὐχή, -ῆς, ἡ, prayer

ἥλιος, -ου, ὁ, sun (cp. *helium*, *heliotrope*, L. *sol*)

θόρυβος, -ου, ὁ, noise

ἱστίον, -ου, τό, sail

ἱστός, -οῦ, ὁ, mast

κάλως, -ω, ὁ, rope, cable

κεραίᾱ, -ας, ἡ, yardarm

κυβερνήτης, -ου, ὁ, helmsman, pilot (cp. *cybernetics*)

ναύτης, -ου, ὁ, sailor (cp. *astronaut*)

ὅρμος, **-ου, ὁ**, anchorage, haven

παιᾱνισμός, **-οῦ, ο**, chanting of the παιάν, paean, or solemn song; sailors' chanty

πλοῖον, **-ου, τό**, ship, sea-vessel

ADJECTIVES

οὔριος, **-α, -ον**, favorable, having a fair wind

σφοδρός, **-ά, -όν**, strong, violent

ADVERBS, PREPOSITIONS, IDIOMS

ἄνω, above

ἔτι, still, yet

ἤδη, already

οὐκέτι, no longer, no more

κατὰ μικρόν, little by little

κατὰ τὸ πλοῖον, around the ship, near the ship

κάτω, below, down, downward

ὡς, to, toward (+ acc); used for approaching a person

ὡς, how! (exclamation)

Notes on the vocabulary

You already know χωρέω with the sense "hold, contain." This is an extension of its basic meaning, which is "make way, make space," then later simply "go." The compound ἀνα-χωρέω takes its meaning from the basic meaning of the simple verb.

ἀποκρίνομαι is compounded from the middle voice of κρίνω; this compound can also be used in the active, meaning "separate, choose," but the middle is more common, and has an idiomatic meaning.

γίγνομαι properly means "become" or "come into a state of being," but is often used as almost a synonym of εἰμι. Note the idiom τί γίγνεται; or τί ἐγένετο; for "what's happening? what happened?"

Verbs that end in -εω with one-syllable stems, like πλε- "sail" or θε- "run" or πνε- "breathe," only have contracted forms when there are two -ε- together; when the ending starts with -ο- the forms are not contracted. Thus the present indicative active of πλέω is πλέω, πλεῖς, πλεῖ, πλεῖτον, πλεῖτον, πλέομεν, πλεῖτε, πλέουσι. Compounds of these verbs work the same way, so διαθέω, περιπλέω "sail around," ἀναπνέω "breathe out," and so on.

When δοκέω means "seem," the subject is usually who or what seems, and there is a complementary infinitive. For example, οὗτος ὁ ἄνθρωπος μοι δοκεῖ εἶναι σοφός, "this man seems wise to me"; δοκεῖς μοι ἁμαρτάνειν, "you seem to me to be making a mistake." Sometimes the infinitive is the subject, in a construction close to the English "it seems that...." A common idiom is ἔδοξε τῇ βουλῇ, with infinitive subject; for example ἔδοξε τῇ βουλῇ τὸν νόμον ἀναγράψαι, "to post this law seemed right to the Boule," which is the normal way to say "the Boule resolved to post this law (in a public place)." Particularly in Athens, decrees may also read ἔδοξε τῇ βουλῇ καὶ τῷ δήμῳ, "it seemed right to the Boule and to the People." The Boule was the planning body for the Athenian government, responsible for the agenda for meetings of the Assembly of citizens (ἐκκλησία) and for financial affairs.

The future θρέξω and aorist ἔθρεξα from the verb τρέχω also occur but the suppletive forms from δραμ- are more common.

The aorist active of χαίρω is rare.

The noun κάλως is a contracted second-declension noun with stem κάλω-; its forms look just like ordinary second-declension nouns except that they have long -ω- instead of -o-, -ου-. Don't confuse this noun with καλῶς, the regular adverb from καλός.

ἱστός is related to ἵστημι: the mast stands on the ship. ἱστίον is a diminutive: the sail is the smaller thing attached to the mast.

παιανισμός is from παιάν, -ᾶνος, a choral song, especially a hymn to Apollo Paean, god of healing.

The neuter accusative plural of σφοδρός, but with recessive accent, σφόδρα, is used as an adverb meaning "very much, exceedingly," in a good or a bad sense.

You have already seen ὡς in the sense "as, as though"; in this meaning it can also be strengthened by -περ. You have also seen it as a conjunction introducing indirect discourse, like ὅτι. It can also be a preposition, taking the accusative, meaning "to, toward." In this sense the object of the preposition is a person; for going toward a thing or a place, use ἐπί, πρός, or even the accusative alone. Another use of ὡς is to introduce exclamations, as ὡς καλόν!, "how pretty! what a pretty thing!"

X.7 Reading

1. ἔχαιρον τὸ πρῶτον, ὁρῶν τὴν θάλατταν, ὄντος ἐν τῷ ὅρμῳ ἔτι τοῦ πλοίου. ὡς δ᾽ ἔδοξεν οὔριος εἶναι πρὸς ἀναγωγὴν ὁ ἄνεμος, θόρυβος ἦν εὐθὺς κατὰ τὸ πλοῖον, τῶν ναυτῶν διαθεόντων, τοῦ κυβερνήτου κελεύοντος, ἑλκομένων τῶν κάλων· ἡ κεραία περιήγετο, τὸ ἱστίον καθίετο, τὸ πλοῖον ἀπεσάλευε, τὰς ἀγκύρας ἀνέσπων, ὁ ὅρμος κατελείπετο· τὴν γῆν ὁρῶμεν ἀπὸ τοῦ πλοίου κατὰ μικρὸν ἀναχωροῦσαν, ὥσπερ αὐτὴν πλέουσαν. παιανισμὸς ἦν καὶ εὐχή, θεοὺς δ᾽ ἐκάλουν, εὐφημοῦντες αἴσιον τὸν πλοῦν γενέσθαι· ὁ ἄνεμος ᾔρετο σφοδρότερον, τὸ ἱστίον ἐκυρτοῦτο καὶ ἔτρεχε τὸ πλοῖον ἤδη.

> ἀπο-σαλεύω, ride at anchor, with predictable principal parts; αἴσιος, -α, -ον, lucky, prosperous; κυρτόομαι, belly out, become convex (present system only). This passage comes from an ancient novel, *Leucippe and Cleitophon*, by Achilles Tatius; it is book 2 chapter 32. Cleitophon is speaking.

2. τὸ λεγόμενον τοῦτ' ἐστὶ νῦν· τἄνω κάτω, τὰ κάτω δ' ἄνω.

> Note crasis, τἄνω = τὰ ἄνω. The participle λεγόμενον can idiomatically be used as a neuter noun, "something said," hence "saying, proverb."

3. ὡς αἰεὶ τὸν ὅμοιον ἄγει θεὸς ὡς τὸν ὅμοιον.

4. ὁ Λεωνίδας στρατηγὸς ἦν τῶν Λακεδαιμονίων. ἐπὶ τῷ μετὰ τῶν Περσῶν πολέμῳ στρατιώτης τις ἔφη "ἀπὸ τῶν οἰστῶν τῶν βαρβάρων οὐκ ἔχομεν τὸν ἥλιον ἰδεῖν." "οὐκοῦν" ἔφη ὁ Λεωνίδας, "ὑπὸ σκιὰν αὐτοῖς μαχεσόμεθα."

> **οἰστός, -οῦ, ὁ**, arrow. **σκιά, -ᾶς, ἡ**, shadow, shade. Adapted from Plutarch's life of Leonidas.

5. πόλεμός ποτε ἦν μετὰ δύο στρατώ. ὁ μὲν στρατὸς ἀνδρεῖος ἦν, ὁ δὲ δειλός. οἱ ἀνδρεῖοι, ἐθέλοντες μαχέσασθαι, σημεῖον ἦραν ἵνα οἱ ἄλλοι αὐτὸ ἴδωσι, ἡγούμενοι ὅτι νικήσουσι. οἱ δὲ δειλοί, ἐν ἀπορίᾳ ὄντες, ηὐφήμησαν. ἔπειτα στρατιώτης τις τοῦ δειλοῦ στρατοῦ εἶπε, "πῶς ἔχομεν μαχέσασθαι τούτοις τοῖς γίγασι; δοκεῖ μοι φυγεῖν. εἰ τρέχομεν, τὸν βίον καὶ τὴν ὑγίειαν ἕξομεν. εἰ δὲ μαχόμεθα, οὗτοι ἡμᾶς ἀποκτείνουσι. ἐγὼ μὲν οὐκ ἐθέλω ἀποθνήσκειν, ὑμεῖς δέ μοι δοκεῖτε τοῦτο οὐκ ἐθέλειν. κρίνω οὖν τὸ φυγεῖν εἶναι τὸ ἄριστον."

ἄλλος στρατιώτης ἀπεκρίνετο. "τί γίγνεται;" ἔφη. "τί ποιεῖτε, ὦ ἑταῖροι; εἰ λείπομεν τήνδε τὴν γῆν, καὶ φεύγομεν πρὸς τὴν θάλατταν, καὶ ἐκεῖνοι ἡμᾶς πέτραις βάλλουσι, τί ἄρα ποιήσομεν; τὸ μαχέσασθαι ἔμοιγε δοκεῖ." πάντες ἔλεγον, ὁ μὲν ἐθέλων φυγεῖν, ὁ δὲ μαχέσασθαι, ὁ δὲ δραμεῖν εὐθὺς πρὸς τὸν ἄλλον στρατόν. τέλος δὲ ἔκριναν· ἔδοξε μαχέσασθαι μᾶλλον ἢ φυγεῖν.

ὁ δὲ ἀνδρεῖος στρατὸς ἔδραμε πρὸς τὸν δειλόν. οἱ στρατιῶται τοῖς ἄλλοις ἀπήντησαν. εὖ ἐμαχέσαντο. τί οὖν ἐγένετο; οἱ δειλοί, οὐκέτι δειλοὶ ὄντες, ἐνίκησαν.

> **σημεῖον, -ου, τό**, sign, flag, standard. **τέλος, -ους, τό**, end; **τέλος δέ**, in the end, finally.

6. ὁμολογῶ, εἶπε ὁ Σωκράτης, περί γε παιδείας· τοῦτο γὰρ ἴσασιν ἐμοὶ μεμεληκός. περὶ δὲ ὑγιείας τοῖς ἰατροῖς μᾶλλον οἱ ἄνθρωποι πείθονται ἢ τοῖς γονεῦσι· καὶ ἐν ταῖς ἐκκλησίαις γε πάντες δήπου οἱ Ἀθηναῖοι τοῖς φρονιμώτατα λέγουσι πείθονται μᾶλλον ἢ τοῖς προσήκουσιν. οὐ γὰρ δὴ καὶ στρατηγοὺς αἱρεῖσθε καὶ πρὸ πατέρων καὶ πρὸ ἀδελφῶν, καὶ ναὶ μὰ Δία γε ὑμεῖς πρὸ ὑμῶν αὐτῶν, οὓς ἂν ἡγῆσθε περὶ τῶν πολεμικῶν φρονιμωτάτους εἶναι;

οὕτω γάρ, εἶπε ὁ Μέλητος, ὦ Σώκρατες, καὶ συμφέρει καὶ νομίζεται.

> This passage is from Xenophon's *Apology*; Meletus is prosecuting Socrates on charges of impiety.
>
> **ὁμολογέω**, agree. **παιδεία, -ας, ἡ**, education. **ἴσασιν** "they know," 3rd pl perf indicative active of οἶδα, a verb with only perfect forms (chapter 17). **μεμεληκός, μεμεληκυῖα, μεμεληκός**, relevant, of concern; formally, perfect participle from μέλει (chapter 11). **γονεύς, -έως, ὁ**, parent (chapter 16). **ἐκκλησία, -ας, ἡ**, assembly. **δήπου**, particle, indicating that the speaker expects the hearer to agree. **φρονιμώτατα**, most thoughtful, most prudent. **προσήκων, προσήκουσα, προσῆκον**, related, kinsman; participle of προσήκω, come near, be at hand, be appropriate. **πολεμικός, -ή, -όν**, having to do with war, warlike. **συμφέρω**, be useful, be profitable.

7. οἳ δ’ ὅτε δὴ λιμένος πολυβενθέος ἐντὸς ἵκοντο
ἱστία μὲν στείλαντο, θέσαν δ’ ἐν νηῒ μελαίνῃ,
ἱστὸν δ’ ἱστοδόκῃ πέλασαν προτόνοισιν ὑφέντες
καρπαλίμως, τὴν δ’ εἰς ὅρμον προέρεσσαν ἐρετμοῖς.
ἐκ δ’ εὐνὰς ἔβαλον, κατὰ δὲ πρυμνήσι’ ἔδησαν·
ἐκ δὲ καὶ αὐτοὶ βαῖνον ἐπὶ ῥηγμῖνι θαλάσσης,
ἐκ δ’ ἑκατόμβην βῆσαν ἑκηβόλῳ Ἀπόλλωνι·
ἐκ δὲ Χρυσηὶς νηὸς βῆ ποντοπόροιο.

> *Iliad* 1.432-439. The subject (οἱ δέ in the first line) is a group of men led by Odysseus, bringing Chryses his daughter back.
>
> **λιμήν, -ένος, ὁ** = ὅρμος. **πολυβενθέος** = πολυβενθοῦς, genitive of πολυβενθής, deep. **ἱκνέομαι, ἵξομαι, ἱκόμην, – , ἷγμαι, – ,** come, arrive. **στείλαντο** = ἐστείλαντο, aorist of στέλλω, arrange, make ready. As often in epic, the augment is omitted; similarly θέσαν = ἔθεσαν, πέλασαν = ἐπέλασαν, προ-έρεσσαν = προήρεσσαν, βαῖνον = ἔβαινον. **νηί** is dative sg of ναῦς, ship, and νηός is genitive (Ionic dialect form); see chapter 14 for this noun. **ἱστοδόκη, -ης, ἡ** is a support to receive the mast when it is taken down. **πελάζω**, bring near to. **πρότονος, -ου, ὁ**, forestay, one of the ropes supporting the mast. **ὑφ-ίημι**, lower, let down. **καρπαλίμως**, rapidly. **προ-ἐρέσσω**, row forward, related to the noun ἐρετμός, -οῦ, ὁ, oar. **εὐνή, -ῆς, ἡ**, heavy stone (for an anchor). **πρυμνήσια, -ων, τά**, stern cables, to fasten the ship to a mooring. **ἔδησαν** aorist from δέω, bind, tie. **βαίνω, βήσομαι, ἔβην, βέβηκα, – , – ,** step, go; ἔβαινον is imperfect and ἔβησαν is aorist, both 3rd pl, and ἔβη is 3rd sg aorist indicative active. **ῥηγμίν, -ῖνος, ὁ**, surf, breakers. **θαλάσσης** = θαλάττης; some dialects use -σσ- in words where Attic Greek has -ττ-. **ἑκατόμβη, -ης, ἡ**, hecatomb, a large sacrifice; here referring to the animals who will be sacrificed. **ἑκηβόλος**, a traditional epithet for Apollo, probably meaning "the one who shoots arrows at will and hits his target," related to ἑκών, but often taken to mean "one who shoots from afar." **ποντοπόρος, -ον**, sea-going; the form is an archaic genitive.
>
> Prose paraphrase: ὅτε δὴ ἐν τοῦ ὅρμου πολυβενθοῦς ἀφίκοντο, τὰ μὲν ἱστία ἔθεσαν ἐν τῷ πλοίῳ μέλανι, τὸ δὲ ἱστόν καλῶς ὑφέντες ἐν τῇ ἱστοδόκῃ τάχα ἔθεσαν, καὶ τὸ πλοίων ἐρετμοῖς εἰς τὸν ὅρμον προήρετταν. τὰς δὲ εὐνὰς ἐξέβαλον, αἵ εἰσι ἡ ἄγκυρα, τὰ δὲ πρυμνήσια ἔδησαν, ἅ ἐστι κάλως. ἐξέβαινον ἐπὶ τοῖς τῆς θαλάττης ῥηγμῖνι. τὰ ζῷα, τὴν ἑκατόμβην τῷ Ἀπόλλωνι, ἐξήγαγον. ὁ δὲ Χρυσηὶς ἐκ τοῦ ποντοπόρου πλοίου ἐξέβη.

8. *περὶ τοῦ Τρωικοῦ πολέμου, τέταρτον μέρος*

οἱ Ἕλληνες, οὐρίου ὄντος τοῦ ἀνέμου, τὴν ἄγκυραν ἦραν καὶ ἐξ Αὐλίδος ἔπλευσαν εἰς Τένεδον. ὁ Τένης, βασιλεὺς ὢν τοῦ Τενέδου, τοὺς Ἕλληνας ὁρῶν πέτρας ἔβαλλε.

"παύετε! μὴ προσέρχεσθε!" εἶπε. "αὕτη ἡ γῆ ἐμοί ἐστι. τίνες ἐστέ, ποῖ καὶ πόθεν ἔρχεσθε;"

"πλέομεν πρὸς τὸν Ἴλιον," ἀπεκρίνατο ὁ Ἀγαμέμνων. "Ἀγαμέμνων μὲν εὔχομαι εἶναι, ὁ τοῦ Ἀτρέως, στρατηγὸς δὲ τῶν Ἑλλήνων. ἐθέλοιμεν ἂν ταύτῃ τῇ νυκτὶ ἐνθάδε μένειν. ἆρα ἐάσεις;"

"οὐκ ἐῶ. ἀπέρχεσθε, ἀποπλεῖτε, καταλείπετε τὴν γῆν. εἰ δὲ μή, πόλεμον ἕξομεν."

"εἰ πόλεμον ἔχειν ἐθέλεις, πόλεμον σοὶ δώσομεν," ἀπεκρίναντο οἱ Ἕλληνες. ἐμάχοντο οὖν δύο ὥρας. τέλος δὲ ὁ Ἀχιλλεὺς ὡς τὸν Τένην ἦλθε. "εὖ οἶδα," ἐνόμισε, "ὅτι, τὸν Τένην ἀποκτείνας, ἐγὼ ἀποθανοῦμαι ὑπὸ Ἀπόλλωνος. ἡ δὲ Θέτις ἐμοὶ τοῦτο εἶπε. ἀλλὰ εἰ μὴ ἀποκτείνω, πάντες ἀποθανούμεθα. δοκεῖ μέντοι μοι αὐτὸν ἀποκτείνειν." τοῦτο νομίσας, τὸν Τένην ἀποκτείνας, τοῦ πολέμου ἔπαυσε.

οἱ δὲ Ἕλληνες ἔχαιρον. τῷ δὲ Ἀπόλλωνι ἔθυσαν. δράκων δὲ ἐκ τοῦ βωμοῦ προσῆλθε. "ἰδού!" εἶπε στρατιώτης τις, Φιλοκτήτης ὀνόματι. "οὗτος ὁ δράκων πρὸς τὴν θυσίαν ἔρχεται ἵνα αὐτὴν φάγῃ. ἄπελθε, ὦ δράκων." τὸν δὲ δράκοντα οὐκ ἀπελθόντα ὁ Φιλοκτήτης πέτρᾳ ἔβαλε. ὁ δὲ τὸν Φιλοκτήτην ἔδακνε.

ὁ δὲ Φιλοκτήτης μεγάλην λύπην εἶχε. πᾶσαν τὴν νύκτα ἐβόα. αὔριον, οἱ Ἕλληνες πλεύσαντες ἀφίκοντο εἰς τὸν Λῆμνον. ἀθεραπεύτου τοῦ ἕλκους, τῆς τε ὀδμῆς οὐκ ἀνεχομένου τοῦ στρατοῦ, ὁ Ὀδυσσεὺς καὶ ὁ Ἀγαμέμνων τὸν Φιλοκτήτην ἐξετίθετον ἐπὶ τῇ νήσῳ μετὰ τῶν τοῦ Ἡρακλέους τόξων, καὶ αὐτὸν ἐλίπετον. ὁ μὲν Φιλοκτήτης ἐκεῖ τοὺς ὄρνιθες τοξεύων ἐπὶ τῆς νήσου ἑαυτὸν ἔθρεψε. οἱ δὲ ἄλλοι πρὸς τὸν Ἴλιον ἐξέπλεον.

> βασιλεύς, -έως, ὁ, king (chapter 16). εὔχομαι, boast, claim. νύξ, νυκτός, ἡ, night. ἐάω, ἐάσω permit, allow. ὥρα, -ας, ἡ, time, hour. οἶδα, know; this verb only has perfect forms: see chapter 17. δράκων, -οντος, ὁ, snake, serpent, dragon. βωμός, -οῦ, ὁ, altar. δάκνω, δήξομαι, ἔδακον, – , δέδηγμαι, ἐδήχθην, bite. ἀθεράπευτος = ἰατροὶ οὐκ ἔχουσι θεραπεύειν τὸ ἀθεράπευτον ἕλκον. ἕλκος, -ους, τό, wound, sore. βοάω, βοήσω, ἐβόησα, βεβόηκα, βεβόημαι, ἐβοήθην, shout, cry out. ὀδμή, -ῆς, ἡ, smell, odor. ἀνέχω, hold up; middle, put up with, endure. νῆσος, -ου, ἡ, island. τόξα, -ων, τά, bow and arrows. τοξεύω (predictable parts), shoot a bow, hunt with a bow. ὄρνις, ὄρνῑθος, ὁ, ἡ, bird.

X.8 Conversation

1. (reading 1) διὰ τί ἔχαιρον ὁ Κλειτοφῶν; τί εἶδε; διὰ τί εἶδε ὁ Κλειτοφῶν πρῶτος τὴν θάλατταν; ποῖος ἦν ὁ θόρυβος κατὰ τὸ πλοῖον; τί ἐγένετο; τί ἐποίησαν οἱ ναῦται; and so on in the usual way.

2. (reading 2) τί λέγεται; τὰ ἄνω κάτω εἶναι λέγεται. τί δ’ ἄλλο; τὰ κάτω ἄνω εἶναι, καὶ τοῦτο λέγεται. ἆρα ταὐτό ἐστι τοῦτ’ ἐκείνῳ; οὐ ταὐτό, ἀλλ’ ὅμοιον.

3. (reading 4) διὰ τί οὐκ ὁρῶσι οἱ στρατιῶται τὸν ἥλιον; πόσους οἰστοὺς ἔχουσι οἱ Πέρσαι; πῶς μαχεσόνται οἱ Λακεδαιμόνιοι, κατὰ τὸν Λεωνίδην;
   Similar questions for the other readings.

4. (use of the passive) τίς ἄγει; τίς δ’ ἄγεται; ποῖ δ’ ἄγεται ὁ ὅμοιος; πότε δέ;

X.9 Writing

1. Do the change-number exercise with the following sentences, and say what voice all the verbs are.

     a. φιλούμεθα ὑπὸ τῶν φίλων.

     b. οὗτος ὑπὸ τῶν ἄλλων φιλεῖται.

     c. οὗτος τοὺς ἄλλους φιλεῖται.

     d. τοὺς φίλους φιλεῖσθε.

     e. τὰ παιδία ἐφιλοῦ.

     f. ὁ διδάσκαλος τὰ παιδία ἐφιλήσατο.

     g. ὑπὸ ἀδίκου οὐ φιλεῖ, ὦ ἑταῖρε.

     h. ὁ λόγος ὑπὸ τῶν ποιητῶν ἀεὶ λέγεται.

     i. ὁ λόγος ὑπὸ τῶν ποιητῶν ἀεὶ ἐλέγετο.

     j. ὁ πολίτης τὸν αἰσχρὸν γράφεται.

     k. ὁ κακὸς πολίτης τὸν ἀγαθὸν ἀδίκως ἐγράψατο.

     l. τὼ δένδρω ὑπὸ τοῦ λέοντος βλέπεσθον.

     m. οἱ λόγοι ὑπὸ τοῦ μαθητοῦ ἐμανθάνοντο.

     n. τὰ ζῷα φιλούμενοι ἐτρεφόμεθα.

     o. τὼ ἀδελφὼ ἡγησάσθην τὴν τεκοῦσαν καλήν.

     p. πρὸς τὴν κώμην πέμπῃ, ὦ ἄγγελε, ἵνα τοῦ πολέμου παύσῃς.

     q. ὁ μαθητὴς τὸ βιβλίον ἐλάβετο ἵνα μανθάνῃ.

     r. τοῦ στρατοῦ ἐρχομένου, οἱ πολῖται ἐφύγοντο.

     s. τῷ διδασκάλῳ εἰπόντι τὼ μαθητὰ ἀπεκρινάσθην.

     t. εἰς τὴν οἰκίαν ἔρχομαι.

     u. ὁ στρατὸς εὖ ἐμαχέσατο καὶ ἐνίκησε.

     v. ὁ στρατὸς εὖ μαχεσάμενος ἐνίκησε.

     w. ὅστις ἂν εὖ ποιῇ ἀγαθὸς γίγνεται.

     x. ἐπεὶ ὁ στρατηγὸς ἀπέθανε, σὺ στρατηγὸς ἐγένου.

     y. ἡγούμενος τὸ πλοῖον πλευσόμενον, ὁ ναύτης ἔδραμε πρὸς τὸν ὅρμον.

2. In each of the following sentences, change the main verb from active to passive, or from passive to active, making whatever other changes are required to keep roughly the same meaning. For example, from ὁ ἄνθρωπος τὸν ἑταῖρον φιλεῖ make ὁ ἑταῖρος ὑπὸ τοῦ ἀνθρώπου φιλεῖται.

     a. ὁ κυβερνήτης τὸ πλοῖον ἄγει.

     b. ὁ ἄνθρωπος τὸν πέτασον καταλείπει.

     c. οἱ παῖδες ὑπὸ σοῦ τρέφονται.

     d. οἱ ναῦται τὸν κάλων ἕλκουσι.

     e. ὁ ἱστὸς ὑπὸ τῶν ναυτῶν αἴρεται.

     f. ὁ γίγας τὴν πέτραν ᾖρε.

g. οἱ παῖδες ὑφ᾽ ἡμῶν ἐτρέφοντο.

h. τὴν ἀλήθειαν ἐλέγετε.

i. τὼ δούλω ὑπὸ τοῦ δεσπότου ἐπωλείτην.

j. τὸ βιβλίον ὑπ᾽ ἐμοὶ εἴχετο.

3. Rewrite the following sentences, turning the participial phrases into subordinate clauses. You may use whatever kind of clause fits the sense. For example, from ὁ μαθητὴς, σοφὸς ὤν, εὖ μανθάνει make ὁ μαθητὴς εὖ μανθάνει, ἐπεὶ σοφός ἐστι.

a. τὸ πλοῖον, ἐπὶ τῆς θαλάττης πλέοντα, ὑπὸ τοῦ ἀνέμου ἤγετο.

b. τοῦ ἰατροῦ ἁμαρτόντος, ὁ παῖς τυφλὸς ἐγένετο.

c. παρὰ τῷ δένδρῳ ἐρχομένη τὸ θηρίον εἶδον.

d. ὁ στρατιώτης, κλεινὸς γενόμενος, οὐκέτι ἤθελε μαχέσασθαι.

e. οἱ θεοὶ ἀγαθὰ τῷ εὐφημησαμένῳ διδόντες τιμῶνται.

f. τοῦ κυβερνήτου ἄγγελον ἱέντος, οἱ ναῦται πάλιν πρὸς τὸν πλοῖον ἔρχονται.

g. μεγάλου γιγνομένου τοῦ θορύβου, οὐκ ἠκούσαμεν τὸν λόγον.

h. τῶν μαθητῶν οὐκ ἀποκρινομένων, ὁ διδάσκαλος αὖθις ἠρώτησε.

i. ὁ παῖς οὐ φιλεῖ τὸν ἰατρὸν φάρμακα διδόντα.

j. ὁ φάρμακα διδοὺς ἰατρὸς ὑπὸ τοῦ παιδὸς οὐ φιλεῖται.

4. Rewrite reading 1 in the present tense.

5. Rewrite reading 5 using indirect statement instead of direct.

6. Write a paragraph about a ship setting sail.

CHAPTER XI

Protesilaus

XI.1 Present middle/passive: remaining moods

Every tense and mood exists in all three voices, though as you already know the middle and the passive may be identical in form. These are the forms of the remaining finite moods in the present system in the middle and passive.

	Imperative	Subjunctive	Optative
singular			
1st		λύ-ωμαι	λῡ-οίμην
2nd	λύ-ου	λύ-ῃ	λύ-οιο
3rd	λῡ-έσθω	λύ-ηται	λύ-οιτο
dual			
2nd	λύ-εσθον	λύ-ησθον	λύ-οισθον
3rd	λῡ-έσθων	λύ-ησθον	λῡ-οίσθην
plural			
1st		λῡ-ώμεθα	λῡ-οίμεθα
2nd	λύ-εσθε	λύ-ησθε	λύ-οισθε
3rd	λῡ-έσθων	λύ-ωνται	λύ-οιντο

For contract verbs, as always, the endings contract with the stem vowels. Here are the singular forms to give you the idea; the dual and plural are exactly as you would expect.

	Imperative	Subjunctive	Optative
α	τιμῶ, τιμάσθω	τιμῶμαι, τιμᾷ, τιμᾶται	τιμῴμην, τιμῷο, τιμῷτο
ε	ποιοῦ, ποιείσθω	ποιῶμαι, ποιῇ, ποιῆται	ποιοίμην, ποιοῖο, ποιοῖτο
ο	δηλοῦ, δηλούσθω	δηλῶμαι, δηλοῖ, δηλῶται	δηλοίμην, δηλοῖο, δηλοῖτο

As in the active, the subjunctive middle/passive of α-contracts is identical to the indicative.

The future optative middle is formed from the future stem just as the present optative middle is formed from the present; of course future subjunctive and future imperative do not exist in any voice.

Exercise

Write the three third-person forms of the present subjunctive middle/passive and the present optative middle/passive of φέρω, γράφω, λέγω, νικάω, βάλλω, τίκτω, ἀξιόω, φιλέω, ἄγω and πέμπω. Write the present infinitive middle/passive and the masculine nominative singular of the present participle middle/passive for all 10 of these verbs.

XI.2 Aorist middle

In these moods, just as in the indicative, the strong (second) aorist middle is conjugated in the same way as the present. For example, here are forms from γίγνομαι, aorist ἐγενόμην:

Imperative (2nd sg.)	Subjunctive (1st sg.)	Optative (1st sg.)	Infiniive	Participle
γενοῦ	γένωμαι	γενοίμην	γενέσθαι	γενόμενος

Note accents in γενοῦ and γενέσθαι.

The first aorist is similar, but with the characteristic aorist α instead of the theme vowel:

	Indicative	Imperative	Subjunctive	Optative
singular				
1st	ἐ-λῡσ-άμην		λύσ-ωμαι	λῡσ-αίμην
2nd	ἐ-λύσ-ω	λῦσ-αι	λύσ-ῃ	λύσ-αιο
3rd	ἐ-λύσ-ατο	λῡσ-άσθω	λύσηται	λύσ-αιτο
dual				
2nd	ἐ-λύσ-ασθον	λῦσ-ασθον	λύσ-ησθον	λύσ-αισθον
3rd	ἐ-λῡσ-άσθην	λῡσ-άσθων	λύσ-ησθον	λῡσ-αίσθην
plural				
1st	ἐ-λῡσ-άμεθα		λῡσ-ώμεθα	λῡσ-αίμεθα
2nd	ἐ-λύσ-ασθε	λύσ-ασθε	λύσ-ησθε	λύσαισθε
3rd	ἐ-λύσ-αντο	λῡσ-άσθων	λύσ-ωνται	λύσαιντο

The aorist passive comes from the sixth principal part, not the third; you will learn this in chapter 13.

You have now learned the third of the three nearly identical forms in -σαι, namely the second singular aorist imperative middle, as πίστευσαι. Don't confuse this with the third singular aorist optative active πιστεύσαι or the aorist infinitive active πιστεῦσαι. The infinitive does not have recessive accent, but the two finite forms do, like all finite forms. But because the -αι counts as long in the optative, the optative form cannot be accented on the antepenult. From a verb like λύω with a one-syllable stem, two of those forms fall together: λύσαι is third singular aorist optative active, but λῦσαι is both aorist infinitive active and second singular aorist imperative middle.

Exercise

Write out the following forms: aorist imperative middle of πέμπω, aorist subjunctive middle of φέρω, aorist optative middle of λαμβάνω, aorist subjunctive middle of μανθάνω, aorist optative middle of ποιέω.

XI.3 Neuter nouns in -μα

A large group of nouns ends in -μα in the nominative, with stem in -ματ-. Many of these are abstract nouns formed from verb roots, as πρᾶγμα "thing being done" from πράττω "do." They are regular third declension nouns, so they have the same endings as ὄν (neuter of participle ὤν). Because they are all neuter, they are identical in nominative and accusative in all three numbers.

σῶμα, -ατος, τό, **body**

	Singular	Dual	Plural
nom., voc., acc.	σῶμα	σώματε	σώματα
gen.	σώματος	σωμάτοιν	σωμάτων
dat.	σώματι	σωμάτοιν	σώμασι(ν)

XI.4 S-stem nouns

Another group of third-declension nouns has a stem ending in -εσ-. Virtually all of them are neuter except for those that are proper names. They use the same endings as all third-declension nouns, but because of changes early in the history of Greek, the endings are disguised. The σ of the stem disappears when it is between vowels, and (in Attic Greek) the two vowels then contract with each other — so these S-stem nouns usually *don't* have an audible "s" in them. An example is γένος, -ους, τό, "family, race, kind."

singular

nom., voc., acc.	γένος	(pure stem, no ending, o-grade of the stem vowel)
gen.	γένους	(from γένεσ-ος, γένεος)
gen. dat.	γένει	(from γένεσ-ι)

dual

nom., voc., acc.	γένει	(from γένεσ-ε)
dat.	γενοῖν	(from γενέσ-οιν)

plural		
nom., voc., acc.	γένη	(from γένεσ-α)
gen.	γενῶν	(from γενέσ-ων)
dat.	γένεσι(ν)	(from γένεσ-σι, with the double consonant simplified)

The genitive plural and genitive and dative dual have circumflex on the last syllable because they are contracted from forms with an acute on the first of the two merging vowels.

Early in the history of Greek, the "s" sound between vowels disappeared; later on, the speech community changed its collective mind and accepted that sound again, which is why there *are* lots of forms with "s" between vowels in the language as we know it. But the S-stem nouns were affected by the change.

Although most of the S-stems are neuter nouns, there are also adjectives. Most of them are compounds, so have the same forms for masculine and feminine (see vocabulary in chapter 7). The masculine and feminine forms are only different from the neuter in the nominative, accusative, and vocative. Here is an example: εὐγενής, εὐγενές "noble, well born."

	Masc. and Fem.	Neu.
singular		
nom.	εὐγενής	εὐγενές
gen.	εὐγενοῦς	
dat.	εὐγενεῖ	
acc.	εὐγενῆ	εὐγενές
voc.	εὐγενές	
dual		
nom., voc., acc.	εὐγενεῖ	
gen., dat.	εὐγενοῖν	
plural		
nom., voc., acc.	εὐγενεῖς	εὐγενῆ
gen.	εὐγενῶν	
dat.	εὐγενέσι(ν)	

Note the accent: in the adjectives, it is on the -έσ- of the stem, whereas in most of the nouns it is earlier in the word.

These adjectives have regular comparative and superlative: εὐγενέσ-τερος "more noble"; εὐγενέσ-τατος "most noble." The associated adverbs are also formed in the regular way with -ως instead of the -ων in the genitive plural, so εὐγενῶς, "nobly."

There are also S-stem proper names, most of which are compounds, typically ending in -κράτης from κράτος "strength," or -κλης from κλέος "fame." They work just like the adjectives:

nom.	Σωκράτης
gen.	Σωκράτους
dat.	Σωκράτει
acc.	Σωκράτη (or Σωκράτην)
voc.	Σώκρατες (note accent)

One of the few common feminine S-stem nouns is τριήρης "trireme"; a trireme is a type of ship with three banks of oars. It is just like εὐγενής except that its vocative can be τριῆρες or τριήρης (for those rare instances when one talks to a ship).

Exercise

Write out the complete declension (all cases and numbers) of the phrases τὸ καλὸν σῶμα, ἡ μεγάλη τριήρης, ὁ εὐγενὴς ναύτης.

XI.5 Purpose with participles

Besides the purpose clause introduced by ἵνα, ὅπως, or ὡς, purpose can also be expressed with a future participle, often introduced by ὡς. For example, ἔλεγεν ὡς βλάψων, "he spoke in order to do harm."

Sometimes ὥστε plus infinitive can express purpose, as πᾶν ποιοῦσιν ὥστε δίκην μὴ διδόναι "they do everything in order not to incur punishment" (Plato, *Gorgias* 479c); this is roughly the same as πᾶν ποιοῦσιν ἵνα δίκην μὴ διδῶσι. More usually ὥστε indicates the result expected or predicted from an action; see chapter 17.

XI.6 Vocabulary

VERBS

ἀκμάζω, ἀκμάσω, ἤκμασα, ἤκμακα, – , – , be in one's prime, be ripe (cp. *acme*)

ἀπο-τείνω, stretch, extend

ἀπο-φέρω, carry off, take away

ἀφ-ικνέομαι, come, arrrive

βαστάζω, βαστάσω, ἐβάστασα, – , βεβάσταγμαι, ἐβαστάχθην, lift, carry

ἐγ-χέω, pour in

ἐκ-καθαίρω, cleanse

ἐμ-βάλλω, put in

ἐπείγω, ἐπείξω, ἤπειξα, – , – , ἠπείχθην, urge; in middle, hasten, hurry

ἐπι-σκευάζω, prepare

ἕρπω, ἕρψω, ἧρψα, – , – , – , creep, go (cp. *herpetology*, L. *serpo*) θλίβω, θλίψω, ἔθλῑψα, τέθλῐφα, τέθλιμμαι, ἐθλίβην, crush

ἱκνέομαι, ἵξομαι, ἱκόμην, – , ἷγμαι, – , come, arrive, reach

μέλει, μελήσει, ἐμέλησε, μεμέληκε, – , – , be an object of care (usually impersonal)

παρα-σκευάζω, prepare

πατέω, πατήσω, ἐπάτησα, πεπάτηκα, πεπάτημαι, ἐπατήθην, tread, walk on

πλέκω, πλέξω, ἔπλεξα, πέπλοχα, πέπλεγμαι, ἐπλέχθην, weave, braid (cp. *flax, plait, pleach*, L. *plecto*)

σκευάζω, σκευάσω, ἐσκεύασα, ἐσκεύακα, ἐσκεύασμαι, ἐσκευάσθην, prepare

στρέφω, στρέψω, ἔστρεψα, – , ἔστραμμαι, ἐστράφην, turn, twist (cp. *strophe, apostrophe*)

τείνω, τενῶ, ἔτεινα, τέτακα, τέταμαι, ἐτάθην, stretch (cp. *thin*, L. *tendo*)

χέω, χέω, ἔχεα, κέχυκα, κέχυμαι, ἐχύθην, pour

NOUNS

ἀγρός, -οῦ, ὁ, field, country (cp. L. *ager*)

αἴξ, αἰγός, ὁ, ἡ, goat

ἄμπελος, -ου, ἡ, vine

ἀρχή, -ῆς, ἡ, beginning

γένος, -ους, τό, family, race, kind (cp. *kin*, L. *genus*)

ἔτος, -ους, τό, year (cp. *etesian, wether*, L. *vetus*)

θάνατος, -ου, ὁ, death

κλέος, τό, fame, nominative and accusative only (cp. *listen*)

κλῆμα, -ατος, τό, tendril, branch

κράτος, -ους, τό, strength (cp. *democracy*)

λίθος, -ου, ὁ, stone (cp. *monolith*)

λύγος, -ου, ἡ, flexible twig or branch, withy; willow tree

νύξ, νυκτός, ἡ, night (cp. L. *nux*)

ὅπλον, -ου, τό, weapon, usually plural

ὀπώρᾱ, -ᾱς, ἡ, autumn, fruit

πίθος, -ου, ὁ, wine-jar

ποτόν, -οῦ, τό, drink

πρόβατον, -ου, τό, sheep

σπάργανα, -ων, τά, swaddling clothes, baby blanket

σταφυλή, -ῆς, ἡ, cluster, bunch, grapes

σῶμα, σώματος, τό, body (cp. *somatic*)

τεῖχος, -ους, τό, wall

τέλος, -ους, τό, end, goal (cp. *telic, talisman*)

τομή, -ῆς, ἡ, cut, act of cutting (cp. *atom*)

τριήρης, **-ους**, **ἡ**, trireme

τροφή, **-ῆς**, **ἡ**, food

φάος, φάους, τό, and φῶς, φωτός, light (cp. *photo, phosphorus*)

χρῆμα, **-ατος**, **τό**, thing; in plural sometimes "money"

ὠφέλεια, **-ας**, **ἡ**, help

ADJECTIVES

ἀληθής, **-ές**, true

ἀλλήλων, each other (cp. *allele*)

εὐγενής, **-ές**, noble, well born (cp. *eugenic*)

ξηρός, **-ή**, **-όν**, dry (cp. *xerography*)

μετέωρος, **-ον**, high, uplifted, raised (cp. *meteor, meteorology*)

παλαιός, **-ά**, **-όν**, old

ADVERBS, ETC.

ἄρτι, just, lately

νύκτωρ, by night

μέχρι, prep + gen, until

Notes on the vocabulary

ἐπείγω, despite appearences, is not a compound with ἐπι-, so the augment goes at the beginning, as in aorist ἤπειξα or imperfect ἤπειγον.

The simple verb ἱκνέομαι is poetic; Attic prose prefers the compound ἀφικνέομαι, which means the same thing. Other compounds of this verb are ἐφικνέομαι "reach," καθικνέομαι "come down," συνικνέομαι "come together; interest, be relevant to."

The construction of μέλει is like οὗτος ἐμοὶ μέλει, literally "he is an object of care to me." This is the reverse of the English idiom, "I care for him."

The simple verb τείνω is almost never used in Attic prose; ἀποτείνω is used instead.

χέω is like πλέω. Once again, the simple verb is not as common in prose as the various compounds, like ἐγ-χέω here, or συγ-χέω "pour together," ἐκ-χέω "pour out," κατα-χέω "pour down," and others.

Dictionaries may list the s-stem nouns either in the form τέλος, -ους, τό, showing the contraction used in Attic Greek, or in the form τέλος, -εος, τό, without contraction (just as verbs like ποιέω or ἱκνέομαι are listed without their contraction). The vocabulary lists in this book use the contracted form.

The base meaning of ὀπώρα is autumn, or late summer. Because this is the time fruit ripens on trees, the word also comes to mean "fruit."

πρόβατον is much more common in the plural than in the singular. It is derived from προ-βαίνω: sheep are wealth that can walk around.

The form φάος is poetic; Attic prose writers use φῶς, φωτός.

ἀλλήλων, the **reciprocal pronoun**, has no nominative and no singular; its dual and plural forms are just like those of καλός. It is derived from ἄλλος - ἄλλος, though the second double -λ- has been simplified.

XI.7 Reading

1. Vintage

   ἤδη δ' ὀπώρας ἀκμαζούσης καὶ ἐπείγοντος τοῦ τρυγητοῦ, πᾶς ἦν κατὰ τοὺς ἀγροὺς ἐν ἔργῳ· ὁ μὲν ληνοὺς ἐπεσκεύαζεν· ὁ δὲ πίθους ἐξεκάθαιρεν· ὁ δὲ ἀρρίχους ἔπλεκεν· ἔμελέ τινι δρεπάνης μικρᾶς ἐς σταφυλῶν τομήν, καὶ ἑτέρῳ λίθου ἵνα θλίψαι τὰ ἔνοινα τῶν σταφυλῶν, καὶ ἄλλῳ λύγου ξηρᾶς ἵνα ὑπὸ φάους νύκτωρ τὸ γλεῦκος φέροιτο. ἀμελήσαντες οὖν καὶ ὁ Δάφνις καὶ ἡ Χλόη τῶν προβάτων καὶ τῶν αἰγῶν, ὠφέλειαν ἀλλήλοις μεταδιδόασιν. ὁ μὲν ἐβάσταζεν ἐν ἀρρίχοις σταφυλάς, καὶ ἐπάτει ταῖς ληνοῖς ἐμβαλών, καὶ εἰς τοὺς πίθους ἔφερε τὸν οἶνον. ἡ δὲ τροφὴν παρεσκεύαζε τοῖς τρυγῶσι, καὶ ἐνέχει ποτὸν αὐτοῖς πρεσβύτερον οἶνον, καὶ τῶν ἀμπέλων τὰς ταπεινοτέρας ἀπετρύγα. πᾶσα γὰρ ἡ κατὰ τὴν Λέσβον ἄμπελος ταπεινή, οὐ μετέωρος, καὶ κάτω τὰ κλήματα ἀποτείνει, ἕρπουσα ὥσπερ κιττός· καὶ παιδίον ἂν ἐφίκοιτο σταφυλῆς ἄρτι ἐκ σπαργάνων γενόμενον.

   This is the opening of book 2 of Longus's *Daphnis and Chloe*.

   τρυγάω, τρυγήσω, ἐτρύγησα, – , – , – , pluck fruit, take the vintage (also ἀπο-τρυγῶ, with no difference in meaning), related to the noun τρύγητος, -ου, ὁ "vintage"; both are derived from the base noun τρύγη, "crop, vintage." Derived from the verb is the agent noun τρυγητής. **ληνός, -οῦ, ἡ,** wine-vat, treading-vat. **δρεπάνη, -ης, ἡ,** sickle. **γλεῦκος, -ους, τό,** freshly pressed grape juice, new wine. **ἄρριχος, -ου, ὁ,** basket. **ἔνοινος, -ον,** containing wine. **ταπεινός, -ή, -όν,** low, close to the ground, humble. **πρεσβύτερος, -α, -ον,** older; comparative of πρέσβυς, old. **κιττός, -οῦ, ὁ,** ivy.

2. ἐπὶ τῇ νυκτὶ τὸ φῶς οὐχ ὁρῶμεν. οἴκαδε ἀναχωρήσαντες, ἀφικόμενοι, χαίρομεν. ἐν γὰρ τῇ οἰκίᾳ, μετὰ τὰ τείχη, φῶς ποιούμεθα. ἐκεῖ τροφὴν ποτὸν τε ἔχομεν. τὰ παιδία ἐν σπαργάνοις εἰσὶ ὥσπερ μικρὰ κλήματα ἐπὶ τὸ δένδρον ὅ ἐστι τὸ γένος. λέγομεν μετ' ἀλλήλοις καὶ ἀμελοῦμεν τὴν νύκτα.

3. ἄκουε λόγον παλαιόν. ἦν ποτε κόρη καλὴ ᾗ ἤτην δύο ἀδελφὰ κακά. τὼ ἀδελφὰ τὴν κόρην ἐκελεύετον πάντα τὰ ἔργα πράττειν· τὴν οἰκίαν ἐκκαθαίρειν, τὴν τροφὴν παρασκευάζειν, τὰ πρόβατα τρέφειν. ἡ κόρη, Τεφρανίσκη ὀνόματι, τὰ χρήματα ἐποίει ἑκοῦσα. νυκτί τινι, ἑορτῆς οὔσας ἐν τῇ κώμῃ, τὼ ἀδελφὰ ἦλθετον. ἡ δὲ Τεφρανίσκη ἠθέλησε πρὸς τὴν ἑορτὴν ἐλθεῖν, ἀλλ' οὐδ' ἔσχε ἄμαξαν οὐδὲ καλὸν ἱμάτιον. "εἴθε πρὸς τὴν ἑορτὴν ἔλθοιμι," ἑαυτῇ εἶπε. ἡ θεὰ Ἀθηνᾶ αὐτὴν ἀκούσασα ἄμαξαν καὶ ἱμάτιον εὐθὺς ἐποίησε. "ἀγαθὴ εἶ καὶ εὐγενής, ὦ Τεφρανίσκη," εἶπε ἡ θεά. "σοὶ οὖν δίδωμι ταύτην τὴν ἄμαξαν καὶ τοῦτο τὸ ἱμάτιον. ἀπελθὲ πρὸς τὴν ἑορτήν. ἀλλὰ ἐπεὶ τὸ τῆς νυκτὸς τέλος ἀφικνεῖται, ἐλθὲ εὐθὺς οἴκαδε." ἡ Τεφρανίσκη ἔχαιρε καὶ τῇ ἀμάξᾳ πρὸς τὴν ἑορτὴν ἤλασε. ἐκεῖ εἶδε κόρον τινὰ καλὸν καὶ ἀγαθόν. εὐθὺς ἐφιλείτον ἀλλήλω. τοῦ δὲ τῆς νυκτὸς τέλους ἀφικομένου ἡ Τεφρανίσκη ἀπῆλθε. ὁ κόρος εἶπε ἑαυτὸν τὴν κόρην εὑρήσειν. ἆρα τοῦτο ἔπραξε; τί νομίζεις; ἡ Ἀθηνᾶ αὐτῷ ὠφέλειαν ἔδωκε. ἐν τῷ τοῦ λόγου τέλει τί γίγνεται; πάντες ἀγαθὸν βίον ἀεὶ ἔχουσιν.

ἑορτή, -ῆς, ἡ, festival.

This story may be familiar: the name Τεφρανίσκη is from τέφρα, -ας, ἡ, ash, cinder.

4. κράτος μὲν ἔχει ὁ στρατηγός, φιλοσοφίαν δὲ ὁ διδάσκαλος. ἐκεῖνος τῷ σώματι, οὗτος τῷ νῷ διαφέρει. ὁ μὲν ὅπλοις μάχεται, ὁ δὲ βιβλία λέγει καὶ γράφει. ἀμφοτέρω τὸ κλέος λαβεῖν ἐθέλετον. ὁ μὲν στρατηγὸς λέγει τοὺς θεοὺς ἀληθὲς κλέος διδόναι τοῖς ἀνδρείοις. ὁ δὲ ἀποκρίνεται τοὺς σοφοὺς ἑαυτοῖς κλέος ποιεῖν τῷ γράφειν. ὁ διδάσκαλος ἄνευ κράτους καὶ ὁ στρατηγὸς ἄνευ φιλοσοφίας ἀλλήλους τιμῶσιν, ἀλλὰ ἕκαστος χαίρει ὅτι οὔκ ἐστι ὅμοιος τῷ ἄλλῳ.

5. γνήσιός εἰμι φίλος καὶ τὸν φίλον ὡς φίλον οἶδα,
      τοὺς δὲ κακοὺς διόλου πάντας ἀποστρέφομαι.
   οὐδένα θωπεύω πρὸς ὑπόκρισιν· οὓς δ᾽ ἄρα τιμῶ,
      τούτους ἐξ ἀρχῆς μέχρι τέλους ἀγαπῶ.

   Phocylides, from the Greek Anthology 10.117.

   γνήσιος, -α, -ον, genuine, legitimate. οἶδα, know, 1st sg; see chapter 16. διόλου, altogether, entirely. θωπεύω, flatter. ἀγαπάω = φιλέω.

6. μήτηρ γάρ τέ μέ φησι θεὰ Θέτις ἀργυρόπεζα
   διχθαδίας κῆρας φερέμεν θανάτοιο τέλος δέ.
   εἰ μέν κ᾽ αὖθι μένων Τρώων πόλιν ἀμφιμάχωμαι,
   ὤλετο μέν μοι νόστος, ἀτὰρ κλέος ἄφθιτον ἔσται·
   εἰ δέ κεν οἴκαδ᾽ ἵκωμι φίλην ἐς πατρίδα γαῖαν,
   ὤλετό μοι κλέος ἐσθλόν, ἐπὶ δηρὸν δέ μοι αἰὼν
   ἔσσεται, οὐδέ κέ μ᾽ ὦκα τέλος θανάτοιο κιχείη.

   Iliad 9.410-416. Achilles is speaking to Odysseus, Ajax, and Phoenix, who are trying to convince him to return to battle.

   Prose paraphrase: ἡ γὰρ Θέτις ἀργυρόπεζα, μήτηρ οὖσα, ἐμέ φησι δύο θανάτω φέρειν. ἐὰν μὲν ἐνθάδε μένω καὶ τὴν πόλιν ἀμφιμάχωμαι, οἴκαδε οὔποτε ἀφίξομαι, ἀλλὰ κλέος ἀεὶ ἕξω. ἐὰν δὲ ἀφίκωμι οἴκαδε εἰς τὴν φίλην πατρίδα γῆν, κλέος οὐχ ἕξω, ἀλλὰ μακρὸς ἔσεται ὁ βίος, καὶ τὸ τέλος θανάτου οὐ ταχὺ ἐμὲ εὑρήσει.

   ἀργυρόπεζος, -α, -ον, having silver feet. διχθάδιος, -α, -ον, double, two-fold. κήρ, κηρός, ἡ, fate. φερέμεν = φέρειν, an epic dialect form. θανάτοιο = θανάτου, an earlier form of the genitive ending. κε = ἄν, an epic dialect equivalent for the particle, so εἰ κε = ἐάν. The particle has the sandhi form κέν before a vowel. αὖθι, here. μένω, μενῶ, ἔμεινα, μεμένηκα, – , – , stay, remain. ἀμφι-μάχομαι τὴν πόλιν = μάχομαι ἀμφὶ τὴν πόλιν. ὄλλυμι, ὀλῶ, ὤλεσα, ὀλώλεκα, – , –, destroy, lose; in middle, perish, die. The form ὤλετο comes from the alternate second aorist middle ὠλόμην, used here with gnomic sense (present, for a permanent fact; see chapter 14) rather than as a past tense. νόστος, -ου, ὁ, home-coming. ἀτάρ = ἀλλά. ἄφθιτος, -ον, indestructible, imperishable. ἔσται, ἔσσεται = ἔσεται, epic dialect forms. γαῖαν = γῆν. δηρός, -ά, -όν = μακρός. αἰών, -ῶνος, ὁ, lifetime, period of time. ὦκα, quickly. κιχάνω, find, meet up with.

7a. ὦ παῖ, γένοιο πατρὸς εὐτυχέστερος,
τὰ δ᾽ ἄλλ᾽ ὅμοιος· καὶ γένοι᾽ ἂν οὐ κακός.

> Sophocles, *Ajax* 550-551, Ajax speaking. This scene between Ajax and his wife and son imitates or responds to the scene in *Iliad* 6 between Hector and his family; the lines relevant to these lines follow. **εὐτυχής, -ες** = ὃς ἀγαθὴν τύχην ἔχει.

b. Ζεῦ ἄλλοι τε θεοὶ δότε δὴ καὶ τόνδε γενέσθαι
παῖδ᾽ ἐμὸν ὡς καὶ ἐγώ περ ἀριπρεπέα Τρώεσσιν,
ὧδε βίην τ᾽ ἀγαθόν, καὶ Ἰλίου ἶφι ἀνάσσειν·
καί ποτέ τις εἴποι πατρός γ᾽ ὅδε πολλὸν ἀμείνων
ἐκ πολέμου ἀνιόντα· φέροι δ᾽ ἔναρα βροτόεντα
κτείνας δήϊον ἄνδρα, χαρείη δὲ φρένα μήτηρ.

> *Iliad* 6.476-482, Hector speaking.
>
> **δότε** is 2nd pl, aorist imperative active, from δίδωμι (see chapter 16). **τόνδε** modifies παῖδα ἐμόν in the next line. **ἐμός, -ή, -όν**, my. **ἀριπρεπής, -ές**, splendid, pre-eminent. **βίην** = βίαν, from βία, -ᾱς, ἡ, strength, force; this form is from the Ionic dialect, where the sound-shift of ᾱ to η occurs everywhere, even after ε, ι, ρ. **ἶφι**, strongly, powerfully. **ἀνάσσω**, rule, be king. **ἀμείνων, -ον**, better, stronger. **ἄν-ειμι**, return, from εἶμι (chapter 15), not εἰμί; ἀνιών is pres. ppl. active. **ἔναρα, -ων, τά** = ὅπλα. **βροτόεις, -εσσα, -εν**, bloody, gory. **κτείνω** = ἀποκτείνω. **δάϊος, -α, -ον**, hostile, enemy; note another Ionic form. **ἀνήρ, ἀνέρος, ὁ**, man (chapter 15). **χαρείη** is 3rd sg aorist optative passive from χαίρω (chapter 13). **φρήν, φρενός, ἡ**, mind, heart.

8. *περὶ τοῦ Τρωικοῦ πολέμου, πέμπτον μέρος*

τέλος δὲ οἱ Ἕλληνες ἀφίκοντο παρὰ τῷ Ἰλίῳ. ἔπεμψαν τὸν Ὀδυσσέα καὶ τὸν Μενέλαον ὡς ἀπαιτήσοντε τὴν Ἑλένην. οἱ δὲ Τρῶες οὐ μόνον τὴν Ἑλένην οὐκ ἀποδιδόναι ἀλλὰ καὶ τούτω ἀποκτείνειν ἤθελον. τοῖν δὲ ἀγγέλοιν φυγόντοιν, οἱ Ἕλληνες ἀναλαβόντες τὰ ὅπλα ἔπλεον ἐπὶ τοῖς Τρωσί.

οἱ δὲ, πυθόμενοι τὸν στρατὸν ἐπιπλεῖν, σὺν ὅπλοις ἐπὶ τὴν θάλατταν ὥρμησαν καὶ βάλλοντες πέτραις ἀποβῆναι ἐκώλυον. ἦν ἡ ἀρχὴ τοῦ πράγματος.

ὁ πρῶτος τῶν Ἑλλήνων ἀπέβη ἀπὸ τῆς τριήρους Πρωτεσίλαος. εὖ μὲν ἐμάχετο, τέλος δὲ ὁ Ἕκτωρ αὐτὸν ἀπέκτεινε. ὁ Πρωτεσίλαος πρῶτος οὖν ἀπέθανε παρὰ τοῖς τοῦ Ἰλίου τείχεσι.

Λαοδάμεια, γυνὴ οὖσα τοῦ Πρωτεσιλάου, καὶ μετὰ θάνατον αὐτὸν ἐφίλει. εἴδωλον τοῦ ἀνθρώπου ἐποίησε ὃν ἐφίλει ὥσπερ τὸν ἀληθῆ Πρωτεσίλαον. οἱ δὲ θεοὶ ταῦτα ἰδόντες τὴν γυναῖκα ἠλέησαν. μεγάλη γὰρ ἐγένετο ἡ τῆς Λαοδαμείας λύπη. ταύτῃ δὲ τῇ νυκτὶ ὁ Ἑρμῆς κατῆλθε εἰς Ἅιδου, τὸν Πρωτεσίλαον λαβών, καὶ πρὸς τὴν Λαοδάμειαν ἀφίκετο. ἡ δὲ ἰδοῦσα ἐνόμισε αὐτὸν ἔτι βιοῦντα, καὶ πολὺ ἔχαιρε. ὁ Πρωτεσίλαος καὶ ἡ Λαοδάμεια εἰς ἀλλήλω ἐβλεπέτην. τέλος δὲ ὁ Πρωτεσίλαος εἶπε, "χαῖρε, ὦ Λαοδάμεια. οὐκέτι μὲν βιῶ· ἀπέθανον δὲ ἐπὶ τῷ Ἰλίῳ. ὕστατον μέντοι καὶ σὲ καὶ τὸ τοῦ ἡλίου φῶς ἰδών, νῦν ἀπέρχομαι. ἀεὶ σὲ ἐφίλησα." ταῦτα εἰπὼν πρὸς Ἅιδου ἀπῆλθε. ἡ δὲ Λαοδάμεια, πολὺ λυποῦσα, αὐτὴ ἀπέθανε.

ἀπ-αιτέω, ask for. ἀνα-λαμβάνω, take up, retrieve. πυνθάνομαι, πεύσομαι, ἐπυθόμην, – , πέπυσμαι, – , learn. ὁρμάω, ὁρμήσω, ὥρμησα, ὥρμηκα, ὥρμημαι, ὡρμήθην, hurry. ἀπο-βαίνω, come down from, disembark; ἀποβῆναι is aorist infinitive active and ἀπέβη is 3rd sg aorist indicative active (see chapter 13). κωλύω, prevent, hinder. γυνή, γυναικός, ἡ, woman, wife. εἴδωλον, -ου, τό, image, effigy. ἐλεέω, ἐλεήσω, ἠλέησα, – , – , – , pity, have pity for. Ἅιδης is god of the underworld, which can be called Ἅιδου, "Hades's (place)." Note that iota is not written subscript under a capital letter. βιόω, be alive, live. ὕστατον, for the last time.

XI.8 Conversation

Questions about the readings and the new vocabulary as usual, for example:

1. (reading 1) πότε ἐποίησαν τοῦτο τὸ ἔργον; πότε τοῦτο τὸ ἔργον ἐποιήθη; ποῦ ἐποιήθη; τίνας πλέκονται; τίνων ἠμελησάτην ὁ Δάφνις καὶ ἡ Χλόη; and so on, using active, middle, and passive verbs.

2. (reading 3) ποιά ἔστον τὼ ἀδελφά; τί ποιεῖτον τὼ ἀδελφὰ τῇ Τεφρανίσκῃ; τί ἐθέλει ἡ Τεφρανίσκη; τίς αὐτῇ ἱμάτιον δίδωσι; and so on.

3. (vocabulary) τί ἐσθίουσι οἱ αἶγες; ἆρα οἱ αἶγες σταφυλὰς ἐσθίουσι; ἆρα λίθους; ἆρα ἄρτους; ποίαν τροφὴν ἐσθίουσι; καὶ τί ἐσθίει τὰ πρόβατα; καὶ τί ἐσθίουσι οἱ ἄνθρωποι; ἆρα οἱ ἄνθρωποι τὰ πρόβατα ἐσθίουσι; ἆρα τοὺς αἶγας; τίνι τροφῇ τὸ σῶμα τρέφεις; and so on.

XI.9 Writing

1. Do the change-number exercise with the following sentences.
   a. ἀποκρίνου τῷ διδασκάλῳ, ὦ μαθητά.
   b. ὁ στρατὸς μαχέσθω ὅταν ὁ στρατηγὸς κελεύῃ.
   c. ἀφίκεσθε εἰς τὴν πατρίδα, ὦ πολῖται.
   d. εἴθε τριήρη ἔχοιμεν ἵνα τὰ μικρὰ πλοῖα νικῶμεν.
   e. εἰ τὴν τροφὴν μὴ ἐπισκευάζῃ, οὐκ ἔδῃ.
   f. εἰ ὁ παῖς τοῦ διδασκάλου ἀκούοι, ἀγαθὸς ἂν γίγνοιτο.
   g. τὸν πόλεμον μάχοντο ἵνα ἐλεύθεροι γίγνωνται.
   h. εἰ γὰρ τὼ παῖδε οἴκαδε ἀφικνεῖσθον.
   i. ὅστις ἂν τὸ σῶμα εὖ τρέφῃ κράτος λαμβάνει.
   j. ἥδε ἡ τριήρης τρία ἔτη ἔπλευσε.
   k. αἱ μὲν ἀρχαὶ κακαί, τὰ δὲ τέλη ἦν ἀγαθά.
   l. τί ἔχοιτε ἂν μᾶλλον, τὰ χρῆμα ἢ τὸ κλέος;

2. Each of these sentences contains a clause to which the OOO rule may apply. Change the main verb of the sentence to an appropriate past tense, and apply the OOO rule to the subordinate clause. For example, from λέγω ὅτι γράφεις make εἶπον ὅτι γράφοις.

    a. ὁ μαθητὴς ἀποκρίνεται ὅτι τὸ φῶς οὐκ ὁρᾷ.

    b. αἱ κόραι τὰ σπάργανα παρασκευάζουσι ἵνα ἀστεῖα γίγνηται τοῖς παιδίοις.

    c. ὅταν αἱ σταφυλαὶ ἀκμάζωσι, αὐτὰς ἀπὸ τῶν δένδρα ἀποφέρομεν.

    d. ἐὰν ὁ στρατὸς νικήσας οἴκαδε ἀφίκηται, ὁ λεὼς χαιρήσει.

    e. ὁ δεσπότης ἐρωτᾷ ὅστις τὴν τροφὴν ἐπισκευάζει.

    f. ὁ παῖς ἐρωτᾷ ὁπότε ἀφίξονται οἱ φίλοι.

    g. ὁ στρατηγὸς ἐρωτᾷ εἰ οἱ στρατιῶται κλέος λήψονται.

    h. ὁ μαθητὴς ἐρωτᾷ εἰ τοῦτο τὸ βιβλίον ἑαυτῷ συνικνεῖται.

    i. ὁ διδάσκαλος ἀποκρίνεται ὅτι τὸ βιβλίον κλεινὸν γίγνεται.

    j. οἱ αἶγες ἐκ τοῦ ἀγροῦ τρέχουσι ἵνα τὰ τῶν ἀμπέλων κλήματα ἐσθίωσι.

3. Rewrite the following sentences, turning the participial phrases into subordinate clauses. You may use whatever kind of clause fits the sense. For example, from ὁ μαθητής, σοφὸς ὤν, εὖ μανθάνει make ὁ μαθητὴς εὖ μανθάνει, ἐπεὶ σοφός ἐστι.

    a. τριήρη ποιοῦμεν τὰ ἄλλα πλοῖα νικήσοντες.

    b. οἱ ἀνδρεῖοι μάχοντο ὡς τὴν πατρίδα ἐλευθέραν πράξοντες.

    c. τῶν φίλων ἀφικομένων, οἱ παῖδες σκόλια ἀκούσονται.

    d. οὗτος, εὐγενὴς ὤν, κλέος ἕξει καὶ μετὰ τὸν θάνατον.

    e. ἀμελήσαντες τῶν προβάτων, οἱ ἄνθρωποι ὠφέλειαν ἀλλήλοις μεταδιδόασιν.

    f. τῶν προβάτων φευγόντων, ὁ γεωργὸς τεῖχος ἔπραξε.

4. Rewrite the following sentences, turning the purpose clauses into phrases with future participles. For example, from βιβλίον ἐπώλησε ἵνα τρεῖς ὀβολοὺς ἔχει make βιβλίον ἐπώλησε τρεῖς ὀβολοὺς ἕξων.

    a. ἡ Χλόη τὴν τροφὴν ἐπισκευάζεται ἵνα ἐσθίῃ.

    b. ὁ δοῦλος εἰς τὴν ἀγορὰν ἀφίκετο ὅπως οἶνον ἀγοράζῃ.

    c. ἐκεῖνος ὁ αἲξ πρὸς τὴν ἄμπελον ἔδραμε ἵνα τὰς σταφυλὰς ἐσθίῃ.

    d. ὁ ἰατρὸς τῷ παιδὶ φάρμακα δίδωσι ὅπως αὐτὸν θεραπεύῃ.

    e. ὁ νεανίας δῶρον τῇ κόρῃ δίδωσι ἵνα τὴν φιλίαν δηλοῖ.

    f. αἱ κόραι ἔπλεκον ἵνα ἱμάτια ἔχοιντο.

5. Write a paragraph about the animals or plants on a farm.

CHAPTER XII

The Wrath of Achilles

XII.1 Future middle and passive

The future middle (like the future active) is formed from the second principal part exactly as the present middle is formed from the first. In other words, use the future stem (for example, λυσ- from λύω, or ποιησ- from ποιέω) and add the same endings as the present middle of the appropriate mood — indicative, optative, infinitive, or participle. Of course there is no future subjunctive or future imperative in any voice.

The future passive is formed from the sixth principal part, with an additional suffix -ησ- similar to the -σ- suffix that often forms the future active/middle stem. The sixth principal part is the first singular aorist indicative passive, as ἐλύθην from λύω; we will discuss the aorist passive in the next chapter. To form the future passive stem from the sixth principal part, remove the past indicative augment and the ending -ην, then add the suffix: λυθ-ησ-. Then the endings are exactly the same as for the future middle (and, thus, the same as for the present middle). Here are the future indicative middle and passive of λύω.

	Middle	Passive
singular		
1st	λύσ-ομαι	λυθήσ-ομαι
2nd	λύσ-ῃ, λύσ-ει	λυθήσ-ῃ, -ει
3rd	λύσ-εται	λυθήσ-εται
dual		
2nd	λύσ-εσθον	λυθήσ-εσθον
3rd	λύσ-εσθον	λυθήσ-εσθον
plural		
1st	λῡσ-όμεθα	λυθησ-όμεθα
2nd	λύσ-εσθε	λυθήσ-εσθε
3rd	λύσ-ονται	λυθήσ-ονται

The other moods are formed just the same way:

Optative (1st sg.)	Infinitive	Participle
λῡσοίμην	λύσεσθαι	λῡσόμενος
λυθησοίμην	λυθήσεσθαι	λυθησόμενος

The other persons and numbers of the future optative, both middle and passive, have the same endings as the present optative middle/passive.

Several verbs have future middle forms but not future active; you will recognize them because their second principal part ends in -ομαι instead of -ω. If the second principal part ends in -οῦμαι, the future middle is contracted, as ἀποθανοῦμαι; in this case the forms are as for the middle of an e-contract present. Just as for active futures, all contracted middle futures are e-contracts (so formed like the present system of ποιέω).

Exercise

Write out the future indicative middle and passive of πράττω, ἀκούω, and the future indicative middle of πυνθάνομαι, γίγνομαι, θύω. Write out the future infinitive middle, future infinitive passive, and the three nominative singular forms of the future participle middle and future participle passive for ἔχω, μανθάνω, γράφω, ποιέω, φέρω, ἄγω, δίδωμι.

XII.2 Use of the future optative

The future optative is rare. It is used when the OOO rule is applied to an indirect statement. For example, ὁ διδάσκαλος λέγει ὅτι ὁ μαθητὴς ἐπιστολὴν γράψει. If we look back on this the next day, we may say ὁ διδάσκαλος εἶπε ὅτι ὁ μαθητὴς ἐπιστολὴν γράψει, with the indicative, or, applying the OOO rule, ὁ διδάσκαλος εἶπε ὅτι ὁ μαθητὴς ἐπιστολὴν γράψοι. This is just about the only construction where a future optative makes sense; occasionally, it will turn up in another subordinate clause, through the OOO rule. The future optative essentially never appears in a main clause.

XII.3 Third declension nouns in ι and υ

A small but important group of nouns in the third declension has a stem ending in ι or υ. While the third declension is generally the declension of consonant stems, these vowels are sometimes much like consonants; they can be called **semi-vowels**. Compare English "y" (the consonant version of "i") and "w" (the consonant version of "u"). If you know Latin, you will also recognize that "i" and "u" can be consonants in that language (and, when they are, they might be written as "j" and "v"); similar things happen in Sanskrit as well.

These nouns, of course, have the same endings as all third declension nouns, but, as usual, there are complications arising from internal sandhi. Most obviously, the accusative singular for masculine and feminine nouns of this group ends in -ν instead of -α like the consonant stems. This is actually the original ending for all the third declension nouns, but when -ν follows a consonant, it ends up pronounced as "a." You've already seen other examples of this sound change: consider ἕπτα, which is cognate with Latin *septem* and English *seven*. The inherited Indo-European form is roughly *sept-m*. Similarly, the negative prefix α-, as in ἀθάνατος "immortal, undying," is originally *n-*, which becomes αν- before a vowel and α- before a consonant in Greek, *un-* in Germanic, and *in-* in Latin. Sanskrit shares this sound shift with Greek: it has *sapta* and *a-, an-* for the number and the negative prefix respectively.

The more complicated sandhi change in the ι-stem nouns and one group of υ-stem nouns is **quantitative metathesis**, just as we saw in nouns like νεώς in the "Attic declension" (chapter 7). In these nouns, too, just as in the Attic declension, the position of the accent is fixed before the long and short quantities change places, with the result that some forms have accent on the third-to-last syllable even though the final syllable contains a long vowel.

Here are three paradigmatic nouns: πόλις, πόλεως, ἡ, "city"; πῆχυς, πήχεως, ὁ, "forearm, cubit"; ἰχθύς, ἰχθύος, ὁ, "fish" (which does not have quantitative metathesis).

singular

nom.	πόλις	πῆχυς	ἰχθύς
gen.	πόλεως	πήχεως	ἰχθύος
dat.	πόλει	πήχει	ἰχθύι
voc.	πόλιν	πῆχυν	ἰχθύν
acc.	πόλι	πῆχυ	ἰχθύ

dual

nom., acc., voc.	πόλει	πήχει	ἰχθύε
gen., dat.	πολέοιν	πηχέοιν	ἰχθύοιν

plural

nom., voc.	πόλεις	πήχεις	ἰχθύες
gen.	πόλεων	πήχεων	ἰχθύων
dat.	πόλεσι(ν)	πήχεσι(ν)	ἰχθύσι(ν)
acc.	πόλεις	πήχεις	ἰχθύας, ἰχθῦς

ἰχθύς is the commoner type of υ-stem, *without* quantitative metathesis. Note that this word has long ῡ in its two-syllable forms (ἰχθῡ́ς, ἰχθῡ́ν, ἰχθῡ́, ἰχθῦς) and short ῠ in all the others.

There are neuter nouns of this class as well: ἄστυ, ἄστεως, τό "city" is like πῆχυς, with nominative/accusative plural ἄστη; and δάκρυ, δάκρυος, τό "tear, teardrop" is like ἰχθύς, with nominative/accusative plural δάκρυα.

Exercise

Write out the complete declension of the phrases ὁ ἄξιος μάντις, τὸ ἐλεύθερον ἄστυ.

XII.4 Time and space

A particular point in time is expressed with the dative (**of time**): ταύτῃ τῇ ἡμέρᾳ ἦλθε "he came on that day." A point in space can also be expressed with the dative, though this is poetic; in prose, the dative **of place** normally isn't used alone but with a suitable preposition. Thus ἱμάτιον ὤμοις ἔχει is a poetic equivalent for what would in plain prose be ἱμάτιον ἐπὶ τοῖς ὤμοις ἔχει.

Extent of time or **extent of space** is expressed with the accusative: ἔλεγε πέντε ὥρας "he spoke for five hours" (time); ἤλαυνε ἕκατον στάδια "he marched for 100 stades" (space). No preposition is required.

An action or circumstance that starts in the past and extends into the present is expressed with the present tense, for example δέκα ἔτη νοσῶ "I have been ill for ten years." Note that English uses the perfect here, but Greek does not. The Greek construction is similar to the Latin: *decem annos laboro* (not *laboravi*).

XII.5 Vocabulary

VERBS

ἀγγέλλω, ἀγγελῶ, ἤγγειλα, ἤγγελκα, ἤγγελμαι, ἠγγέλθην, announce, report, send a messenger

αἰτέω, αἰτήσω, ᾔτησα, ᾔτηκα, – , – , ask, request

ἀν-έρομαι, ask

δια-φθείρω, destroy

δράω, δράσω, ἔδρᾱσα, δέδρᾱκα, δέδρᾱμαι, ἐδράσθη, do (cp. *drama*)

ἕπομαι, ἕψομαι, ἑσπόμην, – , – , – , follow (cp. L. *sequor*)

ἔρομαι, ἐρήσομαι, ἠρόμην, – , – , – , ask (a question)

κατ-έχω, restrain, hold down

ξενίζω, ξενιῶ, ἐξένισα, ἐξένικα, – , – , receive as a guest, entertain

οἴομαι, οἰήσομαι, – , – , – , ᾠήθην, think, suppose

πυνθάνομαι, πεύσομαι, ἐπυθόμην, – , πέπυσμαι, – , ask, learn, inquire, ascertain

συγ-γίγνομαι, associate with, be with (+ dative)

σῴζω, σώσω, ἔσωσα, σέσωκα, σέσωμαι, ἐσώθην, save, rescue, keep safe

ταράττω, ταράξω, ἐτάραξα, τέτρηχα, τετάραγμαι, ἐταράχθην, confuse, disturb

τελευτάω, τελευτήσω, ἐτελεύτησα, τετελεύτηκα, τετελεύτημαι, ἐτελευτήθην, end, complete, often specifically end one's life, die

φθείρω, φθερῶ ἔφθειρα, ἔφθορα, ἔφθαρμαι, ἐφθάρην, destroy

NOUNS

ἀβουλίᾱ, -ας, ἡ, foolishness

ἄστυ, ἄστεως, τό, town, city

γέρας, -ως, τό, reward, prize

δάκρυ, δάκρυος, τό, tear, teardrop (cp. L. *lacrima*)

δημοκρατίᾱ, -ας, ἡ, democracy

δῆμος, -ου, ὁ, deme, a district or administrative area in Athens; the people, the populace

θεωρίᾱ, -ᾱς, ἡ, spectacle; act of viewing

ἰχθύς, ἰχθύος, ὁ, fish (cp. *icthyology*)

κύκλος, -ου, ὁ, circle (cp. *cycle, wheel*)

μάντις, -εως, ὁ, prophet, seer.

ξένος, -ου, ὁ, stranger, guest (cp. *xenophobia*)

ὄνομα, ὀνόματος, τό, name (cp. L. *nomen*)

πῆχυς, πήχεως, ὁ, forearm, cubit

πόλις, -εως, ἡ, city (cp. *politics*)

σκηνή, -ῆς, ἡ, stage; tent (cp. *scene*)

στάδιον, -ου, τό, stade, unit of measure roughly 200 meters (cp. *stadium*)

υἱός, -οῦ, ὁ, son

φόρος, -ου, ὁ, tribute, tax

χωρίον, -ου, τό, place, farm

ὥρα, -ας, ἡ, hour, time

ADJECTIVES

ἅπᾱς, ἅπᾱσα, ἅπαν, all, stronger form of πᾶς

ἕτερος, -α, -ο, one or other of two (cp. *heterodox*)

παντοδαπός, -ή, -όν, from all sources, of all kinds

συν-άπᾱς, all together, σύν + ἅπας

ADVERBS

αὐτίκα, at once, for example

εἶέν, well then, so be it

ἕνεκα, because of, for the sake of (postposition + gen.)

ἐνταῦθα, here

σχεδόν, almost

τάχα, quickly; with ἄν, perhaps

Notes on the vocabulary

The compounds ἀνέρομαι and διαφθείρω mean the same as the simple verbs they are compounded from. As usual, the compound verb διαφθείρω is more common than the simple φθείρω, particularly in prose.

The imperfect of οἴομαι is ᾤμην. In Attic prose a contracted present οἶμαι can be used as a parenthetical remark, especially in the first person, just as we might qualify a statement in English with "I think."

Recall that the final consonant of σύν undergoes assimilation when σύν is a prefix; thus συγγίγνομαι (guttural nasal to match γ-, aorist συνεγενόμην (original dental nasal retained before vowel).

γέρας has stem γερασ- and is declined like γένος, with loss of -σ- and contraction. Because the stem vowel is α rather than ε, the resulting contracted vowels are different: genitive γέρως, not -ους, and so on.

A σκηνή is any sort of temporary structure, like a tent, shed, or hut. The word comes to mean "stage" because the original backdrop for performance in the theater at Athens looked like a shed.

The noun υἱός is usually a regular o-stem noun, but can also have third-declension u-stem forms, from υἱεύς.

The interjection εἶέν is one of very few words in Greek with a rough breathing or *h*-sound *inside* the word; another is ὁ ταῶς, peacock.

ἕνεκα is just like a preposition, except it comes after the word it governs rather than before, for example δίκης ἕνεκα, "for justice."

XII.6 Reading

1. ἐγὼ δ' ὄνομα τὸ μὲν καθ' ἑκάστην αὐτίκα
   λέξω, συνάπασαι δ' εἰσὶ παντοδαπαὶ πόλεις,
   αἳ νῦν ἀνοηταίνουσι πολὺν ἤδη χρόνον.
   τάχ' ἄν τις ὑποκρούσειεν ὅτι ποτ' ἐνθάδε
   νῦν εἰσι κἀνέροιτο· παρ' ἐμοῦ πεύσεται.   5
   τὸ χωρίον μὲν γὰρ τόδ' ἐστὶ πᾶν κύκλῳ
   Ὀλυμπία, τηνδὶ δὲ τὴν σκηνὴν ἐκεῖ
   σκηνὴν ὁρᾶν θεωρικὴν νομίζετε.
   εἶέν. τί οὖν ἐνταῦθα δρῶσιν αἱ πόλεις;
   ἐλευθέρι' ἀφίκοντο θύσουσαί ποτε,   10
   ὅτε τῶν φόρων ἐγένοντ' ἐλεύθεραι σχεδόν.
   κἄπειτ' ἀπ' ἐκείνης ἡμέρας διέφθορεν
   αὐτὰς ξενίζουσ' ἡμέραν ἐξ ἡμέρας
   Ἀβουλία κατέχουσα πολὺν ἤδη χρόνον.
   γυναῖκε δ' αὐτὰς δύο ταράττετόν τινε   15
   ἀεὶ συνοῦσαι· Δημοκρατία θατέρᾳ
   ὄνομ' ἐστίν, ἀλλ' Ἀριστοκρατία θατέρᾳ.

> This extensive fragment is quoted in an anthology; it is from a play by Heniochus whose title the anthologist does not give.
>
> In line 1, τὸ καθ' ἑκάστην is adverbial, "one by one," the same as if there were no article; note the contrast, τὸ μὲν καθ' ἑκάστην ... συνάπασαι δέ.
>
> Line 2, ἀνοηταίνω, be senseless, foolish; present system only.
>
> Line 4, ὑπο-κρούω, object, interrupt, break in.
>
> Line 7: τηνδί is τήνδε with the emphatic suffix -ί. This can be added to any form of a demonstrative, replacing the final -ε if there is one. The suffix always has the accent.

Line 8: θεωρικός, -ή, -όν, connected with a θεωρία

Line 10: ἐλευθέρια, -ων, τά, a sacrifice in thanksgiving for freedom; the accent tells you this is not the noun ἐλευθερίᾱ, freedom

Line 15: γυναῖκε is fem. nom. dual of the irregular noun γυνή, γυναικός, ἡ "woman"; see chapter 14.

Line 16: θατέρᾳ = τῇ ἑτέρᾳ by crasis. Any form of the article ending in a vowel may contract with ἕτερος, as ὁ ἕτερος = ἅτερος, ἡ ἑτέρα = ἁτέρα, τὸ ἕτερον = θάτερον. Of course if the article ends in a consonant no crasis is possible.

Line 17: ἀριστοκρατίᾱ, -ας, ἡ, aristocracy

2. ἄνθρωπός τις καὶ οἱ υἱοὶ πλέουσι ἐπὶ τῇ θαλάττῃ ἰχθύων ἕνεκα. τοῦτ᾽ ἐστί, πλέουσι ἵνα ἰχθύας λάβωσι. ἐὰν ἰχθύας λάβωσι, οἱ ἰχθύες τελευτῶσι. οἱ ἄνθρωποι οὐδένα δάκρυα ἴᾱσι, καίπερ τοὺς ἰχθύας φιλοῦντες. οἱ γὰρ ἰχθύες οὔκ εἰσι φίλοι ἀλλὰ τροφή. οἱ ἄνθρωποι ξενίζουσι οὐ τοὺς ἰχθύας ἀλλὰ τοῖς ἰχθύσιν.

3. μαθητής τις ἤθελε μαθεῖν. ἐπύθετο οὖν, "τί λέγεις, ὦ διδάσκαλε;" ὁ δὲ ἀπεκρίνατο, "ἆρ᾽ ἀνέρου ὁ τι λέγω; οὐκ ἀκούεις, οἶμαι. εἴ που μάντις εἶ, οἱ θεοί σε πάντα ἀγγελοῦσι. εἰ δὲ μή, ὥρα ἐστὶ ἐμοῦ ἀκούειν, ἵνα μάθῃς." ὁ δὲ μαθητής, παιδίον ὤν, μικρὸν δάκρυ ἐκ τοῦ ὀφθαλμοῦ ἐξεκάθαιρε. "νῦν ὁ διδάσκαλος οὐκ οἴεται ἐμὲ ἐργαστικὸν εἶναι. οἴεται δὲ ἐμὲ ἀργόν. εἰ ὁ διδάσκαλος ἄδικός ἐστι, τί ποιήσομαι; οὐδὲν μαθήσομαι. φθαρήσομαι καὶ τελευτήσω. ὦ τάλας ἐγώ." ταῦτα οἰόμενος, ὁ μαθητὴς οἴκαδε ἦλθε καὶ τούτῳ τῷ διδασκάλῳ οὐκέτι συνεγένετο. οἱ δὲ ἄλλοι μαθηταὶ οὐχ ἕσποντο. ἀεὶ τοῦ διδασκάλου ἀκούοντες, εὖ ἐμάνθανον, ἀλλὰ τὸν ἑταῖρον οὐκ ἔσωσαν.

4. ξένος τις πρὸς τὴν οἰκίαν ἦλθε. "χαῖρε, ὦ ξένε," εἶπε ὁ τῆς οἰκίας δεσπότης. "ὥρα ἐστὶ ἀριστᾶν. ἆρ᾽ ἐθέλεις ἐσθίειν;" ὁ δὲ ξένος ἀπεκρίνετο, "ναί, πεινῶ γάρ. δοκεῖτέ μοι πλουτεῖν· εὖ ἔχετέ με ξενίζειν." "οὐ μὰ τὸν Δία, οὐ πλουτοῦμεν," ἀπεκρίνετο ὁ δεσπότης, "ἀλλὰ ἅπαντες ἡγούμεθα τὸ ξενίζειν καλὸν καὶ ἀγαθόν. ξένος μὲν εἶ, φίλος δὲ ἔσει. ἐλθέ, ἕπου μοι εἰς τὴν οἰκίαν." ὁ δὲ ξένος καὶ οἱ ἄλλοι μίαν ὥραν ἤσθιον.

μετὰ δὲ ταῦτα εἶπε ὁ δεσπότης, "νῦν, ἐπεὶ ἐφάγομεν, σὲ ἔρομαι ὅστις εἶ. τί ἐστι τὸ ὄνομα; ποῖ καὶ πόθεν ἐνταῦθα ἀφίκου;" ὁ δὲ ξένος εἶπε, "εἶπες ὅτι φίλος ἐσοίμην. τοῦτο οὐκ ἂν λέγοις ἐπεὶ ἀκούσει ὅ τι ἐποίησα. εἰς τὴν πόλιν ἀφικόμην ἵνα τὴν θεωρίαν ὁρῶ. πολλοὶ ἄνθρωποι εἰς τὴν σκηνὴν ἔβλεπον. ἐγὼ μὲν εἰς τὸν κύκλον ἦλθον ἵνα καὶ ἐγὼ βλέποιμι. ἄλλος τις δὲ εἶπε, 'τί ἡμᾶς ταράττεις; οὐκ εἶ πολίτης ταύτης τῆς πόλεως, οἶμαι. ἀπελθέ.' ταῦτα κακῶς φέρων τῷ ἀνθρώπῳ προσέβαλλον. οἱ ἄλλοι οὔ με κατεῖχον, καὶ αὐτὸν διέφθειρα. τάχα ἀπὸ τῆς σκηνῆς ἔδραμον ἵνα ἐμαυτὸν σώζω. μετὰ δὲ πολλὰς ὥρας, ἐνταῦθα ἀφικόμην."

ὁ δεσπότης ἀπεκρίνετο, "ἆρα σύγε τὸν Πολύστρατον ἀπέκτεινες; τοῦτον τὸν ἄνθρωπον οὐκ ἐφίλουν. ἐπεὶ εἶπες ὅτι οὐ σέ φιλήσοιμι, ἥμαρτες. νῦν φίλτατός μοι εἶ ἀνθρώπων." ὁ ξένος καὶ ὁ δεσπότης οὖν φίλοι ἐγένοντο.

Recall (from chapter 4) that ὅ τι is neuter accusative singular of ὅστις. φίλτατος is superlative of φίλος.

5. νύκτα μέσην ἐποίησε τρέχων ποτὲ Μάρκος ὁπλίτης,
    ὥστ᾽ ἀποκλεισθῆναι πάντοθε τὸ στάδιον.
    οἱ γὰρ δημόσιοι κεῖσθαί τινα πάντες ἔδοξαν
    ὁπλίτην τιμῆς εἵνεκα τῶν λιθίνων.
    καὶ τί γάρ; εἰς ὥρας ἠνοίγετο· καὶ τότε Μάρκος
    ἦλθε προσελλείπων τῷ σταδίῳ στάδιον.

> *Greek Anthology* 11.85. The race in hoplite armor was a feature of the Panathenaia and other festivals. Here **στάδιον** is both the length of the race and the place where it is held. **μέσος, -η, -ον**, middle. **ὁπλίτης**, -ου, ὁ = στρατιώτης ὃς ὅπλα ἔχει. **ἀποκλεισθῆναι** is aorist infinitive passive of ἀποκλήω which means the same as κλήω. **δημόσιοι** εἰσι οἱ ἐν τῷ δήμῳ. **κεῖμαι**, lie, be put; an athematic verb with only middle forms. **εἵνεκα**, Ionic dialect form of ἕνεκα. **λίθινος, -η, -ον·** ἐάν τινα ποιῇς ἐκ λίθου, λίθινόν ἐστι. **ἀνοίγνυμι**, open; the form ἠνοίγετο is imperfect indicative middle, with irregular augment. **προσ-ελ-λείπω**, be still lacking, still need.

> Prose paraphrase: ὁ Μάρκος ἔδραμε ὡς ὁπλίτης. ὁ κριτὴς τὸ στάδιον ἀπέκλησε, νυκτὸς μέσης οὔσας, ἀλλὰ ὁ Μάρκος ἔτι ἔτρεχε. πάντες οἱ τοῦ δήμου πολῖται, αὐτὸν ὁρῶντες, ἐνόμισαν ὅτι ἦν ἄγαλμα ὁπλίτου λίθινον. ὁ γὰρ Μάρκος μετὰ τοὺς ἄλλους ὁπλίτας ἦν σταδίῳ.

6. ὁ Πεισίστρατος τοῦτον ἐμηχανᾶτο ἵνα τὴν τυραννίδα ἔχῃ. ἐν τῷ δήμῳ τῷ Παιανιεῖ ἦν γυνὴ ἧς ὄνομα ἦν Φύη, μέγεθος ἀπὸ τεττάρων πήχεων ἀπολείπουσα τρεῖς δακτύλους καὶ ἄλλως εὐειδής. ὁ Πεισίστρατος καὶ οἱ φίλοι ταύτην τὴν γυναῖκα σκευάσαντες πανοπλίᾳ, εἰς ἅρμα εἰσβιβάσαντες καὶ προδέξαντες σχῆμα οἷόν τι ἔμελλε εὐπρεπέστατον φανέεσθαι ἔχουσα, ἤλαυνον ἐς τὸ ἄστυ, προδρόμους κήρυκας προπέμψαντες, οἳ τοὺς τοῦ Πεισιστράτου λόγους ἠγόρευον ἀφικόμενοι εἰς τὸ ἄστυ, λέγοντες τοιάδε· "ὦ Ἀθηναῖοι, δέχεσθε ἀγαθῷ νόῳ Πεισίστρατον, ὃν αὐτὴ ἡ Ἀθηνᾶ τιμήσασα ἀνθρώπων μάλιστα κατάγει εἰς τὴν ἑαυτῆς ἀκρόπολιν." οἱ μὲν δὴ ταῦτα διαφοιτῶντες ἔλεγον, αὐτίκα δὲ εἴς τε τοὺς δήμους φάτις ἀφίκετο ὡς Ἀθηνᾶ Πεισίστρατον κατάγει, καὶ οἱ ἐν τῷ ἄστει πειθόμενοι τὴν γυναῖκα εἶναι αὐτὴν τὴν θεὸν προσεύχοντό τε τὴν ἄνθρωπον καὶ ἐδέχοντο Πεισίστρατον.

> Herodotus 1.60, slightly adapted. At the time of this incident Athens was not yet a democracy.

> **μηχανάομαι, μηχανήσομαι, ἐμηχανησάμην, – , μεμηχάνημαι, – ,** contrive, devise. **τυραννίς, τυραννίδος, ἡ**, rule, kingship. **γυνή, γυναικός, ἡ**, woman (see chapter 14). **μέγεθος, -ους, τό**, size, magnitude. **εὐειδής, εὐειδές** = καλός. **πανοπλία, -ας, ἡ**, full set of weapons and armor. **ἅρμα, -ατος, τό**, war chariot. **εἰσβιβάζω**, cause to go in, put in, send in. **προδείκνυμι**, show, point out beforehand; προδέξας is aorist participle active. **σχῆμα, -ατος, τό**, form, shape. **μέλλω, μελλήσω, ἐμέλλησα, – , – , –**, intend. **εὐπρεπής, -ες**, attractive, suitable. **πρόδρομος, -ον**, going on ahead, running in front. **κῆρυξ, κήρυκος, ὁ**, herald. **ἀγορεύω, ἀγορεύσω, ἠγόρευσα, ἠγόρευκα, ἠγόρευμαι, ἠγορεύθην**, proclaim, speak in public. **δέχομαι, δέξομαι, ἐδεξάμην, – , δέδεγμαι, ἐδέχθην**, receive. **φάτις, -εως, ἡ**, rumor. **κατ-άγω**, lead down, bring down. **δια-φοιτάω**, wander around.

7. μῆνιν ἄειδε θεὰ Πηληιάδεω Ἀχιλῆος
   οὐλομένην, ἣ μυρί' Ἀχαιοῖς ἄλγε' ἔθηκε,
   πολλὰς δ' ἰφθίμους ψυχὰς Ἄϊδι προΐαψεν
   ἡρώων, αὐτοὺς δὲ ἑλώρια τεῦχε κύνεσσιν
   οἰωνοῖσί τε πᾶσι, Διὸς δ' ἐτελείετο βουλή,
   ἐξ οὗ δὴ τὰ πρῶτα διαστήτην ἐρίσαντε
   Ἀτρεΐδης τε ἄναξ ἀνδρῶν καὶ δῖος Ἀχιλλεύς.

> *Iliad* 1.1-7, the beginning of the poem.
>
> **μῆνις, -εως, ἡ**, wrath, anger. **ἀείδω** = ᾄδω, sing. **Πηληιάδεω** = Πηληιάδου, genitive of Πηληιάδης = υἱὸς τοῦ Πηλέως. Note the form **Ἀχιλῆος**, dating from before quantitative metathesis. **οὐλόμενος, -η, -ον**, destructive; this is a variant of the aorist participle middle of ὄλλυμι. **ἄλγος, -ους, τό**, pain, trouble. **ἴφθιμος, -η, -ον**, strong. **προ-ιάπτω**, throw; the diaeresis tells you that οι is not a diphthong in this verb. **ἑλώριον, -ου, τό**, prey, spoils. **οἰωνός, -οῦ, ὁ**, bird, especially a bird of prey. **τελέω** = τελευτάω. **βουλή, -ῆς, ἡ**, will, desire. **διαστήτην** is διεστήτην without its augment (often omitted in epic). **ἐρίζω, ἐρίσω, ἤρισα, –, –, –**, quarrel. **ἄναξ, ἄνακτος, ὁ**, lord, king. **ἀνήρ, ἀνδρός, ὁ**, man (chapter 15). **δῖος, -α, -ον,** brilliant.
>
> Prose paraphrase: ᾆδε, ὦ θεά, τὴν οὐλομένην μῆνιν τοῦ Ἀχιλλέως τοῦ Πηλέως, ἣ μυρία ἄλγεα τοῖς Ἀχαιοῖς ἔθηκε. ψυχὰς μὲν πολλὰς ἰφθίμους ἡρώων τῷ Ἅιδι προσέβαλε, τοὺς δὲ ἥρωας αὐτοὺς ἐποίει ἑλώρια τοῖς τε κυσὶ καὶ πᾶσι τοῖς ὄρνισι. ἡ δὲ Διὸς βουλὴ ἐτελεῖτο. ᾆδε δὴ ἐξ οὗ τὰ πρῶτα διεστήτην ἐρίσαντε ὁ μὲν Ἀγαμέμνων Ἀτρεΐδης ἄναξ ἀνθρώπων καὶ ὁ δῖος Ἀχιλλεύς.

8. *περὶ τοῦ Τρωικοῦ πολέμου, ἕκτον μέρος*

ἐννέα ἔτη ἐμάχοντο. οἱ Ἕλληνες πολλὰ μικρὰ ἄστεα ἐνίκησαν, ἐν οἷς ἡ Θήβη παρὰ τῷ Ἰλίῳ. οἱ Ἕλληνες τοὺς τῆς Θήβης πολίτας ἔλαβον καὶ τοὺς αἰχμαλώτους πάλιν πρὸς τὸν στρατόπεδον ἤγαγον.

δύο τῶν αἰχμαλώτων ἦτον ἡ μὲν Χρυσηὶς ἡ δὲ Βρισηίς. ὁ τῆς Χρυσηίδος πατήρ, μάντις ὢν τοῦ Ἀπόλλωνος, τὸν θεὸν ᾔτησε τοὺς Ἕλληνας διαφθείρειν. τοῦ Ἀπόλλωνος νόσον πέμψαντος, πολλῶν στρατιωτῶν θανόντων, ὁ Ἀγαμέμνων τῷ μάντι τὸ τέκνον, τὴν Χρυσηίδα, ἀπέδοσαν.

ἀλλὰ ἡ Χρυσηὶς ἦν τὸ τοῦ Ἀγαμέμνονος αὐτοῦ γέρας. ὁ δὲ εἶπε, "ἐπεὶ τὸ γέρας ἀπέδωκα, νῦν λήψομαι τὸ τοῦ ἄλλου τινὸς γέρας. σύ, ὦ Ἀχιλλεύς, δός μοι τὸ σὸν γέρας, τὴν κόρην Βρισηίδα."

"οὐχί," ἀπεκρίνατο ὁ Ἀχιλλεύς. "ἡ μὲν Χρυσηὶς ἦν τὸ σὸν γέρας, ἡ δὲ Βρισηὶς τὸ ἐμόν. οἱ μὲν ἄλλοι στρατιῶται ἐμὲ τούτῳ τῷ γέραι ἐτίμησαν. σὺ δὲ ἄδικος γίγνει καὶ ἐμὲ οὐ τιμᾷς. ὅτε τὸν Ἴλιον νικήσομεν, πολλὰ γέρη λήψει, ὁπόσα ἄν ἐθέλοις. τὴν δὲ Βρισηίδα ἐγὼ ἕξομαι."

ὁ δὲ Ἀγαμέμνων, σφόδρα ὀργιζόμενος, πάλιν ἐκέλευσε τὸν Ἀχιλλέα τὴν κόρην διδόναι. ὁ δὲ Ἀχιλεὺς εἶπε, "πῶς τίς τῶν Ἀχαιῶν τοῖς σοῖς λόγοις πείθεται; οὐκ ἐνθάδε ἦλθον γερῶν ἕνεκα οὐδὲ στρατιωτῶν Τρωικῶν ἕνεκα. σοί ἐστι οὗτος ὁ πόλεμος, καὶ τῷ ἀδελφῷ, οὐκ ἐμοί. τὴν κόρην ἣν παρά μου ἔλαβες ἐφίλουν, ὥσπερ σὺ καὶ ὁ ἀδελφὸς τὰς γυναῖκας. νῦν δὲ ἐπανέρχομαι πρὸς τὴν πατρίδα Φθίαν. οὐκέτι μαχοῦμαι."

καὶ εὐθὺς ἀνεχώρησε ὁ Ἀχιλλεὺς εἰς τὴν σκηνήν.

οἱ δὲ ἄλλοι ἔτι ἐμάχοντο. οἱ δὲ Τρῶες, τοῦ Ἀχιλλέως ἀπόντος, τοῖς Ἀχαιοῖς πολλάκις προσέβαλλον. ὁ Ἕκτωρ ἦν στρατηγὸς τῶν Τρώων καὶ υἱὸς τοῦ βασιλέως Πριάμου. "νῦν μαχώμεθα, ἵνα τοὺς Ἕλληνες ἐκ τοῦ Ἰλίου ἐκπέμπωμεν," εἶπε ὁ Ἕκτωρ.

ἡ Ἀνδρομάχη, γυνὴ οὖσα τοῦ Ἕκτορος, αὐτῷ ἀπεκρίνατο, "μὴ πρὸς τὸν πόλεμον πάλιν ἔλθῃς, ὦ φίλε. καίπερ τοῦ Ἀχιλλέως ἀπόντος, οἱ Ἕλληνες ἰσχυρότεροί εἰσι ἡμῶν."

ὁ δὲ ἀπεκρίνατο, "δεῖ ἐμὲ μάχεσθαι.

εὖ γὰρ ἐγὼ τόδε οἶδα κατὰ φρένα καὶ κατὰ θυμόν·
ἔσσεται ἦμαρ ὅτ᾽ ἄν ποτ᾽ ὀλώλῃ Ἴλιος ἱρὴ
καὶ Πρίαμος καὶ λαὸς ἐυμμελίω Πριάμοιο.

ἀποθανοῦμαι μέν, οὐ δὲ δειλὸς ἔσομαι. καίπερ τὴν πόλιν μὴ σώσων, μαχοῦμαι." τοῦτο εἰπών, πάλιν δὴ εἰς τὴν μάχην ἀπῆλθε.

οἱ μὲν Τρῶες εὖ ἐμάχοντο, οἱ δὲ Ἀχαιοὶ νῦν ἐφοβοῦντο. "τί ποιήσομεν ἄνευ τοῦ Ἀχιλλέως;" ἔλεγον. πολλάκις μὲν ᾔτουν τὸν Ἀχιλλέα μάχεσθαι, πολλάκις δὲ ὁ Ἀχιλλεὺς "οὐχί" ἔλεγε. τέλος δὲ ὁ Πάτροκλος, φίλτατος ὢν τοῦ Ἀχιλλέως, τὰ τοῦ Ἀχιλλέως ὅπλα ἔλαβε καὶ εἰς τὴν μάχην εἰσῆλθε.

"ἰδού! Ἀχιλλεύς ἐστι," ἔλεγον οἱ Τρῶες, τὸν Πάτροκλον ὁρῶντες. πολὺ καὶ εὖ ἐμάχοντο. ὁ Ἕκτωρ πρὸς τὸν Πάτροκλον ἦλθεν. τὼ μὲν ἀγαθὼ ἐμαχέσθην. ὁ δὲ Ζεὺς καὶ ὁ Ἀπόλλων τῷ Ἕκτορι τὴν νίκην ἔδωκαν. ὁ δὲ Πάτροκλος ἀπέθανε.

ὁ δὲ Ἀχιλλεὺς, πυνθανόμενος τὸν τοῦ Πατρόκλου θάνατον, μεγάλην λύπην εἶχε· πολὺ γὰρ ἐφίλει τὸν Πάτροκλον. νῦν δὲ ἐθέλει μάχεσθαι. νῦν ἐθέλει δίκην λαβεῖν τοῦ Ἕκτορος.

ὁ Ἀχιλλεὺς τὸν Ἕκτορα ἀπέκτεινε μετὰ μακρὰν μάχην. πάντες δὲ οἱ Τρῶες ἔκλαιον, εὖ ἰδόντες τὸ τέλος τὸ τοῦ πολέμου καὶ τοῦ Ἰλίου ἄφυκτον νῦν εἶναι.

The verse is *Iliad* 6.447-449. Paraphrase of the verse: εὖ οἶδα παντὶ τῷ νῷ ὅτι ἡμέρα γενήσεται ὅτε οἱ Ἕλληνες τὴν ἱερὰν πόλιν διαφθεροῦσι καὶ ἀποκτενοῦσι τὸν Πρίαμον καὶ τὸν λεών.

αἰχμάλωτος, -ου, ὁ, captive, prisoner of war. στρατόπεδον, -ου, τό, military camp. νόσος, -ου, ἡ, sickness, disease. δός is 2nd sg aorist imperative active of δίδωμι (chapter 16), and ἔδοκαν is 3rd pl aorist indicative active. σός, σή, σόν, your, and ἐμός, ἐμή, ἐμόν, my, are possessive adjectives (chapter 20). ὀργίζω, anger, make angry (predictable principal parts). προσ-βάλλω, attack. βασιλεύς, -εως, ὁ, king (chapter 16). γυνή, γυναικός, ἡ, wife, woman. ἰσχυρός, -ά, -όν, strong. δεῖ, it is necessary (infinitive subject). οἶδα, know (perfect only, see chapter 17). φρήν, φρενός, ἡ, mind, heart. θυμός, -οῦ, ὁ = ψυχή. ἔσσεται = ἔσεται, epic form. ἦμαρ, -ατος, τό = ἡμέρα. ὄλλυμι, destroy; ὀλώλῃ is 3rd sg perfect subjunctive middle; the perfect means "perish." ἱρή = ἱερά, epic dialect form, from ἱερός, sacred, holy. λᾱός = λαός, another epic form. ἐυμμελίω = ἐυμμελίου, from ἐυμμελής, warrior with a good spear. Πριάμοιο = Πριάμου, an old form. φοβέομαι, fear (predictable principal parts). φίλτατος is superlative of φίλος. μάχη, -ης, ἡ, battle. ἄφυκτος, -ον· τὸ ἄφυκτόν ἐστι τοῦτον ὁ τι οὐκ ἔχεις φυγεῖν.

XII.7 Conversation

Questions about the readings in the regular way, for example:

1. (reading 1) τίς πεύσεται; ἐγὼ πεύσομαι. τί δὲ πεύσῃ; πεύσομαι ὅτι ποτ᾽ εἰσὶν ἐνθάδε αἱ πόλεις. ποῦ δέ εἰσίν; ἐνταῦθα ἐν κύκλῳ εἰσὶν αἱ πόλεις. τί δὲ χωρίον ἐστιν; Ὀλυμπίαν εἶναι νόμιζε δή. τί δρῶσιν ἐν Ὀλυμπίᾳ; διὰ τί θύσουσιν; τίς ξενίζει αὐτάς; τίς ταράττει; τί δρᾷ ἡ Ἀβουλία;

2. (reading 5) τί ἐποίει ὁ Μάρκος; ἆρα εὖ ἔτρεχε ὁ Μάρκος; ἆρα τάχα ἔτρεχε; τί ἐνόμισαν οἱ δημόσιοι, τὸν Μάρκον ὁρῶντες;

3. (reading 6) τί ἤθελε ἔχειν ὁ Πεισίστρατος; τίς ἦν ἡ Φύη; ποία ἦν; διὰ τί ἡ Φύη πανοπλίαν εἶχε;

   And so on.

XII.8 Writing

1. Do the change-number exercise with the following sentences.
   a. οἱ διδάσκαλοι τῶν μαθητῶν ἀκούσονται.
   b. ταῦτα τὰ γέρα τῷ ξένῳ δώσομεν.
   c. ὅστις ἂν πυνθάνηται τὴν ἀβουλίαν φθείρει.
   d. ὁ ἄνθρωπος τοῖς λίθοις θλιβήσεται.
   e. εἰ τοῦτο δράσεις, πάντας ἡμᾶς εἴτε σώσεις εἴτε φθερεῖς.
   f. οὗτοι οἱ ἰχθύες ὑφ᾽ ἡμῶν ληφθήσονται.
   g. ἡ πόλις τεῖχος δέκα πήχεων ἔχει ἐν κύκλῳ.
   h. τὸ ἄστυ διαφθαρήσεται εἰ τὸν φόρον Ἀθήναζε μὴ ληψόμεθα.
   i. ὁ ξένος γέρας ὑμῖν αἰτεῖ διὰ τὸ κλέος.
   j. αὔριον μὲν ἡ θεωρία ἀχθήσεται, τήμερον δὲ ἡ σκηνὴ ποιεῖται.
   k. εἰ ὁ μαθητὴς πεύσεται ὁπότερον ὥρα ἐστὶ ἀριστᾶν, ὁ διδάσκαλος ἀποκρινεῖται ὅτι ὥρα ἐστὶ ἀβουλίαν οὐκέτι λέγειν.
   l. εἷς πολίτης τὴν πόλιν ἔσωσε.
   m. τὼ παῖδε ᾐτησάτην τὸν διδάσκαλον δῶρα διδόναι.
   n. τοῖς φίλοις ἀεὶ συγγιγνόμεθα.
   o. ὁ υἱὸς τοῖς αἰξὶ αὔριον ἕψεται.

2. In each of the following sentences, change the main verb from active to passive, or from passive to active, making whatever other changes are required to keep roughly the same meaning. For example, from ὁ ἄνθρωπος τὸν ἑταῖρον φιλεῖ make ὁ ἑταῖρος ὑπὸ τοῦ ἀνθρώπου φιλεῖται.
   a. ὁ γεωργὸς τὸν αἶγα ἐπὶ τοῖν ὤμοιν οἴσει.
   b. ἡ ἄνθρωπος υἱὸν τέξει.
   c. ὁ στρατιώτης τὰ ὅπλα ἀρεῖ ἵνα μάχηται.
   d. ἡ τριήρης ὑπὸ τῶν δούλων νικήσεται.
   e. κύκλος ἐπὶ τῆς γῆς ὑπὸ τοῦ σχολαστικοῦ γραψάτω.

    f. δύο μὲν ὥρα τὸν γίγαντα κατεῖχε, τέλος δὲ ὑπὸ τοῦ γίγαντος ἐνικήθη.

    g. ὁ ἄνθρωπος, μεγάλῳ κράτει, τὰ πρόβατα καὶ τοὺς αἶγας σώσει.

    h. οἱ παρασκευάζοντες ὑπὸ τῶν παίδων ταράξουσι.

    i. οἱ ναῦται τὰ ἱστία ἀροῦσιν ἵνα πλέωσι.

    j. τὼ μάντει λόγους σοφοὺς λέξετον.

    k. τοὺς φίλους ξενιεῖτε.

    l. ἐξ ἀβουλίας ὑπὸ τοῦ μαθεῖν σωθησόμεθα.

    m. ὁ μάντις τὸ γενησόμενον ἀγγελεῖ.

3. Each of the following sentences is a direct quotation. Rewrite as indirect using ὅτι or ὡς, or a suitable indirect question word if it is a question rather than a statement. If the OOO rule applies, write the sentence both with optional optative and with retained indicative; if the OOO rule does not apply, write the sentence only once. For example, ὁ διδάσκαλος εἶπε, "οἱ μαθηταὶ γράψουσι." becomes first ὁ διδάσκαλος εἶπε ὅτι οἱ μαθηταί γράψουσι, then ὁ διδάσκαλος εἶπε ὅτι οἱ μαθηταί γράψοιεν.

    a. ὁ στρατηγὸς ἤγγειλε, "αὕτη ἡ πόλις οὐ διαφθαρήσεται."

    b. ὁ υἱὸς ἤρετο "ἆρα ἡ τεκοῦσα τελευτήσει εἰ ὁ ἰατρὸς πρὸς αὐτὴν μὴ πεμφθήσεται;"

    c. οἱ πολῖται εἶπον, "γέρα δώσομεν αὐτοῖς οἳ τὴν δημοκρατίαν τήν τε ἐλευθερίαν σῴζουσι."

    d. εἴπομεν, "ἡμεῖς οὐ σὲ ταράξομεν εἰ σὺ ἡμᾶς μὴ ταράττεις."

    e. ὁ μάντις τοῖς παισὶ λέγε, "ὑπ' ἐμοῦ τάχα σωθήσεσθε."

    f. τοῖς ζῴοις εἶπον, "ὑπ' ἐμοῦ αὐτίκα σωθήσεσθε."

    g. οἱ πολῖται εἶπον, "θεωρίαν ὀψόμεθα ἐπὶ τῇ σκηνῇ."

    h. χθὲς εἴπετε, "αὔριον ἱξόμεθα," ἀλλὰ τήμερον λέγετε, "οὐκ ἱκνούμεθα."

    i. τὼ ἀδελφὼ εἰπέτην, "οὗτος οἴκαδε ἀναχωρήσεται, ἡμᾶς καταλείπων."

    j. ὁ ξένος εἶπε, "δύο ἔτει πρὸς τὸ ἄστυ ἤλασα."

4. Write a prose paraphrase of reading 1 in the third person.

5. Write a paragraph on the topic of a city-state (or nation-state) and its government.

CHAPTER XIII

Penthesileia

XIII.1 Subordinate moods of εἰμι

You already know the present active infinitive εἶναι of εἰμι "be," along with the participle ὤν. These are the remaining forms of the present system of εἰμι.

	Imperative	Subjunctive	Optative
singular			
1st		ὦ	εἴην
2nd	ἴσθι	ᾖς	εἴης
3rd	ἔστω	ᾖ	εἴη
dual			
2nd	ἔστον	ἦτον	εἶτον
3rd	ἔστων	ἦτον	εἴτην
plural			
1st		ὦμεν	εἶμεν
2nd	ἔστε	ἦτε	εἶτε
3rd	ἔστων	ὦσι(ν)	εἶεν

This verb has only active forms in the present system, and only middle forms in the future. The future is regular: indicative ἔσομαι, ἔσῃ, ἔσται, ἔσεσθον, ἔσεσθον, ἐσόμεθα, ἔσεσθε, ἔσονται; optative ἐσοίμην, ἔσοιο, etc.; infinitive ἔσεσθαι; participle ἐσόμενος. It has no aorist and no perfect. Thus you now have its complete conjugation.

XIII.2 Aorist passive

The aorist passive is formed from the sixth principal part, as is the future passive. It is the same for all verbs, whether they have a first aorist, a second aorist, or a root aorist in the aorist active/middle system.

	Indicative	Imperative	Subjunctive	Optative
singular				
1st	ἐ-λύ-θη-ν		λυ-θῶ	λυ-θείην
2nd	ἐ-λύ-θη-ς	λύ-θη-τι	λυ-θῇ-ς	λυ-θείης
3rd	ἐ-λύ-θη	λυ-θή-τω	λυ-θῇ	λυ-θείη
dual				
2nd	ἐ-λύ-θη-τον	λύ-θη-τον	λυ-θῆ-τον	λυ-θεῖτον
3rd	ἐ-λυ-θή-την	λυ-θή-των	λυ-θῆ-τον	λυ-θείτην
plural				
1st	ἐ-λύ-θη-μεν		λυ-θῶ-μεν	λυ-θεῖμεν
2nd	ἐ-λύ-θη-τε	λύ-θη-τε	λυ-θῆ-τε	λυ-θεῖτε
3rd	ἐ-λύ-θη-σαν	λυ-θέ-ντων	λυ-θῶ-σι(ν)	λυ-θεῖεν

The original ending for the second singular aorist imperative passive was -θι, but it becomes -τι by **dissimilation**, to avoid successive aspirate consonants -θη-θι.

The aorist infinitive passive is λυ-θῆ-ναι and the participle is λυ-θείς, -εῖσα, -έν (first- and-third declension).

As you can see, the endings of the aorist passive are not like any of the other passive or middle endings in Greek: in fact, they look like *active* endings. Note that the subjunctive and optative endings, after the -θ- suffix that makes the stem, are just the same as the forms of the subjunctive and optative of εἰμί. The indicative endings are similar to the imperfect of εἰμί, except that the second singular ends in -ης instead of -ησθα and the third singular has no -ν.

To form the sixth principal part, verbs normally add the suffix -θ- to their root. Some verbs use no suffix at all, as γράφω forms ἐ-γράφ-ην. Contract verbs lengthen the stem vowel and take the -θ- suffix, as ἐ-τιμή-θ-ην, ἐ-ποιή-θ-ην, ἐ-δηλώ-θ-ην. Once you have the stem, the endings are exactly the same for all verbs, so for example the infinitives are γραφῆναι, τιμηθῆναι, and so on.

Exercise

Write out the three third-person forms of the aorist passive of ἐπιτιμάω, θεραπεύω, βάλλω, πλουτέω, λαμβάνω, τάττω, φωνέω. Write out the aorist infinitive passive and the three nominative singular forms of the aorist participle passive of γράφω, λέγω, πράττω, τιμάω, κρίνω.

XIII.3 Root aorist

A small group of verbs forms the aorist *active* with endings exactly like those of the aorist *passive*. For these verbs, the stem is just the verb root, so this formation is called the **root aorist**; perhaps it should have been "third aorist," since the other two are "first" and "second," but that name never caught on. Here are some examples. All forms in this table are aorist active:

Verb	1st sg. indic.	2nd sg. imper.	1st sg. subj.	1st. sg. pt.	Inf.	Participle
βαίνω "step, go"	ἔβην	βῆθι	βῶ	βαίην	βῆναι	βάς βᾶσα βάν (with α for ε throughout)
γιγνώσκω "know"	ἔγνων	γνῶθι	γνῶ	γνοίην	γνῶναι	γνούς γνοῦσα γνόν (with ο for ε)
διδράσκω "run away, escape"	ἔδρᾱν	δρᾶθι	δρῶ	δραίην	δρᾶναι	δράς δρᾶσα δράν

Some of the forms of διδράσκω are only used in compound verbs, such as ἀποδιδράσκω, διαδιδράσκω, and ἐκδιδράσκω, all meaning much the same as the base verb.

The verb φύω, "be, be by nature," has aorist indicative active ἔφῡν, infinitive φῦναι, and participle φύς φῦσα φύν. In the present system the middle is more common than the active in this sense; the active can be transitive, "beget, produce."

Some μι- verbs also form their aorist this way, notably ἔστην from ἵστημι.

Verbs with a root aorist do not have an aorist middle.

Exercise

Write out the three third-person forms of the aorist indicative active of βαίνω, γιγνώσκω, διδράσκω, φύω, and ἵστημι.

XIII.4 Negation

In addition to οὐ and μή, the simple negative words, Greek has a group of compound negative words: οὐδείς "no one, nobody, nothing"; οὔποτε, οὐδέποτε, οὐδεπώποτε "never"; οὐδαμῶς "in no way, by no means"; οὐδέ "and not, not even"; οὐκέτι "no longer, not any more"; οὔπω "not yet"; οὔτις "nobody, no one." Each of these has a corresponding version compounded with μή to be used in the clauses where μή is the appropriate negation.

When a compound negative follows a simple one, the negation is strengthened. For example, οὐχ ὁρᾷ οὐδείς οὐδεπώποτε, "no one ever sees at all." Note that there's normally at least one other word between the simple οὐ and the following compound. But if the compound negative comes first, the negatives cancel out, as οὐδείς οὐχ ὁρᾷ "no one doesn't see, no one fails to see" (that is, everyone sees perfectly well).

In English an emphatic double negative can be colloquial or even ungrammatical: the first example might be expressed as "nobody never sees nothing." In Greek simple-then-compound negation is not particularly colloquial, but a fairly normal way to add emphasis. The compound-then-simple form, in which the two negatives cancel out, is used roughly the same way in Greek and in English. Often it is an understatement or **litotes** (as we might say "not bad" meaning "rather good," or "not unaware" meaning "entirely aware").

XIII.5 Indirect discourse with participle

You already know two ways to express a quotation without directly quoting the speaker's exact words: with ὅτι or ὡς and a finite verb (OOO rule applicable), or with the infinitive. There is a third construction used in the similar situation when the main verb is not one of saying but one of knowing or perceiving, such as οἶδα "know" (see chapter 17), νομίζω, ἀκούω, ὁράω, εὑρίσκω, μανθάνω, αἰσθάνομαι "perceive," μέμνημαι "remember" (see chapter 15). With these verbs we use a participle rather than an infinitive.

Here are some examples: ἀκούω τὸ παιδίον λέγοντα "I hear the child speaking," or "I hear that the child is speaking." ὁ ἄνθρωπος ὁρᾷ τὸν Σωκράτη γράφοντα "The man sees Socrates writing." οἶδα ὤν "I know that I am"; the participle is nominative here because it modifies the subject of the main verb. οἶδα ὑμᾶς ὄντας (plural) or οἶδά σ’ ὄντα (singular), "I know that you are."

The tense of the participle tells when the action happens relative to the time of the main verb. So: ὁρῶ τὸν Σωκράτη γράφοντα, seeing and writing at the same time, both right now. εἶδον τὸν Σωκράτη γράφοντα, seeing and writing at the same time, both in the past. ὁρῶ τὸν Σωκράτη γράψαντα, writing before the seeing, which is going on now; εἶδον τὸν Σωκράτη γράψαντα, writing before seeing, which was in the past. ὁρῶ τὸν Σωκράτη γράψοντα and εἶδον τὸν Σωκράτη γράψοντα, writing comes after the seeing ("I see (saw) that S. is about to write, is going to write"), and the seeing is respectively present and past.

XIII.6 Vocabulary

VERBS

αἰσθάνομαι, αἰσθήσομαι, ᾐσθόμην, – , ᾔσθημαι, – , perceive (cp. *aesthetic*, L. *audio*)

βαίνω, βήσομαι, ἔβην, βέβηκα, – , – , step, go (cp. *come, base*, L. *venio*)

βούλομαι, βουλήσομαι, – , – , βεβούλημαι, ἐβουλήθην, wish, intend

γιγνώσκω, γνώσομαι, ἔγνων, ἔγνωκα, ἔγνωσμαι, ἐγνώσθην, recognize, learn to know (cp. *know*, L. *gnosco*)

διδράσκω, δράσομαι, ἔδρᾱν, δέδρᾱκα, – , – , run away, escape

δύναμαι, δυνήσομαι, – , – , δεδύνημαι, ἐδυνήθην, be able (cp. *dynamic*)

ἐπι-τιμάω, blame

ζητέω, ζητήσω, ἐζήτησα, ἐζήτηκα, – , ἐζητήθην, seek, look for

λαλέω, λαλήσω, ἐλάλησα, λελάληκα, – , – , talk, chatter, babble

νοσέω, νοσήσω, ἐνόσησα, νενόσηκα, – , – , be ill

πάσχω, πείσομαι, ἔπαθον, πέπονθα, – , – , suffer, experience, undergo

πείθω, πείσω, ἔπεισα, πέποιθα, πέπεισμαι, ἐπείσθην, persuade

πίνω, πῠ́ομαι, ἔπιον, πέπωκα, πέπομαι, ἐπόθην, drink (cp. L. *bibo*) προσ-αγορεύω, προσαγορεύσω, προσηγόρευσα, προσηγόρευκα, προσηγόρευμαι, προσηγορεύθην, address, speak to (compound of ἀγορεύω)

σῑτέω, σῑτήσω, ἐσίτησα, – , – , ἐσῑτήθην, feed

συμ-παθέω, συμπαθήσω, συνεπάθησα, συμπεπάθηκα, συμπεπάθημαι, feel with, sympathize

συν-τάττομαι, bargain, make a compact

φύω, φύσω, ἔφῡν, πέφῡκα, – , – , beget, produce; be, be by nature (cp. *be, physics,* L. *fui*)

NOUNS

ἐπήρεια, -ας, ἡ, insult

ἱερεῖον, -ου, τό, victim for a sacrifice

καιρός, -οῦ, ὁ, right time, nick of time

μισθός, -οῦ, ο, pay, reward

μῖσος, -ους, τό, hate, hateful thing (cp. *misanthrope*)

οὐσίᾱ, -ας, ἡ, property

πρᾶγμα, πράγματος, τό, thing, action, matter, business; in plural sometimes "trouble" (cp. *pragmatic*)

συμφορά, -ᾶς, ἡ, misfortune

τρυφή, -ῆς, ἡ, luxury

φθόνος, -ου, ὁ, hate, envy

ADJECTIVES

διπλάσιος, -α, -ον, double, twice as big

μυρίοι, -αι, -α, countless (cp. *myriad*)

οὐδείς, οὐδεμία, οὐδέν, none, no one, nothing (from οὐδέ + εἷς)

ADVERBS AND CONJUNCTIONS

εἰκότως, probably, reasonably, as you would expect

οὐδαμῶς, in no way, by no means

οὔποτε, never

οὐδέποτε, never

οὐδεπώποτε, never

οὔπω, not yet

Notes on the vocabulary

The verb βούλομαι has an aorist passive rather than an aorist middle, though it has a future middle.

The verb δύναμαι is athematic, since it has no -o- before its ending; it has only passive forms, including the irregular second person singular present indicative δύνη or δύνᾳ used in verse, though the regular form δύνασαι is used in prose. Aside from the missing theme vowel, its forms are otherwise like those of thematic verbs; see chapter 20 for more details on the passive forms of athematic verbs.

ἔπιθον is a poetic alternative for ἔπεισα. In the perfect the verb can mean "trust": to be in a persuaded state is to trust the person who persuaded you. Note that the future middle πείσομαι is identical to the future middle of πάσχω; this seems confusing but it is generally clear from context which verb it is.

φύω in its transitive sense ("beget, bring forth") can also have an ordinary first aorist, ἔφυσα. When it means "be, be by nature" it is usually middle in the present system, φύομαι, with the root aorist ἔφυν.

οὐσία is derived from οὖσα, the present participle active of εἰμι in the feminine.

μυρίοι "countless" and μύριοι "10,000" are the same word, as we might say "a hundred" or "a million" simply meaning "a lot." Traditionally the two uses of μύριοι are pronounced with different accent.

Along with the οὐ-forms of negatives, also learn the matching μη-forms.

XIII.7 Reading

1. ἀεὶ τὸ πλουτεῖν συμφορὰς πολλὰς ἔχει,
   φθόνον τ' ἐπήρειάν τε καὶ μῖσος πολύ,
   πράγματα δὲ πολλὰ κἀνοχλήσεις μυρίας·
   ἔπειτα μετὰ ταῦτ' εὐθὺς εὑρέθη θανών,
   ἄλλοις καταλείψας εἰς τρυφὴν τὴν οὐσίαν.

   > ἐνόχλησις, -εως, ἡ, annoyance; note crasis. θανών is like ἀποθανών, the aorist participle from θνήσκω; note participle used with εὑρέθη.

   > Selections 1 through 4 are fragments from comedies by Philemon.

2. λίθον γενέσθαι τὴν Νιόβην, μὰ τοὺς θεούς,
   οὐδέ ποτ' ἐπείσθην, οὐδὲ νῦν πεισθήσομαι
   ὡς τοῦτ' ἐγένετ' ἄνθρωπος· ὑπὸ δὲ τῶν κακῶν
   οὐδὲν λαλῆσαι δυναμένη πρὸς οὐδένα,
   προσηγορεύθη, διὰ τὸ μὴ φωνεῖν, λίθος.

3. στρατιῶτα, κοὐκ ἄνθρωπε, καὶ σιτούμενε
   ὥσπερ ἱερεῖον, ἵν' ὅταν ᾖ καιρός, τυθῇς.

4. ἐκ τοῦ παθεῖν γίγνωσκε καὶ τὸ συμπαθεῖν·
   καὶ σοὶ γὰρ ἄλλος συμπαθήσεται παθών.

5. Σχολαστικὸς νοσῶν συνετάξατο τῷ ἰατρῷ, εἰ θεραπευθείη, μισθὸν δώσειν. ὡς οὖν οἶνον πίνοντι αὐτῷ ἐπετίμα ἡ γυνή, "βούλει δὲ σύ," ἔφη, "ὑγιαίνοντά με τῷ ἰατρῷ δοῦναι τὸν μισθόν;"

   > γυνή, γυναικός, ἡ = ἡ ἄνθρωπος

6. δίκαιος ἴσθι καὶ φίλοισι καὶ ξένοις.

   > This line and the next reading are attributed to lost plays by Menander.

7. οὐκ ἔστιν οὐδείς, ὅστις οὐχ αὑτὸν φιλεῖ.

8. οὔτοι συνέχθειν, ἀλλὰ συμφιλεῖν ἔφυν.

> Sophocles, *Antigone* 523; Antigone is speaking. **ἔχθω**, hate; the two συν-compounds suggest reciprocal feelings.

9. τίνα μὲν γὰρ ἐπίστασθε ἧττον ἐμοῦ δουλεύοντα ταῖς τοῦ σώματος ἐπιθυμίαις; τίνα δὲ ἀνθρώπων ἐλευθεριώτερον, ὃς παρ᾽ οὐδενὸς οὔτε δῶρα οὔτε μισθὸν δέχομαι; δικαιότερον δὲ τίνα ἂν εἰκότως νομίσαιτε τοῦ πρὸς τὰ παρόντα συνηρμοσμένου, ὡς τῶν ἀλλοτρίων μηδενὸς προσδεῖσθαι; σοφὸν δὲ πῶς οὐκ ἄν τις εἰκότως ἄνδρα φήσειεν εἶναι ὃς ἐξ ὅτουπερ συνιέναι τὰ λεγόμενα ἠρξάμην οὐπώποτε διέλειπον καὶ ζητῶν καὶ μανθάνων ὅ τι ἐδυνάμην ἀγαθόν;

> Xenophon, *Apology* 16; Socrates is speaking.
>
> **ἐπίσταμαι, ἐπιστήσομαι, – , – , – , ἠπιστήθην**, understand. **ἥττων, -ον**, less, comparative of ὀλίγος or μικρός, here an adverb. **ἐπιθυμία, -ας, ἡ**, desire, passion. **δέχομαι**, receive. **συνηρμοσμένος, -η, -ον**, appropriate, well adapted; perfect participle middle from συν-αρμόζω, adapt, fit together. **ἀλλότριος, -α, -ον**, belonging to someone else, foreign. **προσ-δέω**, need, need in addition (+ gen.). **ἀνήρ, ἀνδρός, ὁ** = ἄνθρωπος (chapter 15).

10. ἐν τοῖς ὀρθογωνίοις τριγώνοις τὸ ἀπὸ τῆς τὴν ὀρθὴν γωνίαν ὑποτεινούσης πλευρᾶς τετράγωνον ἴσον ἐστὶ τοῖς ἀπὸ τῶν τὴν ὀρθὴν γωνίαν περιεχουσῶν πλευρῶν τετραγώνοις.

ἔστω τρίγωνον ὀρθογώνιον τὸ ΑΒΓ ὀρθὴν ἔχον τὴν ὑπὸ ΒΑΓ γωνίαν· λέγω, ὅτι τὸ ἀπὸ τῆς ΒΓ τετράγωνον ἴσον ἐστὶ τοῖς ἀπὸ τῶν ΒΑ, ΑΓ τετραγώνοις.

ἀναγεγράφθω γὰρ ἀπὸ μὲν τῆς ΒΓ τετράγωνον τὸ ΒΔΕΓ, ἀπὸ δὲ τῶν ΒΑ, ΑΓ τὰ ΗΒ, ΘΓ, καὶ διὰ τοῦ Α ὁποτέρᾳ τῶν ΒΔ, ΓΕ παράλληλος ἤχθω ἡ ΑΛ· καὶ ἐπεζεύχθωσαν αἱ ΑΔ, ΖΓ. καὶ ἐπεὶ ὀρθή ἐστιν ἑκατέρα τῶν ὑπὸ ΒΑΓ, ΒΑΗ γωνιῶν, πρὸς δή τινι εὐθείᾳ τῇ ΒΑ καὶ τῷ πρὸς αὐτῇ σημείῳ τῷ Α δύο εὐθεῖαι αἱ ΑΓ, ΑΗ μὴ ἐπὶ τὰ αὐτὰ μέρη κείμεναι τὰς ἐφεξῆς γωνίας δυσὶν ὀρθαῖς ἴσας ποιοῦσιν· ἐπ᾽ εὐθείας ἄρα ἐστὶν ἡ ΓΑ τῇ ΑΗ.

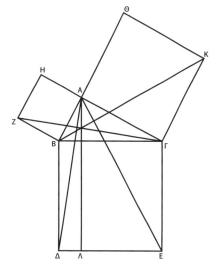

διὰ τὰ αὐτὰ δὴ καὶ ἡ ΒΑ τῇ ΑΘ ἐστιν ἐπ᾽ εὐθείας.

καὶ ἐπεὶ ἴση ἐστὶν ἡ ὑπὸ ΔΒΓ γωνία τῇ ὑπὸ ΖΒΑ (ὀρθὴ γὰρ ἑκατέρα), κοινὴ προσκείσθω ἡ ὑπὸ ΑΒΓ. ὅλη ἄρα ἡ ὑπὸ ΔΒΑ ὅλῃ τῇ ὑπὸ ΖΒΓ ἐστιν ἴση. καὶ ἐπεὶ ἴση ἐστὶν ἡ μὲν ΔΒ τῇ ΒΓ, ἡ δὲ ΖΒ τῇ ΒΑ, δύο δὴ αἱ ΔΒ, ΒΑ δύο ταῖς ΖΒ, ΒΓ ἴσαι εἰσὶν ἑκατέρα ἑκατέρᾳ· καὶ γωνία ἡ ὑπὸ ΔΒΑ γωνίᾳ τῇ ὑπὸ ΖΒΓ ἴση· βάσις ἄρα ἡ ΑΔ βάσει τῇ ΖΓ ἴση, καὶ τὸ ΑΒΔ τρίγωνον τῷ ΖΒΓ τριγώνῳ ἐστὶν ἴσον.

καὶ τοῦ μὲν ΑΒΔ τριγώνου διπλάσιον τὸ ΒΛ παραλληλόγραμμον· βάσιν τε γὰρ τὴν αὐτὴν ἔχουσι τὴν ΒΔ καὶ ἐν ταῖς αὐταῖς εἰσι παραλλήλοις ταῖς ΒΔ, ΑΛ. τοῦ δὲ ΖΒΓ τριγώνου διπλάσιον τὸ ΗΒ τετράγωνον· βάσιν τε γὰρ πάλιν τὴν αὐτὴν ἔχουσι τὴν ΖΒ καὶ ἐν ταῖς αὐταῖς εἰσι παραλλήλοις ταῖς ΖΒ, ΗΓ. ἴσον ἄρα ἐστὶ καὶ τὸ ΒΛ παραλληλόγραμμον τῷ ΗΒ τετραγώνῳ.

ὁμοίως δὴ ἐπιζευγνυμένων τῶν ΑΕ, ΒΚ δειχθήσεται καὶ τὸ ΓΛ παραλληλόγραμμον ἴσον τῷ ΘΓ τετραγώνῳ.

ὅλον ἄρα τὸ ΒΔΕΓ τετράγωνον δυσὶ τοῖς ΗΒ, ΘΓ τετραγώνοις ἴσον ἐστίν. καὶ ἐστι τὸ μὲν ΒΔΕΓ τετράγωνον ἀπὸ τῆς ΒΓ ἀναγραφέν, τὰ δὲ ΗΒ, ΘΓ ἀπὸ τῶν ΒΑ, ΑΓ. τὸ ἄρα ἀπὸ τῆς ΒΓ πλευρᾶς τετράγωνον ἴσον ἐστὶ τοῖς ἀπὸ τῶν ΒΑ, ΑΓ πλευρῶν τετραγώνοις.

ἐν ἄρα τοῖς ὀρθογωνίοις τριγώνοις τὸ ἀπὸ τῆς τὴν ὀρθὴν γωνίαν ὑποτεινούσης πλευρᾶς τετράγωνον ἴσον ἐστὶ τοῖς ἀπὸ τῶν τὴν ὀρθὴν γωνίαν περιεχουσῶν πλευρῶν τετραγώνοις· ὅπερ ἔδει δεῖξαι.

Euclid, *Elements* 1.47, called the Pythagorean theorem. See figure.

γωνία, -ας, ἡ, corner or angle; many of the geometrical terms are derived from this word, as τὸ ὀρθογώνιον, right angle. **ὑπο-τείνω**, stretch under, stretch across, subtend. **πλευρά, -ᾶς, ἡ**, side, rib. **ἴσος, -η, -ον**, equal. **περι-έχω**, enclose, surround. **ἀνα-γράφω** = γράφω, and ἀναγεγράφθω is 3rd singular, perfect imperative passive, meaning very roughly the same as ἀναγραφήτω. **ἐπι-ζεύγνυμι**, join together; ἐπεζεύχθωσαν is another perfect imperative passive, this time 3rd plural. **σημεῖον, -ου, τό**, point (in geometry). **εὐθεία, -ας, ἡ**, straight line. **μέρος, -ους, τό**, part. **κεῖμαι**, lie, be placed, athematic verb with only a present and a future system (chapter 16). **πρόσ-κειμαι**, lie on, lie near. **ὅλος, -η, -ον**, whole, entire. **βάσις, -εως, ἡ**, base. **δεῖ**, it is necessary, with infinitive as subject. **δείκνῡμι, δείξω, ἔδειξα, δέδειχα, δέδειγμαι, ἐδείχθην**, show, prove; the phrase ὅπερ ἔδει δεῖξαι may also be familiar in its Latin version, *quod erat demonstrandum*.

11. *περὶ τοῦ Τρωικοῦ πολέμου, ἕβδομον μέρος*

Πενθεσίλεια ἦν Ἀμαζών, θυγάτηρ οὖσα τοῦ Ἄρεος. ἐθήρα ὥσπερ αἱ Ἀμαζόνες ἀεὶ ποιοῦσι. ἡμέρᾳ τινὶ θηρᾶσα, ἐθέλουσα ἔλαφον λαβεῖν, τῆς ἀδελφῆς ἔτυχε καὶ ἀπέκτεινε. ὅτε τὴν θανοῦσαν ἀδελφὴν ᾐσθάνετο, λύπην δὲ καὶ αἰδῶ εἶχε, αἰτία οὖσα τοῦ τῆς ἀδελφῆς θανάτου. "ἐμαυτῇ ἐπιτιμῶ," εἶπε, "ὡς τὴν ἀδελφὴν ἀποκτεινούσῃ ἀντὶ τοῦ ἐλάφου. ἡ τάλαινα οὐκ ἐδύνατο δρᾶναι. μῖσος νῦν φύομαι πᾶσι· οὐδείς μοι συμπαθεῖ. οὐκ ἐγὼ οὐδεπώποτε οὐδαμῶς ἐκ τῆς λύπης λυθήσομαι, ἐάν με μὴ οἱ θεοὶ ὠφελῶσιν." ἠρώτησε οὖν τοῖς θεοῖς ὅπως ἐκ τῆς λύπης λυθήσοιτο. οἱ δὲ θεοὶ ἀπεκρίναντο ὅτι, εἰ πρὸς τὸν Ἴλιον ἔρχοιτο καὶ τοὺς Τρωικοὺς ὠφέλοι, οὐδὲ λύπην οὐδὲ αἰδῶ ἕξοι.

ἡ Πενθεσίλεια οὖν τὸν Ἴλιον ἐζήτησε ἵνα πολεμοίη τοῦ τῆς ἀδελφῆς θανάτου ἕνεκα. σύμμαχος δὲ τῶν Τρώων ἐγένετο. ἐνταῦθα οἱ Ἕλληνες τοῖς Τρωσὶ ἐμάχοντο παρὰ τοῖς τείχεσι. ὁ δὲ Ἀχιλλεὺς πρῶτος καὶ ἄριστος ἐμάχετο. ἡ δὲ Ἀμαζὼν οὖν, τὸν Ἀχιλλέα αἰσθανομένη, πρὸς αὐτὸν ἔβη. "ἐγὼ μὲν Ἀμαζὼν φύομαι," εἶπε ἡ Πενθεσίλεια, "σύμμαχος οὖσα τῶν Τρωικῶν. σὺ δὲ δοκεῖς ἄριστος Ἀχαιῶν εἶναι. μάχην ζητῶ· σοὶ οὖν προσβάλλω," καὶ ἐποίησε. μακρὸν χρόνον ἡ μὲν Πενθεσίλεια ὁ δὲ Ἀχιλλεὺς ἐμαχέσθην. τέλος δὲ οὗτος αὐτὴν ξίφει ἔτρωσε. κακῶς ἐβλάβη ἡ Πενθεσίλεια. εἰς τὼ τοῦ Ἀχιλλέως ὀφθαλμὼ ἔβλεψε. "νῦν ἀποθανοῦμαι," ἔφη. "τόν τε βίον καὶ τὴν λύπην τελευτῶ. πρὸς τὸν Ἴλιον ἑκοῦσα ἦλθον, τῶν θεῶν κελευσάντων, ἀλλ᾽ οὐκ ἐδυνήθην τὸν Ἴλιον σῴζειν. ἐμὲ ἐνίκησας.”

ὁ δὲ Ἀχιλλεὺς εἰς τὴν ἀποθνήσκουσαν ἔβλεψε. οὔπω αὐτὴν ἀληθείᾳ ᾔσθετο, ἀλλὰ νῦν εὖ εἶδε. καλὴ ἦν καὶ ἀγαθή, καὶ ἀξία τοῦ Ἀχιλλέως. εὐθὺς αὐτὴν ἐφίλησε, ἀλλὰ ὕστερος· ἡ γὰρ Πενθεσίλεια ἀπέθανε.

> θυγάτηρ, θυγατρός, ἡ, daughter. θηράω, hunt. ἔλαφος, -ου, ὁ, ἡ, deer. τυγχάνω, τεύξομαι, ἔτυχον, τετύχηκα, – , – , hit (+ gen.). αἰδῶς, -ους, ἡ, shame; stem αἰδοσ-. αἰτία, -ας, ἡ, cause. ὠφελέω, help, assist. πολεμέω = πόλεμον ποιέω, μάχομαι. σύμμαχος, -ου, ὁ, ally. προσ-βάλλω, attack. ξίφος, -ους, τό, sword. τιτρώσκω, τρώσω, ἔτρωσα, – , τέτρωμαι, ἐτρώθην, wound. ὕστερος, -α, -ον, later; too late.

XIII.8 Conversation

Questions on the readings in the usual way, for example:

1. (reading 1) τι ἔχει τὸ πλουτεῖν; τί γίγνεται θανόντος τοῦ πλουσίου; τίνι καταλείψει τὴν οὐσίαν; πρὸς τί;

2. (reading 5) τί συνετάξατο ὁ Σχολαστικός; ποῖός τις ἐστιν ὁ στρατιώτης;

3. (reading 10) τί σημαίνει ἀγγλιστὶ τὸ "τρίγωνος" καὶ τὸ "παραλληλόγραμμον" καὶ τὰ λοιπά; διὰ τί εἰσι ἡ ΒΑ καὶ ἡ ΑΘ ἐπὶ μιᾶς εὐθείας; and so on, making the details explicit as necessary.

XIII.9 Writing

1. Do the change-number exercise with the following sentences.

   a. εἰς τὴν ἀγορὰν ἔβη, νέον ἱμάτιον ζητοῦν.

   b. ὅστις ἂν ᾖ εὐγενής, μήτε λαλείτω μήτε ἀβουλίαν λεγέτω.

   c. οὐκ ἔγνωτε οὐδὲν περὶ τοῦτο τοῦ πράγματος.

   d. λόγος σοφὸς εἰκότως ὑπὸ τῶν παιδίων ἐλέχθη.

   e. εἰ φιλεῖσθαι βούλει, ἀξία τῆς φιλίας ἴσθι.

   f. οἱ στρατιῶται ἐν κύκλῳ ἔστησαν, τὰ ὅπλα φέροντες.

   g. εἰς τὸ ἄστυ ἔδραμεν καὶ καιρῷ ἀφικόμεθα.

   h. τὸ ἐκ τοῦ δωματίου ληφθὲν βιβλίον τριῶν ὀβολῶν ἐπωλήθη.

   i. τὼ ἀνθρώπω εἰπέτην ὅτι, οὐ δυναμένω ἐκεῖ βῆναι, οὐκ εἴτην χρησίμω.

   j. ὁ μαθητὴς, ζητήσας, πυθόμενος, γνούς, νῦν σοφὸς ἂν εἴη.

   k. ὁ δοῦλος τῷ δεσπότῃ ἔπεισε μισθὸν διδόναι.

   l. οἱ διδάσκαλοι ἀκουσθῆναι ἐβουλήθησαν.

   m. ἐὰν ὁ παῖς νοσῇ, ὁ ἰατρὸς ζητεῖται.

   n. ἐπεὶ ξένοι φύεσθε, ὑπ᾽ ἐμοῦ σιτηθήσεσθε.

   o. εἰ συμφορὰν ζητεῖς, αὐτὴν εὑρήσεις.

   p. ὁ κυβερνήτης ᾔσθετο τοὺς ἰχθύας τὸ πλοῖον ἑπομένους.

2. In each of the following sentences, change the main verb from active to passive, or from passive to active, making whatever other changes are required to keep roughly the same meaning. For example, from ὁ ἄνθρωπος τὸν ἑταῖρον φιλεῖ make ὁ ἑταῖρος ὑπὸ τοῦ ἀνθρώπου φιλεῖται.

    a. μισθὸς τοῖς στρατιώταις ὑπὸ τοῦ στρατηγοῦ ἠνέχθη.

    b. ὁ οἶνος ὑφ' ἡμῶν ἐπόθη.

    c. οἱ φιλάργυροι μισθὸν ἀεὶ ἐζήτησαν.

    d. οἱ πεινῶντες φθόνον ἔχουσι τῶν πλουτούντων.

    e. ἐπήρειαι τοῖς ξένοις ὑπὸ τοῦ ἀγαθοῦ οὔποτε ἐλέχθησαν.

    f. τὴν πόλιν σώσαντες μισθὸν καὶ γέρας ἔλαβον.

    g. ὁ ἐπὶ τὴν σκηνὴν βαίνων ὑπὸ πάντων ὤφθη.

    h. πεισθέντες τοῖς σοφοῖς λόγοις οἱ πολῖται οὐκ ἐφθάρησαν.

    i. ὑπ' οὐδενὸς τὸ ἔργον ἐποιήθη.

    j. ὁ ναύτης οἰκίαν ἔχει διπλασίαν οὖσαν τῆς ἄλλης.

3. Create complex sentences from the following parts. For each sentence, choose one main clause and one subordinate clause; you may need to add a suitable subordinate conjunction or make other changes to the subordinate clause to fit in with what is required by your main clause. If the OOO rule is applicable, use it. Create at least 10 new sentences. For example, if the main clause is ἡ διδασκάλη λέγει and the subordinate clause is οἱ μαθηταί εἰσι ἀγαθοί, you would create ἡ διδασκάλη λέγει ὅτι οἱ μαθηταί εἰσι ἀγαθοί or ἡ διδασκάλη λέγει τοὺς μαθητὰς εἶναι ἀγαθούς.

    Main clauses:

    a. μανθάνομεν

    b. οὗτος εὗρε

    c. τίς ἐνόμισε;

    d. οἱ ναῦται ἔγνωσαν

    e. τὸ ἱερεῖον αἰσθάνεται

    f. ἡ ἄνθρωπος οὐκ εἶπε

    Subordinate clauses:

    a. τυθήσεται

    b. οὐ δύναται ἀποδιδράσκειν

    c. οἱ παῖδες λαλοῦσι

    d. κακὰ ἔπαθε

    e. τὰ ζῷα ἐσιτήσατε

    f. καιρός ἀφίξεται

4. Rewrite reading 2 in straightforward prose.

5. Using the vocabulary from reading 9, write a paragraph containing more facts from geometry. You may choose to state and prove a theorem, or you may simply list some observations about geometric figures.

6. Write a paragraph about someone very rich, and how other people feel about this person.

CHAPTER XIV

The Death of Achilles

XIV.1 Perfect active system: forms

The perfect active system comes from the fourth principal part. This stem is created by **reduplication** of the verb root. Reduplication means doubling a syllable; in Greek verbs, reduplication makes a new syllable at the beginning of a word, normally created from the first consonant of the root and an inserted vowel. In the perfect system, that vowel is ε. For example, from λύω, the reduplicated perfect active form is λέ-λυ-κα. Most verbs also have a suffix at the end of the perfect stem, typically -κ- as in this example; it may also be aspiration of the final consonant, or there might not be a suffix at all. When possible, the verb usually takes o grade of its root, as πέπομφα from πέμπω. So the perfect active stem is: reduplication, verb root in o grade, possible -κ- suffix or aspiration. The perfect has its own set of endings, different from those of the present and aorist systems.

The perfect middle/passive system comes from the fifth principal part, and you will meet this in the next chapter.

There are three forms of reduplication for Greek perfect stems:

(1) If the verb stem begins with a single consonant, other than ρ, or a cluster consisting of a stop consonant followed by a liquid, the reduplication syllable is the first consonant plus ε. Thus:

λύ-ω	λέ-λυ-κα
πέμπω	πέπομφα
πράττω	πέπραχα
θύ-ω	τέθυ-κα
θνήσκω	τέ-θνη-κα

If the consonant is aspirated, the reduplication uses the un-aspirate form; as you've already seen, Greek avoids having two successive syllables beginning with aspirate consonants. Thus from θύω we have τέθυκα.

(2) If the stem begins with two or more consonants (except as above), or with a double consonant (ζ, ξ, ψ), or with ρ, the reduplication syllable is just ἐ-. An initial ρ also gets doubled.

πταί-ω "stumble"	ἔ-πται-κα
ψαύ-ω "touch"	ἔ-ψαυ-κα
ζητέω	ἐ-ζήτη-κα
ῥί-π-τω "throw"	ἔ-ρρι-φα

(3) If the stem begins with a vowel, the reduplication is once again just ε-, which contracts with the vowel. In other words, for these verbs reduplication is exactly the same as the past indicative augment.

ἀγγέλ-λω	ἤγγελ-κα

Contract verbs generally use the same long vowel in the perfect stem as in the future and the aorist, with the characteristic -κ- suffix and, of course, reduplication. For example, τε-τίμη-κα, πε-ποίη-κα, δε-δούλω-κα.

Very rarely, a verb will have two perfects, one with the -κ- suffix and one without. In this case the form with the suffix is often transitive and the one without is intransitive. The most common examples are ἵστημι, which has 3rd plural perf. indic. active ἑστήκασι or ἑστᾶσι, and βαίνω, which has βεβήκασι and βεβᾶσι.

More often, a verb has no perfect at all, or has a perfect middle or passive but no perfect active. This may mean that the perfect forms were never used, or that they were used but don't happen to appear in any of the texts that we have. The perfect system in general is markedly less common than the present or aorist.

Reduplication in the perfect always uses ε for the vowel, while verbs with reduplication in the present always have ι. Thus even if a verb has reduplication in both systems, you can tell the stems apart by the vowel of the reduplication syllable. For example, from δίδωμι we have present infinitive active διδόναι and perfect infinitive active δεδωκέναι, both infinitives ending in -ναι with the accent on the previous syllable, both from reduplicated stems, but with different reduplication vowels.

In the perfect active system we have two tenses of the indicative, the perfect (which is a type of present) and the pluperfect (which is a type of past, so is augmented). The perfect also has an infinitive and a participle. Imperative, subjunctive, and optative can be formed but are quite rare.

Once you have the stem, all verbs take the same endings for the perfect system, and these are different from the endings of the present, future, or aorist systems.

Indicative Active:	Perfect	Pluperfect
singular		
1st	λέ-λυκ-α	ἐ-λε-λύκ-η
2nd	λέ-λυκ-ας	ἐ-λε-λύκ-ης
3rd	λέ-λυκ-ε(ν)	ἐ-λε-λύκ-ει(ν)

Indicative Active:	Perfect	Pluperfect
dual		
2nd	λε-λύκ-ατον	ἐ-λε-λύκ-ετον
3rd	λε-λύκ-ατον	ἐ-λε-λυκ-έτην
plural		
1st	λε-λύκ-αμεν	ἐ-λε-λύκ-εμεν
2nd	λε-λύκ-ατε	ἐ-λε-λύκ-ετε
3rd	λε-λύκ-ασι(ν)	ἐ-λε-λύκ-εσαν *or* ἐλελύκεισαν

The perfect infinitive active is λελυκέναι and the participle is λελυκώς. Note the accents: as for all the verbal nouns and adjectives, these forms have persistent accent, and, unlike the present infinitive and participle, this accent is not recessive.

To form the perfect subjunctive active or perfect optative active, add the same endings as for present or second aorist to the perfect stem, as λελύκω, λελύκῃς, and so on (subjunctive); λελύκοιμι, λελύκοις, and so on (optative). These are not common. The perfect imperative active is almost never used, but also uses the same endings as for the present. You will recognize these three rare moods, if you ever see them, because they show the perfect stem, with the unmistakable reduplication, but have the endings of these other moods rather than of the perfect indicative.

The perfect participle active is a first-and-third declension adjective like the other active participles. Its masculine and neuter stem is λελυκ-οτ- and its feminine stem is λελυκ-υια-. It is accented on the last syllable of the stem.

	Masc.	Fem.	Neu.
singular			
nom.	λελυκώς	λελυκυῖα	λελυκός
gen.	λελυκότος	λελυκυίας	λελυκότος
dat.	λελυκότι	λελυκυίᾳ	λελυκότι
acc.	λελυκότα	λελυκυῖαν	λελυκός
dual			
nom., acc.	λελυκότε	λελυκυίᾱ	λελυκότε
gen., dat.	λελυκότοιν	λελυκυίαιν	λελυκότοιν
plural			
nom.	λελυκότες	λελυκυῖαι	λελυκότα
gen.	λελυκότων	λελυκυιῶν	λελυκότων
dat.	λελυκόσι(ν)	λελυκυίαις	λελυκόσι(ν)
acc.	λελυκότας	λελυκυία-ς	λελυκότα

One fairly common verb has an irregular perfect participle active: (ἀπο-)θνῄσκω. The expected form τεθνήκως is not used, but instead we have τεθνεώς, -ῶσα, -ός, masculine genitive singular τεθνεῶτος. The accent is always on the syllable -ωτ- before the ending.

Exercise

Determine what the perfect active stem should be for each of the following verbs. Check the result against the vocabulary listing. (Work it out for yourself *first* rather than simply looking up the principal parts.) Then write out the perfect indicative active for any three of them.

παύω, stop, cause to stop; πορεύω, transport; παιδεύω, instruct; κελεύω, bid; πιστεύω, believe; ὀργίζω, anger; κλήω, shut; κωλύω, hinder; στεφανόω, crown; φυτεύω, plant; στερέω, deprive.

XIV.2 Uses of the perfect

The perfect tense has **stative** aspect. That is, it refers to a state that the subject is in, typically as a result of a prior action. Another way to look at it is that the perfect denotes the continuing consequences of a previous act. Thus τὸ βιβλίον γέγραφα means something like "I have the status of writer: I wrote the book and am therefore now a writer." English does not always distinguish between "I am in the writer's state," γέγραφα, and "I wrote," ἔγραψα, simple past (aorist). The perfect is a primary tense, so the OOO rule does not apply to subordinate clauses when the main verb is perfect.

What's called the perfect in English is a past tense compounded with *have*, as "I have written." Sometimes this has a similar meaning to the Greek perfect, but not always; in particular, in questions ("Have you written that letter yet?") it is usually a simple past (same as "Did you write that letter yet?"), for which Greek would use the aorist.

The pluperfect tense is an anterior past, past-in-the-past. It is the same as the English pluperfect, the tense compounded with *had*. Thus ἐγεγράφει is "he had written." There is no difficulty about the pluperfect: it's easy to recognize, because it is the only form that is both augmented (since it's a past tense) and reduplicated with -ε- (since it comes from the perfect system), and it works just like the similarly named tense in English.

In your own speaking and writing, though, do not forget that English and Greek have different tense rules for subordinate clauses. In English we say "He said that he had written the letter," using the pluperfect because the main verb is past tense. In Greek, this would be εἶπε ὅτι τὴν ἐπιστολὴν ἔγραψε or (with the OOO rule) εἶπε ὅτι τὴν ἐπιστολὴν γράψαι. The pluperfect would not make sense: it would mean "he said, 'I had written the letter'" rather than "he said, 'I wrote the letter.'"

XIV.3 Third declension: liquid stems

A group of third declension nouns ends in -ν. The nominative singular will have a long vowel, but the stem may have a long vowel or a short one; the genitive case will tell you. There are also a few stems in -ρ and one or two in -λ.

Examples: Ἕλλην, Ἕλληνος, ὁ or ἡ, Greek (stem Ἕλλην-); λιμήν, λιμένος, ὁ, harbor (stem λιμεν-).

singular

nom., voc.	Ἕλλην	λιμήν
gen.	Ἕλληνος	λιμένος
dat.	Ἕλληνι	λιμένι
acc.	Ἕλληνα	λιμένα

dual

nom., acc., voc.	Ἕλληνε	λιμένε
gen., dat.	Ἑλλήνοιν	λιμένοιν

plural

nom., voc.	Ἕλληνες	λιμένες
gen.	Ἑλλήνων	λιμένων
dat.	Ἕλλησι(ν)	λιμέσι(ν)
acc.	Ἕλληνας	λιμένας

So δελφίς, δελφῖνος, ὁ, ἡ "dolphin," dative plural δελφῖσι(ν).

Similarly these stems in -ων- and -ον-:

> λειμών, λειμῶνος, ὁ "meadow," λειμῶσι(ν).

> γείτων, γείτονος, ὁ "neighbor," γειτόσι(ν).

The declension of other stems is similar. In each of these nouns, the genitive singular will show whether the stem vowel is long or short. The vowel is long in the nominative singular because the -ς ending has combined with the final consonant of the stem; the vowel is lengthened to ensure that the syllable remains long: λιμήν, for example, was originally λιμένς. When the consonant cluster was simplified, the vowel was changed by **compensatory lengthening**, as if to "make up" for the lost sound, giving λιμήν.

Here are more nouns that work the same way, with their principal parts and dative plural forms:

> ὁ θήρ "beast," θηρός, θηρσί(ν) — (ρ-stem).

> ὁ ῥήτωρ "orator," ῥήτορος, ῥήτορσι(ν) — (ρ-stem).

> ὁ ἅλς "salt," ἁλός, ἁλσί(ν) — (the only λ-stem).

Nouns whose stems end in dental consonants also show cluster simplification in the nominative singular, from -τς or -δς to just -ς. In a noun whose stem ends in a labial or guttural stop, the stop is assimilated to the unvoiced -ς of the nominative singular, but does not entirely disappear. Thus -κ-ς and -γ-ς both produce -ξ in the nominative singular, while -π-ς and -β-ς both produce -ψ.

> ὁ, ἡ αἴξ "goat," αἰγός, αἰξί(ν) — (guttural stem).

> ὁ γύψ "vulture," γυ-πός, γυ-ψί(ν) — (labial stem).

> ὁ, ἡ φυγάς "fugitive," φυγάδος, φυγάσι(ν) — (dental stem).

ὁ θής "laborer," θητός, θησί(ν) — (dental stem). Also like this are declined all the feminine abstract nouns in -της formed from adjectives, for example ἡ χρηστότης "honesty," χρηστότητος, or ταχυτής, ταχυτῆτος "speed" from ταχύς "fast."

The forms of θήρ, θηρός contradict the rule that accent in nouns is persistent. In fact, there is a special rule for third declension nouns of one syllable: in these words, the genitive and dative always have the accent on their last syllable. Thus τοῦ θηρός, αἰγός, γυπός, and so on.

XIV.4 Irregular nouns (third declension)

Several common words are irregular.

First is the name Ζεύς, an ancient name cognate with Latin *Iuppiter* and Sanskrit *dyaus*. Its oblique cases are regular. In the nominative and vocative, the δι- cluster has become ζ- before the diphthong ευ.

nom.	Ζεύς
gen.	Διός
dat.	Διί
acc.	Δία
voc.	Ζεῦ

Next comes the word for "woman," γυνή. The stem is γυναικ-; only the nominative and vocative singular are irregular. We might have expected something like γυναίξ, but instead all the consonants have disappeared. Be careful: the nominative singular looks like it belongs to a *first* declension noun, but it doesn't.

	Singular	Dual	Plural
nom.	γυνή	γυναῖκε	γυναῖκες
gen.	γυναικός	γυναικοῖν	γυναικῶν
dat.	γυναικί	γυναικοῖν	γυναιξί(ν)
acc.	γυναῖκα	γυναῖκε	γυναῖκας
voc.	γύναι	γυναῖκε	γυναῖκες

The remaining nouns in this group have stems ending in vowels: ναῦς, νεώς, ἡ, "ship"; γραῦς, γρᾱός, ἡ, "old woman"; βοῦς, βοός, ἡ, ὁ "cow, ox."

singular

nom.	ναῦς	γραῦς	βοῦς
gen.	νεώς	γρᾱός	βοός
dat.	νηΐ	γρᾱΐ	βοΐ
acc.	ναῦν	γραῦν	βοῦν
voc.	ναῦ	γραῦ	βοῦ

dual

nom., acc., voc.	νῆε	γρᾶε	βόε
gen., dat.	νεοῖν	γρᾱοῖν	βοοῖν

plural

nom., voc.	νῆες	γρᾶες	βόες
gen.	νεῶν	γρᾱῶν	βοῶν
dat.	ναυσί(ν)	γραυσί(ν)	βουσί(ν)
acc.	ναῦς	γραῦς	βοῦς

Don't confuse the forms of ναῦς with those of νεώς "temple." Note the dative singular forms νηΐ, γρᾱΐ, and βοΐ. Each of these is two syllables, not one syllable with a diphthong. The **diaeresis** on the ϊ indicates this; *diaeresis* means "separation, taking away," from διαιρέω, divide, separate.

Exercise

Write out the complete declension of the following phrases: ἡ εὐγενὴς γυνή, ὁ μέγας λειμών, ὁ ἀγαθὸς ῥήτωρ, ἡ λευκὴ βοῦς.

XIV.5 Gnomic aorist

The aorist tense can be used to express a habit or a general rule. This is called the **gnomic aorist** because it is the typical tense for a γνώμη, a proverb or maxim. For example, ὁ Ἔρως διαφθείρει τε πολλὰ καὶ ἠδίκησεν, "love destroys (present) many things and is unjust (aorist)" (Plato, *Symposium* 188a); this is, in context, a general truth, not a statement about the past. The aorist is used for these because it is the most general tense, not necessarily denoting a particular aspect (as the present and perfect do). If there were a present tense in the aorist system, it would be exactly right for gnomic statements.

XIV.6 Words for ability

There are several ways to say someone can do something, or is able to do it. You have seen ἔχω and δύναμαι, each with a complementary infinitive: ὁ μαθητὴς ἔχει γράψαι, ὁ μαθητὴς δύναται γράψαι. The idiom οἷός τ' εἰμί is another way: ὁ μαθητὴς οἷός τ' ἐστὶ γράψαι. A fourth is with the adjective ἱκανός, "sufficient, competent": ὁ μαθητὴς ἱκανός ἐστι γράψαι. Yet one more is the impersonal verb ἔξεστι, taking an infinitive as subject: ἔξεστι τὸν μαθητὴν γράψαι.

XIV.7 Vocabulary

VERBS

ᾄδω, ᾄσω, ᾖσα, –, –, ᾔσθην, sing, crow

ἀνα-φέρω, lift up, bring back; praise

ἀρόω, ἀρόσω, ἤροσα, ἀρήροκα, ἀρήρομαι, ἠρόθην, plow (cp. L. *arare, aratrum*)

βοάω, βοήσω, ἐβόησα, βεβόηκα, βεβόημαι, ἐβοήθην, shout, cry out

γεωργέω, γεωργήσω, ἐγεώργησα, –, –, –, farm, be a farmer

δεῖ, δεήσει, ἐδέησε, –, –, –, it is necessary (impersonal)

δέχομαι, δέξομαι, ἐδεξάμην, –, δέδεγμαι, ἐδέχθην, receive (cp. *synecdoche, xenodochia*, L. *decus, decet*)

εἴωθα, be accustomed, do habitually (perfect system only)

ἐκ-πίπτω, fall out, be sent ashore

ἔξεστι, it is possible, usually with infinitive as subject

ἐρέττω, ἐρέσω, ἤρεσα, –, –, –, row

ἡττάομαι, ἡττήσομαι, –, –, ἥττημαι, ἡσσήθην, be less (than someone, in genitive), be beaten, lose

κατηγορέω, accuse (κατά + ἀγορεύω)

μέλλω, μελλήσω, ἐμέλλησα, –, –, –, intend

νέμω, νεμῶ, ἔνειμα, νενέμηκα, νενέμημαι, ἐνεμήθην, tend (cattle or the like), pasture; share out, allot, distribute

πίπτω, πεσοῦμαι, ἔπεσον, πέπτωκα, –, –, fall (cp. *symptom*)

ὑπερ-βάλλω, surpass

ὑπό-κειμαι, lie beneath

φθέγγομαι, φθέγξομαι, ἐφθεγξάμην, –, ἔφθεγμαι, –, utter a voice or sound, articulate

ὠφελέω, ὠφελήσω, ὠφέλησα, ὠφέληκα, ὠφέλημαι, ὠφελήθην, help, assist

NOUNS

ἀγέλη, -ης, ἡ, herd

αἰθρίᾱ, -ᾱς, ἡ, fine weather

ἀλεκτρυών, -όνος, ὁ, rooster, fowl

ἅλς, ἁλός, ὁ, salt (cp. *salt*, L. *sal*)

ἀμέλεια, -ας, ἡ, carelessness, disregard

ᾆσμα, -ατος, το, song, chanty

αὐλών, -ῶνος, ὁ, ditch, ravine, hollow

βοῦς, βοός, ἡ, ο, cow, ox, bull (cp. *cow*, L. *bos*)

γαλήνη, -ης, ἡ, calm weather

γείτων, -ονος, ὁ, ἡ, neighbor

γνώμη, -ης, ἡ, thought, judgement, intention; proverb, maxim

γραῦς, γρᾶός, ἡ, old woman

γυνή, γυναικός, η, woman (cp. *queen, quean, gynecology*)

γύψ, γῦπός, ὁ, vulture

δελφίς, δελφῖνος, ὁ, ἡ, dolphin

Ἕλλην, Ἕλληνος, ὁ, Greek

θήρ, θηρός, ὁ, beast (cp. *theriomorphic, treacle*, L. *ferus*)

θής, θητός, ὁ, laborer, thete

κάματος, -ου, ὁ, toil, effort

κώπη, -ης, ἡ, oar

λειμών, λειμῶνος, ὁ, meadow

λιμήν, λιμένος, ὁ, harbor

μάρτυς, μάρτυρος, ο, witness (cp. *martyr*)

μιμητής, -οῦ, ὁ, imitator (cp. *mimic*)

ναῦς, νεώς, ἡ, ship

ὄργανον, -ου, τό, instrument, tool (cp. *organ*)

ῥήτωρ, ῥήτορος, ὁ, orator (cp. *rhetoric*)

σῖτος, -ου, ὁ, grain, food in general

τράγος, -ου, ὁ, he-goat, male goat

φυγάς, φυγάδος, ὁ, ἡ, fugitive, exile

χορός, -ου, ὁ, body of dancers or singers (cp. *chorus*)

ᾠδή, -ῆς, ἡ, song (cp. *ode*)

ADVERBS

ἐν ᾧ (χρόνῳ), while

ἰδίᾳ, separately (cp. *idiot, idiosyncratic*)

ADJECTIVES

ἄμεμπτος, -ον, blameless

ἐρρωμένος, -η, -ον, strong

ἱερός, -ά, -όν, sacred, holy (cp. *hieroglyphic*)

ἱκανός, -ή, -όν, capable, sufficient

κοῖλος, -ν, -ον, hollow

λοιπός, -ή, -όν, left, remaining

ναυτικός, -ή, -όν, relating to a ship, nautical

οἷος, -α, -ον, as, such

ὁμόφωνος, -ον, in harmony, harmonious (cp. *homophony*)

πρότερος, -α, -ον, prior, former, earlier

σαφής, -ές, clear, distinct

τρισχίλιοι, -αι, -α, 3000

φαῦλος, -η, -ον, miserable, contemptible

Notes on the vocabulary

ἄδω is contracted from ἀείδω. Attic prose uses the contracted form, while the uncontracted form is used in epic and in other dialects. The nouns ᾆσμα and ᾠδή are also related.

ἀναφέρω can mean "praise" just as we might use "build up" in English.

The forms of δεῖ are just like those of πλέω except that this verb only exists in third person singular and only in the present system. It takes an infinitive as its subject (which may have a subject, object, and so on of its own), as δεῖ γράψαι "writing is necessary, it is necessary to write" or δεῖ σὲ γράψαι "it is necessary that you write" or δεῖ σὲ τὴν ἐπιστολὴν γράψαι "it is necessary that you write the letter."

εἴωθα is an isolated perfect, with no present in use in Attic. It takes a complementary infinitive, as γράφειν εἴωθα, "I am in the habit of writing, I'm used to writing."

Although ἔξεστι is compounded from ἐξ + εἰμι, it is not enclitic. Only the 3rd singular forms are used, generally with an infinitive as subject.

The active ἡττάω that goes with ἡττάομαι comes into use relatively late; in classical Attic Greek the verb is only passive.

μέλλω may have ἠ- instead of ἐ- for its augment in the imperfect. The verb takes a complementary infinitive, often a future infinitive: μέλλω γράφειν or μέλλω γράψειν both mean "I intend to write." Because sometimes what one *intends* to do does not actually get done, μέλλω can also mean "hesitate, hold off, defer."

The θῆτες made up the fourth and lowest social class in classical Athens. They were free men, but relatively poor; they could not afford horses or hoplite armor. They were typically paid workers.

λειμών and λιμήν sound similar because they are related to each other.

σῖτος is masculine in the singular, but its plural is τὰ σῖτα.

XIV.8 Reading

1. *Sailors' Chanties*

ἐσθιόντων δ᾽ αὐτῶν ναῦς ὤφθη παραπλέουσα. ἄνεμος μὲν οὐκ ἦν, γαλήνη δ᾽ ἦν καὶ ἐρέττειν ἐδόκει· καὶ ἤρεττον ἐρρωμένως· ἠπείγοντο γάρ. οἷον οὖν εἰώθασι ναῦται δρᾶν ἐς καμάτων ἀμέλειαν, τοῦτο κἀκεῖνοι δρῶντες τὰς κώπας ἀνέφερον. εἰς μὲν αὐτοῖς κελευστὴς ναυτικὰς ᾖδεν ᾠδάς, οἱ δὲ λοιποί, ὥσπερ χορός, ὁμοφώνως κατὰ καιρὸν τῆς ἐκείνου φωνῆς ἐβόων. ἐν ᾧ δὲ ταῦτα ἔπραττον, πολλὴ μὲν ἠκούετο βοή, σαφῆ δ᾽ ἐξέπιπτεν εἰς τὴν γῆν τὰ τῶν κελευστῶν ᾄσματα. κοῖλος γὰρ τῷ πεδίῳ αὐλὼν ὑποκείμενος, καὶ τὴν ἠχὴν εἰς αὐτὸν ὡς ὄργανον δεχόμενος, πάντων τῶν φθεγγομένων μιμητὴν φωνὴν ἀποδίδωσιν, ἰδίᾳ μὲν τῶν κωπῶν τὴν ἠχήν, ἰδίᾳ δὲ τὴν φωνὴν τῶν ναυτῶν.

From *Daphnis and Chloe*, 3.21.

Remember **ὤφθην** is the sixth principal part of ὁράω. **κελευστής, -οῦ, ὁ,** coxswain, boatswain. **βοή, -ῆς, ἡ,** sound. **ἠχή, -ῆς, ἡ,** sound; generally a poetic word.

2. *A Proposal of Marriage*

ἐμοὶ δὸς Χλόην γυναῖκα. ἐγὼ καὶ συρίζειν οἶδα καλῶς, καὶ κλᾶν ἄμπελον, καὶ φυτὰ κατορύττειν· οἶδα καὶ γῆν ἀροῦν, καὶ λικμῆσαι πρὸς ἄνεμον. ἀγέλην δ' ὅπως νέμω μάρτυς Χλόη· πεντήκοντ' αἶγας παραλαβὼν διπλασίους πεποίηκα· ἔθρεψα καὶ τράγους μεγάλους καὶ καλούς. καὶ νέος εἰμὶ καὶ γείτων ὑμῖν ἄμεμπτος. τοσοῦτον δὲ τοὺς ἄλλους ὑπερβάλλων οὐδὲ δώροις ἡττηθήσομαι. ἐκεῖνοι δώσουσιν αἶγας καὶ πρόβατα καὶ ζεῦγος φαύλων βοϊδίων, καὶ σῖτον οὐδ' ἀλεκτρυόνας οἷόν τε θρέψαι· παρ' ἐμοῦ δ' αἵδε αἱ τρισχίλιαι δραχμαί.

Daphnis and Chloe, 3.29.

δός is 2nd sg aorist imperative active of δίδωμι; see chapter 16. **συρίζω**, whistle, play the syrinx (σῦριγξ) or pan-pipe. **οἶδα**, 1st sg, "know"; this verb has only a perfect system. See chapter 17. **κλάω**, pluck, break off. **κατορύττω**, plant, bury. **λικμάω**, winnow, blow away the chaff or husks from grain (predictable principal parts). **τὸ ζεῦγός** ἐστι δύο ἵππω ὑπὸ τῷ αὐτῷ ζυγῷ. **βοΐδιον, -ου, τό** is a diminutive from βοῦς, like παιδίον from παῖς.

3. ὁ δελφίς ἐστι θὴρ τῆς θαλάττης. ἰχθὺς οὔκ ἔστι, καίπερ τὴν θάλατταν οἰκῶν. δελφῖνες οὐκ οἷοί τ' εἰσὶ λέγειν ὥσπερ οἱ ἄνθρωποι, ἀλλὰ ᾄδουσιν. σοφοὶ οἱ δελφῖνες. πολλὰς γνώμας γιγνώσκουσι, οἶμαι, ἃς ἡμεῖς οὐδεπώποτε ἀκουσόμεθα, διότι οὐ μανθάνομεν τὰς τῶν δελφίνων ᾠδάς. ἀλλ' εἰ ἐκ τοῦ λιμένος πλέομεν, οἱ δελφῖνες, γείτονες ἡμῶν ὄντες, εἰκότως ἡμᾶς δέξονται. τί μέλλομεν; πλέωμεν εὐθὺς ἵνα τοὺς δελφῖνας ὁρῶμεν. ἑπώμεθα τούτοις τοῖς θηρσὶ διὰ τῆς θαλάττης.

4. βόες ἐν λειμῶσι οὐ νέμονται, ἀλλὰ ἐν ἀγροῖς. τὰ γὰρ φυτὰ τῶν λειμώνων οὔκ εἰσι ἱκανὰ τοὺς βοῦς τρέφειν. οἱ δὲ βόες οὐκ ἐσθίουσι τοιαῦτα φυτά. δεῖ τοὺς βοῦς πόαν φαγεῖν. οἱ μὲν βόες τὴν πόαν φαγεῖν, οἱ δὲ γῦπες τοὺς τεθνεῶτας βοῦς, ἢ τὰ τῶν ἀλλῶν ζῴων σώματα. τοῖς μὲν βουσὶ σῖτον δίδομεν, ἡμῖν δὲ οἱ βόες γάλακτα διδόασι. καὶ δὴ καὶ ἄλον τοῖς βουσὶ δίδομεν, πάντων ζῴων τὸν ἄλον ἐσθιόντων. οἱ βόες φθέγγονται, "μοῦ μοῦ" λέγοντες. ἐπειδὰν αἰθρία ᾖ, οἱ βόες χαίρουσι.

πόα, -ας, ἡ, grass. **γάλα, γάλακτος, τό**, milk.

5. οἱ θῆτες οὔκ εἰσι δοῦλοι, ἀλλ' ἐλεύθεροι. ἔξεστι αὐτοὺς ἀπὸ τῆς πόλεως ἀναχωρεῖν καὶ ἐπανέρχεσθαι, εἰ ἐθέλουσι· φυγάδες οὐκ ἂν εἶεν. οὐ πλουτοῦσι. ἔργα δὲ καὶ καμάτους πράττουσι τοῖς ἄλλοις, μισθὸν δεχόμενοι. γεωργοῦσι μὲν τοὺς ἀγρούς, ἐν δὲ ναυσὶ ναῦται γίγνονται, στρατιῶται δ' εἰσί, οἰκίας δὲ ποιοῦσι καὶ νεώς. πέντε ἢ ἓξ ὀβολοὺς καθ' ἡμέραν διδόασι οἱ δεσπόται τοῖς θησίν. οἱ ῥήτορες εἰώθασι λέγειν τοὺς θῆτας ἀγαθοὺς εἶναι, καίπερ νομίζοντες αὐτοὺς φαύλους. ἐπὶ τῇ δημοκρατίᾳ οἱ θῆτες, πολλοὶ ὄντες, πολλὰ δύνανται.

6. ἀλλὰ γὰρ οὐ τὰ μέλλοντα ἔσεσθαι βούλομαι λέγειν, τὰ πραχθέντα ὑπὸ τούτων οὐ δυνάμενος εἰπεῖν. οὐδὲ γὰρ ἑνὸς κατηγόρου οὐδὲ δυοῖν ἔργον ἐστίν, ἀλλὰ πολλῶν. ὅμως δὲ τῆς ἐμῆς προθυμίας οὐδὲν ἐλλέλειπται, ὑπέρ τε τῶν ἱερῶν, ἃ οὗτοι τὰ μὲν ἀπέδοντο τὰ δ᾽ εἰσιόντες ἐμίαινον, ὑπέρ τε τῆς πόλεως, ἣν μικρὰν ἐποίουν, ὑπέρ τε τῶν νεωρίων, ἃ καθεῖλον, καὶ ὑπὲρ τῶν τεθνεώτων, οἷς ὑμεῖς, ἐπειδὴ ζῶσιν ἐπαμῦναι οὐκ ἐδύνασθε, ἀποθανοῦσι βοηθήσατε.

οἶμαι δ᾽ αὐτοὺς ἡμῶν τε ἀκροᾶσθαι καὶ ὑμᾶς εἴσεσθαι τὴν ψῆφον φέροντας, ἡγουμένους, ὅσοι μὲν ἂν τούτων ἀποψηφίσησθε, αὐτῶν θάνατον κατεψηφισμένους ἔσεσθαι, ὅσοι δ᾽ ἂν παρὰ τούτων δίκην λάβωσιν, ὑπὲρ αὐτῶν τιμωρίας πεποιημένους.

παύσομαι κατηγορῶν. ἀκηκόατε, ἑωράκατε, πεπόνθατε, ἔχετε· δικάζετε.

This is the conclusion of Lysias speech 12, against Eratosthenes.

κατήγορος, -ου, ὁ = ἄνθρωπος ὃς κατηγορεῖ. **προθυμία, -ας, ἡ**, good will, zeal. **ἐκ-λείπω**, leave out, omit, abandon. **τὸ ἱερόν** = ὁ νεώς, from ἱερός. **μιαίνω**, desecrate, pollute. **νεώριον, -ου, τό**, dockyard, shipyard. **καθεῖλον**, 3rd pl aorist indicative active of **καθ-αιρέω**, take down, destroy (chapter 15). **ζάω** = βιόω, βίον ἔχω. **ἐπαμύνω** = ὠφελέω, **βοηθέω** = ὠφελέω. **ἀκροάομαι** = ἀκούω. **εἴσεσθαι** is future infinitive middle of οἶδα, know (chapter 17). **ψῆφος, -ου, ἡ**, vote; ψῆφον φέρειν, to vote, to give one's vote; ἀποψηφίζομαι, acquit, vote to acquit, vote a charge away; καταψηφίζομαι, vote against, vote to condemn. **τιμωρία, -ας, ἡ**, vengeance, retribution. **δικάζω**, judge, adjudicate.

7. ὁ θεὸς Πᾶν λέγει·

τῆς Ἀττικῆς νομίζετ᾽ εἶναι τὸν τόπον,
Φυλήν, τὸ νυμφαῖον δ᾽ ὅθεν προέρχομαι
Φυλασίων καὶ τῶν δυναμένων τὰς πέτρας
ἐνθάδε γεωργεῖν, ἱερὸν ἐπιφανὲς πάνυ.
τὸν ἀγρὸν δὲ τὸν ἐπὶ δεξί᾽ οἰκεῖ τουτονὶ   5
Κνήμων, ἀπάνθρωπός τις ἄνθρωπος σφόδρα
καὶ δύσκολος πρὸς ἅπαντας, οὐ χαίρων τ᾽ ὄχλῳ.
"ὄχλῳ" λέγω; ζῶν οὗτος ἐπιεικῶς χρόνον
πολὺν λελάληκεν ἡδέως ἐν τῷ βίῳ
οὐδενί, προσηγόρευκε πρότερος δ᾽ οὐδένα,   10
πλὴν ἐξ ἀνάγκης γειτνιῶν παριών τ᾽ ἐμὲ
τὸν Πᾶνα· καὶ τοῦτ᾽ εὐθὺς αὐτῷ μεταμέλει,
εὖ οἶδ᾽. ὅμως οὖν, τῷ τρόπῳ τοιοῦτος ὤν,
χήραν γυναῖκ᾽ ἔγημε, τετελευτηκότος
αὐτῇ νεωστὶ τοῦ λαβόντος τὸ πρότερον   15
υἱοῦ τε καταλελειμμένου μικροῦ τότε.
...
ὁ γέρων δ᾽ ἔχων τὴν θυγατέρ᾽ αὐτὸς ζῇ μόνος   30
καὶ γραῦν θεράπαιναν, ξυλοφορῶν σκάπτων τ᾽, ἀεὶ
πονῶν, ἀπὸ τούτων ἀρξάμενος τῶν γειτόνων
καὶ τῆς γυναικὸς μέχρι Χολαργέων κάτω
μισῶν ἐφεξῆς πάντας.

This is the opening of Menander's play *Δύσκολος*, lines 1-16 and 30-34.

νομίζετε is imperative, to the audience, establishing the scene. **τόπος, -ου, ὁ**, place. **νυμφαῖον, -ου, τό**, shrine to the nymphs. **προ-έρχομαι**, come forward, come near. **ἐπιφανής, -ές**, apparent, conspicuous, outstanding. **δεξιός, -ά, -όν**, right; ἐπὶ δεξιά, on the right; in the verse line, because the last syllable of δεξιά is elided and δεξιά is not a particle, preposition, or the like, the accent moves back to the previous syllable so the word will not lose its accent altogether. **τουτονί** = τοῦτον, with the emphatic suffix -ι. **ἀπάνθρωπος** = ἀπὸ τῶν ἀνθρώπων, ὃς ἀνθρώποις οὐ συγγίγνεται. **δύσκολος, -ον**, grouchy, bad-tempered. **ὄχλος, -ου, ὁ**, crowd, throng, mob. **ζάω** = βιόω, βίον ἔχω. **ἐπιεικῶς**, moderately, fairly. **ἡδέως**, pleasantly. **ἀνάγκη, -ης, ἡ**, necessity. **γειτνιάω** = γείτων εἰμί. **παριών** is present participle active of πάρειμι from εἶμι, go past, go by. **μεταμέλει**, 3rd person only, cause regret, cause sorrow, be an object of regret. **οἶδα**, know, 1st sg; this verb has only a perfect system. **τρόπος, -ου, ὁ**, way, way of doing something, way of life. **χῆρος, -α, -ον**, bereaved, widowed. **γαμέω, γαμῶ, ἔγημα, γεγάμηκα, γεγάμημαι, ἐγαμήθην**, marry. **νεωστί**, recently. **γέρων, -οντος, ὁ**, old man. **θυγάτηρ, θυγατρός, ἡ**, daughter. **θεράπαινα, -ας, ἡ** = οἰκετὴς ἢ δοῦλος ἥ ἐστι γυνή. **ξυλοφορέω**, carry wood. **σκάπτω**, dig. **πονέω** = ἔργον πράττω.

8a. τί χρῆμ' ἀλύω, πνεῦμ' ἀνεὶς ἐκ πλευμόνων;
     ποῖ ποῖ ποθ' ἡλάμεσθα δεμνίων ἄπο;
     ἐκ κυμάτων γὰρ αὖθις αὖ γαλήν' ὁρῶ.

Euripides, *Orestes* 277-279. Orestes speaks; he has just had a vision or hallucination.

ἀλύω, be distraught, have one's mind wander. **πνεῦμα, -ατος, τό**, breath. **ἀνείς** is present participle active, masc. nom. sg., from ἀν-ίημι, send out. **πλεύμων, -ονος, ὁ**, lung. **ἡλάμεσθα** = ἡλάμεθα, from ἅλλομαι, ἁλοῦμαι, ἡλάμην, spring, jump; Orestes simply means himself. **δέμνια, -ων, τά**, bedding. **κῦμα, κύματος, τό**, waves, stormy sea. **γαληνός, -ή, -όν**, calm. The accent on ἄπο is on the first syllable because the object of the preposition comes before it rather than after. The accent of **γαλήν'** (= τὰ γαληνά) has moved because of the elision, just as for δεξιά in reading 7.

Prose paraphrase: διὰ τί ἀλύω, τὸ πνεῦμα ἀνεὶς ἐκ τῶν πλευμόνων; ποῖ ἀπὸ τῶν δεμνίων ἄλλομαι; ἐκ τῶν κυμάτων γὰρ αὖθις τὴν γαλήνην ὁρῶ. When this play was performed at the City Dionysia festival of 408, Hegelochus took the role of Orestes and mispronounced a crucial word. Comic poets recalled the incident for the next several years:

b. τί οὖν γενόμενος εἰς ὀπὴν ἐνδύσομαι;
    ζητητέον· φέρ' εἰ γενοίμην μυγαλῆ.
    ἀλλ' Ἡγέλοχος οὗτός με μηνύσειεν ἄν
    ὁ τραγικὸς ἀνακράγοι τ' ἂν εἰς ἐχθροὺς μέγα
    "ἐκ κυμάτων γὰρ αὖθις αὖ γαλῆν ὁρῶ."

A fragment from the comedy *Danae* by Sannyrion.

ὀπή, -ῆς, ἡ, opening in the roof for a chimney. ἐνδύομαι, go into, put on (clothes). ζητητέος, -α, -ον, needing to be sought or looked into. μυγαλῆ, -ῆς, ἡ, field mouse, shrew. μηνύω, reveal, betray, make known. ἀνα-κράζω = βοάω. ἐχθρός, -ά, -όν, enemy, hostile. γαλῆ, -ῆς, ἡ, weasel; contracted like γῆ.

c. θάρρει· πάντ᾽ ἀγαθὰ πεπράγαμεν,
ἔξεστί θ᾽, ὥσπερ Ἡγέλοχος, ἡμῖν λέγειν,
"ἐκ κυμάτων γὰρ αὖθις αὖ γαλῆν ὁρῶ."

Aristophanes, *Frogs* 302-304, referring to the same incident, three years later. θαρρέω, be brave, be courageous.

9. *περὶ τοῦ Τρωικοῦ πολέμου, ὄγδοον μέρος*

δέκατον ἔτος νῦν ἐγίγνετο τοῦ πολέμου. τοῦ Ἕκτορος θανομένου, οἱ Τρῶες κακῶς εἶχον. καθ᾽ ἡμέραν μὲν οἱ Ἕλληνες πρὸς τὰ τείχη ἤρχοντο, καθ᾽ ἡμέραν δὲ πολλοὶ στρατιῶται Τρωικοὶ ἀπέθνησκον.

ἡμέρα τινὶ ὁ Ἀχιλλεὺς εὖ ἐμάχετο. τοὺς δὲ Τρῶας ἐδίωξε εἰς τὴν πόλιν. ἐνθάδε ὁ Πάρις αὐτὸν ἀνέμενε, τὰ τόξα ἔχων. "εὖ οἶδα ὅτι ἔγωγε αἴτιός εἰμι τούτου τοῦ πολέμου," εἶπε. "εἰ τὸν Ἀχιλλέα ἀποκτείνειν δύναμαι, τοὺς Ἕλληνας μαχομένους παύσω καὶ τὴν πόλιν σώσω. ὠφελοῖς ἄν μοι, ὦ Ἀπόλλω, εἰ σοὶ δοκεῖ. οὐ μὲν οἷός τ᾽ εἰμὶ αὐτὸν ἀποκτείνειν ἄνευ ὠφελείας· σὺν δὲ τοῖς θεοῖς πᾶν ἔξεστι."

ὁ δὲ Ἀπόλλων ἤκουσε. ὅτε ὁ Πάρις ἐτόξευε, ὁ θεὸς τὸν οἰστὸν ἔλαβε καὶ πρὸς τὸν Ἀχιλλέα ἤγαγε. ὁ δὲ Ἀχιλλεὺς ἔπεσε.

οἱ μὲν Τρῶες ἔχαιρον, οἱ δὲ Ἀχαιοὶ οὔ. οἱ μὲν "νῦν νενίκαμεν," οἱ δὲ "νῦν ἐνικήθημεν," ἐνόμισαν.

ὁ δὲ Ὀδυσσεὺς τοῖς ἄλλοις Ἀχαιοῖς εἶπε, "μὴ ἀπογνῶτε. δυνάμεθα ἔτι τὴν πόλιν λαβεῖν· οὔπω ὁ πόλεμος τέλος ἔχει. οὐ γὰρ ἡττώμεθα τῶν Τρώων. πρῶτον μὲν οὖν δεῖ τὸ τοῦ Ἀχιλλέως σῶμα ἀναλαβεῖν ἵνα θάπτωμεν. ἔπειτα δὲ πάλιν μαχούμεθα. τίς οὖν τὸ σῶμα ἀναλήψεται; τίς οἷός τ᾽ ἐστὶ τὸ τοῦ ἑταίρου σῶμα σῴζειν;"

"ἔγωγε," ἔφη ὁ Αἴας, καὶ εἰς τὴν πόλιν εἰσῆλθε. μετὰ μεγάλην καὶ μακρὰν μάχην τὸ σῶμα ἀνέλαβε. οἱ δὲ Ἕλληνες προέθεσαν τὸ σῶμα. ἡ δὲ Θέτις, μήτηρ οὖσα τοῦ Ἀχιλλέως, τὸ σῶμα ἀφεῖλε πρὸς τὴν Λευκὴν Νῆσον, οὗ οἰκοῦν οἱ ἥρωες. οἱ δὲ ἥρωες τὸν Ἀχιλλέα ἐδέξαντο ὡς καὶ αὐτὸν ἥρωα ὄντα.

οἱ Ἕλληνες ἀγῶνα ἔθεσαν ἐπὶ τῷ Ἀχιλλέι. ἔπειτα πάλιν ἐμάχοντο.

διώκω, διώξω, ἐδίωξα, δεδίωχα, δεδίωγμαι, ἐδιώχθην, chase. ἀνα-μένω, wait for. τόξα, -ων, τά, bow and arrows. αἴτιος, -α, -ον, responsible for, causing, guilty of. τοξεύω = οἰστῷ βάλλω. οἰστός, -οῦ, ὁ, arrow. ἀπο-γιγνώσκω, despair, give up hope. ἀνα-λαμβάνω, retrieve, take up. θάπτω, bury. μάχη, -ης, ἡ, battle. προ-τίθημι, lay out (a body before burial), display. νῆσος, -ου, ἡ, island. ἥρως, ἥρωος, ὁ, hero.

XIV.9 Conversation

1. (reading 1) ποῖος ἦν ὁ οὐρανός; αἰθρία δή· ἆρ᾽ ἄνεμος ἦν; τί ἐφαίνετο; πότε; πῶς ἐπορεύετο; τί ἐποίουν οἱ ναῦται; διὰ τί; πῶς ἤκουσεν ὁ Δάφνις;

2. (reading 2) τί οἶδε ὁ Δάφνις; τί ἔχει; τί ζητεῖ; πόσους αἶγας ἔχει; τί δώσει; πρὸς τί; and so on, as usual.

XIV.10 Supplement: Weather

Following are words related to weather and climate. They may be used in conversation or writing.

οὐρανός, -οῦ, ὁ, sky, climate (cp. *Uranus*)

ἀήρ, ἀέρος, ὁ, air

αἰθρίᾱ, -ᾱς, ἡ, clear weather

νεφέλη, -ης, ἡ, cloud (cp. *nebula*)

νεφελώδης, -ες, cloudy

ὀμίχλη, -ης, ἡ, mist, fog

ἀστραπή, -ῆς, ἡ, lightning

ἀστράπτω, ἀστράψω, ἤστραψα, –, –, –, lighten

βροντή, -ῆς, ἡ, thunder (cp. *brontosaur*)

βροντάω, βροντήσω, ἐβρόντησα, –, –, –, thunder

νιφετός, -οῦ, ὁ, snow storm

νιφάς, νιφάδος, ἡ, snow flake (cp. *snow*, L. *nix*)

νίφει, νίψει, ἔνιψε, snow (3rd person only) (cp. L. *ninguit*)

χιών, -ονος, ἡ, snow, especially snow lying on the ground (cp. *hibernate*, *Himalaya*, L. *hiems*)

ὑετός, -οῦ, ὁ, rain

ὕω, ὕσω, ὕσα, –, –, –, rain

χάλαζα, -ας, ἡ, hail

λάμπω, λάμψω, ἔλαμψα, λέλαμπα, –, –, shine, be bright; λάμπει ὁ ἥλιος. (cp. *lamp*)

φέγγω, make bright; in passive, shine, gleam; present system only. ἡ σελήνη φέγγει.

σελήνη, -ης, ἡ, moon

The following time idioms are also useful:

τῆτες, this year (formed like τήμερον)

πέρυσι(ν), last year

προπέρυσι(ν), the year before last

ἐς νέωτα, next year

τρίτον ἤδη ἔτος, two years ago

XIV.11 Writing

1. Rewrite the sentences of chapter 6, writing exercise 1, changing the main verbs into the perfect tense, then again into the pluperfect.

2. Rewrite the following sentences, turning the participial phrases into subordinate clauses. You may use whatever kind of clause best captures the sense of the participle. For example, from ὁ μαθητής, σοφὸς ὤν, εὖ μανθάνει, you might make ὁ μαθητὴς εὖ μανθάνει, ἐπεὶ σοφός ἐστι.

   a. βεβλεφὼς τοὺς μαθητάς, ὁ διδάσκαλος βιβλίον ἔλαβε.

   b. δεῖ σέ, ἐρρωμένον ὄντα, τὴν ναῦν ἐρέσαι.

   c. οἱ κριταὶ γέρας διδόασι τοῖς εὖ πεποιηκόσι.

   d. τοὺς καλάμους εἰληφότες, νῦν γράφειν δυνάμεθα.

   e. ὁ ἐγνωκὼς οὐ πάλιν ἥμαρτε.

   f. τὰς κώπας ἐνηνοχὼς ὁ ναύτης ἤρεττε.

   g. τῷ Δαφνίδι αἰτοῦντι ἡ Χλόη γυνὴ δοθήσεται.

   h. τὰ πραχθέντα ἑωρακὼς καὶ τῶν μαρτύρων ἀκηκοώς, τὴν ἀλήθειαν ἐπύθου.

   i. ἐκεῖνος ὁ στρατὸς ἥττωται τοῦ νενικηκότος.

   j. ὠφεληκότες τοὺς βοήσαντας φίλους, νῦν τὸν κάματον πεπαύκαμεν.

3. Do the change-number exercise with the following sentences.

   a. οἱ ναῦται τὸν τῆς νεὼς κάλων λελύκασι.

   b. αὕτη ἡ γυνὴ εἴωθε τὰ παιδία τρέφειν.

   c. ὁ βοῦς οὐ γίγνεται ἄνθρωπος, ἀλλὰ θήρ.

   d. οἱ φυγάδες ἐκ τῆς πόλεως πεφεύγασι.

   e. ἐπεὶ ὁ ῥήτωρ τοὺς πολίτας ἐπεποίθει, ἐκέλευσε τοῖς θεοῖς θῦσαι.

   f. ἐπὶ τῇ σκηνῇ τὼ χορὼ ᾠδὰς ᾄδετον.

   g. ἔμελλον τοῦτο ποιεῖν, ἀλλ’ οὐκ οἷά τ’ ἦν.

   h. οὗτοι οἱ Ἕλληνες τοὺς ξένους δέχονται ὡς φίλους.

   i. ὁ ῥήτωρ πᾶσαν ὥραν λελάληκε, καίπερ οὐδενὸς ἀκούοντος.

   j. δὶς μὲν τὼ νέα γυναῖκε ἐκείνας τὰς γραῦς ἐσεσώκετην, αὖθις δὲ οὐκ ἐδυνηθήτην.

   k. ἱερὰ τοῖς θεοῖς ἐν τοῖς νεῷς ἀνατίθεμεν.

   l. ὁ ἄμεμπτος δεσπότης τὸν σῖτον τοῖς δούλοις νέμει.

4. Rewrite each of the following sentences as an indirect quotation, first using the infinitive and then again using ὅτι or ὡς. If the OOO rule applies, write the sentence both with optional optative and with retained indicative.

   a. οἱ ῥήτορες εἶπον, "οὗτος ὁ ἄνθρωπος τὴν πόλιν ὠφέληκε."

   b. ὁ γείτων ἡμῖν ἀποκρίνεται, "οἱ παῖδες ἐκ τοῦ δένδρου πεπτώκασι."

   c. ἐν τῷ βιβλίῳ γέγραφε ὁ διδάσκαλος, "οἱ ἀλεκτρυόνες ᾄδουσι καθ’ ἡμέραν."

  d. ἐγεγράφεμεν, "ὁ ἄνθρωπος τοὺς ἀγροὺς ἀρήροκε, ἀλλ᾽ οὐ γεωργεῖ."

  e. τὼ μαθητὰ ἀπεκρινάσθην, "ὁ δελφὶς τοὺς ἰχθύας ὑπερβέβληκε."

5. Rewrite reading 2 from the point of view of Chloe's father (to whom Daphnis is speaking).

6. Rewrite reading 7 in prose, using normal prose word order and simple vocabulary.

7. Try to invent two or three sentences of your own like the one from Euripides that the actor Hegelochus mispronounced (reading 8): sentences where two words that sound similar both fit grammatically, but only one makes good sense.

8. Using the vocabulary from the supplement, write a paragraph about the weather in your home town.

CHAPTER XV

The Arms of Achilles

XV.1 Perfect middle and passive system

In the perfect system, as in the present system, middle and passive are the same. They are formed from the fifth principal part. This principal part has reduplication exactly as for the fourth, e grade of the stem vowel if applicable (unlike the fourth which has o grade), and no suffix. Watch out for internal sandhi between the stem and the endings, to be discussed in more detail in the next chapter. All verbs form this principal part the same way, and all verbs take the same endings. As in the perfect active, so in the perfect middle/passive there are two tenses of the indicative, an infinitive, and a participle.

These are the indicative forms:

Indicative Active:	Perfect	Pluperfect
singular		
1st	λέ-λυ-μαι	ἐ-λε-λύ-μην
2nd	λέ-λυ-σαι	ἐ-λέ-λυ-σο
3rd	λέ-λυ-ται	ἐ-λέ-λυ-το
dual		
2nd	λέ-λυ-σθον	ἐ-λέ-λυ-σθον
3rd	λέ-λυ-σθον	ἐ-λε-λύ-σθην
plural		
1st	λε-λύ-μεθα	ἐ-λε-λύ-μεθα
2nd	λέ-λυ-σθε	ἐ-λέ-λυ-σθε
3rd	λέ-λυ-νται	ἐ-λέ-λυ-ντο

The perfect infinitive middle/passive is λελύσθαι and the perfect participle middle/passive is λελυμένος. Note the accent in each of these forms.

When the verb root ends in a consonant, the third plural perfect and pluperfect indicative would have an impossible cluster consisting of the consonant from the root plus the -ντ- of the ending, for example βέβλεπ-νται from βλέπω. These forms are therefore not used; instead, the perfect participle middle is used with εἰσι or ἦσαν, as βεβλεμμένοι εἰσί. (This is not quite the whole story of these forms; see chapter 16 for the details.) In these periphrases the participle modifies the subject, so must agree with it: οἱ ἄνδρες βεβλεμμένοι εἰσί, αἱ γυναῖκες βεβλεμμέναι εἰσί.

The subjunctive and optative are rare. If they are needed, they are normally formed periphrastically: use the perfect participle middle/passive with the subjunctive or optative of εἰμι, as λελυμένος ὦ, λελυμένος εἴην, and so on. In these forms too, as in all the periphrastic forms, the participle modifies the subject and therefore agrees with it.

The perfect imperative passive is also rare, though you have seen examples in reading 10 of chapter 12. It is formed with the perfect passive stem and the endings of the present imperative passive.

Some verbs form a future perfect from this stem: λελύσομαι "I shall have loosed for myself" (middle) or "I shall have been loosed" (passive), conjugated like λύσομαι. This is not common, but it is vastly more common than the future perfect active, formed for only four verbs (and those four forms are used only rarely in verse, almost never in prose). If you ever see it, you will recognize the future perfect — active, middle, or passive — because it has the perfect stem, the -σ- suffix typical for futures, and the ordinary future endings.

Exercise

Figure out the fifth principal part of the following verbs, and check against the vocabulary. Write out the perfect and pluperfect indicative middle/passive for two of them.

παύω, make stop, check; πορεύω, transport; πιστεύω, trust; παιδεύω, teach; κελεύω, order; κωλύω, hinder; κλήω, shut; φυτεύω, plant; ὀργίζω, pray.

XV.2 Nouns in R

A small but important group of nouns ends in -ρ in the nominative singular. Many of these are names of family members, as πᾰτήρ, πατρός, ὁ, "father." Another is ἀνήρ, ἀνδρός, ὁ, "man."

singular

nom.	πατήρ	ἀνήρ
gen.	πατρός	ἀνδρός
dat.	πατρί	ἀνδρί
acc.	πατέρα	ἄνδρα
voc.	πάτερ	ἄνερ

dual

nom., acc., voc.	πατέρε	ἄνδρε
gen., dat.	πατέροιν	ἀνδροῖν

plural		
nom., voc.	πατέρες	ἄνδρες
gen.	πατέρων	ἀνδρῶν
dat.	πατράσι(ν)	ἀνδράσι(ν)
acc.	πατέρας	ἄνδρας

Like πατήρ are declined μήτηρ "mother," θυγάτηρ "daughter," and γαστήρ "stomach." In all these nouns, when the -ε- of the stem is present, it is accented, and the genitive and dative singular have accent on the last syllable.

The difference between ἀνήρ and ἄνθρωπος is that the former is exclusively male, while the latter can refer to any human being, male or female. Thus the opposite of ἀνήρ is γυνή, and the opposite of ἄνθρωπος is ζῷον.

XV.3 The verb "go"

You already know the present system of εἰμί "be." Similar, but *not* enclitic, is the verb εἶμι meaning "go." In Attic it has a future sense; the corresponding present is ἔρχομαι, and the aorist is ἦλθον. All forms of εἶμι are active; it has no middle and, since it is intransitive, no passive.

	Present ("Future") Indicative	Imperfect Indicative	Imperative	Subjunctive	Optative
singular					
1st	εἶ-μι	ᾖ-α		ἴ-ω	ἴ-οιμι
2nd	εἶ	ᾔ-εισθα	ἴ-θι	ἴ-ῃς	ἴ-οις
3rd	εἶ-σι(ν)	ᾔ-ει(ν)	ἴ-τω	ἴ-ῃ	ἴ-οι
dual					
2nd	ἴ-τον	ᾖ-τον	ἴ-τον	ἴ-ητον	ἴ-οιτον
3rd	ἴ-τον	ᾔ-την	ἴ-των	ἴ-ητον	ἰ-οίτην
plural					
1st	ἴ-μεν	ᾖ-μεν		ἴ-ωμεν	ἴ-οιμεν
2nd	ἴ-τε	ᾖ-τε	ἴ-τε	ἴ-ητε	ἴ-οιτε
3rd	ἴ-ᾱσι(ν)	ᾖ-σαν, ᾔ-εσαν	ἰ-ό-ντων	ἴ-ωσι(ν)	ἴ-οιεν

The present ("future") infinitive active is ἰέναι and the participle is ἰών, ἰοῦσα, ἰόν.

Although the present system of this verb has a future sense in Attic Greek, it can be a true present in other dialects and in compounds, which is why it has an imperfect tense and a subjunctive mood.

The two verbs εἰμί "be" and εἶμι "go" are similar (and some forms of οἶδα "know" are similar as well; see chapter 17). Here are some pointers to keep them straight.

εἰμί — root is ἐσ-, and the -σ- disappears between vowels. Most forms in the present indicative are enclitic. Most forms in other moods look like naked endings.

εἶμι — root is εἰ-. *Every* form has an -ι- somewhere, possibly subscript. No forms are enclitic.

οἶδα — root is ϝειδ-, and the digamma disappeared long ago (see vocabulary note, chapter 9). Every form has an -ι-, possibly part of a diphthong, followed by either a -δ- or a cluster with -σ- resulting from sandhi. The singular of the indicative has o grade of the root (ϝοιδ-, οἰδ-), the subjunctive and optative have e grade (ϝειδ-, εἰδ-), and the imperative and the dual and plural of the indicative have zero grade (ϝιδ-, ἰδ-).

XV.4 Supplementary participles

The following verbs take a supplementary participle instead of a complementary infinitive: τυγχάνω "I happen to be, I chance"; κινδυνεύω "I dare, I venture, I take a risk"; παύω "I stop, I cause to stop" (also as middle, παύομαι "I cease"); λανθάνω "I escape notice, I get away with" (like Latin *fallo*); φθάνω, "I do first, I come before, I overtake"; εὑρίσκω "I find."

That is, we have παύομαι γράφων "I stop writing," with a participle where you might have expected an infinitive. This is a bit similar to the construction with verbs of knowing, perceiving, and feeling (chapter 13).

More examples: ἔτυχον ὤν ἐν τῷ κήπῳ "I happened to be in the field." ἔτυχον γράφων "I happened to be writing." ἔλαθεν τοῦτον ἰδών "he saw it unobserved," in other words he escaped notice while seeing, or got away with looking. φθάνει ἐλθών "he comes in first," or he is the first to come in.

The verbs τυγχάνω, λανθάνω, and φθάνω may seem odd because in English we prefer adverbs or phrases to express the same idea.

When τυγχάνω is used without a supplementary participle, it means "hit, touch, bump into," and in this sense it normally takes a genitive complement instead of an accusative direct object: ὁ παῖς τοῦ ἑταίρου πέτρᾳ τυγχάνει, "the child hits his friend with a rock" (not τὸν ἑταῖρον). This genitive is normal with verbs of touching or hitting, as ἅπτεται τοῦ δένδρου, ψαύει τοῦ δένδρου, θιγγάνει τοῦ δένδρου.

XV.5 More about commands

You already know that the negative with an imperative is μή, as for example μὴ λέγε "don't speak." Idiomatically, the imperative is used for positive commands with either durative or punctual aspect, so λέγε or εἰπέ, but for negative commands, Greek normally uses the present imperative (μὴ λέγε, don't keep speaking, do not habitually speak) but the aorist subjunctive (μὴ εἴπῃς, don't speak, as a simple action).

Verbs that take an indirect command, like κελεύω, also have μή for the negative of the command: κελεύω αὐτὸν μὴ λέγειν, "I order him not to speak." (Contrast οὐ κελεύω αὐτὸν λέγειν, "I do not order him to speak, I do not give an order that he speak," where the negative negates the main verb, not the command.)

Verbs of forbidding, hindering, and preventing usually also take this μή even though the negative is built in to the meaning of the main verb. Thus ἀπεῖπον μὴ ἐλθεῖν, "I forbade him to come, told him not to come." The μή is logically redundant but helps remind the hearer that this is a prohibition.

The subjunctive by itself can make up for the absence of a first-person imperative form, as γράφωμεν "let's write," τοῦτο ποιήσωμεν, "let's do it." The negative, as for all the command-like constructions, is μή. This use is called the **hortatory subjunctive**. The subjunctive can also be used for the sort of question that expresses doubt, often when the speaker is talking to himself or herself; for example, Hamlet might say ἆρ᾽ ὦ, ἢ μὴ ὦ; — "to be, or not to be: that is the question" (*Hamlet* III.i). As you see, the negative is μή. The traditional name for this use is the **deliberative subjunctive**.

XV.6 Vocabulary

VERBS

ἄγχω, ἄγξω, ἦγξα, –, –, –, throttle, strangle (cp. *angina*, L. *ango*)

αἱρέω, αἱρήσω, εἷλον, ᾕρηκα, ᾕρημαι, ᾑρέθην, take, grasp, catch

ἀπ-αγορεύω, ἀπειρῶ, ἀπεῖπον, ἀπείρηκα, –, –, forbid

ἀπο-χωρέω, go away, depart; give something up

ἅπτομαι, ἅψομαι, ἡψάμην, –, ἧμμαι, ἥφθην, touch (+ gen.) (cp. *haptic*)

ἁρπάζω, ἁρπάσω, ἥρπασα, ἥρπακα, ἥρπασμαι, ἡρπάσθην, seize, grab, plunder (cp. *harpy*)

ᾄττω, ᾄξω, ᾖξα, –, –, –, rush, move quickly

ἀφ-αιρέω, carry off

διαιτάομαι, διαιτηθήσομαι, –, –, δεδιῄτημαι, διῃτήθην, dwell, lead one's life (cp. *diet*)

δια-φεύγω, flee in different directions

εἶμι, go (suppletive future to ἔρχομαι) (cp. L. *eo, īre*)

ἐκ-φέρω, carry out; also ἐκφορέω

ἐπ-αν-ήκω, return, come back

ἐπ-εισ-πηδάω, leap in upon

ἐπ-έχω, stop (intransitive, like παύομαι)

καθ-οράω, catch sight of

κατα-βάλλω, throw down

κατα-λαμβάνω, find, catch

κινδῡνεύω, κινδυνεύσω, ἐκινδύνευσα, κεκινδύνευκα, κεκινδύνευμαι, ἐκινδυνεύθην, dare, venture

λανθάνω, λήσω, ἔλαθον, λέληθα, λέλησμαι, ἐλήσθην, escape notice

μιμνήσκω, μνήσω, ἔμνησα, –, μέμνημαι, ἐμνήσθην, remind; in middle, especially perfect middle μέμνημαι, remember (cp. *mind*, L. *memini*)

πηδάω, πηδήσω, ἐπήδησα, –, –, –, jump, leap

τυγχάνω, τεύξομαι, ἔτυχον, τετύχηκα, – , – , happen

τύπτω, τυπτήσω, ἐτύπτησα, – , τέτυμμαι, – , strike

φθάνω, φθήσομαι, ἔφθασα, – , – , – , be first, overtake, anticipate

NOUNS

ἀνήρ, ἀνδρός, ὁ, man (cp. *android*)

ἀρετή, -ῆς, ἡ, excellence, virtue

αὐλή, -ῆς, ἡ, courtyard

βραχίων, -ονος, ὁ, upper arm (cp. *bracelet*)

γαστήρ, γαστρός, ὁ, stomach (cp. *gastric*)

θεράπαινα, -ας, ἡ, maidservant

θυγάτηρ, θυγατρός, ἡ, daughter (cp. *daughter*)

ἱππόδρομος, -ου, ὁ, race course

καρπός, -οῦ, ὁ, wrist (cp. *carpal*)

κόλπος, -ου, ὁ, bosom, lap, fold of a garment usable as a pocket

κυμβίον, -ου, το, cup

μειράκιον, -ου, το, boy

μήτηρ, μητρός, ἡ, mother (cp. *mother*, L. *mater*)

οἰκέτης, -ου, ὁ, servant, house slave

πατήρ, πατρός, ὁ, father (cp. *father*, L. pater)

πρέσβυς, πρέσβεως, ὁh, old man, ambassador, envoy (cp. *presbyter, presbyopia*)

πύργος, -ου, ὁ, tower

πονηρίᾱ, -ᾱς, ἡ, wickedness

σοφία, -ας, ἡ, wisdom, intelligence, skill

σκεῦος, -ους, τό, article, utensil

τράχηλος, -ου, ὁ, neck

χείρ, χειρός, ἡ, hand, arm (cp. *enchiridion, chiropractor, surgeon*)

ADJECTIVES

εὔνους, -ον, friendly; contracted like νοῦς

πιστός, -ή, -όν, faithful, trusty

ὑπόλοιπος, -ον, left over, remaining

ὕφαιμος, -ον, bloodshot, bloody, bruised

ADJECTIVE, CONJUNCTION

ἔνδον, inside

ἕως, until, while

Notes on the vocabulary

ἀπ-αγορεύω can also use a future from the same root, ἀπαγορεύσω; the other forms are from the same roots as the suppletive forms of λέγω.

The active forms of ἅπτω can mean "affix, fasten."

διαιτάομαι comes from the noun δίαιτα, -ας, ἡ, daily life, way of life, and our word *diet* is taken from this noun as well.

μιμνήσκω means "remind," as ὁ στρατηγὸς τοὺς στρατιώτας τῆς νίκης μιμνήσκει, the general reminds the soldiers of victory. But the verb is more common in the middle in the sense "remember," particularly in the perfect μέμνημαι.

φθάνω also has a root aorist ἔφθην.

βραχίων is formally the comparative of βραχύς "short," because the upper arm is shorter than the forearm.

πρέσβυς is almost always a masculine noun, but can also form a comparative and superlative, πρεσβύτερος, πρεσβύτατος, like an adjective.

χείρ has some forms with ει and some with just ε. The genitive/dative dual is χεροῖν and the dative plural is χερσί; the oblique cases in the singular may use ε.

XV.7 Reading

1. γεωργῶ μὲν πρὸς τῷ ἱπποδρόμῳ, καὶ οἰκῶ ἐνταῦθ' ἐκ μειρακίου. ὁ οὖν Θεόφημος καὶ Εὔεργος ὁ ἀδελφὸς αὐτοῦ, εἰσελθόντες εἰς τὸ χωρίον, πρῶτον μὲν ἐπὶ τοὺς οἰκέτας ᾖξαν. ὡς δὲ οὗτοι διαφεύγουσιν αὐτούς, καὶ ἄλλος ἄλλῃ ἀπεχώρησεν, ἐλθόντες εἰς τὴν οἰκίαν καὶ καταβαλόντες τὴν θύραν τὴν εἰς τὸν κῆπον φέρουσαν, καὶ ἐπεισελθόντες ἐπὶ τὴν γυναῖκά μου καὶ τὰ παιδία, ἐξεφορήσαντο ὅσα ἔτι ὑπόλοιπά μοι ἦν σκεύη ἐν τῇ οἰκίᾳ. πρὸς δὲ τούτοις, ἔτυχεν ἡ γυνή μου μετὰ τῶν παίδων ἀριστῶσα ἐν τῇ αὐλῇ. καὶ μετ' αὐτῆς τίτθη τις ἐμὴ γεγενημένη πρεσβυτέρα, ἄνθρωπος εὔνους καὶ πιστή, καὶ ἀφειμένη ἐλευθέρα ὑπὸ τοῦ πατρὸς τοῦ ἐμοῦ. συνῴκησε δὲ ἀνδρί, ἐπειδὴ ἀφείθη ἐλευθέρα· ὡς δ' οὗτος ἀπέθανε, καὶ αὐτὴ γραῦς ἦν, καὶ οὐκ ἦν αὐτὴν ὁ θρέψων, ἐπανῆκεν αὐτὴ ὡς ἐμέ. ἐν ᾧ δ' ἐγὼ ἀπεδήμουν, τῇ γυναικὶ βουλομένῃ ἦν τοιαύτην οἰκουρὸν μετ' αὐτῆς με καταλιπεῖν. ἀριστώντων δ' ἐν τῇ αὐλῇ, ὡς ἐπεισπηδῶσιν οὗτοι, καὶ καταλαμβάνουσιν αὐτάς, καὶ ἥρπαζον τὰ σκεύη, αἱ μὲν ἄλλαι θεράπαιναι (ἐν τῷ πύργῳ γὰρ ἦσαν, οὗπερ διαιτῶνται) ὡς ἤκουσαν τῆς κραυγῆς, κλῄουσι τὸν πύργον, καὶ ἐνταῦθα μὲν οὐκ εἰσῆλθον, τὰ δὲ ἐκ τῆς ἄλλης οἰκίας ἐξέφερον σκεύη, ἀπαγορευούσης τῆς γυναικὸς μὴ ἅπτεσθαι αὐτῶν· οἱ δ' οὐχ ὅπως ἐπέσχον, ἀλλὰ καὶ τῆς τίτθης τὸ κυμβίον λαβούσης, ἐξ οὗ ἔπινε, καὶ ἐνθεμένης εἰς τὸν κόλπον, ἵνα μὴ οὗτοι λάβοιεν, ἐπειδὴ εἶδεν ἔνδον ὄντας αὐτούς, κατιδόντες αὐτὴν οὕτω διέθεσαν ἀφαιρούμενοι τὸ κυμβίον Θεόφημος καὶ Εὔεργος ἀδελφὸς αὐτοῦ οὑτοσί, ὥστε ὕφαιμοι μὲν οἱ βραχίονες καὶ οἱ καρποὶ τῶν χειρῶν αὐτῆς ἐγένοντο, ἀμυχὰς δὲ ἐν τῷ τραχήλῳ εἶχεν ἀγχομένη· εἰς τοῦτο δ' ἦλθον πονηρίας, ὥστε, ἕως ἀφείλοντο τὸ κυμβίον ἐκ τοῦ κόλπου αὐτῆς, οὐκ ἐπαύσαντο ἄγχοντες καὶ τύπτοντες τὴν γραῦν.

> Demosthenes 47.53 ff. Although this speech is attributed to Demosthenes, it was probably written by his contemporary Apollodorus. The speaker is prosecuting Euergos.

ἐπ-εισ-έρχομαι, come in upon. τίτθη, -ης, ἡ, nurse, nursemaid. ἐπ-αν-ίημι, let go back, relax. οἰκουρός, -όν, keeping house, watching the house, domestic. κραυγή, -ῆς, ἡ din, noise. ἀμυχή, -ῆς, ἡ, tear, scratch. οὐχ ὅπως, idiom: so far from, not only did they not; usually followed by ἀλλά as here.

2. Οἰδίπους, ἐπεὶ νέον μειράκιον ἦν, ἐνόμιζε τὸν Πόλυβον ὄντα τὸν πατέρα καὶ τὴν Μερόπην τὴν μητέρα. οὐκ ἦν ἀλήθεια, ἀλλὰ τοῦτο ἐπίστευε ὁ Οἰδίπους. ἡμέρα τινὶ εἰς Θήβας ἐλθὼν ἔτυχε. ἡ Σφίγξ, μέγας θὴρ οὖσα, τὴν πόλιν ἐξήτασε, πολλὰ ἐρωτῶσα καὶ κελεύουσα τοῖς Θηβαίοις ἢ ἀποκρίνεσθαι ἢ ἐσθίεσθαι. ὁ Οἰδίπους ἐκινδύνευσε τὸν θῆρα μαχόμενος, οὐ ὅπλοις ἀλλὰ σοφίᾳ. εὖ ἀπέκρινε καὶ τὴν Σφίγγα ἀπέκτεινε. ὁ δὲ Θηβαίων βασιλεὺς ἄρτι ἀποθανὼν ἔτυχε. διότι ὁ Οἰδίπους τὴν πόλιν ἐσεσώκει, οἱ Θηβαῖοι αὐτὸν βασιλέα ἐποίησαν καὶ αὐτῷ τὴν τοῦ τεθνεῶτος βασιλέως γυναῖκα ἔδοσαν, Ἰοκάστην ὀνόματι.

ὁ δὲ Οἰδίπους καὶ ἡ Ἰοκάστη πολλὰ ἔτη ἐδιαιτάσθην, ἀλλήλω φιλοῦντε. τέτταρας παῖδας ἔτεκε ἡ Ἰοκάστη, δύο μὲν υἱὼ δύο δὲ θυγατέρε. ὁ πατήρ, ἡ μήτηρ, καὶ οἱ παῖδες εὖ εἶχον, ἕως ἄγγελός τις ἦλθε ἀπὸ τῆς Κορίνθου. ὁ ἄγγελος εἶπε, "χαῖρε, ὦ Οἰδίπους. ὁ Πόλυβος ἀπέθανε· σὺ οὖν εἶ βασιλεὺς τῆς Κορίνθου." ὁ δὲ Οἰδίπους ἀπεκρίνατο, "ἆρ' ὁ ἐμὸς πατὴρ ἀπέθανε; τί λέγεις περὶ τῆς μητρὸς Μερόπης; ἆρα τὸν ἥλιον ἔτι ὁρᾷ;" "ναί, εὖ ἔχει ἡ Μερόπη," ἐφὴ ὁ ἄγγελος.

"τί λέγεις;" ἠρώτησε ὁ Οἰδίπους. "ἀλλὰ ὁ θεὸς εἶπε ὅτι τὸν πατέρα ἀποκτεῖναι ἔμελλον καὶ τὴν μητέρα γυναῖκα ἔχειν. εἰ τὸν Πόλυβον μὴ ἐγὼ ἀπέκτεινα, ἆρα ὁ θεὸς ἥμαρτε;"

"μὴ πυνθάνου," ἐβόησε ἡ Ἰοκάστη. "μὴ ἐρωτήσῃς περὶ τοῖν πατέροιν." ἔγνω γὰρ ὅστις ἦν ἀληθείᾳ ὁ τοῦ Οἰδίπου πατήρ. ὁ Ἀπόλλων τῇ Ἰοκάστῃ καὶ τῷ ἀνδρὶ εἶπέ ποτε, "εἰ τέκνον τέξεις, τοῦτο τὸ τέκνον τὸν πατέρα ἀποκτενεῖ καὶ τὴν μητέρα γυναῖκα ἕξει." ἀλλὰ ἡ Ἰοκάστη, τέκνον τετοκυῖα, αὐτὸ ἀφῆκε. τοῦτο τὸ τέκνον ἦν ὁ Οἰδίπους. ἡ Ἰοκάστη ἔλαθε μήτηρ οὖσα ἕως ὁ Οἰδίπους πρέσβυς ἐγένετο.

"βούλομαι γνῶναι," εἶπε ὁ Οἰδίπους. "σύ, λέγε μοι· ἆρ' ἀληθῆ ἔλεγες; ἆρα ὁ Πόλυβος, ὁ πατήρ, ἀπέθανε;"

ὁ δὲ ἄγγελος εἶπε, "ἀλλὰ ὁ Πόλυβός σοι οὐκ ἦν πατήρ, οὐδὲ ἡ Μερόπη μήτηρ. δεῖ σοι μιμνήσκειν ὅτι δοῦλός τις τοῦ Πολύβου σὲ εὗρε, παιδίον ὄντα."

νῦν δὴ ὁ Οἰδίπους πάντα ἔγνω· οἱ παῖδες ἄρα ἦσαν ἀδελφοί, ἡ γυνὴ ἦν μήτηρ. ἔβλαψε τὼ ὀφθαλμὼ ἵνα αὐτὴν μὴ αὖθις ἴδοι. ἡ δὲ Ἰοκάστη αὐτὸν ἔφθασε, ἑαυτὴν ἀποκτείνουσα.

βασιλεύς, -εως, ὁ, king. ἐμός, -ή, -όν, my.

3. ἐάν τινα πίνωμεν ἢ ἐσθίωμεν, εἰς τὸν γαστρὰ πίπτει. κυμβίον οἴνου ἕλε τῇ χειρὶ καὶ πίνε. οὐχ ὅπως σε διαφθερεῖ ἀλλὰ σε σώσει, κατὰ τὸν Διόνυσον. θεὸς δέ ἐστι τοῦ οἴνου. μὴ ἄκουε· ὁ θεὸς ἀνθρώπους πείθει ἑαυτοῖς κακὰ ποιεῖν. ὁ Διόνυσος πηδᾷ καὶ ᾄδει σὺν σατύροις. οἱ δὲ σάτυροι οὐδὲ θῆρες οὐδὲ ἄνθρωποί εἰσι, ἀλλὰ ὥσπερ ἀμφότεροι. χορὸς τοῦ Διονύσου εἰσί. οἶνον ἀεὶ πίνουσι. τὸ κυμβίον αἴρουμεν, αἴρομεν, καὶ τὸν οἶνον πίνομεν, τοῦ Διονύσου μιμνησκόμενοι.

4. ἀνὴρ γὰρ ἄνδρα καὶ πόλις σῴζει πόλιν.
χεὶρ χεῖρα νίπτει, δάκτυλός τε δάκτυλον.

From a lost play by Menander. νίπτω or νίζω, wash.

5. ἐν δορὶ μέν μοι μᾶζα μεμαγμένη, ἐν δορὶ δ᾽ οἶνος
   Ἰσμαρικός· πίνω δ᾽ ἐν δορὶ κεκλιμένος.

   > Archilochus, frag. 2.

   > **δόρυ, δορός, τό**, spear. **μᾶζα, -ας, ἡ**, bread made from barley. **μάττω**, knead.
   > **κλίνω**, lean, recline.

6. παῖς μὲν ἄνηβος ἐὼν ἔτι νήπιος ἕρκος ὀδόντων
       φύσας ἐκβάλλει πρῶτον ἐν ἕπτ᾽ ἔτεσιν.
   τοὺς δ᾽ ἑτέρους ὅτε δὴ τελέσῃ θεὸς ἕπτ᾽ ἐνιαυτούς,
       ἥβης ἐκφαίνει σήματα γεινομένης.
   τῇ τριτάτῃ δὲ γένειον ἀεξομένων ἔτι γυίων
       λαχνοῦται, χροιῆς ἄνθος ἀμειβομένης.
   τῇ δὲ τετάρτῃ πᾶς τις ἐν ἑβδομάδι μέγ᾽ ἄριστος
       ἰσχύν, ᾗ τ᾽ ἄνδρες σήματ᾽ ἔχουσ᾽ ἀρετῆς.
   πέμπτῃ δ᾽ ὥριον ἄνδρα γάμου μεμνημένον εἶναι
       καὶ παίδων ζητεῖν εἰσοπίσω γενεήν.
   τῇ δ᾽ ἕκτῃ περὶ πάντα καταρτύεται νόος ἀνδρός,
       οὐδ᾽ ἔρδειν ἔθ᾽ ὁμῶς ἔργ᾽ ἀπάλαμνα θέλει.
   ἑπτὰ δὲ νοῦν καὶ γλῶσσαν ἐν ἑβδομάσιν μέγ᾽ ἄριστος
       ὀκτώ τ᾽ · ἀμφοτέρων τέσσαρα καὶ δέκ᾽ ἔτη.
   τῇ δ᾽ ἐνάτῃ ἔτι μὲν δύναται, μαλακώτερα δ᾽ αὐτοῦ
       πρὸς μεγάλην ἀρετὴν γλῶσσά τε καὶ σοφίη.
   τὴν δεκάτην δ᾽ εἴ τις τελέσας κατὰ μέτρον ἵκοιτο,
       οὐκ ἂν ἄωρος ἐὼν μοῖραν ἔχοι θανάτου.

   > Solon, poem 19.

   > **ἄνηβος, -ον**, not grown up, not yet adolescent. **ἐών** = ὤν, epic form. **νήπιος, -ου**,
   > foolish, childish. **ἕρκος, -ου, τό**, barrier, enclosure. **τελέω, τελέσω, ἐτέλεσα,**
   > **τετέλεκα, τετέλεσμαι, ἐτελέσθην** = τελευτάω, τέλος ποιοῦμαι. **ἐνιαυτός, -οῦ,**
   > **ὁ** = ἔτος. **ἥβη, -ης, ἡ**, youth, young manhood. **ἐκ-φαίνω**, bring out, show. **σῆμα,**
   > **-ατος, τό**, sign, indication. **γείνομαι** = γίγνομαι, be born. **γένειον, -ου, τό**, chin.
   > **ἀέξω**, grow, increase (present system only). **γυῖον, -ου, τό**, limb. **λαχνόομαι**,
   > grow downy, become hairy. **χροιά, -ᾶς, ἡ**, skin, complexion; χροιῆς, gen. sg.,
   > is an epic form. **ἄνθος, -ους, τό**, bloom, flower. **ἀμείβω**, change, exchange,
   > take a turn. **ἑβδομάς, -άδος, ἡ**, group of seven. **ἰσχύς, ἰσχύος, ἡ**, strength.
   > **ὥριος, -ον**, seasonable, timely. **γάμος, -ου, ὁ**, marriage, wedding. **εἰσοπίσω**,
   > hereafter, in the future. **γενεά, -ᾶς, ἡ**, birth; τὴν γενεήν is another epic form.
   > **καταρτύω**, prepare, arrange. **νόος** = νοῦς, without contraction. **ἔρδω**, work.
   > **ἀπάλαμνος, -ον**, helpless, undisciplined, foolish. **θέλει** = ἐθέλει, a variant form
   > of the verb. **μαλακός, -ή, -όν**, weak, gentle, soft. **σοφίη** = σοφία. **μέτρον, -ου,**
   > **τό**, measure, standard of measurement. **ἄωρος, -ον**, untimely, unseasonable,
   > too early. **μοῖρα, -ας, ἡ**, fate.

7. *περὶ τοῦ Τρωικοῦ πολέμου, ἐννέατον μέρος*

   ὁ Ἀγαμέμνων ἐνόμισε τὰ τοῦ Ἀχιλλέως ὅπλα τῷ ἀρίστῳ διδόναι. ὁ Ὀδυσσεὺς καὶ
   ὁ Αἴας ἠθέλετον ταῦτα φέρεσθαι. ὁ δὲ Ἀγαμέμνων ἄκων κρίνειν ἐκάλεσε πάντας

τοὺς Ἀχαιοὺς ἵνα κρίνωσι. "εἰπέ ὦ Αἴας, πρῶτος, καὶ σύ, ὦ Ὀδυσσεύς, δεύτερος εἰπέ. εἴπετε περὶ τῆς ἀρετῆς· εἰπέτω ἕκαστος ὅ τι τὰ τοῦ Ἀχιλλέως ὅπλα ἄξιός ἐστι."

τοῦ Ἀγαμέμνονος οὕτως κελεύσαντος, ὁ Αἴας πρῶτος ἔλεγε. εἶπε ὅτι ἀνδρεῖος καὶ ἰσχυρός ἐστι· μεμάχηται εὖ καί, τοῦ τέλους ἐγγὺς ὄντος, διὰ ἑαυτὸν οἱ Ἕλληνες νικήσουσι· ἄξιος οὖν ἐστι τῶν ὅπλων διὰ τὴν ἀρετήν.

ὁ δὲ Ὀδυσσεὺς ἀπεκρίνατο ὅτι σοφώτερός ἐστι τοῦ Αἴαντος· ὁμολογεῖ τὸν Αἴαντα ἰσχυρὸν εἶναι, ἀλλὰ ἡ σοφία καὶ ἡ βουλὴ ἐπὶ τῷ πολέμῳ μᾶλλον διαφέρουσι· διὰ τὴν ἑαυτοῦ σοφίαν νικήσουσι· ἀξιώτερος οὖν ἐστι τῶν ὅπλων.

οἱ ἄλλοι ἀκηκοότες ψῆφον ἤνεγκαν. τῆς μὲν ἀρετῆς τοῦ Αἴαντος ἐμέμνηντο, τὴν δὲ βουλὴν τοῦ Ὀδυσσέως εὖ ἔγνωσαν. τέλος δὲ πάντες ἐνόμισαν τὸν Ὀδυσσέα ἀξιώτερον καὶ αὐτῷ τὰ ὅπλα ἔδοσαν.

ὁ δὲ Αἴας μεγάλην λύπην εἶχε. διὰ τὴν ὀργὴν ἐμήνατο. ἤθελε ἀποκτεῖναι τὸν μὲν Ὀδυσσέα, τὸν δὲ Ἀγαμέμνονα, τὸν δὲ Μενέλαον, πολλοὺς δὲ ἄλλους. ἐκ τῆς σκηνῆς νυκτὶ ἐξῆλθε, τὸ ξίφος φέρων. "νῦν ἐκεῖνοι ἴασι εἰς Ἅιδου. οὐ μὲν τετίμημαι, ἰσχυρότερος δὲ ἐκείνων ἔτι ὢν τυγχάνω. ἆρ' ἄγξω ἢ τυπτήσω ἢ τέμω; πῶς αὐτοὺς ἀποκτείνω;"

ἡ δὲ Ἀθηνᾶ, αὐτὸν ὁρᾶσα, οὐκ ἐβούλετο τοὺς ἄλλους ἀποθνήσκειν· οἱ γὰρ Τρῶες νικῷεν ἄν. ἤγαγε οὖν τὸν Αἴαντα πρὸς τὰ πρόβατα καὶ αὐτῷ εἶπε, "ἰδού· ἔχεις τοὺς στρατηγούς. οὐκ ἀπαγορεύω μὴ αὐτοὺς ἀποκτεῖναι· οὐ σὲ κωλύσω μὴ τοῦτο ποιεῖν."

ὁ δὲ ἀπέκρινατο, "εὖ μοι ὠφέλεις, ὦ θεά. τὸν μὲν Ἀγαμέμνονα νῦν ἀποκτείνω, τὸν δὲ Ὀδυσσέα βραδέως καὶ λυπηρῶς ἀποκτενῶ, ὃν μάλιστα μισῶ." καὶ ἁρπάζων τὰ πρόβατα ἀπέκτεινε ὥσπερ εἰ οἱ τῶν Ἑλλήνων στρατηγοὶ εἴησαν.

ἐπεὶ ὁ ἥλιος πάλιν ἔλαμψε, ἡ μανία ἀπῆλθε, καὶ ὁ Αἴας εἶδε τὰ τῶν προβάτων σώματα. "τί ἐποίησα;" ἐνόμισε. "οὐκέτι οἷός τ' εἰμὶ μετὰ τοῖς ἄλλοις στρατιώταις ζῆν. ἀλλὰ εἰ οἴκαδε πρὸς τὸν πατέρα ἴοιμι, οὗτος ἄν με διαφθείροι. οὐκέτι ἄξιός εἰμι τοῦ βίου." ἀπέκτεινε οὖν ἑαυτὸν ξίφει.

> ἄκων = οὐχ ἑκών. ἐγγύς, close, near. ὁμολογέω, agree. βουλή, -ῆς, ἡ, will, plan, advice. ψῆφος, -ου, ἡ, vote. ὀργή, -ῆς, ἡ, anger, passion. μαίνομαι, μανοῦμαι, ἐμηνάμην, μέμηνα, μεμάνημαι, ἐμάνην, be crazy, rage, go mad. ξίφος, -ους, τό, sword. τέμνω, τεμῶ, ἔτεμον, τέτμηκα, τέτμημαι, ἐτμήθην, cut. ἰδού, here, look. κωλύω, κωλύσω, ἐκώλυσα, κεκώλυκα, κεκώλυμαι, ἐκωλύθην, hinder. βραδέως, slowly. λυπηρῶς, painfully. μισέω, hate. μανία, -ας, ἡ, madness. ζάω = βιόω, βίον ἔχω.

XV.8 Conversation

Some examples:

1. (reading 1) ποῦ εἰσι οἱ ἀγροί; ποῦ γεωργεῖ ὁ ἄνθρωπος; τίς ἐστι ὁ Εὔεργος; τίνος ἀδελφός ἐστι ὁ θεόφημος; τίνες τίνας διαφεύγουσιν; διὰ τί;

2. (reading 2) τίς ἀληθείᾳ ἐστὶ ἡ τοῦ Οἰδίπου μήτηρ; τί εἶπε ὁ θεὸς Ἀπόλλων; πόσα τέκνα εἶχον ὁ Οἰδίπους καὶ ἡ Ἰοκάστη;

3. (reading 4) τί σημαίνει ὁ λόγος; τίς νίπτει; διὰ τί;

XV.9 Writing

1. Do the change-number exercise with the following sentences.

   a. ὁ ἀνὴρ εἶσι εἰς τὴν πόλιν.

   b. μὴ ἄγξῃς τὴν θεράπαιναν.

   c. οἱ πλοῖ ὑπὸ τοῦ ναύτου πεποίηνται.

   d. ἐλεύθεροι ἐγεγενήμεθα, ἀλλὰ ἐμελλήσαμεν πάλιν δοῦλοι γενήσεσθαι.

   e. τέτυψαι, ὦ γραῦ, ὑπὸ τοῦ γείτονος.

   f. ὁ παῖς ἐπαύσατο τὰς πέτρας βάλλων καὶ ἀπεχώρησε ἀπὸ τῆς αὐλῆς.

   g. ὁ ἀνὴρ τὼ τῆς μητρὸς χεῖρε αἴρει καὶ ὠφέλειαν αἰτεῖ.

   h. ὁ ἵππος ἐπὶ τῷ ἱπποδρόμῳ δραμόμενος ἔτυχε.

   i. αἱ θυγατέρες οὐ κινδυνεύουσι ἰοῦσαι εἰς τὸν λειμῶνα.

   j. τὼ ξένω ὑπὸ τοῦ εὔνου ἀνδρὸς τετίμησθον.

   k. ὁ ἀδελφὸς ἐπὶ τοὺς διαφεύγοντας οἰκέτας ᾖξε.

   l. πολλαὶ θεράπαιναι ἐν τῷ πύργῳ δεδιῄτηνται.

   m. οἱ κακοὶ οὐκ ἐπαύσαντο ἄγχοντες καὶ τύπτοντες τὴν γραῦν.

   n. ὁ στρατιώτης πίνει ἐν δορὶ κεκλιμένος.

2. In each of the following sentences, change the main verb from active to passive, or from passive to active, making whatever other changes are required to keep roughly the same meaning.

   a. ὁ τῆς νεὼς κάλος ὑπὸ τοῦ ναύτου λέλυται.

   b. τὸ παιδίον τῷ πατρὶ ὑπὸ τῆς μητρὸς δεδήλωται.

   c. τὸ κυμβίον ἑοράκασι καὶ ᾑρήκασι.

   d. ὁ πατὴρ τοὺς παῖδας πεφίληκε.

   e. τὸ ἱμάτιον ὑπὸ τοῦ γεωργοῦ ἠνήνεκτο.

   f. ᾠὰ τοῖν χειροῖν βέβληκας.

3. Create complex sentences from the following parts. For each sentence, choose one main clause and one subordinate clause. You will need to change the subordinate clause to a participial phrase, and you may need to adjust the number of the participle to match the main clause. Create at least 10 new sentences. For example, if the main clause is ἐπαύσετο and the subordinate clause is τοῦ διδασκάλου ἀκούει, you would create ἐπαύσετο τοῦ διδασκάλου ἀκούων.

   Main clauses:

   a. ὁ παῖς ἔλαθε

   b. ὁ γείτων ἔτυχε

   c. ἡ μήτηρ φθάνει

   d. τυγχάνομεν

   e. παύσεσθε

   Subordinate clauses:

   a. τὸν οἶνον πίνει.

    b. τὸν μειράκιον ἐτύπτησε.

    c. ἐκ τοῦ δένδρου ἐπήδησε.

    d. λαλεῖ.

    e. τὰ πρόβατα νέμει.

4. Rewrite reading 1 as told by the old woman, or by Theophemus, or by a slave.

5. Write a paragraph on the theme of country life in Greece. The weather words from the last chapter may be useful.

6. Write a paragraph similar to reading 5 about the phases or stages of a woman's life, ancient or modern.

CHAPTER XVI

The Return of Philoctetes

XVI.1 Consonant verb stems

Many of the verbs we have seen so far have a vowel at the end of their roots, like ἀκούω. In these verbs there is usually no problem with adding endings to the various stems: vowels will contract, if the present stem ends in ε, α, or ο, or if the future stem ends in ε, but consonants cause no problems. When the verb's root ends in a consonant, however, and the ending or the tense-system suffix begins with another consonant, internal sandhi takes place: assimiliation of one consonant to the other.

The first rule for internal sandhi in verbs is that voicing must match: the first consonant will gain or lose voicedness to match the second one. The second rule is that aspiration propagates through an entire consonant cluster: if any consonant is aspirate, they all are. For example:

λέγ-ω	λεκ-τός (adjective)	ἐλέχ-θην
βλάβ-η (noun)	βλάπ-τω	ἐβλάφ-θην

These rules do not apply merely to verbs: consider the ordinal numbers ἕβ-δομος from ἑπτά and ὄγ-δοος from ὀκτώ.

Voicing assimilation also occurs before μ: —

βλάβ-η	βέβλαμ-μαι
τύπ-τω strike, hit	τέτυμ-μαι
πλέκ-ω	πέπλεγ-μαι

Dentals are dropped before κ and ς: —

| πιθ-: | πείθ-ω | πεί-σω | πέπει-κα |

Before other consonants they become ς (by **dissimilation**): —

| πιθ-: | πισ-τός | ἐπείσ-θην | πέπεισ-μαι |

Nasals are assimilated partially to labials and gutturals, wholly to liquids: —

ἐμ-βάλλω   ἐγ-καλῶ

συλ-λαμβάνω   συρ-ράπτω

Gutturals + ς become ξ: —

λέγ-ω   λέξω

πλέκ-ω   πλέξω

βρέχ-ω (moisten, sprinkle)   βρέξω

Similarly, labials + ς become ψ. In both cases this is another form of voicing assimilation, as ς is unvoiced.

βλαβ-   βλάψω,   τρέπ-ω   τρέψω

There are some irregular forms which have to be learned as they come up. Often the apparent irregularity happens because of the order of various sound changes in the earlier history of Greek.

In this chapter we will consider the rules and the typical patterns for principal parts of verbs whose roots end in stops. The patterns for verbs ending in liquids are different; we will look at those in chapter 18. See also Appendix 1 sections 1 and 6.

XVI.2 Principal parts of consonant stems

Verbs with roots ending in a labial often take aspiration rather than -κ- as a suffix to form the perfect active, for example πέπομφα from root πεμπ-.

Verbs whose first principal part ends in -ττω, such as πράττω, come from roots ending in a guttural; the root of πράττω is πραγ-. The present system is made with a suffix -ι-, which assimilates in a complicated way. The guttural consonant is clearly audible in the remaining principal parts. In Attic these verbs have -ττ- in the present; in other dialects, they have -σσ-. This sound change is characteristic of Attic and applies to other words as well, for example θάλαττα "sea" is θάλασσα in the other dialects.

When the verb root ends in a dental, there are no special considerations beyond the sandhi principles discussed in the previous section.

The following chart shows how the stems of these verbs are formed.

Root	Present	Future	Perfect Active	Perfect Indic. Middle	Perfect Inf. Middle	Aorist Passive
βλαβ- (labial)	βλάπ-τω	βλάψω	βέ-βλαφ-α	βέ-βλαμ-μαι	βε-βλάφ-θαι	ἐ-βλάφ-θην
τριβ- (labial)	τρίβ-ω	τρί-ψω	τέ-τριφ-α	τέ-τρῐμ-μαι	τε-τρῐφ-θαι	ἐ-τρῐφ-θην
πραγ- (guttural, present with -ι- suffix)	πράττω	πράξω	πέ-πραχ-α	πέ-πραγ-μαι	πε-πρᾶχ-θαι	ἐ-πράχ-θην
πλεκ- (guttural, no suffix)	πλέκ-ω	πλέξω	πέ-πλεχ-α	πέ-πλεγ-μαι	πε-πλέχ-θαι	ἐ-πλέχ-θην
πειθ- (dental)	πείθ-ω	πείσω	πέ-πει-κα or πέ-ποιθ-α	πέ-πεισ-μαι	πε-πεῖσ-θαι	ἐ-πείσ-θην

When the stem of the fifth principal part ends in a consonant, the third person plural perfect and pluperfect indicative middle/passive are not used; instead, we use the perfect participle middle with εἰσί(ν) or ἦσαν. This is roughly because the regular form would be hard to pronounce: πέ-πειθ-νται, πέ-πλεχ-νται, and so on. In fact it's a bit more complicated. The -ν- between consonants originally became -α-, exactly as in the accusative singular ending of third declension nouns, giving forms like πέπειθαται or πέπλεχαται, but these look like *singular* forms, which is confusing; thus, the forms dropped out of use early, and only the periphrastic forms are used.

The following chart shows all the sandhi combinations in the perfect indicative passive, using πλέκω, πείθω, and τρίβω as sample verbs. Note how the final consonant of the root changes to match the initial consonant of the ending.

	root πλεκ-		root πειθ-		root τριβ-	
	Perfect	Pluperfect	Perfect	Pluperfect	Perfect	Pluperfect
singular						
1st	πέπλεγμαι	ἐπεπλέγμην	πέπεισμαι	ἐπεπείσμην	τέτρῑμμαι	ἐτετρίμμην
2nd	πέπλεξαι	ἐπέπλεξο	πέπεισαι	ἐπέπεισο	τέτρῑψαι	ἐτέτρῑψο
3rd	πέπλεκται	ἐπέπλεκτο	πέπεισται	ἐπέπειστο	τέτρῑπται	ἐτέτρῑπτο
dual						
2nd	πέπλεχθον	ἐπέπλεχθον	πέπεισθον	ἐπέπεισθον	τέτρῑφθον	ἐτέτρῑφθον
3rd	πέπλεχθον	ἐπεπλέχθην	πέπεισθον	ἐπεπείσθην	τέτρῑφθον	ἐτετρίφθην
plural						
1st	πεπλέγμεθα	ἐπεπλέγμεθα	πεπείσμεθα	ἐπεπείσμεθα	τετρίμμεθα	ἐτετρίμμεθα
2nd	πέπλεχθε	ἐπέπλεχθε	πέπεισθε	ἐπέπεισθε	τέτρῑφθε	ἐτέτρῑφθε
3rd	πεπλεγμένοι εἰσί(ν)	πεπλεγμένοι ἦσαν	πεπεισμένοι εἰσί(ν)	πεπεισμένοι ἦσαν	τετρῑμμένοι εἰσί(ν)	τετρῑμμένοι ἦσαν

The perfect infinitives and participles passive of these verbs are:

	infinitive	participle
πλέκω	πεπλέχθαι	πεπλεγμένος
πείθω	πεπεῖσθαι	πεπεισμένος
τρίβω	τετρῖφθαι	τετρῑμμένος

Exercises

1. Predict the principal parts for verbs made from the following roots. Do not look in a dictionary to find them, but determine yourself what they must be, based on the patterns in this section. ἑλικ- "roll, whirl"; τρῑβ- "rub, grind"; στειβ- "tread, walk on" (with second aorist); βριθ- "be heavy, load, press"; ἐπείγ- "hurry, cause to hurry" (not a compound).

2. Identify the following forms and determine the root of each verb. If there are several possibilities, give all of them. For example, given γεγραμμένη, identify the form as "perfect participle middle/passive, feminine nominative singular," and identify the possible roots as γραπ-, γραφ-, γραβ-, and γραμ-; of course you know this is from γράφω with root γραφ-, but the goal of the exercise is to identify all the ways a given form *might* arise. Do not consult a dictionary or other tool. γέγονε, λέλεκται, δέδειξαι, τεθλιμμένη, ἔγνωσται, κεχάρηνται, πεφύλαγμαι, ἐτετρόφει, τετάρακται, πεπλόχασι.

XVI.3 Verbs in -μι: active forms

In chapter 9 we saw the present indicative active of athematic verbs. The imperfect indicative active uses slightly different endings from those of thematic verbs (note the first person singular and plural and the third person plural in particular), and, like the present, has both long and short quantities of the stem vowel. The present subjunctive active is largely regular; the optative and imperative are nearly so.

Imperfect indicative active:

singular

1st	ἐ-τί-θη-ν	ἐ-δί-δουν	ἵ-στη-ν
2nd	ἐ-τί-θεις	ἐ-δί-δους	ἵ-στη-ς
3rd	ἐ-τί-θει	ἐ-δί-δου	ἵ-στη

dual

2nd	ἐ-τί-θε-τον	ἐ-δί-δο-τον	ἵ-στα-τον
3rd	ἐ-τι-θέ-την	ἐ-δι-δό-την	ἱ-στά-την

plural

1st	ἐ-τί-θε-μεν	ἐ-δί-δο-μεν	ἵ-στα-μεν
2nd	ἐ-τί-θε-τε	ἐ-δί-δο-τε	ἵ-στα-τε
3rd	ἐ-τί-θε-σαν	ἐ-δί-δο-σαν	ἵ-στα-σαν

The other finite moods are:

Imperative

singular

2nd	τίθει	δίδου	ἵστη
3rd	τιθέτω	διδότω	ἱστάτω

dual

2nd	τίθετον	δίδοτον	ἵστατον
3rd	τιθέτων	διδότων	ἱστάτων

plural

2nd	τίθετε	δίδοτε	ἵστατε
3rd	τιθέντων	διδόντων	ἱστάντων

Subjunctive

singular

1st	τιθῶ	διδῶ	ἱστῶ
2nd	τιθῇς	διδῷς	ἱστῇς
3rd	τιθῇ	διδῷ	ἱστῇ

dual

2nd	τιθῆτον	διδῶτον	ἱστῆτον
3rd	τιθῆτον	διδῶτον	ἱστῆτον

plural

1st	τιθῶμεν	διδῶμεν	ἱστῶμεν
2nd	τιθῆτε	διδῶτε	ἱστῆτε
3rd	τιθῶσι(ν)	διδῶσι(ν)	ἱστῶσι(ν)

Optative

singular

1st	τιθείην	διδοίην	ἱσταίην
2nd	τιθείης	διδοίης	ἱσταίης
3rd	τιθείη	διδοίη	ἱσταίη

dual

2nd	τιθεῖτον	διδοῖτον	ἱσταῖτον
3rd	τιθείτην	διδοίτην	ἱσταίτην

plural

1st	τιθεῖμεν	διδοῖμεν	ἱσταῖμεν
2nd	τιθεῖτε	διδοῖτε	ἱσταῖτε
3rd	τιθεῖεν	διδοῖεν	ἱσταῖεν

ἵημι is like τίθημι, so for example 3rd sg subjunctive is ἱῇ and 3rd sg optative is ἱείη.

The aorists of these four verbs also show the alternation between long and short vowel forms. In τίθημι, ἵημι, and δίδωμι the singular of the indicative has long root vowel, and the dual and plural have short. The singular also ends in -κα, not -σα, but the -κ- disappears in the dual and plural, and in the other moods.

ἵστημι has two different aorists that differ in meaning: the root aorist ἔστην is intransitive, "I stood," while the first aorist ἔστησα is transitive, "I placed, set up." Note the smooth breathing. The rough breathing of the present and perfect stems comes from reduplication: root στη- forms reduplicated present σίστημι, and then initial σ- changes to rough breathing (early in the history of Greek). Similarly for the perfect, which was once σέστηκα. Because the aorist is *not* reduplicated, its augment has the usual smooth breathing.

These are the forms of the aorist indicative active for the four verbs.

singular

1st	ἔθηκα	ἔδωκα	ἧκα	ἔστην
2nd	ἔθηκας	ἔδωκας	ἧκας	ἔστης
3rd	ἔθηκε	ἔδωκε	ἧκε	ἔστη

dual

2nd	ἔθετον	ἔδοτον	εἷτον	ἔστητον
3rd	ἐθέτην	ἐδότην	εἵτην	ἐστήτην

plural

1st	ἔθεμεν	ἔδομεν	εἷμεν	ἔστημεν
2nd	ἔθετε	ἔδοτε	εἷτε	ἔστητε
3rd	ἔθεσαν	ἔδοσαν	εἷσαν	ἔστησαν

The other moods of the aorist active system are formed from the same stems as the plural forms of the indicative. Some of the imperative forms are irregular (like θές instead of the expected θέτι) but the other moods are all regularly formed.

Imperative	Subjunctive	Optative	Infinitive	Participle
θές, θέτω … θέντων	θῶ, θῇς, …	θείην, θείης, …	θεῖναι	θείς, θεῖσα, θέν
δός, δότω … δόντων	δῶ, δῷς, …	δοίην, δοίης, …	δοῦναι	δούς, δοῦσα, δόν
ἕς, ἕτω … ἕντων	ὧ, ἧς, …	εἵην, εἵης, …	εἷναι	εἵς, εἷσα, ἔν
στῆθι, στήτω … στάντων	στῶ, στῇς, …	σταίην, σταίης, …	στῆναι	στάς, στᾶσα, στάν

Note that the aorist subjunctive active is just like the present subjunctive active, except that it does not have the characteristic reduplication of the present system: διδῷ, δῷ. Similarly for the optative, διδοίη, δοίη, and for most of the imperative, διδότω, δότω.

The aorist participle active εἵς from ἵημι has stem ἑντ- in the masculine and neuter; the masculine nominative singular has a long vowel by **compensatory lengthening**, just like λέων. Don't confuse εἵς, ἕντος with εἷς, ἑνός, the number one, or with the preposition εἰς, a proclitic with a smooth breathing.

XVI.4 Third declension nouns in -εύς

A large class of nouns, often naming an agent or person who does an action, ends in -εύς. This is the third and final group of nouns with quantitative metathesis (compare chapter 7 and chapter 12). They have -υ- in nominative and vocative singular and dative plural, but lose it in all the other forms, where the endings begin with vowels. They always have -ε-, possibly contracted with the ending. The accusative singular ends in -α, not -ν as you might expect, because the stem originally ended in a consonant, βασιλῆϝ- (see vocabulary note, chapter 9). The accusative singular was thus originally βασιλῆϝα, then after loss of digamma βασιλῆα, and finally after quantitative metathesis βασιλέα. Contrast nouns like πῆχυς (in chapter 12), the true -υ-stems, ending in -υς in the nominative rather than -εύς, and having no digamma.

These are the forms of βασιλεύς, βασιλέως, ὁ, "king":

singular

nom.	βασιλεύς
gen.	βασιλέως
dat.	βασιλεῖ
acc.	βασιλέᾱ
voc.	βασιλεῦ

dual

nom., voc., acc.	βασιλεῖ
gen., dat.	βασιλέοιν

plural

nom., voc.	βασιλῆς (or, later, βασιλεῖς)
gen.	βασιλέων
dat.	βασιλεῦσι(ν)
acc.	βασιλέᾱς

Exercise

The following nouns follow the same pattern: χαλκεύς "smith, bronze-worker," ἱππεύς "horseman," ἱερεύς "priest," γονεύς "parent." Write out the complete declension of each one, including the article.

XVI.5 Remembering and forgetting

Verbs of remembering and forgetting take a complement in the genitive instead of an accusative direct object. Thus ἀναμιμνήσκεται τοῦ πολέμου, "he remembers the war"; μέμνημαι τῆς τελευτῆς τοῦ Σωκράτους βίου, "I remember the end of Socrates's life" (Xen. *Apol.* 1). Similarly, ἐλάθετο τοῦ ὀνόματος, "he has forgotten the name."

Latin and Sanskrit have the same rule: *belli meminit*; *yuddhasya smarati*; "he remembers the war." It may help to think of expressions like "be mindful/forgetful *of*" in English.

XVI.6 Idioms with ἄλλος

In English, to say that each of a group of subjects does something different, we have constructions like "one goes one way, the other goes the other way." The equivalent idiom in Greek is similar but with only one phrase rather than two coordinated phrases, so ἄλλος ἄλλοσε ἔρχεται. Any form of ἄλλος or any of the various adverbs derived from ἄλλος can be used this way: ἄλλος ἄλλην θυγατρὰ τρέφει "each feeds one of the daughters"; ἄλλον ἄλλοτε λέγω "I speak sometimes to one man, sometimes to another"; ἄλλῳ ἄλλως δίδωτι "He gives differently to each person"; and so on. The succinct Greek expression is fairly common.

Another idiom singles out one member of a group: τά τε ἄλλα βιβλία ἔχω καὶ τὸ τοῦ Σοφοκλέους. The sense is not just that one of the speaker's books is by Sophocles, but that he has this book in particular. Similarly ἐν Τροίᾳ τετελευτήκασιν οἵ τε ἄλλοι καὶ ὁ τῆς Θέτιδος υἱός, "in particular the son of Thetis died at Troy" (Plato *Apol.* 28c), or perhaps "many died at Troy, especially the son of Thetis." Although formally the ἄλλοι and the specifically named book, hero, or whatever it might be are simply coordinated, in fact the named member of the group is marked as special, without any need for an adverb meaning "specially" or "particularly."

XVI.7 Vocabulary

VERBS

ἀνα-βλύζω, -βλύσω, -ἔβλυσα, – , – , – , bubble up

ἀνα-ζητέω, seek

ἀνά-κειμαι, be dedicated

ἀνα-μιμνήσκω, remind; in middle, remember

ἀνθέω, ἀνθήσω, ἤνθησα, ἤνθηκα, – , – , bloom, blossom, flower

ἀπ-άρχομαι, begin, make a beginning of

ἄρχω, ἄρξω, ἦρξα, ἦρχα, ἦργμαι, ἤρχθην, begin; rule (+ gen.) (cp. *archaic, archaeology, monarch*)

γυμνόω, γυμνώσω, ἐγύμνωσα, – , – , ἐγυμνώθην, lay bare, strip naked

ἐάω, ἐάσω, εἴασα, εἴακα, εἴαμαι, εἰάθην, permit, allow

ἐρεθίζω, ἐρεθίσω, ἠρέθισα, – , – , – , provoke, challenge

θερμαίνω, θερμανῶ, ἐθέρμηνα, – , τεθέρμαμμαι, ἐθερμάνθην, heat, warm (cp. *thermometer*)

καθίζω, καθιῶ, ἐκάθισα, – , – , – , cause to sit, set; sit

κεῖμαι, κείσομα, lie, be placed (present and future systems only)

μειδιάω, μειδιάσω, ἐμείδησα, – , – , – , smile

ὀρχέομαι, ὀρχήσομαι, ὠρχησάμην, – , – , – , dance (cp. *orchestra*)

ῥέω, ῥεύσομαι, ἔρρευσα, ἐρρύηκα, – , ἐρρύην, flow (cp. *stream, rheostat*)

τρίβω, τρίψω, ἔτριψα, τέτριφα, τέτριμμαι, ἐτρίβην, rub (cp. *diatribe, thread,* L. *tero*)

ὑπ-ανθέω, begin to flower

ὑπο-φθέγγομαι, utter, voice

ψεύδω, ψεύσω, ἔψευσα, – , ἔψευσμαι, ἐψεύσθην, falsify, cheat; in middle, lie, tell a lie (cp. *pseudonym*)

NOUNS

ἀηδών, -όνος, ἡ, nightingale

ἀνάθημα, -ατος, τό, offering (cp. *anathema*)

ἄνθος, -ους, τό, flower (cp. *anthology, chrysanthemum*)

ἄντρον, -ου, τό, cave

αὐλός, -οῦ, ὁ, aulos, a musical instrument like an oboe or shawm

αὐχήν, -ένος, ὁ, neck

βασιλεύς, βασιλέως, ὁ, king (cp. *basilica, basil*)

γάλα, γάλακτος, τό, milk (cp. *milk, galaxy*, L. *lac*)

γονεύς, -έως, ὁ, parent

δρόμος, -ου, ὁ, running, race

δρῦς, δρυός, ἡ, oak (cp. *tree, trust, Druid, drupe*, L. *durus*)

ἔαρ, ἦρος, τό, springtime

ζῶμα, -ατος, τό, girdle, belt

θέρος, -ους, τό, summer, harvest time

ἱερεύς, -έως, ὁ, priest

ἰξύς, -ύος, ἡ, waist

ἴον, ἴου, τό, violet, pansy

κάλαμος, -ου, ὁ, pipe, reed

κόμη, -ης, ἡ, hair

μειδίᾱμα, -ατος, τό, smile

νάρκισσος, -ου, ὁ, narcissus-flower

νομεύς, -έως, ὁ, herdsman

νομή, -ῆς, ἡ, pasturage

νύμφη, -ης, ἡ, nymph, bride (cp. *nuptial*, L. *nubo*)

οἶς, οἰός, ὁ, ἡ, sheep (cp. *ewe*, L. *ovis*)

ὀφρύς, -ύος, ἡ, brow (cp. *brow*)

πηγή, -ῆς, ἡ, spring of water (cp. *Pegasus*)

πόᾱ, -ᾱς, ἡ, grass

πούς, ποδός, ὁ, foot; dat. pl. ποσίν (cp. *podiatrist, foot*, L. *pes*)

ποιμήν, -ένος, ὁ, shepherd

σιωπή, -ῆς, ἡ, silence

σῦριγξ, σύριγγος, ἡ, syrinx, Pan's pipes

σχῆμα, -ατος, τό, form, shape, guise (cp. *scheme*)

ὕδωρ, ὕδατος, τό, water (cp. *hydrate, water*, L. *unda*)

ὑπόδημα, -ατος, τό, shoe

χιών, -ονος, ἡ, snow (cp. *hibernate, Himalaya*, L. *hiems*)

χορείᾱ, -ᾱς, ἡ, dance

ADJECTIVES

γυμνός, -ή, -όν, bare, naked (cp. *gymnast, naked*, L. *nudus*)

μαλακός, -ή, -όν, soft, weak, gentle

περιφερής, -ές, vaulted, arched, round, rolling (cp. *periphery*)

ADVERBS AND CONJUNCTIONS

ἄλλοθεν, from another place

ἄλλοθι, in another place

ἄλλοσε, to another place

ἄλλοτε, at another time

ἔνδοθεν, within, inside, from inside

ἔξωθεν, without, outside, from outside

ἐντεῦθεν, after that, from there

καὶ δὴ καί, and in particular

Notes on the vocabulary

ἀναμιμνήσκω is not different from the simple verb μιμνήσκω.

ἄρχω is frequently used in the middle rather than the active. It takes a genitive complement, ἄρχομαι τοῦ ἔργου, ἄρχομαι τῆς γῆς, "I begin work, I rule the land."

κεῖμαι is an athematic present middle with a regular future. It is used instead of the ordinary passive forms of τίθημι.

καθίζω is originally a compound, κατά + ἵζω, but it is no longer treated that way: in particular, in past indicative tenses the augment goes first, as if the καθ- is not a prefix, so imperfect ἐκάθιζον and aorist ἐκάθισα. The underlying simple verb ἵζω is cognate with English *sit* and Latin *sedeo*.

The aorist ἐρρύην is a root aorist active rather than an aorist passive; because ῥέω is intransitive it has no passive. The future ῥυήσομαι is more common than ῥεύσομαι in Attic Greek. The present is like πλέω.

The base meaning of αὐλός is a pipe or tube, but the word commonly refers to a particular wind instrument with a double reed, called "aulos" in English. Older books will call an αὐλός a "flute," but it's more like an oboe.

You already know κάλαμος in the sense "pen." This is an extension from the basic meaning "reed," since a pen can be made from a reed.

οἶς is an Attic form; in other dialects you will see the word in three syllables, ὄϊς, ὄιος.

XVI.8 Reading

1. *Springtime*

   ἤδη δὲ ἦρος ἀρχομένου καὶ τῆς μὲν χιόνος λυομένης, τῆς δὲ γῆς γυμνουμένης καὶ τῆς πόας ὑπανθούσης, οἵ τ᾽ ἄλλοι νομῆς ἦγον τὰς ἀγέλας ἐς νομὴν καὶ δὴ καὶ Δάφνις καὶ Χλόη. εὐθὺς οὖν δρόμος ἦν ἐπὶ τὰς Νύμφας καὶ τὸ ἄντρον, ἐντεῦθεν ἐπὶ τὸν Πᾶνα καὶ τὴν πίτυν, εἶτ᾽ ἐπὶ τὴν δρῦν, ὑφ᾽ ἣν καθίζοντες τὰς ἀγέλας ἔνεμον. ἀνεζήτησαν δὲ ἄνθη ἐθέλοντες στεφανῶσαι τοὺς θεούς· τὰ δ᾽ ἄρτι ὁ Ζέφυρος τρέφων καὶ ὁ ἥλιος θερμαίνων ἐξῆγεν· ὅμως δὲ εὑρέθη καὶ ἴα καὶ νάρκισσος καὶ ὅσα ἦρος πρῶτα γίγνεται. ἡ μὲν Χλόη καὶ ὁ Δάφνις ἀπ᾽ αἰγῶν καὶ ἀπ᾽ οἰῶν ἔπινον γάλα νέον· ἀπήρξαντο καὶ σύριγγος, ὥσπερ τὰς ἀηδόνας ἐς τὴν μουσικὴν ἐρεθίζοντες· αἱ δ᾽ ὑπεφθέγγοντο ἐν ταῖς λόχμαις, ὥσπερ ἀναμιμνησκόμεναι τῆς ᾠδῆς ἐκ μακρᾶς σιωπῆς.

   > **πίτυς, πίτυος, ἡ**, pine. **στεφανόω**, crown (predictable principal parts). **Ζέφυρος, -ου, ὁ**, west wind. **λόχμη, -ης, ἡ**, bush, thicket.

2. *Another Spring*

   Νυμφῶν ἄντρον ἦν, πέτρα μεγάλη, τὰ ἔνδοθεν κοίλη, τὰ ἔξωθεν περιφερής· ἐνῆν δὲ ἀγάλματα τῶν Νυμφῶν αὐτῶν λίθινα, ὧν πόδες ἀνυπόδητοι, χεῖρες εἰς ὤμους γυμναί, κόμαι μέχρι τῶν αὐχένων λελυμέναι, ζῶμα περὶ τὴν ἰξύν, μειδίαμα περὶ τὴν ὀφρύν, τὸ πᾶν σχῆμα χορεία ἦν ὀρχουμένων. ἐκ δὲ τῆς πηγῆς ὕδωρ ἀναβλύζον ἔρρει, ὥστε καὶ λειμὼν πάνυ καλὸς ἦν πρὸ τοῦ ἄντρου, πολλῆς καὶ μαλακῆς πόας ὑπὸ τῆς νοτίδος τρεφομένης. ἀνέκειντο δὲ καὶ γαυλοὶ καὶ αὐλοὶ καὶ σύριγγες καὶ κάλαμοι, πρεσβυτέρων ποιμένων ἀναθήματα.

   > Selections 1 and 2 are from *Daphnis and Chloe*.

   > **ἄγαλμα, ἀγάλματος, τό**, statue. **λίθινος** = ἐκ λίθου πεποιημένος. **ἀνυπόδητος πούς** = πούς ἄνευ ὑποδημάτων, πούς γυμνός. **γαυλός, -οῦ, ὁ**, milk-pail. **νοτίς, -ίδος, ἡ**, moisture.

3. ὁ βασιλεὺς ὀνομάζεται ποιμὴν λεῶν. ὁ γὰρ λεώς τῷ βασιλεῖ μέλει ὥσπερ οἱ οἶες τῷ ποιμένι.

4. ἡ γυνὴ τρίβει τὸν σῖτον ἵνα ἄρτον ποιῇ. τοῦ σίτου εὖ τετριμμένου, ὕδωρ καὶ ἅλα ἐντίθησι. ἐντεῦθεν τὸν σῖτον θερμαίνει. τέλος δὲ τὸν ἄρτον ἐσθίομεν.

5. ὁ δρῦς δένδρον ἐστί. πολλὰ μὲν φυτὰ ἀνθοῦσιν, ὁ δὲ δρῦς οὔ. ὁ νάρκισσος καὶ ὁ ἴον ἄνθη εἰσί. ἄλλα ἄνθη ἄλλοτε γίγνονται, τὰ μὲν ἦρι, τὰ δὲ θέρει, τὰ δὲ ὀπώρᾳ. καὶ ἄλλα ἄλλοθί εἰσι· παρὰ ταῖς πηγαῖς, ἐν τοῖς λειμῶσι, ἐν τοῖς κήποις. οὐδὲν δὲ ἄνθος ἐν ἄντρῳ γίγνεται. ἄνθη γὰρ τοῦ ἡλίου χρῄζουσι.

6. ἦν ποτε νεανίας, Νάρκισσος ὀνόματι, καλὸς ὢν ἀλλ᾽ ὢν σοφός. ὁ δὲ Νάρκισσος ποιμὴν ἦν. ἡμέρᾳ τινί, τῶν προβάτων ἐν νομῇ ὄντων, ὁ νεανίας πρὸς πηγὴν ἐρχόμενος ἐπὶ τῇ πόᾳ ἔκειτο. εἰς τὸ τῆς πηγῆς ὕδωρ ἔβλεψε. ἐκεῖ ἄλλον νεανίαν ἑώρα. "ὡς καλὸς ὁ νεανίας," ἐνόμισε. "χαῖρε, ὦ φίλε," εἶπε ὁ Νάρκισσος τῷ ἐν τῷ ὕδατι μειρακίῳ. "τίς εἶ καὶ τίνων γονέων; ἆρα ἐᾷς μέ σε ἅπτεσθαι; ἐᾷς μέ σε φιλεῖν;" ὁ δὲ ἄλλος οὐδὲν ἀπεκρίνατο, ἀλλὰ ἐμειδία. ὁ δὲ Νάρκισσος, τὸ μειδίαμα ὁρῶν, πάλιν εἶπε, "καλός ἐστι, ὦ νεανία, τὸ σχῆμα, ἐκ κεφαλῆς ἐπὶ πόδα. ἡ μὲν μέλαινα κόμη μαλακή ἐστι, ὡς ἔοικε, τὼ δὲ χεῖρε λευκά, τὼ δὲ ὤμω μεγάλω. τί ἐθέλεις; σοὶ πάντα δώσω." ἀλλὰ ὁ ἄλλος οὐδὲν ἀπεκρίνατο.

ὁ δὲ Νάρκισσος πολλὰς ἡμέρας παρὰ τῇ πηγῇ ἐκαθίζετο τὸν νεανίαν ὁρῶν. οὐδὲ ἤσθιε οὐδὲ ἔπιε. οἱ οἶες, τοῦ Ναρκίσσου οὐκέτι νέμοντος, ἄλλος ἄλλοθεν ἀπεχώρει. τέλος δὲ ὁ Νάρκισσος ἀπέθανε, καὶ ἐκ τοῦ σώματος ἄνθος ὑπήνθησε, ὃ νῦν ὀνομάζομεν νάρκισσον.

7. ὦ ξεῖν᾽, ἀγγέλλειν Λακεδαιμονίοις ὅτι τῇδε
   κείμεθα τοῖς κείνων ῥήμασι πειθόμενοι.

> This is the epitaph for the 300 Spartan dead at Thermopylae, as reported by Herodotus.
>
> **κείνων** is a dialect form for ἐκείνων, and ξεῖνε for ξένε from ξένος. Note use of infinitive ἀγγέλλειν instead of imperative. **ῥῆμα, -ατος, τό** = λόγος.

8. χαίρετε συμπόται ἄνδρες ὁμήλικες· ἐξ ἀγαθοῦ γὰρ
   ἀρξάμενος τελέω τὸν λόγον εἰς ἀγαθόν·
   χρὴ δ᾽, ὅταν εἰς τοιοῦτο συνέλθωμεν φίλοι ἄνδρες
   πρᾶγμα, γελᾶν παίζειν χρησαμένους ἀρετῇ,
   ἥδεσθαί τε συνόντας, ἐς ἀλλήλους τε φλυαρεῖν
   καὶ σκώπτειν τοιαῦθ᾽ οἷα γέλωτα φέρειν.
   ἡ δὲ σπουδὴ ἑπέσθω, ἀκούωμέν τε λεγόντων
   ἐν μέρει· ἥδ᾽ ἀρετὴ συμποσίου πέλεται.
   τοῦ δὲ ποταρχοῦντος πειθώμεθα· ταῦτα γάρ ἐστιν
   ἔργ᾽ ἀνδρῶν ἀγαθῶν, εὐλογίαν τε φέρειν.

> This poem is preserved on a papyrus fragment from Elephantine; it probably comes from the 5th century, but its author is unknown.
>
> **συμπότης, -ου, ὁ**, fellow drinker, party companion. **ὁμῆλιξ, -ικος, ὁ, ἡ**, age-mate, person of the same age. **τελέω** = τέλος ποιῶ, note uncontracted form. **παίζω**, play. **χράομαι, χρήσομαι, ἐχρησάμην, –, κέχρημαι, ἐχρήσθην**, use (+ dative). **ἥδομαι**, enjoy oneself, take pleasure. **φλυαρέω**, fool around, talk nonsense. **σκώπτω**, joke, have fun. **γέλως, -ωτος, ὁ**, laughter. **σπουδή, -ῆς, ἡ**, earnestness, seriousness. **μέρος, -ους, τό**, part. **πέλεται** = ἐστι. **ποταρχέω** = τοῦ συμποσίου ἄρχω, ἄρχων εἰμὶ τῶν πινόντων. **εὐλογία, -ας, ἡ**, praise.

9. *περὶ τοῦ Τρωικοῦ πολέμου, δέκατον μέρος*

ἤδη δὲ ὄντος τοῦ πολέμου δέκα ἐτῶν οἱ Ἀχαιοὶ ἐν ἀπορίᾳ ἦσαν. ὁ μὲν Ἕκτωρ, υἱὸς ὢν τοῦ βασιλέως Τρωικοῦ, ἀπέθανε, ὁ δὲ Ἀχιλλεύς, ἄριστος στρατιώτης ὢν τῶν Ἑλλήνων, καὶ αὐτὸς ἀπέθανε. ἀλλὰ οὐδέτερος στρατὸς ἐδύνατο νικᾶν.

ἐν μάχῃ ὁ Ὀδυσσεὺς τὸν Ἕλενον ἔλαβε, ἱερέα καὶ μάντιν ὄντα τῶν Τρώων. τῷ Ὀδυσσεῖ ἐρωτῶντι εἶπε ὁ μάντις, "ὑμεῖς οὐκ ἄλλως τὸν Ἴλιον αἱρήσετε ἢ τοῖς τοῦ Ἡρακλέους τόξοις. ἐὰν μὴ τὰ τόξα ἔχητε, οὔποτε νικήσετε. ἐκείνοις μὲν τοῖς τόξοις μόνον ἡ πόλις αἱρεῖσθαι δύναται, ἄλλῳ δὲ ὅπλῳ οὔ."

διότι οἱ Ἕλληνες τοὺς μάντεις τιμῶσι, ὁ Ὀδυσσεὺς τὸν Ἕλενον ἀπελθεῖν εἴασε, καὶ ὁ μάντις πάλιν ὑπὸ τὰ τείχη ἀπῆλθε.

ὁ δὲ Ἀγαμέμνων, τὸν τοῦ μάντεως λόγον πυνθανόμενος, ἠρώτησε ὅπου εἴη τὰ τόξα καὶ ὅστις αὐτὰ ἔχοι.

"ὁ Φιλοκτήτης ἔχει ἐκεῖνα τὰ τόξα. Λήμνῳ ἐστὶ οὗ αὐτὸν κατελίπομεν πρὶν ἐνθάδε ἐλθεῖν. δεῖ που αὐτὸν ἀναφέρειν."

"ναί," ἀπεκρίνατο ὁ στρατηγός. "ἴθι εἰς Λῆμνον αὐτὸν ληψόμενος ἵνα τὴν πόλιν νικῶμεν."

ὁ Ὀδυσσεὺς οὖν ναῦν παρασκευάσας ἐκάλεσε Νεοπτόλεμον, υἱὸν ὄντα τοῦ Ἀχιλλέως. ἐβούλετο τὸν νεανίαν λαβεῖν ὡς τὸν Φιλοκτήτην. ἐλθόντε ἐπὶ τῇ νήσῳ ὁ Ὀδυσσεὺς καὶ ὁ Νεοπτόλεμος δόλον ηὑρέτην. εἰ μὲν ὁ Ὀδυσσεὺς τῷ Φιλοκτήτῃ λέγοι, ὁ ἄλλος αὐτὸν ἀποθνῄσκοι ἄν. εἰ δὲ ὁ Νεοπτόλεμος αὐτῷ λέγοι, μὴ τὸν Ὀδυσσέα δηλούντων, ὁ Φιλοκτήτης πρὸς τὸν Ἴλιον ἔρχοιτο ἄν. ὁ γὰρ Φιλοκτήτης τὸν Ὀδυσσεὺς ἐμίσει διότι ὁ Ὀδυσσεὺς τοῖς ἄλλοις ἔπεισε αὐτὸν ἐπὶ τῷ Λήμνῳ καταλιπεῖν.

ὁ Νεοπτόλεμος οὖν τῷ Φιλοκτήτῃ ἔλεγε. ἀλλὰ, οὐχ ἑκὼν ψεύδειν, τὴν ἀληθείαν εἶπε. ὁ Φιλοκτήτης μὲν ὠργίσθην, ὁ δὲ Ὀδυσσεὺς καὶ αὐτός. τέλος δὲ ὁ Φιλοκτήτης ἐπείθετο καὶ τὰ τοῦ Ἡρακλέους τόξα πρὸς τὸν Ἴλιον ἀνήνεγκε.

ὁ δὲ Μαχάων, ἰατρὸς ὢν τῶν Ἀχαιῶν, ἐθεράπευσε τὸ τοῦ Φιλοκτήτου ἕλκος. ὁ δὲ Νεοπτόλεμος τοῖς τόξοις τὸν Ἀλέξανδρον ἔβαλε καὶ ἀπέθανε.

> **οὐδέτερος, -α, -ον**, neither. **τόξα, -ων, τά**, bow and arrows. **πρίν**, before. **δόλος, -ου, ὁ**, trick, deceit. **μισέω**, hate. **ὀργίζομαι**, become angry, predictable principal parts. **ἕλκος, -ους, τό**, wound, sore.

XVI.9 Conversation

1. (reading 1) διὰ τί γυμνοῦται ἡ γῆ τῷ ἦρι; ποῦ εἰσι ὁ Δάφνις καὶ ἡ Χλόη; τί ποιοῦσιν; ποῖα ζῷα ἐν ἀγέλῃ εἰσί; and so on as usual.

2. (reading 2) ποῖα εἰσι τὰ τῶν νυμφῶν ἀγάλματα; ἆρα τὸ ἄγαλμα πέτασον φέρει ἐπὶ τῇ κόμῃ; ἆρα ὑποδήματα φέρει; ποῦ ἐστι τὰ ἄγαλμα; and so on.

XVI.10 Writing

1. Do the change-number exercise with the following sentences.
   a. ὁ ἱερεὺς τὰ ἀναθήματα τῇ θεᾷ ἐδίδου.
   b. οἱ ναῦται τὸν ἱστὸν ἵστασαν ἵνα πλέωσι.
   c. ὁ ἀγαθὸς ποιμὴν τῶν οἰῶν ἀναμιμνήσκεται.
   d. τὼ κόρα τὴν κόμην πέπλεχθον.
   e. τὼ γονεῖ τοῖς παισὶ γάλα ἐδιδότην.
   f. τὰ ὑποδήματα ἐπὶ τοὺς πόδας φέρομεν.
   g. ὁ βασιλεὺς ἔμνησε τῆς ἀηδόνος νύκτωρ ᾀδούσης.
   h. εἰ ἐν τῇ χιόνι ὀρχοίμεθα γυμνοὶ ὄντες, ἀποθνήσκοιμεν ἄν.
   i. τρῖψον τὸν λίθον ἑνὶ δακτύλῳ καὶ τὸ θελκτήριον εἰπέ.
   j. ὁ ποιμὴν ἐν τῇ πόᾳ ὑπὸ δρυὶ ἔκειτο.
   k. ὁ βασιλεὺς οὐκ ἐάσει τοὺς δούλους ᾄδειν.
   l. εἰ γυμνὸς εἴης τοὺς πόδας, οὗτος ὁ ἀνήρ σοι ἄν ὑποδήματα διδοίη.

2. Rewrite the following sentences, turning the participial phrases into subordinate clauses. You may use whatever kind of clause fits the sense. For example, from ὁ μαθητής, σοφὸς ὤν, εὖ μανθάνει make ὁ μαθητὴς εὖ μανθάνει, ἐπεὶ σοφός ἐστι.

    a. δόντες τοῖς ζῴοις σῖτον οἱ ποιμένες τῆς χορείας ἦρχον.

    b. τῶν μαθητῶν ὑπὸ τοῦ διδασκάλου ἐξητασμένων, οἱ γονῆς ἐθαύμαζον.

    c. οὐ πειθόμεθα τῷ ἀεὶ ψεύδοντι.

    d. ἡ βοῦς ἅπαξ ἐφθεγμένη σιωπῇ ἔφαγε.

    e. τὰ ἀναθήματα ἐν τῷ νεῴ| τιθεὶς ὁ ἱερεὺς ἐκέλευσε τὰ ἱερεῖα φέρεσθαι.

    f. τοῦ ἱερέως τὰ ἀναθήματα ἐν τῷ νεῴ νεῴ| τιθέντος, οἱ θῆτες τὰ ἱερεῖα ἤνεγκαν.

    g. οἱ παῖδες, οὐ δυνάμενοι σιωπὴν σῴζειν, μετ' ἀλλήλοις ἐλάλουν.

    h. τὰ τόξα μὴ ἔχοντες, οὔποτε τὴν πόλιν αἱρήσουσι.

    i. τὰ οὔπω πεπραγμένα ἔργα πρᾶξον.

    j. τὰ μήπω πεπραγμένα ἔργα πρᾶξον.

    k. τὴν ἅμαξαν τοῖς λευκοῖς ἵπποις εἱλκυσμένην ἐβεβλέφειμεν.

    l. τοὺς στρατιώτας περὶ τῶν τειχῶν στάντε τὼ στρατηγὼ τῆς τοῦ πολέμου ἀρχῆς ἀναμέμνησθον.

    m. οἱ πολῖται τοῦ τὴν φωνὴν ἐντὸς ῥήτορος ἀκούουσι.

    n. τὰ ζῷα γάλα διδόντα εἰσι βόες, οἶες, αἶγες.

3. Write two or three different completions for each of the following sentences.

    a. τὸ ὕδωρ τεθερμαμμένον _____.

    b. οἱ γονεῖς τὰ τέκνα ἐῶσι _____.

    c. ἄλλη ἄλλοτε _____.

    d. ἡ χιὼν τῷ ἦρι _____.

    e. ἡ μὲν ἀηδὼν _____, ὁ δὲ ἀλεκτρυὼν _____.

4. Rewrite reading 8 in straightforward prose.

5. Write a paragraph about the springtime; you may find the first two reading selections in this chapter and the supplement to chapter 14 useful for vocabulary.

Chapter XVII

How the Greeks Enter Troy

XVII.1 The verb οἶδα

The verb οἶδα "I know" is perfect in form but present in meaning (like Latin *cognovi*). It is the perfect from the same root as the aorist εἶδον "I saw"; the idea is that what you have seen, you know. Its past tense is formally a pluperfect. It forms a future middle from εἴσομαι, with the regular middle endings. These are the finite forms of the present (perfect) system:

	Present Perfect	Past	Imperative	Subjunctive	Optative
singular					
1st	οἶδ-α	ᾔδη		εἰδ-ῶ	εἰδ-είην
2nd	οἶσ-θα	ᾔδησ-θα	ἴσ-θι	εἰδ-ῇς	εἰδ-είης
3rd	οἶδ-ε(ν)	ᾔδ-ει(ν)	ἴσ-τω	εἰδ-ῇ	εἰδ-είη
dual					
2nd	ἴσ-τον	ᾖσ-τον	ἴσ-τον	εἰδ-ῆ-τον	εἰδ-εῖτον
3rd	ἴσ-τον	ᾖσ-την	ἴσ-των	εἰδ-ῆ-τον	εἰδ-είτην
plural					
1st	ἴσ-μεν	ᾖσ-μεν		εἰδ-ῶ-μεν	εἰδ-εῖμεν
2nd	ἴσ-τε	ᾖσ-τε	ἴσ-τε	εἰδ-ῆ-τε	εἰδ-εῖτε
3rd	ἴσ-α-σι(ν)	ᾖσαν	ἴσ-των	εἰδ-ῶ-σι(ν)	εἰδ-εῖεν

The present (perfect) infinitive active is εἰδέναι and the participle is εἰδώς, εἰδυῖα, εἰδός, declined like any other perfect participle (masc. gen. sg. εἰδότος and so on).

Note the internal sandhi: dental before dental becomes σ, so οἶσθα from οἶδ-θα; similarly for ἴστε and other forms. Note, too, that this verb has o grade in the singular of the indicative, as you would expect for a perfect stem, but zero grade in the dual and plural (and the imperative), and e grade in the subjunctive and optative; this is different from any other perfect tense in Greek. See chapter 15 section 3 for pointers on distinguishing forms of this verb from those of εἶμι and εἰμί.

XVII.2　The verb φημί

In chapter 9 you met the verb φημί "I say," which is enclitic in the present indicative active, just like εἰμί. Its imperfect is ἔφη, ἔφησθα, ἔφη, ἔφατον ἐφάτην, ἔφαμεν, ἔφατε, ἔφασαν. Its present infinitive active is φάναι. Its other finite moods are predictable:

> Imperative: φαθί, φάτω . . . φάντων
>
> Subjunctive: φῶ, φῇς . . . φῶσι(ν)
>
> Optative: φαίην, φαίης . . . φαῖεν

Although it has a present participle active φάς, φᾶσα, φάν, you will not see it in Attic Greek texts, where the participle from φάσκω is normally used instead.

The future φήσω and aorist ἔφησα are regular. There is no perfect, and there is no middle or passive in any tense.

XVII.3　Contract verbs with -η-

A few common contracted verbs in -άω conjugate with η wherever the others have ᾱ, as ζάω, ζῶ, ζῇς, ζῇ "live," πεινάω "I am hungry," διψάω "I thirst," χράομαι, χρῶμαι, χρῇ, χρῆται "use."

Note that χράομαι "use" takes a dative complement rather than an accusative direct object — really an instrumental dative. Thus καλάμῳ χρῶμαι, "I use a pen." If you know Latin, you will recognize this as exactly like *utor* with instrumental ablative.

XVII.4　Verbs in -νῡμι

Most of the athematic verbs we have seen so far have reduplicated present stems. Another group of athematic verbs ends in -νῡμι, with suffix -νῡ- added to the root to form the present stem. This suffix does not appear in the other tense systems.

For example, δείκνῡμι "show, point out" has root δεικ- and principal parts δείκνῡμι, δείξω, ἔδειξα, δέδειχα, δέδειγμαι, ἐδείχθην. (The perfect active stem is arguably slightly irregular, since we would have expected o grade of the root, but it uses the regular endings.)

These are the forms of the -νῡμι verbs:

	Pres. Indic. Act.	Pres. Indic. Mid.	Impf. Indic. Act.	Impf. Indic. Mid.
singular				
1st	δείκνῡμι	δείκνῡμαι	ἐδείκνῡν	ἐδεικνύμην
2nd	δείκνῡς	δείκνυσαι	ἐδείκνῡς	ἐδείκνυσο
3rd	δείκνῡσι	δείκνυται	ἐδείκνῡ	ἐδείκνυτο

	Pres. Indic. Act.	Pres. Indic. Mid.	Impf. Indic. Act.	Impf. Indic. Mid.
dual				
2nd	δείκνυτον	δείκνυσθον	ἐδείκνυτον	ἐδείκνυσθον
3rd	δείκνυτον	δείκνυσθον	ἐδεικνύτην	ἐδεικνύσθην
plural				
1st	δείκνυμεν	δεικνύμεθα	ἐδείκνυμεν	ἐδεικνύμεθα
2nd	δείκνυτε	δείκνυσθε	ἐδείκνυτε	ἐδείκνυσθε
3rd	δεικνύᾱσι	δείκνυνται	ἐδείκνυσαν	ἐδείκνυντο

The present infinitive active is δεικνύναι and middle δείκνυσθαι. The present participle active is δεικνύς, δεικνῦσα, δεικνύν and middle δεικνύμενος, -η, -ον.

The rest of the present system is more like the thematic verbs: the imperative active is δείκνῡ, δεικνύτω, and so on; the subjunctive δεικνύω, δεικνύῃς, and so on; and the optative δεικνύοιμι, δεικνύοις, and so on; and similarly for the middle.

Exercise

Write out the three third-person forms of the present indicative active, and the present infinitives active and middle, of ἀνοίγνυμι "open" (= ἀνα- + οἴγνυμι), ζεύγνυμι "yoke, harness," μίγνυμι "mix."

XVII.5 General or indefinite past constructions

As you know (Chapter 8, section 7), general expressions are made with relative or other subordinators, the particle ἄν, and a subjunctive verb. The OOO rule applies, but the particle ἄν must be dropped if the verb becomes optative. This is because an optative with ἄν means a potential, something that *might* happen, not the same as a general statement of what *always* happens.

Thus the regular way to express indefiniteness or a generalization in the past is with a relative subordinator and the optative mood.

Examples:

εἰ γένοιτο = "if it ever happened" (compare present or future ἐὰν γένηται, "if it ever happens").

ὅστις ἔλθοι = "whoever came" (pres. or fut. ὃς ἂν ἔλθῃ, "whoever comes").

ὁπότ᾽ ἴδοι = "whenever she saw" (pres. or fut. ὁπόταν ἴδῃ, "whenever she sees").

XVII.6 Result constructions

To express a result we use ὥστε. If the result is natural, or to be expected, the verb is in the infinitive and ὥστε is an adverb:

οὕτως καλὸς ἦν ὥστε θαυμάζειν πάντας, "he was so beautiful that all admired him" (natural result). Note that the subject of the infinitive, as always, is in the accusative. In English we might also say "so beautiful that everyone would admire him," or even "so beautiful as to be universally admired."

The negative is μή, as οὕτως κακὸς ἦν ὥστε μηδὲν φιλεῖν, "he was so evil that no one could love him."

If the result is a fact, the verb is in the indicative and ὥστε is a subordinating conjunction:

οὕτως καλὸς ἦν ὥστε πάντες ἐθαύμαζον, "he was so beautiful that all admired him" (fact).

Here the negative is οὐ.

The infinitive means that the result is what you would expect from the circumstance in the main clause, but does not necessarily mean that the result has actually taken place in this particular instance. The indicative means that the result has taken place, whether it was expected or unusual. This seems like a subtle distinction because it is one that English typically does not make.

The main clause will often have a word like οὕτως ("so," adverb), τοιοῦτος ("such"), or τοσοῦτος ("so large"). The adjectives have variant forms τοῖος, τοιόσδε, τόσος, τοσόσδε.

XVII.7 Vocabulary

VERBS

ἀν-άπτω, kindle (from ἅπτομαι)

ἀν-οίγνῡμι, ἀν-οίξω, ἀν-έῳξα, ἀν-έῳχα, ἀν-έῳγμαι, ἀν-εῴχθην, open

ἀπο-σβέννῡμι, extinguish

βαδίζω, βαδιοῦμαι, ἐβάδισα, βεβάδικα, – , – , walk, go

δείκνῡμι, δείξω, ἔδειξα, δέδειχα, δέδειγμαι, ἐδείχθην, show, point out (cp.
    index, token, teach, L. *dico*)

δυσκολαίνω, δυσκολανῶ, – , – , – , – , be annoyed, be discontented

ἐπι-δείκνυμι, exhibit, show

ζάω, ζήσω, ἔζησα, – , – , – , live

ἥκω, I have come, am arrived (present system only)

θηλάζω, θηλάσω, ἐθήλασα, τεθήλακα, τεθήλαγμαι, ἐθηλάσθην, nurse, suckle

καθεύδω, καθευδήσω, – , – , – , – , sleep

κατα-βαίνω, come down

κλαίω, κλαύσομαι, ἔκλαυσα, – , κέκλαυμαι, – , weep, cry

λούω, λούσω, ἔλουσα, – , λέλουμαι, ἐλούσθην, wash (cp. *lather*, L. *lavo*)

λῡπέω, λῡπήσω, ἐλύπησα, λελύπηκα, λελύπημαι, ἐλυπήθην, vex, hurt, cause
    pain

μίγνῡμι, μίξω, ἔμιξα, – , μέμιγμαι, ἐμίχθη, mix (cp. L. *misceo*)

οἶδα, εἴσομαι, know (perfect and future systems only) (cp. *wit, wisdom*, L. *video*)

παίζω, παίξομαι, ἔπαισα, πέπαικα, πέπαισμαι, – , play, sport, cavort

πρό-ειμι, go on (from εἶμι)

προσ-ποιέομαι, pretend

σβέννῡμι, σβέσω, ἔσβεσα, ἔσβηκα, – , ἐσβέσθην, extinguish, quench (cp. *asbestos*)

σύν-οιδα, be aware, be in on the secret

φάσκω, say, assert (present system only)

χράομαι, χρήσομαι, ἐχρησάμην, – , κέχρημαι, ἐχρήσθην, use

ψοφέω, ψοφήσω, ἐψόφησα, ἐψόφηκα, – , – , make noise, slam, bang

NOUNS

ἀνδρωνῖτις, -ίδος, ἡ, men's rooms

γυναικωνῖτις, -ίδος, ἡ, women's rooms

δεῖπνον, -ου, το,supper

θυρίς, -ίδος, ἡ, window

κλείς, κλειδός, ἡ, key (cp. L. *clavis*)

κλέπτης, -ου, ὁ, thief (cp. *kleptomania*)

κλῖμαξ, -ακος, ἡ, ladder, stair (cp. *climax*)

λύχνος, -ου, ὁ, light, lamp (cp. L. *lux, lumen*)

οἰκίδιον, -ου, τό, little house

ADJECTIVES

ἄσμενος, -η, -ον, willing, glad

διπλοῦς, -ῆ, -οῦν, double

δυσ-, prefix for adjectives, un-, mis-, ill-

ἐπιτήδειος, -α, -ον, suitable, convenient

ἴσος, -η, -ον, equal (cp. *isosceles, isogloss, isotope*)

ὕστερος, -α, -ον, later; **ὕστατος, -η, -ον**, latest. (cp. *out*)

ADVERBS

ἀ-προσ-δοκήτως, unexpectedly

ἐπίτηδες, on purpose

Notes on the vocabulary

The simple verb οἴγνυμι does exist, as does the thematic present οἴγω, but the compound ἀνοίγνυμι (sometimes ἀνοίγω) is much more common.

As usual, the compound ἀποσβέννυμι means the same as the uncompounded verb; κατασβέννυμι does too.

βαδίζω is related to βαίνω.

ἥκω only has a present system; its meaning is much like a perfect.

In Attic Greek prose, κλαίω is sometimes written κλάω (with no contractions), which should not be confused with the less common verb κλάω "pluck." Note the difference in vowel quantity.

The middle of μίγνυμι can be used idiomatically to mean "make love, have sex," as ὁ ἀνὴρ τῇ γυναικὶ μίγνυται. This is polite, rather than slangy, obscene, or clinical.

ἀνδρωνῖτις and γυναικωνῖτις refer to parts of the house reserved for male and female occupation, not to bathrooms.

θυρίς is related to θύρα: a window is like a little door.

ὕστερος and ὕστατος are comparative and superlative forms with no positive degree in use in Greek. The neuter accusatives singular can be used as adverbs, ὕστερον, "later on, too late"; ὕστατον "at last."

The adverb ἐπίτηδες comes from ἐπὶ τάδε, "for that (purpose, reason)," and the adjective ἐπιτήδειος is derived from the adverb.

XVII.8 Reading

1. οἰκίδιόν ἐστί μοι διπλοῦν, ἴσα ἔχον τὰ ἄνω τοῖς κάτω, κατὰ τὴν γυναικωνῖτιν καὶ κατὰ τὴν ἀνδρωνῖτιν. ἐπειδὴ δὲ τὸ παιδίον ἐγένετο ἡμῖν, ἡ μήτηρ αὐτὸ ἐθήλαζεν· ἵνα δὲ μή, ὁπότε λούεσθαι δέοι, κινδυνεύῃ κατὰ τῆς κλίμακος καταβαίνουσα, ἐγὼ μὲν ἄνω διῃτώμην, αἱ δὲ γυναῖκες κάτω. καὶ οὕτως ἤδη συνειθισμένον ἦν, ὥστε πολλάκις ἡ γυνὴ ἀπῄει κάτω καθευδήσουσα ὡς τὸ παιδίον, ἵνα μὴ βοᾷ. καὶ ταῦτα πολὺν χρόνον οὕτως ἐγίγνετο. προϊόντος δὲ τοῦ χρόνου, ἧκον μὲν ἀπροσδοκήτως ἐξ ἀγροῦ, μετὰ δὲ τὸ δεῖπνον τὸ παιδίον ἐβόα καὶ ἐδυσκόλαινεν, ὑπὸ τῆς θεραπαίνης ἐπίτηδες λυπούμενον, ἵνα ταῦτα ποιῇ· ἦν γὰρ κλέπτης ἔνδον, ἐκείνης συνειδυίας· ὕστερον γὰρ ἅπαντα ἐπυθόμην. καὶ ἐγὼ τὴν γυναῖκα ἀπιέναι ἐκέλευον ὡς τὸ παιδίον, ἵνα παύσηται κλαίων. ἡ δὲ ἀναστᾶσα καὶ ἀπιοῦσα προστίθησι τὴν θύραν, προσποιουμένη παίζειν, καὶ τὴν κλεῖν ἐφέλκεται. κἀγὼ ἐκάθευδον ἄσμενος, ἥκων ἐξ ἀγροῦ. ἐπειδὴ δ᾽ ἦν πρὸς ἡμέραν, ἧκεν ἐκείνη καὶ τὴν θύραν ἀνέῳξεν. ἐρομένου δέ μου τί αἱ θύραι νύκτωρ ψοφοῖεν, ἔφασκε τὸν λύχνον ἀποσβεσθῆναι τὸν παρὰ τῷ παιδίῳ, εἶτα ἐκ τῶν γειτόνων ἀνάψαι.

> Lysias 1.9-14. The speaker is the defendant in a murder case.
>
> συνειθισμένον, perfect participle passive from συν-εθίζω, accustom. ἐφ-έλκω, pull out, pull away.

2. φιλόσοφός τίς ποτε ἐβάδιζε διὰ τὴν ἀγοράν. παῖδες πέτραις ἔπαιζον. ὁ φιλόσοφος, τοὺς παῖδας ὁρᾶν, εἶπε, "θαυμάζω ὅτι παίζουσι πέτραις μόναις. αἱ πέτραι ἔμοιγε ἐπιτήδειαι οὐ δοκοῦσιν. τί οὖν ποιοῦσι;" εἷς τῶν παίδων ἀπεκρίνατο, "μὴ θαύμαζε, ὦ ἄνθρωπε, εἰ παίζομεν ταῖς πέτραις. τί ἄλλον ἔχομεν;" ὁ δὲ φιλόσοφος ἔφη, "οἶδα ἄλλως παίζειν, οὕτως καλῶς ὥστε μήποτε ταῖς πέτραις ὑμᾶς παίξεσθε. καί, εἰ ἐθέλετε, ὑμῖν ἐρῶ." τῶν παίδων "ναί" λεγόντων, ὁ φιλόσοφος εἶπε, "ἔγωγε τῇ φιλοσοφίᾳ παίζω. τοῖς λόγοις χρῶμαι ὥσπερ ὑμεῖς ταῖς πέτραις. νῦν σύνιστε." οἱ παῖδες ἐθαύμαζον. "ἆρα λόγοις δεῖ παίζειν; πῶς ποιοῦμεν; οὐκ ἴσμεν οὐδὲν περὶ τῆς φιλοσοφίας." ὁ δέ, "ἔπεσθέ με" φάσκων, ἐκ τῆς ἀγορᾶς ἐβάδιζε. οἱ παῖδες εἴποντο. ὁ δὲ φιλόσοφος ἔδειξε τοὺς ἀνθρώπους. "πολλοὶ μὲν κακῶς ζῶσι, τὴν φιλοσοφίαν οὐκ εἰδότες. ἄλλοτε λυποῦνται, ἄλλοτε χαίρουσι, ἄλλοτε γελῶσι, ἄλλοτε κλαίουσι, οὐδέποτε τὰς τοῦ βίου μεταβολὰς

συνιᾶσι. ἡμεῖς δὲ οἱ φιλόσοφοι εὖ ζῶμεν. οὐκ ἄγαν χαίρομεν, οὐκ ἄγαν λυπούμεθα, οὐ δυσκολαίνομεν. τὴν ἀλήθειαν ἀεὶ ζητοῦμεν. τὸν οἶνον πολλῷ ὕδατι μίγνυμεν. τὴν τρυφὴν φεύγομεν. εἰ ἐθέλετε φιλόσοφοι γενέσθαι, ὦ παῖδες, γνῶτε ὑμᾶς αὐτούς." οἱ παῖδες ἐγέλασαν. "τοῦτο οὖκ ἔστι παίζειν, ἀλλὰ ἔργον καὶ κάματον ποιεῖν. μᾶλλον ταῖς πέτραις ἢ τῇ φιλοσοφίᾳ παιξόμεθα." καὶ ἀπέδρασαν.

> ἄγαν, too much

3. πόλλ᾽ οἶδ᾽ ἀλώπηξ, ἀλλ᾽ ἐχῖνος ἓν μέγα.

> Archilochus frag. 201.
>
> ἀλώπηξ, ἀλώπεκος, ἡ, ὁ, fox. ἐχῖνος, -ου, ὁ, hedgehog.

4. εἷρπε δράκων καὶ ἔπινεν ὕδωρ· σβέννυντο δὲ πηγαί,
   καὶ ποταμὸς κεκόνιστο, καὶ ἦν ἔτι διψαλέος θήρ.

> *Greek Anthology* 9.128.
>
> δράκων, -οντος, ὁ, snake, serpent, dragon. ποταμός, -οῦ, ὁ, river. κονίω, κονίσω, ἐκόνισα, κεκόνικα, κεκόνιμαι, – , cover with dust, make dusty; κεκόνιστο = ἐκεκόνιστο and σβέννυντο = ἐσβέννυντο, unaugmented in epic style. διψαλέος, -α, -ον, thirsty.
>
> Prose paraphrase: δράκων τοσοῦτο ὕδωρ ἔπινεν ὥστε αἱ πηγαὶ ξηραὶ ἐγένοντο, ἀλλ᾽ ἔτι ἐδίψαν.

5. ἥκω Διὸς παῖς τήνδε Θηβαίων χθόνα
   Διόνυσος, ὃν τίκτει ποθ᾽ ἡ Κάδμου κόρη
   Σεμέλη λοχευθεῖσ᾽ ἀστραπηφόρῳ πυρί·
   μορφὴν δ᾽ ἀμείψας ἐκ θεοῦ βροτησίαν
   πάρειμι Δίρκης νάματ᾽ Ἰσμηνοῦ θ᾽ ὕδωρ.

> This is the opening of Euripides' play *Bacchae*.
>
> χθών, χθονός, ἡ = ἡ γῆ. λοχευθεῖσα = τεκοῦσα. ἀστραπηφόρος = ὃς τὴν ἀστραπὴν φέρει. πῦρ, πυρός, τό, fire. μορφή, -ῆς, ἡ = τὸ σχῆμα. ἀμείβω, change. βροτήσιος, -α, -ον = θνητός, ὥσπερ ἄνθρωπος. νᾶμα, -ατος, τό, stream.
>
> Prose paraphrase: Διόνυσός εἰμι, παῖς Διός, καὶ ἥκω εἰς τήνδε τὴν Θηβαίων γῆν. ἡ Κάδμου κόρη Σεμέλη ποτέ με ἔτεκε ἐν τῷ πυρὶ καὶ τῇ ἀστραπῇ. νῦν μεταβολὴν τῆς μορφῆς ἐποίησα· μορφὴν ἀνθρώπου ἔχω ἀντὶ θεοῦ, ἵνα μηδεὶς εἰδῇ ἐμὲ θεὸν εἶναι. πάρειμι παρὰ τὰ τῆς Δίρκης νάματα καὶ τὸ τοῦ Ἰσμηνοῦ ὕδωρ.

6. *περὶ τοῦ Τρωικοῦ πολέμου, ἐνδέκατον μέρος*

   νῦν οἱ Ἕλληνες, εἰς τὴν πόλιν εἰσελθεῖν βουλόμενοι, δόλῳ ἐχρήσαντο. ὁ Ὀδυσσεὺς τὸν δόλον ηὗρε, καὶ Ἐπειός, ἀρχιτέκτων ὤν, τὸ πρᾶγμα ἔπραξε. τοῦ Ὀδυσσέως κελεύοντος, ὁ Ἐπειὸς μέγαν ἵππον ἐποίησε ξύλῳ, κοῖλον ἔνδοθεν. τοσοῦτος ἦν ὁ ἵππος ὥστε πολλοὺς ἀνθρώπους εἰσελθεῖν. οὐδὲ θύρας οὐδὲ θυρίδας εἶχε, ἵνα μηδεὶς τοὺς ἔνδον ὁρᾷ. ὁ Ὀδυσσεὺς ἔπειθε πεντήκοντα στρατιώτας εἰς τὸν ἵππον εἰσελθεῖν. ἐπὶ δὲ τῷ ἵππῳ σημεῖον ἔγραψαν· "οἱ Ἕλληνες τῇ Ἀθηνᾷ ἀνατιθέασι." ἔπειτα τὸν ἵππον, στρατιώτας χωροῦντα, παρὰ τοῖς τείχεσι ἔθεσαν. οἱ δὲ ἄλλοι, πλὴν τοῦ Σίνωνος, ἐπανῆλθον ἐπὶ ταῖς ναυσί.

   τῇ ὑστέρᾳ ἡμέρᾳ, παῖς τις Τρωικὸς τὸν ἵππον εἶδε παρὰ τοῖς τείχεσι. τοὺς ἄλλους ἐκάλεσε καὶ τὸν ἵππον αὐτοῖς ἐπέδειξε. οἱ Τρῶες, τὸν ἵππον μὲν ἰδόντες, τοὺς

Ἀχαιοὺς δὲ οὐκέτι ἰδόντες, πολὺ ἔχαιρον. ἐβουλεύοντο ὅ τι δεῖ ποιεῖν τῷ ἵππῳ. τοῖς μὲν ἐδόκει αὐτὸν διαφθεῖραι, τοῖς δὲ τῇ Ἀθηνᾷ διδόναι. ἡ Κασσάνδρα, μάντις οὖσα καὶ θυγάτηρ τοῦ βασιλέως Πριάμου, εἶπε στρατιώτας εἶναι ἐν τῷ ἵππῳ καὶ μέγαν κίνδυνον εἶναι. οὐδεὶς δὴ ἐπείσατο πλὴν τοῦ Λαοκόωντος, ἄλλου μάντεως ὄντος, ὃς ὡμολόγει τῇ Κασσάνδρᾳ. ἔπειτα δὲ ὁ Ἀπόλλων δύο δράκοντας ἔπεμψε ἐκ τῆς θαλάττης οἳ τὸν Λαοκόωντα καὶ τοὺς υἱοὺς αὐτοῦ διέφθειραν. οἱ δὲ Τρῶες ἐνόμισαν, "θεός τις τὸν Λαοκόωντα ἀπέθανε. ὁ δὲ Λαοκόων οὖν οὐκ ὀρθῶς εἶπε. οὐκ οὖν ἐστι κίνδυνος." ἀλλ᾽ οὐκ ᾖσαν τὴν ἀλήθειαν.

τὸν ἵππον οὖν εἰς τὴν πόλιν εἷλξαν. ὁ δὲ Σίνων, τοῦτο ὁρᾶν, σημεῖον ἐποίησε τοῖς ἄλλοις Ἕλλησι ἐπὶ ταῖς ναυσί. οἱ ἐν τῷ ἵππῳ στρατιῶται κατέβησαν καὶ τοῖς Τρῶσι κατέβαλον. τούτῳ τῷ δόλῳ οἱ Ἕλληνες τὴν πόλιν εἷλον.

> δόλος, -ον, ὁ, trick. ξύλον, -ου, τό, wood. σημεῖον, -ου, τό, sign, indication. βουλεύω, βουλεύσω, ἐβούλευσα, βεβούλευκα, βεβούλευμαι, ἐβουλεύθην, plan, consider, decide. δεῖ, it is necessary (infinitive subject). κίνδυνος, -ου, ὁ, danger, risk. ὁμολογέω, ὁμολογήσω, ὡμολόγησα, ὡμολόγηκα, ὡμολόγημαι, ὡμολογήθην, agree. δράκων, -οντος, ὁ, snake, serpent, dragon.

XVII.9 Conversation

1. The usual questions and answers on the readings, as ποῖον ἐστι τὸ οἰκίδιον; τί θηλάζει τὸ παιδίον; ἆρα τροφὸς (nurse) ἢ μήτηρ τὸ παιδίον τρέφει; τίς ἄνω διητᾶται καὶ τίς κάτω; ἆρα τὰ ἄνω τοῦ οἰκιδίου μείζονά ἐστι τῶν κάτω;

2. Questions and answers based on activity in the classroom, for example:

   Κάρολε, ἄνοιξον τὴν θυρίδα· τί δρᾷς;

   Charles, speaking as he does it: ἀνοίγνυμι τὴν θυρίδα (or ἀνοίγω). τί ἔδρασα; ἀνέῳξα τὴν θυρίδα. Γουλιέλμε, τί ἔδρασεν ὁ Κάρολος;

   William answers: ἀνέῳξε τὴν θυρίδα ὁ Κάρολος.

   He or another may then ask, Λυδία, τί φησίν ὁ Γουλιέλμος; and Lydia answers ἀνοῖξαι τὴν θυρίδα φησὶ τὸν Κάρολον (or ὅτι ἀνέῳξεν).

   Similarly with κλῆσον τὴν θύραν, κατάβηθι (κατάβα)κατὰ τῆς κλίμακος καὶ φέρε μοι τὸ βιβλίον, etc. Use questions like τί δράσεις; ποῖ πορεύσῃ; and so on.

XVII.10 Supplement: the kitchen

The following verses, quoted by Athenaeus (14.60) from a work by Aristotle's student Clearchus, supply vocabulary for talking about food and cooking. Most of the words are regular; see the main vocabulary for principal parts if there is any question. Some of the words, like λήκυθος, are fairly common; others, like ἀκταία, are decidedly rare. It is not necessary to memorize these lists. For further information, with pictures, see "The Greek Kitchen" by B. A. Sparkes, *Journal of Hellenic Studies* 82 (1962), 121-137 with plates IV-VIII, and the "Addendum," *JHS* 85 (1965), 162-163 with plates XXIX and XXX.

In the Kitchen

τρίπους, χύτρα, λυχνεῖον, ἀκταία, βάθρον,
σπόγγος, λέβης, σκαφεῖον, ὅλμος, λήκυθος,
σπυρίς, μάχαιρα, τρύβλιον, κρατήρ, ῥαφίς.

tripod, ramekin or little pot, lamp-stand, marble mortar, stand,
sponge, cauldron, bowl, mortar, oil-flask,
basket, knife, cup, mixing-bowl, needle.

In the Pantry

ἔτνος, φακῆ, τάριχος, ἰχθύς, γογγυλίς,
σκόροδον, κρέας, θύννειον, ἅλμη, κρόμμυον,
σκόλυμος, ἐλαία, κάππαρις, βολβός, μύκης.

soup, lentils or pea-soup, dried fish, fish, turnip,
garlic, meat, tuna, brine, onion,
artichoke, olive, caper, plant bulb, mushroom.

In the Storeroom

ἄμης, πλακοῦς, ἔντιλτος, ἴτριον, ῥόα,
ᾠόν, ἐρέβινθος, σησάμη, κοπτή, βότρυς,
ἰσχάς, ἄπιος, περσεία, μῆλ’ , ἀμύγδαλα.

milk-cake, flat-cake, fish-cake, honey-cake, pomegranate,
egg, chick-pea, sesame, pounded sesame, grapes,
dried fig, pear, Egyptian plum, apples, almonds.

Other relevant vocabulary

μάγειρος, -ου, ὁ, cook

μαγειρική, -ῆς, ἡ, cookery, the cook's art

ὄψον, -ου, τό, the food that goes along with bread, often meat or vegetables

ὀπτάνιον, -ου, τό, kitchen

ἰπνός, -οῦ, ὁ, oven

πέπτω, πέψω, ἔπεψα, – , πέπεμμαι, ἐπέφθην, cook (general word); also πέττω

ὀπτάω, ὀπτήσω, ὤπτησα, ὤπτηκα, ὤπτημαι, ὠπτήθην, bake, roast, cook with
   dry heat

ἕψω, ἑψήσω, ἥψησα, ἥψηκα, ἥψημαι, ἡψήθην, boil, cook in liquid

XVII.11 Writing

1. Write an answer to each of the following questions using a result construction. For example, given πόσον ἐστὶ τὸ δένδρον; you might write τόσον ἐστὶ τὸ δένδρον ὥστε οὐ δύναμαι αὐτὸν ἀναβαίνειν.

   a. πόσας δραχμὰς ἔχεις;

   b. ποία ἦν ἡ γυνή;

   c. πῶς παίζουσι οἱ νεανίαι;

   d. πόσοις δείκνυς τὰ ἄνθη;

   e. ποῖοι τοῦτο ἴσασι;

2. Do the change-number exercise with the following sentences.

    a. οἱ Ἕλληνες τὸν οἶνον ἀεὶ ὕδατι μιγνύασι.

    b. τὼ κλέπτα ζῆτον, ἐπεὶ ἐλάθετον τὰ χρῆμα λαμβάνοντε.

    c. ὁ γράφων τῷ καλάμῳ χρῆται.

    d. ὁ ἱερεὺς οἶδε θῦσαι.

    e. τὴν θύραν κλειδὶ ἀνοίγνυμι.

    f. αἱ γρᾶες τὸν λύχνον ἀπέσβεσαν ἵνα καθεύδωσι.

    g. ἆρα ἐπίτηδες τὴν θυγατέρα ἐλύπησας;

    h. οἱ ποιμένες κατὰ τῆς κλίμακος εἰς τὴν ἀνδρωνῖτιν κατέβησαν.

    i. ἀπροσδοκήτως ἥκει ὁ βασιλεύς.

    j. τῇ μητρὶ τὴν ἐπὶ τῷ δένδρῳ ἀηδόνα δείκνυς.

    k. ἡ μήτηρ τὸ παιδίον λούεται καὶ θηλάζει.

    l. ἡ θεράπαινα τὸ παιδίον ἐπίτηδες ἐλύπησε ἵνα τοῦτο δυσκολαίνῃ.

    m. ἡ θεράπαινα λανθάνει τὸν πατέρα, τὸ παιδίον λυποῦσα.

3. Each of these sentences contains a clause to which the OOO rule may apply. Change the main verb of the sentence to an appropriate past tense, and apply the OOO rule to the subordinate clause. For example, from λέγω ὅτι γράφεις make εἶπον ὅτι γράφοις.

    a. ἐὰν τὸ παιδίον δυσκολαίνῃ, κλαίει.

    b. ἐπειδὰν τοὺς λύχνους ἀποσβεννύωμεν, οὐδὲν ὁρῶμεν.

    c. οἵτινες ἄν παίζωσιν εὖ μαθήσονται.

    d. ὅταν τὸ παιδίον θηλάζηται, καθεύδει.

    e. ἐὰν τὸ ἔλαιον καὶ τὸ ὕδωρ μιγνύῃς, ἄλληλα φεύγουσιν.

4. Rewrite the following sentences, changing participial phrases to subordinate clauses or subordinate clauses to participial phrases, as appropriate.

    a. δεικνὺς τὴν θυρίδα, ὁ ἀνὴρ τὸν λύχνον σβέννυσι.

    b. ἐπεὶ οἱ παῖδες ψοφοῦσι, οἱ γονῆς οὐκ ἀκούουσι.

    c. τῆς θυρίδος ψοφούσας, ὁ ἀνὴρ τὸν κλέπτην ἐν τῷ οἰκιδίῳ ᾔσθετο.

    d. ὁ θὴρ ἕρπει πρὸς τὴν πηγὴν τὸ ὕδωρ πιόμενος.

    e. ὁ Διόνυσος, ὃν ἔτεκε ἡ Σεμέλη, ἥκει εἰς τὰς Θήβας.

    f. ἡ Σεμέλη, τὸν Διόνυσον τετοκυῖα, ἀπέθανε.

5. Describe your own house, as the speaker of reading 1 describes his.

6. Write a paragraph about a meal, using the vocabulary from the supplement.

7. The character in Athenaeus's book who quotes the lines from Clearchus in the supplement says they come from his *On Riddles*. It is just possible, however, that they come from a comedy by a different Clearchus, who was a playwright, since they are in the proper meter for comedy; the philosopher Clearchus may also have taken the lines from a play. Suppose they do come from a comedy, and write a short scene in Greek (prose) in which a character says them.

CHAPTER XVIII

The Sack of Troy

XVIII.1 Verbs with liquid stems

Most of the verbs whose roots end in a liquid or nasal have a suffix -ιο- in the present system. But after internal sandhi, this suffix generally appears as either a double final consonant or a long stem vowel. These verbs usually form their future with -εσ-, but as usual, the -σ- between vowels dropped out long ago, making a contraction just like the present of ποιέω; as you recall, all contracted futures are ε-contracts. In the aorist active system, these verbs have a first aorist, but the -σ- of the ordinary suffix has been lost after the liquid consonant, and the stem vowel undergoes **compensatory lengthening** to "make up" for the lost sound. Thus in these verbs the root is most easily recognized from the second principal part, not the first or third. Here are some examples.

Present	Future act.	Future mid.	Aorist act.	Aorist mid.
φαίν-ω	φαν-ῶ	φαν-οῦμαι	ἔ-φην-α	ἐ-φην-άμην
κρίν-ω	κριν-ῶ	κριν-οῦμαι	ἔ-κρῑν-α	ἐ-κρῑν-άμην
ἀγγέλλ-ω	ἀγγελ-ῶ	ἀγγελ-οῦμαι	ἤ-γγειλ-α	ἠγγειλ-άμην
φθείρ-ω	φθερ-ῶ	φθερ-οῦμαι	ἔ-φθειρ-α	ἐ-φθειρ-άμην

The future active and middle forms are exactly like the forms of ε-contract presents.

	Indic. Act.	Indic. Mid.	Opt. Act.	Opt. Mid.
singular				
1st	φανῶ	φανοῦμαι	φανοίην	φανοίμην
2nd	φανεῖς	φανεῖ	φανοίης	φανοῖο
3rd	φανεῖ	φανεῖται	φανοίη	φανοῖτο

	Indic. Act.	Indic. Mid.	Opt. Act.	Opt. Mid.
dual				
2nd	φανεῖτον	φανεῖσθον	φάνοιτον	φάνοισθον
3rd	φανεῖτον	φανεῖσθον	φανοίτην	φανοίσθην
plural				
1st	φανοῦμεν	φανούμεθα	φανοῖμεν	φανοίμεθα
2nd	φανεῖτε	φανεῖσθε	φανοῖτε	φανοῖσθε
3rd	φανοῦσι(ν)	φανοῦνται	φανοῖεν	φανοῖντο

The future infinitive active is φανεῖν and the middle is φανεῖσθαι. The participles are φανών, φανοῦσα, φανοῦν (masc. gen. sg. φανοῦντος) and φανούμενος.

Exercise

Write the three third-person forms of the future and aorist indicative active and middle of φαίνω, κρίνω, ἀγγέλλω, τείνω "stretch," αἰσχύνω "disgrace," σημαίνω "signal, show," δυσχεραίνω "be impatient." Write out the present, future, and aorist active and middle infinitives of the same verbs, and finally give the root of each verb.

XVIII.2 Adjectives in -υς

Some first-and-third declension adjectives end in -υς in the nominative singular. An example is ἡδύς "sweet" (cognate with English *sweet*, Latin *suavis*, and Sanskrit *svādu*).

	Masc.	Fem.	Neu.
singular			
nom., voc.	ἡδύς	ἡδεῖα	ἡδύ
gen.	ἡδέος	ἡδείας	ἡδέος
dat.	ἡδεῖ	ἡδείᾳ	ἡδεῖ
acc.	ἡδύν	ἡδεῖαν	ἡδύ
dual			
nom., voc., acc.	ἡδέε	ἡδείᾱ	ἡδέε
gen., dat.	ἡδέοιν	ἡδείαιν	ἡδέοιν
plural			
nom., voc.	ἡδεῖς	ἡδεῖαι	ἡδέα
gen.	ἡδέων	ἡδειῶν	ἡδέων
dat.	ἡδέσι(ν)	ἡδείαις	ἡδέσι(ν)
acc.	ἡδεῖς	ἡδείᾱς	ἡδέα

Similar are ταχύς "fast, swift"; βραχύς "short"; ὀξύς "sharp, pointy, keen"; βαρύς "heavy"; θῆλυς "female"; εὐρύς "broad, wide"; and γλυκύς "sweet."

XVIII.3 Comparatives in -ων

Many of the -υς adjectives form the comparative with -ίων instead of -ότερος, and the superlative with -ιστος instead of -ότατος. Some suppletive or irregular comparatives also end this way. The superlatives are declined like καλός; the comparatives are third declension forms with two endings (that is, with masculine and feminine identical).

	Masc./Fem.	Neu.
singular		
nom., voc.	ἡδίων	ἥδῑον
gen.	ἡδίονος	
dat.	ἡδίονι	
acc.	ἡδίονα, ἡδίω	ἥδῑον
dual		
nom., voc., acc.	ἡδίονε	
gen., dat.	ἡδῑόνοιν	
plural		
nom., voc.	ἡδίονες, ἡδίους	ἡδίονα, ἡδίω
gen.	ἡδῑόνων	
dat.	ἡδίοσι(ν)	
acc.	ἡδίονας, ἡδίους	ἡδίονα, ἡδίω

Along with the adjectives in -υς, these are the most important adjectives that form their comparative this way.

Positive	Comparative	Superlative
ἡδύς	ἡδίων	ἥδιστος
αἰσχρός	αἰσχίων	αἴσχιστος
ἀγαθός	βελτίων, κρείττων, ἀμείνων	βέλτιστος, κράτιστος, ἄριστος
κακός	κακίων	κάκιστος
καλός	καλλίων	κάλλιστος
μικρός	ἐλάττων	ἐλάχιστος
ὀλίγος	ἥττων	ὀλίγιστος
πολύς	πλείων	πλεῖστος
μέγας	μείζων	μέγιστος
ῥάδιος	ῥᾴων	ῥᾷστος

ταχύς forms θάττων instead of ταχίων, but has the regular superlative τάχιστος.

Exercise

Write the complete declension of ὁ βελτίων στρατηγός, ἡ καλλίων ἀηδών, τὸ ῥᾷον ἔργον.

XVIII.4 Impossible wishes

A wish that can be fulfilled normally refers to the future, and uses the optative. A wish referring to the past, or even to the present, is impossible: the wish expresses regret about a fact that cannot now be changed. These use the *indicative* in Greek, and their negative is μή. They are introduced by εἴθε just like ordinary wishes with the optative. So for example εἴθε λέων ἦν, "I wish I were a lion," or εἴθε τὸ παιδίον μὴ ἐδυσκόλαινε, "if only the child wasn't fretful."

The imperfect indicates an on-going situation, or a wish about the present, while the aorist indicates a wish about the past. Thus:

> εἴθε βιβλίον ἔγραφες "if only you were writing a book," present or
> continuing; εἴθε βιβλίον ἔγραψας "if only you had written a book," past.
> Note the difference in tenses for a past wish: English typically uses the
> pluperfect, but Greek uses the aorist.

Wishes can also be expressed with the aorist ὤφελον "owe, ought" (from ὀφείλω) and a complementary infinitive. The particle ὡς is optional. Thus: ὤφελεν πιστὸς εἶναι "he ought to be trustworthy, if only he were trustworthy, I wish he were trustworthy," same as εἴθ' ἦν πιστός. Or ὤφελες βιβλίον γράψαι, same as εἴθε βιβλίον ἔγραψας. The tense of the infinitive denotes relative time.

The indicative is also used for impossible conditions. For example, εἰ ὁ διδάσκαλος δραχμὴν εἶχε, βιβλία ἠγόραζε ἄν. Here the particle ἄν marks the conclusion as counterfactual: in fact, the teacher is not buying books, because he has no money. The verbs are in the imperfect to indicate that the action would be going on right now, if it were going on at all. Similarly, εἰ ὁ διδάσκαλος δραχμὴν ἔσχε, βιβλία ἠγόρασε ἄν tells us about a past situation: at some past point, the teacher could not afford to buy books and so did not do so. The particle ἄν is always in the conclusion or then-clause, and the verb of that clause is always past indicative, normally imperfect or aorist. Note that if the particle ἄν is *not* in the sentence, it is a simple past conditional: εἰ ὁ διδάσκαλος δραχμὴν εἶχε, βιβλία ἠγόραζε, if the teacher had money (at some point in the past), then he bought books. This form of condition implies that the situation described probably did happen, or could have happened. It's not quite as strong as the generalizing conditional ἐὰν ὁ διδάσκαλος δραχμὴν ἔχῃ, βιβλία ἠγόραζε, which says he always bought books with every spare drachma, but it's not the counterfactual version either. The difference among these three is the position of ἄν — in the if-clause for the generalization (attached to εἰ to make ἐάν, and requiring a subjunctive verb), in the then-clause for the counterfactual, not in the sentence at all for the simple conditional.

XVIII.5 Vocabulary

VERBS

ἁλιεύω, ἁλιεύσω, ἡλίευσα, ἡλίευκα, – , – , fish, go fishing

ἀρτάω, ἀρτήσω, ἤρτησα, ἤρτηκα, ἤρτημαι, ἠρτήθην, fasten (usually with ἀπό, fasten onto, or ἐξ, hang off from) (cp. *arm, article*, L. *artus, arma, ars*)

ἀσκέω, ἀσκήσω, ἤσκησα, ἤσκηκα, ἤσκημαι, ἠσκήθην, practice, exercise; deck out, adorn (cp. *ascetic*)

δέδοικα, fear; normally only in perfect

δι-αιρέω, pull apart, open

ἐν-ηβάω, enjoy oneself in

ἡβάω, ἡβήσω, ἥβησα, ἥβηκα, – , – , enjoy life, be merry, be young

ὁρμίζω, ὁρμιῶ, ὥρμισα, – , ὥρμισμαι, ὡρμίσθην, bring to anchor, make fast; middle, come to anchor, rest

ὀφείλω, ὀφειλήσω, ὤφελον, ὠφείληκα, – , ὠφειλήθην, owe; second aorist ὤφελον, ought

παρ-έχω, provide

φαίνω, φανῶ, ἔφηνα, πέφηνα, πέφασμαι, ἐφάνθην, show, reveal; in middle, appear, seem (cp. *phenomenon, phantom*)

NOUNS

ἄγκιστρον, -ου, τό, hook (cp. *ankle*)

ἄγρᾱ, -ᾱς, ἡ, chase, hunt

ἁλιεύς, -έως, ὁ, fisherman

ἄλσος, -ους, τό, grove of trees

βρόχος, -ου, ὁ, noose

δίκτυον, -ου, τo, net

κύων, κυνός, ὁ, ἡ, dog (cp. *hound*, L. *canis*)

λαγώς, λαγώ, ὁ, hare, rabbit (cp. L. *lepus*)

λίνον, -ου, τό, string, thread (cp. *line, linen*, L. *linum*)

λουτρόν, -οῦ, τό, bath

νῆττα, -ας, ἡ, duck (cp. L. *anas*)

οἴκησις, -εως, ἡ, dwelling

ὄρνῑς, ὄρνῑθος, ὁ, ἡ, bird (cp. *ornithology*)

παράδεισος, -ου, ὁ, park (cp. *paradise*)

στέγη, -ης, ἡ, roof (cp. *thatch*, L. *tego, toga*)

στῆθος, -ους, τό, breast (cp. *stethoscope*)

τέρψις, -εως, ἡ, enjoyment (cp. *Terpsichore*)

τέχνη, -ης, ἡ, art, skill (cp. *technique*)

τράπεζα, -ης, ἡ, table (cp. *trapezoid*)

φρήν, φρενός, ἡ, mind, heart (cp. *frenzy, schizophrenia*)

φυή, -ῆς, ἡ, bodily nature, stature, growth

φύσις, -εως, ἡ, nature

ADJECTIVES

ἄγριος, -α, -ον, wild

ἄδολος, -ον, sincere, honest

ἄρρην, ἄρρεν, male, masculine (gen. ἄρρενος)

ἀσφαλής, -ές, safe

βαρύς, -εῖα, ὑ, heavy (cp. *barometer*, L. *gravis*)

βραχύς, -εῖα, -ύ, short (cp. *brachylogy*, L. *brevis*)

γλυκύς, -εῖα, ὑ, sweet (cp. *glycerine, glucose*, L. *dulcis*)

εὐρύς, -εῖα, ὑ, broad, wide (cp. *aneurysm, eurypterid*)

ἡδύς, -εῖα, -ύ, sweet, pleasant (cp. *sweet, hedonist*, L. *suavis*)

θεῖος, -α, -ον, godly, divine

θῆλυς, -εια, -υ, female (cp. L. *femina, fecundus*)

θνητός, -η, -ον, mortal

λεπτός, -ή, -ον, lightweight, slight, delicate (cp. *light, lepton*, L. *levis*)

ὀξύς, -εῖα, -υ, sharp, keen, pointy (cp. *oxygen, edge*, L. *acer*)

πλούσιος, -α, -ον, rich, wealthy

ταχύς -εῖα, -ύ, fast, swift (cp. *tachycardia*)

χειμέριος, -ον, stormy, wintry

φίλος, -η, -ο, friendly

ADVERB

ἐγγύς, close, near

Notes on the vocabulary

Also learn the suppletive comparatives in section 3.

δέδοικα is perfect from δείδω, and future δείσομαι and aorist ἔδεισα do exist, but in classical Attic only the perfect is used, with the sense "be in a fearing state, fear." The usual construction with this verb is μή plus subjunctive (called a **fear clause**); the OOO rule applies. Thus: δέδοικα μὴ οὗτος βιβλίον γράφῃ, "I'm afraid he's going to write a book," or δέδοικα μὴ οὐκ ἀκούωσι, "I fear they aren't listening," or ἐδεδοίκη μὴ οὗτος βιβλίον γράφοι, "I was afraid he was going to write a book." The verb has the regular perfect participle δεδοικώς but also has δεδιώς, δεδιυῖα, δεδιός.

Both ἡδύς (somewhat more common) and γλυκύς can mean "sweet-tasting" or, by extension, "pleasant, friendly, delightful." The root from which γλυκύς is derived apparently began with *d-*, as in the Latin cognate *dulcis*, and the initial consonant changed its place of articulation to assimilate to the -κ-.

You already know φίλος as a noun, but (like δοῦλος and other words) it is originally an adjective.

Although ἐγγύς is an adverb, the comparative ἐγγίων and superlative ἐγγύτατος are adjectives. The basic form can be used with a genitive, as τὸ δένδρον ἐστι ἐγγὺς τοῦ τείχεως, "near the wall."

XVIII.6 Reading

1. *A Pleasure Trip*

   Νέοι τινὲς πλούσιοι, ναῦν μικρὰν καθελκύσαντες καὶ οἰκέτας προσκώπους καθίσαντες, τοὺς ἀγροὺς περιέπλεον τοὺς παραθαλαττίους. εὐλίμενός τε γὰρ ἡ παραλία καὶ οἰκήσεσιν ἠσκημένη πολλαῖς, καὶ λουτρὰ συνεχῆ, καὶ παράδεισοι καὶ ἄλση· τὰ μὲν φύσεως ἔργα, τὰ δ᾿ ἀνθρώπων τέχνη· πάντα ἐνηβῆσαι καλά. παραπλέοντες οὖν καὶ προσορμιζόμενοι, κακὸν μὲν ἐποίουν οὐδέν, τέρψεις δὲ πολλὰς εἶχον, ποτὲ μὲν ἀγκίστροις καλάμων ἀπηρτημένοις ἐκ λίνου λεπτοῦ ἰχθῦς ἁλιεύοντες, ποτὲ δὲ κυσὶ καὶ δικτύοις λαγῶς λαμβάνοντες. καὶ δὴ καὶ ὀρνίθων ἄγρας ἐμέλησεν αὐτοῖς, καὶ ἔλαβον βρόχοις χῆνας ἀγρίους καὶ νήττας· ὥσθ᾿ ἡ τέρψις αὐτοῖς καὶ τραπέζης ὠφέλειαν παρεῖχεν· εἰ δέ τινος προσέδει, παρὰ τῶν ἐν τοῖς ἀγροῖς ἐλάμβανον, πλείους τῆς ἀξίας ὀβολοὺς καταβάλλοντες. ἔδει δὲ μόνον ἄρτου καὶ οἴνου καὶ στέγης· οὐ γὰρ ἀσφαλὲς ἐδόκει μετοπωρινῆς ὥρας ἐνεστώσης ἐνθαλαττεύειν· ὥστε καὶ τὴν ναῦν ἀνεῖλκον ἐπὶ τὴν γῆν, νύκτα χειμέριον δεδοικότες.

   Daphnis and Chloe 2.12.

   καθ-έλκω, drag down; launch (ship). **πρόσκωπος, -ον**, at the oars. **παραθαλάττιος** = παρὰ τῇ θαλάττῃ. **εὐ-λίμενος, -ον** = ἀγαθὸν λιμένα ἔχων. **παραλίᾱ, -ας, ἡ**, beach, sea-coast. **συνεχής, -ές**, continuous. **προσορμίζω** = ὁρμίζω. **προσ-δέω**, need in addition. **μετοπωρινός, -η, -ον**, of autumn. **ἐν-θαλαττεύω**, stay on the sea.

2. *Skolia* (convivial songs), PMG 889 and 890

A. εἴθ᾿ ἐξῆν ὁποῖός τις ἦν ἕκαστος,
   τὸ στῆθος διελόντ᾿, ἔπειτα τὸν νοῦν
   ἐσιδόντα, κλήσαντα πάλιν,
   ἄνδρα φίλον νομίζειν ἀδόλῳ φρενί.

B. ὑγιαίνειν μὲν ἄριστον ἀνδρὶ θνητῷ,
   δεύτερον δὲ φυὴν καλὸν γενέσθαι,
   τὸ τρίτον δὲ πλουτεῖν ἀδόλως,
   καὶ τὸ τέταρτον ἡβᾶν μετὰ τῶν φίλων.

3. ὁ βίος βραχὺς, ἡ δὲ τέχνη μακρά.

   This is the first of the Hippocratic aphorisms.

4. πάντων ζῴων, αἱ μὲν θηλεῖαι τὰ παιδία τίκτουσι καὶ θηλάζουσι, οἱ δ᾿ ἄρρενες οὔ. εἰ πάντα ζῷα ἄρρενα ἦν, οὐδεπώποτε ἂν νέα ζῷα ἐγίγνετο. ἡ μὲν ἄνθρωπος θηλεία

καλεῖται γυνή, ὁ δὲ ἄρρην ἀνήρ. ὁ μὲν γονεὺς θῆλύς ἐστι μήτηρ, ὁ δὲ ἄρρην πατήρ. τὸ ἄρρεν ζῷον πολλάκις ἐστὶ μεῖζον, βάριον, ἰσχυρότερον ἢ τὸ θῆλυ ζῷον.

ἰσχυρός, -ά, -όν, strong.

5. οἱ ἁλιεῖς ἁλιεύουσι ἐν θαλάττῃ. ὀξέσι ἀγκίστροις καὶ εὑρέσι δικτύοις χρῶνται. τὸν δὲ δίκτυον ἐκ τοῦ πλοίου βάλλει ὁ ἁλιεὺς ἵνα ἰχθύες εἰσέλθωσι. ἔπειτα τὸν ἰχθύας ἔχοντα δίκτυον ἕλκει πάλιν εἰς τὸ πλοῖον. εἰ ἰχθύες ἐπὶ τὴν γῆν ζῆν ἐδύναντο, τὸν δίκτυον ἔφευγον ἄν. ἀλλὰ οὐ δύνανται ζῆν ἄνευ τοῦ ὕδατος. ἀποθνήσκοντες οὖν ἐν τοῖς τῶν ἁλιέων δικτύοις σῖτον ἀνθρώποις γίγνονται. οἱ Ἀθηναῖοι νομίζουσι τοὺς ἰχθύας τὸν γλύκιστον καὶ ἥδιστον βέλτιστον σῖτον. ἐὰν ἰχθὺς ἐπὶ τῇ τραπέζῃ ᾖ, τέρψις καὶ ἡδονὴ ἐγγίονέ ἐστον.

6. λαγώς, ζῷον ἄγριον ὤν, τρέχει διὰ τοὺς ἀγρούς. ἐὰν κύων λαγὼν ὁρᾷ, ἐθέλει αὐτὸν λαβεῖν. τρέχει οὖν πρὸς τὸν λαγὼν ἵνα λάβῃ. ὁ λαγὼς δέδοικε τὸν κύνα. δέδοικε γὰρ μὴ ὁ κύων αὐτὸν ἀποκτείνῃ καὶ ἐσθίῃ. οἶδε ὅτι ὁ κύων ὀξεῖς ὀδόντας ἔχει. ἐὰν κύων τῷ λαγῷ φαίνηται, ὁ λαγὼς φεύγει. ταχὺς μὲν ὁ κύων, ταχίων δὲ ὁ λαγώς. ὑπὸ τῶν δένδρων τρέχετον πρὸς τὴν τοῦ λαγὼ οἴκησιν. ὁ μὲν κύων μείζων ἐστι τοῦ λαγὼ καὶ οὐ δύναται εἰς τὴν οἰκίαν εἰσέρχεσθαι. ὁ δὲ λαγώς, μικρότερος ὤν, ῥᾳδίως εἰσέρχεται. τέλος δὲ ὁ λαγὼς ἀσφαλής οἴκαδε ἔρχεται, ὥσπερ ναῦς ὡρμισμένη.

7. ἔοικας, ὦ Ἀντιφῶν, τὴν εὐδαιμονίαν οἰομένῳ τρυφὴν καὶ πολυτέλειαν εἶναι. ἐγὼ δὲ νομίζω τὸ μὲν μηδενὸς δεῖσθαι θεῖον εἶναι, τὸ δ᾽ ὡς ἐλαχίστων ἐγγυτάτω τοῦ θείου, καὶ τὸ μὲν θεῖον κράτιστον, τὸ δ᾽ ἐγγυτάτω τοῦ θείου ἐγγυτάτω τοῦ κρατίστου.

Xenophon, *Memorabilia* 1.6.10. Socrates is speaking.

ἔοικας οἰομένῳ = ἔοικας ἀνθρώπῳ τινὶ ὃς οἴεται, δοκεῖς οἴεσθαι. **εὐδαιμονία, -ας, ἡ** = τὸ ἀγαθὴν τύχην ἔχειν. **πολυτέλεια, -ας, ἡ** = τρυφή, τὸ πολλὰ ἀγοράζειν. **τὸ μηδενὸς δεῖσθαι θεῖον εἶναι·** ὁ Σωκράτης λέγει, "εἰ ἄνθρωπος μηδενὸς χρῄζει, ὁ βίος θεῖός ἐστι, ὥσπερ ὁ τῶν θεῶν βίος." **δέω, δεήσω, κτλ.** = χρῄζω.

ἔοικας is a second-person form from the same verb as ἔοικε, which is in fact a perfect.

8. νεανίας τις ἔθηλε πλείω λέγειν ἢ ἀκούειν. ὁ δὲ Ζήνων πρὸς αὐτὸν εἶπεν· ἡ φύσις ἡμῖν γλῶτταν μὲν μίαν, δύο δὲ ὦτα παρέσχεν, ἵνα διπλασίονα ὧν λέγομεν ἀκούωμεν.

οὖς, ὠτός, τό: τοῖν ὠσὶν ἀκούομεν.

9. ὡς κέδρου βραχὺ φύλλον, ἔχει δ᾽ ἡδεῖαν ὀδωδήν,
   οὕτως λουτρὰ τάδε μικρὰ μέν, ἀλλὰ φίλα.

Greek Anthology 9.612.

κέδρος, -ου, ἡ, cedar. **φύλλον, -ου, τό**, leaf. **ὀδωδή, -ῆς, ἡ**, scent, fragrance.

10. ἀσπίδι μὲν Σαΐων τις ἀγάλλεται, ἣν παρὰ θάμνῳ,
    ἔντος ἀμώμητον, κάλλιπον οὐκ ἐθέλων·
    αὐτὸν δ᾽ ἐξέσωσα. τί μοι μέλει ἀσπὶς ἐκείνη;
    ἐρρέτω· ἐξαῦτις κτήσομαι οὐ κακίω.

Archilochus fragment 5.

ἀσπίς, -ιδος, ἡ, shield. ἀγάλλω, adorn, ornament. θάμνος, -ου, ὁ = μικρὸν δένδρον. ἀμώμητος, -ον, blameless. **κάλλιπον** = κατέλιπον; this is a **syncopated** form, with a syllable dropped out: κατ᾽ λιπον, κάλλιπον. ἔρρω, go, often in a bad sense, like English "get lost!" ἐξαῦτις = αὖθις, πάλιν. **κτάομαι, κτήσομαι, ἐκτησάμην, – , κέκτημαι, – ,** get, acquire.

Prose paraphrase: ἐμαχόμην Σαίωνί τινι. ἀσπίδα μὲν παρὰ θάμνῳ κατέλιπον, καίπερ ἀμώμητον καὶ ἀγαθὴν οὖσαν. ἐμαυτὸν δὲ ἐξεσῶσα. τί μοι μέλει ἐκείνη ἡ ἀσπίς; ἐρρέτω ἡ ἀσπίς. ἄλλο τι κτήσομαι οὐ κακίω.

11. ὁπόσα διὰ κινδύνων, πεπασμοὺς τῶν ἀπιόντων πάντας πάντοθεν ἐπικαίρους, ἢ καλὰς καὶ κρισίμους ἀποστάσεις, σκοπεῖσθαι. πεπασμοὶ ταχυτῆτα κρίσεως καὶ ἀσφάλειαν ὑγιείας σημαίνουσιν. ὠμὰ δὲ καὶ ἄπεπτα, καὶ ἐς κακὰς ἀποστάσεις τρεπόμενα, ἀκρισίας, ἢ πόνους, ἢ χρόνους, ἢ θανάτους, ἢ τῶν αὐτῶν ὑποστροφάς. ὅ τι δὲ τουτῶν ἔσται μάλιστα, σκεπτέον ἐξ ἄλλων· λέγειν τὰ προγενόμενα, γιγνώσκειν τὰ παρόντα, προλέγειν τὰ ἐσόμενα, μελετᾶν ταῦτα. ἀσκεῖν, περὶ τὰ νοσήματα, δύο· ὠφελεῖν, ἢ μὴ βλάπτειν. ἡ τέχνη διὰ τριῶν, τὸ νόσημα, ὁ νοσῶν, καὶ ὁ ἰατρός· ὁ ἰατρός, ὑπηρέτης τῆς τέχνης· ὑπεναντιοῦσθαι τῷ νοσήματι τὸν νοσοῦντα μετὰ τοῦ ἰατροῦ χρή.

Epidemics 1.2, from the Hippocratic corpus.

κίνδυνος, -ου, ὁ, danger, risk. **πεπασμός, -οῦ, ὁ,** secretion (of urine or other wastes), digestion. **ἐπίκαιρος, -ον,** at a suitable time, timely. **κρίσιμος, -ον,** decisive, critical. **ἀπόστασις, -εως, ἡ,** separation, standing apart; in a medical context, abscess or collection of pus in a wound. **σκοπέω,** look at, look into. **ταχυτής, -ῆτος, ἡ,** speed, rapidity. **κρίσις, -εως, ἡ,** crisis. **ἀσφάλεια, -ας, ἡ,** safety, certainty. **σημαίνω,** show, mean. **ὠμός, -ή, -όν,** raw, crude. **ἄπεπτος, -ον,** uncooked, undigested. **τρέπω,** turn. **σκεπτέος, -α, -ον,** needing to be looked at. **νόσημα, -ατος, τό,** sickness. **ὑπηρέτης, -ου, ὁ,** helper, assistant, servant. ἄπεπτος and πεπασμός are derived from πέπτω, cook; digestion was considered a kind of cooking.

12. ὁ πατὴρ Στρεψιάδης καὶ ὁ υἱὸς Φειδιππίδης λέγετον.

Στρ· Φειδιππίδη. Φειδιππίδιον. **Φει·** τί, ὦ πάτερ;
Στρ· κύσον με καὶ τὴν χεῖρα δὸς τὴν δεξιάν.
Φει· ἰδού. τί ἔστιν; **Στρ·** εἰπέ μοι, φιλεῖς ἐμέ;
Φει· νὴ τὸν Ποσειδῶ τουτονὶ τὸν ἵππιον.
Στρ· μὴ ᾽μοί γε τοῦτον μηδαμῶς τὸν ἵππιον·
οὗτος γὰρ ὁ θεὸς αἴτιός μοι τῶν κακῶν.
ἀλλ᾽ εἴπερ ἐκ τῆς καρδίας μ᾽ ὄντως φιλεῖς,
ὦ παῖ, πιθοῦ. **Φει·** τί οὖν πίθωμαι δῆτά σοι;
Στρ· ἔκστρεψον ὡς τάχιστα τοὺς σαυτοῦ τρόπους,
καὶ μάνθαν᾽ ἐλθὼν ἂν ἐγὼ παραινέσω.
Φει· λέγε δή, τί κελεύεις; **Στρ·** καί τι πείσει; **Φει·** πείσομαι
νὴ τὸν Διόνυσον. **Στρ·** δεῦρό νυν ἀπόβλεπε.
ὁρᾷς τὸ θύριον τοῦτο καὶ τῳκίδιον;
Φει· ὁρῶ. τί οὖν τοῦτ᾽ ἐστὶν ἐτεόν, ὦ πάτερ;

Στρ· ψυχῶν σοφῶν τοῦτ᾽ ἐστὶ φροντιστήριον.
ἐνταῦθ᾽ ἐνοικοῦσ᾽ ἄνδρες, οἳ τὸν οὐρανὸν
λέγοντες ἀναπείθουσιν ὡς ἔστιν πνιγεύς,
κἄστιν περὶ ἡμᾶς οὗτος, ἡμεῖς δ᾽ ἄνθρακες.
οὗτοι διδάσκουσ᾽, ἀργύριον ἤν τις διδῷ,
λέγοντα νικᾶν καὶ δίκαια κἄδικα.

...

εἶναι παρ᾽ αὐτοῖς φασιν ἄμφω τὼ λόγω,
τὸν κρείττον᾽, ὅστις ἐστί, καὶ τὸν ἥττονα.
τούτοιν τὸν ἕτερον τοῖν λόγοιν, τὸν ἥττονα,
νικᾶν λέγοντά φασι τἀδικώτερα.
ἢν οὖν μάθῃς μοι τὸν ἄδικον τοῦτον λόγον,
ἃ νῦν ὀφείλω διὰ σέ, τούτων τῶν χρεῶν
οὐκ ἂν ἀποδοίην οὐδ᾽ ἂν ὀβολὸν οὐδενί.
Φει· οὐκ ἂν πιθοίμην· οὐ γὰρ ἂν τλαίην ἰδεῖν
τοὺς ἱππέας τὸ χρῶμα διακεκναισμένος.

Aristophanes, *Clouds* 80-99, 112-120. Pheidippides has run up a rather large debt with his stable, and his father hopes to get out of paying it.

Φειδιππίδιον, diminutive of the son's name, as a pet name. **κυνέω, κυνήσομαι, ἔκυσα, –, –, –**, kiss. **δεξιός, -ά, -όν**, right (side). **ἰδού**, here, look (interjection). **νὴ τὸν θεὸν** = ναί μὰ τὸν θεὸν. **ἵππιος, -α, -ον**, relating to horses, equestrian; Ποσειδῶν ἵππιος is a horse god. **καρδίᾱ, -ᾱς, ἡ**, heart. **δῆτα**, particle marking that a question follows along from what's just been said. **ἐκ-στρέφω**, turn away, turn aside. **τρόπος, -ου, ὁ**, direction, turning, way. **παρ-αινέω**, advise, recommend. **δεῦρο**, here, this way, hither. **ἀπο-βλέπω**, look at steadily. **θύριον** = μικρὰ θύρα. **ἐτεός, -ά, -όν**, true, real; ἐτεόν as adverb, truly, really. **φροντιστήριον, -ου, τό**, a word invented for this play and explained in the next couple of lines. **ἐν-οικέω** = οἰκέω. **οὐρανός, -οῦ, ὁ**, sky. **ἀνα-πείθω**, persuade. **πνιγεύς, -έως, ὁ**, oven. **ἄνθραξ, ἄνθρακος, ὁ**, coal. **ἀργύριον, -ου, τό**, piece of silver, coin. **ἔτλην**, aorist system only, endure, put up with. **ἱππεύς, -εως, ὁ**, horseman, cavalry soldier, rider. **χρῶμα, -ατος, τό**, color. **δια-κναίω**, wear away, erode, rub out.

13. *περὶ τοῦ Τρωικοῦ πολέμου, δωδέκατον μέρος*

οἱ Ἕλληνες εἰς τὴν νενικημένην πόλιν ἥκουσι. μετὰ δέκα ἔτη τὸν Ἴλιον ἔχουσι. οἱ μὲν Τρῶες πεπτωκότες ἀμφὶ τὰ τῶν ἄνδρων καὶ τῶν ἀδελφῶν σώμασιν βοᾶσιν καὶ λυποῦσιν. οἱ δὲ Ἀχαιοὶ εὑρίσκουσι τροφὴν ἵνα ἀριστῶσι, ἀλλὰ ἡ πόλις οὕτως διεφθαρμένη ἐστὶ ὥστε οὐδὲν εὑρίσκουσι. ἐθέλοντες δὲ λείαν λαβεῖν διὰ τὴν πόλιν διατρέχουσιν ἵνα διαφθείρειν.

ὁ μὲν Μενέλαος τὴν Ἑλένην ἐπὶ τὴν ναῦν ἄγει. ὁ δὲ Αἴας ὁ τοῦ Οἰλέως τὴν Κασσάνδραν ὁρᾷ παρὰ τῷ τῆς Ἀθηνᾶς ἀγάλματι ἐν τῷ νεῴ. ἡ δὲ Κασσάνδρα θυγάτηρ ἐστὶ τοῦ Πριάμου καὶ ἱερεία τῶν θεῶν. ὁ δὲ Αἴας, καίπερ ἱερείαν οὖσαν, αὐτὴν βιάζεται. ἔπειτα δὲ ὁ Ἀγαμέμνων τὴν Κασσάνδραν λαμβάνει ὡς τὸ ἑαυτοῦ γέρας.

ὁ δὲ Νεοπτόλεμος τὸν Πρίαμον ἀποκτείνει παρὰ τῷ τοῦ Διὸς βωμῷ. ἡ Ἀνδρομάχη γίγνεται γέρας τοῦ Νεοπτολέμου, ἣ γυνὴ ἦν τοῦ Ἕκτορος. ἡ δὲ Ἑκάβη, μήτηρ τοῦ Ἕκτορος καὶ γυνὴ τοῦ Πριάμου, γέρας ἐστὶ τοῦ Ὀδυσσέως.

ὁ δὲ Ἀστυάναξ ἦν υἱὸς τοῦ τε Ἕκτορος καὶ τῆς Ἀνδρομάχης. οἱ δὲ Ἕλληνες νομίζουσι αὐτὸν βασιλέα γενήσεσθαι καὶ τὴν Ἑλλάδα πολεμήσειν. δοκεῖ οὖν αὐτὸν ἀποκτείνειν, καίπερ μικρὸν παιδίον ὄντα. ὁ δὲ Ὀδυσσεὺς τὸ παιδίον ἀπὸ τῶν πύργων καταβάλλει.

ἔπειτα τὸ τοῦ Ἀχιλλέως εἴδωλον φαίνεται τῷ Ἀγαμέμνονι λέγων ὅτι ὁ Ἀχιλλεὺς γέρας λαβεῖν ἐθέλει. "εἴθε ἔτι ἔζων," εἶπε τὸ εἴδωλον. "ὤφελον δοῦλος εἶναι ὃς τὸν ἥλιον ὁρᾷ μᾶλλον ἢ βασιλεὺς ἐν τοῖς τεθνηκόσι. νῦν δέ, τῶν ἄλλων Ἀχαιῶν γέρα λαμβανόντων, ἔγωγε γέρας ἔχειν ὀφείλω. δός μοι καλὴν κόρην." ταῦτα εἰπών, τὸ εἴδωλον ἀπῆλθε.

ὁ δὲ Ἀγαμέμνων τοῖς ἄλλοις ἀγγέλει ὅτι ὁ Ἀχιλλεύς ἐφήνατο, γέρας αἰτοῦν. οἱ Ἀχαιοὶ οὖν κρίνουσι Πολυξένην ἱκανὴν εἶναι. ἡ δὲ Πολυξένη ἄλλη θυγάτηρ ἦν τοῦ Πριάμου, νέα καὶ καλή. τῷ Ἀχιλλεῖ τὴν κόρην θύουσιν ἐπὶ τὸν τάφον. νῦν πάντες ἐκ τῆς βασιλικῆς οἰκίας ἢ τεθνήκασι ἢ αἰχμάλωται γεγόνασι.

οἱ δὲ Ἕλληνες τὴν πόλιν πέρσαντες τὰς ναῦς παρασκευάζουσι. τοῖς θεοῖς οὐ θύουσιν. ἱερέας καὶ παῖδας ἀπεκτόνεσαν. οἱ δὲ θεοὶ βουλεύονται τοὺς Ἕλληνας διαφθείρειν διὰ τὴν ἀσέβειαν. ἀλλὰ οἱ Ἕλληνες, ταῦτα οὐκ ἰδόντες, οὐδὲν δεδοίκασι.

> **λεία, -ας, ἡ,** booty, spoils. **ἄγαλμα, ἀγάλματος, τό,** statue. **ἱερεία** = ἱερεὺς θῆλυς. **βιάζομαι, βιάσομαι, ἐβιασάμην, – , βεβίασμαι, – ,** overpower, assault forcibly. **βωμός, -οῦ, ὁ,** altar. **πολεμέω** = πόλεμον ποιέω, μαχάομαι. **εἴδωλον, -ου, τό,** apparition, image, picture, ghost. **τάφος, -ου, ὁ,** tomb, grave. **βασιλικός, -ά, -όν,** royal, kingly. **αἰχμάλωτος, -ου, ὁ,** captive, prisoner of war. **πέρθω, πέρσω, ἔπερσα, πέπορθα, – , – ,** sack, ravage (a city). **ἀσέβεια, -ας, ἡ,** impiety, disrespect for the gods.

XVIII.7 Conversation

1. (reading 1) τίνες εἰσι πλούσιοι; ποῖά ἐστι ἡ ναῦς; ἆρα μικρὰ ἢ μακρὰ ἡ ναῦς; τίνες τὴν ναῦν καθέλκουσι; ποῦ πλέουσι; and so on.

2. (reading 2) ἀληθείᾳ, ἔξεστι τὸ στῆθος διαιρεῖν ἵνα τὸν νοῦν ἴδωμεν; τίς ἄδολον φρένα ἔχει; and so on.

3. (reading 12) ἆρα ὁ υἱὸς τὸν πατέρα φιλεῖ; τίς θεὸς αἴτιός ἐστι τῶν τοῦ Στρεψιάδου κακῶν; τί κελεύει ὁ πατὴρ τῷ υἱῷ; τίνες εἰσὶ ἐν τῷ φροντιστηρίῳ; and so on.

XVIII.8 Writing

1. Here are several groups of words, each containing an adjective and some nouns. Write sentences ranking the nouns by how much they have the property named by the adjective. For example, given μέγας, δένδρον, παιδίον, μήτηρ you might write: τὸ παιδίον ἐστὶ μέγα. ἡ μήτηρ ἐστὶ μείζονα τοῦ παιδίου. τὸ δένδρον ἐστὶ μεῖζον τῆς μητέρος. τὸ δένδρον ἐστὶ μέγιστον. You could also begin τὸ παιδίον οὔκ ἐστι μέγα if this makes more sense.

   a. ἡδύς, ὕδωρ, οἶνος, γάλα

   b. ἀγαθός, τρυφή, τέχνη, σοφία

   c. ταχύς, Ἀχιλλεύς, κύων, ἵππος

   d. αἰσχρός, κλέπτης, ῥήτωρ, ναύτης

   e. ῥάδιος, μουσικὴ τέχνη, πλοῦς ἐπὶ χειμερίαν θάλατταν, ἄγρα τῶν λαγῶν

2. Each of these sentences is in aorist, present, or future tense. Change the main verb to each of the other two tenses, making all other changes necessary for grammar or sense.

   a. ὁ ἄγγελος ἀγγελεῖ τὸν στρατὸν ἐγγὺς τῆς πόλεως νικηθῆναι.

   b. οἱ κριταὶ τοὺς καλοὺς κύνας ἔκριναν.

   c. ἐκεῖνος ὁ ἀνὴρ ἴσος τοῖς θεοῖς φαίνεται.

   d. ὁ μαθητὴς τὸν λόγον τῷ ἑταίρῳ ἔφηνε.

   e. εἰς τὴν πόλιν ταχέοιν ἵπποιν ἠλάσαμεν.

   f. οἱ πολῖται τὸ ἄλσος διέφθειραν ἵνα ἀγροὺς καὶ κήπους ποιήσαιεν.

   g. τέσσαρες ὄρνιθες πρὸς τῷ μάντει ἐφήναντο.

   h. ὁ στρατηγὸς τοῖς δεδιόσι ξένοις ἐμαχέσατο.

   i. τὼ κακίονε παιδίω πέτραις τὸν λαγὼν βάλλετον.

   j. ὁ κύων κατὰ τῆς κλίμακος τρέχει.

   k. ὁ στρατιώτης τὸ σῶμα ἀσκεῖ.

   l. ὁ ἥλιος οὐ φαίνεται διὰ τὰς νεφέλας.

3. Do the change-number exercise with the following sentences.

   a. ὁ παῖς δέδοικε μὴ ἡ μήτηρ αὐτὸν καταλείπῃ.

   b. εἰ λίνον καὶ ἄγκιστρον εἶχον, οἱ ἄνδρες ἠλίευον.

   c. ὁ μὲν κόρος ἡβᾷ καὶ οὐδὲν δέδοικε.

   d. ὁ γλυκὺς οἶνος ἡδὺς γίγνεται τοῖς θνητοῖς.

   e. αἱ μὲν νῆτται, θήλειαι οὖσαι, ᾠὰ τίκτουσι, οἱ δὲ ἀλεκτρυόνες, ἄρρενες ὄντες, οὐ τίκτουσι.

   f. ἡ θεὰ τοῖς θνητοῖς καλλίων φαίνεται ἢ ἡμεῖς.

   g. οἱ ναῦται βαρὺν λίθον παρέσχον ὅπως ἄγκυραν ἔχωμεν.

   h. τὼ ἁλιεῖ ὠφελέτην ἰχθύας λαβεῖν.

   i. πότε, ὦ παῖς, τὸ ἄγκιστρον εἰς τὸ ὕδωρ βαλεῖς;

j. ὁ ἄδολος καὶ φανεῖται καὶ ἔσεται φίλος.

k. ῥᾳδίως κρινοῦμεν ὁπότερος ποιητὴς βελτίων ἐστί.

l. οἱ ταχεῖς ἵπποι τὴν βαρεῖαν ἄμαξαν εἵλκυσαν.

4. Form conditional sentences from the following pairs of clauses. For each pair make a simple conditional statement, a generalizing statement ("whenever, always if"), a potential or hypothetical statement ("if this were true, which it might or might not be") and a contrary-to-fact statement ("if this were true, but it isn't"). If the OOO rule applies to any of your sentences, write both versions. For example, given ὁ διδάσκαλος λέγει as hypothesis and ὁ μαθητὴς ἀκούει as conclusion, you would write the simple conditional εἰ ὁ διδάσκαλος λέγει, ὁ μαθητὴς ἀκούει, the generalizing statement ἐὰν ὁ διδάσκαλος λέγῃ, ὁ μαθητὴς ἀκούει, the hypothetical statement εἰ ὁ διδάσκαλος λέγοι, ὁ μαθητὴς ἀκούοι ἄν, and the counterfactual εἰ ὁ διδάσκαλος ἔλεγε, ὁ μαθητὴς ἤκουε ἄν.

    a. Hypothesis: τὸ παιδίον κλαίει. Conclusion: ἡ μήτηρ θεραπεύει.

    b. H: τὸ παιδίον ἔκλαιε. C: ἡ μήτηρ ἐθεράπευε.

    c. H: ὁ οἶς φαίνεται. C: ὁ ποιμὴν χαίρει.

    d. H: τὸ σῶμα ἀσκεῖς. C: σῶμα λεπτὸν οὐκ ἔχεις.

    e. H: ὁ ἁλιεὺς τὸ δίκτυον ἐκ τῆς νεὼς βάλλει. C: ἰχθύας λαμβάνει.

    f. H: ὁ ἁλιεὺς τὸ δίκτυον ἐκ τῆς νεὼς ἔβαλε. C: ἰχθύας ἔλαβε.

5. Summarize reading 12 in straightforward prose.

6. Write a paragraph about a day in the country.

CHAPTER XIX

Homecomings: Menelaus and Agamemnon

XIX.1 Verbs in -ζω

Some verb roots ending in -δ form a present in -ζω. This is originally an -ι- suffix that combines with the voiced dental, just as inherited *Dyaus* becomes Ζεύς in Greek. Internal sandhi makes the root difficult to discern; the dental disappears before σ or κ and becomes σ before θ or μ. For example, from the root φραδ- "say" we have the following principal parts:

φράζω, φράσω, ἔφρασα, πέφρακα, ἐφράσθην, πέφρασμαι.

In Attic Greek, verbs in -ίζω form the future in -ιῶ, contracted, rather than in -ίσω as you might expect; the -ίσω forms are used in other dialects. Remember contract futures are all ε-contracts. Thus from root νομιδ- we have:

νομίζω, νομιῶ, ἐνόμισα, νενόμικα, νενόμισμαι, ἐνομίσθην "believe, think."
The third-person singular future indicative and optative active are νομιεῖ,
νομιοίη and the future infinitive active is νομιεῖν.

Exercise

Form the principal parts of κομίζω "carry, convey"; φροντίζω "think"; ἁρπάζω "grab"; ἐλπίζω "expect, hope." Write out the present and future infinitives active and middle for these verbs. Identify the root of each verb.

XIX.2 Temporal clauses with πρίν

The conjunction πρίν normally takes the infinitive, as λούομαι πρὶν καθεύδειν, "I wash before I sleep, before sleeping." But when the main verb is negative, or has a negative idea, then πρίν takes a finite mood. It takes indicative when the sentence refers to a specific incident, as ὁ παῖς οὐ καθηῦδε πρὶν ἔλουσε, "the child did not sleep before washing, did not sleep until he had washed" (note the back-shifted tense in English, unlike the Greek). The OOO rule does not apply to πρίν clauses with indicative. A clause with πρίν takes subjunctive with ἄν in a general statement, as οὐδέποτε καθεύδω πρὶν ἄν λούωμαι, and here the OOO rule does apply, as οὐδέποτε καθηῦδον πρὶν λουοίμην, "I never used to go to sleep before washing." A clause with πρίν can also take optative when the main clause has a potential optative, in a construction similar to a hypothetical conditional, as ὁ παῖς οὐκ ἂν καθεύδοι πρὶν λούοιτο, "the child presumably would not sleep before washing, not until he washed."

XIX.3 Negation of emotional statements

Normally the negative of an indirect statement uses the same adverb as the direct statement, οὐ or μή as the case may be. For example, ὁ ἄνθρωπος λέγει τὸ παιδίον οὐ κακὸν εἶναι, declarative statement with οὐ, or ὁ ἄνθρωπος λέγει ὅτι ὁ παῖς μὴ τὸν κύνα βλαπτέτω, imperative with μή. But if the verb of saying implies a feeling of any kind, as ἐλπίζω "hope" or ὄμνυμι "swear," and the construction is the infinitive (rather than a clause with ὅτι), the negative is often μή. For example, ὁ βασιλεὺς λέγει πόλεμον οὐ μαχεῖσθαι, but ὁ βασιλεὺς ὄμνυσι πόλεμον μὴ μαχεῖσθαι. This is similar to the use of μή with verbs of fearing, as δέδοικα μὴ ὁ βασιλεὺς τοῦτο ἔβλεψε, "I am afraid the king has seen that."

Verbs of swearing always have μή as the negative, as in the example above.

But an oath that merely strengthens a statement doesn't call for μή Thus: ναὶ μὰ Δία "yes, by Zeus," as an answer to a question; οὐ μὰ Δία "no, by Zeus" similarly. Here μὰ Δία is parenthetical; there is no main verb of swearing explicit or understood in these sentences.

XIX.4 Necessity

There are several ways in Greek to express necessity. Simplest is the adjective ἀναγκαῖος, -α, -ο, as ἀναγκαῖος οὗτος ὁ πόλεμος, "this war is necessary." The adjective is derived from the noun ἀνάγκη.

The imperative can convey the idea that someone must do something, as ὁ παῖς γράψατο, roughly the same as κελεύω τὸν παῖδα γράψαι. More usually, when the speaker is not giving an order but simply recognizing what must happen, writers will use δεῖ or χρή. These verbs take an infinitive as subject, so they are always third-person singular: δεῖ γράψαι. As always, the infinitive may have a subject or object of its own: δεῖ τὸν παῖδα γράψαι, δεῖ τὸν παῖδα τὴν ἐπιστολὴν γράψαι, δεῖ τοὺς παῖδας τὴν ἐπιστολὴν γράψαι, and so on. Recall from chapter 14 that the forms of δεῖ are regular, exactly like those of πλέω: present indicative active δεῖ, imperfect ἔδει, subjunctive δέη or δῇ, optative δέοι, and infinitive δεῖν. Because the subject is always an infinitive, the present participle active only has neuter singular forms (to agree with the subject), δέον, δέοντος, and so on. The future δεήσει and aorist ἐδέησε can also be used. The verb only has active forms.

The verb χρή is used just like δεῖ and, similarly, is always third-person singular and active. It has only a present system, forms: χρή, ἐχρῆν, χρῇ, χρείη, χρῆναι. The neuter nominative/accusative singular participle is χρεών; the other cases are rare.

Both δεῖ and χρή can also indicate need of a thing, as δεῖ σοὶ καλάμου, χρὴ σὲ καλάμου. What is needed is in the genitive, while the person who needs it may be either dative or accusative.

XIX.5 Vocabulary

VERBS

ἀδικέω, ἀδικήσω, ἠδίκησα, ἠδίκηκα, ἠδίκημαι, ἠδικήθην, do wrong

αἰτιάομαι, αἰτιάσομαι, ᾐτιασάμην, – , ᾐτίαμαι, ᾐτιάθην, accuse

ἀλλάττω, ἀλλάξω, ἤλλαξα, ἤλλαχα, ἤλλαγμαι, ἠλλάχην, change

ἀπ-εσθίω, eat away

ἀπ-όλλῡμι, destroy; in middle, perish, be ruined

βλαστάνω, βλαστήσω, ἔβλαστον, βεβλάστηκα, – , – , grow (cp. *blastoma*)

βόσκω, βοσκήσω, ἐβόσκησα, – , – , – , feed, drive to pasture (cp. *proboscis*)

δακρῡω, δακρῡσω, ἐδάκρῡσα, δεδάκρῡκα, δεδάκρῡμαι, ἐδακρύθην, weep, cry, weep for, lament

δέω, δήσω, ἔδησα, δέδεκα, δέδεμαι, ἐδέθην, bind

διά-κειμαι, be situated, be in a condition (with an adverb)

διδάσκω, διδάξω, ἐδίδαξα, δεδίδαχα, δεδίδαγμαι, ἐδιδάχθην, teach

διώκω, διώξω, ἐδίωξα, δεδίωχα, δεδίωγμαι, ἐδιώθχην, chase, pursue, prosecute

ἐπι-δακρῡω, weep also

θηράω, θηράσω, – , – , – , – , hunt

κατα-φρονέω, despise (+ gen.)

ὄλλῡμι, ὀλῶ, ὤλεσα, ὀλώλεκα, – , – , destroy, lose; aorist middle ὠλόμην; alternate perfect ὄλωλα, perish.

ὄμνῡμι, ὀμοῦμαι, ὤμοσα, ὀμώμοκα, – , – , swear

παιδεύω, παιδεύσω, ἐπαίδευσα, πεπαίδευκα, πεπαίδευμαι, ἐπαιδεύθην, instruct, train, educate

πρέπει, it is fitting, it is appropriate

ὑλακτέω, ὑλακτήσω, ὑλάκτησα, – , – , – , bark (with dog as subject)

ὑπ-άγομαι, attract

φράζω, φράσω, ἔφρασα, πέφρακα, πέφρασμαι, ἐφράσθην, say, declare (cp. *phrase, periphrasis*)

φρονέω, φρονήσω, ἐφρόνησα, πεφρόνηκα, πεφρόνημαι, ἐφρονήθην, think; be sane, be wise

χρή, must

NOUNS

ἀκτή, -ῆς, η, shore

ἀνάγκη, -ης, ἡ, necessity

βουκόλος, -ου, ὁ, herdsman

δικαιοσύνη, -ης, ἡ, justice

θήρᾱ, -ᾱς, ἡ, hunt

κυνηγέτης, -ου, ὁ, huntsman, hunter

κωμήτης, -ου, ὁ, villager

λύκος, -ου, ο, wolf (cp. *wolf, lycanthrope*, L. *lupus*)

νόμος, -ου, ὁ, law, custom (cp. *economy, binomial*)

οἶκτος, -ου, ὁ, pity

ὅρκος, -ου, ὁ, oath, vow

ὄρος, -ους, τό, mountain, hill

πληγή, -ῆς, ἡ, blow, strike

πνεῦμα, -ατος, τό, wind, breath (cp. *sneeze, pneumatic*)

πῦρ, πῠρός, τό, fire (cp. *fire, pyrotechnics*)

χειμών, -ῶνος, ο, storm, winter

ψάμμος, -ου, ἡ, sand (cp. *psammophile*)

ADJECTIVES

ἀγροῖκος, -ον, rustic, boorish

ἀναγκαῖος, -α, -ον, necessary

περιττός, -ή, -όν, excessive, very great (often in a bad sense)

πονηρός, -ά, -όν, bad, wicked, causing pain

σύντομος, -ον, brief

χλωρός, -ά, -όν, green (cp. *chlorophyll, chlorine*)

ADVERBS, CONJUNCTIONS, PARTICLES

οὔκουν, then ... not, not therefore

πρίν, before, until

ὧδε, here, thus

Notes on the vocabulary

As usual, the compound ἀπόλλυμι is prefered to the simple verb ὄλλυμι in Attic prose.

Don't confuse δέω "bind" and δεῖ "be necessary." They are the same in the present but not in the other tenses, and only "bind" has a passive.

ὄμνυμι can take an accusative denoting what is sworn, as ὅρκον ὄμνυμι "I swear an oath," or indirect statement, normally with infinitive, as ὄμνυμι τοῦτο ποιεῖν. It can also take an accusative of the god to or by whom one swears, as τὸν Δία ὄμνυμι. A dative with this verb is an ordinary indirect object, as τὸν Δία σοι ὄμνυμι, roughly "as Zeus is my witness, I tell you on oath."

πρέπει normally has an infinitive as subject, often with a dative rather than a subject of the infinitive (which would be accusative), as πρέπει σοὶ τὴν ἀλήθειαν λέγειν instead of πρέπει σὲ τὴν ἀλήθειαν λέγειν. It is generally used only in the present in this sense.

The derivation of χρή is uncertain. Traditionally it is said to be a noun that gets somehow attached to forms of εἰμι, but it would be an unusual noun (in particular, it would be neuter, not feminine) and the "attached" or "contracted" forms are not exactly what we would expect. It could also be an old verb form, perhaps an isolated root (as if we had θή from τίθημι), later re-interpreted as a third-person form.

The noun κυνηγέτης means ἄνθρωπος ὃς τὸν κύνα ἄγει, and is the agent noun from ἄγω compounded with the root of κύων.

The particle οὔκουν is roughly a negative version of οὐκοῦν, used in an affirmative statement as a strong negative, or used in a question to express surprise or impatience, as οὔκουν γιγνώσκεις; "but don't you realize ...?"

XIX.6 Reading

1. *A Rustic Trial*

δικαστὴν καθίζουσι Φιλητᾶν τὸν βουκόλον· πρεσβύτατος γὰρ ἦν τῶν παρόντων καὶ κλέος εἶχεν ἐν τοῖς κωμήταις δικαιοσύνης περιττῆς. πρῶτοι δὲ κατηγόρουν οἱ Μυτιληναῖοι σαφῆ καὶ σύντομα. "ἤλθομεν εἰς τούτους τοὺς ἀγροὺς θηρᾶσαι ἐθέλοντες. τὴν μὲν οὖν ναῦν λόγῳ χλωρᾷ δήσαντες, ἐπὶ τῆς ἀκτῆς κατελίπομεν· αὐτοὶ δὲ μετὰ τῶν κυνῶν θήραν ἐποιούμεθα. ἐν τούτῳ πρὸς τὴν θάλατταν αἱ αἶγες τούτου κατελθοῦσαι, τήν τε λύγου κατεσθίουσι, καὶ τὴν ναῦν ἀπολύουσιν. ἀνθ᾽ ὧν ἀξιοῦμεν ἄγειν τοῦτον πονηρὸν ὄντα βουκόλον, ὃς ἐπὶ τῆς θαλάττης νέμει τὰς αἶγας ὡς ναύτης."

τοσαῦτα οἱ Μυτιληναῖοι κατηγόρησαν. ὁ δὲ Δάφνις διέκειτο μὲν κακῶς ὑπὸ τῶν πληγῶν, Χλόην δ᾽ ὁρῶν παροῦσαν, πάντων κατεφρόνει, καὶ ὧδ᾽ εἶπεν· "ἐγὼ νέμω τὰς αἶγας καλῶς. οὐδέποτ᾽ ἠτιάσατο κωμήτης οὐδὲ εἷς, ὡς ἢ κῆπόν τινος αἴξ ἐμὴ κατεβοσκήσατο ἢ ἄμπελον βλαστάνουσαν κατέκλασεν· οὗτοι δ᾽ εἰσὶ κυνηγέται πονηροὶ καὶ κύνας ἔχουσι κακῶς πεπαιδευμένους, οἵτινες τρέχοντες καὶ ὑλακτοῦντες κατεδίωξαν αὐτὰς ἐκ τῶν ὀρῶν καὶ τῶν πεδίων ἐπὶ τὴν θάλατταν, ὥσπερ λύκοι. ἀλλ᾽ ἀπέφαγον τὴν λύγον· οὐ γὰρ εἶχον ἐν ψάμμῳ πόαν ἢ κόμαρον ἢ θύμον. ἀλλ᾽ ἀπώλετο ἡ ναῦς ὑπὸ τοῦ πνεύματος καὶ τῆς θαλάττης. ταῦτα χειμῶνος, οὐκ αἰγῶν, ἔργα ἐστιν."

τούτοις ἐπεδάκρυσεν ὁ Δάφνις, καὶ εἰς οἶκτον ὑπηγάγετο τοὺς ἀγροίκους πολύν· ὥσθ᾽ ὁ Φιλητᾶς ὁ δικαστὴς ὤμνυε Πᾶνα καὶ Νύμφας μηδὲν ἀδικεῖν Δάφνιν.

Daphnis and Chloe 2.15-16

θήραν ἐποιούμεθα = ἐθηρῶμεν; a verbal idea can be paraphrased with the middle of ποιοῦμαι and a suitable noun. **ἄγειν τὸν βουκόλον**, with the implication ὡς δίκην ληψόμενοι τοῦ βουκόλου, ἄγειν πρὸς τὴν δίκην. **κατα-βόσκω** = βόσκω, **κατα-διώκω** = διώκω, **κατα-κλάω** = κλάω, break off. **κόμαρος, -ου, ἡ**, arbutus or strawberry-tree. **θύμον, -ου, τό**, the herb thyme.

2. οἱ πατέρες τοὺς παῖδας τοὺς νόμους διδάσκουσι. δεῖ δὲ τοὺς πατέρας διδάσκειν, διότι οἱ παῖδες οὐ δύνανται αὐτοὺς διδάσκειν. οἱ ἀγαθοὶ πατέρες ἀεὶ φράζουσι τοῖς παισὶ εὖ πράττειν. τί πρέπει παιδί; οὔκουν οἶσθα; λέγω δή· πρέπει μὲν τῶν πατέρων ἀκούειν καὶ αὐτοῖς πείθεσθαι. πρέπει δὲ τοὺς θεοὺς τιμᾶν. πρέπει δὲ τοὺς ξένους εὔνως δέχεσθαι. ταῦτα ποιεῖν παιδὶ πρέπει.

3. ὁ κυνηγέτης τὰ ζῷα κυσὶ θηρᾷ. οὐδὲ βοῦς οὐδὲ πρόβατα θηρᾷ, οὐδὲ ἄλλα ζῷα ἃ ἄνθρωποι βόσκουσι καὶ νέμουσι, ἀλλὰ ζῷα ἄγρια, ὡς ἀλώπεκα, λέοντα, ἔλαφον, λαγών. οἱ κύνες τὰ ἄγρια διώκουσι, τοῦ κυνηγέτου ἑπομένου. ὅτε ζῷον λαμβάνουσι, ὑλακοῦσι, φράζοντες τῷ κυνηγέτῃ ὅτι ζῷον ἔχουσι. οἱ μὲν ἔλαφοι φρονοῦσι τοὺς κύνας ἀδικεῖν, οἱ δὲ κύνες παίζουσι. οὐ συνιᾶσι ὅτι οἱ ἔλαφοι δεδοίκασι. οἱ δὲ λέοντες οὐ δεδοίκασι, ἀλλ᾽ οὐκ ἐθέλουσι ὄλλυσθαι· φεύγουσι οὖν. οἱ δὲ ἀλώπεκες, δεινοὶ καὶ σοφοὶ ὄντες, τρέχουσι, τῶν κυνῶν διωκόντων, ἕως ἂν οἱ κύνες παύωνται διώκειν.

   ἀλώπηξ, ἀλώπεκος, ἡ, ὁ, fox. **ἔλαφος, -ου, ὁ, ἡ,** deer.

4. πλαστὸν ἔχεις τὸν ἔρωτα, φόβῳ δὲ φιλεῖς καὶ ἀνάγκῃ·
      τοῦ δὲ φιλεῖν οὕτως οὐδὲν ἀπιστότερον.

   Greek Anthology 11.385.

   πλαστός, -ή, -όν, made, modelled; counterfeit. **ἔρως, ἔρωτος, ὁ,** love. **φόβος, -ου, ὁ,** fear. **ἄπιστος, -ον,** untrustworthy, unbelievable.

5. εἰ καὶ δακρυόεις, Εὐριπίδη, εἷλέ σε πότμος,
      καί σε λυκορραῖσται δεῖπνον ἔθεντο κύνες,
   τὸν σκηνῇ μελίγηρυν ἀηδόνα, κόσμον Ἀθηνῶν,
      τὸν σοφίᾳ Μουσῶν μιξάμενον χάριτα,
   ἀλλ᾽ ἔμολες Πελλαῖον ὑπ᾽ ἠρίον, ὡς ἂν ὁ λάτρις
      Πιερίδων ναίῃς ἀγχόθι Πιερίης.

   Greek Anthology 7.44, by Ion of Chios.

   πότμος, -ου, ὁ, destiny, fate, death. **λυκορραίστης, -ου, ὁ,** destroyer of wolves. **μελίγηρυς, -υος, ὁ, ἡ,** sweet-voiced. **κόσμος, -ου, ὁ,** ornament, adornment (also, good order; the world). **βλώσκω, μολοῦμαι, ἔμολον, μέμβλωκα, – , – ,** go, come. **ἠρίον, -ου, τό,** mound, burial-mound. **λάτρις, λάτριος, ὁ** = δοῦλος, θεράπων. **ναίω** = οἰκέω. **ἀγχόθι,** near, close to.

   Prose paraphrase: ὁ θάνατος σὲ εἷλε, ὦ Εὐριπίδη, ἑκόντα ἢ μή. οἱ κύνες, οἳ λύκους διαφθείρουσι, νῦν τὸ σὸν σῶμα ἐσθίουσι. ὁ θάνατος ἀφεῖλε ἀπὸ τῆς σκηνῆς τὴν σὴν φωνή, ἣν οἱ Ἀθηναῖοι ἐφίλουν. οἱ σοὶ λόγοι ἀεὶ χάριτα ἐμίγνυσαν τῇ τῶν Μουσῶν σοφίᾳ. ἀλλὰ νῦν κεῖσαι παρὰ τῷ Πελλαίῳ. διότι θεράπων ἦσθα τῶν Μουσῶν, οἰκεῖς Πιερίᾳ σὺν ταῖς Πιερίσι Μούσαις.

6. **Μενέλαος·** ἀλλὰ ὕδωρ μέν σε γενέσθαι, ὦ Πρωτεῦ, οὐκ ἀπίθανον, ἐνάλιόν γε ὄντα, καὶ δένδρον, ἔτι φορητόν, καὶ εἰς λέοντα δὲ εἰ ἀλλαγείης, ὅμως οὐδὲ τοῦτο ἔξω πίστεως· εἰ δὲ καὶ πῦρ γίγνεσθαι δυνατὸν ἐν τῇ θαλάττῃ οἰκοῦντά σε, τοῦτο πάνυ θαυμάζω καὶ ἀπιστῶ.

   Πρωτεύς· μὴ θαυμάσῃς, ὦ Μενέλαε· γίγνομαι γάρ.

   Μενέλαος· εἶδον καὶ αὐτός· ἀλλά μοι δοκεῖς — εἰρήσεται γὰρ πρὸς σέ — γοητείαν τινὰ προσάγειν τῷ πράγματι καὶ τοὺς ὀφθαλμοὺς ἐξαπατᾶν τῶν ὁρώντων αὐτὸς οὐδὲν τοιοῦτο γιγνόμενος.

   Πρωτεύς· καὶ τίς ἂν ἡ ἀπάτη ἐπὶ τῶν οὕτως ἐναργῶν γένοιτο; οὐκ ἀνεῳγμένοις τοῖς ὀφθαλμοῖς εἶδες, εἰς ὅσα μετεποίησα ἐμαυτόν; εἰ δὲ ἀπιστεῖς, καὶ τὸ πρᾶγμά σοι ψευδὲς εἶναι δοκεῖ, φαντασία τις πρὸ τῶν ὀφθαλμῶν ἱσταμένη, ἐπειδὰν πῦρ γένωμαι, προσένεγκέ μοι, ὦ γενναῖε, τὴν χεῖρα· εἴσῃ γάρ, εἰ ὁρῶμαι μόνον, ἢ καὶ τὸ κάειν τότε μοι πρόσεστιν.

Μενέλαος· οὐκ ἀσφαλὴς ἡ πεῖρα, ὦ Πρωτεῦ.

Πρωτεύς· σὺ δέ μοι, ὦ Μενέλαε, δοκεῖς οὐδὲ πολύπουν ἑορακέναι πώποτε οὐδὲ εἰδέναι ὅ τι πάσχει ὁ ἰχθῦς οὗτος.

Μενέλαος· ἀλλὰ τὸν μὲν πολύπουν εἶδον, ἅττα δὲ πάσχει, ἡδέως ἂν μάθοιμι παρὰ σοῦ.

Πρωτεύς· ὁποίᾳ ἂν πέτρᾳ προσελθὼν ἁρμόσῃ τὰς κοτύλας καὶ προσφὺς ἔχηται κατὰ τὰς πλεκτάνας, ἐκείνῃ ὅμοιον ἐργάζεται ἑαυτὸν καὶ μεταβάλλει τὴν χροιὰν μιμούμενος τὴν πέτραν, ὡς ἂν λάθῃ τοὺς ἁλιέας μὴ φανερὸς ὢν διὰ τοῦτο, ἀλλὰ ἐοικὼς τῷ λίθῳ.

Μενέλαος· φασὶ ταῦτα· τὸ δὲ σὸν πολλῷ παραδοξότερον, ὦ Πρωτεῦ.

Πρωτεύς· οὐκ οἶδα, ὦ Μενέλαε, ᾧτινι ἂν ἄλλῳ πιστεύσειας, τοῖς σεαυτοῦ ὀφθαλμοῖς ἀπιστῶν.

Μενέλαος· εἶδον· ἀλλὰ τὸ πρᾶγμα τεράστιον, ὁ αὐτὸς πῦρ καὶ ὕδωρ.

This dialogue comes from Lucian's *Dialogues of the Sea Creatures*.

ἀπίθανος, -ον, unbelievable, implausible. ἐνάλιος, -α, -ον, marine, of the sea. φορητός, -ή, -όν, bearable, tolerable. πίστις, -εως, ἡ, trust, belief. δυνατός, -ή, -όν, able, powerful. ἀπιστέω, doubt, disbelieve. γοητεία, -ας, ἡ, witchcraft, magic. προσ-άγω, furnish, supply, add, employ. ἐξαπατάω, ἐξαπατήσω, ἐξηπάτησα, ἐξηπάτηκα, –, – , cheat, deceive. ἀπάτη, -ης, ἡ, fraud, deceit, trickery. ἐναργής, -ές, visible, clear, bright. μετα-ποιέω, alter, change. φαντασίᾱ, -ᾱς, ἡ, appearance, display, apparition. προσ-φέρω, bring forward. γενναῖος, -α, -ον, noble, classy. καίω, καύσω, ἔκαυσα, κέκαυκα, κέκαυμαι, ἐκαύθην, burn. πεῖρα, -ας, ἡ, experiment, attempt. πολύπους, πολύποδος, ὁ, octopus. ἁρμόττω, ἁρμόσω, ἥρμοσα, ἥρμοκα, ἥρμοσμαι, ἡρμόσθην, fit together, join. κοτύλη, -ης, ἡ, cup, socket. προσ-φύω, grow on, cling to. πλεκτάνη, -ης, ἡ, coil, anything twisted or braided. ἐργάζομαι, ἐργάσομαι, εἰργασάμην, – , εἴργασμαι, – , work, be busy, accomplish. μιμέομαι, μιμήσομαι, ἐμιμησάμην, – , μεμίμημαι, – , mimic, imitate. παράδοξος, -η, -ον, unexpected, strange. τεράστιος, -α, -ον, monstrous, scary.

7. **Κρέων·** καὶ δῆτ᾽ ἐτόλμας τούσδ᾽ ὑπερβαίνειν νόμους;
   Ἀντιγόνη· οὐ γάρ τί μοι Ζεὺς ἦν ὁ κηρύξας τάδε,   450
   οὐδ᾽ ἡ ξύνοικος τῶν κάτω θεῶν Δίκη
   τοιούσδ᾽ ἐν ἀνθρώποισιν ὥρισεν νόμους.
   οὐδὲ σθένειν τοσοῦτον ᾠόμην τὰ σὰ
   κηρύγμαθ᾽, ὥστ᾽ ἄγραπτα κἀσφαλῆ θεῶν
   νόμιμα δύνασθαι θνητὸν ὄνθ᾽ ὑπερδραμεῖν.   455
   οὐ γάρ τι νῦν γε κἀχθές, ἀλλ᾽ ἀεί ποτε
   ζῇ ταῦτα, κοὐδεὶς οἶδεν ἐξ ὅτου 'φάνη.
   τούτων ἐγὼ οὐκ ἔμελλον, ἀνδρὸς οὐδενὸς
   φρόνημα δείσασ᾽, ἐν θεοῖσι τὴν δίκην
   δώσειν· θανουμένη γὰρ ἐξῄδη, τί δ᾽ οὔ;   460
   κεἰ μὴ σὺ προὐκήρυξας. εἰ δὲ τοῦ χρόνου
   πρόσθεν θανοῦμαι, κέρδος αὔτ᾽ ἐγὼ λέγω.
   ὅστις γὰρ ἐν πολλοῖσιν ὡς ἐγὼ κακοῖς

ζῆ, πῶς ὅδ᾽ οὐχὶ κατθανὼν κέρδος φέρει;
οὕτως ἔμοιγε τοῦδε τοῦ μόρου τυχεῖν   465
παρ᾽ οὐδὲν ἄλγος· ἀλλ᾽ ἄν, εἰ τὸν ἐξ ἐμῆς
μητρὸς θανόντ᾽ ἄθαπτον ἠνσχόμην νέκυν,
κείνοις ἂν ἤλγουν· τοῖσδε δ᾽ οὐκ ἀλγύνομαι.
σοὶ δ᾽ εἰ δοκῶ νῦν μῶρα δρῶσα τυγχάνειν,
σχεδόν τι μώρῳ μωρίαν ὀφλισκάνω.   470

Sophocles, *Antigone* 449-470.

δῆτα, particle marking that a question follows along from what's just been said. τολμάω, τολμήσω, ἐτόλμησα, τετόλμηκα, – , – , dare, venture. ὑπερβαίνω, ὑπερτρέχω, go beyond, transgress (law). κηρύττω, κηρύξω, ἐκήρυξα, κεκήρυχα, κεκήρυγμαι, ἐκηρύχθην, announce, proclaim, act as a herald; προ-κηρύττω means the same. ξύνοικος, -ον, common, communal, living together; also σύν-οικος, but Attic Greek frequently uses ξυν- for συν-. ὁρίζω, ὁριῶ, ὥρισα, ὥρικα, ὥρισμαι, ὡρίσθην, determine, settle, demarcate. σθένω, present system only, be strong, have power. κήρυγμα, -ατος, τό, proclamation, public notice. ἄγραπτος = οὐ γεγραμμένος. νόμιμος, -η, -ον = κατὰ τοὺς νόμους, τὰ νόμιμα = οἱ νόμοι. ἐχθές = χθές. φρόνημα, -ατος, τό = ὁ νοῦς, ἡ φρήν, ἡ ψυχή. δείσασα is aorist participle active, fem. nom. sg., from δείδω. ἔξ-οιδα, know thoroughly. πρόσθεν, before, sooner. κέρδος, -ους, τό, profit, advantage. κατα-θνήσκω = ἀπο-θνήσκω. μόρος, -ου, ὁ, fate, normally a bad fate. ἄθαπτος, -ον, not buried. ἄλγος, -ους, τό, pain; ἀλγύνω, cause pain, grieve. ἠνσχόμην = ἀνεσχόμην, an epic form with augment before the prefix rather than before the actual verb stem, from ἀν-έχω, endure. νέκυς, νέκυος, ὁ, corpse, dead body. κείνοις = ἐκείνοις. μωρία, -ας, ἡ, foolishness. ὀφλισκάνω, ὀφλήσω, ὤφληκα, – , – , – , incur a debt, bring something on oneself.

8. *περὶ τοῦ Τρωικοῦ πολέμου, τρισκαιδέκατον μέρος*

τοῦ πολέμου τελευτηθέντος, ἀναγκαῖόν ἐστι οἴκαδε ἐλθεῖν. ἀπὸ τοῦ Ἰλίου οὖν ἐξέπλεον οἱ Ἀχαιοί. ὁ μὲν Διομήδης, ὁ δὲ Νέστωρ, ὁ δὲ Λεόντευς, πολλοὶ καὶ ἄλλοι οἴκαδε ἀσφαλεῖς ἀφίκοντο. τῶν ἄλλων δὲ χαλεποὶ ἦσαν οἱ νόστοι.

ὁ δὲ Μενέλαος σὺν τῇ Ἑλένῃ χειμῶνι περιέπεσε. χαλεπὸν μὲν τὸ πλοῦν, τέλος δὲ εἰς Αἴγυπτον ἀφίκετο. ὁ Πρωτεύς, γέρων τὴν θάλατταν οἰκῶν, βασιλεὺς ἦν ἐκείνου τοῦ τόπου. ὁ δὲ τοὺς ξένους ἐμίσει. τὸν Μενέλαον ἀποκτείνοι ἂν εἰ λάβοι. χρὴ δόλον εὑρεῖν, ἀλλὰ πῶς; ἡ δὲ Εἰδοθεΐα, θυγάτηρ οὖσα τοῦ Πρωτέως, τῷ Μενελάῳ ὠφέλειαν ἔδοκε, εἰποῦσα τὸν πατέρα τὴν μορφὴν ἀλλάττειν ἔχειν. "ὁ δὲ Πρωτεύς πάντα ζῷα γίγνεται, ἅτινα ἂν ἐπὶ τὴν γῆν ἔρπονται ἢ ἐν τῇ θαλάττῃ οἰκῶσι. χρὴ σὲ μένειν· μὴ αὐτῷ μάχου πρὶν ἂν ἄνθρωπος γίγνηται. ἔπειτα ἕξεις αὐτῷ εἰπεῖν."

ὁ Μενέλαος οὖν ἑαυτὸν τῷ δέρματι φώκης ἐκάλυψε καὶ μετὰ τῶν φώκων ἔκειτο. αἱ δὲ φῶκαι εἰσὶ τὰ τοῦ Πρωτέως πρόβατα. μία φώκη ὑλάκτησε τὸν Μενέλαον, ξένον ὄντα, ἀλλ᾽ ἔπειτα πᾶσαι καθηῦδον. ἐπεὶ ὁ Πρωτεὺς ἦλθε, ὁ Μενέλαος ἔστη καὶ εἶπε, "ἐθέλω οἴκαδε ἐλθεῖν, ὦ Πρωτεύς, καὶ σὺ μόνος δύνασαί με ὠφελεῖν." ὁ δὲ Πρωτεὺς ἑαυτὸν ἤλλαξε εἰς μὲν πάνθηρα, εἰς δὲ ἰχθύν, εἰς δὲ λέοντα, εἰς δὲ μῦν, εἰς δὲ πολλὰ ἄλλα ζῷα, ὁ δὲ Μενέλαος ἀεὶ ἔμεινε καί, ἐπεὶ τέλος ὁ Πρωτεὺς ἄνθρωπος πάλιν ἐγένετο, αὖθις εἶπε, "ὠφελοίης μοι ἄν."

"τί σὲ ὠφελοίμην ἄν; ξένος εἶ· οὔ σε γιγνώσκω. τί ἐμοὶ δώσεις;" ὁ δὲ Μενέλαος ἀπεκρίνατο, "πρέπει πᾶσι τοὺς ξένους ὠφελεῖν· οὗτός ἐστι ὁ πάντων Ἑλλήνων νόμος. ἐγὼ μέν εἰμι θνητὸς ἄνθρωπος, σὺ δ᾽ εἶ θεός· οὐδὲν ἔχω ἄξιον σοὶ δοῦναι. οὔκουν σοι δῶρα δώσω, ἀλλὰ τοῦτο ποιήσω· ὄμνυμι μηδένα Ἕλληνα φώκας θηρᾶν, εἰ οἴκαδε ἀσφαλὴς ἀφίξομαι. τοῦτον τὸν ὅρκον ὄμνυμι."

διὰ τὸν ἀγαθὸν ὅρκον, ὁ δὲ Πρωτεὺς αὐτὸν ὠφέλησε καὶ ὁ Μενέλαος καὶ ἡ Ἑλένη οἴκαδε ἠλθέτην.

ὁ δὲ Ἀγαμέμνων πλοῦν μὲν χαλεπὸν οὐκ ἔσχε, νόστον δὲ χαλεπώτατον. ἡ δὲ Κλυταίμηστρα ἔτι ὀργιζομένη περὶ τὴν τῆς Ἰφιγενείας θυσίας αὐτὸν ἀπέκτεινε.

> **νόστος, -ου, ὁ**, home-coming, voyage home. **χαλεπός, -ή, -όν**, difficult. **περιπίπτω**, fall around, fall foul of, fall into. **γέρων, -οντος, ὁ**, old man. **τόπος, -ου, ὁ**, place. **μισέω**, hate (predictable principal parts). **δόλος, -ον, ὁ**, trick. **μορφή, -ῆς, ἡ**, shape. **δέρμα, -ατος, τό**, skin. **φώκη, -ης, ἡ**, seal, sea-lion. **καλύπτω**, cover, conceal. **μένω, μενῶ, ἔμεινα, μεμένηκα, – , –** , stay, remain. **ὀργίζω**, anger, make angry. **θυσία, -ας, ἡ**, sacrifice.

XIX.7 Conversation

The usual questions and answers on the readings and the vocabulary, for example:

1. (reading 1) τίς ἐστι ὁ Φιλητᾶς; διὰ τί ποιοῦσιν αὐτὸν δικαστήν; τί λέγουσιν οἱ Μυτιληναῖοι; τίνα κατηγόρουσι; and so on through the passage.

2. (reading 3) τίς θηρᾷ; τίνα θηρᾷ; ποῖα ζῷα θηρᾷ ὁ κυνηγέτης; τί ποιοῦσι οἱ κύνες; ἆρα οἱ κύνης φοβοῦνται τοὺς ἐλάφους; ἆρα οἱ ἔλαφοι τοὺς κύνας φοβοῦνται; and so on.

XIX.8 Writing

1. Rewrite each of the following sentences using a different expression for necessity. For example, you might change δεῖ με γράψαι to χρή με γράψαι, or to ἀναγκαῖόν ἐστί με γράψαι.
   a. χρὴ τῷ διδασκάλῳ δῶρα διδόναι.
   b. ὁ μαθητὴς τῷ διδασκάλῳ δῶρα διδότω.
   c. εἰ ὁ φίλος δακρύει, δεῖ σε ἐπιδακρύειν.
   d. ἀναγκαῖα ἡ μεταβολή.
   e. ἀναγκαῖόν ἐστι τὸ πνεῦμα τοῦ βίου.
   f. ἔδει τοὺς κυνηγέτας πῦρ ἀποσβεννύναι.
   g. ὁ βασιλεὺς ἐνόμισε ὅτι δέοι βελτίονας νόμος ποιεῖν.
   h. ὁ βασιλεὺς ἐνόμισε ἀναγκαῖον εἶναι τὸν πόλεμον παῦσαι.
   i. ἴδμεν τοὺς στρατιώτας μάχεσθαι χρῆναι.
   j. δεῖ ἡμᾶς ὅρκον ὀμνύναι.

2. Do the change-number exercise with the following sentences.

   a. οἱ βουκόλοι φράζουσι ὅτι λύκοι παρὰ τῇ κώμῃ εἰσί.

   b. οἱ θεοὶ ἀπολλύασι τοὺς ἀδικοῦντας.

   c. ὁ βασιλεὺς πάντας τοὺς θεοὺς ὀμνὺς εἶπε δίκην τοῦ κακοῦ λήψεσθαι.

   d. τὼ κύνε ὑλακτεῖτον δεδιότε τοὺς λύκους.

   e. ὁ ἀδικηθεὶς παῖς δακρύει.

   f. ὁ βουκόλος διέκειτο κακῶς ὑπὸ τῶν πληγῶν.

   g. εὖ πεπαίδευνται οἱ τῶν κυνηγετῶν κύνες.

   h. εἰ εἰς ὕδωρ ἀλλαγείης, οὐκ ἂν πῦρ εἴης.

   i. ἡμεῖς γε, ἄνθρωποι ὄντες, οὐκ ἔχομεν πῦρ γενέσθαι.

   j. ὁ μὲν λύκος δικαιοσύνῃ κρῖναι ὄμνυσι, ὁ δὲ οἷς οὐ πιστεύει.

   k. τίς, ὦ ἑταῖρε, σ᾽ ἀδικεῖ;

   l. αἱ ἄμπελοι ἐβλάστανον ἐν τοῖς ὄρεσι.

3. Each of these sentences is in aorist, present, or future tense. Change the main verb to each of the other two tenses, making all other changes necessary for grammar or sense.

   a. οἱ κομῆται νομίζουσι ὅτι διὰ ἀνάγκην πολὺ εὑρίσκομεν.

   b. ὁ παῖς τῷ ἐν τῇ ἀκτῇ ψάμμῳ παίξεται.

   c. τοῦτον τὸν κομήτην εὔνως ξενιοῦμεν.

   d. οἱ ἁλιῆς ἠρέθισαν, καίπερ δέοντος τὴν ναῦν ὁρμίσαι.

   e. οἱ ναῦται χειμῶνα ἐλπίζουσι.

   f. ὁ μὲν κυνηγέτης ἐβάδισε, οἱ δὲ κύνες ἔδραμον.

4. Each of the following sentences contains a subordinate clause to which the OOO rule has been applied. Rewrite the sentences, changing the main verb to present tense and the subordinate verb to indicative or subjunctive, as appropriate. For some sentences there will be more than one possibility; write them all. Be sure to adjust conjunctions and add ἄν when necessary. For example, given εἶπε ὅτι γράφοις, make λέγει ὅτι γράφεις.

   a. ὁ στρατηγὸς τὸν πόλεμον οὐκ ἐπαύσατο πρὶν τὴν πόλιν διαφθεῖραι.

   b. οἱ Μυτιληναῖοι εἶπον ὅτι οἱ αἶγες τὴν λύγου καταφάγοιεν.

   c. ὁ Πρωτεὺς ἑαυτὸν ὕδωρ ἐποίησε ἵνα ὁ Μενέλαος μὴ αὐτὸν λαμβάνοι.

   d. εἰ ὁ Πρωτεὺς τὸ σχῆμα ἀλλάττοι, ὁ Μενέλαος ἐθαύμαζε.

   e. ἐχρῆν σε οὐ δακρύειν πρὶν ἀδικοῖο.

   f. ἐνομίσαμεν ὅτι δέοι τὸν οἶνον ὕδατι μιγνύναι.

5. Summarize Antigone's argument in reading 7, in a short paragraph in Greek.

6. Write a paragraph on the theme of coming home, νόστος.

CHAPTER XX

Homecoming: Odysseus

XX.1 Athematic verbs: present middle/passive

The present middle/passive of the μι-verbs has the short stem vowel in all forms. The endings are nearly the same as for thematic verbs. Here are the forms of δίδωμι:

	Pres. Indic.	Imperf. Indic.	Imper.	Subj.	Opt.
singular					
1st	δίδομαι	ἐδιδόμην		διδῶμαι	διδοίμην
2nd	δίδοσαι	ἐδίδοσο	δίδοσο	διδῷ	διδοῖο
3rd	δίδοται	ἐδίδοτο	διδόσθω	διδῶται	διδοῖτο
dual					
2nd	δίδοσθον	ἐδίδοσθον	δίδοσθον	διδῶσθον	διδοῖσθον
3rd	δίδοσθον	ἐδιδόσθην	διδόσθων	διδῶσθον	διδοίσθην
plural					
1st	διδόμεθα	ἐδιδόμεθα		διδώμεθα	διδοίμεθα
2nd	δίδοσθε	ἐδίδοσθε	δίδοσθε	διδῶσθε	διδοῖσθε
3rd	δίδονται	ἐδίδοντο	διδόσθων	διδῶνται	διδοῖντο

The present infinitive middle/passive is δίδοσθαι and the participle is διδόμενος.

The others are similar. These are the first-person singular forms for the middle/passive for ἵστημι, τίθημι, and ἵημι:

Pres. Indic.	Imperf. Indic.	Subj.	Opt.
ἵσταμαι	ἱστάμην	ἱστῶμαι	ἱσταίμην
τίθεμαι	ἐτιθέμην	τιθῶμαι	τιθείμην
ἵεμαι	ἱέμην	ἱῶμαι	ἱείμην

The present middle/passive infinitives are ἵστασθαι, τίθεσθαι, and ἵεσθαι and the participles are ἱστάμενος, τίθεμενος, ἱέμενος.

Exercise

Write out the three third-person forms of the present indicative middle/passive of ἵστημι, τίθημι, δύναμαι, δείκνυμι, κεῖμαι. Write the three third-person forms of the imperfect indicative middle/passive of ἀνατίθημι, ἀφίημι, ἀποδίδωμι, ἀνοίγνυμι. Write the three second-person forms of the present imperative middle/passive of δύναμαι, ἐπιδείκνυμι, ἀπόλλυμι.

XX.2 Aorist middle

Some athematic verbs have ordinary first aorists, as ἔμιξα from μίγνυμι. In this case the aorist middle is the same as for any other first aorist. Verbs with root aorists, whether athematic like ἵστημι (aorist ἔστην) or thematic like γιγνώσκω (aorist ἔγνων), do not have an aorist middle at all. The rest of the athematic verbs have second aorist forms in the middle, using the short vowel in the verb stem; when the ending begins with a vowel, the stem vowel and the ending vowel contract. These are the forms:

δίδωμι: third principal part ἔδωκα, aorist infinitive active δοῦναι, aorist infinitive middle δόσθαι, aorist participle middle δόμενος, -η, -ον.

τίθημι: third principal part ἔθηκα, aorist infinitive active θεῖναι, aorist infinitive middle θέσθαι, aorist participle middle θέμενος, -η, -ον.

ἵημι: third principal part ἧκα, aorist infinitive active εἷναι, aorist infinitive middle ἕσθαι, aorist participle middle ἕμενος, -η, -ον. Most of the aorist forms of this verb are only used in compounds, like συνίημι and so on.

	Indicative			Imperative		
singular						
1st	ἐδόμην	ἐθέμην	εἵμην			
2nd	ἔδου	ἔθου	εἷσο	δοῦ	θοῦ	οὗ
3rd	ἔδοτο	ἔθετο	εἷτο	δόσθω	θέσθω	ἕσθω
dual						
2nd	ἔδοσθον	ἔθεσθον	εἷσθον	δόσθον	θέσθον	ἕσθον
3rd	ἐδόσθην	ἐθέσθην	εἵσθην	δόσθων	θέσθων	ἕσθων
plural						
1st	ἐδόμεθα	ἐθέμεθα	εἵμεθα			
2nd	ἔδοσθε	ἔθεσθε	εἷσθε	δόσθε	θέσθε	ἕσθε
3rd	ἔδοντο	ἔθεντο	εἷντο	δόσθων	θέσθων	ἕσθων

The subjunctive and optative are as you would expect:

	Subjunctive			Optative		
singular						
1st	δῶμαι	θῶμαι	ὧμαι	δοίμην	θείμην	εἵμην
2nd	δῷ	θῇ	ἧ	δοῖο	θεῖο	εἷο
3rd	δῶται	θῆται	ἧται	δοῖτο	θεῖτο	εἷτο

and so on. Just as in the active, the aorist subjunctive, optative, and imperative middle are just like the corresponding present tense forms, except that they are formed from the aorist stem instead of from the reduplicated present stem. For example, compare δίδωται, διδοῖτο, διδόσθω and δῶται, δοῖτο, δόσθω.

Exercise

Write out the aorist infinitive middle and the three nominative singular forms of the aorist participle passive of ὑποτίθημι, συντίθημι, ἵημι, ἀπόλλυμι, ὄμνυμι.

XX.3 Possessive adjectives

In English, the **possessive adjectives** *my, your, her,* and so on are **determiners**, used in places where the definite or indefinite article would also be grammatically correct, as *I have my book* alongside *I have a book* or *I have the book*. In contexts like this, English would not use an adjective by itself: *I have black book* is not correct, but *I have the black book* or *I have my black book* is correct. And there cannot be two determiners for the same noun: *I have the my book* is not correct. Thus the possessive adjectives behave like the articles, and differently from other adjectives, in English.

In Greek, on the other hand, possessive adjectives work like ordinary adjectives rather than like the definite article: they are *not* determiners. They can be used with the article, just as an ordinary adjective like μέλας would be, or they can be used without the article if the noun phrase is indefinite. Thus we may write τὸ ἐμὸν βιβλίον ἔχω or τὸν ἐμὸν μέλαν βιβλίον ἔχω. A sentence like ἐμὸν βιβλίον ἔχω implies "I've got one of my books, a book of mine," since the noun phrase is not definite: there is no determiner to make it definite.

Greek generally does not use a possessive adjective if it's clear from context who the possessor is: given τὸ βιβλίον ἔχω, we normally assume it's the speaker's own book. Thus when Greek *does* use a possessive adjective, there is generally a sense of emphasis or contrast: τὸ ἐμὸν βιβλίον ἔχω implies something like "the book in my hand isn't yours" or "I'm prepared for class even if the rest of you aren't." Of course without context it's hard to tell exactly what is implied.

The possessive adjectives are all first-and-second declension adjectives like καλός. They are ἐμός, ἡμέτερος, σός, ὑμέτερος, ὅς, and σφέτερος. The third-person form ὅς ("his, her, its") is poetic, not used in Attic prose, so you should not use it in your own writing. The forms for a dual possessor are also poetic, νωίτερος ("our" when there are two of us) and σφωίτερος ("your" for two of you); there is no attested form for "their" with two owners.

Like any other adjective, the possessive adjectives agree with the noun they modify in gender, case, and number. Do not confuse the "number" of the owner with the number of the adjective: τὸν ὑμέτερον ἀδελφὸν ὁρῶ (one brother of several people), τὸν σὸν ἀδελφὸν ὁρῶ (one brother of one person), τοὺς ὑμετέρους ἀδελφοὺς ὁρῶ (several brothers of several people), τοὺς σοὺς ἀδελφοὺς ὁρῶ (several brothers of one person).

It is also possible to use the genitive case of a personal pronoun to indicate possession, in predicate position: τὸ βιβλίον μοῦ ἔχω. The short form μοῦ is normal in this sense, rather than the ordinary form ἐμοῦ, and the enclitic form μου is also common.

XX.4 Vocabulary

VERBS

διακονέω, διακονήσω, ἐδιακόνησα, δεδιακόνηκα, δεδιακόνημαι, ἐδιακονήθην, wait on, serve, supply (cp. *deacon*)

θάπτω, θάψω, ἔθαψα, τέθαφα, τέθαμμαι, ἐτάφην, bury

καίω, καύσω, ἔκαυσα, κέκαυκα, κέκαυμαι, ἐκαύθην, burn (cp. *caustic*)

κατ-άγω, lead down, bring down

πορεύω, πορεύσω, ἐπόρευσα, πεπόρευκα, πεπόρευμαι, ἐπορεύθην, transport, bring; in middle, go, travel

στορέννῡμι, στορῶ, ἔστρωσα, – , ἔστρωμαι, – , spread out, strew (cp. *strew, straw*)

συμ-βαίνω, happen; κατὰ συμβεβηκός, by chance.

NOUNS

ἄκυρον, -ου, τό, straw

ἡδονή, -ῆς, ἡ, pleasure

θυμός, -οῦ, ὁ, spirit, consciousness, heart, breath, life (cp. L. *fumus*)

κόλαξ, -ακος, ὁ, flatterer

μηχανή, -ῆς, ἡ, contrivance, invention, machine (L. *machina* is a derivative)

πάθος, -ους, τό, anything that happens to one, what one experiences; feeling, emotion (cp. *pathos, pathetic*)

πόντος, -ου, ὁ, sea (cp. *Hellespont*)

τυρός, -οῦ, ὁ, cheese (cp. *tyrosine*)

χθών, χθονός, ἡ, earth, land (cp. *chthonic*, L. *humus, homo*)

ADJECTIVES

ἀθάνατος, -ον, immortal, undying

ἁπλοῦς, ἁπλῆ, ἁπλοῦν, simple

ἀφανής, -ές, invisible, vanished

ἐμός, -ή, -όν, my

ἔνορκος, -ον, sworn, bound by oath

ἡμέτερος, -α, -ον, our

ὀλίγος, -η, -ον, small, little, few (cp. *oligarchy*)

πολιός, -ά, -όν, white; serene; hoary, old

σός, σή, σόν, your, thy (belonging to one person)

σφέτερος, -α, -ον, their

ὑμέτερος, -α, -ον, your (belonging to more than one person)

χαλεπός, -ή, -όν, difficult, severe

ADVERBS

ἅμα, at the same time, together

Notes on the vocabulary

From κόλαξ are derived the verb κολακεύω and the noun κολακεία.

The adjective ἁπλοῦς is contracted, like χρυσοῦς.

XX.5 Reading

1. *Winter*

γίγνεται δὲ χειμών, Δαφνίδι καὶ Χλόῃ τοῦ πολέμου πικρότερος. ἐξαίφνης γὰρ περιπεσοῦσα χιὼν πολλὴ πάσας μὲν ἀπέκλησε τὰς ὁδούς, πάντας δὲ κατέκλησε τοὺς γεωργούς. λάβροι μὲν οἱ χείμαρροι κατέρρεον, ἐπεπήγει δὲ κρύσταλλος· τὰ δένδρα πλήρη ἦν χιόνος, ἡ γῆ πᾶσα ἀφανὴς ἦν πλὴν περὶ πηγάς που καὶ ῥεύματα. οὔτ᾽ ἀγέλην ἐς νομὴν ἦγεν οὐδείς, οὔτ᾽ αὐτὸς προὔβαινε τῶν θυρῶν, ἀλλὰ πῦρ καύσαντες μέγα περὶ ᾠδὰς ἀλεκτρυόνων, οἱ μὲν λίνον ἔστρεφον, οἱ δ᾽ αἰγῶν τρίχας ἔκρεκον, οἱ δὲ παγίδας ὀρνίθων ἠργάζοντο. τότε βοῶν ἐπὶ φάτναις φροντὶς ἦν ἄχυρον ἐσθιόντων, αἰγῶν καὶ προβάτων ἐν τοῖς σηκοῖς φυλλάδας, ὑῶν ἐν τοῖς συφεοῖς βαλάνους. τῇ δὲ Χλόῃ ἀεὶ συνῆν ἡ μήτηρ, ἔριά τε ξαίνειν διδάσκουσα καὶ ἀτράκτους στρέφειν.

> *Daphnis and Chloe* 3.3.
>
> ἐξαίφνης, suddenly. περι-πίπτω, fall around. ἀπο-κλήω, close up, close off. ὁδός, -οῦ, ἡ, road. λάβρος, -ον, vehement, blustery, violent. χείμαρρος, -ου, ὁ, torrent, flood, specifically of a stream swollen with melted snow. πήγνῡμι, πήξω, ἔπηξα, πέπηγα, – , ἐπήχθην, freeze, fasten. κρύσταλλος, -ου, ὁ, ice. πλήρης, -ες, full. ῥεῦμα, -ατος, τό, stream. παγίς, παγίδος, ἡ, trap. φάτνη, -ης, ἡ, manger. φροντίς, -ίδος, ἡ, concern, care, thought. σηκός, -οῦ, ὁ, sheepfold. φυλλάς, φυλλάδος, ἡ, foliage, leafiness. ὗς, ὑός, ὁ, ἡ, pig. συφεός, -οῦ, ὁ, pigsty. βάλανος, -ου, ἡ, acorn. ἔριον, -ου, τό, wool. ξαίνω, ξανῶ, ἔξηνα, – , – , – , card (wool), comb out, scratch.

2. Ἴσθμια καὶ Πυθοῖ Διοφῶν ὁ Φίλωνος ἐνίκα
   ἅλμα, ποδωκείαν, δίσκον, ἄκοντα, πάλην.

> An epigram by Simonides for an athletic victor. The five events in the second line make up the pentathlon.
>
> ἅλμα, -ατος, τό, jump. ποδωκεία, -ας, ἡ, speed; sprint race. δίσκος, -ου, ὁ, discus. ἄκων, -οντος, τό, javelin (don't confuse with the adjective ἄκων, unwilling). πάλη, -ης, ἡ, wrestling.

3. ἐν δὲ τῷ αὐτῷ χειμῶνι, Ἀθηναῖοι, τῷ πατρίῳ νόμῳ χρώμενοι, δημοσίᾳ ταφὰς
   ἐποιήσαντο τῶν ἐν τῷδε τῷ πολέμῳ πρώτων ἀποθανόντων τρόπῳ τοιῷδε. τὰ μὲν
   ὀστᾶ προτίθενται τῶν ἀπογενομένων πρότριτα σκηνὴν ποιήσαντες, καὶ ἐπιφέρει τῷ
   αὑτοῦ ἕκαστος ἤν τι βούληται. ἐπειδὰν δὲ ἡ ἐκφορὰ ᾖ, λάρνακας κυπαρισσίνας ἄγουσιν
   ἅμαξαι, φυλῆς ἑκάστης μίαν. ἔνεστι δὲ τὰ ὀστᾶ ἧς ἕκαστος ἦν φυλῆς. μία δὲ κλίνη
   κενὴ φέρεται ἐστρωμένη τῶν ἀφανῶν, οἳ ἂν μὴ εὑρεθῶσιν ἐς ἀναίρεσιν. συνεκφέρει
   δὲ ὁ βουλόμενος καὶ ἀστῶν καὶ ξένων, καὶ γυναῖκες πάρεισιν αἱ προσήκουσαι ἐπὶ τὸν
   τάφον ὀλοφυρόμεναι. τιθέασιν οὖν ἐς τὸ δημόσιον σῆμα, ὅ ἐστιν ἐπὶ τοῦ καλλίστου
   προαστείου τῆς πόλεως, καὶ αἰεὶ ἐν αὐτῷ θάπτουσι τοὺς ἐκ τῶν πολέμων, πλήν γε
   τοὺς ἐν Μαραθῶνι· ἐκείνων δὲ διαπρεπῆ τὴν ἀρετὴν κρίναντες αὐτοῦ καὶ τὸν τάφον
   ἐποίησαν. ἐπειδὰν δὲ κρύψωσι γῇ, ἀνὴρ ᾑρημένος ὑπὸ τῆς πόλεως, ὃς ἂν γνώμῃ τε
   δοκῇ μὴ ἀξύνετος εἶναι καὶ ἀξιώσει προήκῃ, λέγει ἐπ’ αὐτοῖς ἔπαινον τὸν πρέποντα·
   μετὰ δὲ τοῦτο ἀπέρχονται. ὧδε μὲν θάπτουσιν· καὶ διὰ παντὸς τοῦ πολέμου, ὁπότε
   συμβαίη αὐτοῖς, ἐχρῶντο τῷ νόμῳ. ἐπὶ δ’ οὖν τοῖς πρώτοις τοῖσδε Περικλῆς ὁ
   Ξανθίππου ᾑρέθη λέγειν. καὶ ἐπειδὴ καιρὸς ἐλάμβανε, προελθὼν ἀπὸ τοῦ σήματος
   ἐπὶ βῆμα ὑψηλὸν πεποιημένον, ὅπως ἀκούοιτο ὡς ἐπὶ πλεῖστον τοῦ ὁμίλου, ἔλεγε.

   Thucydides 2.34.

   δημόσιος, -α, -ον, public; δημοσίᾳ, at public expense. ταφή, -ῆς, ἡ, burial,
   funeral. προ-τίθημι, lay out (a body before burial), display. πρότριτα, for three
   days, three days beforehand. ἐκφορά, -ᾶς, ἡ, act of carrying out the body
   for burial. λάρναξ, λάρνακος, ἡ, box, coffin. κυπαρίσσινος, -η, -ον, made of
   cypress wood. φυλή, -ῆς, ἡ, tribe, one of the ten divisions of the Athenian
   people. κενός, -ή, -όν, empty. ὀλοφύρομαι, ὀλοφυροῦμαι, ὠλοφυράμην, – ,
   – , – , wail, lament, weep. σῆμα, -ατος, τό, sign, indication; tomb, gravestone.
   προάστειον, -ου, τό, suburb, outlying neighborhood. διαπρεπής, -ές, excellent,
   outstanding. κρύπτω, κρύψω, ἔκρυψα, κέκρυφα, κέκρυμμαι, ἐκρύφθην, hide,
   cover. ἀξύνετος, -ον, stupid, unintelligent. ἀξίωσις, -εως, ἡ, worth, value. προ-
   ήκω, be first, come forth. ἔπαινος, -ου, ὁ, praise, eulogy. βῆμα, -ατος, τό, step,
   platform. ὑψηλός, -ή, -όν, high. ὅμιλος, -ου, ὁ, crowd, group.

4. πολλὰ τὰ δεινὰ κοὐδὲν ἀνθρώπου δεινότερον πέλει.
   τοῦτο καὶ πολιοῦ πέραν   335
   πόντου χειμερίῳ νότῳ
   χωρεῖ, περιβρυχίοισιν
   περῶν ὑπ’ οἴδμασιν. θεῶν
   τε τὰν ὑπερτάταν, Γᾶν
   ἄφθιτον, ἀκαμάταν, ἀποτρύεται
   ἰλλομένων ἀρότρων ἔτος εἰς ἔτος
   ἱππείῳ γένει πολεύων.   340

   κουφονόων τε φῦλον ὀρ-
   νίθων ἀμφιβαλὼν ἄγει
   καὶ θηρῶν ἀγρίων ἔθνη   345
   πόντου τ’ εἰναλίαν φύσιν
   σπείραισι δικτυοκλώστοις,
   περιφραδὴς ἀνήρ· κρατεῖ
   δὲ μηχαναῖς ἀγραύλου

θηρὸς ὀρεσσιβάτα, λασιαύχενά θ᾽   350
   ἵππον ὀχμάζεται ἀμφὶ λόφον ζυγῷ
οὔρειόν τ᾽ ἀκμῆτα ταῦρον.

καὶ φθέγμα καὶ ἀνεμόεν   355
   φρόνημα καὶ ἀστυνόμους
ὀργὰς ἐδιδάξατο καὶ δυσαύλων
πάγων ὑπαίθρεια καὶ
δύσομβρα φεύγειν βέλη
παντοπόρος· ἄπορος ἐπ᾽ οὐδὲν ἔρχεται
   τὸ μέλλον· Ἄιδα μόνον   360
φεῦξιν οὐκ ἐπάξεται·
νόσων δ᾽ ἀμηχάνων φυγὰς
ξυμπέφρασται.

σοφόν τι τὸ μηχανόεν   365
   τέχνας ὑπὲρ ἐλπίδ᾽ ἔχων
τοτὲ μὲν κακόν, ἄλλοτ᾽ ἐπ᾽ ἐσθλὸν ἕρπει,
νόμους γεραίρων χθονὸς
   θεῶν τ᾽ ἔνορκον δίκαν,
ὑψίπολις· ἄπολις ὅτῳ τὸ μὴ καλὸν   370
   ξύνεστι τόλμας χάριν.
μήτ᾽ ἐμοὶ παρέστιος
γένοιτο μήτ᾽ ἴσον φρονῶν   375
ὃς τάδ᾽ ἔρδει.

Sophocles, *Antigone* 333-375. Each line is a colon (not a period); see Appendix 4.

First strophe: **πέλω** = εἰμί. **πέρᾱν**, across, beyond (prep. + gen., but here after its object). **νότος, -ου, ὁ**, south wind. **περιβρύχιος, -ον**, engulfing, overwhelming. **οἶδμα, -ατος, τό**, wave, swell of the sea. **ὑπέρτατος, -η, -ον**, highest, uppermost (superlative formed from ὑπέρ). **ἄφθιτος, -ον**, indestructible, imperishable. **ἀκάματος, -η, -ον**, untiring, indefatigable. **ἀποτρύω**, rub away, wear out. **ἴλλω**, roll, cause to revolve (present system only). **ἵππειος, -α, -ον**, equestrian, relating to horses. **πολεύω, πολεύσω, ἐπόλευσα, –, –, –**, turn up, turn over.

First antistrophe: **κουφόνοος, -ον**, light-minded, unthinking, flighty. **φῦλον, -ου, τό**, race, tribe. **ἀμφι-βάλλω**, throw (something) around, embrace, ensnare. **ἔθνος, -ους, τό**, type, nation, species. **εἰνάλιος** = ἐνάλιος, -α, -ον, marine, of the sea, Ionic dialect form. **σπείρω, σπερῶ, ἔσπειρα, ἔσπαρκα, ἔσπαρμαι, ἐσπάρην**, sow, scatter. **δικτυόκλωστος, -ον**, mesh, woven like a net. **περιφραδής, -ές**, thoughtful, skillful. **κρατέω, κρατήσω, ἐκράτησα, κεκράτηκα, κεκράτημαι, ἐκρατήθην**, be strong, be powerful, rule, conquer, master. **ἄγραυλος, -ον**, field-dwelling, rustic. **ὀρεσσιβάτης, -ου, ὁ**, one who roams the mountains; ὀρεσσιβάτᾱ has a Doric genitive ending. **λασιαύχην, λασιαύχενος, ὁ**, one with a shaggy neck or mane (λάσιος, -α, -ον, shaggy). **ὀχμάζω, ὀχμάσω, ὤχμασα, –, –, –**, grip, hold on to, rein in, control. **λόφος, -ου, ὁ**, back of the neck, nape. **ὄρειος, -α, -ον**, mountain-dwelling, from the mountains; οὔρειον is an epic dialect form. **ἀκμής, -ές**, untiring, unwearied.

Second strophe: **φθέγμα, -ατος, τό**, voice, sound. **ἠνεμόεις, -εσσα, -εν**, windy; ἀνεμόεν is a Doric form. **ἀστυνόμος, -ον**, city-protecting. **ὀργή, -ῆς, ἡ**, character, disposition, natural passion. **δύσαυλος, -ον**, inhospitable, not like a palace hall. **πάγος, -ου, ὁ**, frost, ice. **ὑπαίθρειος, -ον**, under the sky, out in the open. **δύσομβρος, -ον**, stormy. **βέλος, -ους, τό**, dart, shaft, thrown weapon. **ἄπορος, -ον**, at a loss, unable to find a way (**πόρος, -ου, τό**, way to pass, means of doing something); **παντόπορος, -ον** is the opposite. **φεῦξις, -εως, ἡ**, refuge, escape; **φυγή, -ῆς, ἡ** below is a synonym. **ἐπ-άγω**, bring in, procure. **νόσος, -ου, ἡ**, sickness, illness. **συμ-φράζομαι**, consider, take counsel with; **ξυν-** is an Attic form of the prefix, as also in **ξύνεστι** = **σύνεστι** below.

Second antistrophe: **μηχανόεις, -εσσα, -εν**, ingenious, able to contrive things. **γεραίρω, γεραρῶ, ἐγέρηρα, – , – , –**, reward. **ὑψίπολις** and **ἄπολις** are compounds formed just for this lyric. **παρέστιος, -ον**, at one's hearth, in one's house, domestic. **ἔρδω, ἔρξω, εἶρξα, ἔοργα, – , –**, do.

5. ἡ δὲ τῶν νέων φιλία δι᾽ ἡδονὴν εἶναι δοκεῖ· κατὰ πάθος γὰρ οὗτοι ζῶσι, καὶ μάλιστα διώκουσι τὸ ἡδὺ αὐτοῖς καὶ τὸ παρόν· τῆς ἡλικίας δὲ μεταπιπτούσης καὶ τὰ ἡδέα γίγνεται ἕτερα. διὸ ταχέως γίγνονται φίλοι καὶ παύονται· ἅμα γὰρ τῷ ἡδεῖ ἡ φιλία μεταπίπτει, τῆς δὲ τοιαύτης ἡδονῆς ταχεῖα ἡ μεταβολή. καὶ ἐρωτικοὶ δ᾽ οἱ νέοι· κατὰ πάθος γὰρ καὶ δι᾽ ἡδονὴν τὸ πολὺ τῆς ἐρωτικῆς· διόπερ φιλοῦσι καὶ ταχέως παύονται, πολλάκις τῆς αὐτῆς ἡμέρας μεταπίπτοντες. συνημερεύειν δὲ καὶ συζῆν οὗτοι βούλονται· γίγνεται γὰρ αὐτοῖς τὸ κατὰ τὴν φιλίαν οὕτως.

τελεία δ᾽ ἐστὶν ἡ τῶν ἀγαθῶν φιλία καὶ κατ᾽ ἀρετὴν ὁμοίων. οὗτοι γὰρ τἀγαθὰ ὁμοίως βούλονται ἀλλήλοις ᾗ ἀγαθοί, ἀγαθοὶ δ᾽ εἰσὶ καθ᾽ αὑτούς. οἱ δὲ βουλόμενοι τἀγαθὰ τοῖς φίλοις ἐκείνων ἕνεκα μάλιστα φίλοι· δι᾽ αὑτοὺς γὰρ οὕτως ἔχουσι, καὶ οὐ κατὰ συμβεβηκός. διαμένει οὖν ἡ τούτων φιλία ἕως ἂν ἀγαθοὶ ὦσιν, ἡ δ᾽ ἀρετὴ μόνιμον.

καὶ ἔστιν ἑκάτερος ἁπλῶς ἀγαθὸς καὶ τῷ φίλῳ. οἱ γὰρ ἀγαθοὶ καὶ ἁπλῶς ἀγαθοὶ καὶ ἀλλήλοις ὠφέλιμοι. ὁμοίως δὲ καὶ ἡδεῖς· καὶ γὰρ ἁπλῶς οἱ ἀγαθοὶ ἡδεῖς καὶ ἀλλήλοις. ἑκάστῳ γὰρ καθ᾽ ἡδονήν εἰσιν αἱ οἰκεῖαι πράξεις καὶ αἱ τοιαῦται, τῶν ἀγαθῶν δὲ αἱ αὐταὶ ἢ ὅμοιαι.

ἡ τοιαύτη δὲ φιλία μόνιμος εὐλόγως ἐστίν· συνάπτει γὰρ ἐν αὐτῇ πάνθ᾽ ὅσα τοῖς φίλοις δεῖ ὑπάρχειν. πᾶσα γὰρ φιλία δι᾽ ἀγαθόν ἐστιν ἢ δι᾽ ἡδονήν, ἢ ἁπλῶς ἢ τῷ φιλοῦντι, καὶ καθ᾽ ὁμοιότητά τινα· ταύτῃ δὲ πάνθ᾽ ὑπάρχει τὰ εἰρημένα καθ᾽ αὑτούς· ταύτῃ γὰρ ὅμοια καὶ τὰ λοιπά, τό τε ἁπλῶς ἀγαθὸν καὶ ἡδὺ ἁπλῶς ἐστίν, μάλιστα δὲ ταῦτα φιλητά· καὶ τὸ φιλεῖν δὴ καὶ ἡ φιλία ἐν τούτοις μάλιστα καὶ ἀρίστη. σπανίας δ᾽ εἰκὸς τὰς τοιαύτας εἶναι· ὀλίγοι γὰρ οἱ τοιοῦτοι.

Aristotle, *Nichomachean Ethics* 8, 1156a-b

κατὰ πάθος ζῶσι = οἱ νέοι τοῦ βίου ἄρχουσι τοῖς πάθεσι. **ἡλικία, -ας, ἡ**, age, time of life. **μετα-πίπτω**, undergo a change, fall into something different. **ἐρωτικός, -ή, -όν**, having to do with love, erotic. **συνημερεύω**, pass the day with (+ dative, predictable principal parts). **συ-ζάω**, live with. **τέλειος, -α, -ον**, complete, perfect. **δια-μένω**, remain, continue. **μόνιμος, -ον**, steadfast, constant. **πρᾶξις, -εως, ἡ**, deed, act of doing, business, matter, action. **εὔλογος, -ον**, reasonable, probable. **συν-άπτω**, fasten together, unite. **ὑπ-άρχω**, exist. **ὁμοιότης, ὁμοιότητος, ἡ**, similarity, likeness. **φιλότης, -ητος, ἡ**, friendship. **σπάνιος, -α, -ον**, rare.

6. διάλογος Διὸς καὶ Γανυμήδους

Ζεύς· ἄγε, ὦ Γανύμηδες — ἥκομεν γὰρ ἔνθα ἐχρῆν — ὁρᾷς με νῦν οὐκέτι ῥάμφος ἀγκύλον ἔχοντα οὐδ᾽ ὄνυχας ὀξεῖς οὐδὲ πτερά, οἷος ἐφαινόμην σοι πτηνὸς εἶναι δοκῶν.

Γανυμήδης· ἄνθρωπε, οὐκ ἀετὸς ἄρτι ἦσθα καὶ καταπτάμενος ἥρπασάς με ἀπὸ μέσου τοῦ ποιμνίου; πῶς οὖν τὰ μὲν πτερά σοι ἐκεῖνα ἐξερρύηκε, σὺ δὲ ἄλλος ἤδη ἀναπέφηνας;

Ζεύς· ἀλλ᾽ οὔτε ἄνθρωπον ὁρᾷς, ὦ μειράκιον, οὔτε ἀετόν, ὁ δὲ πάντων βασιλεὺς τῶν θεῶν οὗτός εἰμι πρὸς τὸν καιρὸν ἀλλάξας ἐμαυτόν.

Γανυμήδης· Τί φής; σὺ γὰρ εἶ ὁ Πὰν ἐκεῖνος; εἶτα πῶς σύριγγα οὐκ ἔχεις οὐδὲ κέρατα οὐδὲ λάσιος εἶ τὰ σκέλη;

Ζεύς· μόνον γὰρ ἐκεῖνον ἡγῇ θεόν;

Γανυμήδης· ναί· καὶ θύομέν γε αὐτῷ ἔνορχον τράγον ἐπὶ τὸ σπήλαιον ἄγοντες, ἔνθα ἔστηκε· σὺ δὲ ἀνδραποδιστής τις εἶναί μοι δοκεῖς.

Ζεύς· εἰπέ μοι· Διὸς δὲ οὐκ ἤκουσας ὄνομα, οὐδὲ βωμὸν εἶδες ἐν τῷ Γαργάρῳ τοῦ ὕοντος καὶ βροντῶντος καὶ ἀστραπὰς ποιοῦντος;

Γανυμήδης· σύ, ὦ βέλτιστε, φῂς εἶναι, ὃς πρῴην κατέχεας ἡμῖν τὴν πολλὴν χάλαζαν, ὁ οἰκεῖν ὑπεράνω λεγόμενος, ὁ ποιούμενος τὸν ψόφον, ᾧ τὸν κριὸν ὁ πατὴρ ἔθυσεν; εἶτα τί ἀδικήσαντά με ἀνήρπασας, ὦ βασιλεῦ τῶν θεῶν; τὰ δὲ πρόβατα ἴσως οἱ λύκοι διαρπάσονται ἤδη ἐρήμοις ἐπιπεσόντες.

Ζεύς· ἔτι γὰρ μέλει σοι τῶν προβάτων, ἀθανάτῳ γεγενημένῳ, καὶ ἐνταῦθα συνεσομένῳ μεθ᾽ ἡμῶν;

Γανυμήδης· τί λέγεις; οὐ γὰρ κατάξεις με ἤδη ἐς τὴν Ἴδην τήμερον;

Ζεύς· οὐδαμῶς· ἐπεὶ μάτην ἀετὸς ἂν εἴην ἀντὶ θεοῦ γεγενημένος.

Γανυμήδης· οὐκοῦν ἐπιζητήσει με ὁ πατὴρ καὶ ἀγανακτήσει μὴ εὑρίσκων, καὶ πληγὰς ὕστερον λήψομαι καταλιπὼν τὸ ποίμνιον.

Ζεύς· ποῦ γὰρ ἐκεῖνος ὄψεταί σε;

Γανυμήδης· μηδαμῶς· ποθῶ γὰρ ἤδη αὐτόν. εἰ δὲ ἀπάξεις με, ὑπισχνοῦμαί σοι καὶ ἄλλον παρ᾽ αὐτοῦ κριὸν τυθήσεσθαι λύτρα ὑπὲρ ἐμοῦ. ἔχομεν δὲ τὸν τριετῆ, τὸν μέγαν, ὃς ἡγεῖται πρὸς τὴν νομήν.

Ζεύς· ὡς ἀφελὴς ὁ παῖς ἐστι καὶ ἁπλοῦς καὶ αὐτὸ δὴ τοῦτο παῖς ἔτι. — ἀλλ᾽, ὦ Γανύμηδες, ἐκεῖνα μὲν πάντα χαίρειν ἔα καὶ ἐπιλάθου αὐτῶν, τοῦ ποιμνίου καὶ τῆς Ἴδης. σὺ δὲ — ἤδη γὰρ ἐπουράνιος εἶ — πολλὰ εὖ ποιήσεις ἐντεῦθεν καὶ τὸν πατέρα καὶ πατρίδα, καὶ ἀντὶ μὲν τυροῦ καὶ γάλακτος ἀμβροσίαν ἔδῃ καὶ νέκταρ πίῃ. τοῦτο μέντοι καὶ τοῖς ἄλλοις ἡμῖν αὐτὸς παρέξεις ἐγχέων. τὸ δὲ μέγιστον, οὐκέτι ἄνθρωπος, ἀλλ᾽ ἀθάνατος γενήσῃ, καὶ ἀστέρα σου φαίνεσθαι ποιήσω κάλλιστον, καὶ ὅλως εὐδαίμων ἔσῃ.

Γανυμήδης· ἐὰν δὲ παίζειν ἐπιθυμήσω, τίς συμπαίξεταί μοι; ἐν γὰρ τῇ Ἴδῃ πολλοὶ ἡλικιῶται ἦμεν.

Ζεύς· ἔχεις κἀνταῦθα τὸν συμπαιξόμενόν σοι τουτονὶ τὸν Ἔρωτα καὶ ἀστραγάλους μάλα πολλούς. θάρρει μόνον καὶ φαιδρὸς ἴσθι καὶ μηδὲν ἐπιπόθει τῶν κάτω.

Γανυμήδης· τί δαὶ ὑμῖν χρήσιμος ἂν γενοίμην; ἢ ποιμαίνειν δεήσει κἀνταῦθα;

Ζεύς· οὔκ, ἀλλ' οἰνοχοήσεις καὶ ἐπὶ τοῦ νέκταρος τετάξῃ καὶ ἐπιμελήσῃ τοῦ συμποσίου.

Γανυμήδης· τοῦτο μὲν οὐ χαλεπόν· οἶδα γὰρ ὡς χρὴ ἐγχέαι τὸ γάλα καὶ ἀναδοῦναι τὸ κισσύβιον.

Ζεύς· ἰδού, πάλιν οὗτος γάλακτος μνημονεύει καὶ ἀνθρώποις διακονήσεσθαι οἴεται· ταυτὶ δ' ὁ οὐρανός ἐστι, καὶ πίνομεν, ὥσπερ ἔφην, τὸ νέκταρ.

Γανυμήδης· ἥδιον, ὦ Ζεῦ, τοῦ γάλακτος;

Ζεύς· εἴσῃ μετ' ὀλίγον καὶ γευσάμενος οὐκέτι ποθήσεις τὸ γάλα. νῦν δὲ ἄπαγε αὐτόν, ὦ Ἑρμῆ, καὶ πιόντα τῆς ἀθανασίας ἄγε οἰνοχοήσοντα ἡμῖν διδάξας πρότερον ὡς χρὴ ὀρέγειν τὸν σκύφον.

This is an excerpt from Lucian's *Dialogues of the Gods.*

ῥάμφος, -ους, τό, beak of a bird. ἀγκύλος, -η, -ον, curved. ὄνυξ, ὄνυχος, ὁ, claw, talon, fingernail, fingertip. πτερόν, -οῦ, τό, wing, feather. πτηνός, -ή, -όν, winged. ἀετός, -οῦ, ὁ, eagle. κατα-πέτομαι, κατα-πτήσομαι, κατ-επτάμην, – , – , – , fly down. ποίμνιον, -ου, τό, flock. ἐκ-ρέω, flow out, disappear. ἀνα-φαίνω, show, appear, reveal. κέρας, κέρατος, τό, horn. λάσιος, -α, -ον, shaggy, hairy. σκέλος, -ους, τό, leg. ἔνορχος, -ον, uncastrated. σπήλαιον, -ου, τό, cave. ἀνδραποδιστής, -οῦ, ὁ, slave-dealer, kidnapper. βωμός, -οῦ, ὁ, altar. πρῷος, -α, -ον, early. κατα-χέω, pour down. ὑπερ-άνω, up above. ψόφος, -ου, ὁ, noise, sound. κρῑός, -οῦ, ὁ, ram. ἐρῆμος, -η, -ον, empty, deserted, solitary. ἐπι-πίπτω, fall on, attack. μάτην, in vain. ἐπι-ζητέω, seek, wish for, miss. ἀγανακτέω, ἀγανακτήσω, ἠγανάκτησα, ἠγανάκτηκα, ἠγανάκτημαι, ἠγανακτήθην, be irritated. ποθέω, ποθήσω, ἐπόθησα, – , – , – , long for, miss, desire; ἐπι-ποθέω is a synonym. ἀπ-άγω, lead away, bring home. ὑπ-ισχνέομαι, ὑπο-σχήσομαι, ὑπ-εσχόμην, – , ὑπ-έσχημαι, – , promise. λύτρον, -ου, τό, ransom. τριετής, -ές, three years old; occurring every three years. ἐπι-λήθομαι, ἐπι-λήσομαι, ἐπελαθόμην, – , ἐπι-λέλησμαι, – , forget. ἐπουράνιος, -ον, heavenly, in heaven. ἀμβροσία, -ας, ἡ, ambrosia, a divine food. νέκταρ, -αρος, τό, nectar, a divine beverage. ἀστήρ, ἀστέρος, ὁ, star. εὐδαίμων, -ον, fortunate, happy, blessed. ἐπι-θυμέω, ἐπι-θυμήσω, ἐπι-εθύμησα, – , – , – , desire, want, covet. συμ-παίζω, play with. ἡλικιώτης, -ου, ὁ, person of the same age. ἀστράγαλος, -ου, ὁ, vertebra, knucklebone; gaming die. θαρρέω, θαρρήσω, ἐθάρρησα, τεθάρρηκα, – , – , be brave, bold, cheerful. δαί, particle expressing surprise or curiosity, used in questions. οἰνοχοέω, -ήσω, – , – , – , – , pour wine. συμπόσιον, -ου, τό, drinking party. κισσύβιον, -ου, τό, drinking cup made of ivy wood. γεύω, γεύσω, ἔγευσα, – , γέγευμαι, – , give a taste; in middle, taste. ὀρέγω, ὀρέξω, ὤρεξα, – , – , – , stretch out, reach out. σκύφος, -ου, ὁ, cup.

7. *περὶ τῆς κολακείας*

τὴν δὲ κολακείαν ὑπολάβοι ἄν τις ὁμιλίαν αἰσχρὰν εἶναι, συμφέρουσαν δὲ τῷ κολακεύοντι, τὸν δὲ κόλακα τοιοῦτόν τινα, ὥστε ἅμα πορευόμενον εἰπεῖν· "ἐνθυμῇ, ὡς ἀποβλέπουσι πρὸς δὲ οἱ ἄνθρωποι; τοῦτο δὲ οὐδενὶ τῶν ἐν τῇ πόλει γίγνεται πλὴν σοί." "ηὐδοκίμεις χθὲς ἐν τῇ στοᾷ." πλειόνων γὰρ ἢ τριάκοντα ἀνθρώπων καθημένων καὶ ἐμπεσόντος λόγου, τίς εἴη βέλτιστος, ἀπ' αὐτοῦ ἀρξαμένους πάντας ἐπὶ τὸ ὄνομα αὐτοῦ κατενεχθῆναι. καὶ ἄλλα τοιαῦτα λέγων ἀπὸ τοῦ ἱματίου ἀφελεῖν κροκύδα, καὶ ἐάν τι πρὸς τὸ τρίχωμα τῆς κεφαλῆς ὑπὸ πνεύματος προσενεχθῇ ἄχυρον, καρφολογῆσαι. καὶ ἐπιγελάσας δὲ εἰπεῖν· "ὁρᾷς; ὅτι δυοῖν σοι ἡμερῶν οὐκ ἐντετύχηκα, πολιῶν ἔσχηκας τὸν πώγωνα μεστόν, καίπερ εἴ τις καὶ ἄλλος ἔχεις πρὸς τὰ ἔτη μέλαιναν τὴν τρίχα." καὶ λέγοντος δὲ αὐτοῦ τι τοὺς ἄλλους σιωπᾶν κελεῦσαι, καὶ ἐπαινέσαι δὲ ἀκούοντος, καὶ ἐπισημήνασθαι δέ, εἰ παύσαιτο, "ὀρθῶς," καὶ σκώψαντι ψυχρῶς ἐπιγελάσαι τό τε ἱμάτιον ὦσαι εἰς τὸ στόμα ὡς δὴ οὐ δυνάμενος κατασχεῖν τὸν γέλωτα. καὶ τοὺς ἀπαντῶντας ἐπιστῆναι κελεῦσαι, ἕως ἂν αὐτὸς παρέλθῃ. καὶ τοῖς παιδίοις μῆλα καὶ ἀπίους πριάμενος εἰσενέγκας δοῦναι ὁρῶντος αὐτοῦ, καὶ φιλήσας δὲ εἰπεῖν· "χρηστοῦ πατρὸς νεοττία." καὶ συνωνούμενος ἐπὶ κρηπῖδας τὸν πόδα φῆσαι εἶναι εὐρυθμότερον τοῦ ὑποδήματος. καὶ πορευομένου πρός τινα τῶν φίλων προδραμὼν εἰπεῖν ὅτι "πρὸς σὲ ἔρχεται," καὶ ἀναστρέψας ὅτι "προσήγγελκα." ἀμέλει δὲ καὶ τὰ ἐκ γυναικείας ἀγορᾶς διακονῆσαι δυνατὸς ἀπνευστί. καὶ τῶν ἑστιωμένων πρῶτος ἐπαινέσαι τὸν οἶνον καὶ παραμένων εἰπεῖν· "ὡς μαλακῶς ἐσθίεις," καὶ ἄρας τι τῶν ἀπὸ τῆς τραπέζης φῆσαι· "τουτὶ ἄρα ὡς χρηστόν ἐστι," καὶ ἐρωτῆσαι, μὴ ῥιγοῖ, καὶ εἰ ἐπιβάλλεσθαι βούλεται, καὶ εἴ τι περιστείλῃ αὐτόν· καὶ μὴν ταῦτα λέγων πρὸς τὸ οὖς προσπίπτων διαψιθυρίζειν· καὶ εἰς ἐκεῖνον ἀποβλέπων τοῖς ἄλλοις λαλεῖν. καὶ τοῦ παιδὸς ἐν τῷ θεάτρῳ ἀφελόμενος τὰ προσκεφάλαια αὐτὸς ὑποστρῶσαι. καὶ τὴν οἰκίαν φῆσαι εὖ ἠρχιτεκτονῆσθαι καὶ τὸν ἀγρὸν εὖ πεφυτεῦσθαι καὶ τὴν εἰκόνα ὁμοίαν εἶναι.

Theophrastus, *Characters* 2, the flatterer.

ὑπο-λαμβάνω, assume, understand. ὁμιλία, -ας, ἡ, interaction, association. ἐν-θυμέομαι, ἐν-θυμήσομαι, – , – , ἐν-τεθύμημαι, ἐν-εθυμήθην, take to heart, consider. ἀπο-βλέπω, look at. εὐδοκιμέω, εὐδοκιμήσω, ηὐδοκίμησα, ηὐδοκίμηκα, – , – , have a good reputation, be famous. στοά, -ᾶς, ἡ, colonnade, columned walkway, building that has a colonnade. κάθημαι, sit, be seated (athematic, present system only). ἐμ-πίπτω, fall in; of words, come to mind, be heard. κατα-φέρω, bring down, carry down. κροκύς, κροκύδος, ὁ, lint, bit of fluff. τρίχωμα, -ατος, τό, hair, growth of hair. καρφο-λογέω, gather twigs, pick off bits of lint (predictable principal parts). ἐν-τυγχάνω, meet, meet up with, fall in with. πώγων, πώγωνος, ὁ, beard. θρίξ, τριχός, ἡ, hair. σιωπάω, σιωπήσομαι, ἐσιώπησα, σεσιώπηκα, – , ἐσιωπήθην, be silent. ἐπ-αινέω, praise, approve, agree. ἐπι-σημαίνω, mark, signify, give a sign, indicate approval. σκώπτω, σκώψομαι, ἔσκωψα, – , ἔσκωμμαι, ἐσκώφθην, mock, laugh at, make fun of. ὠθέω, ὤσω, ἔωσα, – , ἔωσμαι, ἐώσθην, push, shove. στόμα, στόματος, τό, mouth. γέλως, γέλωτος, ὁ, laughter. παρ-έρχομαι, pass, go by. μῆλον, -ου, τό, apple. ἄπιος, -ου, ἡ, pear. ἐπριάμην, buy; aorist system only. νεοττίον, -ου, τό, chick, little bird. συν-ωνέομαι, buy up. κρηπίς, -ίδος, ἡ, shoe. εὔρυθμος, -ον, in good rhythm, well-proportioned, graceful. ἀνα-στρέφω, invert, turn over, turn away. γυναικεῖος, -α, -ον, feminine, womanly. ἀ-πνευστί, without breathing, holding one's breath. ἑστιάω, ἑστιάσω, εἱστίασα, εἱστίακα, εἱστίαμαι, εἱστιάθην, entertain, hold a dinner party. ῥιγέω, ῥιγήσω, ἐρρίγησα, ἔρριγα, – , – , shiver, shudder (with cold or with emotion). περι-στέλλω, dress, wrap up. προσ-πίπτω, fall against, fall onto. δια-ψιθυρίζω, -ιῶ, -ισα, – , – , – , whisper together. προσκεφάλαιον, -ου, τό, pillow. ὑπο-στορέννυμι, spread out under. ἀρχιτεκτονέω, be architect, construct. φυτεύω, φυτεύσω, ἐφύτευσα, πεφύτευκα, πεφύτευμαι, ἐφυτεύθην, plant. εἰκών, εἰκόνος, ἡ, image, portrait, pattern.

8. ἄνδρα μοι ἔννεπε, μοῦσα, πολύτροπον, ὃς μάλα πολλὰ
πλάγχθη, ἐπεὶ Τροίης ἱερὸν πτολίεθρον ἔπερσεν.
πολλῶν δ᾽ ἀνθρώπων ἴδεν ἄστεα, καὶ νόον ἔγνω,
πολλὰ δ᾽ ὅ γ᾽ ἐν πόντῳ πάθεν ἄλγεα ὃν κατὰ θυμόν,
ἀρνύμενος ἥν τε ψυχὴν καὶ νόστον ἑταίρων.

    Odyssey 1.1-5

    ἐννέπω, ἐνέπω = λέγω, ἀγγέλλω. πολύτροπος, -ον, having many turns, wily, versatile, well-travelled. πλάζω, πλάγξω, ἔπλαγξα, – , – , ἐπλάγχθην, cause to wander, lead astray; πλάγχθη = ἐπλάγχθη, unaugmented as often in epic (as also ἴδεν = εἶδεν, πάθεν = ἔπαθεν). πτολίεθρον = πόλις, πύργος. πέρθω, πέρσω, ἔπερσα, πέπορθα, – , – , sack, ravage (a city). ἄλγος, -ους, τό, pain. ἄρνυμαι, present system only, gain, win; try to gain. νόστος, -ου, ὁ, homecoming.

9. *περὶ τοῦ Τρωικοῦ πολέμου, τέταρτον καὶ δέκατον μέρος*

ὁ δὲ Ὀδυσσεὺς μετὰ τοῖς ἄλλοις ἐκ τοῦ ὅρμου ἐξέπλει. περιέπεσε τῷ αὐτῷ χειμῶνι ὡς ὁ Μενέλαος. ἐπὶ νῆσόν τινα ἐπῆλθον ὅπου ἦσαν πρόβατα, φυτά, μέγα ἄντρον.

ὁ οὖν Ὀδυσσεὺς καὶ οἱ ναῦται πρόβατον θύσαντας καὶ φαγόντες ἐν τῷ ἄντρῳ καθηῦδον. νύκτωρ ἦλθε ὁ τοῦ ἄντρου δεσπότης, Πολύφημος ὀνόματι, γίγας ὤν, ὃς ἕνα μόνον ὀφθαλμὸν ἔχει. τοὺς ναύτας ὁρῶν ἠρώτασε, "τίνες ἐστέ; τί ἐν τῷ ἐμῷ ἄντρῳ καθεύδετε; ἴστε ὅτι τοὺς ξένους ἀεὶ ἐσθίω."

ὁ δὲ Ὀδυσσεὺς ἀπεκρίνατο, "Οὖτις ἐστὶ τὸ ὄνομά μου. οὐκ ἤδη σὸν εἶναι τὸ ἄντρον. οἶνον ἀγαθὸν ἔχω, ὃν σοὶ δώσω εἰ μὴ ἡμᾶς ἐσθίεις."

ὁ δὲ Πολύφημος ἐγέλασε. "εἶέν, ὦ Οὖτις, σέ ὕστατον ἐσθίω. δός μοι πότον." καὶ δύο ναῦτα λαβὼν ἔφαγε.

ὁ δὲ Ὀδυσσεὺς οἶνον τῷ γίγαντι ἔδωκε. ὁ δὲ εὐθὺς καθηῦδε, ὁ γὰρ οἶνος οὕτως ἰσχυρός ἦν. ὁ δὲ Ὀδυσσεὺς βουλὴν ἐμηχανήσατο. μέγας μοχλὸς ἦν ἐν τῷ ἄντρῳ, ὥσπερ ἱστὸν νέως. ὁ δὲ Ὀδυσσεὺς τὸν μοχλὸν εἰς τὸ πῦρ ἔθηκε ἕως σκληρός ἐγένετο. ἔπειτα τὸν μοχλὸν εἰς τὸν τοῦ Πολυφήμου ὀφθαλμὸν ἐνήρεισε. νῦν ὁ Πολύφημος ἦν τυφλός. ὁ Ὀδυσσεὺς καὶ οἱ ναῦται ἐκ τοῦ ἄντρου ὥρμησαν.

ὁ δὲ γίγας ἐγειρόμενος πολὺ ἐβόει. οἱ φίλοι ἀκούοντες ἠρώτησαν, "τί γίγνεται; τίς σε ἀδικεῖ, ὦ Πολύφημε;" ὁ δὲ ἀπεκρίνατο, "Οὖτις ἐμὲ βλάπτει. Οὖτις ἐμὲ τυφλὸν ἐποίησε." οἱ ἄλλοι γίγαντες εἶπον, "οὐκ οὖν ἐβλάβης. οὖτις οὐδὲν ἐποίησε. εἰ μήτις σε βλάπτει, εὖ οὖν ἔχεις." καὶ πάλιν ἀπῆλθον.

ὁ δὲ Ὀδυσσεύς, νῦν ἐν τῇ νηί ὤν, ἐλάλησε, "ἐλεύθερός εἰμι, ὦ Πολύφημε. τὸ Οὖτις οὔκ ἐστι τὸ ἐμὸν ὄνομα ἀληθείᾳ. Ὀδυσσεύς εἰμι. οὐκέτι ἔχεις με βλάπτειν."

ὁ δὲ Πολύφημος τὸν πατέρα ἐκάλεσε, τὸν θεὸν Ποσειδῶνα. "ὤφελει μοι, ὦ πάτερ," εἶπε. "οὗτος ὁ Ὀδυσσεὺς ἐμὲ τυφλὸν ἐποίησε." ὁ δὲ Ποσειδῶν τῷ Ὀδυσσέι ἐδίωξε περὶ πάσης τῆς θαλάττης καὶ τὸν νόστον χαλεπὸν ἔπραττε. ἀλλὰ μετὰ δέκα ἔτη, πολλὰ πάθη πεπονθώς, τέλος, οἴκαδε ἦλθε καὶ τὴν γυναῖκα Πηνελόπειαν αὖθις εἶδε. ὁ δὲ Ὀδυσσεὺς ὕστατος πάντων τῶν Ἑλλήνων μετὰ τὸν πόλεμον οἴκαδε ἦλθε.

νῆσος, -ου, ὁ, island. ἰσχυρός, -ά, -όν, strong. μηχανάομαι, μηχανήσομαι, ἐμηχανησάμην, – , μεμηχάνημαι, – , contrive, devise. μοχλός, -οῦ, ὁ, bar, stake, pole. σκληρός, -ή, -όν, hard. ἐν-ερείδω, ἐν-ερείσω, ἐν-ήρεισα, ἐν-ήρεικα, ἐν-ήρεισμαι, ἐν-ηρείσθην, thrust in, shove in. ἐγείρω, ἐγερῶ, ἤγειρα, ἐγρήγορα, ἐγήγερμαι, ἠγέρθην, wake up, awaken.

XX.6 Conversation

The usual questions and answers, for example (reading 1) τίς πικρότερός ἐστι, ὁ χειμὼν ἢ ὁ πόλεμος; ἆρα ὁ Δάφνις τὴν χιόνα φιλεῖ; ποῖά ἐστι ἡ γῆ τῷ χειμῶνι; Or (reading 2) τί ἐποίησε ὁ Διοφῶν; τίς ἐστι ὁ τοῦ Διοφῶνος πατήρ; And so on.

XX.7 Writing

1. In each of the following sentences, change the main verb from active to passive, or from passive to active, making whatever other changes are required to keep roughly the same meaning. For example, from ὁ ἄνθρωπος τὸν ἑταῖρον φιλεῖ make ὁ ἑταῖρος ὑπὸ τοῦ ἀνθρώπου φιλεῖται.

    a. βιβλίον τῷ μαθητῇ ὑπὸ τῆς διδασκάλης δίδοται.

    b. πέτραν χαμαὶ τίθησι ὁ γεωργός.

    c. οἱ ῥήτορες χαλεποὺς λόγους ἵᾱσι.

    d. τὸ πῦρ ὑπὸ τοῖν διδασκάλοιν κεκαυμένον σβέννυται.

    e. δοῦλός τις τὴν θύραν ἀνοίγνυσι.

    f. οὗτος, κόλαξ ὤν, σοι δῶρα δίδωσι.

    g. ὁ τυρὸς τοῖς λαχάνοις ὑπ' ἐμοῦ μίγνυται.

    h. ὁ ἄνεμος τὴν ψάμμον εἰς τὴν θάλατταν ἵησι.

    i. πολλὰ καὶ καλὰ ἐν τῷ νεῷ ἀνατίθεμεν.

    j. ταύτην τὴν μηχανὴν ἵστατε.

    k. οἱ πολῖται τὰ τῶν τεθνεώτων στρατιωτῶν ὀστᾶ προτίθενται.

    l. ὁ βασιλεὺς μέγαν ὅρκον ὄμνυσι.

2. Do the change-number exercise with the following sentences.

    a. τὸν μὲν ἐμὸν πατέρα φιλῶ, τὸν δὲ σὸν οὔ.

    b. ὁ ἀνὴρ τοῖς παισὶ σῖτον δίδοται.

    c. ἆρα δύνασαι τὸν σὸν κύνα θρέψαι;

    d. αἱ γυναῖκες τὴν κλίνην ἀκύρῳ στορεννύᾱσι.

    e. τίνες μὲν τὸν λόγον συνεῖντο, τίνες δὲ τὴν ἀλήθειαν οὐκ ἔγνωσαν.

    f. τὼ παῖδε τὰ βιβλία ἐπὶ τῇ τραπέζῃ ἐθέσθην.

    g. ἡ ἀδελφὴ ὤμοσε τὸν ἀδελφὸν θάψαι.

    h. ἐὰν μὴ τὸ πῦρ ἀποσβεννύῃς, πάντες ἀπολοῦνται.

    i. ἱστάμενοι ἐπὶ τῆς ἀκτῆς λίθους ἵεμεν εἰς τὸν πόντον.

    j. τὰ δῶρα χαμαὶ θέμενος, τὼ χεῖρε ἀνίστᾱς, ὁ ἱερεὺς εὐχὰς τοῖς θεοῖς ᾖσε.

3. Each of these sentences is in aorist, present, or future tense. Change the main verb to each of the other two tenses, making all other changes necessary for grammar or sense.

    a. ὁ ἁλιεὺς πολλὰς ἰχθύας τούτῳ τῷ ἀγκίστρῳ λαβεῖν δυνήσεται.

    b. τὼ στρατηγὼ ἐν τῇ ἀγορᾷ μετὰ τῶν ξένων ἵστασθον.

    c. ὁ μὲν φιλόσοφος ἀπωλέσατο, τὸ δὲ κλέος ἀθάνατον ἦν.

    d. αἱ διδασκάλαι τὰ νέα βιβλία ἔδειξαν τοῖς πατράσι.

    e. ἴα καὶ ναρκίσσους ἐκ τοῦ ὄρους πορεύσας, ποῦ θήσῃ;

    f. τὴν οἰκίαν τετταράκοντα μνῶν ἀπεδόμην.

4. Rewrite the following sentences, changing participial phrases to subordinate clauses or subordinate clauses to participial phrases, as appropriate.

    a. τοῦ χειμῶνος γιγνομένου, οἱ βόες ἄκυρον οὐκ ἐδύναντο φαγεῖν.

    b. οἱ νέοι τοῖς φίλοις συγγίγνονται ἵνα ἡδονὴν ἀλλήλοις διδῶνται.

    c. ὅταν ἄφηται ὁ ἄνθρωπος κόλακα, τρεῖς ἄλλοι πρὸς αὐτὸν ἀνίασι.

    d. ὁ κυνηγέτης δίκτυα ἐπὶ τὴν χθόνα ἐτίθετο ὡς ζῷα ληψόμενος.

    e. ὁ δεσπότης τοὺς δούλους παραδιδομένους ὑπὸ τοῦ φίλου τῷ γείτονι ἐπώλεσε.

    f. κλέπτης τις τὰ δῶρα ἀνατιθέμενα ἐν τῷ νεῴ ἀπέστησε.

    g. πάθη παθὼν ὁ σοφὸς ἔμαθον.

5. Rewrite reading 3 from the point of view of an Athenian whose son is among the war dead being honored.

6. Summarize reading 6 as a narrative, rather than a dialogue, using indirect quotation as necessary. Your summary might begin ὁ Ζεύς, τὸν Γανυμήδην πρὸς τὸν Ὄλυμπον λαβών, ...

7. Choose a story from mythology and re-tell it in straightforward Greek.

Appendix 1

Forms

In this appendix are references to all the form charts in the various chapters, along with information about derivation within Greek.

1. Basic sandhi rules

Sandhi means the way sounds change when they are put together. Greek has internal sandhi and external sandhi: respectively changes inside words and between words.

External sandhi

There are three main kinds of external sandhi: different forms of a word, elision, and crasis.

Some words have different forms in different sound contexts. In Greek, the change in form always comes at the end of the word, depending on the first sound of the next word. Two common examples are οὐ, which becomes οὐκ before smooth vowels and οὐχ before rough vowels; and ἐκ, which becomes ἐξ before vowels. Certain third-person verb forms may have **movable nu** before vowels, as λύουσι τοῦτον but λύουσιν ἐκεῖνον. The affected forms are the ones that end in -σι (even if it is spelled -ξι or -ψι) and most of those that end in -ε. Noun forms ending in -σι also take movable nu: these are the dative plural forms of third declension nouns, adjectives, and participles.

Elision takes place when a word ends with a short vowel and the next word begins with a vowel. Elision is optional in prose: a writer may choose whether or not to elide the vowel. In verse it almost always takes place. The elided vowel is replaced by an apostrophe, as ἀλλ᾽ ἔχω for ἀλλὰ ἔχω. Only short vowels may be elided.

Crasis is another possibility when one word ends with a vowel and the next word begins with a vowel. This is a contraction or mixing of the two vowels (compare κρατήρ, "mixing bowl," and κεράννυμι "mix"), generally following the regular rules for contraction as given below. Crasis is always marked in writing with a **coronis**, identical to a smooth breathing, over the resulting long vowel; thus, a word that appears to have a breathing inside, not on the first sound of the word, is really two words joined by crasis at the spot where the coronis appears. For example, κἀν is καὶ ἐν, or τἄνω is τὰ ἄνω. When the initial vowel of the second word has a rough breathing, the consonant that ends up next to it is aspirated, as τὸ ἱμάτιον becomes θοἰμάτιον. Forms of ἕτερος become ἅτερ- in crasis, so that τὸ ἕτερον ends up as θἅτερον instead of the expected θοὔτερον. Note the vocative phrases ὦνερ = ὦ ἄνερ, ὦνθρωπε = ὦ ἄνθρωπε, used in comedy. Note also ἁνήρ = ὁ ἀνήρ; when a word that normally has a smooth breathing appears with a rough breathing, this is a crasis with the definite article.

Internal sandhi: vowels

Attic Greek avoids two successive simple vowels. When two vowels come together, therefore, they contract. If the first vowel sound is actually a diphthong, though, there is no contraction, because the diphthong is like a vowel followed by a semi-vowel. For example, in ἀκούει, the diphthong ου behaves like o followed by a sound like *w*. Or in ποῖος, the diphthong οι is like o followed by *y*. Vowels that aren't diphthongs, on the other hand, can't be "broken up" into a vowel and a semi-vowel, so end up contracting with a following vowel.

Contraction occurs in verbs whose stems end in ε, α, or ο in the present (like καλέω) or in the future (like βαλῶ, future stem βαλε-); in a small group of nouns with stems ending in these vowels (like γῆ); in s-stem nouns, since the *s* disappeared early in the history of Greek, leaving a vowel behind (for example, γένος); in the addition of the past indicative augment to a verb stem that begins with a vowel (as ἤκουον); in reduplication of verbs that begin with a vowel (as ἤγγελκα); and in crasis. Wherever it occurs, it always follows the same rules.

The main principle for contraction is that *o*-sounds dominate everything, and *a*-sounds dominate *e*-sounds. The other two vowels, *i* and *u*, don't participate in contraction if they come before another vowel, and produce a diphthong if they come second. The result of contraction is always a long vowel or a diphthong.

This chart shows all the combinations. Where α is not marked long or short, the rule applies to both long and short α.

first + second	becomes
α + α, α + ε, α + η	ᾱ
α + ει, α + ᾳ, α + ῃ, ᾱ + ι	ᾳ
α + αι, ᾰ + ι	αι
α + ο, α + ου, α + ω	ω
α + οι, η + οι	ῳ
ε + ε, ε + ι	ει
ε + ο	ου
ε + υ	ευ
ε + any long vowel or diphthong	that long vowel or diphthong (ε is absorbed)
η + ε, η + ει	η
η + ι	ῃ
ο + ε, ο + ο, ο + ου	ου
ο + α, ο + η, ο + ω	ω
ο + ει, ο + ῃ, ο + ι, ο + οι	οι

This table shows how a contracted vowel might have arisen:

form	could come from
α	α + α, α + ε, α + η
ᾳ	α + ει, α + ῃ, α + ᾳ, ᾱ + ι
ει	ε + ε, ε + ει
η	ε + η
ῃ	ε + ῃ, η + ι
οι	ο + ει, ο + ῃ, ο + οι, ε + οι
ου	ε + ο, ε + ου, ο + ο, ο + ε, ο + ου
ω	ο + η, ο + ω, ε + ω, α + ο, α + ου, α + ω
ῳ	α + οι, η + οι

Internal sandhi: consonants

Consonants can come together when a suffix beginning with a consonant is added to a root ending with a consonant, when an ending beginning with a consonant is added to a stem ending with a consonant, and when an infix is inserted into a root. They can also come together when a prefix ending in a consonant is added to a form beginning with a consonant. Usually the resulting consonant cluster undergoes **assimilation**, as one of the consonants changes to become similar to the others.

When a suffix or ending starting with σ is added to a form ending in a labial stop, the labial is de-voiced and de-aspirated, resulting in π-σ, always written with ψ. Similarly, when σ is added to a velar stop, the result is ξ = κ-σ. For example, consider the futures γράψω = γραφ-σ-ω, βλάψω = βλαβ-σ-ω, ἄξω = ἄγ-σ-ω. But when σ is added to a dental, the cluster becomes just σ, as if the dental stop disappears: φράσω = φραδ-σ-ω, future of φράζω, ἐλπίς = ἐλπίδ-ς, nominative singular of the noun.

When two stops come together, the first one becomes voiced or unvoiced as necessary to assimilate to the voicing of the second. A stop before μ similarly becomes voiced, and if it is a labial it becomes another μ. If any consonant in a cluster is aspirated, all of them become aspirated together. Thus βλαβ-τω = βλάπτω, ἐ-βλαβ-θην = ἐβλάφθην, βε-βλαβ-μαι = βέβλαμμαι, all from root βλαβ-, and πε-πλεκ-μαι = πέπλεγμαι.

Dental stops are simply dropped before κ or σ, and become σ before other consonants, as πειθ-σω = πείσω, πε-πειθ-κα = πέπεικα, but πε-πειθ-μαι = πέπεισμαι, all from πείθω.

Nasals, for example in the prefix συν-, are assimilated, becoming μ before labials (συμ-βαίνω, συμ-φέρω), the guttural nasal before gutturals (συγ-γίγνομαι, συγ-χέω), and λ and ρ before those sounds (συλ-λέγω, συρ-ράπτω). The same assimilation occurs in the present stem of verbs in the nasal infix present class, which have -ν- inserted before the final consonant of the root, followed by -αν- as a suffix: root μαθ- forms μανθάνω, λαβ- forms λαμβάνω, θιγ- forms θιγγάνω.

Some large clusters are simplified with **compensatory lengthening** of the preceding vowel. This happens in the nominative singular of the third declension, as λέοντ-ς = λέων, in the dative plural of the same declension, as λέοντ-σι = λέουσι, and in the aorist stem of verbs ending in liquid consonants, as ἐ-αγγελ-σ-α = ἤγγειλα or ἐ-φθερ-σ-α = ἔφθειρα. The vowel becomes long to "compensate" or "make up" for the lost consonant sounds, so that the syllable will still be long (see Appendix 4 section 1 for the definition of **long syllable**).

The remaining consonant sandhi rule is **dissimilation of aspirates**, sometimes called **Grassmann's Law** after the 19th-century scholar who first explained it. One environment where dissimilation takes place is reduplication, when the original syllable begins with an aspirate consonant. It also happens in some aorist passive forms, and in other forms as well. In reduplication, whether for present stems (with ι) or for perfect stems (with ε), normally the first consonant of the stem is duplicated, as λέλυκα. When that consonant is aspirated, the added consonant is the corresponding non-aspirate consonant, as τέθυκα or τίθημι. The aorist passive of θύω is ἐ-θυ-θην, dissimilated in exactly the same way to produce ἐτύθην. Dissimilation of aspirates is not restricted to verbs, but can happen in nouns as well; an example is τρίχα, the accusative of θρίξ. The root of this noun is θριχ-. In the nominative, the -ς ending causes the final consonant to become unaspirated, so the first consonant can keep its aspiration, but in the other cases, it cannot.

2. Nouns, adjectives, pronouns: forms

There are three declensions of nouns.

- First declension: a-stem nouns ending in -η II.2; ending in -ā III.2; ending in -ă IV.4; masculine nouns VII.1; contracted nouns VII.2
- Second declension: o-stem nouns, masculine II.2, neuter II.2; contracted nouns VII.2; Attic declension with quantitative metathesis VII.3
- Third declension: stems in -οντ-, -αντ- VIII.1; neuters in -μα XI.3; s-stem XI.4; i-stem and u-stem nouns with quantitative metathesis XII.3; liquid stems XIV.4; irregular nouns XIV.4; r-stem nouns XV.2; nouns in -ευς XVI.4

Irregular nouns: third declension XIV.4

Adjectives have the same forms as nouns.

- Definite article: II.4
- First and second declension: II.3
- Third declension: S-stems XI.4
- First and third declension: participle ὤν, οὖσα, ὄν VIII.1; adjectives in -ας VIII.1; active participles in -ντ- VIII.2; perfect active participles XIV.1; adjectives in -υς, -εια, -υ XVIII.2; comparatives in -ων XVIII.3

Irregular adjectives: πολύς II.3; μέγας VIII.1; irregular comparatives XVIII.3

Comparison: regular III.5, irregular and suppletive XVIII.3

Regular adverbs: formation and comparison III.5

Pronouns have their own forms, usually different from those of nouns. Most Greek pronouns, except ἐγώ and σύ, can also be adjectives.

- Personal pronouns: ἐγώ (νώ, ἡμεῖς) IV.1; σύ (σφώ, ὑμεῖς) IV.1; αὐτός, αὐτή, αὐτό IV.1

- Relative pronoun ὅς, ἥ, ὅ II.4
- Demonstratives: οὗτος, αὕτη, τοῦτο III.1; ὅδε, ἥδε, τόδε III.1; ἐκεῖνος, -η, -ο VI.4
- Interrogative: direct τίς, τί IV.2; indirect ὅστις, ἥτις, ὅ τι II.1, VIII.5
- Indefinite τις, τι IV.2
- Reflexive pronouns IV.5
- Reciprocal pronoun ἀλλήλων XI.7

The basic question words, like ποῦ or πότε, are indeclinable. They have associated indirect forms, indefinite forms, and relative forms, just as τίς is associated with ὅστις, τις, and ὅς. The chart of correlated forms is in section II.1.

3. Numerals

The cardinal numbers are adjectives; numbers 1, 2, 3, 4 are declinable, and so are those from 200 up, but the rest are not. Ordinals are regular first-and-second declension adjectives. The numeral adverbs mean "once," "twice," and so on. The forms of 1, 2, 3, and 4 are in IV.3.

	Cardinals	Ordinals	Adverbs
1	εἷς, μία, ἕν	πρῶτος, -η, -ον	ἅπαξ
2	δύο	δεύτερος	δίς
3	τρεῖς, τρία	τρίτος	τρίς
4	τέτταρες, -α	τέταρτος	τετράκις
5	πέντε	πέμπτος	πεντάκις
6	ἕξ	ἕκτος	ἑξάκις
7	ἑπτά	ἕβδομος	ἑπτάκις
8	ὀκτώ	ὄγδοος	ὀκτάκις
9	ἐννέα	ἔνατος	ἐνάκις
10	δέκα	δέκατος	δεκάκις
11	ἕνδεκα	ἑνδέκατος	ἑνδεκάκις
12	δώδεκα	δωδέκατος	δωδεκάκις
13	τρεῖς καὶ δέκα	τρίτος καὶ δέκατος	τρισκαιδεκάκις
14	τέτταρες καὶ δέκα	τέταρτος καὶ δέκατος	τετταρεσκαιδεκάκις
15	πεντεκαίδεκα	πέμπτος καὶ δέκατος	πεντεκαιδεκάκις
16	ἑκκαίδεκα	ἕκτος καὶ δέκατος	ἑκκαιδεκάκις
17	ἑπτακαίδεκα	ἕβδομος καὶ δέκατος	ἑπτακαιδεκάκις
18	ὀκτωκαίδεκα	ὄγδοος καὶ δέκατος	ὀκτωκαιδεκάκις
19	ἐννεακαίδεκα	ἔνατος καὶ δέκατος	ἐννεακαιδεκάκις

	Cardinals	Ordinals	Adverbs
20	εἴκοσι(ν)	εἰκοστός	εἰκοσάκις
30	τριᾱ́κοντα	τριᾱκοστός	τριᾱκοντάκις
40	τεττᾰράκοντα	τετταρακοστός	τετταρακοντάκις
50	πεντήκοντα	πεντηκοστός	πεντηκοντάκις
60	ἑξήκοντα	ἑξηκοστός	ἑξηκοντάκις
70	ἑβδομήκοντα	ἑβδομηκοστός	ἑβδομηκοντάκις
80	ὀγδοήκοντα	ὀγδοηκοστός	ὀγδοηκοντάκις
90	ἐνενήκοντα	ἐνενηκοστός	ἐνενηκοντάκις
100	ἑκατόν	ἑκατοστός	ἑκατοντάκις
200	διᾱκόσιοι, -αι, -α	διᾱκοσιοστός	διᾱκοσιάκις
300	τριᾱκόσιοι	τριᾱκοσιοστός	τριᾱκοσιάκις
400	τετρακόσιοι	τετρακοσιοστός	τετρακοσιάκις
500	πεντακόσιοι	πεντακοσιοστός	πεντακοσιάκις
600	ἑξακόσιοι	ἑξακοσιοστός	ἑξακοσιάκις
700	ἑπτακόσιοι	ἑπτακοσιοστός	ἑπτακοσιάκις
800	ὀκτακόσιοι	ὀκτακοσιοστός	ὀκτακοσιάκις
900	ἐνακόσιοι	ἐνακοσιοστός	ἐνακοσιάκις
1,000	χῑ́λιοι	χῑλιοστός	χῑλιάκις
2,000	δισχῑ́λιοι	δισχῑλιοστός	δισχῑλιάκις
10,000	μῡ́ριοι	μῡριοστός	μῡριάκις
20,000	δισμῡ́ριοι	δισμῡριοστός	δισμῡριάκις

4. Verbs: forms

There are two conjugations of verbs, classified by how they form their present system from their present stem: thematic (like λύω) and athematic (like δίδωμι).

- Present system:

  indicative active, thematic: present II.5, imperfect V.2

  indicative middle/passive, thematic, present and imperfect X.2

  indicative active, athematic: present IX.1, imperfect XVI.3

  indicative middle/passive, athematic, present and imperfect XX.1

  imperative active, thematic VIII.3

  imperative middle/passive, thematic XI.1

  imperative active, athematic XVI.3

  imperative middle/passive, athematic XX.1

> subjunctive active, thematic VIII.3
> subjunctive middle/passive, thematic XI.1
> subjunctive active, athematic XVI.3
> subjunctive middle/passive, athematic XX.1
> optative active, thematic VIII.3
> optative middle/passive, thematic XI.1
> optative active, athematic XVI.3
> optative middle/passive, athematic XX.1
> infinitive active, thematic III.3
> infinitive middle/passive, thematic X.2
> infinitive active, athematic IX.1
> infinitive middle/passive, athematic XX.1
> participle active, thematic VIII.2
> participle middle/passive, thematic X.2
> participle active, athematic IX.1
> participle middle/passive, athematic XX.1
> athematic in -νῡμι XVII.4

- Future active/middle system:
  > indicative active VI.1
  > optative active VIII.3
  > infinitive active VI.1
  > participle active VIII.2
  > indicative middle XII.1
  > optative middle XII.1
  > infinitive middle XII.1
  > participle middle XII.1

- Aorist active/middle system:
  > first aorist indicative active VI.2
  > first aorist imperative active VIII.3
  > first aorist subjunctive active VIII.3
  > first aorist optative active VIII.3
  > first aorist infinitive active VI.2
  > first aorist participle active VIII.2
  > first aorist indicative middle X.3
  > first aorist imperative middle XI.2
  > first aorist subjunctive middle XI.2
  > first aorist optative middle XI.2
  > first aorist infinitive middle X.3

first aorist participle middle X.3

second aorist indicative active V.3

second aorist imperative active VIII.3

second aorist subjunctive active VIII.3

second aorist optative active VIII.3

second aorist infinitive active V.4

second aorist participle active VIII.2

second aorist indicative middle X.3

second aorist imperative middle XI.2

second aorist subjunctive middle XI.2

second aorist optative middle XI.2

second aorist infinitive middle X.3

second aorist participle middle X.3

root aorist, all moods, XIII.3

aorist of athematic verbs with long and short grade stems XVI.3

- Perfect active system:

perfect indicative, pluperfect indicative XIV.1

perfect subjunctive, perfect optative XIV.1

perfect infinitive, perfect participle XIV.1

- Perfect middle/passive system:

perfect indicative, pluperfect indicative XV.1

perfect subjunctive, perfect optative formed periphrastically XV.1

perfect infinitive, perfect participle XV.1

- Aorist passive system:

all moods XIII.2

- Future passive:

all moods XII.1

Irregular or unusual verbs: εἰμι III.4, XIII.1; φημι IX.1, XVII.2; εἶμι XV.3; οἶδα XVII.1

5. How to write a verbal synopsis

A **synopsis** (from σύνοψις, -εως, ἡ, overview, general view) of a verb is a list of all the forms of a given person and number, through all the tenses, moods, and voices. It is a convenient way to compare endings (primary vs. secondary, active vs. middle/passive, and so on), and to review morphology. When you are asked to write a synopsis, you will be given a person and number for the finite forms, and a gender, number, and case for the participles. The forms in a synopsis include all the stems of the verb, and show all the moods in the standard order.

Here is the procedure:

1. First, write the Standard Six Principal Parts, and write a short gloss for the verb (in English at first; in Greek if you know a synonym).

2. Then work through the forms, *in order* by Principal Part. That is, first write the forms that are made from the stem of the first Principal Part (present system), then those that come from the second Principal Part (future active and middle system), and so on through all six. Write the forms for each Principal Part (that is, for each tense system) *in the standard order* by moods: indicative, imperative, subjunctive, optative, infinitive, participle. Write the active voice, then the middle, then the passive (as appropriate: as you know, sometimes middle and passive are identical, and sometimes the three voices do not all come from the same Principal Part). Give the finite forms for the specified person and number, and give the participles in the specified gender, case, and number. Note that there are no first-person imperatives in Greek, so if you are doing a synopsis in the first person, this mood will not appear. In three of the six tense systems there will be more than one tense in the indicative — put them together at the head of your list. Some tense systems do not form all four finite moods (though they do all have both non-finite moods), so do not write forms that do not exist.

You may wish to lay out the synopsis with three columns, for active, middle, and passive, and a row for each combination of tense and mood.

As you are learning, write only the forms you have learned so far. Your synopses will grow as the year goes on.

Here is a complete synopsis, showing all the forms in the correct order.

Synopsis of γράφω in 3rd plural, participles in feminine nominative singular.

γράφω, γράψω, ἔγραψα, γέγραφα, γέγραμμαι, ἐγράφην — write
Present system:

    present indicative active γράφουσι, middle/passive γράφονται

    imperfect indicative active ἔγραφον, middle/passive ἐγράφετο

    present imperative active γραφόντων, middle/passive γραφέσθων

    present subjunctive active γράφωσι, middle/passive γράφωνται

    present optative active γράφοιεν, middle/passive γράφοιντο

    present infinitive active γράφειν, middle/passive γράφεσθαι

    present participle active, feminine nominative singular γράφουσα, middle/passive γραφομένη

Future active system:

    future indicative active γράψουσι, middle γράψονται

    future optative active γράψοιεν, middle γράψοιντο

    future infinitive active γράψειν, middle γράψεσθαι

    future participle active, feminine nominative singular γράψουσα, middle γραψομένη

Aorist active system:

   aorist indicative active ἔγραψαν, middle ἐγράψατο

   aorist imperative active γραψάντων, middle γραψάσθων

   aorist subjunctive active γράψωσι, middle γράψωνται

   aorist optative active γράψειαν, middle γράψαιντο

   aorist infinitive active γράψαι, middle γράψασθαι

   aorist participle active, feminine nominative singular γράψασα, middle γραψαμένη

Perfect active system:

   perfect indicative active γεγράφασι

   pluperfect indicative active ἐγεγράφεσαν

   perfect imperative active γεγραφότες ὄντων

   perfect subjunctive active γεγραφότες ὦσι

   perfect optative active γεγραφότες εἴησαν

   perfect infinitive active γεγραφέναι

   perfect participle active, feminine nominative singular γεγραφυῖα

Perfect middle system:

   perfect indicative middle/passive γεγραμμένοι εἰσι

   pluperfect indicative middle/passive γεγραμμένοι ἦσαν

   perfect imperative middle/passive γεγραμμένοι ὄντων

   perfect subjunctive middle/passive γεγραμμένοι ὦσι

   perfect optative middle/passive γεγραμμένοι εἴησαν

   perfect infinitive middle/passive γεγράφθαι

   perfect participle middle/passive, feminine nominative singular γεγραφομένη

Aorist passive system:

   aorist indicative passive ἐγράφησαν

   future indicative passive γραφήσονται

   aorist imperative passive γραφέντων

   aorist subjunctive passive γραφῶσι

   aorist optative passive γραφείησαν

   future optative passive γραφήσοιντο

   aorist infinitive passive γραφῆναι

   future infinitive passive γραφήσεσθαι

   aorist participle passive, feminine nominative singular γραφεῖσα

   future participle passive, feminine nominative singular γραφησομένη

6. Verb stems and principal parts

A Greek verb has six principal parts, representing the six tense/voice systems:

- present
- future active and middle
- aorist active and middle
- perfect active
- perfect middle/passive
- aorist passive and future passive

Some verbs may not be used in all voices or in all tenses, as for example εἰμι has no aorist or perfect, and has only middle forms in the future. But in general a normal verb has all six principal parts. Moreover, there are standard patterns for the formation of the six stems from the root. Learning these patterns makes it easier to recognize forms from new verbs, when you meet them in reading. Most verbs conform to one of the typical patterns, and the irregular verbs are common enough that they are in this book: thus, new verbs you will learn later are almost certainly regular and predictable.

Either the present or the aorist (active) typically shows the more or less unadorned root. Identifying the root helps you see how the other principal parts are formed, and helps you find related words, whether within Greek (see section 7 in this appendix) or in English, Latin, and other Indo-European languages, which may give you an idea what the verb means.

It is convenient to introduce some terminology. **Ablauting roots** are those that undergo **ablaut**, which means they can be in e grade, o grade, or zero grade. Such roots usually have one of the shapes CeC, CeRC, or CReC, where C denotes any consonant (and the C at start and end do not have to be the same) and R denotes a **resonant**: a liquid λ, μ, ν, ρ or a semi-vowel ι, υ. For example, λείπω has root λειπ-, which is shaped CeRC. This root appears in e grade in the present λείπω, in o grade in the perfect λέλοιπα, and in zero grade in the aorist ἔλιπον. Other words from the same root may also use any grade, as λειπτέος "needing to be left"; λοιπός "left over"; ἐλλιπής "defective, with something left out." An example of a CeC-shape root is γεν-, with e grade in the aorist ἐγενόμην, zero grade in the present γίγνομαι (with reduplication, as γί-γν-ο-μαι), and o grade in the noun γόνος. And θρεφ- is CReC-shaped, with e grade in the present τρέφω and o grade in the perfect τέτροφα. (Although it may not be obvious, this root also shows zero grade in the aorist passive ἐτράφην: in Greek, a liquid consonant either adds an α or changes to α if there would not otherwise be a vowel in the syllable.)

In principle, verbs can form their various tenses in any combination of ways. That is, two verbs that form their present in the same way may form their aorist differently. But there are certain combinations that are more common, and certain combinations that do not occur: for example, verbs with contracted presents never have second aorists.

The present system can be formed as follows:

1. Simple thematic present: the present system is just the root, in e grade, with theme vowel before endings. Example: λείπω

2. Contracted present, always thematic: the present system is the root, which ends in ε, ο, or α. That vowel contracts with the theme vowel. These are often denominative.

They always have future type 3 or 4 and aorist type 1b. Example: φιλέω, denominative from φίλος.

3. Reduplicated thematic present: present system is reduplicated with ι and often has zero grade of the root. Example: γίγνομαι

4. SK suffix, always thematic. Two varieties:
   a. reduplicated, with ι, example γιγνώσκω
   b. without reduplication, sometimes denominative, example εὑρίσκω

5. I suffix, always thematic. There is always sandhi between the suffix and the root. Four varieties:
   a. root ending in guttural produces -ττω, as πραγ-, πραγ-ι-ω, πράττω. (Note that -ττ- here is an Attic sound; other dialects have -σσ-. Some of these verbs have poetic variants with -ζω instead.)
   b. root ending in λ produces -λλω, as βαλ-, βαλ-ι-ω, βάλλω. These usually have future type 2 and may have aorist type 1c.
   c. root ending in ν or ρ has metathesis, giving -ινω, -ιρω, and making a diphthong with the original root vowel, as φθερ-, φθερ-ι-ω, φθείρω. If the vowel of the root is ι or υ it is lengthened, as κρῐν-, κριν-ι-ω, κρῑνω. These usually have future type 2 and aorist type 1c.
   d. root ending in dental produces -ίζω, as ἐλπιδ-, ἐλπιδ-ι-ω, ἐλπίζω; many of these are denominative

6. N suffix, thematic or athematic. Four varieties:
   a. simple suffix, thematic, as τέμνω
   b. nasal infix, always with additional -αν- suffix as well, thematic; the nasal assimilates to the final consonant of the root. Example: λαβ-, λα-μ-β-αν-ω, λαμβάνω. These normally have future type 1 and always have aorist type 2 (second aorist).
   c. NE suffix, usually thematic, as ἱκ-, ἱκνέομαι
   d. NU suffix, athematic, as δεικ-, δείκνῡμι

7. T suffix, thematic, rather rare. Example: τεκ-, τι-τκ-τ-ω, τίκτω; this verb is reduplicated with zero grade, and the consonant cluster -τκτ- is simplified.

8. Root athematic. Two varieties:
   a. reduplicated, with ι, as δω-, δίδωμι; several of these have aorist type 3 (root aorist).
   b. not reduplicated, as εσ-, εἰμι

The future active system can be formed as follows. All futures have the same endings as thematic presents.

1. S suffix, as λειπ-σ-ω, λείψω

2. ES suffix, with loss of intervocalic sigma followed by contraction. This is typical for roots ending in a liquid, as βαλ-, βαλ-εσ-ω, βαλέω (βαλῶ)

3. ĒS suffix, without contraction, also common for liquid roots. This is the usual future for contracts in ε and α. Example: εὑρ-, εὑρήσω

4. ŌS suffix, without contraction, typical for contracts in o, as δηλώσω

The aorist active system can be formed as follows.

1. First aorist, with aorist endings (-α, -ας, -ε, -αμεν, and so on)
   a. S suffix, as πεμπ-, ἔπεμψα
   b. S suffix with preceding vowel, as ἐφίλησα, typical for verbs with future type 3 or 4
   c. Lengthened root vowel, typical for liquid roots, as ἀγγελ-, ἤγγειλα. Actually this is the same as type (a) with simplification of the consonant cluster and compensatory lengthening: ἀγγελ-, ἤγγελ-σ-α, ἤγγειλα.

2. Second aorist, with endings like a thematic present; normally zero grade of ablauting roots. Example: λειπ-, ἔλιπον

3. Root aorist, with no affixes and no theme vowel, and root aorist endings (-ν, -ς, – , -μεν, and so on), as γνω-, ἔγνων.

The perfect active system can be formed as follows. The stem is always reduplicated with ε and ablauting roots take o grade. All perfects use the same endings.

1. K suffix, sometimes also -εκ- or -ηκ-, as λυ-, λέλυκα

2. Aspiration of final consonant, as πεμπ-, πέπομφα; voiced consonants would be devoiced first, as πραγ-, πέπραχα.

3. No suffix at all, as λειπ-, λέλοιπα

The perfect middle/passive system is always formed the same way. The stem is reduplicated exactly as in the perfect active, and ablauting roots take e grade. As there is no theme vowel or tense vowel before the endings, there will be internal sandhi with roots ending in consonants. Examples: λειπ-, λέλειμμαι, πραγ-, πέπραγμαι.

The aorist passive system can be formed as follows. Ablauting roots take e grade.

1. Θ suffix; a final consonant becomes unvoiced and aspirated for assimilation, and an initial aspirate is dissimilated. Examples: λειπ-, ἐλείφθην, θυ-, ἐτύθην

2. No suffix. Example: γραφ-, ἐγράφην

Exercise

Identify the root and the formation of the tense stems for several different verbs. For example, for γράφω, we have root γραφ-, present type 1, future type 1, aorist type 1a, perfect active type 2, and aorist passive type 2.

7. Word families and derivation

Greek, like English, can have several different words formed from the same root. For example, English has *play, player, playful, plaything, replay, byplay, misplay, wordplay,* and others, all from the base word *play.* Learning the most common patterns of word formation can help you recognize new words related to familiar ones.

This list of derivation patterns is not intended to be exhaustive. Many of these patterns are **productive** during the classical period; that is, speakers of classical Greek would use these patterns to invent new words as necessary. An example of productive derivation in English is the *-ize* suffix (itself derived from the Greek -ίζω verbs) to make verbs from nouns, as *equalize,* "make equal." The productive patterns are particularly useful for word play: a poet can invent a new word for a joke, knowing that the audience will understand it at once (as we might invent *Nutellize,* which might mean "turn into chocolate sauce" or "cover with Nutella" or anything along those lines, depending on context).

Making nouns and adjectives

Nouns and adjectives can be derived from other nouns and adjectives, or from verbs. One of the easiest ways to derive an adjective is to add the negative prefix ἀν- (or ἀ- before consonants), as ἀνάξιος, opposite of ἄξιος. Adjectives with this prefix are considered compounds and have the same forms for masculine and feminine, so ἡ ἀνάξιος γυνή.

The prefixes εὐ- "good" and δυσ- "bad" make opposite pairs, as εὐτυχής, δυστυχής, "fortunate" and "unfortunate" (literally, with good or bad τύχη).

An abstract noun referring to the quality described by an adjective can be derived with the suffix -ίᾱ, as σοφία, -ας, ἡ, the quality that ὁ σοφός has. Another suffix with a similar meaning is -σύνη, as δικαιοσύνη, -ης, ἡ, the quality of being δίκαιος.

An adjective meaning that someone or something is like something else can be derived with the suffix -ικός, as μουσικός, -ή, -όν, "like the Muses, associated with the Muses." The feminine singular can be used by itself, with τέχνη understood, to refer to an art or skill, as ἡ μουσική, "the Muses' art." Another suffix that forms adjectives is -αιος, as ἀναγκαῖος "necessary" from ἀνάγκη "necessity," or πάλαιος "ancient" from πάλαι "long ago."

To denote a small version of a noun, often as a pet name, use the **diminutive** suffixes -ίον or -ίδιον, as παιδίον, -ου, τό or οἰκίδιον, -ου, τό. These diminutives are always neuter, no matter what the original gender was, and even if the noun denotes a person.

An abstract noun referring to the action named by a verb can be derived with the suffix -σις added to the verb root, as φύσις, -εως, ἡ from φύω, or κίνησις, -εως, ἡ "movement" from κινέω "move." These are always feminine.

Some neuters ending in -μα denote the result of a verbal action, as πρᾶγμα, πράγματος, τό, "thing done, action, business," from the root of πράττω.

An agent noun, naming the person who does the action of the verb, can be derived with -της or -τηρ added to the root of the verb, as ποιητής, -οῦ, ὁ from ποιέω or σωτήρ, σωτῆρος, ὁ from σῴζω. Some nouns in -ευς are also agent nouns, like γονεύς from γίγνομαι; note o-grade of the root, which is common in nouns. These agent nouns may also come from nominal roots, as ἱερεύς from ἱερός.

Sometimes a noun or adjective will be formed directly from the same root as the verb, often in o grade, as λόγος and λέγω.

Many verbs have associated adjectives in -τός, as θαυμαστός, -ή, -όν from θαυμάζω, or χρηστός, -ή, -όν from χράομαι. These may indicate that the action of the verb is possible (χρηστός, able to be used, usable) or that it has happened (πλαστός, -ή, -όν, made, modelled, from πλάττω, make).

Another type of adjective derived from verbs ends in -τέος and indicates that the action of the verb must be done, as ζητητέος, -α, -ον, needing to be sought or looked into. Both the -τός adjectives and the -τέος adjectives often come from the aorist passive stem, though not invariably. The accent for both of these types of adjective is on the suffix.

Making verbs

Verbs can be compounded with adverbs or prepositions, as you saw in chapter 8 section 8. In Attic prose compound verbs are often more common than the simple versions, as ἀφικνέομαι is more common than plain ἱκνέομαι.

Many verbs are **denominative**, meaning that they are derived from nouns or adjectives. A large number of contract verbs (though not all of them) are denominative, as φιλέω is from φίλος, νικάω from νίκη, and ἀξιόω from ἄξιος.

Verbs in -ίζω and -άζω are also often denominative, as ἐλπίζω from ἐλπίς, or σκευάζω from σκεῦος.

The suffix -εύω forms denominative verbs that often mean "be (noun)," as βασιλεύω "be a king, rule" or δολεύω "be a slave."

Verbs can also be derived from other verbs, though these are not as common as **primary verbs** (not derived from anything) or those derived from nouns. A **desiderative** verb, meaning to desire to do the action of the original verb, can be formed with the suffix -σείω, as δρασείω "want to do, intend to do" from δράω, or ἀλλαξείω "want to change" from ἀλλάττω. Some verbs in -άω and -ιάω are also desideratives, as θανατάω "want to die." These generally have only a present system.

The suffix -έω, added to the o-grade of the root, can make a **frequentative** verb, meaning to do the action of the original verb frequently or repeatedly. For example, from φέρω is formed φορέω "carry around, wear."

Exercises

1. Figure out how each of the following words is formed, what its principal parts are, and what it should mean, without using a dictionary. For example, σοφία is the abstract noun from σοφός, derived with suffix -ία, so its principal parts are σοφία, σοφίας, ἡ, and it means "quality of being wise, wisdom." Words: μάθησις, εὔξενος, ἱερωσύνη, ἄνελπις, ἐρώτημα, λιθίδιον, τυφλόω, εἰρηναῖος, δωτήρ, ἄσκευος, ἀκουστέος, πικρία, ἱππεύς, φωνέω, δυσπόλεμος, ἀνθρωπικός, στρατεύω, λέξις, γράμμα, κριτής, πομπή, θαυμαστός, μερίζω

2. For each of the following words, identify as many derivatives or related words within Greek as you can, and say how each is derived and what it means. Words: φίλος, δίδωμι, ποιέω, ἔχω, λέγω, πόλις.

APPENDIX 2

Syntax

Syntax is the group of rules explaining how words relate to each other to form phrases, clauses, and sentences. Syntax tells you what it means that a given noun is in the dative case, say, or that a given verb is aorist optative. To **parse** a word is to explain its syntax, naming the construction or giving the reason why the word has the form it has within the sentence, rather than any of its other possible forms.

The basic rules of classical Greek syntax are summarized in this appendix. The lists of constructions with their traditional names are not intended to be exhaustive; some less common constructions are omitted. More details and examples can be found in the main text where the constructions are introduced.

1. Agreement

The primary rules of agreement are the **Three Concords**:

- A finite verb and its subject agree in person and number.
- An adjective agrees with the noun it modifies in gender, case, and number.
- A pronoun agrees with its antecedent in gender and number.

The first rule has two exceptions. A neuter plural subject takes a singular verb, and a first-person dual subject takes a plural verb (because there are no first-person dual verb forms).

2. The Nominal System

Words in the nominal system have gender, case, and number. These words are the nouns, adjectives, and pronouns. Pronouns are a **closed class**, which means there is a given, fixed list of words that are pronouns, and no others. They include ἐγώ, αὐτός, οὗτος, τίς, and so on. Adjectives are words that may have any gender, like καλός: ὁ καλὸς ἄνθρωπος, ἡ καλὴ γῆ, τὸ καλὸν δένδρον. Everything else in the nominal system is a noun.

Nominal words use whatever case is appropriate for their function in their own clause.

A **noun phrase** is a noun along with its article (if any) and any modifiers between the article and the noun. The noun is called the **head** of the noun phrase. Modifiers may be adjectives, other noun phrases in the genitive, prepositional phrases, and the like. Modifiers after the article are in **attribute position** and are considered part of the noun phrase, while modifiers in **predicate position**, outside the article-noun group, are a separate noun phrase. Thus a sentence like ὁ ἄνθρωπός ἐστι ἀγαθός (or ὁ ἄνθρωπος ἀγαθός, or ἀγαθὸς ὁ ἄνθρωπος) has two noun phrases, one which modifies the other in predicate position. The modifiers of a noun may be adjectives, other noun phrases in the genitive case (as for example ἡ τοῦ ἀνθρώπου θυγάτηρ), or prepositional phrases (for example, οἱ ἐν τῇ πόλει ἄνθρωποι). A noun phrase works as a unit to fill a syntactic role, such as "subject" or "direct object." That is, in a sentence like ἡ γυνὴ τὴν θυγατέρα φιλεῖ, strictly speaking the subject is the phrase ἡ γυνή, not just γυνή alone. Modifiers may be quite complicated, as ἡ ἀγαθὰ βιβλία γράψασα γυνὴ τὴν ἐν τῇ οἰκίᾳ θυγατέρα φιλεῖ. Here the noun γυνή is modified by a participle γράψασα, which has a direct object, ἀγαθὰ βιβλία, that is itself a noun phrase including an adjective. The noun θυγατέρα is modified by a prepositional phrase. An English speaker might expect something like ἡ γυνὴ, ἢ ἀγαθὰ βιβλία ἔγραψε, φιλεῖ τὴν θυγατέρα, ἥ ἐστι ἐν τῇ οἰκίᾳ, but that is not as graceful in Greek.

If the modifier is particularly long, the article may be repeated after the noun, as ἡ γυνὴ ἡ ἀγαθὰ βιβλία γράψσα. This creates a sort of "extended" attribute position, allowing the listener or reader to know what the noun is before the modifiers come along.

The **nominative** is the subject of a finite verb: ἡ γυνὴ γράφει. It may also be the predicate after a linking verb: οὗτός ἐστι ὁ πατήρ. If the subject of that linking verb is not nominative, however, the predicate noun or adjective is the same case as the subject: λέγω τοῦτον εἶναι τὸν πατέρα (accusative), τοῦ ἀνθρώπου, τοῦ πατρὸς ὄντος, ἀκούω (genitive), δῶρον τῷ ἀνθρώπῳ, τῷ πατρὶ ὄντι, δίδωμι (dative).

The **genitive** has two main groups of uses. In one group, nouns in the genitive depend on other nouns; in the other group, the main idea has to do with separation.

These are the major uses for genitives depending on other nouns. First of all, the genitive can indicate **possession**: ἡ γυνή ἐστι μήτηρ τοῦ παιδός.

Especially with numbers and superlatives, the genitive can indicate the whole of which a part is singled out (**partitive genitive** or **genitive of the whole**): τρεῖς τῶν ἀνθρώπων, ὁ ἄριστος τῶν Ἀχαιῶν.

With a noun denoting a verbal or verb-like idea, the genitive may show the doer of the verbal action (**subjective genitive**), as τῶν Ἑλλήνων πόλεμος (that is, οἱ Ἕλληνες πολεμοῦσι) or the object of the verbal action (**objective genitive**), as ὁ ποιητὴς τοῦ ᾄσματος (that is, τὸ ᾆσμα ποιεῖ).

The **genitive of material** indicates what something is made of, as οἰκία ξύλου. The **genitive of price** indicates its value, as βιβλίον τριῶν ὀβολῶν. The **genitive of measure** is similar to both of these, as τεῖχος πέντε πήχεων.

The following are the uses where the genitive has a sense of separation.

Verbs meaning "stop," "need," or "lack" take a genitive complement, as χρημάτων χρήζομεν.

The **genitive of comparison** goes along with comparative adjectives, as ὁ λέων ἐστὶ μείζων τοῦ μυός.

The genitive can indicate the **source** something comes from, as θυγάτηρ τοῦ πατρός, or τοῦ διδασκάλου ἀκούω (source of sound).

It can indicate **time or space within which** something happens, as καθεύδω τῆς νυκτός.

Verbs meaning "touch" or "hit" generally take a genitive complement, as ὁ παῖς τοῦ ἑταίρου πέτρᾳ τυγχάνει.

The **genitive absolute** is a phrase in the genitive case, typically a participle and its subject noun, loosely connected to the rest of the sentence, as τοῦ στρατοῦ μαχομένου, ὁ βασιλεὺς καθηῦδε.

Finally, many prepositions can take the genitive, particularly when their meaning is related to one of the usual genitive uses.

The **dative** has three major uses: indirect object of a verb, location in time or space, and means or instrument.

The **indirect object** is someone or something secondarily affected by the action of the verb, for example the recipient of a gift, as τῷ ἀνθρώπῳ βιβλίον δίδωμι. The **dative of advantage** (or **of disadvantage,** as appropriate) is similar, except that while some verbs need an indirect object, no verb *requires* a dative of advantage. An example is ὁ πατὴρ τοῖς τέκνοις πονεῖ, works on his children's behalf. The **possessive dative**, used with linking verbs, is also in this group of functions: ἡ οἰκία ἐστί μοι means roughly the same as τὴν οἰκίαν ἔχω.

The dative can also indicate **place where** or **time when**, as ἡμέρᾳ τινὶ ξένος ἦλθε. Dative of place where is poetic; prose would use a preposition.

The **dative of means** is an instrument (not a person) by which something is done, as καλάμῳ γράφω. The **dative of manner** tells how something is done, as σιωπῇ ἀναγιγνώσκομεν. The **dative of degree of difference** tells how much bigger, smaller, or whatever a compared object is to the standard of comparison, as ὁ λέων ἐστι μείζων τοῦ μυός τέτταρσι ποσί, "bigger by four feet," that is, "four feet bigger."

Prepositions can take the dative as well.

The **accusative** is primarily the case for the **direct object**, as τὸν λόγον λέγω. Some verbs take two accusatives, as ὁ διδάσκαλος τοὺς μαθητὰς τὴν τέχνην διδάσκει.

The **subject of an infinitive** is in the accusative, as λέγω τὸν ἄνθρωπον εἶναι ἀγαθόν.

The accusative of **extent of time** or **extent of space** tells how large something is or how long it takes, as ἀναγιγνώσκομεν τρεῖς ὥρας.

The **accusative of respect** qualifies or limits an action or a description, for example specifying a part of the body that is affected. For example, ὁ ἄνθρωπός ἐστι τυφλὸς τὸν ἀριστερὸν ὀφθαλμόν, "blind with respect to his left eye," that is, "blind in his left eye." The **adverbial accusative** is similar, as τέλος ἡ γυνὴ ἦλθε, "in the end, with respect to the end." Note in particular the neuter accusative singular τί; meaning "why?"

The accusative can indicate **place to which**, as τὴν κώμην ἔρχεται, though this is a poetic construction, and prose would use a preposition.

Prepositions may take the accusative as well.

The **vocative** is the case of direct address: χαῖρε, ὦ φίλε.

Although the **locative** case no longer really exists in Greek, there are several productive suffixes that make place adverbs from nouns: -δε, -φι, -ι, -θεν. Of these, -φι and -ι indicate a location, as οἴκοι "at home"; these are vestiges of the original locative. The suffix -δε denotes a destination, as οἴκαδε "homeward," and -θεν denotes motion away, as οἴκοθεν "from home."

The **antecedent** of a pronoun is the noun that the pronoun seems to stand in for. The pronoun has the gender and number of its antecedent but takes its case from its function in its own clause. The antecedent may or may not ever be explicitly stated. Consider for example a question like τίς τοῦτο ἐποίησε; The speaker presumably does not know who did it, the antecedent of τίς, though we may find out that antecedent in the answer to the question. As for τοῦτο, its antecedent may have been explained earlier, or may be something the speaker is pointing at (something knocked over, perhaps) which never gets put into words.

An adjective may be used alone without a noun, as ὁ ἀγαθὸς τὸν κακὸν μισεῖ. In this case the noun will be clear from context, for example if the text so far has identified a good man and a bad one, or if the adjective has general reference, making a general statement about any good man and any bad one. In fact, anything that could modify a noun can be used as a noun phrase, with an article, with or without an actual noun to be the head of the phrase: ἡ ἐν τῇ οἰκίᾳ is just as acceptable as ἡ ἐν τῇ οἰκίᾳ γυνή. Whereas English uses placeholder words like "one" in such contexts, Greek does not. Sometimes adjectives used this way are called **substantivized adjectives**. This comes from an older way of naming the words of the nominal system: older grammar books may refer to **nouns substantive** and **nouns adjective** for what we now usually call nouns and adjectives respectively. In that system "nouns" are all the words of the nominal system; "nouns substantive" are those that have a single given gender; "nouns adjective" are those that can modify another noun, and agree with it in gender: the name indicates that the modifier is generally *adjacent* to the noun.

3. The verbal system

Words in the verbal system have tense, mood, and voice. Finite verb forms also have person and number; non-finite forms do not. A **verb phrase** is a verb with its modifiers; the direct object or other essential arguments, typically not including the subject, may also be considered part of the verb phrase. Thus in ὁ ἄνθρωπος τὸ δένδρον ὁρᾷ, the smallest verb phrase is ὁρᾷ, which has no modifiers. The group τὸ δένδρον ὁρᾷ is the larger verb phrase consisting of the verb itself and its object. A **clause** is a finite verb with its subject (if explicitly expressed), objects and other complements, and modifiers; if the clause is a **subordinate clause**, it also includes a **subordinating conjunction** or other word (a relative pronoun, for example) to mark it as subordinate and indicate its relationship to the main clause. A verb phrase with a non-finite verb (an infinitive or participle) is usually not called a clause.

The subject of a Greek verb does not need to be explicit in a sentence. Finite verbs are marked for person and number, so there is no need for subject pronouns like English "I, you, she" except for clarity or to mark a change of subject.

The **tenses** in Greek are present, imperfect, future, aorist, perfect, pluperfect, and future perfect; the future perfect is rare enough to ignore. The **moods** are indicative, imperative, subjunctive, optative, infinitive, and participle. Of these, the **finite moods** are the indicative, imperative, subjunctive, and optative: these moods have different forms for different persons and numbers. The **infinitives** of each tense are verbal nouns and the **participles** are verbal adjectives.

The **person** of a verb indicates who the subject is. The first person is the speaker (singular) or a group including the speaker (plural); Greek does not have first-person dual verb forms. The second person is the listener, or a pair or group including the listener. The third person is everyone else. The **number** of a verb tells whether the subject is one person or thing (singular), or two (dual), or more (plural).

The **tense** of a verb more or less indicates the time when the action takes place. For example, ἡ γυνὴ γράφει, she is writing now; ἡ γυνὴ ἔγραψε, she wrote in the past; ἡ γυνὴ γράψει, she will write later. For verbs in the indicative in main clauses, the aorist, present, and future tenses simply indicate past, present, and future time from the point of view of the speaker.

But tense can also indicate **aspect**, which is a view of an action as either continuing (or habitual, or a process) or completed (or a unit of action rather than a process). In the imperative, for example, the difference between γράφε and γράψον is entirely aspect: the aorist imperative γράψον gives a simple command, telling the listener to perform a single act of writing, but the present imperative γράφε tells the listener to write habitually, or to take up a process of writing.

In the indicative, tense generally indicates time, especially in main clauses. The difference between the imperfect and the aorist, however, is one of aspect: both tenses indicate past time, but the imperfect considers a past action as a process, or makes a point of its duration, while the aorist says only that it is past.

In the imperative, as noted above, tense indicates aspect. In participles, tense generally indicates time relative to the time of the main verb, so in γράφουσα ᾖσε, "she sang while writing," the writing is going on at the same time as the singing. The singing is in the past (the main verb is aorist indicative), so the writing is also in the past, but the present participle indicates that the action is going on concurrently with the action of the main verb.

The tense of an infinitive may indicate either time or aspect, depending on how it is used. An infinitive in indirect statement generally indicates time from the point of view of the original speaker; it will have the same tense as the indicative that would have been in the speaker's exact words. Thus εἶπε τὴν στρατίαν νικήσειν corresponds to εἶπε, "ἡ στρατία νικήσει". The speaker said the conquering was going to happen in the future, subsequent to the time when he was making this statement. On the other hand, an infinitive may also indicate aspect. For example, the difference between κελεύω σε γράφειν and κελεύω σε γράψαι is exactly the same as the difference between γράφε and γράψον.

In the subjunctive, tense usually indicates aspect. In the optative, tense normally indicates aspect, but when the optative replaces an indicative in indirect statement (by the **OOO rule**), tense indicates time just as for the infinitive in indirect statement.

The pluperfect tense is a past anterior, past before the past; it exists only in the indicative and always refers to time. The perfect tense is slightly outside the tense/aspect system framed by the present system and the aorist system. It is **stative**, referring to the present consequences of a past action, or to the state that action has produced. For example, τοῦτον ἔλυσα just says that the action happened, while τοῦτον λέλυκα is not just "I set him free" but more like "I am his liberator."

The **voice** of a verb form indicates the subject's relationship to the action. When the subject is the doer of the action the verb is active: ὁ ἄνθρωπος τὸ πρᾶγμα πράττει. When the subject is the undergoer, recipient, or patient, the verb is passive: τὸ πρᾶγμα ὑπὸ τοῦ ἀνθρώπου πράττεται. The middle voice has this name because it is sort of in between the active and the passive: the subject does the action, but for himself or herself, or arranges the action for his or her benefit, or does it to himself or herself. Thus ὁ ἄνθρωπος τὸ πρᾶγμα πράττεται means roughly the same as ὁ ἄνθρωπος τὸ πρᾶγμα πράττει but with the additional idea that the person is doing this deed for himself.

Some verbs only have middle forms, or only have middle forms in some tenses (for example, in the future). For such verbs the "self-interested" or "involved" sense may seem natural, intrinsic to the meaning of the verb. An example is ἡγέομαι, since thinking is certainly an action that involves its subject intimately. On the other hand, νομίζω has a similar meaning but is active. It is not always possible to identify a specifically middle meaning in a verb that *only* has middle forms; the middle meaning mainly comes through when it can be contrasted with the meaning of active forms of the same tense system of the same verb.

The following paragraphs summarize some of the main uses of the moods. See also the next section, on sentence constructions.

The **indicative** is the mood of ordinary statements and questions. It appears in main clauses and subordinate clauses when there is no special reason to use another mood. It is also the mood for counterfactual statements or impossible wishes, as for example ὁ ἄνθρωπος, εἰ θυγατέρα ἢ υἱὸν ἔσχε, πατὴρ ἦν ἄν, implying that the man has neither a daughter nor a son and therefore is not a father.

The **imperative** gives a command. Tense indicates aspect: aorist imperative for a simple command, present imperative commanding a habitual action or a longer process. There are no first-person imperative forms.

The **subjunctive** makes a generalization, normally in a subordinate clause with ἄν, as ὅντινα ἂν βλέπῃ, τρέφει "anyone he sees, he feeds; whenever he sees anyone, he feeds him." It can also be used in place of the imperative, in the first person where there are no imperative forms (this can be called **hortatory subjunctive**), or in a negative command, especially in the aorist. The subjunctive can be used for a question expressing doubt, almost always in the first person, as τί ποιήσωμεν; "what should we do?" This is called **deliberative subjunctive**. In addition to general clauses, two other types of subordinate clause require a subjunctive: **fear clauses**, as φοβεῖται μὴ ὁ ἀνὴρ ἄλλην φιλῇ, "She is afraid her husband loves somebody else"; and **purpose clauses**, as λέγω ἵνα ἀκούῃς, "I speak for you to hear."

The **optative** is primarily used to mark a subordinate clause in past tense. Many kinds of subordinate clauses (though not all) may take the optative instead of the normal mood (the indicative or subjunctive) when the main verb of the main clause is in a past tense. As this is an option for the writer, not a requirement, we call it the **OOO rule**, for "or optional optative, in secondary sequence." The **sequence of moods** is the set of rules about which moods in a subordinate clause follow which tenses in a main clause: primary sequence means the ordinary mood for the type of clause, when the main verb is in a primary tense, and secondary sequence means the ordinary mood or the optional optative, when the main verb is in a secondary tense. Primary tenses are the present, the future, and (normally) the perfect; the future perfect is also primary. Secondary tenses are the aorist, the imperfect, and the pluperfect.

The optative can be used for hypothetical statements or conditions, always with the particle ἄν if it is in a main clause. This is the **potential optative**. In a hypothetical conditional, the optative may appear in both the if-clause and the main clause; then the particle will be only in the main clause. For example, εἰ γράψαιμι, πάντες ἀναγιγνώσκοιεν ἄν, "if I were to write (hypothetically, but it probably isn't going to happen), then everybody would read."

The optative can also express a wish, often along with the particles εἴθε or εἰ γάρ, as εἴθε εὖ γένοιτο, "may it turn out well."

The **infinitive** is a verbal noun. As a noun, it is always neuter singular; since it does not have different case forms, its case is shown by an accompanying article if necessary. A Greek verb has ten different infinitives: present active, present middle/passive, future active, future middle, future passive, aorist active, aorist middle, aorist passive, perfect active, perfect middle/passive. The subject of an infinitive is in the accusative case. The infinitive may also have a direct object or whatever other complements the verb normally takes.

The **complementary infinitive** is required to complete the meaning of various verbs, as ἐθέλω γράφειν. The infinitive can also be the subject, as δεῖ γράφειν, "writing is necessary." Some verbs, like δεῖ, almost always have an infinitive as subject, but the infinitive can be the subject of other verbs as well, as γράφειν ἀγαθόν ἐστι, "writing is good" (subject of ἐστι).

The infinitive can have other noun functions, as μανθάνετε τῷ ἀναγιγνώσκειν, dative of means. When the infinitive is primarily a noun and accompanied by an article it can be called an **articular infinitive**. If an articular infinitive has an object or other complement, or is modified by an adverb, those words may come after the article, as μανθάνετε τῷ βιβλία ἀναγιγνώσκειν.

The infinitive is one way to express an **indirect statement**, as λέγω τὸν διδάσκαλον βιβλία γράφειν. Here tense denotes time: the tense of the infinitive is the same as whatever tense of the indicative the speaker used in the actual statement being quoted.

To express **natural result**, or the result normally expected from a state of affairs, Greek uses the infinitive with ὥστε, as οὕτως σοφός ἐστι ὥστε ἡμᾶς αὐτοῦ ἀκούειν, "he is so wise that we listen to him," as a general rule, not necessarily referring to a particular incident. But an actual result clause takes the indicative; it does refer to a particular incident.

The conjunction πρίν takes the infinitive when the sentence makes a positive statement, as οἱ μαθηταὶ ἀκούουσιν πρὶν λέγειν. When the main verb is negative, temporal clauses of this type take a finite verb.

The infinitive may limit the sense of certain adjectives or nouns, as οὗτός ἐστι ἄριστος μάχεσθαι, "best at fighting." The adjectives and nouns that use this construction often imply ability or suitability, as ἡ πέτρα ἦν ἱκανὴ βάλλειν, "the rock was suitable for throwing."

Sometimes the infinitive is used instead of the imperative as a command, as in chapter 16 reading 7.

The **participle** is a verbal adjective. A verb has ten participles, with the same tenses and voices as the ten infinitives. The tense almost always indicates time relative to the time of the main verb of the sentence. Each participle inflects for number, gender, and case like any other adjective. The subject of a participle is the noun it modifies; participles may be substantivized like other adjectives, however, so the noun need not be present in the sentence, as οἱ βλέποντες ἐχαίρησαν, "the spectators, the ones watching." If the participle is in attribute position, including a case like the previous example in which the participle itself is the head of the noun phrase, it is called an **attributive participle**; otherwise, it is in predicate position and is called a **circumstantial participle**. The participle may have an object or other complements of its own, as οἱ τὸν ἀγῶνα βλέποντες, "those watching the game," or ἡ γυνή, τὸν ἀγῶνα βλέπουσα, τοῦ ἀνδρὸς οὐκ ἀκούει, "the woman, while (or because, or if) she is watching the game, isn't listening to her husband."

The relationship of a circumstantial participle to the action of the main verb may be specified by adverbs like καίπερ or ὡς, but is often left vague. The relationship may be temporal ("while, when, earlier, later"), causal (the participle gives a reason for the main action), conditional (the participle is like an if-clause), or concessive ("although, even though").

One particular case of a circumstantial participle is a future participle, often with ὡς, indicating an intention or purpose, as ὁ ἀνὴρ ἦλθε ὡς βλέψων, "he came to see, intending to see."

Some verbs take a **supplementary participle** instead of a complementary infinitive, as ὁ παῖς παύει γράφων.

A participle may be used instead of an infinitive in indirect discourse, especially with verbs that refer to knowing, seeing, thinking, hearing, or the like. For example, μέμνημαι τὸν διδάσκαλον τοῦτο εἰπόντα, "I remember the teacher said this." Here τὸν διδάσκαλον is both direct object of μέμνημαι and subject of εἰπόντα.

The perfect participle middle/passive forms periphrases for third-person plural indicative forms with impossible consonant clusters, as γεγραμμένοι εἰσί corresponding to singular γέγραπται. The perfect subjunctive and optative middle and passive are also made periphrastically with this participle and the present subjunctive or optative of εἰμι.

The **genitive absolute** is a phrase, normally a participle and its subject, in the genitive case, giving another piece of information somehow related to the rest of the sentence. The noun of the genitive absolute phrase does not appear elsewhere in the sentence. For example, τῆς γυναικὸς τὸν ἀγῶνα βλεπούσας, ὁ ἀνὴρ καθεύδει. The sentence does not specify whether he goes to sleep because she is busy, or falls asleep even though he could be watching alongside his wife, or simply happens to be sleeping at the same time.

4. Sentence-level constructions

In the previous section we considered verbal syntax from the point of view of the verb forms. In this section we will look at the syntax of types of clauses and sentences.

A sentence has a main clause and may also have subordinate clauses (or subordinate participial phrases or infinitive phrases). The main clause normally has a finite verb, most often in the indicative, though any finite mood is possible. A **clause** is a finite verb phrase plus its subject if the subject is expressed. In a **subordinate clause**, there is a marker of subordination, which may be a subordinating conjunction like ἐπεί or a relative pronoun like ὅς or ὅστις. A subordinate clause cannot be a complete sentence. A **main clause** is a clause without a subordinator; such a clause can stand alone as a grammatically complete sentence. These may be declarative sentences or questions (typically in the indicative), commands (imperative or subjunctive), or wishes (optative or indicative).

Syntax permits the phrases that make up a Greek sentence to be arranged in any order. That is, a sentence like λύπης ἰατρός ἐστιν ἀνθρώποις λόγος (chapter 3 reading 1, from Menander) could also be written as ὁ λόγος ἐστὶ ἀνθρώποις ἰατρός λύπης, or as ἀνθρώποις ἐστὶ λύπης ὁ λόγος ἰατρός, or in any other order, and still be grammatically correct Greek. What determines the order of a particular sentence is its connection with other sentences, so we will discuss word order in the next section. In general, though, a rule of thumb is that something already known or established in the context comes first, the new information the sentence has to tell about that something comes next, and everything else follows along behind. Often this means an explicit subject comes first, and the verb comes last, but these are tendencies rather than rules.

In **nominal sentences** there is no finite verb, as if it has been omitted. A nominal sentence consists of a noun phrase and either a modifier in predicate position or another noun phrase, and the missing finite verb would be a linking verb. Thus διδάσκαλος οὗτος or ἀγαθὸς ὁ ἄνθρωπος are nominal sentences which could be written with finite verbs as οὗτός ἐστι διδάσκαλος and ἀγαθός ἐστι ὁ ἄνθρωπος. The tense to be understood will depend on context.

As noted above, occasionally an infinitive will be used in place of an imperative and will thus be the main verb of a main clause, but this is an exception to the general rule about finite verbs.

Greek has two negative words, οὐ and μή, along with their compound forms like οὐδείς, μηδείς, and so on, each used in different situations. Most clauses and verb phrases are negated with οὐ. The following types take μή instead:

- Commands of all sorts: imperatives, commands in the subjunctive, indirect command
- Deliberative subjunctive
- The if-clause of a conditional sentence
- Purpose clause
- Natural result (with infinitive)
- Wishes (with optative or with indicative)
- Indirect quotation of oaths or of emotional statements
- Indirect questions with εἰ
- Any participial phrase behaving like a clause that would take μή
- Any infinitive phrase except in indirect discourse

In addition, μή is a subordinator with verbs of fearing, and optionally with verbs of forbidding, preventing, or hindering. When those clauses are negated, the negative is οὐ, resulting in μὴ οὐ together. To strengthen or emphasize a negation, Greek uses more than one negative word together, always putting the simple οὐ (or μή) first. But in a sentence with a compound negative followed by a simple one, the negatives cancel out, as in οὐπότε οὐ μαθήσεται, "he will never fail to learn, he will positively always learn."

Each type of subordinate clause calls for a verb in a particular mood. When the main verb of the main clause is in a secondary tense, certain subordinate clauses allow an optional optative instead of the expected mood. This **OOO rule**, "Or Optional Optative in secondary sequence," applies to the following types of clause:

- Indirect statement with finite verb
- Indirect question
- Purpose clause
- General subjunctive clause with ἄν (but that particle is not used with the optative)
- Fear clause

A **conditional sentence** has a subordinate clause introduced by εἰ, giving the hypothesis, and a main clause giving the conclusion that follows from that hypothesis. Traditionally the if-clause is called the **protasis** and the then-clause the **apodosis**. Depending on the moods in the protasis and apodosis, a conditional sentence can imply that the hypothesis is likely, unlikely, or impossible, or make no special claim one way or another. These are the various combinations:

- Simple conditional: nothing implied about the probability of the hypothesis, only that the conclusion follows. Indicative in both clauses; no ἄν in either clause.

- Generalizing conditional: stronger statement that *whenever* the hypothesis holds, the conclusion results. Subjunctive with ἄν in protasis (always in crasis, ἐάν), indicative in apodosis; OOO rule applies.

- Potential conditional: suggests that the hypothesis is uncertain or unlikely. Optative in the protasis, optative with ἄν in the apodosis (potential optative).

- Contrary-to-fact conditional: implies that the hypothesis is actually not true, and says what would have happened if it had been. Indicative in both clauses, imperfect or aorist, with ἄν in apodosis.

Observe that only the generalizing conditional uses ἐάν, because only this form has the subjunctive in the protasis. In the apodosis, ἄν goes with the potential optative in the potential conditional, and with the impossible indicative in the contrary-to-fact conditional.

Several other families of subordinate clauses have the same structure as the family of conditionals: an ordinary version using indicatives; a generalizing version in which the subordinate clause has the subjunctive with ἄν, and the OOO rule applies; and a potential or hypothetical version in which both main clause and subordinate clause have the optative, with ἄν in the main clause. In particular, relative clauses and temporal clauses work this way.

Two forms of conditional sentence have traditional names beyond the plain description of their formation. A general conditional with the future indicative in the apodosis can be called **future more vivid**. A potential conditional is called **future less vivid**.

The simplest form of the crasis εἰ + ἄν is ἐάν, but you will also see the contracted forms ἄν and ἤν. The form ἤν is effectively unambiguous; there is an exclamatory particle ἤν but context will always make it clear whether the clause containing this form is a conditional (necessarily a subordinate clause) or an exclamation. The form ἄν that is a contraction from ἐάν has a long vowel, while the original particle ἄν has a short vowel; unfortunately, this is not much help in telling them apart in a prose text. What *is* useful is that the particle ἄν is post-positive, never first in its clause, usually either second or next to the verb, while the contraction ἄν = ἐάν typically *is* first in the clause.

Indirect quotation includes **indirect statement** (quotation of a plain statement), **indirect question** (quotation of a question), and **indirect command** (quotation of an order). Of these, indirect command is the simplest: it is the complementary infinitive with verbs like κελεύω, as ὁ πατὴρ κελεύει τὸν παῖδα ἐλθεῖν. Tense indicates aspect; the negative is μή.

An indirect question is a clause with a finite verb, introduced by an indirect question word like ὅπου, or by εἰ if the direct question might have had ἄρα, or by πότερον for either-or questions. The verb is in the indicative; the OOO rule applies; the negative is the same as for the direct form, normally οὐ.

There are three different ways to express an indirect statement: with a finite verb, with an infinitive, or with a participle. Indirect statement with a finite verb uses ὅτι or ὡς as subordinator. The tense and mood of the verb are the same as in the direct version of the statement, and the same negative would be used. Note that the person of the quoted verb may change. For example, the direct statement ὁ ἄνθρωπος λέγει, "βιβλίον ἔχω" would become ὁ ἄνθρωπος λέγει ὅτι βιβλίον ἔχει in indirect discourse, since the subjects of the two verbs are in fact the same. The OOO rule applies, unless the optative would mean something different. In particular, if the quotation is a contrary-to-fact conditional or an impossible wish, it must stay in the indicative. If the quoted statement has subordinate clauses of its own, and its main clause is changed to optative by the OOO rule, the subordinate clauses may be changed as well if they happen to be in primary tenses, but will not be changed if they are not. For example, ὁ ἄνθρωπος εἶπε, "ὁ παῖς, ἐπεὶ τὴν φωνὴν ἤκουσε, ἐχαίρησε." In indirect discourse this could be ὁ ἄνθρωπος εἶπε ὅτι ὁ παῖς, ἐπεὶ τὴν φωνὴν ἤκουσε, ἐχαίρησε or it could be ὁ ἄνθρωπος εἶπε ὅτι ὁ παῖς, ἐπεὶ τὴν φωνὴν ἤκουσε, χαιρήσαι. In either version the subordinate verb ἤκουσε stays in the aorist indicative.

In the infinitive form of indirect statement, the tense of the quoted verb is maintained, but the mood is changed to infinitive, and therefore the case of the subject, if present, must be accusative rather than nominative. If the subject of the quotation is the same as the subject of the main sentence, however, an adjective modifying that subject will stay in the nominative, so ὁ ἄνθρωπος λέγει, "ἀγαθός εἰμι" would become ὁ ἄνθρωπος λέγει ἀγαθὸς εἶναι. If there are subordinate clauses within the quotation, they keep their original moods, as ὁ ἄνθρωπος λέγει τὸν παῖδα, ἐπεὶ τὴν φωνὴν ἤκουσε, χαιρῆσαι.

In the participle form, the tense of the quoted verb is maintained but the mood is changed to participle. The subject of the quotation becomes a complement of the main verb, in the appropriate case (usually the accusative), and the participle agrees with it. This form is typical for verbs of knowing or perception, as ὁ ἄνθρωπος οἶδε τὸν παῖδα ἐρχόμενον. The same idea could be expressed as ὁ ἄνθρωπος οἶδε ὅτι ὁ παῖς ἔρχεται or even ὁ παῖς ἔρχεται. ὁ ἄνθρωπος τοῦτο οἶδε.

A **relative clause** is a subordinate clause introduced by a relative pronoun, either the ordinary relative ὅς, ἥς, ὅ or the generalizing relative ὅστις, ἥτις, ὅ τι. Such a clause is adjectival, modifying its antecedent. For example, in τὸν παῖδα ὁρῶ, ᾧ βιβλίον ἔδωκας, the relative clause modifies παῖδα, which is the antecedent of the pronoun ᾧ. The pronoun and the antecedent are in different cases, because the noun is direct object of ὁρῶ but the pronoun is the indirect object of ἔδωκας. Ordinary relative clauses take the indicative, or whatever other mood is required by sense, as τὸν παῖδα ὁρῶ, ὅς τὸ βιβλίον λαμβανέτω, roughly "I see the child, who must take the book," or "I see the child, and he'd better take the book." Generalizing clauses take the subjunctive with ἄν, and their negative is μή.

A variety of subordinating conjunctions introduce different kinds of **temporal clauses**, telling the time relationship between the subordinate clause and the main clause. The simplest is ὅτε, which follows roughly the same rules as εἰ. A simple temporal clause uses the indicative; a generalizing clause uses the subjunctive with ἄν (always in crasis, ὅταν), and the OOO rule applies to this form.

The conjunctions ἐπεί and ἐπειδή indicate that the circumstance in the subordinate clause is relevant to that in the main clause, but without specifying whether the relationship is purely temporal, purely causal, or some combination of the two. The constructions of the clauses are just as for clauses with ὅτε, and in the generalizing form they also require crasis of ἄν, so ἐπειδάν or ἐπήν or ἐπάν.

To say that the main idea comes before the subordinate idea, Greek uses πρίν, which is both an adverb and a conjunction. As a conjunction, πρίν normally takes the infinitive, as ὁ παῖς γράφει πρὶν τὸν διδάσκαλον ἔρχεσθαι, "the child writes before the teacher comes." But when the main verb is negative, πρίν takes a finite verb: indicative for a specific incident, subjunctive plus ἄν for a general statement (the OOO rule applies here), optative if the main verb is a potential optative. This is roughly the same as the distinction in English between "main happens *before* subordinate" and "main doesn't happen *until* subordinate."

To say that the main idea goes on while the subordinate action does, or as long as the subordinate action does, Greek uses ἕως or μέχρι, for example ὁ διδάσκαλος ἔλεγε ἕως οἱ μαθηταὶ ἤκουον, "the teacher spoke while the students listened, spoke as long as the students were listening." The verb of the subordinate clause has durative aspect (from the present system), because the important idea is the continuation of this action. These conjunctions can also have the sense that the main clause goes on until the subordinate action happens, as ὁ διδάσκαλος ἔλεγε ἕως οἱ μαθηταὶ ἀπῆλθον, "the teacher spoke until the students left." In this sense, the verb of the subordinate clause has punctual aspect (from the aorist system), because the subordinate action is viewed as a single point in time that marks a change in the main action. Like many other subordinate clauses, clauses with ἕως or μέχρι may take ἄν plus subjunctive for a general statement, or the other constructions of conditional or relative clauses.

To indicate purpose, Greek uses ἵνα, ὅπως, or ὡς with subjunctive; the OOO rule applies, and the negative is μή. An older name for a **purpose clause** is a **final clause**.

There are two kinds of **result clauses** in Greek, those denoting the actual result of something (**actual result**) and those denoting the usual or expected result (**natural result**); the latter are not exactly clauses, since they use the infinitive rather than a finite verb. An older term for a result clause is a **consecutive clause**. The negative of a natural result phrase is μή; that of an actual result clause is οὐ.

5. Beyond the sentence

In this section we look briefly at the grammar of discourse in classical Greek: how sentences relate to each other. This idea goes beyond what is usually considered syntax to touch on **pragmatics** and **style**. Pragmatics means the practical aspect of language, or how people use it to communicate. Style means the way one speaker or writer uses language differently from another. Just as a word does not have its full meaning until it is combined with other words into a sentence, so sentences are not really meaningful without context. Here, then, we look at how context gives meaning to sentences.

As we noted in the previous section, syntax does not restrict the order of the phrases that constitute a Greek sentence. Any order is grammatically allowable. The choice of word order is not random, however, but communicative. Typically, what comes first is what the sentence is about, a person, thing, or action already established in the context; this is the **Topic**. Next is the new information the sentence is intended to convey, the **Focus**. Everything else follows along behind; if the verb is not the Topic or the Focus, it typically comes next, and less essential information comes at the end.

The (grammatical) subject can generally be taken for granted: if it is the same from one sentence to the next, it is not repeated. When two subjects alternate, as in a report of a conversation ("Socrates said ... Then Phaedrus said ... And Socrates replied ..." or the like), the particle δέ can mark the alternation, sometimes even without a noun (for example, ὁ Σωκράτης εἶπε ... ὁ δὲ Φαῖδρος εἶπε ... ὁ δὲ ἀπεκρίνατο ...). The two participants have already been introduced into the story; here δέ marks a shift in Topic within the same over-all subject of discussion, from one established participant to another.

Sentences are connected by conjunctions and particles, particularly in more formal style. If a new sentence begins without any connector at all (called **asyndeton**, unconnectedness), listeners and readers will notice a break. In conversation, as in drama or in dialogues, the break may be insignificant; in narrative, the break may indicate a change of subject and may be deliberately abrupt.

These are some of the major sentence connectors. They are post-positive (never first in the sentence, often second) except as noted.

- δέ is common and relatively neutral; it says roughly "within the same general area of discussion, consider this topic"
- δή is a like strengthened version of δέ, and tends to emphasize the previous word or give it focus
- μέν as a sentence connector is much like δέ with the additional idea of contrast, so "consider first this topic, then another which will be contrasted with it"
- οὖν indicates that this sentence states a conclusion that follows from what has gone before. ἄρα can do this as well (though with the imperfect, ἄρα has a sense like "so *that's* the way it is," or "but in fact it's been like *this* all along")
- γάρ indicates that this sentence gives a reason or explanation for what has come before
- καί comes first when it connects sentences; it makes the second sentence a peer of the first
- ἀλλά also comes first, and indicates that the second sentence is a peer of the first one, but with some unexpected point
- μέντοι can mark emphasis, can indicate agreement, and can mark the next step in a logical argument
- οὐκοῦν also indicates the next step in an argument or a narrative
- οὔκουν can be a strong negative or, in a question, can indicate surprise or impatience
- γε emphasizes or limits the word it follows
- τοι calls for the listener's attention

Although all the ancient Greek literature we have is written (necessarily, since there was no other way to record literature in the classical age), some of this literature imitates conversation. In tragedy, characters speak and sing in verse, and they may speak in strict, constrained patterns, for example alternating speeches of exactly one line each (this is **stichomythia**) or exactly two lines (**distichomythia**). In comedy, although the dialogue is still in verse, the meter and the construction of speeches are more flexible, so the dialogue seems closer to the way people must really have spoken. Prose genres, like Plato's dialogues or Lucian's, are free to imitate speech even more closely. In all these conversational forms, speakers may not use complete, textbook-like sentences, but may leave words out, throw in exclamations, interrupt each other, change their minds half-way through a sentence, or even get so snarled up in a complicated construction that the sentence ends up ungrammatical. This can be confusing at first, even though the same sorts of things happen in English, indeed in all languages.

For example, consider these lines, Sophocles' *Antigone* 44-46:

> Ἰσμήνη· ἦ γὰρ νοεῖς θάπτειν σφ᾽ , ἀπόρρητον πόλει;
> Ἀντιγόνη· τὸν γοῦν ἐμὸν καὶ τὸν σόν ἢν σὺ μὴ θέλῃς
> ἀδελφόν· οὐ γὰρ δὴ προδοῦσ᾽ ἁλώσομαι.
>
> γοῦν = γε οὖν, θέλω = ἐθέλω, a variant primarily used in verse.

Antigone's reply is elliptical; she expands on her sister's bare pronoun σφέ with τὸν ἐμὸν ἀδελφόν, using the accusative as if to replace Ismene's word. Then, the participle προδοῦσα is missing a direct object, but it is clear that she means ἀδελφόν again; the word is not in the same clause, so cannot actually be the object of the participle, but there is no need to repeat it as the sense is clear.

In reading, then, it is necessary to consider the context: a sentence that might make no sense, or be incomplete, if seen in isolation, takes its meaning from its relationship to the rest of the passage and the situation. The sentences of grammar exercises, with explicit subjects, verbs, and objects, are somewhat artificial; connected language, particularly in conversation, leaves much implicit, to be understood by the speakers from the context.

APPENDIX 3

Accents

These are the rules for accents in ancient Greek. The main principles come first, followed by details and examples. Accents govern pronunciation of Greek words, and there are many minimal pairs of words that differ only in the position or type of accent.

The Rules

1. A normal word, in normal circumstances, has exactly one accent.

2. (Law of limitation) The accent can only be on the last three syllables of a word, never earlier.

3. Nouns have **persistent accent**.

4. Finite verb forms have **recessive accent**.

5. (Last syllable rule) When a word ends with an acute accent, if it is followed by another non-enclitic word, the accent becomes grave; when a word ends in a circumflex, the accent does not change.

6. (Way-back rule) When a word has a circumflex on the penult, or an acute on the antepenult, and it is followed by an enclitic, the word gains a second accent, an acute on its ultima.

7. When a word has an acute on its penult, if it is followed by a two-syllable enclitic, the enclitic gets an acute accent on its second syllable.

8. (Chain rule) An enclitic followed by another enclitic gets an acute on its last syllable.

9. If the word before an enclitic is elided, the second syllable of the enclitic gets an accent.

Definitions

It is convenient to have names for the syllables. The **ultima** is the last syllable of a word (from Latin *ultima syllaba* "last syllable"). The **penult** is the second to last, Latin *paene ultima* "almost last." The **antepenult** is the third to last (from Latin *ante* "before," so "before the almost-last syllable").

The accents, as you know, are the **acute** (ά), denoting raised pitch; the **circumflex** (ᾶ), denoting pitch that rises and falls on the same syllable; and the **grave** (ὰ), used in place of the acute when it falls on the last syllable of a word that is not the end of a sentence.

There are also traditional names for words with various accent patterns. The acute is ὀξύς "sharp." A word with an acute on its last syllable is **oxytone**. A word with acute on its penult is **paroxytone**, and if the acute is on the antepenult, the word is **proparoxytone**. The circumflex is περισπώμενος "bending around," so a word with a circumflex on its ultima is called **perispomenon** and one with a circumflex on the penult is **properispomenon**. If a word has no accent on its ultima (if it is paroxytone, proparoxytone, or properispomenon), it can also be called **barytone**, from βαρύς "heavy."

Exercise

Give examples of words that are oxytone, paroxytone, proparoxytone, perispomenon, and properispomenon.

The Details

1. A normal word, in normal circumstances, has exactly one accent.

Abnormal words are **proclitics** and **enclitics**. Proclitics cannot come last in a sentence, and enclitics cannot come first. A proclitic is a "before-leaning" word and an enclitic is an "on-leaning" word; these words need other words to lean on. A **clitic** is a proclitic or enclitic: this is the more general term.

Strictly, for accent we are concerned with **prosodic** proclitics and enclitics — that is, words that are proclitic or enclitic because they have no accent. There are also **syntactic** proclitics and enclitics. These are words that are pronounced and written with accents, but have restrictions on their position in a sentence: they need words to lean on. Every prosodic clitic is also a syntactic clitic, but not the other way around. For example, καί is a syntactic proclitic (it cannot be last) but not a prosodic proclitic (it has an accent), and ὁ is both a syntactic proclitic and a prosodic one. Similarly, γάρ is a syntactic enclitic (it cannot be first) but not a prosodic enclitic, while τοι is enclitic both syntactically and prosodically.

Proclitics and enclitics are normally written with no accent, except when they earn one from rules 7, 8, or 9. In isolation (in the dictionary, for example) the two-syllable enclitics are often written with an acute on the second syllable, as εἰμί.

The proclitic words are ὁ, ἡ, οἱ, αἱ, ἐν, ἐκ, εἰς, εἰ, ὡς, and οὐ, along with the sandhi forms of ἐκ and οὐ. Note that all the other forms of the article have accents. Sometimes οὐ is not enclitic, for example when it is the entire answer to a question or the entire δέ branch of a contrast. In this case it is written οὔ.

The enclitic words are:

- forms of εἰμι in the present indicative, except for εἶ
- forms of φημι in the present indicative, except for φής
- the particles γε, τε, τοι, περ, also the particles κε, ῥα which are not used in Attic

- the variants νυ, νυν of the adverb νῦν
- the "short" pronoun forms μου, μοι, με, σου, σοι, σε
- the short forms from the poetic third-person pronoun, οὑ, οἱ, ἑ, μιν, νιν, σφε, σφι
- the indefinite pronoun τις in all its forms (not to be confused with the interrogative τίς, which always has an accent)
- the indefinite adverbs ποτε, που, πως, ποι, ποθεν, ποθι, πη

These are the only proclitic and enclitic words in Greek; every other word has an accent.

2. (Law of limitation) The accent can only be on the last three syllables of a word, never earlier.

Furthermore, when the last syllable has a long vowel, the accent cannot be on the antepenult (Long Vowel Rule). A circumflex accent can only go on a long vowel (including diphthongs); an acute can be on a long vowel or a short one. When the accent belongs on the penult, and the vowel of the penult is long, and the vowel of the ultima is short, the accent is a circumflex. For example, the second person singular present imperative active of χαίρω is χαῖρε. But if the accent is on the penult and the ultima has a long vowel, the penult must have acute, as τούτων.

Final -αι and -οι, even though they are diphthongs, count as short for accentuation, except in optative verb forms. But when αι and οι appear before the final syllable, or when the last syllable is one of these sounds followed by a consonant (such as -αις or -οιν), the diphthong counts as long in the usual way. For example, the dative plural of θάλαττα is θαλάτταις: the accent cannot remain on the antepenult. But in the nominative plural θάλατται, the accent does not have to move because the final -αι counts as short.

Circumflex accents often arise from contraction. The position of the accent is fixed first, before contraction happens. Then, if the accent is on the first of the two vowels that contract, the resulting long vowel has a circumflex. If the accent is on the second of the two vowels that contract, the resulting long vowel has an acute. If the accent is not on either of the two vowels that contract, it is unaffected.

In nouns that have **quantitative metathesis**, the position of the accent is fixed first, and is unaffected by the metathesis. The resulting forms have accents that look wrong. For example, the genitive singular of πόλις "city" was originally πόληος, with the usual third-declension genitive singular ending and a normal accent. After quantitative metathesis, the form is πόλεως with accent on the antepenult even though the ultima has a long vowel. There are two groups of nouns with quantitative metathesis, the Attic declension in the second declension and the I-stems and a subset of U-stems in the third; these are the only words where this anomalous accent happens.

3. Nouns have persistent accent.

This rule applies to all words in the nominal system: nouns, pronouns, and adjectives. It also applies to verbal nouns (that is, infinitives) and verbal adjectives (that is, participles). The nominative singular of a noun, or the masculine nominative singular of an adjective, shows where the accent belongs.

By rule 2, the accent on different forms of the noun may be on different syllables. For example, consider ὁ ἄνθρωπος, τοῦ ἀνθρώπου. The ending for the genitive singular has a long vowel, so the last syllable of the genitive singular form has a long vowel, so the accent cannot be on the antepenult. This is difficult for English speakers because in English all forms of a word are normally stressed on the same syllable — but in Greek, it's not that way.

For infinitives and participles, the accent is always the same in a given tense and voice, for all verbs. For example, the present participle active has accent on the last syllable of the stem, like κελεύων, and the second aorist participle active has accent on the first syllable of the ending, like λιπών.

The accent of the genitive plural of the first declension looks like an exception, since it is always on the ultima, but this is in fact a regular form. The ending was originally -άων, which necessarily has an accent on the alpha. In Attic Greek this form contracts, resulting in -ῶν.

A few nouns in the third declension do not have persistent accent. If the nominative singular is one syllable, then the accent is on the stem in the nominative and accusative, but on the ending in the genitive and dative, in all three numbers. For example, θήρ, θηρός, θηρί, θῆρα are the singular forms of "beast." And μήτηρ "mother" and θυγάτηρ "daughter" have mobile accent: nom. sg. θυγάτηρ, gen. sg. θυγατέρος or θυγατρός, voc. sg. θύγατερ, dat. pl. θυγατράσι.

You must learn the accent of a noun or adjective as part of its spelling and pronunciation. There are some general tendencies, though, which you may learn as a group if you like. For example all short-a nouns in the first declension have recessive accent (that is, persistent accent on the earliest possible syllable), and all third declension nouns ending -ις with -ιτος in the genitive, like χάρις, are recessive.

4. Finite verb forms have recessive accent.

That is, the accent on a finite verb form is as early as possible in the word, consistent with rule 1. Non-finite forms, however, are nouns or adjectives and are accented accordingly; see rule 3. Just as with nouns, different forms of the same verb may be accented on different syllables. For example, μανθάνει and ἐμάνθανε are both third-person singular indicative active, respectively present and imperfect tense. The present form has a long vowel in its last syllable, so the accent cannot go back to the antepenult. The imperfect form has a short vowel in its last syllable, so the accent does go back to the antepenult.

In verbs compounded with a prefix, the accent will never be earlier than the past indicative augment or earlier than the reduplication of the perfect system. Thus ἀπῆλθον is accented on the penult, not the antepenult because that syllable is before the augment.

5. (Last syllable rule) When a word ends with an acute accent, if it is followed by another non-enclitic word, the accent becomes grave; when a word ends in a circumflex, the accent does not change.

At the end of a sentence (or, at the editor's option, before any punctuation), a final acute is retained. If the next word is enclitic, the acute is also retained. For example, ὁ μαθητὴς ἦν ἀγαθός shows grave accent on the noun, before the non-enclitic verb form, but acute on the adjective at the end of the sentence. But in ὁ μαθητής ἐστι ἀγαθός, the noun keeps acute before the enclitic.

The interrogative pronoun τίς is the only exception to this rule. Its masculine/feminine nominative singular τίς and neuter nominative/accusative singular τί never have acute. (The other forms of this pronoun have the ordinary accent: they have a circumflex or an accent on the first of two syllables.) Thus τί ποιεῖς;

6. (Way-back rule) When a word has a circumflex on the penult, or an acute on the antepenult, and it is followed by an enclitic, the word gains a second accent, an acute on its ultima.

That is, when the accent is as far back as an accent of this type is ever permitted to go, the word can have a second accent. This is the only circumstance in which a Greek word can have two accents. For example, δῆλόν ἐστι ὅτι ὁ ἄνθρωπός ἐστι ἀγαθός.

7. When a word has an acute on its penult, if it is followed by a two-syllable enclitic, the enclitic gets an acute accent on its second syllable.

That acute probably turns into a grave, by the Last Syllable Rule. For example, ἡ διδασκάλη ἐστὶ ἀγαθή. An example where the Last Syllable Rule does not apply is οὐκ οἶδα ὅπου ἡ διδασκάλη ἐστί.

8. (Chain rule) An enclitic followed by another enclitic gets an acute on its last syllable.

This can happen as many times as necessary, if there are several successive enclitics. Because enclitics tend to cluster in second position in a clause, there often will be. For example, ὁ μαθητής γέ ἐστι ἀγαθός.

The tendency of enclitics to cluster in second position is called **Wackernagel's Law**. It applies both to prosodic enclitics and to syntactic enclitics. It is not a grammatical rule — the only rule is that enclitics cannot be first, not that they must be second.

9. If the word before an enclitic is elided, the second syllable of the enclitic gets an accent.

This only applies to two-syllable enclitics, of course, but the word before a one-syllable enclitic is never elided. Elision is optional in prose, so in writing you may avoid this rule entirely. Here is an example: ἐκεῖνος δέ ἐστι ἀγαθός may also be written ἐκεῖνος δ' ἐστὶ ἀγαθός.

Exercises

1. Look through the readings and find an example demonstrating each rule.

2. Write sentences of your own to demonstrate each of the rules.

Appendix 4

Meter

Poetic **meter** is a pattern using some normal feature of the language in a stylized way. In English, meter is based on stress, so metrical verse has patterns of stressed and un-stressed syllables. In Classical Greek, meter is based on **quantity**, with patterns of long and short syllables. Although many of the same traditional names are used to describe English and Greek meters (like "iambic" and "dactylic"), the two types of meter are quite different and the terms don't refer to the same things.

1. Quantity

By definition, every syllable in Greek is either long or short. In principle the difference is based on how long it takes to pronounce a syllable: long syllables take longer than short ones. For metrical purposes, all long syllables are treated the same way and all short ones are treated the same way — there are only two categories.

To determine which syllables are long and which are short, we must begin by identifying syllables. Each Greek word has as many syllables as it has vowel sounds (counting a diphthong as a single vowel sound). A syllable consists of an **onset**, a **nucleus**, and a **coda**. The onset and coda may be omitted, but the nucleus is always there. The nucleus is the vowel sound; the onset is the consonants that come before the vowel, if any; the coda is the consonants that come after it, if any. For example, the word πᾶς has one syllable, with onset π-, nucleus -ᾶ-, and coda -ς. The word ἀνθρώποις has three syllables, ἀν-θρώ-ποις.

To divide a word into syllables, then, it is necessary to determine which consonants go with which vowels. The basic rule is that a single consonant between vowels is the onset of the following syllable, and a cluster of consonants is divided to form the coda of the preceding syllable and the onset of the following one. Thus in ἄνθρωπος, we divide ἄν-θρω-πος, making the π the onset of the last syllable -πος and splitting the cluster νθρ between the first and second syllables.

The letters ζ, ξ and ψ represent consonant clusters, which will be divided between syllables: ἔγραψε is divided as ἔγ-ραπ-σε, πράξω is divided as πράκ-σω, νομίζω is divided as νο-μίσ-δω. You would never *write* the words this way, but this is how they are divided into syllables.

Aspirate consonants are not double consonants. Beginners are sometimes confused by this because in English words derived from Greek, or in English transliteration of Greek words, an aspirate consonant is represented by two letters, the basic unvoiced consonant and an *h* to represent the aspiration. But an aspirate consonant is a single sound in Greek.

An **open syllable** is one that ends with a vowel. A **closed syllable** is one that ends with a consonant. Every syllable is therefore either open or closed. In the examples above, we have πᾶς, closed; ἀνθρώποις, closed, open, closed; ἔγραψε, closed, closed, open; πράξω, closed, open; νομίζω, open, closed, open.

Exercise 1

Divide the following words into syllables and indicate whether the syllables are open or closed: κάλαμος, ἀγαθή, βλέπει, γράφεις, ὀφθαλμός, βιβλία, βιβλίων, διδάσκαλος, ποῖος, ἀποθνήσκομεν, ἀνθρώπου, ἄλλον, δένδρα, θελκτήριον, ἐβλέψαμεν.

A **short syllable** is an open syllable whose vowel is short. A **long syllable** is a closed syllable or a syllable with a long vowel. Traditionally, syllables with long vowels are called **long by nature**, while closed syllables are called **long by position**. For metrical purposes, there is no difference: both are simply long syllables. The symbol ¯, called **macron**, represents a long syllable, while ˘, a **breve**, represents a short one; in discussion of metrical patterns, these symbols mark positions in the pattern where a long or a short syllable goes.

The vowels η and ω are always long, while ε and ο are always short. Any vowel with a circumflex is necessarily long. Any vowel with iota subscript is a diphthong and therefore long. All diphthongs are long vowels for metrical purposes, even those that are treated as short for accent purposes. Thus in ἄνθρωποι, the final syllable -ποι is a long syllable metrically (because it has a long vowel, the diphthong οι) even though the vowel is treated as short for accentuation and does not cause the accent to move.

The onset does not affect whether a syllable is long or short. That is, the syllables ε, τε, τρε, στρε are all short, even though obviously the fourth one takes rather longer to pronounce than the first.

It is possible to have a long *syllable* with a short *vowel*: that the syllable is closed, and therefore long, does *not* make the vowel long. For example, in ἔγραψε, all the vowels are short, even though the first two syllables are long ("by position"). It is wrong to say "the alpha is long by position"; what is long by position is the *syllable*, not the vowel. If you find this confusing, you may prefer to use the alternate terminology, borrowed from Sanskrit: an open syllable with a short vowel is a **light syllable**, and a closed syllable or one with a long vowel is a **heavy syllable**. On the other hand, you should not be led astray by the Sanskrit terms either: heavy syllables in this sense do *not* have extra stress, and light syllables are *not* automatically unstressed. Ancient Greek meter has nothing to do with stress, and accent in ancient Greek is (primarily) a change of pitch, not of loudness. The accented, acoustically prominent, syllable of a Greek word may be a short (light) syllable, a long (heavy) syllable with a short vowel, or a long (heavy) syllable with a long vowel.

Exercise 2

Divide the following words into syllables and say whether the syllables are long (heavy) or short (light). You may need to look up whether α, ι, and υ are long or short in a particular word. ἐβλέψαμεν, θελκτήριον, ἀποθνήσκομεν, ἄκουε, θάλαττα, θυγατράσι, δήλοις, ποιοῦσιν, γέγραφε, ἔβλεψε, ἁμαρτία, υἱός, παίδευσαι, παιδεῦσαι, παιδεύσαι, σύμμαχος.

In verse, an entire metrical phrase (roughly, a line; technically, a period: see below) is treated as a single word: syllable divisions do not respect word breaks. In other words, consonants at the start of one word may cause the last syllable of the previous word to be closed. For example, consider this line from Menander (chapter 2, reading 1):

τυφλόν τε καὶ δύστηνόν ἐστιν ἡ τύχη.

It is divided into syllables as follows:

τυφ-λόν τε καὶ δύσ-τη-νό-νἐσ-τι-νή τύ-χη

— — — ᴗ — — — ᴗ — — —

Note that the last syllable of δύστηνόν would be long in isolation, but in context the -ν is "captured" by the following vowel to become a syllable onset, leaving the syllable -νό- open. Similarly for ἐστιν.

Here is another example, from the *Iliad* (chapter 10, reading 7):

ἐκ δ᾽ εὐνὰς ἔβαλον, κατὰ δὲ πρυμνήσι᾽ ἔδησαν·

ἐκ δ᾽εὐ-νὰ-σἔ-βα-λον, κα- τὰ δὲπ-ρυμ-νή-σι᾽ ἔ-δη-σαν

— — — ᴗ — — — — ᴗ ᴗ — —

Here the second syllable of εὐνάς is long by nature, since the word is the accusative plural of a first-declension noun. The last syllable of ἔβαλον is long by position because the consonants ν κ are divided between the syllables, making the end of the verb a closed syllable, thus long. The cluster πρ- is also divided, so the previous syllable is δεπ, closed and therefore long (by position). Remember that the vowels ο and ε in these syllables are not long: only the syllables are long, not the vowels.

In many types of verse, the unit that is treated as a single "word" for scansion is the same as the typographic line. In others, a single verse line may extend over several print lines; this depends on the metrical family and on the particular pattern within the family. Specific rules and tendencies for each of the major families will be discussed in the remaining sections of this appendix. For the exercises in the rest of this section, you may assume a print line and a verse line (scanned as one word) are equivalent.

The last syllable of a verse line is always considered long by position. That is, the end of the line **makes position**, or causes the final syllable to be treated as closed.

Exercise 3

Divide the following lines into syllables and mark each syllable as long or short: Chapter 2, reading 2, 3; chapter 3 reading 1 (all 4 lines), reading 19 (both lines); chapter 4, reading 4 (both lines); chapter 5, reading 11 (both lines).

So far, this all seems straightforward enough, but there are exceptions to the tidy rules. Both of the major exceptions involve treating a syllable as short when it could have been long; this is called **correption**, from Latin *corripio* in the sense "squish together, abridge."

The first kind of correption involves consonants. A consonant cluster consisting of a stop and a liquid may, at the poet's option, be kept together as onset of the next syllable rather than being divided. The result is that the prior syllable is short when it might otherwise have been long. For example, in chapter 4 reading 4, the first line is ἀεὶ μὲν εἰρήνη γεωργὸν κἀν πέτραις. The last word could be divided either as πέτ-ραις, two long syllables, or as πέ-τραις, short and long. In this line, because of the metrical pattern in use, it must be short-long, so this is an example of this kind of correption. (For the metrical pattern in question see section 4 of this chapter.) Because Attic poets exploit this option more often than other poets, it is called **Attic correption**. If you are reading Attic verse (drama, in particular), you can expect that a stop-plus-liquid cluster will probably be kept together, though not invariably. If you are reading non-Attic verse (such as epic, or archaic lyric), you may expect that such a cluster will probably be split and close the previous syllable, though, again, not invariably.

Note that the stop and liquid must be in that order. A liquid followed by a stop will always be split, closing the previous syllable, so for example ἔργον must be divided ἔρ-γον. Similarly, if the two consonants are both stops or both liquids, they are split, as δάκ-τυ-λος or ὀφ-θαλ-μός. A cluster of *more* than two consonants always makes position: at least one must always close the previous syllable, as in ἄν-θρω-πος. The sibilant σ is not a liquid, so clusters of σ plus stop always make position (cause the preceding syllable to be closed). Because stops are sometimes called mutes, Attic correption is sometimes called the **mute-and-liquid rule**.

The second type of correption is correption in **hiatus**. Hiatus means a gap, in this case the gap between two vowels. Normally poets try to avoid writing a word that ends with a vowel followed by a word that begins with a vowel, like εἶμι ἐγώ. Sometimes it's sufficient to throw in a particle, like γε or δέ (see chapter 8, reading 8, εἶμι δ᾽ ἐγώ). Sometimes the first word can be elided, as ἔστ᾽ ἄλφα (chapter 1 section 2). Sometimes crasis is possible, as κἀν πέτραις (chapter 4, reading 4). But sometimes two vowels *will* be adjacent, as in θαυμάζειν μοι ἔπεισιν (chapter 6, reading 13). In this case, when the prior vowel is long, it may be treated as short, as it is in this line: μοι is metrically a short syllable, by correption in hiatus before the ε. This kind of correption is more common in epic verse. As with Attic correption, correption of the first of two adjacent vowels is the poet's choice, not the reader's: it will be clear from the metrical pattern whether a syllable that could undergo correption actually does or not. In Greek verse, elision or crasis will always be written in; this is different from the convention for most Latin verse. Thus if you see two adjacent vowels in Greek, you know they are *not* elided, and you have only to determine whether the first is a long vowel that may be treated as short by correption in hiatus.

Exercise 4

Identify positions in the following lines where Attic correption or correption in hiatus *could* occur. (Since you do not yet know the metrical patterns, you cannot tell whether correption actually *does* occur; you may come back to this after you've read the rest of this appendix.) Chapter 2 reading 3, chapter 3 reading 19, chapter 4 reading 2, chapter 18 reading 9.

Less commonly, two syllables in a word may be treated as one, as if contracted; this often happens with forms of θεός. You will recognized this contraction (called **synizesis**) only because it's necessary for the meter to make sense. For example, in these lines from *Bacchae*, the word θεοῦ must be a single long syllable:

διὰ δὲ χειμάρρου νάπης
ἀγμῶν τ᾽ ἐπήδων θεοῦ πνοαῖσιν ἐμμανεῖς.

◡ ◡ ◡ – – – ◡ –

– – ◡ – – – ◡ – – – ◡ –

This passage is in iambic trimeters (see section 4 below). If θεοῦ were ◡ – here, the line would have too many positions and would not be correct.

2. Metrical families

The fundamental metrical patterns of Greek verse are sequences of roughly eight to twelve syllables with particular patterns of long and short elements. These sequences are called **cola** (from κῶλον, -ου, τό, limb). Cola with similar properties make up a metrical family. Each family has its own preferred cola and its own rules for which elements of a colon can vary and in which ways. An **element** is a position in a colon, basically a slot that can be filled by a syllable, or under certain conditions by two syllables.

A **period** is a group of one or more cola taken together into a metrical phrase, optionally connected by **link elements**. Very roughly, a period is a line, and when they are short enough they are printed as separate typographical lines. If a period is too long for a single print line, it will be spread over as many lines as necessary, divided at colon boundaries (and often with all the print lines after the first one indented to indicate the continuation). Within a period, a **link element** is a single position that comes between two recognizable cola. That position might be a long element (always filled by a long syllable), a resolvable long element (one that can be filled by a long or by two shorts; see below), or an **anceps** position, that is, one that can have either a long syllable or a short one. Some period shapes become standard and are re-used by many poets; others are one-off creations for a single poem.

There are four major metrical families in Greek verse: **aeolic**, **iambic** and **trochaic** (which go together), **dactylic**, and **anapestic**. There are two minor families as well, **ionic** and **dochmiac**. Each family has its own major types of colon, its own standard periods and ways of linking cola together, and its own rules for what may vary within a colon. Each family is also associated with particular literary genres, and each literary genre is associated with a dialect of Greek. As a result, there is a rough correlation between metrical family and dialect.

For example, lyric verses to be sung by choruses are generally in aeolic or dactylic meters. Because the choral genre was invented by poets using the Doric dialect, it is conventional for *all* choral lyric to use Doric dialect features, even when the song is part of a play which is otherwise in Attic dialect. (The major Doric dialect feature in drama is the use of α in places where Attic dialect has changed it to η, for example μάτηρ instead of Attic μήτηρ. This is not specifically Doric, since most dialects keep the original long α, but it is recognizably different from Attic.)

The **aeolic** family is named for the Aeolic dialect used by some of the early poets, such as Sappho and Alcaeus. Of all the Greek verse forms, this family is closest to the verse form inherited by Greek from Proto-Indo-European. Aeolic cola allow variation only at the beginning; the end or **cadence** is fixed. A characteristic aeolic colon is the glyconic, ᴑᴑ–◡◡–◡–, where the symbol ᴑ ᴑ represents two syllables that may not both be short.

The **iambo-trochaic** family involves patterns with alternate long and short positions, so that the short elements come one at a time rather than in pairs. In this family some long elements may be **resolved** (that is, replaced by two short syllables), under appropriate conditions, and there may also be anceps positions. A typical colon is −◡−◡−◡−, and a typical period pattern is ×−◡−×−◡−×−◡−, the pattern of a line in drama.

The **dactylic** family has its short elements in pairs. Sometimes those pairs may be **contracted** (that is, replaced by a single long syllable). The most important dactylic colon is −◡◡−◡◡−, called the hemiepes.

The **anapestic** family has pairs of short elements, like the dactylic family. It allows both contraction (like dactylic meter) and resolution (like iambo-trochaic meter). This is the meter for the entrance of a chorus in drama, and almost always for the last lines of a play. A characteristic colon is the paroemiac, ◡◡−◡◡−◡◡− − .

The **ionic** family is used for exotic effects; for example, Aeschylus uses it to give a Persian color to his play *Persians*. It has short syllables in pairs, like anapestic and dactylic meter, but also has long syllables in pairs. Resolution may be allowed but contraction is rare. The characteristic plain colon is ◡◡− − ◡◡− − . A variant, used in non-dramatic lyric, is called the anacreontic, ◡◡−◡−◡− − . In this variation the fourth and fifth positions of the plain ionic colon seem to be swapped.

Finally, the **dochmiac** family consists of the single colon ◡− − ◡−, with many permissible variations. Dochmiacs are used only in the lyric portions of drama, and usually connote high emotion, whether positive or negative.

Some general principles apply to all the metrical families. All Greek meter is made of cola. One or more cola, possibly connected with link elements, make up a period, which is the major metrical phrase. A poem is made up of one or more periods. Sometimes every period has the same metrical shape (allowing for whatever variation is permitted by the metrical family), sometimes each period is different. A poem consisting of one period of moderate length repeated over and over is called **stichic**, from στίχος, -ου, ὁ, a row or line. Epic verse is stichic: each period or line has the same shape, a particular form from the dactylic family. Similarly, the dialogue in drama is stichic, normally using a particular iambic form. You will learn these and other standard stichic forms in the next sections. Verse which is not stichic is divided into **stanzas**. A stanza may be one or more periods long. Sometimes every stanza has the same metrical pattern. For example, one well-known two-period stanza from the dactylic family is called the **elegiac couplet**; the **Sapphic stanza** is a three-period stanza from the aeolic family. Other verse is organized in **strophic pairs**. This means that two stanzas of the same pattern can be followed by two more of a different pattern, then two more of yet another pattern, and so on for as long as the poet wishes to continue. In each pair the first stanza is called the **strophe** and the second the **antistrophe**; strophe and antistrophe in the same pair have the same metrical pattern as each other, but not the same as the other pairs. Strophic pairs are common in the lyrics of drama. A similar organization is into **triads**, groups of three stanzas of which the first two match and the third has a different form. The three parts of the triad are **strophe, antistrophe,** and **epode**. Normally in triadic verse every triad has the same pattern, so if there are two triads in a poem, there are six stanzas, four using one pattern (the strophes and antistrophes) and two using another (the epodes). Typically all the cola of a stanza will come from the same metrical family, but not invariably, and different strophic pairs may draw from different metrical families, especially in tragedy.

In order to make sense of the form or structure of a Greek poem, then, you need to recognize the metrical family and the particular cola and periods in use. The four major metrical families sound different: some have short elements in pairs, some only one at a time, some both; some allow many successive long syllables (through contraction), others allow many successive short syllables (through resolution), others permit less variation. With experience you will learn to recognize the families by ear. You will also learn the most common patterns, such as the iambics of dramatic dialogue, the dactylics of epic, or the elegiac couplet. But to understand lyric verse you must be able to understand patterns you have not heard before: Greek lyric poets (unlike most classical Latin poets) normally invent a new stanza pattern for each new poem.

To determine the structure of a stanza, the next step after identifying the family is to determine where the periods end. The rules for period-end are the same in all families. The end of a period is *always* the end of a word, and often the end of a syntactic group as well. Words may continue across colon boundaries, but never across period boundaries. Thus the first rule for figuring out the period division in a poem is to look for places where there is always word end, in every repetition of the pattern.

Take the following passage from Menander as an example (chapter 3, reading 1).

> λύπης ἰατρός ἐστιν ἀνθρώποις λόγος·
> ψυχῆς γὰρ οὗτος μόνος ἔχει θελκτήρια·
> λέγουσι δ᾿ αὐτὸν οἱ πάλαι σοφώτατοι
> ἀστεῖον εἶναι φάρμακον καὶ χρήσιμον.

The basic pattern is twelve elements per printed line. (There is a **resolution** in the second line, so that one of the elements — the sixth — contains two syllables; more on that in section 4.) The initial scansion is as follows:

$$\text{—} \quad \text{—} \quad \text{∪—∪} \quad \text{—∪} \quad \text{—} \quad \text{—} \quad \text{—} \quad \text{∪—}$$
$$\text{—} \quad \text{—} \quad \text{∪} \quad \text{—} \quad \text{—} \quad \text{∪∪} \quad \text{∪—} \quad \text{—} \quad \text{—} \quad \text{∪∪}$$
$$\text{∪—∪} \quad \text{—∪} \quad \text{—} \quad \text{∪—} \quad \text{∪—∪—}$$
$$\text{—} \quad \text{—} \quad \text{∪} \quad \text{—} \quad \text{—} \quad \text{—∪—} \quad \text{—} \quad \text{—∪—}$$

The basic pattern of each line appears to be ×–∪–×–∪–×–∪×. That is, this pattern is repeated four times. Is it a period, or is it part of a larger structure?

The last element of a period is always long. If a naturally short syllable appears at the end of a period, it becomes long by position. The next criterion for period end, then, is to observe short syllables at the end of cola where you would expect long ones, or where there are long syllables in other repetitions of this pattern in the poem. The criterion is called **brevis in longo**, from the Latin description *syllaba brevis in elemento longo*, a short syllable (in reality) in a long element (of the pattern). Remember that it is only the end of a *period* that makes position, not the end of a print line: in simple stichic forms, a period fits onto a print line and they are the same thing, but in much lyric verse, a period may spread over several print lines.

In our example, the last syllable of the second line is short, but the last syllable of each of the other lines is long (except perhaps the third; see below). That is, in the second line we have brevis-in-longo. This strongly indicates that the end of the second line is the end of a period. We might have two periods, each printed on two typographical lines, or four periods, each being one repetition of the pattern we have observed, and each printed on one line.

Hiatus can also indicate period end. As you saw in section 1, Greek poets avoid hiatus betwen vowels within a period. At the end of a period, however, hiatus is allowed.

In our example, we have hiatus between σοφώτατοι and ἀστεῖον, at the end of the third line and start of the fourth. If the two words were together in a single period, you would expect correption of the diphthong. But if this is period end, then the last syllable of σοφώτατοι is long and the hiatus is permitted. Thus hiatus tells us the end of the third line of the passage is a period end.

We conclude that the quotation consists of four periods. The basic pattern is ×–◡–×–◡–×–◡–, and each print line is a metrical period. The end of this pattern can be marked by brevis-in-longo (as at line 2) or by hiatus (as at line 3). There is no explicit indication of period end at line 1 or line 4, but every instance of a stanza will always have the same period ends. Because each period is the same, and the periods are not very long (they fit on a single print line), we observe that this is stichic verse.

Greek poets like to end periods with more than one long syllable. One way to accomplish this is with **catalexis** (from κατάλεξις, -εως, ἡ, removal, taking away), the removal of a syllable from near the end of a colon. For example, a typical iambic form is ×–◡–×–◡–×–◡–. Its catalectic variant is ×–◡–× –◡–×– – . Similarly, the glyconic colon (mentioned above as typical of aeolic meter) is ∘∘–◡◡–◡–. Its catalectic variant is ∘∘–◡◡–– – . Although catalectic cola may appear anywhere in a period, so catalexis does not guarantee period end, the sound of two or more long syllables together at the same point in the pattern, and always ending with word end, is a clue that this position *might* be the end of a period.

Thus to determine period end, look for places in the metrical pattern where there is always word end, every time the pattern repeats, and where there is brevis-in-longo or hiatus in at least one repetition. Places where there is catalexis along with consistent word end are also possible period ends.

Exercise

> In the following passages, determine where period ends occur, and whether they are marked by brevis-in-longo, by hiatus, or both. Chapter 9 reading 1, chapter 9 reading 2, chapter 10 reading 7, chapter 11 reading 5, chapter 12 reading 1. Slightly more challenging: chapter 18 reading 2 (A and B are separate poems).

3. Aeolic verse

Meters of the aeolic family are used for lyric verse. In this family, each colon begins with a variant portion called the **aeolic base**, or just the **base** for short. The center of the colon is the **nucleus**, and its shape will always be –◡◡– or one of a small number of possible variations on this. After the nucleus comes the **tail**. In each colon, variation is only permitted in the base: one or more elements of the base will be anceps. Neither contraction nor resolution is permitted, so an aeolic colon always has the same number of syllables as there are elements in the pattern. Different cola have different shapes for base and tail, and occasionally also for the nucleus.

The most characteristic aeolic colon is the **glyconic**, ∘∘–◡◡–◡– The notation ∘∘ means that the first two positions, which are the base, can be either long or short, provided that they are not both short. Thus there are exactly three possible realizations of a glyconic line:

—∪—∪∪—∪—

∪— — ∪∪—∪—

— — —∪∪—∪—

Nothing else can vary. The base of the glyconic is just two syllables; the tail is also two, a short and a long.

Many other aeolic cola can be analyzed as variations on the glyconic. The catalectic glyconic is so common that it also has a traditional name, **pherecratean**; it is ∘∘—∪∪— —. The **telesillean** is a glyconic with one less syllable at the beginning, ×—∪∪—∪—. That is, the telesillean is an **acephalic** or "headless" glyconic (from ἀ + κεφαλή). The phalacean hendecasyllable is ∘∘—∪∪—∪—∪— —, a glyconic with three more positions in the tail. Poets can create other new cola in the same kinds of ways, with different tails or different bases, or both.

Variation can also happen in the nucleus. One widely-used variant is a glyconic with a double nucleus, ∘∘ —∪∪— —∪∪— ∪—. Because the —∪∪— pattern is sometimes called a **choriamb**, this variation is called **choriambic expansion**. The traditional name for a glyconic with choriambic expansion is **asclepiad**. In principle choriambic expansion can be applied to any aeolic colon, though usually it is used with glyconics and pherecrateans. Two or even three extra nuclei can be inserted to produce longer and longer cola; often there is word-break between nuclei.

The form ∘∘ —∪∪—∪∪— ∪— has what seems to be a "reduplicated" nucleus: instead of the entire nucleus, only the first three elements are repeated. This is called **dactylic expansion** because the new nucleus —∪∪—∪∪— sounds like the characteristic colon of the dactylic family; in addition, the three repeated elements —∪∪ make up a unit traditionally called a dactyl.

Other standard aeolic cola include —∪—×—∪∪—∪— —, the **sapphic hendecasyllable**; ×—∪—×—∪∪—∪—, the **alcaic hendecasyllable**; and —∪∪— — , the **adonic**, which has no base.

Exercise 1

The following are in aeolic meters. Mark the long and short syllables and identify the cola; they will not necessarily be cola with traditional names. Where possible, determine where the period-ends are. Vocabulary for these texts, and for the rest of the examples and exercises in this appendix, will be found in the main vocabulary list at the back of the book.

a. Chapter 18 reading 2 (both poems).

b.

ἐν Δήλῳ ποτ᾽ ἔτικτε τέκνα Λητώ,
Φοῖβον χρυσοκόμην ἄνακτ᾽ Ἀπόλλω
ἐλαφηβόλον τ᾽ ἀγροτέραν
Ἄρτεμιν, ἣ γυναικῶν μεγ᾽ ἔχει κράτος.   (scolion 886)

c.

ὁ δὲ καρκίνος ὧδ᾽ ἔφη
χηλῇ τὸν ὄφιν λαβών·
"εὐθὺν χρὴ τὸν ἑταῖρον εἶ-
ναι καὶ μὴ σκολιὰ φρονεῖν."   (scolion 892)

d.

ἐν μύρτου κλαδὶ τὸ ξίφος φορήσω,
ὥσπερ Ἁρμόδιος κ' Ἀριστογείτων,
ὅτ' Ἀθηναίαις ἐν θυσίαις
ἄνδρα τύραννον Ἵππαρχον ἐκαινέτην.   (scolion 895)

Although Greek poets normally invented new stanzas for each poem, there are a few forms that became traditional and were re-used. In aeolic meters, the most important stanza forms are the sapphic stanza and the alcaic stanza. There is also a commonly used form consisting of glyconics one after another, usually closed off with a pherecratean (the catalectic glyconic).

The **sapphic stanza** is four cola: three sapphic hendecasyllables followed by an adonic. Although it is traditionally printed as four lines, there is no period-end after the third line, so it might more logically be printed as three lines. The form is named for Sappho, a poet from Lesbos in the 7th century, and one of the only major female writers in classical Greek literature. This is the scheme:

—∪—×—∪∪—∪—   —

—∪—×—∪∪—∪—   —

—∪—×—∪∪—∪—   —

—∪∪—   —

This is an example, Sappho fragment 34.

ἄστερες μὲν ἀμφὶ κάλαν σελάνναν
ἂψ ἀπυκρύπτοισι φάεννον εἶδος
ὄπποτα πλήθοισα μάλιστα λάμπη
γᾶν ἐπι παῖσαν.

Paraphrase in Attic prose: οἱ μὲν ἀστέρες ἀμφὶ τὴν καλὴν σελήνην ἂψ ἀποκρύπτουσι τὸ φαεινὸν εἶδος, ὁπότε πλήθουσα μάλιστα λάμπει ἐπὶ πᾶσαν τὴν γῆν.

The **alcaic stanza** is another four-colon form, this time in four actual periods. It is named for Sappho's contemporary and fellow-countryman Alcaeus. The first two cola are alcaic hendecasyllables. The third is related to iambics, since it has no double-short (no aeolic nucleus). The fourth can be called an aristophanean (—∪∪—∪—   —) with dactylic expansion; it has no base and has the "reduplicated" nucleus form. The schema is as follows:

×—∪—×—∪∪—∪—

×—∪—×—∪∪—∪—

×—∪—×—∪—   —

—∪∪—∪∪—∪—   —

Alcaeus fragment 335 is an alcaic stanza:

οὐ χρῆ κάκοισι θῦμον ἐπιτρέπην,
προκόψομεν γὰρ οὐδὲν ἀσάμενοι,
ὦ Βύκχι, φαρμάκων δ' ἄριστον
οἶνον ἐνεικαμένοις μεθύσθην.

Paraphrase in Attic prose: οὐ χρὴ τὸν θυμὸν κακοῖς ἐπιτρέπειν. οὐ γὰρ προκόψομεν εἰ ἀσώμεθα. τὸ ἄριστον, ὦ Βύκχι, πάντων φαρμάκων ἐστι οἶνον ἐνέγκαι καὶ μεθυσθῆναι.

In addition to the standard stanza patterns, poets invent their own aeolic stanzas. Here is an example from Aristophanes, *Knights* 551-564. This is the strophe; the antistrophe follows a bit later (lines 581-594) and has the same metrical pattern.

> ἵππ᾽ ἄναξ Πόσειδον, ᾧ
>   χαλκοκρότων ἵππων κτύπος
>   καὶ χρεμετισμὸς ἁνδάνει
>   καὶ κυανέμβολοι θοαὶ
>   μισθοφόροι τριήρεις,
> μειρακίων θ᾽ ἅμιλλα λαμ-
>   πρυνομένων ἐν ἅρμασιν
>   καὶ βαρυδαιμονούντων,
> δεῦρ᾽ ἔλθ᾽ ἐς χορόν, ὦ χρυσοτρίαιν᾽, ὦ
>   δελφίνων μεδέων Σουνιάρατε,
> ὦ Γεραίστιε παῖ Κρόνου,
>   Φορμίωνί τε φίλτατ᾽ ἐκ
>   τῶν ἄλλων τε θεῶν Ἀθη-
>   ναίοις πρὸς τὸ παρεστός.

The metrical pattern of this stanza is:

> –⏑⏑–⏑–⏑–　(4 times)
>   –⏑⏑–⏑–　–　(catalexis, so possible period end)
> –⏑⏑–⏑–⏑–　(2 more times)
>   –⏑⏑–⏑–　–　(catalexis again)
> –　–　–⏑⏑–　–　⏑⏑–　–　catalectic asclepiad, twice
> ∘∘–⏑⏑–⏑–　glyconic, three times
>   –　–　–⏑⏑–　–　pherecratean

The colon –⏑⏑–⏑–⏑– which opens this stanza is widely used, and sometimes treated as a kind of variation on the glyconic. Note that words can be split between cola, as λαμπρυνομένων in 556 and Ἀθηναίοις in 593, but never split between periods.

Exercise 2

Identify the cola and, where possible, the stanza forms of the following. The first passage is in Attic dialect, but the other two are in Aeolic. In the Aeolic dialect, accent is always recessive (on all words, not just verbs); there is no rough breathing, not even on initial υ; the diphthong ου is often replaced by οι, as in Μοῖσα for Μοῦσα; the sound σδ is written that way instead of with ζ; and, as you would expect, the Attic change of ᾱ to η has not taken place.

  a. Aristophanes, *Knights* 985-996

> ἀλλὰ καὶ τόδ᾽ ἔγωγε θαυ-
>   μάζω τῆς ὑομουσίας
>   αὐτοῦ· φασὶ γὰρ αὐτὸν οἱ
>   παῖδες οἳ ξυνεφοίτων,
> τὴν Δωριστὶ μόνην ἂν ἁρ-
>   μόττεσθαι θαμὰ τὴν λύραν,
>   ἄλλην δ᾽ οὐκ ἐθέλειν μαθεῖν·
>   κᾆτα τὸν κιθαριστὴν

ὀργισθέντ᾽ ἀπάγειν κελεύ-
ειν, ὡς ἁρμονίαν ὁ παῖς
οὗτος οὐ δύναται μαθεῖν
ἢν μὴ Δωροδοκιστί.

(Attic dialect. Note ξυνεφοίτων from συμφοιτάω, Attic ξυν- for συν-, and crasis κᾆτα = καὶ εἶτα. The last word of the passage, Δωροδοκιστί, is formed like ἑλληνιστί from δωροδοκία, bribery.)

b. Alcaeus fragment 362

ἀλλ᾽ ἀνήτω μὲν περὶ ταῖς δέραισι
περθέτω πλέκταις ὑποθύμιδάς τις
κὰδ δὲ χευάτω μύρον ἆδυ κὰτ τὼ
στήθεος ἄμμι.

(Aeolic dialect. Here ἀνήτω = ἀνήθου, Aeolic genitive form. περθέτω = περιθέτω, with the prefix shortened as may happen in verse. κάδ, κάτ = κατά, sandhi forms before dental consonants. χευάτω = χεάτω, dialect variant of the aorist stem. ἄμμι is Aeolic for ἡμῖν.)

c. Sappho fragment 16, lines 1-4

οἱ μὲν ἰππήων στράτον, οἱ δὲ πέσδων
οἱ δὲ νάων φαῖσ᾽ ἐπὶ γᾶν μέλαιναν
ἔμμεναι κάλλιστον, ἔγω δὲ κῆν᾽ ὄττω τις ἔραται.

(Aeolic dialect. This is the first stanza of a poem that was at least 5 stanzas long. ἰππήων = ἰππήων = ἰππέων, and νάων = νεῶν. φαῖσι = φησι. ἔμμεναι = εἶναι. κῆν᾽ = κῆνο = ἐκεῖνο. ὄττω = ὅ τι, ὅτι.)

4. Iambic and Trochaic Verse

The next major metrical family is the **iambo-trochaic** family. In this family, positions alternate between long and short, or, more accurately, between long and non-long. Spoken dialogue in drama is always in a meter from this family. Iambo-trochaic meters can also be used in lyric, and in lyric iambics the non-long positions may be dropped. Iambic meter is named after ἴαμβος, the genre of lampoon and invective, because this kind of meter was popular in that kind of poetry. Trochaic meter gets its name from τρόχος, running (o-grade noun related to τρέχω), because the meter was considered fast and lively.

In this family, long positions can be resolved. **Resolution** means filling a long element with two short syllables instead of a long one. The last syllable of a period is never resolved. The other characteristic of the iambo-trochaic family is **anceps positions** (normally with a Latin plural, **ancipitia**), which are elements that may contain either a long syllable or a short one. Resolution and ancipitia are the two permissible kinds of variation in iambics and trochaics.

The most common iambic form, and the easiest, is the so-called **iambic trimeter**. This is a period usually made up of two cola, one of five syllables and one of seven. As a stichic meter it is the standard form for dialogue in drama. The pattern is ×–◡–× –◡–×–◡– or, with different colon division, ×–◡–×–◡ –×–◡–. The long elements can be resolved (all except the last one, of course). In tragedy, the ancipitia can be resolved as well, so that an anceps element could contain a single short syllable, two short syllables, or a long syllable, but this is relatively uncommon and generally only used to fit in proper names that would be impossible to use otherwise, like Ἀντιγόνη. Tragic lines don't usually have very many resolutions: although it's possible to have more than one in a line, it isn't common, and most lines in tragedy don't have any resolutions at all.

For example, consider these lines from *Bacchae* (chapter 17 reading 5):

> ἥκω Διὸς παῖς τήνδε Θηβαίων χθόνα
> Διόνυσος, ὃν τίκτει ποθ᾽ ἡ Κάδμου κόρη
> Σεμέλη λοχευθεῖσ᾽ ἀστραπηφόρῳ πυρί·
> μορφὴν δ᾽ ἀμείψας ἐκ θεοῦ βροτησίαν
> πάρειμι Δίρκης νάματ᾽ Ἰσμηνοῦ θ᾽ ὕδωρ.

The second and third lines both begin ◡◡−, with the first anceps resolved, so that the names will fit the verse. There are no other resolutions in the passage.

In comedy, resolution is more common, and there is no restriction on resolving anceps positions. For example, consider chapter 9 reading 1, from Anaxandrides:

> ὁ τὸ σκόλιον εὑρὼν ἐκεῖνος, ὅστις ἦν,
> τὸ μὲν ὑγιαίνειν πρῶτον ὡς ἄριστον ὂν
> ὠνόμασεν ὀρθῶς, δεύτερον δ᾽ εἶναι καλόν,
> τρίτον δὲ πλουτεῖν, τοῦθ᾽, ὁρᾷς, ἔχρῃζέ που·
> μετὰ τὴν ὑγίειαν γὰρ τὸ πλουτεῖν διαφέρει·
> καλὸς δὲ πεινῶν ἐστιν αἰσχρὸν θηρίον.

The scansion of these lines is as follows:

```
◡   −   ◡◡◡   −   −   ◡−◡   −◡−

◡◡   −◡−   −   −◡   −   ◡−◡   −

−◡◡◡   −   −   −◡−   −   ◡−

◡−   ◡   −   −   −   ◡−   ◡−◡   −

◡◡   −   ◡◡−   −   −   −   −   ◡◡◡−

◡−   ◡   −   −   −◡   −   −   −◡−
```

Four of these six lines have resolutions, and the fifth has three of them.

The traditional name **iambic trimeter** comes from an old-fashioned way of analyzing the metrical phrase, as if it were three units of the form ×−◡−. This unit is called an **iambic metron**, and as there are three metra in the line, the line is a trimeter. This analysis is sometimes convenient, since every iambic trimeter line has the same three metra, while the colon boundaries vary from one line to another.

The other standard metrical period for dramatic dialogue is the **trochaic tetrameter**. Its pattern is −◡−×−◡−×   −◡−×−◡−, two cola, of eight and seven positions, with word break between them. Rules for resolution are exactly as in the iambic trimeter, and similarly stricter in tragedy, looser in comedy. The name comes from the observation that there are four instances of the pattern −◡−× in the line, though as the last one is missing its final position, this line should strictly be called trochaic tetrameter catalectic. The unit −◡−× is called the **trochaic metron**. Observe that it is exactly the reverse of the iambic metron.

Here is an example, Sophocles *Oedipus the King* 1524-1527.

ὦ πάτρας Θήβης ἔνοικοι, λεύσσετ᾽ , Οἰδίπους ὅδε,
ὃς τὰ κλείν᾽ αἰνίγματ᾽ ᾔδει καὶ κράτιστος ἦν ἀνήρ,
οὗ τίς οὐ ζήλῳ πολιτῶν ἦν τύχαις ἐπιβλέπων,
εἰς ὅσον κλύδωνα δεινῆς συμφορᾶς ἐλήλυθεν.

Exercise 1

Scan the following lines and identify the metrical pattern. Chapter 2 reading 1, chapter 8 reading 4, chapter 9 reading 6.

So far we have seen stichic forms. Iambics and trochaics can also be used in stanza forms, for example in songs in drama, sometimes in combination with cola from other families. This metrically straightforward song from Aristophanes' *Frogs* (384-393) is purely iambic:

Δήμητερ ἁγνῶν ὀργίων
    ἄνασσα συμπαραστάτει,
    καὶ σῷζε τὸν σαυτῆς χορόν,
καί μ᾽ ἀσφαλῶς πανήμερον παῖσαί τε καὶ χορεῦσαι·

καὶ πολλὰ μὲν γέλοιά μ᾽ εἰ-
    πεῖν, πολλὰ δὲ σπουδαῖα, καὶ
    τῆς σῆς ἑορτῆς ἀξίως
παίσαντα καὶ σκώψαντα νικήσαντα ταινιοῦσθαι.

The metrical scheme is:

```
 –   –   ᴗ–   x–ᴗ–
   x–ᴗ–x–ᴗ–
 –   –   ᴗ–   –   –   ᴗ–
 –   –   ᴗ–   x–ᴗ–   –   –   ᴗ–   ᴗ–   –
```

5. Dactylic verse

In the dactylic family, long elements alternate with paired short elements. The two short elements together are called a **biceps** (pl. **bicipitia**). In this family, a biceps can sometimes be **contracted**, replaced by a single long syllable. The characteristic colon is –ᴗᴗ–ᴗᴗ–, called the **hemiepes** or "half-epic" because, as you will see shortly, the standard stichic form for epic verse is made up of two of these with link elements. One type of dactylic verse, which may be the earliest to have developed, combines this colon with another shorter unit –ᴗ– in various patterns, with link elements in between. The result is called **dactylo-epitrite** meter; the units – – ᴗ– and –ᴗ– – , the three-syllable unit with a long link element before it or after it, are called **epitrite**. Dactylo-epitrite verse is always stanzaic: there is no moderate-sized period that is used in stichic forms.

The name **dactylic** comes from δάκτυλος because the unit –ᴗᴗ looks like the bones of a finger, counting outward from the palm. This unit is called the **dactylic metron**.

In dactylo-epitrite verse, the link elements may be long or anceps (and occasionally may be resolvable long elements). The bicipitia in the hemiepes elements cannot be contracted, so the −⌣⌣−⌣⌣− pattern is always clearly audible. Here is an example of dactylo-epitrite verse, Aristophanes *Knights* 1264-1273 (a strophe, whose antistrophe comes at line 1290):

> τί κάλλιον ἀρχομένοισιν ἢ καταπαυομένοισιν
> ἢ θοᾶν ἵππων ἐλατῆρας ἀείδειν,
> μηδὲν εἰς Λυσίστρατον,
> μηδὲ Θούμαντιν τὸν ἀνέστιον αὖ
> λυπεῖν ἑκούσῃ καρδίᾳ;
> καὶ γὰρ οὗτος ὦ φίλ᾽ Ἄπολλον ἀεὶ
> πεινῇ, θαλεροῖς δακρύοις
> σᾶς ἁπτόμενος φαρέτρας
> Πυθῶνι δίᾳ μὴ κακῶς πένεσθαι.

(θοᾶν ἵππων = ταχειῶν ἵππων (θηλείων). ἀείδειν = ᾄδειν.) To display the metrical pattern it is convenient to introduce the abbreviation D for the hemiepes unit, and e for the smaller unit −⌣−. With this convention the scheme of this stanza is:

> ×D⌣D×
> e−D−
> e×e
> e−D
> ×e−e
> e×D
> −D
> ×D
> −e−e⌣− −

Link elements are marked as anceps when they are different in the strophe and the antistrophe, but if they are the same in both stanzas their actual quantity is given. Note how the stanza is constructed from D and e units connected by link elements. The characteristic sound of dactylo-epitrite meter is the recurring D, −⌣⌣−⌣⌣−.

Epic verse uses a stichic dactylic form which is not dactylo-epitrite. Its scheme can be derived from −⌣⌣−⌣⌣− − −⌣⌣−⌣⌣− − (or D − D −), two hemiepes units, with a link element between them and another one at the end of the period. The final element must be long, because it is the end of the period. The central link element is treated as a resolvable long. Within the hemiepes units, the bicipitia may be contracted, unlike dactylo-epitrite which does not allow contraction. Thus the scheme can also be pictured as −⏖−⏖−⏖−⏖−⏖− −. Because this looks like five of the "dactyl" units −⌣⌣, plus what could be a contracted sixth one, this stichic form is called **dactylic hexameter**.

Here is an example, the opening of the *Iliad* (chapter 12 reading 7):

> μῆνιν ἄειδε θεὰ Πηληιάδεω Ἀχιλῆος
> οὐλομένην, ἣ μυρί᾽ Ἀχαιοῖς ἄλγε᾽ ἔθηκε,
> πολλὰς δ᾽ ἰφθίμους ψυχὰς Ἄϊδι προΐαψεν
> ἡρώων, αὐτοὺς δὲ ἑλώρια τεῦχε κύνεσσιν
> οἰωνοῖσί τε πᾶσι, Διὸς δ᾽ ἐτελείετο βουλή,

ἐξ οὗ δὴ τὰ πρῶτα διαστήτην ἐρίσαντε
Ἀτρεΐδης τε ἄναξ ἀνδρῶν καὶ δῖος Ἀχιλλεύς.

A standard stanza form is the **elegiac couplet**. It is a couplet because it is two periods; it is called "elegiac" because this form was popular for grave inscriptions. In fact the form is used for almost any kind of short poem. The first period of the couplet is the epic line (dactylic hexameter); the second is two hemiepes units with no link elements. In this stanza, the bicipitia can be contracted in the first period and in the first hemiepes of the second, but not in the final hemiepes. There is *always* a word-break between the two hemiepes units in the second line.

For example, consider this poem, from chapter 3 reading 19:

ἐντὸς ἐμῆς κραδίας τὴν εὔλαλον Ἡλιοδώραν
ψυχὴν τῆς ψυχῆς ἔπλασεν αὐτὸς Ἔρως

The scansion is

$$-\cup\ \ \cup-\ \ \cup\cup-\ \ -\ \ -\cup\cup\ \ -\cup\cup--$$

$$-\ \ -\ \ -\ \ -\ \ -\ \ -\cup\cup\ \ -\cup\ \ \cup-$$

All the bicipitia are contracted in the first hemiepes of the second line, and one is contracted in the first line. As in dactylo-epitrite, the final hemiepes of an elegiac couplet always sounds its D pattern clearly.

Exercise 1

Scan the following: chapter 5 reading 11, chapter 7 reading 9, chapter 8 reading 6, chapter 8 reading 8, chapter 12 reading 7. (More difficult) Chapter 20 reading 4 is part aeolic, part dactylo-epitrite, part iambic. Can you identify the cola?

Dactylic stanzas in drama may be dactylo-epitrite or simpler forms with more "dactyls" and fewer "epitrites" (or none at all). In these forms the biceps positions may be contractible, as they are in the epic line, or not, as in dactylo-epitrite. Sometimes it can be hard to tell whether a period is dactylic or aeolic with dactylic expansion of its nucleus. For example, in chapter 20 reading 4, from *Antigone*, the second to last period of the first strophic pair sounds purely dactylic, analyzable as eight dactylic metra (and this is a rare case in which a period ends on a *short* syllable, with ζυγῷ in line 350 scanned as $\cup\cup$ with correption in hiatus). The final period is $-\ -\ -\cup-\cup-\ -$, which is probably iambic but also could be interpreted as aeolic, $-\cup\cup-\cup-\cup-\ -$, provided we allow a "contraction" of the nucleus (first four positions, $-\cup\cup-$ contracted to $-\ -\ -$). On the other hand, the second to last period might also be interpreted as aeolic, ending $-\cup\cup-\cup-$, if ζυγῷ is not correpted and ἔτος in the strophe is also scanned $\cup-$, as *syllaba brevis in elemento longo*.

6. Anapestic verse

The name **anapest** comes from ἀναπαίω "strike, forge." This is the hammer-blow meter, repetitive and constant, suitable for marching to. In tragedy, the chorus will normally sing anapests as it enters and exits. In comedy, anapests are the characteristic meter for the parabasis song (though not the only possible choice). Anapests are the easiest meter to recognize by ear, because they are the only Greek meter that has the same constant rhythm familiar from English meter.

The typical anapestic colon is ◡◡–◡◡–◡◡–◡◡–. As with iambics, trochaics, and dactyls, there is also a traditional analysis by metra; the anapestic metron is ◡◡–◡◡–, so the basic colon is the **anapestic dimeter**. In drama, an anapestic passage is typically a series of dimeters, though sometimes there are longer cola ◡◡–◡◡–◡◡–◡◡–◡◡–◡◡– or shorter ones ◡◡–◡◡–. The passage generally ends with a catalectic dimeter ◡◡–◡◡–◡◡– – , and there may be catalectic cola elsewhere in the passage as well. The traditional name for the catalectic anapestic dimeter is **paroemiac** because it is a common form for a παροιμία or proverb.

In anapestic meter, the paired shorts (bicipitia) can be contracted *and* the long elements can be resolved. In other words, variation is possible at every position. But because there are no anceps positions in anapestic meter, every metron always has the length of eight short syllables. If you think of a long syllable as a quarter note or crotchet, and a short syllable as an eighth note or quaver, then an anapestic metron is like a measure of 4/4 time: four quarter notes, each divisible into eighth notes. This constant rhythm makes them easy to recognize by ear, and easy to march to.

For example, these lines are the end of five different plays by Euripides, *Medea, Alcestis, Andromache, Helen,* and *Bacchae*:

> πολλαὶ μορφαὶ τῶν δαιμονίων
> πολλὰ δ᾽ ἀέλπτως κραίνουσι θεοί·
> καὶ τὰ δοκηθέντ᾽ οὐκ ἐτελέσθη,
> τῶν δ᾽ ἀδοκήτων πόρον ηὗρε θεός.
> τοιόνδ᾽ ἀπέβη τόδε πρᾶγμα.

They are scanned as follows:

> – – – – – –◡◡–
>
> –◡ ◡– – – – ◡ ◡–
>
> – ◡ ◡– – – ◡◡– –
>
> – ◡◡– – ◡◡ –◡ ◡–
>
> – – ◡◡– ◡◡ – –

Exercise

Scan the following passage in anapests, the closing lines of Sophocles' *Antigone* (1347-1353):

> πολλῷ τὸ φρονεῖν εὐδαιμονίας
> πρῶτον ὑπάρχει. χρὴ δὲ τά γ᾽ εἰς θεοὺς
> μηδὲν ἀσεπτεῖν. μεγάλοι δὲ λόγοι
> μεγάλας πληγὰς τῶν ὑπεραύχων
> ἀποτίσαντες
> γήρᾳ τὸ φρονεῖν ἐδίδαξαν.

7. Minor families

Two other metrical families are moderately common and worth knowing about: dochmiacs and ionics.

Dochmiacs are used only in drama, not in other kinds of poetry. The basic colon is ×– –×–, and the longs may be resolved. Although there are 32 possible variations, most dochmiacs take one of the following forms, ⏑− − ⏑−, ⏑⏑⏑−⏑−, or ⏑⏑⏑⏑⏑⏑⏑. Usually each dochmiac colon is marked off by word end, and usually the cola come in pairs.

Characters sing in dochmiacs when they are gripped by strong emotion, whether joy or terror. Every surviving tragedy has at least one dochmiac passage, sung by the chorus or by another character, sometimes an entire stanza, sometimes along with other meters such as iambics. Comedy also uses dochmiacs, and because this meter is so characteristic of tragedy, a lyric in dochmiacs is an easy way for a comic playwright to parody tragedy.

Here is an example, *Antigone* 1307-1311. Creon has just learned that his wife has killed herself, in reaction to the death of their son.

> ἀνέπταν φόβῳ. τί μ' οὐκ ἀνταίαν
> ἔπαισέν τις ἀμφιθήκτῳ ξίφει;
> δείλαιος ἐγώ, αἰαῖ,
> δειλαίᾳ δὲ συγκέκραμαι δύᾳ.

(ἀνέπταν = ἀνέπτην = ἀνεπτόμην. αἰαῖ is an exclamation of distress.) The scansion is:

⏑− − ⏑− ⏑ − −⏑−

⏑ −− ⏑ −⏑− − ⏑−

−⏑⏑ ⏑⏑ ⏑−

− − − ⏑ −⏑− − ⏑−

Note correption inside ἀνταίαν and δείλαιος, and at the end of ἐγώ.

Greek audiences seem to have considered **ionic** meter exotic, evoking Persia or other far-away, foreign lands. The basic ionic colon is ⏑⏑− − ⏑⏑− − , and the traditional analysis is by metra, where the metron is ⏑⏑− − (so the normal colon is an ionic dimeter; trimeters are also used, ⏑⏑− − ⏑⏑− − ⏑⏑− −). Ionics permit relatively little variation: sometimes the two short syllables are contracted, but only at the beginning of a colon that is also the beginning of a word. A period may end with catalexis, ⏑⏑−, or with an additional long syllable, ⏑⏑− − −.

The colon ⏑⏑−⏑−⏑− − is called the **anacreontic** because the poet Anacreon used it in lyrics. It can be a variant of an ionic colon with the fourth and fifth positions swapped, and it is sometimes found in company with ordinary ionics.

This passage, Euripides *Bacchae* 83-88, shows ionics. Each print line is a colon; the only period end is the end of the passage, which is the end of a stanza. Βρόμιος is a title for Διόνυσος.

> ἴτε βάκχαι, ἴτε βάκχαι,
> Βρόμιον παῖδα θεὸν θεοῦ
> Διόνυσον κατάγουσαι
> Φρυγίων ἐξ ὀρέων Ἑλ-
> λάδος εἰς εὐρυχόρους ἀ-
> γυιάς, τὸν Βρόμιον.

It is scanned as follows:

⏑⏑ − − ⏑⏑ − −

⏑⏑ − − ⏑⏑ − −

⏑⏑ − − ⏑⏑ − −

```
⏑⏑ – –   ⏑⏑ – –
⏑⏑ – –   ⏑⏑ – –
⏑⏑– – ⏑⏑–
```

Note **synezesis** of θεοῦ in line 84: the two vowels are treated as contracted, so the word scans as a single long syllable. Also observe the catalexis at the end of the passage.

8. Conclusion

This introduction has laid out the basic principles of Greek meter and introduced the major forms used in epic, epigram, and drama. Much lyric verse, particularly the forms sung and danced by choruses, can be considerably more complicated. The easiest choral lyrics are those in the plays of Aristophanes. Tragedy is next most difficult, and the lyrics of Sophocles are often slightly easier than those of Aeschylus and Euripides, in metrical terms anyway. Bacchylides and Stesichorus may be taken up next, and Pindar's meters are often considered the most complex among major poets.

The study of meter includes interpretation of how the metrical patterns support or enhance the words of a song. Within a play, meters may be used thematically, as rhythmic motifs that the audience will hear over and over. (Playwrights may have used melodic motifs as well, of course, but as we have only very little of the music for the plays, we cannot recover the melodies.)

Meter is not the only difference between verse and prose. In Greek, as in English and many other languages, some words are considered more suitable for verse, others for prose. For example, ποιέω is an ordinary, prosaic word, and δράω is a more poetic synonym. Poets also love periphrases, as ὦ κοινὸν αὐτάδελφον Ἰσμήνης κάρα (Sophocles, *Antigone* line 1), an elaborate way of saying ὦ ἀδελφὴ Ἰσμήνη. It's not unusual to refer to a person this way: Ἰσμήνης κάρα = Ἰσμήνης κεφαλή = Ἰσμήνη, or Ὀδυσσέως βία = Ὀδυσσεύς.

Word order can also be different. In prose, as you know, phrases generally stay together, so the modifiers of a noun or verb will be right next to the modified word. In verse, on the other hand, phrases are often split apart, with the parts placed next to colon boundaries. For example, in chapter 3, reading 1, we have

> λέγουσι δ' αὐτὸν οἱ πάλαι σοφώτατοι
> ἀστεῖον εἶναι φάρμακον καὶ χρήσιμον.

In plain prose this might be οἱ δὲ πάλαι σοφώτατοι λέγουσιν αὐτὸν εἶναι ἀστεῖον καὶ χρήσιμον φάρμακον. The two adjectives are joined by καί, making a single phrase that modifies the predicate noun φάρμακον. In verse, that phrase is pulled apart, with one part placed at the start of the line and the other part at the end. Another example is *Iliad* 6.26: ἣ δ' ὑποκυσαμένη διδυμάονε γείνατο παῖδε. Here διδυμάονε modifies παῖδε, but the noun phrase is interrupted by the verb γείνατο (= ἐγείνατο, ἔτεκε). The adjective is at the start of the second colon of the period, the noun at the end.

Another word order difference concerns prepositions, which may come after the nouns they govern. In this case, a two-syllable preposition will be accented on its first syllable instead of its second. Thus ταύτης ἔπι (Sophocles, *Antigone* 189), τοῦδε τοῦ νεκροῦ πέρι (283), ὀργῆς ὕπο (Euripides, *Bacchae* 758).

The Greek metrical system is related to the systems of Sanskrit and Latin, though in different ways. The major metrical forms used in Sanskrit are like those of aeolic verse in Greek. Each colon has some varying positions near the beginning but a fixed shape at the end, and contraction and resolution are not used. It is generally believed that the Greek and Sanskrit systems developed from a common ancestor.

As for Latin, Roman poets took over the Greek system of versification in about the third century BC; before this, the major form of Latin poetry was the **saturnian** verse, a form somewhat similar to the verse of Old English, not based on quantitative patterns. Because Latin does have long and short vowels like Greek, it is possible to define long and short syllables for Latin exactly as for Greek, and thus to use the same quantitative versification.

Classical Latin poets took over the simplest Greek forms, and sometimes eliminated some of the possible variation. For example, among aeolic forms, Latin poets use the Sapphic stanza, the Alcaic stanza, glyconics, pherecrateans, phalacean hendecasyllables, and asclepiads, but they do not invent complex aeolic stanza forms like those of Greek tragedies. Moreover, some Latin poets treat the aeolic base as invariant (usually making all the variable elements consistently long), and they may insist on word break always at a particular spot in the colon. For example, when Horace (Q. Horatius Flaccus) uses the Sapphic stanza, he always has a long syllable in the fifth element of the long colon (the varying position in the base) and nearly always has word break after that syllable.

Latin poets use the dactylic hexameter for epic, but treat the last biceps position differently from the others, not contracting it except when necessary to fit in a proper name. Greek epic verse has no such restriction. Some Latin poets introduce a new rule for elegiac couplets as well, namely that the second line must end with a two-syllable word; this is difficult enough that it never became a universal rule for Latin elegiacs.

The early comic playwrights Plautus (T. Maccius Plautus) and Terence (P. Terentius Afer) use the same stichic forms for dialogue as Greek playwrights, the iambic trimeter and the trochaic tetrameter catalectic, but treating the short positions as anceps. Thus in the iambic trimeter, the even positions (second, fourth, and so on) are long syllables (that may be resolved into two shorts), and the odd positions may contain a short syllable, a long syllable, or two short syllables from resolution. The last two positions are left alone, so that the line always ends short-long. In practice there are not very many resolutions, but there are lots of long syllables: this is the opposite of what Aristophanes does, as he often treats anceps positions as short and uses lots of resolution.

The lyrics in Plautus's and Terence's plays are complicated, not always built from cola borrowed from Greek meter.

By the time the Romans were adapting Greek quantitative meter to the Latin language, some scholars had begun to analyze verse in terms of "feet," which are small units of two to four syllables. For simple iambic and dactylic meters, this is not very different from the analysis by metra. For more complicated Greek lyrics, this analysis makes almost no sense, since it ignores the cola into which the poems are structured, and tries to fit everything into patterns of the same size. Imagine trying to explain a dochmiac verse by dividing it into groups of four syllables and giving each one a name. It was not until the early twentieth century that scholars once again began to describe Greek verse in terms of its actual building blocks, the cola.

APPENDIX 5

Further Reading

The following books and web sites may be useful for background about the Greek language, for an introduction to literature, and for practice. These are relatively accessible, not too difficult for students finishing up the first year of Greek; more advanced works on the linguistics of Greek have been omitted.

W. Sidney Allen, *Vox Graeca: The Pronunciation of Classical Greek,* Cambridge University Press, third edition 1987. An authoritative discussion of how classical Greek was pronounced, and how we know.

C. D. Buck, *The Greek Dialects,* University of Chicago Press, 1955, and reprint editions. Although some of the historical material here has been superseded, this book is still the most convenient overview of the differences among dialects, with copious examples, taken from inscriptions rather than from literary texts.

John Chadwick, *The Decipherment of Linear B,* Cambridge University Press, 1958. How scholars determined that the clay tablets of Mycenae contained an early form of Greek.

J. D. Denniston, *The Greek Particles,* Oxford University Press, 1950, and various reprints. This is the classic discussion of the discourse particles of Greek, full of examples.

J. D. Denniston, *Greek Prose Style,* Oxford University Press, 1952, and reprints. A short but fairly thorough treatment of how classical writers make their prose work.

P. E. Easterling and B. M. W. Knox, edd., *The Cambridge History of Classical Literature,* Cambridge University Press, 1985. Overview of Greek and Latin literature, with many examples; available in two volumes (Greek is volume 1) or in nine parts (the first four covering Greek).

Richard C. Gascoyne, chair, *Standards for Classical Language Learning,* American Classical League, 1997. This document, produced by the national and regional professional societies, outlines goals for students of Greek or Latin.

M. L. Gasparov, *A History of European Versification,* translated by G. S. Smith and Marina Tarlinskaja, edited by G. S. Smith with L. Holford-Strevens, Oxford University Press, 1996. Covers verse forms in all the European traditions, with an excellent short introduction to classical meters in chapters 4 and 5.

Geoffrey Horrocks, *Greek: A History of the Language and Its Speakers,* Wiley-Blackwell, 2010. An overview of the language from the earliest attested texts to the present day.

Albert Rijksbaron, *Syntax and Semantics of the Verb in Classical Greek,* University of Chicago Press, 2007. A modern presentation of how verbs work.

W. H. D. Rouse and R. B. Appleton, *Latin on the Direct Method,* University of London Press, 1925. How Rouse conducted his own classes.

W. H. D. Rouse, *The Teaching of Greek at the Perse School, Cambridge,* Board of Education pamphlets 28, printed by Eyre and Spottiswoode, 1914. Summary of the methods and results of Rouse's work with his students.

Andrew Sihler, *New Comparative Grammar of Greek and Latin,* Oxford University Press, 1995. Dense and difficult, but a good overview of Greek in relation to Latin and the other Indo-European languages.

Christopher Stray, *The Living Word: W. H. D. Rouse and the Crisis of Classics in Edwardian England,* Bristol Classical Press, 1992. Biography of the master teacher from whose textbook the present book is adapted.

Oliver Taplin, ed., *Literature in the Greek World,* Oxford University Press, 2000. Overview of Greek literature from early epic to the Roman period; also published along with *Literature in the Roman World* in a single volume.

Calvert Watkins, *The American Heritage Dictionary of Indo-European Roots,* Houghton Mifflin Harcourt, 2000; also as an appendix within the *American Heritage Dictionary.* A glossary of roots from Proto-Indo-European that contribute to words in English, whether native words or borrowings from Greek, Latin, or elsewhere, with an introductory essay on Indo-European culture.

Akropolis World News, J. Coderch, http://www.akwn.net/, current events in classical Greek, updated weekly

Ancient Greece in Fiction, Nick Lowe, http://www.rhul.ac.uk/Classics/NJL/novels.html, just for fun

Ancient Greek Tutorials, Donald Mastronarde, http://socrates.berkeley.edu/~ancgreek/ ancient_greek_start.html, exercises on pronunciation and accents, supplementing Mastronarde's *Introduction to Attic Greek*

Ancient World Mapping Center, http://www.unc.edu/awmc/, geography of the ancient world, including downloadable maps

Greek Grammar on the Web, https://perswww.kuleuven.be/~u0013314/greekg.htm, annotated index to web pages about the Greek language

Greek Prose Style, Hardy Hansen, http://web.gc.cuny.edu/Classics/gk701/, course materials including links to texts

The Intelligent Person's Guide to Greek, William Harris, http://community.middlebury. edu/~harris/GreekGrammar.html, overview of morphology; see also http://community. middlebury.edu/~harris/SubIndex/classics.index.html for Harris's other essays on Greek language and literature

Perseus Digital Library, Gregory Crane, ed., http://www.perseus.tufts.edu, library of Greek and Latin texts with tools for reading

Society for the Oral Reading of Greek and Latin Literature, http://www.rhapsodes.fll.vt.edu/, performances of Greek texts and a guide to pronunciation

VOCABULARY

Greek to English

Numbers in parentheses refer to the chapter in which the word is introduced.

Ἀβδηρίτης, -ου, ὁ, a man of Abdera

ἀβουλίᾱ, -ας, ἡ, foolishness (12)

ἀγαθός, -ή, όν, good (2)

ἄγαλμα, -ατος, τό, statue

ἄγαν, too much

ἀγανακτέω, ἀγανακτήσω, ἠγανάκτησα, ἠγανάκτηκα, ἠγανάκτημαι, ἠγανακτήθην, be irritated

ἀγαπάω, ἀγαπήσω, ἠγάπησα, ἠγάπηκα, – , – , love, be fond of

ἀγγέλλω, ἀγγελῶ, ἤγγειλα, ἤγγελκα, ἤγγελμαι, ἠγγέλθην, announce, report, send a messenger (12)

ἄγγελος, -ου, ὁ, messenger (6)

ἀγέλη, -ης, ἡ, herd (14)

ἄγκιστρον, -ου, τό, hook (18)

ἀγκύλος, -η, -ον, curved

ἄγκῡρα, -ας, ἡ, anchor (10)

ἀγμός, -οῦ, ὁ, crag, broken cliff

ἁγνός, -ή, -όν, holy (9)

ἀγορά, -ᾱς, ἡ, market-place (6)

ἀγοράζω, ἀγοράσω, ἠγόρασα, ἠγόρακα, ἠγόρασμαι, ἠγοράσθην, buy (8)

ἀγορεύω, ἀγορεύσω, ἠγόρευσα, ἠγόρευκα, ἠγόρευμαι, ἠγορεύθην, proclaim, speak in public

ἄγρᾱ, -ᾱς, ἡ, chase, hunt (18)

ἄγραπτος, -ον, unwritten

ἄγραυλος, -ον, field-dwelling, rustic

ἄγριος, -α, -ον, wild (18)

ἀγροῖκος, -ον, rustic, boorish (19)

ἀγρός, -οῦ, ὁ, field, countryside (11)

ἀγρότερος, -α, -ον, wild, fond of hunting

ἀγυιά, -ᾶς, ἡ, road

ἀγχόθι, near, close to

ἄγχω, ἄγξω, ἦγξα, – , – , – , throttle, strangle (15)

ἄγω, ἄξω, ἤγαγον, ἦχα, ἦγμαι, ἤχθην, lead (7)

ἀγών, ἀγῶνος, ὁ, contest, game

ἀδελφή, -ῆς, ἡ, sister (7)

ἀδελφός, -οῦ, ὁ, brother (6)

ἄδικος, -ον, wrong, wicked, unjust (7)

ἀδικέω, ἀδικήσω, ἠδίκησα, ἠδίκηκα, ἠδίκημαι, ἠδικήθην, do wrong (19)

ἀδόκητος, -ον, unexpected

ἄδολος, -ον, sincere, honest (18)

ᾄδω, ᾄσω, ᾖσα, – , – , ᾔσθην, sing, crow (14)

ἀεί, αἰεί, always (4)

ἄελπτος, -ον, not hoped for, unexpected

ἀέξω, grow, increase (present system only)

ἀετός, -οῦ, ὁ, eagle

ἄνηβος, -ον, not grown up, not yet adolescent

ἀηδών, -όνος, ἡ, nightingale (16)

ἀήρ, ἀέρος, ὁ, air (14s)

ἀθάνατος, -ον, immortal, undying (20)

ἄθαπτος, -ον, not buried

ἀθεράπευτος, -ον, incurable

Ἀθῆναι, -ῶν, αἱ, Athens; Ἀθήναζε, to Athens, Ἀθήνηθεν, from A., Ἀθήνησι, at A. (9)

ἀθλοφόρος, -ου, ὁ, prize-winning athlete

αἰδῶς, -ους, ἡ, shame; stem αἰδοσ-

αἰθρίᾱ, -ᾱς, ἡ, fine weather (14)

αἴλουρος, -ου, ὁ, ἡ, cat

αἷμα, -ατος, τό, blood

αἰνέω, αἰνέσω, ᾔνεσα, ᾔνεκα, ᾔνημαι, ᾐνέθην, tell, praise

αἴνιγμα, -ατος, τό, riddle, puzzle, mystery

αἴξ, αἰγός, ὁ, ἡ, goat (11)

αἱρέω, αἱρήσω, εἷλον, ᾕρηκα, ᾕρημαι, ᾑρέθην, take, grasp, catch (15)

αἴρω, ἀρῶ, ἦρα, ἦρκα, ἦρμαι, ἤρθην, raise, lift (10)

αἰσθάνομαι, αἰσθήσομαι, ᾐσθόμην, -, ᾔσθημαι, -, perceive (13)

αἴσιος, -α, -ον, prosperous, lucky

αἰσχρός, -ά, -όν, ugly, base, shameful (9)

αἰσχύνω, αἰσχυνῶ, ᾔσχυνα, -, -, ᾐσχύνθην, disgrace

αἰτέω, αἰτήσω, ᾔτησα, ᾔτηκα, -, -, ask, request (12)

αἴτησις, -εως, ἡ, request

αἰτίᾱ, -ᾱς, ἡ, cause

αἰτιάομαι, αἰτιάσομαι, ᾐτιασάμην, -, ᾐτίαμαι, ᾐτιάθην, accuse (19)

αἴτιος, -α, -ον, responsible for, causing, guilty of

αἰχμάλωτος, -ου, ὁ, captive, prisoner of war

αἰών, -ῶνος, ὁ, lifetime, period of time

ἀκάματος, -η, -ον, untiring, indefatigable

ἀκμάζω, ἀκμάσω, ἤκμασα, ἤκμακα, -, -, be in one's prime, be ripe (11)

ἀκμής, -ές, untiring, unwearied

ἀκοή, ἀκοῆς, ἡ, hearing (2)

ἀκούω, ἀκούσομαι, ἤκουσα, ἀκήκοα, -, ἠκούσθην, hear (2)

ἀκροάομαι, ἀκροάσομαι, ἠκροασάμην, -, ἠκρόαμαι, -, hear, listen; obey

ἀκταία, -ας, ἡ, mortar (for grinding) made of marble

ἀκτή, -ῆς, ἡ, shore (19)

ἄκων, ἄκουσα, ἄκον, unwilling

ἄκων, -οντος, τό, javelin

ἄλγος, -ου, τό, pain, trouble

ἀλγύνω, ἀλγυνῶ, ἤλγυνα, -, -, ἠλγύνθην, cause pain, grieve

ἀλεκτρυών, -όνος, ὁ, rooster, fowl (14)

ἀλήθεια, -ας, ἡ, truth (8)

ἀληθής, -έ, true

ἁλιεύς, -έως, ὁ, fisherman (18)

ἁλιεύω, ἁλιεύσω, ἡλίευσα, ἡλίευκα, -, -, fish, go fishing (18)

ἁλίσκομαι, ἁλώσομαι, ἑάλων, -, -, -, be taken, be captured, be caught doing something

ἀλλά, but (1)

ἀλλαξείω, desire to change (present system only)

ἀλλάττω, ἀλλάξω, ἤλλαξα, ἤλλαχα, ἤλλαγμαι, ἠλλάχην, change, alter (19)

ἀλλήλων, each other (dual and plural oblique cases only) (11)

ἄλλοθεν, from another place (16)

ἅλλομαι, ἁλοῦμαι, ἡλάμην, -, -, -, spring, jump

ἄλλος, -η, -ο, other (2)

ἄλλοσε, to another place (16)

ἄλλοτε, at another time (16)

ἅλμα, -ατος, τό, jump

ἅλμη, -ης, ἡ, brine (17s)

ἅλς, ἁλός, ὁ, salt (14)

ἄλσος, -ους, τό, grove of trees (18)

ἀλύω, be distraught, have one's mind wander (present system only)

ἀλώπηξ, ἀλώπεκος, ἡ, ὁ, fox

ἅμα, at the same time, together (20)

ἅμαξα, -ης, ἡ, cart, carriage (6)

ἁμαρτάνω, ἁμαρτήσομαι, ἥμαρτον, ἡμάρτηκα, ἡμάρτημαι, ἡμαρτήθην, err, make a mistake (7)

ἀμβροσία, -ας, ἡ, ambrosia, a divine food

ἀμείβω, ἀμείψω, ἤμειψα, -, -, -, change, exchange, take a turn; in middle, answer

ἀμείνων, -ον, ἄριστος, -η, -ον, better, best; suppletive to ἀγαθός

ἀμέλεια, -ας, ἡ, carelessness (14)

ἀμελέω, ἀμελήσω, ἡμέλησα, ἡμέληκα, -, -, neglect, disregard (8)

ἄμεμπτος, -ον, blameless (14)

ἄμπελος, -ου, ἡ, vine (11)

ἄμης, -ητος, ὁ, milk-cake (17s)

ἄμιλλα, -ης, ἡ, contest, rivalry

ἀμύγδαλον, -ου, τό, almond; also ἀμυγδάλη (17s)

ἀμύνω, ἀμυνῶ, ἤμυνα, – , – , – , ward off, fend off; defend

ἀμυχή, -ῆς, ἡ, scratch, tear, rip

ἀμφί, around, about (+ gen., dat., acc.) (7)

ἀμφι-βάλλω, throw (something) around, embrace, ensnare

ἀμφίθηκτος, -ον, double-edged

ἀμφι-μάχομαι, fight around

ἀμφότερος, -α, -ον, both (7)

ἄν, particle marks general or hypothetical clause (8)

ἀνά, up, along (+ acc.) (6)

ἀνα-παίω, strike, forge, strike back

ἀνα-πείθω, persuade

ἀνα-πέτομαι, fly up, fly away

ἀνα-πνέω, breathe out

ἀν-άπτω, kindle (from ἅπτομαι) (17)

ἀνα-σπάω, ἀνα-σπάσω, ἀνέσπασα, ἀνέσπακα, ἀνέσπασμαι, ἀνεσπάσθην, pull up (10)

ἄνασσα, -ας, ἡ, lady, queen

ἀνάσσω, ἀνάξω, ἤναξα, ἤναχα, ἤναγμαι, ἠνάθην, rule, be king

ἀνα-στρέφω, invert, turn over, turn away

ἀνατίθημι, set up (9)

ἀνα-φαίνω, show, appear, reveal

ἀνα-φέρω, lift up, bring back; praise (14)

ἀνα-χωρέω, retire, retreat

ἀνδάνω, ἀδήσω, ἔαδον, ἄδηκα, – , – , delight, please

ἀνδραποδιστής, -ου, ὁ, slave-dealer, kidnapper

ἀνδρεῖος, -α, -ον, brave (7)

ἀνδριάς, -άντος, ὁ, statue

ἀνδρωνῖτις, -ίδος, ἡ, men's rooms (17)

ἄνεμος, -ου, ὁ, wind (10)

ἄν-ειμι, return, come back (εἶμι)

ἀν-έρομαι, ask (12)

ἀνέστιος, -ον, without a hearth, homeless

ἄνευ, prep + gen., without (7)

ἀν-έχω, hold up; middle, put up with, endure

ἀνα-βλύζω, -βλύσω, -έβλυσα, – , – , – , bubble up (16)

ἀνα-γιγνώσκω, read

ἀναγκαῖος, -α, -ον, necessary (19)

ἀνάγκη, -ης, ἡ, necessity (19)

ἀνα-γράφω, write, draw, write up

ἀναγωγή, -ῆς, ἡ, launching (10)

ἀνα-ζητέω, seek (16)

ἀνάθημα, -ατος, τό, offering (16)

ἀνά-κειμαι, be dedicated (to a god) (16)

ἀνα-κράζω, shout, cry out

ἀνα-λαμβάνω, take up, adopt, retrieve

ἀνα-μένω, wait for

ἀνα-μιμνήσκω, remind; in middle, remember (16)

ἄναξ, ἄνακτος, ὁ, lord, king

ἀνήρ, ἀνδρός, ὁ, man, male person (15)

ἀνθεμώδης, -ες, flowery, blooming

ἀνθέω, ἀνθήσω, ἤνθησα, ἤνθηκα, – , – , bloom, blossom, put forth flowers (16)

ἄνηθον, -ου, τό, anise, dill; also ἄνητον in verse

ἄνθος, -ους, τό, flower (16)

ἄνθραξ, ἄνθρακος, ὁ, coal

ἄνθρωπος, -ου, ὁ, ἡ, man, human being (2)

ἀν-ίημι, send out

ἀν-ίστημι, rise, raise up

ἀνοηταίνω, be foolish (present system only)

ἀν-οίγνῡμι, ἀν-οίξω, ἀν-έῳξα, ἀν-έῳχα, ἀν-έῳγμαι, ἀν-εῴχθην, open (17)

ἀνταῖος, -α, -ον, in front, against

ἀντί, instead of, in return for (+ gen.) (7)

ἀντι-δωρέω, give in return

ἄντρον, -ου, τό, cave (16)

ἀνυπόδητος, -ον, unshod

ἄνω, above (10)

ἀξίᾱ, -ᾱς, ἡ, worth, value (5)

ἄξιος, -α, -ον, worth, worthy (5)

ἀξιόω, ἀξιώσω, ἠξίωσα, ἠξίωκα, ἠξίωμαι, ἠξιώθην, ask, claim; think worthy; expect (8)

ἀξιώσις, -εως, ἡ, worth, value

ἀξύνετος, -ον, stupid, unintelligent

ἀπ-αγορεύω, ἀπειρῶ, ἀπεῖπον, ἀπείρηκα, – , – , forbid (15)

ἀπ-άγω, lead away, bring home

ἀπ-αιτέω, ask for

ἀπάλαμνος, -ον, helpless, undisciplined, foolish

ἀπάνθρωπος, -ον, anti-social, reclusive

ἀπ-αντάω, ἀπ-αντήσομαι, ἀπ-ήντησα, ἀπ-ήντηκα, – , – , meet, go to meet (8)

ἀπ-αρτάω, fasten to (18)

ἀπ-άρχομαι, make a beginning of (16)

ἄπᾱς, ἅπᾱσα, ἅπαν, all (12)

ἀπάτη, -ης, ἡ, fraud, deceit, trickery

ἄπειμι, (εἰμι) be away (9)

ἄπειμι, (εἶμι) go away, depart

ἀπ-εσθίω, eat away (19)

ἄπεπτος, -ον, uncooked, undigested

ἀπίθανος, -ον, unbelievable, implausible

ἄπιος, -ου, ἡ, pear tree, pear (17s)

ἀπιστέω, ἀπιστήσω, ἠπίστησα, ἠπίστηκα, ἠπίστημαι, ἠπιστήθην, doubt, disbelieve

ἁπλοῦς, ἁπλῆ, ἁπλοῦν, simple (20)

ἀ-πνευστί, without breathing, holding one's breath

ἀπό, from, + gen. (6)

ἀπο-βαίνω, come down, dismount, disembark

ἀπο-βλέπω, look at steadily

ἀπο-γιγνώσκω, despair, give up hope

ἀπο-δημέω, be away from home (usually only present system) (8)

ἀπο-διδράσκω, run away

ἀπο-δίδωμι, give up; in middle, sell (9)

ἀπο-θνήσκω, ἀποθανοῦμαι, ἀπέθανον, τέθνηκα, – , – , die (2)

ἀπο-κλήω, close up, close off

ἀπο-κρίνομαι, answer, reply

ἀπο-κρύπτω, hide away, hide something (acc.) from someone (dat.)

ἀπο-κτείνω, kill (8)

ἀπ-όλλυμι, destroy; in middle, perish (19)

ἀπορίᾱ, -ᾱς, ἡ, difficulty (4)

ἀπόρρητος, -ον, forbidden

ἀποσαλεύω, ride at anchor

ἀπο-σβέννυμι, extinguish (17)

ἀπόστασις, -εως, ἡ, separation, standing apart

ἀπο-στρέφω, turn away

ἀπο-τείνω, stretch (11)

ἀπο-τίνω, pay, pay back, give in atonement

ἀπο-τρυγάω, pluck, harvest

ἀπο-τρύω, rub away, wear out (usually only present system)

ἀπο-φέρω, carry off (11)

ἀπο-χωρέω, go away, depart; give something up (15)

ἀπο-ψηφίζομαι, acquit, vote to acquit

ἀπροσδοκήτως, unexpectedly (17)

ἅπτομαι, ἅψομαι, ἡψάμην, – , ἡμμαι, ἥφθην, touch (+ gen.) (15)

ἅπτω, ἅψω, ἧψα, – , ἡμμαι, ἥφθην, affix fasten (15)

ἄρα, particle marking an inference (4)

ἆρα, particle marking a question (3)

ἀρβύλη, -ης, ἡ, boot (4)

ἀργίᾱ, -ᾱς, ἡ, sloth, idleness (7)

ἀργός, -όν, idle, useless (7)

ἀργύριον, -ου, τό, piece of silver, coin

ἀργυρόπεζος, -α, -ον, having silver feet

ἀρετή, -ῆς, ἡ, excellence, virtue (15)

ἀριπρεπής, -ές, splendid, pre-eminent

ἀριστερός, -α, -ον, left, leftward (opp. right, δεξιός)

ἀριστοκρατίᾱ, -ᾱς, ἡ, aristocracy

ἄριστον, -ου, τό, breakfast

ἄριστος, -η, -ον, best (9)

ἀρῑστάω, ἀρῑστήσω, ἠρίστησα, ἠρίστηκα, – , –, eat breakfast (6)

ἄρκτος, -ου, ὁ, bear

ἅρμα, -ατος, τό, war chariot

ἁρμονία, -ᾱς, ἡ, harmony, music, joining or putting together

ἁρμόττω, ἁρμόσω, ἥρμοσα, ἥρμοκα, ἥρμοσμαι, ἡρμόσθην, fit together, join

ἄροτρον, -ου, τό, plow

ἀρόω, ἀρόσω, ἤροσα, – , – , ἠρόθην, plow (14)

ἁρπάζω, ἁρπάσω, ἥρπασα, ἥρπακα, ἥρπασμαι, ἡρπάσθην, seize, grab, plunder (15) ἄρρην, ἄρρεν, male, masculine (gen. ἄρρενος) (18)

ἄρριχος, -ου, ὁ, basket

ἀρτάω, ἀρτήσω, ἤρτησα, ἤρτηκα, ἤρτημαι, ἠρτήθην, fasten (normally compounded) (18)

ἄρτι, lately, just now (11)

ἄρτος, -ου, ὁ, loaf of bread (9)

ἀρχή, -ῆς, ἡ, beginning (11)

ἄρχω, ἄρξω, ἦρξα, ἦρχα, ἦργμαι, ἤρχθην, begin; rule (+ gen.) (16)

ἀρχιτεκτονέω, be architect, construct

ἀσάομαι, ἀσήσομαι, ἀσάμην, –, –, –, grieve, be upset

ἀσέβεια, -ας, ἡ, impiety, disrespect for the gods

ἀσεπτέω, be impious, be disrespectful of the gods (variant of ἀσεβέω)

ἀσκέω, ἀσκήσω, ἤσκησα, ἤσκηκα, ἤσκημαι, ἠσκήθην, practice, exercise; deck out, adorn (18)

ἄσκησις, -εως, ἡ, practice, exercise

ᾆσμα, -ατος, τό, song (14)

ἄσμενος, -η, -ον, willing, glad (17)

ἀστεῖος, -α, -ον, nice, urbane, elegant (3)

ἀστήρ, ἀστέρος, ὁ, star

ἀστράγαλος, -ου, ὁ, vertebra, knucklebone; gaming die

ἀστραπή, -ῆς, ἡ, lightning (14s)

ἀστραπηφόρος, -ον, bringing lightning

ἀστράπτω, ἀστράψω, ἤστραψα, –, –, –, lighten (14s)

ἄστυ, ἄστεως, τό, city (12)

ἀστυνόμος, -ον, city-protecting

ἀσφάλεια, -ας, ἡ, safety, certainty

ἀσφαλής, -ές, safe (18)

ἀτάρ, but (epic only)

ἄττω, ᾄξω, ᾖξα, –, –, –, rush, move quickly (15)

αὖ, again, moreover; also αὖθις (9)

αὖθι, here

αὐλή, -ῆς, ἡ, courtyard (15)

αὐλός, -οῦ, ὁ, oboe, shawm, type of wind instrument (16)

αὐλών, -ῶνος, ὁ, hollow, ditch, ravine (14)

αὔρα, -ας, ἡ, breeze (9)

αὔριον, tomorrow (6)

αὐτάδελφος, -ον, sibling, related as brother or sister

αὐτίκα, at once, for example (12)

αὐτός, -ή, -ό, self (4)

αὐχήν, -ένος, ὁ, neck (16)

ἀφ-αιρέω, carry off (15)

ἀφανής, -ές, invisible, vanished (20)

ἀφ-ίημι, let go (9)

ἀφ-ικνέομαι, come (11)

ἀφ-ίστημι, put away, remove (9)

ἄφθιτος, -ον, indestructible, imperishable

ἄφυκτος, -ον, inevitable, unavoidable

ἄψ, back, backward

ἄωρος, -ον, untimely, unseasonable, too early

ἄχυρον, -ου, τό, straw (20)

βαδίζω, βαδιοῦμαι, ἐβάδισα, βεβάδικα, –, –, walk, go (17)

βάθρον, -ου, τό, stand, pedestal

βαίνω, βήσομαι, ἔβην, βέβηκα, –, –, step, go (13)

βάκχος, -η, -ον, bacchante, devoted to Bacchus (Dionysus)

βάλανος, -ου, ἡ, acorn

βάλλω, βαλῶ, ἔβαλον, βέβληκα, βέβλημαι, ἐβλήθην, throw (5)

βαρυδαίμων, -ον, having a heavy fate, unlucky

βαρύς, -εῖα, ύ, heavy (18)

βασιλεύς -έως, ὁ, king (16)

βασιλεύω, βασιλεύσω, ἐβασίλευσα, βεβασίλευκα, –, ἐβασιλεύθην, be king, rule

βασιλικός, -ά, -όν, royal, kingly

βάσις, -εως, ἡ, base

βαστάζω, βαστάσω, ἐβάστασα, –, βεβάσταγμαι, ἐβαστάχθην, lift, carry (11)

βάτραχος, -ου, ὁ, ἡ, frog

βέλος, -ους, τό, dart, shaft, thrown weapon

βελτίων, -ον, βέλτιστος, -α, -ον, better, best, suppletive to ἀγαθός

βῆμα, -ατος, τό, step, platform

βία, -ᾱς, ἡ, strength, force

βιάζομαι, βιάσομαι, ἐβιασάμην, – ,
βεβίασμαι, – , overpower, assault
forcibly

βιβλίον, -ου, τό, book (2)

βίος, -ου, ὁ, life (6)

βιόω, βιώσομαι, ἐβίωσα, – , – , – , live, be
alive

βλάβη, -ης, ἡ, harm (6)

βλάπτω, βλάψω, ἔβλαψα, βέβλαφα,
βέβλαμμαι, ἐβλάβην, hurt, hinder

βλαστάνω, βλαστήσω, ἔβλαστον,
βεβλάστηκα, – , – , grow (19)

βλέπω, βλέψω, ἔβλεψα, βέβλεφα,
βέβλεμμαι, ἐβλέφθην, see (2)

βλώσκω, μολοῦμαι, ἔμολον, μέμβλωκα,
– , – , go, come

βοή, -ῆς, ἡ, cry, sound

βοηθέω, βοηθήσω, ἐβοήθησα,
βεβοήθηκα, βεβοήθημαι, – , help

βοΐδιον, -ου, τό, ox, cow

βολβός, -οῦ, ὁ, bulb of a plant, root (17s)

βορέας, -ου, ὁ, north wind

βόσκω, βοσκήσω, ἐβόσκησα, – , – , – ,
feed, drive to pasture (19)

βότρυς, -υος, ὁ, cluster of grapes, bunch
of grapes (17s)

βουκόλος, -ου, ὁ, herdsman, cowherd,
neatherd, cowboy (19)

βουλή, -ῆς, ἡ, will, plan, advice, desire;
council, senate

βουλεύω, βουλεύσω, ἐβούλευσα,
βεβούλευκα, βεβούλευμαι,
ἐβουλεύθην, plan, consider, decide

βούλομαι, βουλήσομαι, – , – ,
βεβούλημαι, ἐβουλήθην, wish, intend
(13)

βοῦς, βοός, ὁ, ἡ, ox, cow, bull (14)

βοάω, βοήσω, ἐβόησα, βεβόηκα,
βεβόημαι, ἐβοήθην, shout, cry out
(14)

βραδύς, βραδεῖα, βραδύ, slow

βραχίων, -ονος, ὁ, upper arm, arm in
general (15)

βραχύς, -εῖα, ύ, short (18)

βρέχω, βρέξω, ἔβρεξα, – , βέβρεγμαι,
ἐβρέχθην, moisten, sprinkle

βροντή, -ῆς, ἡ, thunder (14s)

βροντάω, βροντήσω, ἐβρόντησα, – , – ,
– , thunder (14s)

βροτήσιος, -α, -ον, mortal

βροτόεις, -εσσα, -εν, bloody, gory

βρόχος, -ου, ὁ, noose (18)

βωμός, -οῦ, ὁ, altar

γάλα, γάλακτος, τό, milk (16)

γαλῆ, -ῆς, ἡ, weasel, ferret

γαλήνη, -ης, ἡ, calm weather (14)

γαληνός, -ή, -όν, calm

γαμέω, γαμῶ, ἔγημα, γεγάμηκα,
γεγάμημαι, ἐγαμήθην, marry (also
with future and aorist γαμήσω,
ἐγάμησα)

γάμος, -ου, ὁ, marriage, wedding

γάρ, particle indicating a reason (3)

γαστήρ, γαστρός, ὁ, stomach (15)

γαυλός, -οῦ, ὁ, milk-pail

γε, particle giving emphasis (4)

γείνομαι, – , ἐγεινάμην, – , – , – , beget,
give birth

γειτνιάω, be a neighbor, be next to
(present system only)

γείτων, -ονος, ὁ, neighbor (14)

Γελασῖνος, -ου, ὁ, the Laugher (7)

γελαστής, -οῦ, ὁ, laugher, person who
laughs

γελάω, γελάσομαι, ἐγέλασα, – ,
γεγέλασμαι, ἐγελάσθην, laugh, laugh
at (7)

γέλοιος, -α, -ον, humorous, laughable,
silly

γέλως, -ωτος, ὁ, laughter

γενεά, -ᾶς, ἡ, birth

γένειον, -ου, τό, chin

γενναῖος, -α, -ον, noble, classy; innate

γένος, τό, family, race

γεραίρω, γεραρῶ, ἐγέρηρα, – , – , – ,
reward

γέρας, -ως, τό, reward, prize (12)

γέρων, -οντος, ὁ, old man

γεύω, γεύσω, ἔγευσα, – , γέγευμαι, – ,
give a taste; in middle, taste

γεωργός, -οῦ, ὁ, farmer (4)

γεωργέω, γεωργήσω, ἐγεώργησα, – , – ,
– , farm, be a farmer (14)

γῆ, γῆς, ἡ, land, earth (7)

γῆρας, γήρως, τό, old age

γίγας, γίγαντος, ὁ, giant (8)

γίγνομαι, γενήσομαι, ἐγενόμην, γέγονα, γεγένημαι, – , become, be (10)

γιγνώσκω, γνώσομαι, ἔγνων, ἔγνωκα, ἔγνωσμαι, ἐγνώσθην, recognize, learn to know (13)

γλεῦκος, -ους, τό, freshly pressed grape juice, must, new wine

γλυκύς, -εῖα, -ύ, sweet (18)

γλῶττα, -ας, ἡ, tongue (4)

γνήσιος, -α, -ον, genuine, legitimate

γνώμη, -ης, ἡ, thought, judgement, intention (14)

γογγυλίς, -ίδος, ἡ, turnip (17s)

γοητεία, -ας, ἡ, witchcraft, magic

γονεύς, -έως, ὁ, parent (16)

γραμματικός, -οῦ, ὁ, scholar, pedant (7)

γραῦς, γρᾱός, ἡ, old woman (14)

γράφω, γράψω, ἔγραψα, γέγραφα, γέγραμμαι, ἐγράφην, write (2)

γυῖον, -ου, τό, limb

γυμνός, -ή, -όν, bare, naked (16)

γυμνόω, γυμνώσω, ἐγύμνωσα, – , – , ἐγυμνώθην, lay bare, strip naked (16)

γυναικεῖος, -α, -ον, feminine, womanly

γυναικωνῖτις, -ίδος, ἡ, women's rooms (17)

γυνή, γυναικός, ἡ, woman, wife (14)

γύψ, γῡπός, ὁ, vulture (14)

γύψος, -ου, ἡ, chalk

γωνία, -ας, ἡ, corner, angle

δαί, particle expressing surprise or curiosity, used in questions

δάϊος, -α, -ον, hostile, enemy

δάκνω, δήξομαι, ἔδακον, – , δέδηγμαι, ἐδήχθην, bite

δάκρυ, δάκρυος, τό, tear (12)

δακρῡω, δακρῡσω, ἐδάκρῡσα, δεδάκρῡκα, δεδάκρῡμαι, ἐδακρύθην, weep, cry, weep for, lament (19)

δάκτυλος, -ου, ὁ, finger (3)

δέ, but, and, particle marking Topic (3)

δέδοικα, fear, perfect system only (18)

δεῖ, δεήσει, ἐδέησε, – , – , – , it is necessary (impersonal) (14)

δείδω, δείσομαι, ἔδεισα, – , – , – , fear; normally used in perfect, δέδοικα

δεῖγμα, δείγματος, τό, specimen, example, sample

δείκνῡμι, δείξω, ἔδειξα, δέδειχα, δέδειγμαι, ἐδείχθην, show, point out (17)

δείλαιος, -α, -ον, wretched, miserable

δειλός, -ή, -όν, cowardly (7)

δεινός, -ή, -όν, terrible, clever (7)

δεῖπνον, -ου, τό, supper (17)

δέκα, ten (3)

δελφίς, -ῖνος, ὁ, ἡ, dolphin (14)

δέμνια, -ων, τά, bedding

δένδρον, -ου, τό, tree (3)

δεξιός, -ά, -όν, right (opp. left, ἀριστερός)

δέομαι, δεήσομαι, – , – , – , ἐδεήθην, ask for

δέρη, -ης, ἡ, neck, throat

δέρμα, -ατος, τό, skin

δεσπότης, -ου, ὁ, master (7)

δεῦρο, hither, this way, here

δεύτερος, -α, -ον, second

δέχομαι, δέξομαι, ἐδεξάμην, – , δέδεγμαι, ἐδέχθην, receive, accept (14)

δέω, δεήσω, ἐδέησα, δεδέηκα, δεδέημαι, ἐδεήθην, need, lack

δέω, δήσω, ἔδησα, δέδεκα, δέδεμαι, ἐδέθην, bind (19)

δή, connecting particle (4)

δῆλος, -η, -ον, clear, visible

δηλόω, δηλώσω, ἐδήλωσα, δεδήλωκα, δεδήλωμαι, ἐδηλώθην, declare, make plain, show (2)

δημοκρατίᾱ, -ας, ἡ, democracy (12)

δῆμος, -ου, ὁ, deme, one of the administrative divisions of Athens; more generally, the people, populace, the sovereign people (12)

δημόσιος, -α, -ον, belonging to a deme, public; low-level magistrate of a deme; δημοσίᾳ, at public expense

δήπου, particle, indicating that the speaker expects the hearer to agree δηρός, -ά, -όν, long

δῆτα, particle, marking the connection of a question with the previous dialogue, or emphasizing a point in the answer to a question

διά, on account of (+ acc.), through (+ gen.) (6)

δια-διδράσκω, run away

διαδίδωμι, distribute (9)

δια-θέω, run about (other tenses normally not used) (10)

διαθήκη, -ης, ἡ, will (in the legal sense), testament (6)

δι-αιρέω, pull apart, open (18)

δίαιτα, -ας, ἡ, daily life, way of life

διαιτάομαι, διαιτηθήσομαι, – , – , δεδιήτημαι, διῃτήθην, dwell, lead one's life (15)

διά-κειμαι, be situated, be in a condition (with an adverb) (19)

δια-κναίω, wear away, erode, rub out

διακονέω, διακονήσω, ἐδιακόνησα, δεδιακόνηκα, δεδιακόνημαι, ἐδιακονήθην, wait on, serve, supply (20)

δια-λέγω, converse, reason, argue

δια-μένω, remain, continue

διαπρεπής, -ές, excellent, outstanding

δια-τίθημι, distribute, separate; treat (9)

δια-φέρω, differ, be superior (9)

δια-φεύγω, flee in different directions (15)

δια-φθείρω, destroy (12)

δια-φοιτάω, wander around

δια-ψιθυρίζω, -ιῶ, -ισα, – , – , – , whisper together

διδασκάλη, -ης, ἡ, teacher (2)

διδάσκαλος, -ου, ὁ, ἡ, teacher (2)

διδάσκω, διδάξω, ἐδίδαξα, δεδίδαχα, δεδίδαγμαι, ἐδιδάχθην, teach (19)

διδράσκω, δρᾱσομαι, ἔδρᾱν, δέδρᾱκα, – , – , run away, escape (13)

διδυμάων, -ονος, ὁ, twin brother

δίδωμι, δώσω, ἔδωκα, δέδωκα, δέδομαι, ἐδόθην, give (9)

δι-ίστημι, separate (9)

δικάζω, δικάσω, ἐδίκασα, δεδίκακα, δεδίκασμαι, ἐδικάσθην, judge, adjudicate

δίκαιος, -α, -ον, just, upright (7)

δικαιοσύνη, -ης, ἡ, justice (19)

δικαστής, juror, judge (8)

δίκη, -ης, ἡ, lawsuit, justice (6); δίκην τούτου λαμβάνειν, punish him; δίκην διδόναι, pay a penalty, be punished

δικτυόκλωστος, -ον, made of mesh, woven like a net

δίκτυον, -ου, τό, net (18)

διόλου, altogether, entirely

δῖος, -α, -ον, brilliant

διότι, because (7)

διπλάσιος, -α, -ον, double, twice as big (13)

διπλοῦς, -ῆ, -οῦν, double (17)

δίσκος, -ου, ὁ, discus

δίφρος, -ου, ὁ, stool, chair (3)

διχθάδιος, -α, -ον, double, two-fold

διψαλέος, -α, -ον, thirsty

διψάω, διψήσω, ἐδίψησα, – , – , – , thirst, be thirsty

διώκω, διώξω, ἐδίωξα, δεδίωχα, δεδίωγμαι, εδιώθχην, chase, pursue, prosecute (19)

δοκέω, δόξω, ἔδοξα, – , δέδογμαι, ἐδόχθην, seem, think (10)

δόλος, -ον, ὁ, trick, deceit

δόσις, -εως, ἡ, act of giving

δουλεύω, δουλεύσω, ἐδούλευσα, δεδούλευκα, δεδούλευμαι, – , serve, be a slave (7)

δοῦλος, -ου, ὁ, slave (5)

δράκων, -οντος, ὁ, dragon, serpent

δρασείω, desire to do (present system only)

δραχμή, -ῆς, ἡ, drachma (5)

δρεπάνη, -ης, ἡ, sickle

δρόμος, -ου, ὁ, running, race (16)

δρῦς, δρυός, ἡ, oak (16)

δράω, δρᾱσω, ἔδρᾱσα, δέδρᾱκα, δέδρᾱμαι, ἐδράσθη, do (12)

δύναμαι, δυνήσομαι, – , – , δεδύνημαι, ἐδυνήθην, be able (13)

δυνατός, -ή, -όν, able, powerful

δύο, δυοῖν, two (3)

δύσαυλος, -ον, inhospitable, not like a
    palace hall

δυσκολαίνω, δυσκολανῶ, –, –, –, –, be
    annoyed, be discontent (17)

δύσκολος, -ον, grouchy, bad-tempered

δύσομβρος, -ον, stormy

δύστηνος, -ον, miserable (2)

δωμάτιον, -ου, τό, room in a house (3)

δωρέω, δωρήσω, –, –, –, –, give, present
    with

δωροδοκία, -ας, ή, bribery, bribe-taking

δῶρον, -ου, τό, gift (8)

δωρο-φορέω, bring gifts

ἕ, he, she, it (archaic and non-Attic)

ἐάν, if (8)

ἔαρ, ἤρος, τό, springtime (16)

ἑαυτοῦ, himself (reflexive pronoun) (4)

ἐάω, ἐάσω, εἴασα, εἴακα, εἴαμαι, εἰάθην,
    permit, allow (16)

ἑβδομάς, -άδος, ή, group of seven

ἕβδομος, -η, -ον, seventh

ἐγγύς, near, close (adverb, or prep. + gen.)

ἐγείρω, ἐγερῶ, ἤγειρα, ἐγρήγορα,
    ἐγήγερμαι, ἠγέρθην, wake up,
    awaken, arouse

ἐγ-καλέω, call in, bring a charge against

ἐγ-χέω, pour in (11)

ἐγώ, I (4)

ἕδρᾱ, -ᾱς, ή, seat (3)

ἐθέλω, ἐθελήσω, ἠθέλησα, ἠθέληκα, –,
    –, wish, want to (7)

ἐθίζω, ἐθιῶ, εἴθισα, εἴθικα, εἴθισμαι,
    εἰθίσθην, accustom, habituate

ἔθνος, -ους, τό, type, nation, species

εἰ, if (2)

εἶδον, aorist of ὁράω, see

εἶδος, -ους, τό, form

εἴδωλον, -ου, τό, image, effigy, apparition,
    ghost

εἶέν, well, so be it (12)

εἴθε, particle introducing a wish (8)

εἴκοσι(ν), twenty (4)

εἰκότως, probably, reasonably (13)

εἰκών, εἰκόνος, ή, image, portrait, pattern

εἰμί, ἔσομαι, –, –, –, –, be (3)

εἶμι, go, will go (8, 15)

εἰρήνη, -ης, ή, peace (4)

εἰς, into, to, + acc. (6)

εἰσ-βιβάζω, εἰσβιβῶ, –, –, –, –, cause to
    go in, put in

εἰσ-έρχομαι, enter

εἰσοπίσω, hereafter, in the future

εἴτε, or, either (9)

εἴωθα, be accustomed, do habitually;
    perfect only (14)

ἐκ, ἐξ, out of, prep. + gen. (4)

ἕκαστος, -η, -ον, each, every (3)

ἑκάτερος, -α, -ον, each of two, either (8)

ἑκατόν, hundred (4)

ἐκ-διδράσκω, run away

ἐκεῖ, there (2)

ἐκεῖθεν, thence, from there

ἐκεῖνος, -η, -ο, that (6)

ἐκεῖσε, thither

ἐκ-καθαίρω, cleanse (11)

ἐκκλησία, -ας, ή, assembly, particularly
    of citizens

ἐκ-λέγω, pick out, single out, choose

ἐκ-λείπω, leave out, omit, abandon

ἐκ-περάω, ἐκπερήσω, ἐξεπέρησα,
    ἐκπεπέρακα, –, –, cross, go over (9)

ἐκ-πίπτω, fall out, be cast out or banished,
    be sent ashore (14)

ἐκ-ρέω, flow out, disappear

ἐκ-στρέφω, turn away, turn aside

ἐκτός, outside (adverb) (3)

ἐκ-φαίνω, bring out, show

ἐκ-φέρω, carry out (15)

ἐκ-χέω, pour out

ἐκφορά, -ᾶς, ή, act of carrying out the
    body for burial

ἐκ-φορέω, carry out (15)

ἑκών, ἑκοῦσα, ἑκόν, willing (9)

ἔλαιον, -ου, τό, oil

ἐλατήρ, ἐλατῆρος, ὁ, driver, rider

ἐλάττων, -ον, ἐλάχιστος, -η, -ον, smaller,
    smallest; suppletive to μικρός

ἐλαύνω, ἐλῶ, ἤλασα, ἐλήλακα,
    ἐλήλαμαι, ἠλάθην, ride, drive (6)

ἐλαφηβόλος, -ον, shooting deer, hunting
    deer

ἔλαφος, -ου, ὁ, ἡ, deer

ἐλεέω, ἐλεήσω, ἠλέησα, –, –, –, pity, have pity for

ἐλευθερίᾱ, -ᾱς, ἡ, freedom (7)

ἐλευθέρια, -ων, τά, sacrifice in thanksgiving for freedom

ἐλεύθερος, -ᾱ, -ον, free (4)

ἐλέφας, -αντος, ὁ, ἡ, elephant

ἕλκος, -ους, τό, wound, sore

ἕλκω, ἕλξω, εἵλκυσα, εἵλκυκα, εἵλκυσμαι, εἱλκύσθην, draw, pull (6)

Ἕλλην, Ἕλληνος, ὁ, Greek (14)

ἑλληνιστί, in Greek (1)

ἐλπίς, ἐλπίδος, ἡ, hope (9)

ἐλπίζω, ἐλπιῶ, ἤλπισα, –, –, ἠλπίσθην, hope, expect (5)

ἐλώριον, -ου, τό, prey, spoils

ἐμαυτοῦ, myself (reflexive pronoun) (4)

ἐμ-βάλλω, put in (11)

ἐμμανής, ἐμμανές, crazed, manic, raving

ἐμός, -ή, -όν, my (20)

ἐμ-πίπτω, fall in; of words, come to mind, be heard

ἐμ-ποιέω, put in, insert, cause

ἐν, in, prep. + dat. (4)

ἐνάλιος, -α, -ον, marine, of the sea

ἔναρα, -ων, τά, weapons

ἐναργής, -ες, visible, clear, bright

ἐν-δίδωμι, give in, lend (9)

ἔνδοθεν, (from) within (16)

ἔνδον, in, inside (15)

ἐν-δύομαι, ἐν-δύσομαι, ἐν-έδυν, ἐν-δέδυκα, –, –, go into, put on (clothes)

ἕνεκα, for the sake of, because of (post-position + gen.) (12)

ἐν-ερείδω, ἐν-ερείσω, ἐν-ήρεισα, ἐν-ήρεικα, ἐν-ήρεισμαι, ἐν-ηρείσθην, thrust in, shove in

ἐν-ηβάω, enjoy oneself in (18)

ἐνθάδε, here (2)

ἐνθαλαττεύω, stay on the sea (present system only)

ἐνθένδε, hence

ἐν-θυμέομαι, ἐν-θυμήσομαι, –, –, ἐν-τεθύμημαι, ἐν-εθυμήθην, take to heart, consider

ἐνιαυτός, -οῦ, ὁ, year

ἐν-οικέω, inhabit, dwell

ἔνοικος, -ον, inhabiting, residing in, dwelling in

ἔνοινος, -ον, containing wine

ἔνορχος, -ον, uncastrated, having testicles

ἐνόχλησις, -εως, ἡ, annoyance

ἐνταῦθα, here (12)

ἐντεῦθεν, from there, after that (16)

ἐν-τίθημι, put in

ἔντιλτος, -ου, ὁ, fish cake (17s)

ἐντός, inside (adverb) (3)

ἐν-τυγχάνω, meet, meet up with, fall in with

ἕξ, six

ἐξαίφνης, suddenly

ἐξαπατάω, ἐξαπατήσω, ἐξηπάτησα, ἐξηπάτηκα, –, –, cheat, deceive

ἔξεστι, it is possible (14)

ἐξετάζω, ἐξετῶ, ἐξήτασα, ἐξήτακα, ἐξήτασμαι, ἐξητάσθην, examine, test (5)

ἑξήκοντα, sixty

ἔξωθεν, (from) outside (16)

ἔξ-οιδα, know thoroughly

ἔοικεν, it seems (9)

ἑορτή, -ῆς, ἡ, festival

ἐπ-αινέω, praise, approve, agree

ἔπαινος, -ου, ὁ, approval, praise, eulogy

ἐπ-άγω, bring in, procure

ἐπ-αμύνω, help, defend

ἐπ-αν-έρχομαι, return (8)

ἐπ-αν-ήκω, return, come back (15)

ἐπ-αν-ίημι, let go back, relax

ἐπεί, ἐπειδή, since, because, given that (2)

ἐπείγω, ἐπείξω, ἤπειξα, –, –, ἠπείχθην, urge; in middle, hasten, hurry (11)

ἔπ-ειμι, be on, be additional (9)

ἐπ-εισ-έρχομαι, come in upon

ἐπ-εισ-πηδάω, leap in upon (15)

ἔπειτα, next (9)

ἐπ-έχω, stop, cause to stop (15)

ἐπήρεια, -ας, ἡ, insult (13)

ἐπί, on, onto (prep. + gen., dat., acc.) (4, 6)

ἐπι-βλέπω, look at; especially, look at with envy

ἐπι-δακρύω, weep also (19)

ἐπι-δείκνυμι, exhibit, show (17)

ἐπι-δίδωμι, contribute (9)

ἐπιεικῶς, moderately, fairly

ἐπι-ζεύγνυμι, join together

ἐπι-ζητέω, seek, wish for, miss

ἐπι-θυμέω, ἐπι-θυμήσω, ἐπι-εθύμησα, – , – , – , desire, want, covet

ἐπιθυμητής, -οῦ, ὁ, eager person, one who desires

ἐπίκαιρος, -ον, at a suitable time, timely

ἐπι-λήθομαι, ἐπι-λήσομαι, ἐπελαθόμην, – , ἐπι-λέλησμαι, – , forget

ἐπι-πίπτω, fall on, attack

ἐπι-ποθέω, desire, long for

ἐπι-σημαίνω, mark, signify, give a sign, indicate approval

ἐπι-σκευάζω, prepare (11)

ἐπίσταμαι, ἐπιστήσομαι, – , – , – , ἠπιστήθην, understand, know how

ἐπιστήμη, -ης, ἡ, knowledge, understanding

ἐπιστολή, -ῆς, ἡ, letter (8)

ἐπίτηδες, on purpose (17)

ἐπιτήδειος, -α -ον, fit, suitable, convenient (17)

ἐπιτήδευμα, -ατος, τό, exercise, practice

ἐπι-τίθημι, place upon (9)

ἐπι-τιμάω, blame (13)

ἐπι-τρέπω, turn over to, give over to

ἐπιφανής, -ές, apparent, conspicuous, outstanding

ἐπι-φέρω, put on, impose on, attack

ἕπομαι, ἕψομαι, ἑσπόμην, – , – , – , follow (12)

ἐπουράνιος, -ον, heavenly, in heaven, in the sky

ἐπριάμην, buy; aorist system only, suppletive to ὠνέομαι

ἑπτά, seven

ἔραμαι, – , – , – , – , – , ἠράσθην, love, desire

ἐρατός, -ή, -όν, lovely, lovable, beloved

ἐργάζομαι, ἐργάσομαι, εἰργασάμην, – , εἴργασμαι, – , work, be busy, accomplish

ἐργαστικός, -ή, -όν, active, energetic (7)

ἔργον, -ου, τό, work (4)

ἔρδω, ἔρξω, εἷρξα, ἔοργα, – , – , work, do

ἐρέβινθος, -ου, ὁ, chick-pea, garbanzo (17s)

ἐρεθίζω, ἐρεθίσω, ἠρέθισα, – , – , – , provoke, challenge (16)

ἐρέττω, ἐρέσω, ἤρεσα, – , – , – , row

ἐρῆμος, -η, -ον, empty, deserted, solitary

ἐρίζω, ἐρίσω, ἤρισα, – , – , – , quarrel

ἔρις, ἔριδος, ἡ, strife, quarreling

ἔριον, -ου, τό, wool

ἕρκος, -ου, τό, barrier, enclosure

ἔρομαι, ἐρήσομαι, ἠρόμην, – , – , – , ask, question (12)

ἕρπω, ἕρψω, εἷρψα, – , – , – , creep, go (11)

ἐρρωμένος, -η, -ον, strong (14)

ἔρχομαι, εἶμι, ἦλθον, ἐλήλυθα, – , – , come, go (8)

ἐρωτάω, ἐρωτήσω, ἠρώτησα, – , – , –, ask (7)

ἐρωτικός, -ή, -όν, having to do with love, erotic

ἐσθίω, ἔδομαι, ἔφαγον, ἐδήδοκα, ἐδήδεσμαι, – , eat (9)

ἐσθλός, -ή, -όν, good, honest (7)

ἐς νέωτα, next year

ἑστιάω, ἑστιάσω, εἱστίασα, εἱστίακα, εἱστίαμαι, εἱστιάθην, entertain, hold a dinner party

ἑταῖρος, -ου, ὁ, companion, comrade (8)

ἔτνος, -ους, τό, soup (17s)

ἐτεός, -ά, -όν, true, real

ἕτερος, -α, -ον, one or other of two (12)

ἔτι, still, yet (10)

ἔτος, -ους, τό, year (11)

εὖ, well (2)

εὐγενής, -ές, noble (11)

εὐδαιμονία, -ας, ἡ, good fortune, happiness

εὐδαίμων, -ον, fortunate, happy, blessed

εὐδοκιμέω, εὐδοκιμήσω, ηὐδοκίμησα, ηὐδοκίμηκα, – , – , have a good reputation, be famous

εὐειδής, εὐειδές, attractive, shapely

εὐθεία, -ας, ἡ, straight line

εὐθύς, right away, immediately (6)

εὔλαλος, -ον, sweet-voiced, sweetly speaking

εὐλίμενος, -ον, with good harbors

εὐλογία, -ας, ἡ, praise

εὔλογος, -ον, reasonable, probable

εὐμμελίης, -ου, ὁ, good spear-warrior

εὔνους, -ον, friendly (15)

εὐπρεπής, -ες, attractive, suitable

εὑρίσκω, εὑρήσω, εὗρον, εὕρηκα, εὕρημαι, εὑρέθην, find (9)

εὔρυθμος, -ον, in good rhythm, well-proportioned, graceful

εὐρύς, -εῖα, ύ, broad, wide (18)

εὐρύχορος, -ον, having broad dancing-places

εὐτυχής, -ές, lucky, fortunate

εὐφημέω, εὐφημήσω, ηὐφήμησα, – , – , – , utter words of good omen; be silent (10)

εὐχή, -ῆς, ἡ, prayer (10)

εὔχομαι, εὔξομαι, εὐξάμην, – , ηὖγμαι, – , pray, vow; boast

ἐφ-έλκω, pull away, pull out

ἐφ-ικνέομαι, reach (11)

ἐφ-ίστημι, set over (9)

ἐχθές, yesterday (5)

ἐχθρός, -ά, -όν, enemy, hostile

ἔχθω, hate; present system only

ἐχῖνος, -ου, ὁ, hedgehog

ἔχω, ἕξω, ἔσχον, ἔσχηκα, ἔσχημαι, ἐσχέθην, have (2)

ἕψω, ἑψήσω, ἥψησα, ἥψηκα, ἥψημαι, ἡψήθην, boil, cook in liquid (17s)

ἕως, until, while (15)

ζάω, ζήσω, ἔζησα, – , – , – , live, be alive (17)

ζεύγνῡμι, ζεύξω, ἔζευξα, – , ἔζευγμαι, ἐζεύχθην, yoke, harness, join

ζεῦγος, -ους, τό, yoked pair

Ζέφυρος, -ου, ὁ, west wind

ζῆλος, -ου, ὁ, envy, jealousy, rivalry

ζητέω, ζητήσω, ἐζήτησα, ἐζήτηκα, – , ἐζητήθην, seek, look for (13)

ζητητέος, -α, -ον, needing to be sought or looked into

ζυγόν, -οῦ, τό, yoke (6)

ζῶμα, -ατος, τό, girdle, belt (16)

ζώνη, -ης, ἡ, girdle, belt, waistband

ζῷον, -ου, τό, animal (8)

ζωστήρ, -ῆρος, ὁ, sword-belt

ἤ, or, either/or (3)

ἡβάω, ἡβήσω, ἥβησα, ἥβηκα, – , – , enjoy life, be merry, be young (18)

ἥβη, -ης, ἡ, youth, young manhood

ἥδομαι, ἡσθήσομαι, – , – , – , ἥσθην, enjoy, take pleasure

ἡγέομαι, ἡγήσομαι, ἡγησάμην, – , ἥγημαι, – , think, suppose; lead, be in charge (10)

ἡδέως, gladly, pleasantly (6)

ἤδη, already (10)

ἡδονή, -ῆς, ἡ, pleasure (20)

ἡδύς, -εῖα, -ύ, sweet (18)

ἥκω, I am come (present system only) (17)

ἡλικία, -ας, ἡ, age, time of life

ἡλικιώτης, -ου, ὁ, person of the same age

ἥλιος, -ου, ὁ, sun (10)

ἦμαρ, -ατος, τό, day

ἡμιμναῖον, -ου, τό, half-mina (5)

ἡμέρα, day (6)

ἡμέτερος, -α, -ον, our (20)

ἠνεμόεις, -εσσα, -εν, windy

ἠρίον, -ου, τό, mound, burial-mound

ἦρος, gen. of ἔαρ

ἥρως, ἥρωος, ὁ, hero

ἡττάομαι, ἡττήσομαι, – , – , ἥττημαι, ἡσσήθην, be less (than someone, in genitive), be beaten, lose (14)

ἥττων, -ον, smaller, fewer, less; suppletive to ὀλίγος

ἠχή, -ῆς, ἡ, sound

θάλαττα, -ης, ἡ, sea (6)

θαλερός, -ά, -όν, blooming, abundant, vigorous

θαμά, often

θάμνος, -ου, ὁ, bush, shrub

θανατάω, desire to die (present system only)

θάνατος, -ου, ὁ, death (11)

θάπτω, θάψω, ἔθαψα, τέθαφα, τέθαμμαι, ἐτάφην, bury (20)

θαρρέω, θαρρήσω, ἐθάρρησα, τεθάρρηκα, –, –, be brave, courageous, cheerful

θαυμάζω, θαυμάσω, ἐθαύμασα, τεθαύμακα, – ἐθαυμάσθη, wonder, be amazed (6)

θεά, -ᾶς, ἡ, goddess (3)

θελκτήριον, -ου, τό, charm, spell (3)

θεῖος, -α, -ον, divine, godly (18)

θεός, -οῦ, ὁ, ἡ, god, goddess (2)

θεράπαινα, -ας, ἡ, maidservant, female slave or servant (15)

θεραπεύω, θεραπεύσω, ἐθεράπευσα, –, –, ἐθεραπεύθην, tend, care for (6)

θερμαίνω, θερμανῶ, ἐθέρμηνα, –, τεθέρμαμμαι, ἐθερμάνθην, heat, warm (16)

θέρος, -ου, τό, summer, harvest (16)

θεωρία, -ας, ἡ, spectacle, act of viewing (12)

θεωρικός, -ή, -όν, connected with a θεωρία

Θήβη, -ης, ἡ, Thebes, also αἱ Θῆβαι

θηλάζω, θηλάσω, ἐθήλασα, τεθήλακα, τεθήλαγμαι, ἐθηλάσθην, nurse, suckle (17)

θῆλυς, -εια, -υ, female (18)

θήρ, θηρός, ὁ, beast (14)

θήρᾱ, -ᾱς, ἡ, hunt (19)

θηράω, θηράσω, –, –, –, –, hunt (19)

θηρίον, -ου, τό, beast (9)

θής, θητός, ὁ, laborer, thete (14)

θιγγάνω, θίξομαι, ἔθιγον, –, –, –, touch

θλῑβω, θλίψω, ἔθλῑψα, τέθλῑφα, τέθλιμμαι, ἐθλίβην, crush (11)

θνήσκω, θανοῦμαι, ἔθανον, τέθνηκα, –, –, die

θνητός, -η, -ον, mortal (18)

θοός, -ή, -όν, swift

θόρυβος, -ου, ὁ, noise (10)

θρίξ, τριχός, ἡ, hair

θυγάτηρ, θυγατρός, ἡ, daughter (15)

θύμον, -ου, τό, thyme (herb)

θυμός, -οῦ, ὁ, spirit, life, breath, consciousness (20)

θύννειον, -ου, τό, tuna (17s)

θύρᾱ, -ᾱς, ἡ, door (3)

θύριον, -ου, τό, door, small door

θυρίς, -ίδος, ἡ, window (17)

θυσία, -ας, ἡ, sacrifice

θύω, θύσω, ἔθῡσα, τέθῠκα, τέθῠμαι, ἐτύθην, sacrifice (9)

θωπεύω, θωπεύσω, ἐθώπευσα, τεθώπευκα, τεθώπευμαι, ἐθωπεύθην, flatter, fawn on

ἴαμβος, -ου, ὁ, lampoon, invective; iambic verse

ἰάπτω, ἰάψω, ἴαψα, –, –, –, send, shoot out

ἰᾱτρός, -οῦ, ὁ, physician

ἰδίᾳ, separately (14)

ἰδού, look! see! here!

ἱέρεια, -ας, ἡ, priestess

ἱερεῖον, -ου, τό, victim for a sacrifice (13)

ἱερεύς, -έως, ὁ, priest (16)

ἱερός, -ά, -όν, sacred, holy (14)

ἵημι, ἥσω, ἧκα, εἷκα, εἷμαι, εἵθην, send (9)

ἱκανός, -ή, -όν, capable, sufficient (14)

ἱκνέομαι, ἵξομαι, ἱκόμην, –, ἷγμαι, –, come, arrive, reach

ἵλεως, ἵλεων, propitious (7)

ἴλλω, roll, cause to revolve (present system only)

ἱμάτιον, -ου, τό, cloak (4)

ἵνα, in order that (8)

Ἰνδός, -οῦ, ὁ, Indian (7)

ἰξύς, -ύος, ἡ, waist (16)

ἴον, -ου, τό, violet (16)

ἰπνός, -οῦ, ὁ, oven (17s)

ἱππεύς, -εως, ὁ, horseman, cavalry soldier, rider

ἵππιος, -α, -ον, relating to horses, equestrian; also ἵππειος

ἱπποδρόμος, -ου, ὁ, race course (15)

ἵππος, -ου, ὁ, horse (6)

ἴσος, -η, -ον, equal (17)

ἵστημι, στήσω, ἔστησα (ἔστην), ἔστηκα, ἔσταμαι, ἐστάθην, place, set up (9); first aorist transitive, second aorist intransitive

ἱστίον, -ου, τό, sail (10)

ἱστός, -οῦ, ὁ, mast (10)

ἰσχάς, -άδος, ἡ, dried fig (17s)

ἰσχῡρός, -ά, -όν, strong

ἰσχύς, ἰσχύος, ἡ, strength

ἴσχω, hold, restrain; present system only

ἴτριον, -ου, ὁ, honey cake made with sesame seeds (17s)

ἶφι, strongly, powerfully

ἴφθιμος, -η, -ον, strong

ἰχθύς, ἰχθύος, ὁ, fish (12)

καθ-αιρέω, take down, destroy

καθαίρω, καθαρῶ, ἐκάθηρα, – , κεκάθαρμαι, ἐκαθάρθην, cleanse

καθάπερ, like as, just as (8)

καθ-έλκω, drag down; launch (ship)

καθεύδω, καθευδήσω, – , – , – , – , sleep (17)

κάθημαι, sit, be seated (athematic, present system only)

καθίζω, καθεδοῦμαι, ἐκάθισα, – , – , – , cause to sit, set; sit (16)

καθ-ίημι, let down (10)

καθ-ικνέομαι, come down (11)

καθ-ίστημι, place, set up (9)

καθ-οράω, catch sight of (15)

καί, and, both, also (2)

καίνω, κανῶ, ἔκανον, κέκονα, – , – , slay, kill

καίπερ, even though, although (with participle) (9)

καιρός, -οῦ, ὁ, right time, nick of time (13)

καίω, καύσω, ἔκαυσα, κέκαυκα, κέκαυμαι, ἐκαύθην, burn (20)

κακός, -ή, -όν, bad (2)

κακῶς, badly (2)

κάλαμος, -ου, ὁ, reed, pipe, pen, rod (2)

καλός, -ή, -όν, noble, fine, beautiful (2)

καλέω, καλῶ, ἐκάλεσα, κέκληκα, κέκλημαι, ἐκλήθην, call (7)

καλύπτω, καλύψω, ἐκάλυψα, – , κεκάλυμμαι, ἐκαλύφθην, cover, conceal

καλῶς, well

κάλως, -ω, ὁ, rope (10)

κάματος, -ου, ὁ, toil (14)

κἄν = καὶ ἐν,

κάππαρις, -εως, ἡ, caper (17s)

κάπτω, κάψω, ἔκαψα, κέκαφα, κέκαμμαι, ἐκάφθην, bite, snap up, gulp down greedily

κάρα, -ατος, τό, head

καρδίᾱ, -ᾱς, ἡ, heart; Ionic form κραδίη

καρκίνος, -ου, ὁ, crab

καρπός, -οῦ, ὁ, wrist (15)

καρφο-λογέω, -ήσω, -ησα, – , – , – , gather twigs, pick off bits of lint.

κατά, down to (+ acc.); down from (+ gen.) (6)

κατα-βαίνω, come down (17)

κατα-βάλλω, throw down (15)

κατα-βόσκω, feed, bring to pasture

κατ-άγω, lead down, bring down (20)

κατα-διώκω, pursue

κατα-θνήσκω, die

κατα-κλάω, break off

κατα-λαμβάνω, find, catch (15)

κατα-λείπω, leave behind (10)

κατα-παύω, end, finish, bring to an end

κατα-πέτομαι, fly down

κατα-ρρέω, flow down

καταρτύω, καταρτύσω, – , κατήρτυκα, κατήρτυμαι, κατηρτύθην, prepare, arrange

κατα-σβέννυμι, extinguish

κατα-τίθημι, lay down (9)

κατα-φέρω, bring down, carry down

κατα-φρονέω, despise (+ gen.)

κατα-χέω, pour down

κατα-ψηφίζομαι, vote against, vote to condemn

κατ-έχω, restrain, hold down (12)

κατηγορέω, accuse (κατά + ἀγορεύω) (14)

κατήγορος, -ου, ὁ, accuser, prosecutor

κατορύττω, κατορύξω, κατώρυξα, – , κατορώρυγμαι, κατωρύγην, bury, plant, dig down

κάτω, below, down (10)

κεῖμαι, κείσομα, lie, be placed (present and future systems only) (16)

κελευστής, -οῦ, ὁ, coxswain, boatswain

κελεύω, κελεύσω, ἐκέλευσα, κεκέλευκα, κεκέλευσμαι, ἐκελεύσθην, order, command (5)

κενός, -ή, -όν, empty

κεραία, -ας, ἡ, yardarm (10)

κεράννυμι, κεράσω, ἐκέρασα, – , κεκέρασμαι, ἐκράθην, mix

κέρας, κέρατος, τό, horn (of an animal, or musical instrument)

κέρδος, -ους, τό, profit, advantage

κεφαλή, -ῆς, ἡ, head (4)

κῆπος, -ου, ὁ, garden (3)

κήρ, κηρός, ἡ, fate

κήρυγμα, -ατος, τό, proclamation, public notice

κῆρυξ, κήρυκος, ὁ, herald

κηρύττω, κηρύξω, ἐκήρυξα, κεκήρυχα, κεκήρυγμαι, ἐκηρύχθην, announce, proclaim, act as a herald

κιθαριστής, -οῦ, ὁ, cithara-player, lyre-player

κινδῡνεύω, κινδυνεύσω, ἐκινδύνευσα, κεκινδύνευκα, κεκινδύνευμαι, ἐκινδυνεύθην, dare, venture (15)

κίνδυνος, -ου, ὁ, danger, risk

κισσύβιον, -ου, τό, drinking cup made of ivy wood

κιττός, -οῦ, ὁ, ivy

κιχάνω, κιχήσομαι, ἔκιχον, – , – , – , find, meet up with

κλάδος, -ου, ὁ, sprig, branch

κλαίω, κλαύσομαι, ἔκλαυσα, – , κέκλαυμαι, – , weep, cry (17)

κλᾰ́ω, κλάσω, ἔκλασα, – , κέκλασμαι, ἐκλάσθην, pluck, break off

κλεινός, -η, -ον, famous

κλείς, κλειδός, ἡ, key (17)

κλέος, -ους, τό, fame, renown

κλέπτης, -ου, ὁ, thief (17)

κλέπτω, κλέψω, ἔκλεψα, κέκλοφα, κέκλεμμαι, ἐκλάπην, steal

κλῆμα, -ατος, τό, branch, shoot, tendril (11)

κληρονόμος, -ου, ὁ, heir (6)

κλήω, κλήσω, ἔκλησα, κέκληκα, κέκλημμαι, ἐκλείσθην, shut (6)

κλῖμαξ, -ακος, ἡ, ladder, stair (17)

κλίνη, -ης, ἡ, couch, lounge (3)

κλίνω, κλινῶ, ἔκλινα, κέκλικα, κέκλιμαι, ἐκλίθην, lean, recline

κλύδων, -ωνις, ὁ, wave, surge of the sea

κοῖλος, -ν, -ον, hollow (14)

κοινός, -ή, -όν, common, shared (6)

κόλπος, -ου, ὁ, bosom, lap, fold of a garment used for a pocket (15)

κόμαρος, -ου, ἡ, arbutus, strawberry-tree

κόμη, -ης, ἡ, hair (16)

κομίζω, κομιῶ, ἐκόμισα, κεκόμικα, κεκόμισμαι, ἐκομίσθην, carry

κόμπος, -ου, ὁ, brag, boast, vaunt

κόνις, -εως, ἡ, dust

κονίω, κονίσω, ἐκόνισα, κεκόνικα, κεκόνιμαι, – , cover with dust, make dusty

κοπτή, -ῆς, ἡ, pounded sesame, sesame paste (17s)

κόπτω, κόψω, ἔκοψα, κέκοφα, κέκομμαι, ἐκόπην, cut, hammer, strike

κόρη, -ης, ἡ, girl, maiden (9)

κόρος, -ου, ὁ, young man (9)

κόσμος, -ου, ὁ, ornament, adornment; good order; the world, the universe

κοτύλη, -ης, ἡ, cup, half-pint measure

κουφόνοος, -ον, light-minded, unthinking, flighty

κραίνω, κρανῶ, ἔκρανα, – , κέκραμμαι, ἐκράνθην, accomplish

κρατέω, κρατήσω, ἐκράτησα, κεκράτηκα, κεκράτημαι, ἐκρατήθην, be strong, be powerful, rule, conquer, master

κρατήρ, -ῆρος, ὁ, mixing bowl (17s)

κράτος, -ους, τό, strength (11)

κραυγή, -ῆς, ἡ, din, noise

κρέας, κρέως, τό, meat

κρείττων, -ον, κράτιστος, -η, -ον, better, best; suppletive to ἀγαθός

κρηπίς, -ίδος, ἡ, shoe

κρῑ́νω, κρινῶ, ἔκρῑνα, κέκρικα, κέκριμαι, ἐκρίθη, judge, determine (7)

κρῑός, -οῦ, ὁ, ram

κρίσιμος, -ον, decisive, critical

κρίσις, -εως, ἡ, crisis

κριτής, -οῦ, ὁ, judge (7)

κροκύς, κροκύδος, ὁ, lint, bit of fluff

κρόμμυον, -ου, τό, onion (17s)

κρύπτω, κρύψω, ἔκρυψα, κέκρυφα, κέκρυμμαι, ἐκρύφθην, hide, cover

κρύσταλλος, -ου, ὁ, ice

κτείνω, κτενῶ, ἔκτεινα, ἔκτονα, -, -, kill

κτύπος, -ου, ὁ, loud noise, crash, rattle

κυανέμβολος, -ον, having a blue prow

κυβερνήτης, -ου, ὁ, helmsman, pilot (10)

κύκλος, -ου, ὁ, circle (12)

κῦμα, κύματος, τό, waves, stormy sea

κυμβίον, -ου, τό, cup (15)

κυνέω, κυνήσομαι, ἔκυσα, -, -, -, kiss

κυνηγέτης, -ου, ὁ, huntsman, hunter (19)

κυπαρίσσινος, -η, -ον, made of cypress wood

κύριος, -ου, ὁ, lord, master

κυρτόομαι, belly out (present system only)

κύων, κυνός, ὁ, ἡ, dog (18)

κῶλον, -ου, τό, limb, leg

κωλύω, κωλύσω, ἐκώλυσα, κεκώλυκα, κεκώλυμαι, ἐκωλύθην, hinder, prevent

κώμη, -ης, ἡ, village (6)

κωμήτης, -ου, ὁ, villager (19)

κώπη, -ης, ἡ, oar (14)

λάβρος, -ον, vehement, blustery, powerful, violent, furious

λαβή, -ῆς, ἡ, handle

λαγώς, λαγώ, ὁ, hare, rabbit (18)

λαλέω, λαλήσω, ἐλάλησα, λελάληκα, -, -, talk, chatter, babble (13)

λαμβάνω, λήψομαι, ἔλαβον, εἴληφα, εἴλημμαι, ἐλήφθην, take, grasp (5)

λαμπρύνω, λαμπρυνῶ, ἐλάμπρυνα, -, λελάμπρυμμαι, -, make bright, distinguish; in middle, pride oneself on, be distinguished at

λάμπω, λάμψω, ἔλαμψα, λέλαμπα, -, -, shine, be bright (14s)

λανθάνω, λήσω, ἔλαθον, λέληθα, λέλησμαι, ἐλήσθην, escape notice (15)

λάρναξ, λάρνακος, ἡ, box, coffin

λασιαύχην, λασιαύχενος, ὁ, one with a shaggy neck or mane

λάσιος, -α, -ον, shaggy, hairy

λάτρις, λάτριος, ὁ, slave, hired hand

λάχανον, -ου, τό, herb, vegetable (3)

λαχνόομαι, λαχνώσομαι, -, -, -, -, grow downy, become hairy

λέβης, λέβητος, ὁ, cauldron (17s)

λέγω, λέξω, ἔλεξα, -, λέλεγμαι, ἐλέχθην, speak, say (2)

λεία, -ας, ἡ, booty, spoils

λειμών, -ῶνος, ὁ, meadow (14)

λείπω, λείψω, ἔλειψα, λέλοιπα, λέλειμμαι, ἐλείφθην, leave (10)

λεπτός, -ή, -ον, lightweight, slight, delicate (18)

λευκός, -ή, -όν, white (4)

λεύσσω, (present system only) look, behold

λέων, λέοντος, ὁ, lion (8)

λεώς, λεώ, ὁ, people (7)

λήκυθος, -ου, ἡ, oil flask (7)

ληνός, -οῦ, ἡ, wine vat (11)

λίθινος, -η, -ον, of stone

λίθος, -ου, ὁ, stone (11)

λικμάω, λικμήσω, ἐλίκμησα, -, -, -, winnow

λιμήν, λιμένος, ὁ, harbor (14)

λίνον, -ου, τό, string (18)

λόγος, -ου, ὁ, word, speech (3)

λοιπός, -ή, -όν, left, remaining (14)

λουτρόν, -οῦ, τό, bath (18)

λούω, λούσω, ἔλουσα, -, λέλουμαι, ἐλούσθην, wash (17)

λόφος, -ου, ὁ, back of the neck, nape

λοχεύω, λοχεύσω, ἐλόχευσα, -, -, ἐλοχεύθην, bring forth, bear (also passive with same meaning)

λόχμη, -ης, ἡ, bush, thicket

λύγος, -ου, ἡ, flexible twig or branch, withy; willow tree (11)

Λυδός, -ου, ὁ, Lydian (7)

λυκορραίστης, -ου, ὁ, destroyer of wolves

λύκος, -ου, ὁ, wolf (19)

λύπη, -ης, ἡ, grief, pain, sorrow (3)

λυπηρός, -ά, -όν, painful, grievous

λῡπέω, λῡπήσω, ἐλῡπησα, λελῡπηκα, λελῡπημαι, ἐλυπήθην, vex, hurt, cause pain

λύρα, -ας, ἡ, lyre

λύτρον, -ου, τό, ransom

λυχνεῖον, -ου, τό, lamp-stand (17s)

λύχνος, -ου, ὁ, lamp, light (17)

λῦω, λῦσω, ἔλῦσα, λέλυκα, λέλυμαι, ἐλύθην, loose, undo, annul (2)

μά, particle introducing an oath (8)

μαγειρική, -ῆς, ἡ, cookery, the cook's art (17s)

μάγειρος, -ου, ὁ, cook (17s)

μᾶζα, -ας, ἡ, bread made from barley

μαθητής, -ου, ὁ, student (7)

μαίνομαι, μανοῦμαι, ἐμηνάμην, μέμηνα, μεμάνημαι, ἐμάνην, be crazy, rage, go mad

μακρός, -ᾱ, -όν, long (3)

μάλα, much (6)

μαλακός, -ή, -όν, soft, gentle, weak (16)

μάλιστα, very much, especially (4)

μάλιστά γε, yes, certainly (4)

μανθάνω, μαθήσομαι, ἔμαθον, μεμάθηκα, -, -, learn (2)

μανία, -ας, ἡ, madness, insanity

μάντις, -εως, ὁ, prophet, seer (12)

μάρτυς, μάρτυρος, ὁ, witness (14)

μαρτύριον, -ου, τό, evidence (7)

μάτην, in vain

μάττω, μάξω, ἔμαξα, μέμαχα, μέμαγμαι, ἐμάχθην, knead

μάχαιρα, -ας, ἡ, knife (17s)

μάχη, -ης, ἡ, battle, fight

μάχομαι, μαχοῦμαι, ἐμαχεσάμην, -, μεμάχημαι, -, -, fight, contend (10)

μέγας, μεγάλη, μέγα, large, great (8)

μέγεθος, -ους, τό, size, magnitude

μεδέων, -ονος, ὁ, guardian, ruler

μεθίστημι, remove (9)

μεθύσκω, μεθύσω, ἐμέθυσα, -, -, ἐμεθύσθην, cause to be drunk, intoxicate; in passive, get drunk, be drunk

μειδίαμα, -ατος, τό, smile (16)

μειδιάω, μειδιάσω, ἐμείδησα, -, -, -, smile (16)

μείζων, -ον, bigger; suppletive to μέγας

μειράκιον, -ου, τό, boy, lad (15)

μέλᾱς, μέλαινα, μέλαν, black (8)

μέλει, μελήσει, ἐμέλησε, μεμέληκε, -, -, be an object of care (11)

μελίγηρυς, -υος, ὁ, ἡ, sweet-voiced

μέλλω, μελλήσω, ἐμέλλησα, -, -, -, intend (14)

μέμνημαι, remember (perfect of μιμνήσκω)

μέν, particle marking contrast (3)

μέντοι, particle marking emphasis or contrast (9)

μένω, μενῶ, ἔμεινα, μεμένηκα, -, -, stay, remain

μέρος, -ους, τό, part

μέσος, -η, -ον, middle

μετά, after (+ acc.); with (+ gen.); among (+ dat.) (6)

μεταβολή, -ῆς, ἡ, change (2)

μετα-δίδωμι, give, share (9)

μετα-μέλει, be an object of regret, cause regret

μετα-πίπτω, undergo a change, fall into something different

μετα-ποιέω, alter, change

μετέωρος, -ον, raised, poised, balanced, high, (of ships) floating (11)

μετοπωρινός, -η, -ον, of autumn

μέτρον, -ου, τό, measure, standard of measurement

μέχρι, until, unto (conjunction, or prep. + gen.) (11)

μή, not (4)

μηδείς, no one

μῆλον, -ου, τό, apple (17s)

μῆνις, εως, ἡ, anger, wrath

μηνίω, μηνίσω, ἐμήνισα, -, -, -, be angry, become angry

μηνύω, μηνύσω, ἐμήνυσα, μεμήνυκα, μεμήνυμαι, ἐμηνύθην, reveal, betray, make known

μήτηρ, μήτρος, ἡ, mother (15)

μηχανάομαι, μηχανήσομαι, ἐμηχανησάμην, – , μεμηχάνημαι, – , contrive, devise

μηχανή, -ῆς, ἡ, contrivance, invention, machine (20)

μηχανόεις, -εσσα, -εν, ingenious, able to contrive things

μιαίνω, μιανῶ, ἐμίᾱνα, μεμίαγκα, μεμίασμαι, ἐμιάνθην, pollute, desecrate, stain

μίγνῡμι, μίξω, ἔμιξα, – , μέμιγμαι, ἐμίχθη, mix (17)

μῑκρός, -ᾱ, -όν, small

μιμητής, -οῦ, ὁ, imitator (14)

μιμνήσκω, μνήσω, ἔμνησα, – , μέμνημαι, ἐμνήσθην, remind; middle, remember (15)

μιμέομαι, μιμήσομαι, ἐμιμησάμην, – , μεμίμημαι, – , mimic, imitate

μισέω, μισήσω, ἐμίσησα, μεμίσηκα, μεμίσημαι, ἐμισήθην, hate

μισθός, -οῦ, ὁ, pay, reward (13)

μισθοφόρος, -ον, working for hire, receiving pay, mercenary

μῖσος, -ους, τό, hate, hateful thing (13)

μνᾶ, mina, a unit of money (5)

μνῆμα, μνήματος, τό, memorial

μοῖρα, -ας, ἡ, fate

μόνιμος, -η, -ον, steadfast, constant (also as μόνιμος, -ον)

μόνος, -η, -ον, alone (3)

μόρος, -ου, ὁ, fate, destiny, doom (usually bad sense)

μορφή, -ῆς, ἡ, form, shape

μουσικός, -ή, -όν, musical (9)

μοχλός, -οῦ, ὁ, bar, stake, pole

μυγαλῆ, -ῆς, ἡ, field mouse, shrew

μύκης, -ητος, ὁ, mushroom (17s)

μύριοι, ten thousand (4)

μυρίοι, -αι, -α, countless (13)

μύρον, -ου, τό, fragrant oil, perfume

μύρτος, -ου, ἡ, myrtle

μῦς, μυός, ὁ, mouse

μωρία, -ας, ἡ, foolishness

μῶρος, -α, -ον, foolish (8)

ναί, yes (1)

ναίω, dwell, reside (present system only)

νᾶμα, -ατος, τό, stream

νάπη, -ης, ἡ, valley, forest glen, dale

νάρκισσος, -ου, ὁ, narcissus (16)

ναῦς, νεώς, ἡ, ship (14)

ναύτης, -ου, ὁ, sailor (10)

ναυτικός, -ή, -όν, belonging to a ship or to a sailor, nautical (14)

νεανίας, -ου, ὁ, young man, youth (7)

νέκταρ, -αρος, τό, nectar, a divine beverage

νέκυς, νέκυος, ὁ, corpse, dead body

νέμω, νεμῶ, ἔνειμα, νενέμηκα, νενέμημαι, ἐνεμήθην, tend (cattle or the like), pasture; share out, allot, distribute (14)

νέος, νέα, νέον, young, fresh (2)

νεοττίον, -ου, τό, chick, little bird

νεφέλη, -ης, ἡ, cloud (14s)

νεφελώδης, -ες, cloudy

νεώριον, -ου, τό, dockyard, shipyard

νεώς, νεώ, ὁ, temple (7)

νεωστί, recently

νή, particle introducing an oath as a strong affirmation

νήπιος, -ου, foolish, childish

νῆσος, -ου, ὁ, island

νῆττα, -ας, ἡ, duck (18)

νίζω, νίψω, ἔνιψα, – , νένιμμαι, – , wash

νικάω, νικήσω, ἐνίκησα, νενίκηκα, νενίκημαι, ἐνικήθην, conquer (7)

νίκη, -ης, ἡ, victory

νιφάς, νιφάδος, ἡ, snow flake (14s)

νίφει, νίψει, ἔνιψε, snow (3rd person only) (14s)

νιφετός, -οῦ, ὁ, snow storm (14s)

νοέω, νοήσω, ἐνόησα, νενόηκα, νενόημαι, ἐνοήθην, think, intend

νομεύς, -έως, ὁ, herdsman (16)

νομή, -ῆς, ἡ, pasture (16)

νομίζω, νομιῶ, ἐνόμισα, νενόμικα, νενόμισμαι, ἐνομίσθην, believe, think (7)

νόμιμος, -η, -ον, lawful, pertaining to law

νόμος, -ου, ὁ, law, custom (19)

νόσημα, -ατος, τό, sickness

νόσος, -ου, ἡ, sickness

νόστος, -ου, ὁ, home-coming

νοσέω, νοσήσω, ἐνόσησα, νενόσηκα, – ,
– , be ill (13)

νοτίς, -ίδος, ἡ, moisture

νότος, -ου, ὁ, south wind

νοῦς, νοῦ, ὁ, mind (3)

νύκτωρ, by night (11)

νυμφαῖον, -ου, τό, shrine to the nymphs

νύμφη, -ης, ἡ, nymph; bride (16)

νῦν, now (1)

νύξ, νυκτός, ἡ, night (11)

νωΐτερος, -α, -ον, our, of us two

ξαίνω, ξανῶ, ἔξηνα, – , – , – , card (wool),
comb out, scratch

ξενίζω, ξενιῶ, ἐξένισα, ἐξένικα, – , – ,
receive as a guest, entertain (12)

ξένος, -ου, ὁ, guest, stranger (12)

ξηρός, -ά, -όν, dry (11)

ξίφος, -ους, τό, sword

ξύλον, -ου, τό, wood

ξυλοφορέω, carry wood

ξυν-, Attic variant of συν- as prefix

ὁ, ἡ, τό, the, marks noun phrase as
definite

ὀβολός, -οῦ, ὁ, obol, a small coin (5)

ὀδμή, -ῆς, ἡ, smell, odor

ὅδε, ἥδε, τόδε, this (3)

ὁδός, -οῦ, ἡ, road

ὀδούς, ὀδόντος, ὁ, tooth (9)

ὄγδοος, eighth

ὅθεν, whence, from where (7)

οἷ, whither, to where (5)

οἶδα, εἴσομαι, know (perfect and future
systems only) (17)

οἶδμα, -ατος, τό, wave, swell of the sea

οἴκαδε, homewards (6)

οἰκέτης, -ου, ὁ, servant (15)

οἴκησις, -εως, ἡ, dwelling (18)

οἰκίᾱ, -ᾱς, ἡ, house (3)

οἰκίδιον, -ου, τό, small house (17)

οἴκοθεν, from home (6)

οἴκοι, at home (6)

οἰκουρός, -όν, keeping house, domestic

οἶκτος, -ου, ὁ, pity (19)

οἰκέω, οἰκήσω, ᾤκησα, ᾤκηκα, ᾤκημαι,
ᾠκήθην, dwell, inhabit (9)

οἶνος, -ου, ὁ, wine (7)

οἰνοχοέω, -ήσω, – , – , – , – , pour wine

οἴομαι, οἰήσομαι, – , – , – , ᾠήθην, think,
suppose (12)

οἷος, -α, -ον, as, such, of such a kind (14)

οἷός τε, able (14)

οἶς, οἰός, ὁ, ἡ, sheep (16)

ὀιστός, -οῦ, ὁ, arrow; also οἰστός

οἰωνός, -οῦ, ὁ, bird, especially a bird of
prey

ὀκτώ, eight

ὄλβιος, -α, -ον, blessed, fortunate

ὀλίγος, -η, -ον, small, little (20)

ὄλλυμι, ὀλῶ, ὤλεσα, ὀλώλεκα, – , – ,
destroy, lose; in middle, perish, die;
aorist middle also ὠλόμην; perfect
also ὄλωλα with middle sense (19)

ὅλμος, -ου, ὁ, mortar for grinding (17s)

ὅλος, -η, -ον, whole, entire

ὀλοφύρομαι, ὀλοφυροῦμαι,
ὠλοφῦράμην, – , – , – , wail, lament,
weep

ὁμιλίᾱ, -ᾱς, ἡ, interaction, association

ὁμῆλιξ, -ικος, ὁ, ἡ, contemporary, age-
mate, person of the same age

ὅμιλος, -ου, ὁ, crowd, group

ὀμίχλη, -ης, ἡ, mist, fog (14s)

ὄμνῡμι, ὀμοῦμαι, ὤμοσα, ὀμώμοκα, – ,
– , swear (19)

ὅμοιος, -α, -ον, like, similar (6), also
ὁμοῖος

ὁμοιότης, ὁμοιότητος, ἡ, similarity,
likeness

ὁμολογέω, ὁμολογήσω, ὡμολόγησα,
ὡμολόγηκα, ὡμολόγημαι,
ὡμολογήθην, agree (with someone
or something), promise (to do
something)

ὁμόφωνος, -ον, harmonious (14)

ὄνομα, ὀνόματα, τό, name (12)

ὀνομάζω, ὀνομάσω, ὠνόμασα, ὠνόμακα,
ὠνόμασμαι, ὠνομάσθην, name, call
by name (9)

ὄνυξ, ὄνυχος, ὁ, claw, talon, fingernail,
fingertip

340   *First Greek Course*

ὀξύπεινος, -ον, quick to hunger (9)

ὀξύς, -εῖα, -υ, sharp, keen, pointy (18)

ὀπή, -ῆς, ἡ, opening in the roof for a chimney

ὁπλίτης, -ου, ὁ, hoplite, heavily armed infantry soldier

ὅπλον, -ου, τό, weapon, usually plural (11)

ὁπόθεν, whence (2)

ὅποι, whither (2)

ὁποῖος, what kind (2)

ὁπόσος, -η, -ο, so great, so much, how great (5)

ὁπότε, when (2)

ὁπότερος, -α, -ον, which of two (indirect question) (7)

ὅπου, where (2)

ὀπτάνιον, -ου, τό, kitchen (17s)

ὀπτάω, ὀπτήσω, ὤπτησα, ὤπτηκα, ὤπτημαι, ὠπτήθην, bake, roast, cook with dry heat (17s)

ὀπώρᾱ, -ᾱς, ἡ, autumn, fruit (11)

ὅπως, how (2)

ὀρέγω, ὀρέξω, ὤρεξα, –, –, –, stretch out, reach out

ὄρειος, -α, -ον, mountain-dwelling, from the mountains

ὀρεσσιβάτης, -ου, ὁ, one who roams the mountains

ὄργανον, -ου, τό, instrument, tool (14)

ὀργή, -ῆς, ἡ, anger, passion; character, disposition

ὀργία, -ων, τά, rites, rituals, worship (plural only)

ὀργίζω, ὀργιῶ, ὤργισα, ὤργικα, ὤργισμαι, ὠργίσθην, anger, make angry

ὀρθογώνιον, -ου, τό, right angle, square corner

ὀρθός, -ή, -όν, straight (9)

ὅρκος, -ου, ὁ, oath, vow (19)

ὁρμίζω, ὁρμιῶ, ὥρμισα, –, ὥρμισμαι, ὡρμίσθην, bring to anchor, make fast; middle, come to anchor, rest (18)

ὁρμάω, ὁρμήσω, ὥρμησα, ὥρμηκα, ὥρμημαι, ὡρμήθην, hurry

ὅρμος, -ου, ὁ, anchorage, haven (10)

ὄρνις, ὄρνῑθος, ὁ, ἡ, bird (18)

ὄρος, -ους, τό, mountain, hill (19)

ὅρος, -ου, ὁ, boundary, limit

ὀρχέομαι, ὀρχήσομαι, ὠρχησάμην, –, –, –, dance (16)

ὁράω, ὄψομαι, εἶδον, ἑόρακα, ἑόραμαι, ὤφθην, see (2)

ὁρίζω, ὁριῶ, ὥρισα, ὥρικα, ὥρισμαι, ὡρίσθην, determine, settle, demarcate

ὅς, ἥ, ὅ, who, which (2)

ὅς, ἥ, ὅν, his, her, its; poetic

ὅσιος, -α, -ον, holy

ὁσιότης, -τος, ἡ, holiness, piety

ὅσος, -η, -ον, how great, as much (7)

ὅστις, ἥτις, ὅτι, who, what, whoever (4)

ὀστοῦν -οῦ, τό, bone (7)

ὅτε, when (8)

ὅτι, that (7)

οὗ, where (9)

οὐ, οὐκ, οὐχ, not (2)

οὐδαμῶς, in no way, by no means (13)

οὐδέ, not even (5)

οὐδείς, οὐδεμία, οὐδέν, no one (13)

οὐδέποτε, never (13)

οὐδεπώποτε, never (13)

οὐδέτερος, -α, -ον, neither

οὐκέτι, no longer, no more (10)

οὔκουν, then ... not (19)

οὐκοῦν, then (5)

οὖν, therefore; particle marking a logical conclusion (4)

οὔποτε, never (13)

οὔπω, not yet (13)

οὐρά, -ᾶς, ἡ, tail

οὐρανός, -οῦ, ὁ, sky, climate (14s)

οὔριος, -α, -ον, favorable, having a fair wind (10)

οὖς, ὠτός, τό, ear

οὐσίᾱ, -ας, ἡ, property (13)

οὔτε, neither, nor, and not (6)

οὗτος, αὕτη, τοῦτο, this (3)

οὕτως, so, thus (6)

οὐχί, no (answering a question) (2)

ὄχλος, -ου, ὁ, crowd, throng, mob

ὀχμάζω, ὀχμάσω, ὤχμασα, –, –, –, grip, hold on to, rein in, control

ὀφείλω, ὀφειλήσω, ὤφελον, ὠφείληκα, –, ὠφειλήθην, owe; second aorist ὤφελον, ought (18)

ὀφθαλμός, -οῦ, ὁ, eye (2)

ὀφλισκάνω, ὀφλήσω, ὤφληκα, –, –, –, incur a debt, bring something on oneself

ὀφρύς, -ύος, ἡ, brow (16)

ὄψον, -ου, τό, the food that goes along with bread, often meat or vegetables (17s)

παγίς, -ίδος, ἡ, snare, trap

πάγος, -ου, ὁ, rock, hill, crag; frost, ice

πάθος, -ους, τό, what one undergoes or experiences; feeling, emotion, passion (20)

παιάν, -ᾶνος, ὁ, paean, hymn to Apollo

παιᾱνισμός, solemn song, sailor's chanty

παιδεία, -ας, ἡ, education, child-rearing

παιδεύω, παιδεύσω, ἐπαίδευσα, πεπαίδευκα, πεπαίδευμαι, ἐπαιδεύθην, instruct, train, educate (19)

παιδίον, -ου, τό, child (2)

παίζω, παίξομαι, ἔπαισα, πέπαικα, πέπαισμαι, –, play, sport, cavort (17)

παῖς, ὁ, ἡ, child (9)

παίω, παίσω, ἔπαισα, πέπαικα, πέπαισμαι, ἐπαίσθην, strike, smite, hit

πάλαι, of old, in the olden times, long ago (3)

παλαιός, -ά, -όν, old

πάλιν, back again (7)

πάλη, -ης, ἡ, wrestling

πάνθηρ, πάνθηρος, ὁ, panther

πανήμερος, -ον, all day, lasting all day

πανοπλία, -ας, ἡ, full set of weapons and armor

παντοδαπός, -ή, -όν, from all sources, of all kinds (12)

πάνυ, entirely, totally (9)

παρά, along, up to, within (+ acc.); from (+ gen.); beside (+ dat.) (6)

παράδεισος, -ου, ὁ, park (18)

παρα-δίδωμι, hand over (9)

παράδοξος, -η, -ον, unexpected, strange

παραθαλάττιος, -ον, by the sea, at the sea-side

παρα-κατα-τίθημι, deposit (9)

παρα-λαμβάνω, receive, find (8)

παραλίᾱ, -ας, ἡ, beach, sea-coast

παρα-πλέω, sail along

παρα-σκευάζω, prepare (11)

παρα-τίθημι, put beside (9)

πάρδαλις, -εως, ὁ, leopard

πάρ-ειμι, be present, from εἰμί (9)

πάρ-ειμι, go past, go by, from εἶμι

παρ-έρχομαι, pass, go by

παρέστιος, -ον, at one's hearth, in one's house, domestic

παρ-έχω, provide (18)

παρ-ίστημι, set beside, compare (9)

παρθένος, -ου, ἡ, maiden, virgin

παροιμίᾱ, -ᾱς, ἡ, proverb, adage

πᾶς, πᾶσα, πᾶν, all (8)

πάσχω, πείσομαι, ἔπαθον, πέπονθα, –, –, suffer, experience, undergo (13)

πατήρ, πατρός, ὁ, father (15)

πατέω, πατήσω, ἐπάτησα, πεπάτηκα, πεπάτημαι, ἐπατήθην, tread, walk on (11)

πάτρᾱ, -ᾱς, ἡ, fatherland, native land

πατρίς, πατρίδος, ἡ, fatherland, native land, homeland (9)

παύω, παύσω, ἔπαυσα, πέπαυκα, πέπαυμαι, ἐπαύθην, stop, check; in middle, cease (6)

πεδίον, -ου, τό, plain (4)

πέδον, -ου, τό, ground (9)

πεζός, -ή, -όν, on foot; in military context, infantry or foot-soldier

πείθω, πείσω, ἔπεισα, πέποιθα, πέπεισμαι, ἐπείσθην, persuade (13); in middle or in perfect, believe

πεῖνα, -ης, ἡ, hunger (9)

πεινάω, πεινήσω, ἐπείνησα, πεπείνηκα, –, –, be hungry, hunger, starve (intransitive) (9)

πεῖρα, -ας, ἡ, experiment, attempt

πέλω, be, present system only

πέμπω, πέμψω, ἔπεμψα, πέπομφα,
πέπεμμαι, ἐπέμφθην, send (6)

πένομαι, work, have to work for a living,
be poor (present system only)

πεντακότυλος, -ον, holding 5 measures

πέντε, five (3)

πεντήκοντα, fifty

πεπασμός, -οῦ, ὁ, secretion (of urine or
other wastes), digestion, concoction

πέπτω, πέψω, ἔπεψα, – , πέπεμμαι,
ἐπέφθην, cook, boil, digest (17s)

περ, particle for emphasis, enclitic, often
attached, as εἴπερ, ὥσπερ

πέρᾱν, across, beyond (prep. + gen.)

πέρθω, πέρσω, ἔπερσα, πέπορθα, – , – ,
sack, ravage (a city)

περί, around, about (+ gen., dat., or acc.)
(6)

περι-άγω, pull round (10)

περι-αιρέω, take away (all round)

περιβρύχιος, -ον, engulfing,
overwhelming

περι-έχω, enclose, surround

περι-πίπτω, fall around, fall foul of, fall
into

περι-πλέω, sail around

περι-ποιέω, save, protect, stash away

περι-σπώμενος, bending around

περι-στέλλω, dress, wrap up

περι-τίθημι, put around

περιττός, -ή, -όν, excessive, very great
(19)

περιφερής, -ές, vaulted, arched, round,
rolling (16)

περι-φέρω, carry round

περιφραδής, -ές, thoughtful, skillful

περσεία, -ας, ἡ, Egyptian plum, Assyrian
plum, lasura (17s)

Πέρσης, -ου, ὁ, Persian (7)

πέρυσι(ν), last year (14s)

πέτασος, -ου, ὁ, hat (3)

πέτομαι, πτήσομαι, ἐπτόμην, – , – , – ,
fly; aorist also ἔπτην

πέτρᾱ, -ᾶς, ἡ, rock (4)

πῇ, how (interrogative)

πη, somehow

πηγή, -ῆς, ἡ, spring of water (16)

πήγνῡμι, πήξω, ἔπηξα, πέπηγα, – ,
ἐπήχθην, fix, freeze (transitive)

πηδάω, πηδήσω, ἐπήδησα, – , – , – ,
jump, leap (15)

πῆχυς, -πήχεως, ὁ, forearm, cubit (12)

πίθος, -ου, ὁ, jar (11)

πικρός, -ᾱ́, -όν, bitter (3)

πίναξ, -ακος, ὁ, board, notice-board,
blackboard

πῑ́νω, πίομαι, ἔπιον, πέπωκα, πέπομαι,
ἐπόθην, drink (13)

πίπτω, πεσοῦμαι, ἔπεσον, πέπτωκα, – ,
– , fall (14)

πιστεύω, πιστεύσω, ἐπίστευσα,
πεπίστευκα, πεπίστευμαι,
ἐπιστεύθην, believe (7)

πίστις, -εως, ἡ, trust, belief

πιστός, -ή, -όν, faithful, trusty (15)

πίτυς, -υος, ἡ, pine

πλακοῦς, -οῦντος, ὁ, flat cake (17s)

πλάττω, πλάσω, ἔπλασα, πέπλακα,
πέπλασμαι, ἐπλάσθην, shape, form,
make

πλείων, -ον, πλεῖστος, -η, -ον, more,
most; suppletive to πολύς

πλεκτάνη, -ης, ἡ, coil, anything twisted
or braided

πλεκτός, -ή, -όν, woven, twisted

πλέκω, πλέξω, ἔπλεξα, πέπλοχα,
πέπλεγμαι, ἐπλέχθην, weave, plait
(11)

πλεύμων, -ονος, ὁ, lung

πλευρά, -ᾶς, ἡ, side, rib

πλέω, πλεύσομαι, ἔπλευσα, πέπλευκα,
πέπλευσμαι, – , sail (10)

πληγή, -ῆς, ἡ, blow, strike (19)

πλήθω, – , – , πέπληθα, – , – , be full,
become full; of the moon, a tide, or
the like

πλημμελής, -ές, discordant, unmelodic

πλήν, except (prep. + gen.) (7)

πλήρης, -ες, full

πλοῖον, -ου, τό, ship, sea-vessel

πλούσιος, -α, -ον, wealthy, rich (18)

πλοῦς, -οῦ, ὁ, voyage (7)

πλοῦτος, -ου, ὁ, wealth (8)

πλουτέω, πλουτήσω, ἐπλούτησα, πεπλούτηκα, πεπλούτημαι, ἐπλουτήθην, be rich (9)

πνεῦμα, -ατος, τό, wind, breath (19)

πνιγεύς, -έως, ὁ, oven

πνοή, -ῆς, ἡ, breath (poetic)

πόᾱ, -ᾱς, ἡ, grass (16)

ποδωκεία, -ας, ἡ, speed, sprint

πόθεν, whence, from where

ποθέν, from some place

ποθέω, ποθήσω, ἐπόθησα, –, –, –, long for, miss, desire

πόθι, where, to where (poetic)

ποθί, somewhere, some whither (poetic)

ποῖ, to where, whither

ποι, some-whither, to somewhere

ποιητέος, -α, -ον, needing to be done, required

ποιητής, -οῦ, ὁ, poet (7)

ποιμήν, -ένος, ὁ, shepherd (16)

ποίμνιον, -ου, τό, flock

ποῖος, -α, -ον, what kind? (2)

ποιός, of a certain kind

ποιέω, ποιήσω, ἐποίησα, πεποίηκα, πεποίημαι, ἐποιήθην, do, make (2)

πολεμέω, πολεμήσω, ἐπολέμησα, πεπολέμηκα, πεπολέμημαι, ἐπολεμήθην, fight, make war on

πολεμικός, -ή, -όν, having to do with war, warlike

πόλεμος, -ου, ὁ, war (4)

πολεύω, πολεύσω, ἐπόλευσα, –, –, –, turn up, turn over

πολιός, -ά, -όν, white; serene; hoary, old (20)

πόλις, -εως, ἡ, city (12)

πολίτης, -ου, ὁ, citizen (7)

πολλάκις, often (4)

πολύπους, πολύποδος, ὁ, octopus

πολύς, πολλή, πολύ, much (2)

πολυτέλεια, -ας, ἡ, extravagance

πονέω, πονήσω, ἐπόνησα, πεπόνηκα, πεπόνημαι, –, work, labor

πονηρίᾱ, -ᾱς, ἡ, wickedness (15)

πονηρός, -ά, -όν, bad, wicked, causing pain (19)

πόντος, -ου, ὁ, sea (20)

πορεύω, πορεύσω, ἐπόρευσα, πεπόρευκα, πεπόρευμαι, ἐπορεύθην, transport, bring; in middle, go, travel (20)

πόρος, -ου, ὁ, way to pass, means of doing something

πόρρω, onwards, further

πόσος, -η, -ον, how great (2)

ποσός, of a certain size

ποταμός, -οῦ, ὁ, river

ποταρχέω, ποταρχήσω, ἐποτάρχησα, –, –, –, be leader of the drinking (at a symposium)

πότε, when (2)

ποτέ, sometime, at times

πότερος, -α, -ον, which? (of two) (7)

πότμος, -ου, ὁ, destiny, fate, death

ποτόν, -οῦ, τό, drink (11)

ποῦ, where (2)

που, particle that expresses scepticism or softens statement (5)

πούς, ποδός, ὁ, foot (16)

πρᾶγμα, -ατος, τό, thing, matter, action, business; πράγματα ἔχειν, to have trouble; π. παρέχειν, to give trouble (13)

πρᾶξις, -εως, ἡ, deed, act of doing, business, matter, action

πρᾱττω, πρᾱξω, ἔπρᾱξα, πέπρᾱχα, πέπρᾱγμαι, ἐπρᾱχθην, do (present also πρᾱσσω) (4)

πρέπει, it is fitting, it is appropriate (19)

πρέσβυς, πρέσβεως, ὁ, old man, ambassador, envoy (15)

πρίν, before

προ-βαίνω, go in front

πρόβατον, -ου, τό, sheep (11)

πρό, before, in front of (+ gen.) (6)

προάστειον, -ου, τό, suburb, outlying neighborhood

προ-δείκνυμι, show, point out beforehand

πρόδρομος, -ον, going on ahead, running in front

πρό-ειμι, (εἰμι) be in front of (9)

πρό-ειμι,(εἶμι), go on (17)

προ-έρχομαι, come forward, come near

προ-ήκω, be first, come forth

προθυμία, -ας, ἡ, good will, zeal

προ-ιάπτω, throw

προ-ίστημι, set before (9)

προ-κόπτω, cut away in front; move forward, make progress, get somewhere

προπέρυσι, year before last (14s)

πρός, to, toward, for (+ acc.); besides (+ dat.) (6)

προσ-αγορεύω, address (13)

προσ-άγω, furnish, supply, add, employ

προσ-βάλλω, attack

προσ-δέω, need, need in addition

πρόσ-ειμι, be added to (9)

προσ-έχω, have in addition, bring to

προσ-ήκω, be near, be one's business, be fitting

πρόσθεν, before, sooner

πρόσ-κειμαι, lie on, lie near

προσήκων, προσήκουσα, προσῆκον, related, akin

προσκεφάλαιον, -ου, τό, pillow

πρόσκωπος, -ον, at the oars

προσ-ορμίζω, bring to anchor

προσ-πίπτω, fall against, fall onto

προσ-ποιέω, attach to; in middle, pretend, feign (17)

προσ-τίθημι, put to (9)

προσ-φέρω, bring forward, produce, proclaim

προσ-φύω, grow on, cling to

πρόσωπον, -ου, τό, face, mask in the theater

πρότερος, -α, -ον, prior, former, earlier (14)

προ-τίθημι, lay out (body), display

πρότριτα, for three days, three days beforehand

πρῷος, -α, -ον, early

πρῶτος, -η, -ον, first

πταίω, πταίσω, ἔπταισα, ἔπταικα, ἔπταισμαι, ἐπταίσθην, stumble

πτερόν, -οῦ, τό, wing, feather

πτηνός, -ή, -όν, winged

πυνθάνομαι, πεύσομαι, ἐπυθόμην, – , πέπυσμαι, – , ask, learn, inquire, ascertain (12)

πῦρ, πῠρός, τό, fire (19)

πύργος, -ου, ὁ, tower (15)

πώγων, πώγωνος, ὁ, beard

πωλέω, πωλήσω, ἐπώλησα, – , – , ἐπωλήθην, sell, put up for sale (8)

πῶς, how (2)

πως, somehow

ῥάδιος, -α, -ον, easy (9)

ῥάμφος, -ους, τό, beak of a bird

ῥᾷστος, -η, -ον, easiest

ῥαφίς, -ίδος, -ἡ, needle, pin (17s)

ῥεῦμα, -ατος, τό, stream

ῥέω, ῥεύσομαι, ἔρρευσα, ἐρρύηκα, – , ἐρρύην, flow (16)

ῥῆμα, -ατος, τό, word; in grammar, a noun

ῥήτωρ, ῥήτορος, ὁ, orator (14)

ῥιγέω, ῥιγήσω, ἐρρίγησα, ἔρριγα, – , – , shiver, shudder (with cold or with emotion)

ῥίπτω, ῥίψω, ἔρρῑψα, ἔρρῑφα, ἔρρῑμμαι, ἐρρῑφθην, throw

ῥόα, -ας, ἡ, pomegranate, usually ῥοιά

ῥώμη, -ης, ἡ, strength

σαίνω, σανῶ, ἔσηνα, – , – , – , wag the tail, fawn on, nuzzle, flatter

σαφής, -ές, clear, distinct (14)

σβέννῡμι, σβέσω, ἔσβεσα, ἔσβηκα, – , ἐσβέσθην, extinguish (17)

σεαυτοῦ, yourself (reflexive pronoun) (4)

σελήνη, -ης, ἡ, moon (14s)

σηκός, -οῦ, ὁ, sheepfold

σῆμα, -ατος, τό, sign, indication; tomb, tomb-marker

σημεῖον, -ου, τό, sign, portent, signal; in geometry, a point

σημαίνω, σημανῶ, ἐσήμηνα, – , ἐσείμασμαι, ἐσημάνθην, signal, show, mean

σησάμη, -ης, ἡ, sesame (17s)

σθένω, be strong, have power (present system only)

Σιδώνιος, -ου, ὁ, man of Sidon

σιγή, -ῆς, ἡ, silence

σῖτος, -ου, ὁ, grain, food

σῑτέω, σῑτήσω, ἐσΐτησα, – , – , ἐσῑτήθην, feed (13)

σιωπή, -ῆς, ἡ, silence (16)

σιωπάω, σιωπήσομαι, ἐσιώπησα, σεσιώπηκα, – , ἐσιωπήθην, be silent

σκαφεῖον, -ου, τό, bowl (17s)

σκάπτω, σκάψω, ἔσκαψα, ἔσκαφα, ἔσκαμμαι, ἐσκάφην, dig

σκέλος, -ους, τό, leg

σκεπτέος, -α, -ον, needing to be looked at

σκευάζω, σκευάσω, ἐσκεύασα, ἐσκεύακα, ἐσκεύασμαι, ἐσκευάσθην, prepare (11)

σκεῦος, -ους, τό, utensil, tool, implement, furniture (15)

σκηνή, -ῆς, ἡ, stage, tent (12)

σκιά, -ᾶς, ἡ, shadow, shade

σκληρός, -ή, -όν, hard

σκόλιον, -ου, τό, drinking-song (9)

σκολιός, -ή, -όν, crooked, twisting

σκόλυμος, -ου, ὁ, artichoke, edible thistle (17s)

σκοπέω, look at, look into (present system only)

σκόροδον, -ου, τό, garlic (17s)

σκύφος, -ου, ὁ, cup

σκώπτω, σκώψομαι, ἔσκωψα, – , – , ἐσκώφθην, joke, have fun, mock, laugh at

σορός, -οῦ, ἡ, burial urn, coffin

σός, σή, σόν, your (20)

σοφία, -ας, ἡ, wisdom, intelligence, skill (15)

σοφός, -ή, -όν, wise, skillful, clever (3)

σπάνιος, -α, -ον, rare

σπάργανα, -ων, τά, swaddling clothes, baby blanket (11)

σπείρω, σπερῶ, ἔσπειρα, ἔσπαρκα, ἔσπαρμαι, ἐσπάρην, sow, scatter

σπήλαιον, -ου, τό, cave

σπόγγος, -ου, ὁ, sponge (17s)

σπουδαῖος, -α, -ον, serious, earnest, important, good

σπουδή, -ῆς, ἡ, earnestness, seriousness

σπυρίς, -ίδος, ἡ, basket (17s)

στάδιον, -ου, τό, stade, unit of measure roughly 200 meters (12)

σταφυλή, -ῆς, ἡ, bunch of grapes (11)

στέγη, -ης, ἡ, roof (18)

στέλλω, στελῶ, ἔστειλα, ἔσταλκα, ἔσταλμαι, ἐστάλην, prepare, make ready, send

στερέω, στερήσω, ἐστέρησα, ἐστέρηκα, ἐστέρημαι, ἐστερήθην, deprive

στεφανόω, στεφανώσω, ἐστεφάνωσα, ἐστεφάνωκα, ἐστεφάνωμαι, – , crown

στῆθος, -ους, τό, breast, chest (18)

στίχος, -ου, ὁ, line, row; verse line

στοά, -ᾶς, ἡ, colonnade, columned walkway, building that has a colonnade

στόμα, στόματος, τό, mouth

στρατηγός, -οῦ, ὁ, general (7)

στρατιά, -ᾶς, ἡ, army (7)

στρατιώτης, -ου, ὁ, soldier (7)

στρατόπεδον, -ου, τό, military camp

στρατός, -οῦ, ὁ, army (7)

στρέφω, στρέψω, ἔστρεψα, – , ἔστραμμαι, ἐστράφην, turn, twist (11)

στρογγύλος, -η, -ον, round (3)

σύ, you (singular), thou (4)

συγ-γίγνομαι, be with (12)

συγ-κεράννυμι, blend, mix together

συγ-χέω, pour together

συ-ζάω, live with

συλ-λαμβάνω, seize

συλ-λέγω, collect, bring together

συμ-βαίνω, happen; κατὰ συμβεβηκός, by chance (20)

σύμμαχος, -ου, ὁ, ally

συμ-παθέω, συμπαθήσω, συνεπάθησα, συμπεπάθηκα, συμπεπάθημαι, feel with, sympathize (13)

συμ-παίζω, play with

συμ-παρα-στατέω, stand beside, help (predictable principal parts)

συμπόσιον, -ου, τό, drinking party

συμπότης, -ου, ὁ, fellow drinker, party companion

συμ-φέρω, bring together, contribute; be useful; agree

συμ-φοιτάω, go together, frequent together, particularly of going to school

συμφορᾱ́, -ᾶς, ἡ, event, misfortune (13)

συμ-φράζομαι, consider, take counsel with

σύν, with (prep. + dat.) (7)

συνάπας, συνάπασα, συνάπαν, all together (12)

συν-άπτω, fasten together, unite

σύν-ειμι, be with (9)

συν-εθίζω, accustom

συνεχής, -ές, continuous

συνημερεύω, συνημερεύσω, συνημέρευσαι, – , – , – , pass the day with (+ dat.)

συν-ίημι, send together; understand (9)

συν-ικνέομαι, come together; interest, be relevant to (11)

συν-ίστημι, set together, associate (9)

σύν-οιδα, be aware, be in a secret with (17)

σύνοικος, -ον, communal, common, living together

συν-τάττομαι, bargain, make a compact (13)

συν-τίθημι, put together (9)

σύντομος, -ον, brief (19)

συν-ωνέομαι, buy up

σῦριγξ, σύριγγος, ἡ, syrinx, Pan's pipes (16)

συρίζω, συρίξω, ἐσύριξα, – , – , – , whistle, play the panpipe (usual Attic form συρίττω)

συρ-ράπτω, stitch together

συφεός, -οῦ, ὁ, pigsty

σφεῖς, they (poetic)

σφέτερος, -α, -ον, their (20)

σφοδρός, -ά, -όν, strong, violent (10)

σφωῖτερος, -α, -ον, your, of you two

σχεδόν, almost (12)

σχῆμα, -ατος, τό, shape, guise, form (16)

σχολαστικός, -οῦ, ὁ, scholar, pedant, student (6)

σῴζω, σώσω, ἔσωσα, σέσωκα, σέσωμαι, ἐσώθην, save, rescue, keep (12)

σῶμα, σώματος, τό, body (11)

ταινιόω, ταινιώσω, ἐταινίωσα, τεταινίωκα, τεταινίωμαι, ἐταινιώθην, tie a victory garland onto

τάλαντον, -ου, τό, talent, a large weight of silver (5)

τάλᾱς, τάλαινα, τάλαν, wretched, miserable (8)

ταμίᾱς, -ου, ὁ, steward, treasurer (7)

ταμιεύω, ταμιεύσω, ἐταμίευσα, τεταμίευκα, – , – , be a steward

ταπεινός, -ή, -όν, low, humble

ταράττω, ταράξω, ἐτάραξα, τέτρηχα, τετάραγμαι, ἐταράχθην, confuse, disturb (12)

τάριχος, -ου, ὁ, dried fish, smoked fish (17s)

τάττω, τάξω, ἔταξα, τέταχα, τέταγμαι, ἐτάχθην, fix, arrange (6)

ταφή, -ῆς, ἡ, burial, funeral

τάφος, -ου, ὁ, tomb, grave

τάχα, quickly; τάχ᾽ ἄν, perhaps (12)

ταχύς -εῖα, -ύ, fast, swift (18)

ταχυτής, -ῆτος, ἡ, speed, rapidity

ταῶς, ταῶ, ὁ, peacock

τε, and, both (2)

τείνω, τενῶ, ἔτεινα, τέτακα, τέταμαι, ἐτάθην, stretch (11)

τεῖχος, -ους, τό, wall (11)

τέκνον, -ου, τό, child, offspring (8)

τέλειος, -α, -ον, complete, perfect

τελετή, -ησ=, ἡ, mystic rite, ritual, initiation

τελευτάω, τελευτήσω, ἐτελεύτησα, τετελεύτηκα, τετελεύτημαι, ἐτελευτήθην, end, complete, often specifically end one's life, die (12)

τελευτή, -ῆς, ἡ, end

τελέω, τελῶ, ἐτέλεσα, τετέλεκα, τετέλεσμαι, ἐτελέσθην, finish, accomplish

τέλος, -ους, τό, end, goal (11)

τέμνω, τεμῶ, ἔτεμον, τέτμηκα, τέτμημαι, ἐτμήθην, cut

τεράστιος, -α, -ον, monstrous, scary

τέρμα, τέρματος, τό, end, boundary

τέρπω, τέρψω, ἔτερψα, – , – , ἐτέρφθην, delight, please

τέρψις, -εως, ἡ, enjoyment (18)

τέταρτος, -η, -ον, fourth

τέφρα, -ας, ἡ, ash, cinder

τέχνη, -ης, ἡ, art, technique, skill (18)

τεχνικός, -ή, -όν, skillfull

τήμερον, today (5)

τῆτες, this year (14s)

τίθημι, θήσω, ἔθηκα, τέθηκα, – , ἐτέθην, put, place (9)

τίκτω, τέξω, ἔτεκον, τέτοκα, – , ἐτέχθην, produce, bring forth, give birth (6)

τιμάω, τιμήσω, ἐτίμησα, τετίμηκα, τετίμημαι, ἐτιμήθην, honor (5)

τιμωρία, -ας, ἡ, vengeance, retribution

τίνω, τείσω, ἔτεισα, τέτεικα, τέτεισμαι, ἐτείσθην, pay, pay a debt, pay a penalty, reward

τιτρώσκω, τρώσω, ἔτρωσα, – , τέτρωμαι, ἐτρώθην, wound

τίς, who (4)

τις, some one (4)

τίτθη, -ης, ἡ, nurse, nursemaid

τλάω, τλήσομαι, – , – , – , ἔτλην, endure, put up with (not actually used in present)

τοι, indeed (2)

τοῖος, -α, -ον, such, also τοιόσδε, τοιάδε, τοιόνδε

τοιοῦτος, τοιαύτη, τοιοῦτο, such (8)

τολμάω, τολμήσω, ἐτόλμησα, τετόλμηκα, – , – , dare, venture

τομή, -ῆς, ἡ, cutting, cut (11)

τόξα, -ων, τά, bow and arrows

τοξεύω, τοξεύσω, ἐτόξευσα, τετόξευκα, τετόξευται, ἐτοξεύθη, shoot a bow, hunt with a bow

τόπος, -ου, ὁ, place

τόσος, -η, -ον, so much, so big, also τοσόσδε, τοσήδε, τοσόνδε

τοσοῦτος, -η, -ο, so much, so large (7)

τότε, then

τράγος, -ου, ὁ, he-goat (14)

τράπεζα, -ης, ἡ, table (18)

τράχηλος, -ου, ὁ, neck (15)

τρέπω, τρέψω, ἔτρεψα, τέτροφα, τέτραμμαι, ἐτρέφθην, turn

τρέφω, θρέψω, ἔθρεψα, τέτροφα, τέθραμμαι, ἐτράφην, feed, rear, nourish, keep (animals) (4)

τρέχω, δραμοῦμαι, ἔδραμον, δεδράμηκα, δεδράμημαι, – , run (10)

τρέψις, ἡ, enjoyment

τρίβω, τρίψω, ἔτριψα, τέτριφα, τέτριμμαι, ἐτρίβην, rub (16)

τριετής, -ές, three years old; occurring every three years

τριήρης, -ους, ἡ, trireme, ship (11)

τρίπους, τρίποδος, ὁ, tripod (17s)

τρίς, thrice

τρισχίλιοι, -αι, -α, 3000 (14)

τρίτος, -η, -ον, third

τρίχωμα, -ατος, τό, hair, growth of hair

τρόπος, -ου, ὁ, way, way of doing something, way of life

τροφή, -ῆς, ἡ, food (11)

τρόχος, -ου, ὁ, race, run, race course

τρύβλιον, -ου, τό, cup, bowl (17s)

τρύγη, -ης, ἡ, crop, vintage

τρύγητος, -ου, ὁ, vintage

τρυγάω, τρυγήσω, ἐτρύγησα, – , – , – , pluck fruit, gather vintage

τρυφή, -ῆς, ἡ, luxury (13)

τυγχάνω, τεύξομαι, ἔτυχον, τετύχηκα, – , – , happen (15)

τύπτω, τυπτήσω, ἐτύπτησα, – , τέτυμμαι, – , strike (15)

τυραννίς, τυραννίδος, ἡ, rule, kingship

τύραννος, -ου, ὁ, king, ruler, especially a usurper or tyrant

τυφλός, -ή, -όν, blind (2)

τύχη, -ης, ἡ, fortune (2)

ὑγιαίνω, ὑγιανῶ, ὑγίανα, – , – , – , be healthy (9)

ὑγίεια, -ης, ἡ, health (9)

ὕδωρ, ὕδατος, τό, water (16)

ὑετός, -οῦ, ὁ, rain (14s)

υἱός, -οῦ, ὁ, son

ὑλακτέω, ὑλακτήσω, ὑλάκτησα, – , – , – , bark, as a dog (19)

ὑμέτερος, -α, -ον, your (belonging to more than one person) (20)

ὑομουσία, -ας, ἡ, pig-music

ὑπάγομαι, attract

ὑπαίθρειος, -ον, under the sky, out in the open (or ὑπαίθριος)

ὑπ-ανθέω, begin to flower

ὑπ-άρχω, exist, come to be, begin

ὑπέρ, over, beyond (prep. + gen., acc.) (7)

ὑπερ-άνω, up above

ὑπερ-αυχέω, be excessively proud

ὑπερ-βαίνω, go beyond, transgress

ὑπερ-βάλλω, surpass, exceed (14)

ὑπέρτατος, -η, -ον, highest, uppermost (superlative formed from ὑπέρ)

ὑπηρεσία, -ας, ἡ, help, assistance

ὑπηρέτης, -ου, ὁ, helper, assistant, servant

ὑπ-ισχνέομαι, ὑπο-σχήσομαι, ὑπ-εσχόμην, – , ὑπ-έσχημαι, – , promise

ὑπό, by, under (prep. + gen., dat., acc.) (6)

ὑπόδημα, -ατος, τό, shoe (16)

ὑποδύνω, ὑποδύσω, ὑπέδυσα, – , – , – , slip under, slip into, put on (clothing)

ὑποθῡμίς, -ίδος, ἡ, garland worn at parties

ὑπό-κειμαι, lie beneath (14)

ὑπόκρισις, -εως, ἡ, playing a role; hypocrisy

ὑπο-κρούω, ὑποκρούσω, ὑπέκρουσα, – , ὑποκέκρουμαι, – , interrupt

ὑπο-κύομαι, ὑπο-κύσομαι, ὑπεκυσάμην, – , – , – , conceive, become pregnant

ὑπο-λαμβάνω, assume, understand; reply; catch up to, overtake

ὑπόλοιπος, -ον, left over, remaining (15)

ὑπο-στορέννυμι, spread out under

ὑπο-τείνω, stretch under, stretch across, subtend

ὑπο-τίθημι, put under, put down as deposit (9)

ὑπο-φθέγγομαι, utter, voice (16)

ὕς, ὑός, ὁ, ἡ, pig

ὕστερος, -α, -ον, later, too late; ὕστατον latest, for the last time (17)

ὕφαιμος, -ον, bloodshot, bloody, bruised (15)

ὑψηλός, -ή, -όν, high

ὕω, ὕσω, ὕσα, – , – , – , rain (14s)

φαεινός, -ή, -όν, shining, gleaming

φαίνω, φᾰνῶ, ἔφηνα, πέφηνα, πέφασμαι, ἐφάνθην, show, reveal; in middle, appear, seem (18)

φακῆ, -ῆς, ἡ, lentil soup, pea soup (17s)

φαντασίᾱ, -ᾶς, ἡ, appearance, display, apparition; imagination, fantasy

φάος, φάους, τό, light (11)

φαρέτρᾱ, -ᾶς, ἡ, quiver (for arrows)

φάρμακον, -ου, τό, medicine, drug, remedy (3)

φάσκω, assert, say (present system only) (17)

φάτις, -εως, ἡ, rumor

φάτνη, -ης, ἡ, manger

φαῦλος, -η, -ον, miserable, contemptible (14)

φέγγω, shine, make bright, present system only (14s)

φέρω, οἴσω, ἤνεγκα, ἐνήνοχα, ἐνήνεγμαι, ἠνέχθην, carry, bring, bear, lead (4)

φεύγω, φεύξομαι, ἔφυγον, πέφευγα, πέφυγμαι, – , flee; be defendant in a lawsuit (6)

φεῦξις, -εως, ἡ, refuge, escape

φημι, φήσω, ἔφησα, – , – , – , say (9)

φθάνω, φθήσομαι, ἔφθασα, – , – , – , be first, overtake, anticipate (15)

φθέγμα, -ατος, τό, voice, sound

φθέγγομαι, φθέγξομαι, ἐφθεγξάμην, – , ἔφθεγμαι, – , utter a voice or sound, articulate (14)

φθείρω, φθερῶ ἔφθειρα, ἔφθορα, ἔφθαρμαι, ἐφθάρην, destroy (12)

φθόνος, -ου, ὁ, hate, envy (13)

φιάλη, -ης, ἡ, bowl, drinking cup

φιλάργυρος, -ον, miserly

φιλέω, φιλήσω, ἐφίλησα, πεφίληκα, πεφίλημαι, ἐφιλήθην, love (2)

φιλήτης, -ητος, ἡ, friendship

φιλίᾱ, -ᾱς, ἡ, love, friendship

φίλος, -ου, ὁ, friend (5); φίλος, -η, -ον, friendly (18)

φιλοσοφίᾱ, -ᾶς, ἡ, philosophy (7)

φλυαρέω, φλυαρήσω, ἐφλυάρησα, πεφλυάρηκα, – , – , fool around, talk nonsense φοβέω, φοβήσω, ἐφόβησα, πεφόβηκα, πεφόβημαι, ἐφοβήθην, frighten, terrify; passive φοβέομαι, fear, be afraid

φόβος, -ου, ὁ, fear, fright

φοιτάω, φοιτήσω, ἐφοίτησα, πεφοίτηκα, –, –, wander, roam

φορέω, φορήσω, ἐφόρησα, –, –, –, carry around, wear

φορητός, -ή, -όν, bearable, tolerable

φόρος, -ου, ὁ, tribute, tax (12)

φράζω, φράσω, ἔφρασα, πέφρακα, πέφρασμαι, ἐφράσθην, say, declare (19)

φρήν, φρενός, ἡ, mind, heart, guts (18)

φρόνημα, -ατος, τό, mind, spirit

φρόνιμος, -ον, prudent, thoughtful, wise

φροντίζω, φροντιῶ, ἐφρόντισα, πεφρόντικα, πεφρόντισμαι, ἐφροντίσθην, think

φροντίς, -ίδος, ἡ, concern, care, thought

φροντιστήριον, -ου, τό, phrontisterium

φρονέω, φρονήσω, ἐφρόνησα, πεφρόνηκα, πεφρόνημαι, ἐφρονήθην, think; be sane, be wise (19)

φυγάς, -αδος, ὁ, ἡ, fugitive, exile (14)

φυγή, -ῆς, ἡ, escape, refuge

φυή, -ῆς, ἡ, bodily nature, stature, growth (18)

φύλαξ, φύλακος, ὁ, guard, guardian

φυλλάς, φυλλάδος, ἡ, foliage, leafiness

φυλάττω, φυλάξω, ἐφύλαξα, πεφύλαχα, πεφύλαγμαι, ἐφυλάχθην, guard

φυλή, -ῆς, ἡ, tribe, in particular one of the ten divisions of the Athenian people

φῦλον, -ου, τό, race, tribe

φύσις, -εως, ἡ, nature (18)

φυτεύω, φυτεύσω, ἐφύτευσα, πεφύτευκα, πεφύτευμαι, ἐφυτεύθην, plant

φυτόν, -οῦ, τό, plant (4)

φύω, φύσω, ἔφῡν, πέφῡκα, –, –, beget, produce; be, be by nature (13)

φώκη, -ης, ἡ, seal, sea-lion

φωνή, -ῆς, ἡ, voice (2)

φωνέω, φωνήσω, ἐφώνησα, πεφώνηκα, πεφώνημαι, ἐφωνήθην, speak (2)

φῶς, φωτός, τό, light (11)

χαίρω, χαιρήσω, ἐχαίρησα, κεχάρηκα, κεχάρημαι, ἐχάρην, rejoice (10)

χάλαζα, -ας, ἡ, hail (14s)

χαλεπός, -ή, -όν, difficult

χαλκεύς, -έως, ὁ, smith, bronze-worker, metal-worker

χαλκόκροτος, -ον, having bronze hooves, rattling with bronze

χαμαί, on the ground (9)

χάρις, χάριτος, ἡ, favor, thanks, grace (8)

χείμαρρος, -ου, ὁ, torrent, winter flood

χειμέριος, -ον, stormy, wintry (18)

χειμών, -ῶνος, ὁ, winter, storm (19)

χείρ, χειρός, ἡ, hand, arm (15)

χέω, χέω, ἔχεα, κέχυκα, κέχυμαι, ἐχύθην, pour (11)

χηλή, -ῆς, ἡ, talon, claw, hoof

χήν, ὁ, ἡ, gander, goose

χῆρος, -α, -ον, bereaved, widowed

χθές, yesterday (5)

χθών, χθονός, ἡ, earth, land (20)

χίλιοι, -αι, -α, thousand (4)

χιών, -ονος, ἡ, snow (14s, 16)

χλαῖνα, -ας, ἡ, cloak, overall (4)

χλωρός, -ά, -όν, green (19)

χορείᾱ, -ᾱς, ἡ, dance (16)

χορεύω, χορεύσω, ἐχόρευσα, –, κεχόρευμαι, ἐχορεύθην, dance, be part of a chorus, celebrate in dance

χορός, -οῦ, ὁ, body of dancers or singers (14)

χράομαι, χρήσομαι, ἐχρησάμην, –, κέχρημαι, ἐχρήσθην, use (17)

χρεμετισμός, -οῦ, ὁ, neigh, neighing, whinny

χρή, must, have to (19)

χρήζω, lack, need; be poor (present system only) (9)

χρῆμα, -ατος, τό, thing, business; plural, money (11)

χρηματισμός, -οῦ, ὁ, money-making (7)

χρήσιμος, -η, -ον, useful (3)

χρηστότης, -τος, ἡ, honesty

χρηστός, -ή, -όν, honest (4)

χροιά, -ᾶς, ἡ, skin, complexion

χρόνος, -ου, ὁ, time (6)

χρυσοτρίαινος, -ον, having a golden trident

χρυσοῦς, -ῆ, -οῦν, golden (7)

χρῶμα, -ατος, τό, color

χύτρα, -ας, ἡ, earthenware pot (17s)

χώρα, -ας, ἡ, country, place, land

χωρίον, -ου, τό, place, farm (12)

χωρέω, χωρήσομαι, ἐχώρησα, κεχώρηκα, κεχώρημαι, ἐχωρήθην, hold, contain; go (7)

ψάμμος, -ου, ἡ, sand (19)

ψαύω, ψαύσω, ἔψαυσα, ἔψαυκα, ἔψαυσμαι, – , touch

ψεύδω, ψεύσω, ἔψευσα, – , ἔψευσμαι, ἐψεύσθην, tell a lie, falsify, cheat (16)

ψηφίζομαι, ψηφιοῦμαι, ἐψηφισάμην, – , ἐψήφισμαι, – , vote

ψῆφος, -ου, ἡ, vote

ψιττακός, -οῦ, ὁ, parrot

ψοφέω, ψοφήσω, ἐψόφησα, ἐψόφηκα, – , – , make noise, slam, bang (17)

ψόφος, -ου, ὁ, noise, sound

ψυχή, -ῆς, ἡ, life, soul (3)

ὧδε, here, thus (19)

ᾠδή, -ῆς, ἡ, song (14)

ὠθέω, ὤσω, ἔωσα, – , ἔωσμαι, ἐώσθην, push, shove

ὦκα, quickly

ὦμος, -ου, ὁ, shoulder (4)

ὠμός, -ή, -όν, raw, crude

ὠνέομαι, ὠνήσομαι, ἐπριάμην, ἐώνημαι, ἐωνήθην, buy

ᾠόν, ᾠοῦ, τό, egg (6)

ὥρα, -ας, ἡ, hour, time, season (12)

ὥριος, -ον, seasonable, timely

ὡς, as, how; to (prep. + acc.) (6, 7, 10)

ὥσπερ, like, as (5)

ὠφελέω, ὠφελήσω, ὠφέλησα, ὠφέληκα, ὠφέλημαι, ὠφελήθην, help, assist (14)

ὠφέλεια, -ας, ἡ, benefit, help (11)

Appendix

English to Greek

When you look up a word, always look back at the Greek-to-English vocabulary for the principal parts and further information about idioms and constructions. Contracted verbs are cited in their un-contracted forms, but you should use the standard Attic contractions in writing.

able, δυνατός, οἷός τε, δύναμαι, ἔχω

abroad, be, ἀποδημέω (opposite ἐπιδημέω)

accuse, αἰτιάομαι

accustomed, εἴωθα

acorn, βάλανος

active, ἐργαστικός

address, προσαγορεύω

ago, ἤδη, πάλαι

all, πᾶς, ἅπας

almost, σχεδόν

alone, μόνος

already, ἤδη

also, καί

although, καίπερ

always, ἀεί

anchor, ἄγκυρα

anchor, ὁρμίζω, lie at anchor, ὁρμάω

anchorage, ὅρμος

and, καί, δέ

annoyance, ἐνόχλησις, or use πρᾶγμα

arched, περιφερής

aristocracy, ἀριστοκρατία

arm, βραχίων, χείρ

army, στρατιά

arouse, ἐγείρω

arrange, τάττω

art, τέχνη

ascertain, πυνθάνομαι

ask, ἔρομαι, ἀνέρομαι, ἐρωτάω, πυνθάνομαι

autumn, ὀπώρα

aware, be, σύνοιδα

back again, πάλιν

bad, κακός

badly, κακῶς

balanced, μετέωρος

banished, be, ἐκπίπτω

bare, γυμνός, γυμνόω

bargain, make, συντάττομαι

bark, ὑλακτέω (dog)

basket, ἄρριχος

bath, λουτρόν

bear, bring forth, τίκτω

beast, θηρίον

beautiful, καλός

become, γίγνομαι

begin, ἄρχω

believe, πιστεύω, πείθομαι, πέποιθα

below, κάτω

best, ἄριστος

bid, κελεύω

bind, δέω

bird, ὄρνις

bite, δάκνω, κάπτω

bitter, πικρός

blame, ἐπιτιμάω

blameless, ἄμεμπτος

blind, τυφλός

blood, αἷμα
bloodshot, ὕφαιμος
blow, πληγή, strike a blow, πληγὰς ἐντείνω, πληγὰς λαμβάνω
book, βιβλίον
boot, ἀρβύλη
bosom, κόλπος
both, ἀμφότερος, καί, τε
brave, ἀνδρεῖος
breakfast, ἄριστον, ἀριστάω
breast, στῆθος, κόλπος
breath, πνεῦμα
breeze, αὔρα, ἄνεμος
bride, νύμφη
brief, σύντομος
brother, ἀδελφός
brow, ὀφρύς
bunch of grapes, σταφυλή
burn, καίω
bush, λόχμη
but, ἀλλά, δέ
buy, ἀγοράζω, ὠνέομαι
call, καλέω
calm, γαλήνη (weather)
care, φροντίς
care for, μέλει
carelessness, ἀμέλεια
carry, φέρω, βαστάζω
cart, carriage, ἄμαξα
cat, αἴλουρος
cave, ἄντρον
cease, παύομαι
certainly, μάλιστά γε
chair, δίφρος, ἕδρα
change, μεταβολή
charm, θελκτήριον
chatter, λαλέω
cheap, ἄξιος
check, παύω
chick, νεοττίον
child, παῖς, παιδίον, τέκνον
circle, round, κύκλος
city, πόλις, ἄστυ
claim, ἀξιόω
clear, σαφής

clever, δεινός
cloak, χλαῖνα, ἱμάτιον
coin, ὀβολός
color, χρῶμα
come, ἥκω
common, κοινός
companion, ἑταῖρος
confuse, disorder, ταράττω
contain, χωρέω
corn, σῖτος
couch, κλίνη
courtyard, αὐλή
cowardly, δειλός
cowboy, βουκόλος
coxswain, κελευστής
creep, ἕρπω
cross, ἐκπεράω
crow, ᾄδω
crush, θλίβω
cry out, βοάω
cup, φιάλη, κυμβίον
cut, τέμνω
cutting, τομή
dance, ὀρχέομαι
dance, band of dancers, χορός
day, ἡμέρα
declare, δηλόω
democracy, δημοκρατία
deprive, στερέω
despise, καταφρονέω
destroy, ἀπόλλυμι, διαφθείρω
die, ἀποθνήσκω
differ, διαφέρω
difficulty, ἀπορία
dig, σκάπτω
din, κραυγή
discordant, πλημμελής
discus, δίσκος
disgraceful, αἰσχρός
do, ποιέω, πράττω
doer, θύρα
dog, κύων
double, διπλάσιος, διπλοῦς
doubtless, που

drachma, δραχμή
drink, πίνω (verb) ποτόν (noun)
drive, ἐλαύνω
dry, ξηρός
duck, νῆττα
dwell, διαιτάομαι, οἰκέω
each, ἕκαστος
each other, ἀλλήλων
eagle, ἀετός
ear, οὖς
especially, μάλιστα
examine, ἐξετάζω
example, for, αὐτίκα
except, πλήν
excessive, περιττός
experience, πάσχω
eye, ὀφθαλμός
face, πρόσωπον
faith, πίστις
faithful, πιστός
fall, πίπτω
famous, κλεινός
farm, ἀγρός, ἀγροί, χωρίον (nouns),
    γεωργέω (verb)
farmer, γεωργός
fasten, ἅπτω
fear, φοβέομαι, δέδοικα
feed, τρέφω; feed animals, βόσκω
feel with, συμπαθέω
field, ἀγρός
find, εὑρίσκω, παραλαμβάνω
fine, καλός
fine weather, αἰθρία
finger, δάκτυλος
fish, ἰχθύς (noun), ἁλιεύω (verb)
fisher, ἁλιεύς
flee, φεύγω
floating on water, μετέωρος
flow, ῥέω
flower, ἄνθος (noun), ἀνθέω (verb)
food, τροφή, σῖτος
foolish, μῶρος, be foolish, ἀνοηταίνω
foolishness, ἀβουλία, μωρία
foot, πούς
forbid, ἀπαγορεύω

easy, ῥάδιος
east, ἐσθίω
egg, ᾠόν
either, ἑκάτερος
either ... or, ἤ ... ἤ, εἴτε ... εἴτε
enjoy one's self, ἡβάω
enjoyment, τέρψις
entertain, ξενίζω
envy, φθόνος
equal, ἴσος
fortune, τύχη (luck), πλοῦτος (wealth)
free, ἐλεύθερος
freedom, ἐλευθερία
freeze, πήγνυμι
fret, δυσκολαίνω
friend, φίλος
friendly, εὔνους
from, ἀπό
fruit, ὀπώρα, καρπός
full, πλήρης
furious, λάβρος (of floods or the like)
furniture, τὰ σκεύη
garden, κῆπος
gift, δῶρον
girdle, ζῶμα, ζώνη
girl, κόρη, παρθένος
give, δίδωμι
gladly, ἡδέως
go, ἔρχομαι, εἶμι, βαδίζω, ἕρπω, etc.
goat, αἴξ; he-goat, τράγος
god, θεός
goddess, θεός, θεά
good, ἀγαθός
grass, πόα
green, χλωρός
grief, λύπη
ground, πέδον, on the ground, χαμαί
grove, ἄλσος
grow, βλαστάνω
guest, ξένος
hail, χάλαζα
hair, θρίξ
hand, χείρ
handle, λαβή

happen, τυγχάνω

harbor, λιμήν

hard, σκληρός

hare, λαγώς

harm, βλάβη

harmonious, ὁμόφωνος

harvest, θέρος (noun), ἀποτρυγάω (verb)

hat, πέτασος

hate, μῖσος, φθόνος

hateful thing, μῖσος

have, ἔχω

head, κεφαλή

health, ὑγίεια

healthy, be, ὑγιαίνω

hear, ἀκούω

hearing, ἀκοή

heir, κληρονόμος

helmsman, κυβερνήτης

help, ὠφέλεια (noun), βοηθέω, ὠφελέω (verb)

hence, ἐνθένδε

herb, λάχανον

herd, ἀγέλη

herdsman, νομεύς, βουκόλος

here, ἐνθάδε, ἐνταῦθα

hill, ὄρος

hither, δεῦρο

hollow, αὐλών (noun), κοῖλος (adj)

home: at home, from home, homewards, οἴκαδε and so on

honest, ἐσθλός, χρηστός

hook, ἄγκιστρον

hope, ἐλπίς (noun), ἐλπίζω (verb)

horse, ἵππος

house, οἰκία

how, πῶς, ὅπως, ὡς

how great, πόσος, ὁπόσος, ὅσος

humble, ταπεινός

hunger, πεινάω (verb)

hunt, ἄγρα, θήρα (noun), θηράω (verb)

huntsman, κυνηγέτης

husband, ἀνήρ

ice, κρύσταλλος

idle, ἀργός

idleness, ἀργία

ill, be, νοσέω

imitate, μιμέομαι

imitator, μιμητής

in, ἐν

indeed, δή, τοι

indoors, οἰκουρός

in order that, ἵνα, ὅπως

inside, ἐντός

instrument, ὄργανον

interrupt, ὑποκρούω

into, εἰς

invisible, ἀφανής

invite, καλέω

ivy, κιττός

jar, πίθος

javelin, ἄκων

judge, δικαστής, κριτής (nouns), κρίνω (verb)

jump, ἅλμα

just, δίκαιος

justice, δίκη, δικαιοσύνη

key, κλείς

kind, γένος, of all kinds, παντοδαπός

kiss, κυνέω, φιλέω

know, οἶδα, γιγνώσκω

lad, μειράκιον

ladder, κλῖμαξ

land, γῆ

lately, ἄρτι

later, ὕστερον

laugh, γελάω

launch, ἀναγωγή, καθέλκω

lawsuit, δίκη

lead, ἄγω

leafage, φυλλάς

leap, πηδάω

learn, μανθάνω

leave, λείπω, καταλείπω

left (side), ἀριστερός

leg, σκέλος

letter, ἐπιστολή

lie, κεῖμαι (be placed); ψεύδομαι (tell a lie)

life, ψυχή, βίος

lift, βαστάζω

light, (of weight) λεπτός

light, (illumination) φῶς, λύχνος
like, ὅμοιος
like as, καθάπερ
loaf, ἄρτος
long, μακρός
loose, λύω
love, φιλέω
low, ταπεινός
luxury, τρυφή
lyre, λύρα
maidservant, θεράπαινα
make, ποιέω
man, human being, ἄνθρωπος; male,
    ἀνήρ; any one, τις
manger, φάτνη
market-place, ἀγορά
mast, ἱστός
meadow, λειμών
mean, petty, φαῦλος
medicine, φάρμακον
meet, ἀπαντάω
messenger, ἄγγελος
milk, γάλα
mina, μνᾶ
mind, νοῦς, φρήν
miserable, δύστηνος
miserly, φιλάργυρος
misfortune, συμφορά
mistake, ἁμαρτάνω
moisture, νοτίς
money-making, χρηματισμός
mortal, θνητός
much, μάλα, πολύς
musical, μουσικός
must (new wine), γλεῦκος
name, ὄνομα (noun), ὀνομάζω (verb)
narcissus, νάρκισσος
nature, φύσις
necessary, δεῖ, χρή, ἀναγκαῖος
neck, αὐχήν, τράχηλος
neglect, ἀμελέω
neighbor, γείτων
net, δίκτυον
next, ἔπειτα
night, νύξ, by night, νύκτωρ

nightingale, ἀηδών
noble, καλός
noise, ψόφος, θόρυβος, make noise,
    ψοφέω
noose, βρόχος
not, οὐ, οὐκ, οὐχ, μή
now, νῦν
nurse, τίτθη
nymph, νύμφη
oak, δρῦς
oar, κώπη
often, πολλάκις
oil, ἔλαιον
old, παλαιός
old man, γέρων, πρέσβυς
old woman, γραῦς
on, ἐπί
once, ἅπαξ
once, at, αὐτίκα
one or other, ἕτερος
other, ἄλλος
outside, ἐκτός
overcome, κρατέω, νικάω
park, παράδεισος
pasture, νομή
peace, εἰρήνη
pen, κάλαμος
perhaps, τάχα, που
persuade, πείθω
philosophy, φιλοσοφία
physician, ἰατρός
pig, ὕς
pig-sty, συφεός
pilot, κυβερνήτης
pine, πίτυς
pipes, σῦριγξ, κάλαμος
pity, οἶκτος
place, χωρίον, χώρα
plain, πέδιον
plant, φυτόν (noun), φυτεύω (verb)
play, παίζω
pleasant, ἡδύς
please, (with command or request: use
    optative with ἄν)
plough, ἀρόω (verb), ἄροτρον (noun)

pluck, κλάω, pluck fruit, τρυγάω
pocket, κόλπος
pour, χέω, and compounds
practice, ἀσκέω (verb), ἐπιτήδευμα, ἄσκησις (noun)
prayer, εὐχή
prepare, ἐπι-σκευάζω, παρα-σκευάζω
present, be, πάρειμι
pretend, προσ-ποιέομαι
prime, be in one's, ἀκμάζω
produce, bring forth, τίκτω
promise, ὑπισχνέομαι, ὁμολογέω
property, οὐσία
prosecute, διώκω
prosperous, αἴσιος
provide, παρέχω
provoke, ἐρεθίζω
pull, ἕλκω
pull up, ἀνασπάω
punish, δίκην τινὸς λαμβάνω; be punished, δίκην δίδωμι
purpose, on, ἐπίτηδες
pursue, διώκω
push on, ἐπείγω
put, βάλλω, τίθημι, and compounds
quench, σβέννυμι
rabbit, λαγώς
race, ποδωκεία
racecourse, ἱπποδρόμος
raise, αἴρω
reach, arrive, ἐφικνέομαι
rear, τρέφω
receive, δέχομαι, παραλαμβάνω
recognize, γιγνώσκω
reed, κάλαμος
rejoice, χαίρω
remaining, λοιπός
remind, ἀναμιμνήσκω
renown, κλέος
restrain, κατέχω
retire, ἀποχωρέω
return, ἐπανέρχομαι
rich, πλούσιος
ride, ἐλαύνω
right (side), δεξιός

ripe, be, ἀκμάζω
risk, κινδυνεύω
road, ὁδός
rock, πέτρα
rod, κάλαμος
roof, στέγη
room, δωμάτιον
rooster, ἀλεκτρυών
rope, κάλως
round, στρογγύλος
row, ἐρέττω, ἐλαύνω
rule, ἄρχω, κρατέω
run, τρέχω, διαθέω
running, δρόμος
rush, ἄττω
rustic, ἀγροῖκος
sacrifice, θύω
safe, ἀσφαλής
sail, πλέω
sail, ἱστίον
sailor, ναύτης
sample, δεῖγμα
sand, ψάμμος
say, φημί, λέγω
scholar, σχολαστικός, γραμματικός
sea, θάλαττα
season, ὥρα
see, βλέπω, ὁράω
seek, ζητέω
seem, δοκέω
seems, ἔοικεν
seize, ἁρπάζω
sell, πωλέω, ἀποδίδομαι
separately, ἰδίᾳ
servant, οἰκέτης
serve, δουλεύω
shape, σχῆμα
share, μεταδίδωμι, νέμω
sheep, πρόβατον, οἷς
sheepfold, σηκός
shepherd, ποιμήν
shoe, ὑπόδημα
shore, ἀκτή
shoulder, ὦμος

show, procession, θεωρία

shut, κλήω

sickle, δρεπάνη

silence, σιωπή, σιγή (nouns), σιωπάω (verb)

since, ἐπεί, ἐπειδή

sincere, ἄδολος

sing, ᾄδω

sister, ἀδελφή

sit, καθίζω, καθίζομαι

situated, be, διάκειμαι

slave, δοῦλος

sleep, καθεύδω

small, μικρός

smile, μειδιάω (verb), μειδίαμα (noun)

snare, παγίς

snow, χιών

soft, μαλακός

so large, so much, τοσοῦτος

soldier, στρατιώτης

song, ᾆσμα, ᾠδή

song, chanty, παιανισμός

soul, ψυχή

sound, ψόφος, φθέγμα, ἠχή, make a sound, φθέγγομαι, φωνέω

speak, λέγω, φωνέω

speech, λόγος

spring, πηγή

springtime, ἔαρ

stage, σκηνή

stair, κλῖμαξ

start, κλήω

stature, φυή

stone, λίθος

stool, δίφρος

stop, ἐπέχω

storm, χειμών

stormy, χειμέριος

straight, ὀρθός

straight away, εὐθύς

stranger, ξένος

straw, chaff, ἄχυρον

stream, ῥεῦμα

stretch, τείνω and compounds

strike, τύπτω, τυπτήσω, ἐπάταξα, πέπληγα, ἐπλήγην

string, λίνον

strong, violent, ἰσχυρός, σφοδρός, ἐρρωμένος

such, τοιοῦτος, τοιόσδε

suddenly, ἐξαίφνης

suffer, πάσχω

summer, θέρος

superior, be, διαφέρω

supper, dinner, δεῖπνον

surpass, ὑπερβάλλω

swear, ὄμνυμι

table, τράπεζα

take, λαμβάνω

talk, λαλέω, λέγω

tax, φόρος

teach, διδάσκω, παιδεύω

teacher, διδάσκαλος

tend, νέμω (cattle, etc.), θεραπεύω (serve, attend)

tendril, κλῆμα

tent, σκηνή

terrible, δεινός

test, ἐξετάζω

than, ἤ

that, ὅτι (conjunction)

that, ἐκεῖνος (demonstrative)

then, ἄρα, ἔπειτα, τότε, οὐκοῦν

then ... not, οὔκουν

thence, ἐκεῖθεν

there, ἐκεῖ

therefore, οὖν

thief, κλέπτης

thing, πρᾶγμα, χρῆμα

think, νομίζω, οἴομαι, δοκέω

thither, ἐκεῖσε

throttle, ἄγχω

thus, οὕτως

thyme, θύμον

time, χρόνος; right time, nick of time, καιρός; at the right time, ἐς καιρόν

to, πρός, ὡς, ἐπί

toil, κάματος

tool, ὄργανον

today, τήμερον
tomorrow, αὔριον
torrent, χείμαρρος
touch, ψαύω, ἅπτομαι, θιγγάνω
tower, πύργος
tread, πατέω
treasurer, ταμίας
tree, δένδρον
twist, στρέφω
ugly, αἰσχρός
unexpected, ἀπροσδόκητος
unjust, ἄδικος
useful, χρήσιμος
utensil, σκεῦος
value, ἀξία
vat, ληνός
vegetable, λάχανον
very much, μάλιστα
vessel, πλοῖον (ship), σκαφεῖον (bowl)
vex, λυπέω
victim, ἱερεῖον (for a sacrifice)
village, κώμη
villager, κωμήτης
vine, ἄμπελος
vintage, τρύγητος, (ἀπο)τρυγάω
violent, σφοδρός
violet, ἴον
voice, φωνή
voyage, πλοῦς
waist, ἰξύς
want, χρῄζω (lack), ἐθέλω (desire)
war, πόλεμος
warm, θερμαίνω
wash, λούω, νίζω
wealth, πλοῦτος
wealthy, be, πλουτέω
weather, ἀήρ, οὐρανός
weave, πλέκω
weep, δακρύω, κλαίω
well, εὖ, καλῶς
well then, εἶέν
well, be, ὑγιαίνω
what kind, ποῖος, ὁποῖος, οἷος
when, πότε, ὁπότε, ὅτε
whence, πόθεν, ὁπόθεν, ὅθεν

where, ποῦ, οὗ, ὅπου
whistle, συρίττω
white, λευκός
whither, ποῖ, ὅποι, οἷ
who, τίς, ὅς, ὅστις
wicked, ἄδικος, πονηρός
wickedness, πονηρία
wife, γυνή
wild, ἄγριος
will, γνώμη, βουλή, διαθήκη
willing, ἑκών, ἄσμενος
willing, be, βούλομαι
wind, ἄνεμος
window, θυρίς
wine, οἶνος
winter, χειμών
wintry, χειμέριος
wish, ἐθέλω
witness, μάρτυς
wolf, λύκος
woman, γυνή
wonder, θαυμάζω
wool, ἔρια
word, λόγος
work, ἔργον
work, ἐργάζομαι
worth, ἄξιος (adj.), ἀξία (noun)
wrestling, πάλη
wrist, καρπός
write, γράφω
wrong, do, ἀδικέω
yardarm, κεραία
year, ἔτος, ἐνιαυτός
yes, μάλιστά γε, ναί
yesterday, χθές, ἐχθές
yet, moreover, ἔτι
yoke, ζυγόν
young, νέος